VIDEOS
FOR KIDS

VIDEOS FOR KIDS

*The Essential, Indispensable Parent's Guide
to Children's Movies on Video*

**Doug Atkinson
Fiona Zippan**

**Prima Publishing
P. O. Box 1260
Rocklin, CA 95677**

Cover design by The Dunlavey Studio, Sacramento

Library of Congress Cataloging-in-Publication Data

Atkinson, Doug.
    [Check it out!]
      Videos for kids : the essential, indispensable parent's guide to children's movies on video / Doug Atkinson, Fiona Zippan.
      p.   cm.
    Originally published: Check it out! Richmond Hill, Ont. : Scholastic Canada, 1993
      Includes index.
      ISBN 1-55958-635-4
      1. Video recordings for children—Catalogs. 2. Children's films—Catalogs. I. Zippan, Fiona. II. Title.
    PN1992.945.A84 1994   94-27680
    016.79143′ 75′ 083—dc20   CIP

95 96 97 RRD 10 9 8 7 6 5 4 3 2 1
Printed in the United States of America

Note to Parents: This is *not* a book of recommended videos for children; rather, it is intended to provide information on videos that are commonly *perceived* as being intended for children. Especially in the case of sensitive or very young children, the onus is still on the parent or caregiver to preview visual material.

How to Order:
Single copies may be ordered from Prima Publishing, P.O. Box 1260BK, Rocklin, CA 95677; telephone (916) 632-4400. Quantity discounts are also available. On your letterhead, include information concerning the intended use of the books and the number of books you wish to purchase.

Contents

Acknowledgments

A number of people helped to make this book possible.

First and foremost, special thanks to Denise Bolton, Chris Darroch, Mike Darroch and Natasha Zippan for their efforts beyond the call of duty for adding to and checking the reviews and lists, which were enriched by their knowledge and expertise. And to the rest of the dedicated staff of The Original Kids Video Store who have been with us since the beginning and who held down the fort while we spent months with the VCR and the computer—Elsa Denzey and Nancy and Tanya Varley.

Thanks to Stan Zippan, whose love and support, not to mention computer expertise, proved invaluable.

To David Collard and Lisa Bodnarchuk of Fieldview Telepictures Ltd., for their contribution to the glossary.

To Donald J. Flowers, Vice Chairman of the Ontario Film Review Board, for his help with the chapter on ratings and for the information he provided.

To all the studios and reps for their cooperation in providing material, especially Rob Holmes and Joan MacLellan.

To Denise Cherrington for believing in us, and Danielle for starting it all.

Special thanks to Don Sedgwick of Scholastic Canada for his encouragement and to Prima Publishing.

And finally, to the parents, librarians, teachers, and children whose loyal support over the years made this book possible.

Chapter 1

ABOUT THIS BOOK

In an ideal world, parents would be able to prescreen every film their child was about to see. But with films running anywhere between half an hour and two hours, it's simply impossible; no one has the time to do it. Except us. We're professional movie watchers — that's all we do. And with this book we are, effectively, going to enable you to watch a two hour movie in about one minute. That said, it bears mentioning that in many cases we give away the ending — *if* we feel that the ending is a source of concern. (We've heard of parents renting a film like *Old Yeller*, because they heard it was "a nice dog story," to cheer up a child who has lost a pet.)

Understand that, although we ourselves are oriented toward presenting the finest in children's visual entertainment, this is *not* exclusively a book of recommended films. We have included summaries of certain popular movies which children commonly see (or commonly ask to see), which may contain violence, coarse language and/or sexual situations. In these (and, ideally, in all) cases we believe that the onus is on the parent or supervising adult to use discretion when renting. And we have tried to provide the information necessary for making those choices in this book.

How it all began

In 1988 we started a video store specifically for children.
The store was based on a perceived need — a need which was
brought to our attention by a dramatic incident in our own
lives.

One day, Fiona picked up her ten-year-old daughter
Danielle from school. The child's face was deathly white and
she was obviously distracted. Concerned by the change in her
otherwise cheerful child, Fiona asked what was wrong and
after some prodding the answer came, "I'm trying to get those
awful pictures out of my head."

The awful pictures, it turned out, were from the horror
movie she'd seen at school. During a teachers' strike, one of
the interim guardians, in response to the children's request
for a "scary movie," had gone to the local video store and
rented one. It turned out that the "scary movie" was a horror
movie which included a repeated scene of a father drowning
his crippled child — and upon further investigation it was
revealed that other children in the class were equally or more
traumatized by what they had seen.

Fiona decided then and there that something had to be
done to help adults select movies for children. The result was
a store that provided not only access to quality children's
videos, but also complete information about those videos.

What this book doesn't include

There is such a vast number of videos being produced for
children today that it's impractical to include them all, in
detail or otherwise. To this end we have purposely omitted a
number of categories.

We have left out the classic cartoons, which have retained
their popularity with today's children, but which are already
more or less familiar to parents. These include cartoons like
Warner Brothers favorites *Bugs Bunny* and *Daffy Duck*, and

others such as *Casper the Ghost*, *The Flintstones* and so on.

We have not given space to the recycled television shows of the '50s and '60s such as *The Mickey Mouse Club*, Disney's *Zorro*, *Tarzan*, *Lassie*, *Rin Tin Tin*, *The Three Stooges*, *I Love Lucy*, etc. Although they may be enjoyable for children, they are, for the most part, in black and white and have a style and a tempo which are very different from current creations.

We have not included videos known as teacher's aids in this book as we are mainly concerned with video product which is easily available to the home viewer.

We have purposely omitted almost all PG films that we feel have few redeeming features, in that the incidents of violence, sexual suggestion or representation, or derogatory represen- tations of women and minorities negate any features which might otherwise appeal to children and young people. (Though, again, we have included a few which have had such a high profile that many young children expect to see them.)

We have also omitted many PG films with adult storylines, because many PG films are not necessarily made with children in mind.

We have included very few PG-13-rated films, as these represent a conflict between what is viable and useful for children and what begins to touch on strictly adult themes such as serious illness, realistic human evil and sexual awakening.

And omitted for obvious reasons are R-rated films. (At least, the reasons are obvious to us!)

Finally, just because a PG film isn't included doesn't necessarily mean that it's not a decent children's film. We just didn't have space for everything in this edition — we'll catch the others the next time around.

What this book does include

In the chapters that follow, we've divided the book into the following sections:

- ▶ Ages up to 3

- Ages 3 to 6 (pre-K to grade 1)
- Ages 6 to 10 (grade 1 to grade 5)
- Ages 10 to 13 (grade 5 to grade 8)

Each chapter begins with some practical pointers on characteristics of and problems associated with each age group. Summaries of individual videos and series of videos suitable for children within that age category follow.

We tend to err on the conservative side, usually placing a title in a higher age category if there is any doubt about its suitability. This is not to say, however, that all films in the 3 to 6 category, for instance, are unsuitable for children renting from the up to 3 category, or that some films in the 3 to 6 category won't delight your twelve-year-old. There are gray areas, and you will have to use your own discretion based on our reviews to make the final decision about any one film's suitablity.

You will also find the reviews in this book helpful when you are renting for a number of children, all of them of different ages and with different interests. You should be able to find a number of films that fit the bill for the group. The lists in chapter 7 are a good place to start.

How to use our system and what the symbols mean

Every video summary consists of a brief story synopsis which usually describes events in chronological order. This is followed by brief descriptions of potential points of concern and of the strengths of the film. Our concerns (if any) are listed in two categories: **STOP** and **CAUTION**.

STOP denotes a serious consideration and is indicated not only by a **STOP** description, but also by an ✗ character beside the title. **CAUTION** denotes a less serious consideration.

Strengths are described in our **GO** section and include such things as awards information, notable performances and sometimes even the comments of children who frequent our store.

Following the review you may also notice one or more of the following information bullets:

● — out-of-print

■ — based on a book

Please take into consideration the fact that the availability status of videos changes continually. This information is the most up to date available at the time this book was printed.

A typical review might go as follows:

The title

The studio that distributes the video

The year the film or video was made

The director of the film or video

The actors appearing or providing voices

Synopsis

✗BABAR: THE MOVIE

Astral
1989
77 minutes
Directed by: Alan Bunce
Starring the voices of:
  Elizabeth Hanna, Gavin McGrath,
  Gordon Pinsett, Sarah Polley

When the film opens, a mature King Babar is telling his children a bedtime story. In the story, a young Babar receives word from Celeste that the rhinos are attacking villages and snatching elephants. Impatient with the bureaucracy involved in organizing an army, Babar and Ce-leste set out alone. They learn that the rhinos are forcing the kidnapped elephants to labor on a colossal building project and after a couple of daring escapes, Babar and Celeste participate in a final confrontation with the rhino horde.

✗STOP: A rhino raiding party attacks an elephant village, torching the houses and carrying the adult elephants away. Celeste's mother is bound, painfully, and Celeste is thrown into a well.

CAUTION: This is a film about war and viewers can expect to see a great deal of violence.

GO: An exciting and well animated adventure tale that stresses the values of courage, perseverance and inventiveness.

STOP

CAUTION

GO

Got it? Now, on with the show...

Chapter 2

SELECTING A VIDEO FOR YOUR CHILD
Where are all the children's videos?

Even in large cities, with a video store seemingly on every corner, you may have trouble locating a good source of children's videos. Even stores with sizeable children's sections are organized in such a way that making the right choice is often very difficult. The situation is similar in small towns. But you do have options.

More and more libraries are adding video departments. If your library doesn't have a children's video section, tell the librarian that you would be interested in one, especially one with high-quality videos. Librarians are interested in the needs of children, and they have better access to quality children's product than most retail stores.

Another alternative would be to ask your retailer for more or better children's material. A customer request carries a lot of weight because video retailers know that for every customer who asks for a title, there are at least ten others who will also be interested.

Be specific. Don't just ask your retailer or librarian to get better children's titles (their definition of better may differ significantly from yours); name the titles you're interested in and try to provide the name of the studio as well.

You may also consider ordering videos through the mail or through TV offers and video clubs.

Narrowing down the options

Ask yourself questions

Ask yourself: Who is this film for? The answer may seem obvious, but it can radically affect your choice. Is the film for the children to watch by themselves or will you be watching it with them?

▶ If the children are going to be by themselves, what is the age range of the viewers?

▶ Are there both boys and girls? Are there more girls than boys, or vice versa?

▶ Is the oldest a boy or girl? (This will make a big difference in the way the film is received.)

▶ Is the film intended for everyone to watch together or will it be primarily for the adults in the room, with the children present?

If you can think ahead of time about questions like these, they will help both you and your video retailer to zero in on the perfect movie.

Ask your video dealer questions

The question that most perplexes video dealers is: Is this a good movie? What could "good" possibly mean? By asking vague questions like this you are likely to end up with a film that you and your child are unhappy with. The moral: ask specific questions and provide the dealer with as much information about your child's interests as possible. You would probably do well to share the following information (even if it seems obvious):

▶ your child's age and sex

▶ your child's interests (animals, hobbies, etc.)

▶ your child's preferred genres (adventure, mystery, how-to, etc.)

▶ your requirements regarding coarse language, violence, mature content, etc.

Better still, have your child compile a Top Ten list of favorite movies to give the clerk as an indication of preference, and say you're looking for something like them.

Then, after you have chosen a title, take your selection to the clerk and ask even more questions — questions like:

- Are there any really scary scenes in this movie?
- Do any of the characters die?
- Is this film violent? How?

Ask about anything that you think might upset your child or that might not meet with your standards.

Never take the description on the box as indicative of content. It's best to ask someone who has seen the film about his or her impression of it. It's best if this is someone you know well, whose standards and opinions are familiar to you, but even the stranger standing next to you can be of help.

Ask your friends questions

Compile a list of your family's Top Ten favorite films, and have a friend's family do the same thing. Then exchange the lists. Even if you only find one new title to try, the exercise will have been worth it.

You might want to do the same thing with a Caution list as well, naming films you wished you hadn't seen — whether on video or in the theater — and describing exactly why it was that you and your family were disappointed.

Alternative titles

Invariably it happens: you walk into the video store, having done all of your homework, and not one title on your list is available. Then it's time for some lateral thinking. Here are some alternatives you might want to consider.

Films about films

Many children and teens are truly interested in the art of film-making. And aside from being an excellent choice when nothing else can be found, a "Making-of" film video can:

- Cure the "seen-it" syndrome by encouraging viewers to rescreen the original film.

- Satisfy a little one's curiosity about an unsuitable film. (One child we know believed he had seen a whole feature film after seeing an in-depth video describing how that feature was made.)
- Demystify — "that's not a real monster, it's just a clever combination of great animation and inventive special effects."
- Unglamorize, removing the unhealthy fixation some children develop with negative screen characters (for example, thinking "Freddy" from *Nightmare on Elm Street* is "cool.")
- Show children that a variety of fascinating skills are required to make films; this may interest them in new fields of study.

Documentaries

Be very careful when renting or buying documentaries for a child, as many contain potentially disturbing scenes. For instance, friendly looking videos about dolphins, pandas or rhinos (particularly those that deal with the destruction or preservation of a species) may contain some traumatizing footage.

That said, there are all kinds of documentaries that *are* suitable for young viewers. Begin your search by looking for one that is somehow connected to your child's hobbies or interests. (See our helpful lists for ideas.)

Biographies

Some children are very interested in the lives of famous people, and for them a biography or a film based on a real event may be just the thing. Check the ratings before you rent, though, as some real-life stories are hard to take.

Musicals

If your child has an interest in singing, dancing or musical theater there are a number of great feature film videos on the market. (See chapter 7 for some ideas.) There are also compilation tapes of old musicals (for example, *That's Entertainment*) which are sometimes more engaging for children than a musical with a story running through it.

How-to

For the child who is interested in doing and making things, there are countless how-to videos on such topics as: art, magic, dance, animal care, cooking, horseback riding, hockey and even moving house!

Black-and-white movies

How about trying classic black-and-white movies? The children may groan at first, but they'll probably settle down and watch eventually, especially if you make a family event out of watching it, to add to the enthusiasm. Try making popcorn or inviting guests. Or try a colorized version of an old classic.

Remakes of classics

Don't confuse remakes of classics with movies that are restored, rereleased or remastered. Remakes are updated versions, often set in the present day, that may include intense action scenes or explicit sexual situations that did not appear in the original.

Our criteria

After watching thousands of films, we've noticed that certain "destructive elements" occur over and over. The "constructive elements" we have listed below are things we look for in movies to counterbalance any destructive elements which appear. Note that all of these things commonly appear in PG-rated films!

Destructive elements

▶ There is gratuitous (unnecessary) violence.
▶ There is violent aggression (including destruction of

possessions or property).
- Violence is used in a ritual or quasi-religious context.
- Brutalization of a weaker party by a stronger party is shown.
- Bloodletting (including graphic depiction of wounds) is shown.
- There are graphic depictions of death (eyes open, bleeding from the mouth, choking, etc.).
- The movie shows the death or inhumane treatment of animals.
- A parent or grandparent, sibling or close friend dies.
- Traumatic post-death experiences (damnation, deterioration of the body) are depicted.
- Destructive natural phenomena (earthquakes, floods, storms) are shown.
- Women or minorities are portrayed poorly.
- Stereotypes are reinforced.
- Family angst is featured, and relationships remain unresolved.
- Families experience divorce and/or difficulty dealing with separation.
- There is family violence.
- Authority figures are cruel or evil.
- There is a sense of tension or anxiety throughout.
- The film is aurally intense, with a relentless tempo or soundtrack.
- The movie shows tasteless, gross or demeaning behavior.
- Coarse language is used.
- There is a pervasive sense of hopelessness (especially in "visions-of-the-future" films).
- Sex is ridiculed.

Constructive elements

- A strong positive role model is present.
- An underdog wins.
- The protagonist overcomes significant odds.

- Characters experience inner discovery and growth, or affirmation of self.
- Positive images of women (independent, intelligent, capable) are present.
- Positive working relationships are shown.
- Characters overcome racial/national prejudice and/or stereotypes.
- Magical or spiritual power is used in a positive way.
- The film promotes education or revelation (seeing things in a new way).
- The film generates questions or interest in ideas or concepts.

It may be helpful to keep these questions in mind: Is the film useful for my child in any way? If it's just being chosen for entertainment purposes, then are the negative events outweighed by the positive? Is the overall effect at least balanced?

The bottom line is that every film makes an impression on children, whether dramatically or subtly. The above criteria, and your own personal ones, can help you choose films that have a positive effect on your children and avoid films that may be damaging to them.

RATINGS: A WEALTH OF INFORMATION
IN ONE OR TWO LETTERS
Who gives the movies their ratings?

In the United States the movie rating system is sponsored by The Motion Picture Association of America (MPAA) and The National Association of Theater Owners, to provide parents with advance information on films. Films are voluntarily submitted by the filmmaker for a rating.

The board is comprised of volunteers from all walks of life who, after watching a film in its entirety, make an educated estimate as to which rating most parents would consider appropriate.

When you are making a selection, it is important to understand that the ratings that appear on the back of most video boxes in stores are from the MPAA, and are based on criteria developed in the United States.

We do not rate films for children under 6; you may assume that these films are all G-rated. A listing of "Not rated" indicates that the film was not submitted to the rating boards. "No rating" means that we were unable to find a rating for the film.

MPAA ratings

G — general; suitable for viewers of all ages

PG — parental guidance is suggested as some material may not be suitable for children

PG-13 — parents are strongly cautioned as some material may be inappropriate for children under 13

R — restricted; anyone under 17 must be accompanied by a parent or adult guardian. (Age varies in some jurisdictions.)

NC-17 — no children under 17 are admitted. (Age varies in some jurisdictions.)

In our STOP-CAUTION-GO sections we try to be direct about a film's content. We use a variety of phrases to define problematic material for parents. They are:

▸ Coarse language: words such as *son-of-a-bitch, asshole, jerk-off, prick, bitch.*

▸ Gross behavior: urinating, flatulence, burping, vomiting, nose-picking.

▸ Mature theme: terminal illness, mental illness, pregnant teens, abortion, divorce, family violence, etc.

▸ Mature treatment: scenes too intense or difficult to understand, for example, a realistic death-bed scene.

▸ Sexual innuendo: scenes that suggest sexual activity.

▸ Swearing: either obscenity (four-letter words like *shit, fuck* and so on) or profanity (*Jesus Christ! God damn you!* etc.).

What the letters can tell you: the criteria behind the ratings

Rated G

In a G-rated film there should be nothing that the majority of parents would consider offensive for even little ones to see or hear. There is no nudity, and there are no sex scenes or scenes of drug use; violence is minimal; some dialogue may go beyond polite conversation, but it will not go beyond common usage of words.

Rated PG

Because some of the material is for mature viewers, it is recommended that a parent examine or inquire about PG-rated films before allowing children to see them. There will be no explicit sex scenes and no scenes of drug use. If there is nudity it will be brief, and horror and violence do not exceed moderate levels. (Personally, we are not quite sure what "moderate levels" might mean, but to be sure, what may or may not be considered moderate is definitely changing — as a society we are becoming more tolerant.)

Rated PG-13

Parents should be especially careful about letting their younger children attend PG-13-rated films. There is no rough or persistent violence and theoretically no sexually-oriented nudity (though we can give many examples to the contrary); there also can be much use of harsh sexual language.

A film with an PG-13 rating can contain coarse language (sometimes an information piece is added to give further indication); violent prolonged combat resulting in tissue damage; violent sports; blood-letting; murder in non-graphic detail. There can be full nudity, albeit distance shots with no close-ups. Shots should be non-detailed, brief and casual. Sexual activity can include kissing, petting, fondling and implied sexual activity. Horror should be brief and not prolonged. Nor should the film encourage or glamorize drug use or violence. A film with a subject matter of an extreme nature with social or documentary significance could be considered for inclusion in this classification.

For our purposes here it is not necessary to mention the criteria for R-rated or Restricted films. Suffice it to say there are very few restrictions as to what is allowed in this category. Almost anything goes.

A WARNING BEYOND THE RATINGS: WHAT THE BOX DOESN'T TELL YOU

Aside from the ratings, there are other things that should influence your decision when selecting a video for children.

Misleading descriptions

Don't fall for the hype on the box; after all, they want you to rent the movie. Be careful of phrases like "intimate relationship" and "compelling story"; they may lead you astray. A good example of this is the box cover for the film *The Dollmaker*, starring Jane Fonda. The title sounds pleasant enough, and the description on the box says "it's a deeply moving story . . . that will charm and captivate your entire family." However, this film contains scenes of intense duress: in one, a young girl's legs are severed by a train as she sit on the tracks; in another, the mother must perform a tracheotomy on her child with a penknife. Although this is an excellent film, it is certainly not a charming film for the entire family. And to add to the confusion, there is no indication of rating on the box. This should be a clue. If you cannot find the rating on the box, don't show the film to a child without previewing it first. (Naturally, this isn't necessary if a film is obviously for a child, or if it's a classic which came out before the present rating system was developed.)

Don't assume that a movie is benign because it's "based on a true story"; horrific murders are a fact of life in our world, and so are countless other dreadful things you don't want your child to see. And you might also want to watch for "heartwarming story," which often involves the death of a loved one, and "coming of age," which is sometimes used to allude to a first romantic encounter, or the loss of virginity.

You may be wondering what in the world you can rent if you have to watch out for "heartwarming stories." We are not suggesting that you should steer clear of films with these descriptions, but want you to understand that movies described in this way are not necessarily free of anything that would upset your child.

Unrepresentative box art

Don't judge a video by its cover art. Great art on the box doesn't mean there's a wonderful movie inside and, conversely, bad cover art can hide a great film. Too, some cover art may be misleading in that the depicted scene doesn't even appear in the film, or worse, it may give the impression that a film is animated when in fact it is live-action. Try not to choose a film solely for the cover art, but for a combination of reasons such as its description, rating, stars and recommendations.

Misleading titles

Misleading titles can cause you to pass over some good family films. They can also cause you to rent inappropriate ones, so be careful to read more than the title when you rent.

Fully-animated vs. partly-animated

If you're looking for an animated film, then look for the phrase "fully-animated" on the box. If you can't find it described in exactly this way, the video may not be animated at all; rather, it might feature still pictures with narration, or be only partly-animated. Not that this is necessarily bad; some of the most wonderful children's videos are iconographic.

Same title/wrong movie

Watch out! There are X-rated versions of *Cinderella* and *Snow White* available. And you can't simply rely on the studio labels to make your selection, because the studio that released these films may also make children's product. There is a chance that an inattentive clerk may give you or your child a nasty surprise, so always check your movies before leaving the store.

Same company/different styles

There are studio names that are no longer associated solely with children's entertainment. Disney now has affiliated studios called Touchstone and Hollywood Pictures, and a film with one of these labels isn't necessarily a family film.

The ending

The text on the back of the box isn't going to give you the ending of the film, for obvious reasons. But sometimes this information is very important when you are making a choice for your child. Ask someone who has seen the film about the ending, or prescreen the film yourself. Or, if you're really stuck for time, run through the tape in fast-forward, scanning for suspicious-looking events. This could determine whether or not you show the video to your child.

Watch out!

Just because a child actor stars in a film doesn't mean that the film is suitable for children. Children appear in retrospectives of adult lives, as well as in horror movies, where filmmakers use the concept of the child in peril to intensify the worry level for an adult audience.

Trailers for restricted movies can appear at the beginning or the end of PG-rated films. And although the trailer will be approved for viewing by all audiences (trailers are subject to the ratings systems, too), they may interest a child in an unsuitable film.

Chapter 3

VIDEOS FOR AGES UP TO THREE

As extraordinary as it may seem, there are videos that are specifically designed for babies. These videos are not particularly common, but they do exist, and they are for the most part designed to be, in effect, moving mobiles, very often consisting of computer-generated images accompanied by synthesized music. The theory appears to be that, since mobiles work for babies, it should be possible to create successful mobiles on the television screen. However, in our experience, based on parental feedback from hundreds of rentals of such videos, they just don't seem to work.

Other videos for babies employ gentle voices, images of animals, babies or toddlers at play, animation or puppets. Jim Henson, one of the premiere children's entertainers in visual media history, tried something like this for very young children entitled *Peek-A-Boo*. But whether *Peek-A-Boo* or any other such efforts actually fulfill their objectives remains to be seen.

Song videos

Videos that work well with children under three are broadly categorized as song videos. There are two main types: concert videos and those that are set in specific locations or based on certain themes. The success of a particular concert video depends, of course, on the appeal that the performers hold for their young audiences, while the second group must usually possess one of the following features to achieve success:

 ▶ slightly older children engaged in activities like playing games, sight-seeing, singing and dancing
 ▶ a theme popular with most little ones, such as animals, vehicles, clowns and magical events
 ▶ minimal dialogue and rapid transition between songs
 ▶ rapid editing, often with visual images changing every few seconds, usually to the rhythm of the music, without lingering on any particular shot
 ▶ large, bright images, with an emphasis on close-ups

Because the song videos we have included are for the most part excellent, featuring tried-and-true children's entertainers or popular enjoyable themes, the reviews are minimal. We have discovered that most parents, children and grand-parents just want to know exactly which songs are on which videos. And because the video box doesn't always list every title, we have tried to include them all in our synopses.

Quality storybook videos

There is an entire genre of video which is perceived by the public as being for babies or toddlers. These are most often nursery rhyme or story videos, and are fully- or partly-animated. Some feature well-known entertainers as singers or narrators, and all, despite the aforementioned perception, tend to be very appealing to adults, often winning awards as quality videos (which they absolutely are).

The effect of a storybook video is similar to that of having someone read your child a story. However, these videos generally seem to move too slowly to capture the interest of very young children. Most find it much more captivating to actually have a real live person read a story (thank goodness).

Some of these videos have story lines that are too advanced for children under three, and ironically, when children are a bit older and have the attention span to follow these tapes, they would just as soon read the stories themselves.

Little kids and big movies

It's a fact that toddlers with older siblings are likely to watch more advanced television shows at a far younger age than their predecessors did.

In our store, we were suprised when the parents of a two-and-a-half-year-old came to the counter with *Superman*. His mother explained that the toddler watched everything that his revered older brother saw, and since the older boy, now six, watched *Superman* three times a week, so did his little brother. Of course, the older boy had never seen *Superman* even once when *he* was two-and-a-half.

It's not just younger siblings who are being exposed to films that are meant for older children. In general, more and more children under the age of three are watching full-length movies which were created for much older viewers. One of our customers, a first child, was obsessed with dolphins at the age of two-and-a-half. He would sit entranced through *Flipper* and *Tadpole and the Whale*, so focused on the object of his passion that the long and relatively sophisticated stories didn't deter him at all.

This viewer dedication is not unusual with young viewers. Many a small child has suffered through watching the evil tyrannosaur Sharptooth in *The Land Before Time* simply because the film also features the dinosaurs they love. Other favorites with young viewers are dragons, dogs, animals, vehicles (particularly trains and fire engines) and, interestingly enough, Bad Guys.

Children seem to feel a peculiar mixture of terror and fascination toward representations of evil. At the store we've heard more times than we can count that little so-and-so loves to be scared. All well and good, but be careful; this *can* go too far.

One well-meaning parent of our acquaintance, knowing how much his young son loved scary movies, brought home a copy of *The Great Mouse Detective* as a treat. But it was too much. At bedtime that night, the child could not sleep until his father literally took the video out of the house.

Another risk of showing your toddler a movie when he or she is too young to appreciate it is that it may turn the child off to the film for years. One of the great delights of childhood is looking forward to things such as an exciting holiday or a birthday; add to that list "movies I can watch when I get older."

THE ADVENTURES OF SPOT

Walt Disney Home Video
1993
30 minutes each
Featuring the voices of: Corey Burton,
    Linda Gary, Jonathan Taylor Thomas

Simple animation similar in style to the illustrations in the books by Eric Hill. Spot is a little puppy who lives with his parents and has low-key adventures.

Where's Spot?

Where's Spot? It's dinner time but Spot still wants to play. Spot's mother Sally asks, "Where's Spot?" and in answer to each question we see a bear behind a door, a snake in a clock, a hippo in the piano, a lion under the stairs, a crocodile under the bed and a turtle under the rug. Finally Spot is found in a basket.

Spot's First Walk Spot cavorts in the garden but he gets out and finds a scary cat in the shed and a bone in the flower bed. He falls in a pond.

Spot's Birthday Party It's Spot's birthday and he plays hide-and-seek with his animal friends and opens presents.

Spot Goes Splash Spot sees a rainbow and meets his monkey friend Steve. Helen the hippo, Steve and Spot splash in puddles but when it rains Spot has to go home and have a bath.

Spot Finds a Key Spot finds a lost key and surprises his father when he finds what it opens.

Spot Goes to the Farm

Spot Goes to the Farm At the farm Spot looks for baby animals. He finds a cow in the barn, a bunny behind a bush, a hen in a haystack, sheep in a pen, a duck in a pond, an annoyed goose behind a barrel and finally piglets and kittens.

Spot Sleeps Over Spot stays at his friend Steve's house and brings his teddy bear.

Spot Goes to the Circus Spot loses his ball at the circus where all the circus animals play with it.

Spot's Windy Day Spot tries to fly a kite but it gets stuck in a tree.

Spot Goes to the Park Spot and Helen the hippo learn to share the swing.

Also available:

Spot Goes to a Party

GO: Gentle and slow-moving with simple storylines suitable for toddlers.

THE ANIMAL ALPHABET

Scholastic-Lorimar Home Video
1985
30 minutes
Directed by: Geoffrey Drummond

Created to help kids learn about the alphabet, this video features National Geographic footage of animals in the wild. Pictures are accompanied by twenty-seven original songs by Broadway composer/lyricist Elizabeth Swados.

CAUTION: Some families have complained about the insensitivity of the song for the letter B in which a bear is told to go on a diet.

GO: The songs emulate the rhythmic movements of each featured animal.

ANIMAL BABIES IN THE WILD

Karl-Lorimar HomeVideo
1987
30 minutes
Directed by: Nancy Lebrun

Original stories and songs are narrated and accompanied by live footage of animal babies in the wild.

Stories featured are:
The Beaversons
Calhoun the Racoon
Sara and the Lion Club
The Tuxedo Junction

Songs featured are:
Animal Friends Theme Song
Bears Will Be Bears
Elephants of My Dreams
Let's Do the Hop
Monkey See
Splashin' around in the Water

GO: The live, sometimes humorous, footage shows animals in their natural habitats.

BABY ANIMALS JUST WANT TO HAVE FUN

Karl-Lorimar Home Video
1987
30 minutes
Directed by: Amy Jo Divine,
    Geoffrey Drummond

Original stories and songs accompany charming live-action footage of baby barnyard animals and animals in their natural habitats.

Stories featured are:
A Fawn in the Forest
Hortense Fuzzwuffle:
    The Curious Rabbit
Peter Puppy's Perfect Present
Raindance: The Shy Little Pony
The Skunk Children Find a Home

Songs featured are:
Baby Animals Just Wanna Have Fun
Kittens' Admittins
My Little Chickadee
Scholastic's Animal Friends Theme Song

CAUTION: Raindance the pony is stolen in the night.

GO: The songs are sung by children and the stories are told by adults. The animals are not manipulated into acting out the story; instead, stories are made up according to the footage.

BABY'S FIRST WORKOUT

HPG Home Video
1989
60 minutes
Directed by: Vicki L. Metz
Starring: Patti Gerard Hanna

Based on Patti Gerard Hanna's book *Teaching Your Child Basic Body Confidence*, this video demonstrates thirty-eight exercises designed to help babies with their motor skill development. The program requires no special equipment and takes only a few minutes a day.

GO: Patti Gerard Hanna demonstrates the exercises with a number of babies. All of the information is thorough and well-presented.

■

BABYSONGS COLLECTION

This collection includes song videos primarily, and is highly successful with children under five. Each features babies, toddlers, children, animals and adults acting out the lyrics. Excellent claymation, animation and video effects are used to introduce the songs, but most of the footage is live-action. Original songs are by Hap Palmer and, in the case of *John Lithgow's Kid-Size Concert*, by John Lithgow. A songbook is included with each video.

Baby Rock

> Hi-Tops Home Video/ HGV
> 1990
> 30 minutes
> Directed by: Nate Bashor, Keith Fialcowitz,
>   Lynn Hamrick, Allan Kartun, Lynda Taylor

Children dance and play with costumed characters to popular rock songs performed by the original artists. This video has appeal for children as old as eight.

Songs featured are:
Blue Suede Shoes (Carl Perkins)
Come On, Let's Go (Ritchie Valens)
Come Saturday Morning
   (The Sandpipers)
I'm So Excited (The Pointer Sisters)
I'm Walkin' (Fats Domino)
The Loco-Motion (Little Eva)
Pajamas (Livingston Taylor)
Twist and Shout (The Isley Brothers)
Woolly Bully
   (Sam the Sham and the Pharaohs)
You Baby (The Turtles)

Babysongs

> Hi-Tops Home Video/ HGV
> 1987
> 30 minutes
> Directed by: Dorian Walker

This live-action video features babies and children involved in daily activities.

Songs featured are:
Baby's Good Doggy
I Sleep 'til Morning
My Mommy Comes Back
Piggy Toes
Rolling
Rub a Dub
Security
Share
Shout and Whisper
Today I Took My Diapers Off

Babysongs Christmas

> Golden Book Video
> 1991
> 30 minutes
> Directed by: Nate Bashor, Keith Fialcowitz,
>   Rich Kinney, Lynda Taylor
> Starring: Lori Lieberman

Children on horseback and horses pulling old-fashioned sleighs make this a truly special holiday video.

Songs featured are:
Deck the Halls

It Came upon a Midnight Clear
Jingle Bell Rock
Peace on Earth
Sleigh Ride
The Twelve Days of Christmas
Up on the Rooftop
The Wassail Song
We Wish You a Merry Christmas
We're Cooking Supper for Santa

Songs featured are:
Big Kids Scare the Heck out of Me
The Garden Song
  (Inch by inch, row by row...)
I Had a Rooster
Mommy, Daddy
Mr. McCloud
The Runaway Pancake
She'll Be Coming 'round the Mountain

Babysongs Presents: Follow-Along Songs

Golden Book Video
1990
30 minutes
Directed by: Lynn Hamrick,
  Chris Willoughby, Amy Weintraub

In short, live-action segments, children aged three to six use home-made instruments to accompany the songs. Instructions for making a bean bag are featured (adult supervision is recommended).

Songs featured are:
Bean Bag Alphabet Rag
Bean Bag Shake
Homemade Band
Just Fun
Let's All Clap Our Hands Together
The Mice Go Marching
Parade of Colors
Tap Your Sticks
Weekly Rap

Babysongs Presents: Turn on the Music

Hi-Tops Home Video/HGV
1988
30 minutes
Directed by: Lynda Taylor, Nate Bashor,
  Neal Brown, Barbara Dourmashkin

This music video features more sophisticated concepts than the other titles in the series. Recommended for children aged three to seven.

Songs featured are:
Amanda Schlupp
Backwards Land
Chomping Gum
Francie Had a Football
Hurry up Blues
If I Had Wings
Teddy Bear Ball
When Daddy Was a Little Boy
When Things Don't Go Your Way
You Can Do It

Babysongs Presents: John Lithgow's Kid-Size Concert

Hi-Tops Home Video/HGV
1990
32 minutes
Directed by: Greg Gold
Starring: John Lithgow

John Lithgow accompanies himself on guitar and performs both traditional and original songs.

Babysongs: Sing Together

Golden Book Video
1992
25 minutes
Directed by: Gary Halvorson

This live-action video features high-energy music performed by Chic Street Man, Janet and Judy, Dan Crow and Lori Leiberman. They sing to and with a variety of young children. Some segments are fully costumed with elaborate sets.

Songs featured are:
Let's All Sing Together
Everybody Be Yoself [sic]
ABC
Kiss A Cow
Fruits and Vegetables
Monster Man
Follow Me
Oops
Thank a Plant

Even More Babysongs

Hi-Tops Home Video/HGV
1990
30 minutes
Directed by: Nate Bashor,
   Barbara Dourmashkin, Lynn Hamrick,
   C. D. Taylor, Lynda Taylor

Toddlers and parents are shown involved in everyday activities (eating, dressing and playing), accompanied by up-tempo songs with imaginative lyrics.

Songs featured are:
Baby's First
Finger Foods
Getting Up Time
Goodnight Story Time
I Can Put My Clothes on by Myself
Peek-A-Boo
Raggedy Rag Doll Friend
Teddy Bear
Wash Rag Blues
What a Miracle

More Babysongs

Hi-Tops Home Video/HGV
1987
30 minutes
Directed by: Nate Bashor, Lynda Taylor,
   Dorian Walker

Toddlers and their parents are shown venturing out into the world.

Songs featured are:
Crazy Monster
Daddy Be a Horsie
Family Harmony
The Hammer Song
My Baby
Sittin' in a High Chair
Tickly Toddle
Walking
Watch a Witchie Whiz
Wild and Woolly

CAUTION: Because most of the songs in this series will be new to children, young viewers may not be able to sing along right away. The sound track is over-dubbed which is a particular shame on the *Babysongs Christmas* tape, where it would have been delightful to hear the horses and the sleigh bells.

GO: This series is extremely popular with young children. The families shown seem like real families and a variety of ethnic backgrounds are represented. There are definite breaks between each song, giving parents the opportunity to stop the tape if necessary. The songs are excellent and a songbook is packaged with each tape.

BABYVISION

J2
1987
90 minutes
Directed by: Barron Christian

A kind of video mobile, this film was created to entertain and stimulate children aged nine months to three years. Children, animals, colors, shapes, plants and toys appear and are identified by a disembodied voice. Synthesized music by Barron Christian is played throughout.

Filmed in New Zealand. Music by Barron Christian.

CAUTION: All of the music is over-dubbed and there are no lyrics.

GO: This is a gentle, calming video. Different ethnic groups are represented.

Hug a Color
I Love You
I Wish There Was School Every Day
If All the Raindrops Were Lemon Drops
The Shape Song
There Are 7 Days in a Week
The Three Bears Rap
The Weather Riddle Song
The Welcome Song
What I Want to Be
You're a Grand Old Flag

BARNEY AND THE BACKYARD GANG COLLECTION

This collection combines live-action, animation and music to tell the adventures of Barney, a six-foot purple dinosaur who magically comes to life and visits the children in his neighborhood. Some videos in the series also star Sandy Duncan as Mom, who in true make-believe fashion can't see Barney.
Traditional tunes with new lyrics and original songs are included in every video. Songs and rhymes by Sheryl Leach and Kathy Parker, both M.A.s in early childhood education.

Barney Goes to School

Kids Edutainment Video
1990
40 minutes
Directed by: Gary Potts

Tina is sad because there is no school on Saturdays, until Barney transports her to school where the Backyard Gang is waiting to play.

Songs featured are:
ABC Song/Alphabet Chant
Alligator Pie
The Fishing Song
Goodbye Song

Barney in Concert

The Lyons Group
1991
55 minutes
Directed by: Jim Rowley

This live concert from the Majestic theater in Dallas features Barney, The Backyard Gang and a host of costumed characters, including Barney's dino-pal Baby Bop.

Songs featured are:
ABC's
Baby Bop's Song
Baby Bop's Street Dance
Backyard Gang Rap
Barney Theme Song
Bubble Bubble Bath
Down on Grandpa's Farm
Everyone Is Special
French ABC's
Grand Ole Flag
Hebrew ABC's
Hurry, Hurry, Drive the Firetruck
I Love You
Itsy Bitsy Spider
Mr. Knickerbocker
The Noble Duke of York
Pop Goes the Weasel
Pufferbellies
Sally the Camel
We Are Barney and The Backyard Gang
Where is Thumbkin

Barney's Alphabet Zoo

Barney Home Video
1994
30 minutes
Directed By: Jim Rowley

Shawn, Julie, Tina and Derek tell Barney about the animals they saw at the zoo. They waddle like ducks, hop like frogs, fly like eagles, slither like snakes and gallop like horses. Barney explains why there are zoos and they play an animal guessing game. Julie's Aunt Molly (who can see Barney) tells a story using gestures and Jason signs The Alphabet Song and I Love You.

Songs/Rhymes include:
Barney Theme Song
Animals In Motion
Down By The Station
Sally The Camel
Kookaburra
My Aunt Came Back
The Tiger Song
Alphabet Song
I Love You

Barney's Best Manners

Barney Home Video
1994
30 minutes
Directed By: Jim Rowley

Barney, Tina, Min, Michael and Derek go on a picnic and have a bubble splash party with Baby Bop. The lessons in this video are Please and Thank-you, taking turns and being polite. The kids learn that manners are rules for being nice to people.

Songs featured are:
Barney Theme Song
Taking Turns
Swingin' Up To The Stars

Please and Thank You
Snackin' On Healthy Food
I Try To Be Polite
Good Manners
Does Your Chewing Gum Lose Its Flavor
Splashin' In The Bath
Three Little Fishies
I Love You

Barney Rhymes With Mother Goose

Barney Home Video
1994
30 minutes
Directed By: Jim Rowley

When a bookworm eats the pages of Mother Goose's book, Barney, Kathy, Min, Shawn and Michael help her to remember the words to her favorite rhymes. Aired on TV as Let's Help Mother Goose.

Songs include:
Barney Theme Song
Mother Goose Please Appear
I'm Mother Goose
Old King Cole
Polly Put The Kettle On
Little Jack Horner
Do You Know The Muffin Man
Pease Porridge Hot
Three Little Kittens
Jack and Jill
Little Miss Muffet
Little Boy Blue
Mary, Mary Quite Contrary
Mulberry Bush
I Love You

Let's Pretend With Barney

Barney Home Video
1994
30 minutes
Directed By: Bruce Deck

Originally aired on television as An Adventure In Make Believe. Baby

Bop's older brother BJ, a purple-spotted yellow dino, Shawn and Min try to find a make-believe princess in a jungle, look for birds with pretend binoculars, pretend to be cowboys and fly a plane.

Songs include:
Barney Theme Song
The Little Bird
Just Imagine
If I Lived Under The Sea
Home On The Range
Airplane Song
Jungle Adventure
I Love You

Barney's Home Sweet Home

Barney Home Video
1992
30 minutes
Directed by: Jim Rowley

Different kinds of homes are explored for both animals and people. The children play in snow outside an igloo, explore underwater and act out the story of the three pigs.

Songs include:
Barney Theme Song
Home On The Range
That's A Home To Me
Winter's Wonderful
If I Lived By The Sea
The Caterpillar
The Frog On The Log
My Family's Just Right For Me
I Love You

Barney's Birthday

The Lyons Group
1991
30 minutes
Directed by: Jim Rowley

Barney turns two dinosaur years old and gets to wear the birthday crown. The Gang makes decorations and comes up with the perfect present for Barney. This episode features Baby Bop.

Songs featured are:
The Barney Theme Song
Everyone Is Special
Frosting the Cake
Growing
Happy Birthday (Filipino version)
Hey, Hey, Our Friends Are Here
I Love You
Las Mananitas
She'll Be Comin' 'round the Mountain
There Are 7 Days

Barney's Campfire Sing-Along

The Lyons Group
1992
46 minutes
Directed by: Dwin Tavell

When her mother reads her a bedtime story about camping, Tina dreams that she and The Gang camp out.

Songs featured are:
A-Camping We Will Go
The Ants Go Marching
Are You Sleeping?
Clean Up, Clean Up
The Frog on a Log
The Happy Wanderer
I Love You
   (English and Spanish versions)
I'm Being Eaten by a
   Tyrannosaurus Rex
Kookaburra
Little Cabin in the Forest Green
The Other Day I Met A Bear
Sarasponda
S'Mores
Tell Me Why
There Was a Little Turtle

Barney's Magical Musical Adventure

The Lyons Group
1992
40 minutes
Directed by: Jim Rowley

Barney and The Gang use their imaginations to go to a magical forest. There they meet an elf named Twinkle who escorts them to a castle where they fill in for the king while he goes fishing. This video features Baby Bop.

Songs featured are:
Barney Theme Song
Castles So High
Go Round and Round the Village
I Am a Fine Musician
I Love You
If I Had One Wish
It's Good to Be Home
Looby-Loo
The Noble Duke of York
Old King Cole
Silly Sounds
Tea Party Medley (Polly Put the Kettle On, Little Jack Horner, The Muffin Man, Pat-A-Cake, Pease Porridge Hot, Sing a Song of Sixpence)

Rock with Barney: Protect Our Earth

The Lyons Group
1991
30 minutes
Directed by: Jim Rowley

Adam's mom takes The Backyard Gang to visit the film studio where she works. Barney goes too and brings along his shy dinosaur friend, Baby Bop.

Songs featured are:
Apples and Bananas
Barney Theme Song
Boom, Boom Ain't It Great to Be Crazy
Down by the Bay
Frog on a Log
I Can Laugh
I Love You
Manners
Me and My Teddy
Protect Our Earth
Six Little Ducks
There Are 50 Stars on Our Flag
Tingalayo
We Are Barney and The Backyard Gang
The Yankee Doodle Boy

Waiting for Santa

The Lyons Group
1990
30 minutes
Directed by: Dwin Tavell

Derek, the new boy in the neighborhood, is afraid that Santa won't be able to find him at his new address. So, with Derek in tow, Barney whisks The Backyard Gang to Santa's Workshop where Mrs. Claus assures Derek that he is on Santa's list. Then it's home again to see Santa delivering their presents.

Songs and stories featured are:
Deck the Halls
The Elves' Rap
Jingle Bells
Jolly Old St. Nicholas
I Love You
Let's All Do a Little Tapping
S.A.N.T.A.
Skating, Skating
'Twas the Night before Christmas
Up on the Housetop
Waiting for Santa
We Wish You a Merry Christmas
When Santa Comes to Town

CAUTION: Children may be frustrated when they recognize the tunes, but not the changed lyrics of many of the songs.

GO: The series features children from a number of different ethnic backgrounds, stresses positive values and inspires crea-tive expression through dramatic, imagina-tive play. Most videos are winners of the Film Advisory Board's Award of Excellence, American Film & Video Association Honorable Mention and the California Children's Video Award. The series is one of the top ten picks for children in *TV Guide*, *Redbook* and *USA Today*.

CHARLOTTE DIAMOND: DIAMONDS AND DRAGONS

Hug Bug Music, Inc.
1990
30 minutes
Directed by: Tony Wade
Starring: Charlotte Diamond,
    The Hug Bug Band, Jackson Davies

Multi-talented entertainer Charlotte Diamond finds lots of interesting things in Grannie's attic. Charlotte changes costumes, personas and musical styles throughout.

Songs featured are:
Animals Have Personalities
Competition
Dickie, Dickie Dinosaur
A Happy Street
Hug Bug
La Bamba
La Bastrange
The Laundry Monster
Slimy, the Bug
The Unicorn

GO: This is a well paced video, and Diamond is a competent, talented performer.

CHRISTMAS EVE ON SESAME STREET

Random House Home Video
1978
60 minutes
Directed by: Jon Stone
Starring: The Muppets,
    The Sesame Street cast, Holiday on Ice

In this Sesame Street holiday celebration, a little girl helps Big Bird learn to skate; Cookie, the Count, Ernie and Bert barrel jump on skates; Oscar is thrown off the ice in a game of crack-the-whip; Big Bird, Grover and Kermit try to find out how Santa gets down the chimney and Ernie and Bert do some unlucky giftbuying. Skating sequences are performed on the ice rink at Rockefeller Center.

Songs featured are:
Have Yourself a Merry Little Christmas
I Hate Christmas
Keep Christmas with You (sign language)
True Blue Miracle

CAUTION: This video doesn't move as quickly as the television show. Cookie Monster burps at the end of the video.

DISNEY'S SING-ALONG SONGS

Disneyland Fun

Walt Disney Home Video
1990
29 minutes
Directed by: Bruce Healy, Paul Hoen

In this live-action video, Mickey, Minnie, Goofy, Pluto, Donald, Chip 'n Dale, Roger Rabbit and Alice in Wonderland lead kids and grown-ups in a happy sing-along through the Magic Kingdom. The lyrics for the songs run along the bottom of the screen. See ages three to six for more in this series.

Songs featured are:
The Character Parade
Disneyland Is a Magical Place
Following the Leader
The Great Outdoors
Grim Grinning Ghosts
I'm Walkin' Right down the Middle of Main Street, USA
It's a Small World
Making Memories
Rumbly in My Tumbly
Step in Time
When You Wish upon a Star
Whistle While You Work
You Know It's a Thrill
Zip-A-Dee-Doo-Dah

CAUTION: There is no animation in this video; all of the Disney characters featured are people in costumes. Many parents consider the video to be a half-hour advertisement for the Disney theme parks.

GO: Live characters are a big favorite with young children. The pace is peppy and the atmosphere, happy.

FIREMAN SAM ... THE HERO NEXT DOOR

f.h.e./MCA
1987
30 minutes
Directed by: John Walker
Starring the voice of: John Alderton

Brave and friendly, Fireman Sam spends his days helping the people in his community. He does everything from clearing away hazardous fallen telegraph poles to rescuing wayward kites.

CAUTION: There are no songs except the opening theme.

GO: The pixilation is extremely well done. This video is a big hit with young boys.

FRED PENNER: A CIRCLE OF SONGS

Oak Street Music/Sony
1991
40 minutes
Directed by: Tony Dean
Starring: Fred Penner, Len Udow

Singer/banjo player Fred Penner and his piano-playing accompanist, Len Udow, perform an intimate concert for an audience of about thirty children.

Songs featured are:
The Bump
The Cat Came Back
Grandma's Glasses
Hush Little Baby
I Had a Rooster
John Russell Watkins
Land of the Silver Birch
Poco
Rock a Little Baby
Sandwiches

GO: Fred Penner is one of the most popular and talented children's entertainers today. He's very comfortable with his audiences and his performances have a spontaneous quality that most artists never achieve.

FRED PENNER: THE CAT CAME BACK

(continued on next page)

33

> Oak Street Music
> 1990
> 45 minutes
> Directed by: Tony Dean
> Starring: Fred Penner

Singer/banjo player Fred Penner performs with The Cat's Meow Band for a large crowd.

Songs featured are:
The Cat Came Back
Collections
Holiday
A House Is a House for Me
I Am the Wind
Otto the Hippo
Sandwiches
We're Gonna Shine
You Are My Sunshine
You Can Do It If You Try

FRED PENNER: WHAT A DAY!

> Sony
> 1993
> 28 minutes
> Directed by: Charles Lavack
> Starring: Fred Penner, Al Simmons

Fred is left with time on his hands because of a train delay. However, he meets his friend Al Simmons, who has just discovered a magic photo booth. It turns out that the booth is a portal into other dimensions, and Fred and Al make good use of it. They have musical adventures and sing a few songs, and there are guest appearances by Rocki Rolletti and Charlotte Diamond.

Songs featured are:
The Cat Came Back

Counting Feathers
I Collect Rocks
Happy Feet
Do the Rolletti
Animals Have Personality
You've Got To Be Proud
What A Day

INFANTASTIC LULLABYES ON VIDEO (Vol. 1)

> View Video
> 1989
> 25 minutes
> Directed by: Dick Feldman

Synthesized music accompanies computer animation in this video mobile for children aged three months to two years. Music written and arranged by Lou Garisto.

Songs featured are:
The Alphabet Song
Brahms' Lullaby
Count to 10
Hush Little Baby
Pop Goes the Weasel
This Old Man
Three Blind Mice
Twinkle, Twinkle Little Star
Yankee Doodle

CAUTION: Although the pictures do move, the computer animation in this video doesn't come close to the quality of true animation. There are no lyrics to the music.

JUST ME AND MY DAD

Golden Book
1993
25 minutes
Directed by: Jerry Reynolds
Starring the voices of: Kimberly Harris,
   Ellen Kingston, Jerry Reynolds,
   Nicholas Varnau

Little Critter goes camping with Dad and learns some important lessons, including the values of patience, listening, working with others and keeping the site clean. Songs included. From the book by Mercer Mayer.

CAUTION: Little Critter's younger sister is obnoxiously jealous of her brother's camping opportunity, and gives vague answers to avoid telling the whole truth. The musical score is oppressive, and at times spooky. There is one particularly unfunny moment when a map flies in Dad's face while he's driving, and they nearly crash.

GO: The video stresses the value of safety, cleanliness and consideration for others.
■

KIDSONGS MUSIC VIDEO STORIES

Viewmaster Video
1985-1992
25-30 minutes each volume
Directed by: Bruce Gowers

The *Kidsongs Music* Video Stories collection features children and adults singing and dancing to popular, upbeat songs. The music is over-dubbed with no breaks between songs. Each fast-paced video is based on a particular theme and a lyric card is included with every tape.

A Day at Camp

The Kidsongs Kids spend the day at camp, fishing, hiking and singing.

Songs featured are:
The Animal Fair
The Ants Go Marching In
Baa Baa Black Sheep
Boom, Boom, Ain't It Great to Be Crazy?
The Caissons Go Rolling Along
Fishin' Blues
Found A Peanut
The Hokey Pokey
I Had A Rooster
Little Bunny Foo Foo
The More We Get Together
Ninety-Nine Bottles of Pop on the Wall
The Old gray Mare
On Top of Spaghetti
Pop Goes the Weasel
Pussy Cat, Pussy Cat
When the Saints Go Marching In
Whistle While You Work

A Day at the Circus

The Kidsongs Kids see a circus tent go up, watch circus acts rehearsing and take part in an old-fashioned circus parade.

Songs featured are:
The Circus Is Coming to Town
Entry of the Gladiators
If You're Happy and You Know It
The Lion Tamer
The Man on the Flying Trapeze
Polly Wolly Doodle
Put on a Happy Face
The Ringmaster Song
The Sabre Dance
Strolling through the Park

A Day at Old Macdonald's Farm

The Kidsongs Kids take a trip to the farm. Close-ups of live farm animals are featured. Winner of The Video Review Award in 1987.

Songs featured are:
Here We Go 'round the Mulberry Bush
John Jacob Jingleheimer Schmidt
Mary Had a Little Lamb
Old Macdonald Had a Farm
She'll Be Coming 'round the Mountain
Shortenin' Bread
Skip to My Lou
Take Me Out to the Ball Game
This Old Man
Twinkle, Twinkle Little Star

A Day with the Animals

The Kidsongs Kids visit a zoo where they see chimps, dolphins, whales, cats and dogs.

Songs featured are:
BINGO
Do Your Ears Hang Low?
Harmony
Hickory Dickory Dock
How Much Is That Doggie in the Window?
Itsy Bitsy Spider
Little Bo Peep
Little Duckie Duddle
Rockin' Robin
The Wanderer
Water World
Why Don't You Write Me ?

Cars, Boats, Trains and Planes

Mike the dog leads the kids on a merry chase as he rides a number of vehicles in a theme park.

Songs featured are:
The Bus Song
Car, Car Song
Daylight Train
I Got Wheels
I Like Trucks
Round and Round
Up and Down, Round and Round
Up, Up and Away
Where, Oh Where, Has My Little Dog Gone?
Wild Blue Yonder

Good Night, Sleep Tight

Two sandmen listen in on parents as they "sing" their children to sleep.

Songs featured are:
All the Pretty Little Horses
Good Night
Hush Little Baby
Let Us Dance, Let Us Play
Our House
Ring around the Rosy
A Tisket, a Tasket
Tomorrow Is a Dream Away
The Unicorn

Home on the Range: Sing Out America

Uncle Sam invites the Kidsongs Kids to see a Fourth of July parade that takes them on a trip through American history.

Songs featured are:
America's Heroes
Deep in the Heart of Texas
Home on the Range
If I Had a Hammer
I've Been Working on the Railroad
Living in the U.S.A.
Oh Susanna
There's a Hole in My Bucket
Turkey in the Straw
Yankee Doodle Boy
You're a Grand Old Flag

I'd Like to Teach the World to Sing

The Kidsongs Kids travel around the world, learning songs.

Songs featured are:
Day-O
Did You Ever See a Lassie?
Frère Jacques
Funiculi, Funicula
I'd Like to Teach the World to Sing
Kumbaya
London Bridge
Los Pollitos
Sakura, Sakura
Waltzing Matilda

Let's Play Ball: Wonderful World of Sports

The Kidsongs Kids join children as they play basketball, race cars, lead cheers, do gymnastics, ride horses and sail.

Songs featured are:
Bend Me, Shape Me
Catch a Wave
Centerfield
Footloose
I Get Around
It's Not If You Win or Lose
Practice Makes Perfect
Rah, Rah, Sis, Boom, Bah
You Know that You Can Do It

Ride the Roller Coaster

The Kidsongs Kids spend the day at an amusement park.

Songs featured are:
The 1812 Overture
A Pirate's Life
Anything You Can Do
Fast Food
Here We Go Loopty Loo
Let's Twist Again
Little Deuce Coupe
Splish Splash
We're Gonna Get Wet
Whole Lotta Shakin' Going On

Very Silly Songs

The Kidsongs Kids sing practically every silly song ever made when they visit Silly Dilly Ville.

Songs featured are:
Do the Silly Willy
Down by the Bay
Fiddle-I-Dee
Jim along Josie
Mail Myself to You
Michael Finnegan
The Name Game
Purple People Eater
Rig-A-Jig-Jig
The Thing

We Wish You a Merry Christmas

Frosty the Snowman comes alive and joins the Kidsongs Kids on a holiday adventure to visit Santa at the North Pole.

Songs featured are:
All I Want for Christmas Is My Two Front
  Teeth
Deck the Halls
Frosty the Snowman
Jingle Bells
Santa, Please Don't Forget Me
The Pony Song
Rudolph the Red-Nosed Reindeer
Santa Claus Is Coming to Town
The Twelve Days of Christmas
We Wish You a Merry Christmas

CAUTION: These videos contain popular songs and rock songs from the '60s that many children may not be familiar with. The sound is over-dubbed and songs are performed without breaks.

GO: These videos are positive and non-threatening and deal with themes of interest to children. The singing and dancing is high-quality, showing talented, capable children. They are for the most part non-gender specific and non-racist. Excellent for children under four.

LADY AND THE TRAMP

Walt Disney Home Video
1955
75 minutes
Directed by: Hamilton Luske,
   Clyde Geronimi, Wilfred Jackson
Starring the voices of: Peggy Lee,
   Stan Freberg

Lady, a gentle cocker spaniel, leads a pampered life until a new baby is born, and Aunt Polly and her two troublesome siamese cats come to help out. The trouble begins when Lady is wrongly suspected of mischief and is subsequently taken to be fitted for a muzzle. Escaping in terror she meets Tramp, a street-wise mongrel from the wrong side of the tracks. A romance is kindled, but fades when Tramp involves Lady in a chicken-chasing incident and she's caught by dogcatchers. The dogs eventually manage to make their way back to the house where Tramp wins back Lady's affection by killing a vicious rat that's threatening the baby. And in the end, Lady is vindicated and Tramp is adopted into the household, where he and Lady raise a family of their own. Based on a story by Ward Greene.

Songs featured are:
Bella Notte
He's a Tramp
We Are Siamese

CAUTION: The animal parodies can be stereotypical (the Scottish terrier as miserly, for example). Small children may be disturbed by scenes of the baby in jeopardy and by the two intense fight scenes.

GO: The animation is of the highest quality and the songs are some of Disney's best. The relationships are warm and positive.

MICKEY'S FUN SONGS

These videos are live-action sing-alongs. Children from the ages of eight to ten join Disney costumed characters. Virtually non-stop music is featured with words to each song appearing at the bottom of the screen.

Campout at Disney World

Walt Disney Home Video
1994
30 minutes
Directed by: Gary Halvorson

Costumed Disney characters Goofy, Donald, Mickey and Minnie join a group of children as they set-up a campsite at Walt Disney World and take a boat to Discovery Island where they see tropical birds and animals. Then they play games and go to the beach. After a hayride, they watch a country dance show and participate in a talent show.

Songs featured are:
Comin' Round the Mountain
Bare Necessities
The Caissons Go Rolling Along
   (with Chip 'N Dale)

Happy Wanderer
Oh Susanna (with the
  Country Bears Jamboree)
Camptown Races
By The Beautiful Sea
Don't Fence Me In
Turkey In The Straw
Talent Round-Up
Jeepers Creepers
Mountain Greenery
Country Roads
If You're Happy and You Know It
Goodnight [Ladies] Campers

CAUTION: All songs are performed in virtually the same tempo. Purists will cringe. Over-dubbed voices of adults singing like Mickey and Donald overwhelm the children's voices in most songs.

GO: As with all Disney music videos, one can see children with excellent musical theater training.

Let's Go to the Circus

Walt Disney Home Video
1994
32 minutes
Directed by: Gary Halvorson

Mickey, Minnie, Donald, Goofy and the Fun Songs Kids participate in the real Ringling Brothers Barnum & Bailey Circus.

Songs featured are:
Rainbow World
The Circus On Parade
Upside Down (family tumbling act)
Aba Daba Honeymoon (monkey act)
I Wanna Be Like You
The Men On the Flying Trapeze
  (high-wire artists)
Over and Over Again (acrobatics)
These Magnificent Men
  In Their Flying Machines
Make 'Em Laugh (clowns)
The Bells (comedy act)
Animal Calypso (animal acts)
Jump Rope (skipping acrobats)
Be A Clown
Join the Circus

GO: Impressive acrobatics and skipping performed by children.

PETER, PAUL AND MOMMY TOO

Warner Home Video
1993
90 minutes
Directed by: William Cosel

Peter Yarrow, Paul Stookey and Mary Travers perform for a rapt audience of children. From a PBS television special. Recorded live at the Majestic theater on Brooklyn, New York. Lyric book enclosed.

Songs featured are:
Puff The Magic Dragon
The Fox
Somagwaza/Hey, Motswala
Inside
Day Is Done
Garden Song
The Eddystone Light
I Know An Old Lady
  Who Swallowed a Fly
Somos El Barco
Pastures of Plenty
Home On the Range/
  Don't Ever Take Away My Freedom
All Mixed Up
Right Field
Poem for Erika/For Baby
We Shall Overcome
It's Raining
If I Had A Hammer (The Hammer Song)
Blowin' in the Wind
This Land Is Your Land

GO: A straight-ahead concert video of great performers who bring enthusiasm, skill and comedic charm to a professional performance parents can enjoy with their children.

POLKA DOT DOOR

This program is intended for very small children. Episodes are quiet and leisurely-paced, generally featuring the uncomplicated discussion of a particular subject, a story-time, a song of the day, and a visit from an unthreatening costumed dinosaur-dragon called Polkaroo. Titles in the series are:

Fairy Tales

Morningstar Entertainment
1989
29 minutes
Directed by: David Moore
Starring: Robert Lee, Carrie Loring

The Polka Dot Door crew discusses the characters and traits of familiar fairy tales. Polkaroo acts out a fairy tale starring... Polkaroo.

Colors

Morningstar Entertainment
1990
29 minutes
Directed by: David Moore
Starring: Jim Codrington, Cindy Cook

The PDD gang create their own playground and explore the world of colors, with the help of Polkaroo.

Music and Motion

Morningstar Entertainment
1988
29 minutes
Directed by: Doug Williams
Starring: Johnie Chase, Carrie Loring

John and Carrie plant a musical garden and enjoy a parade.

Animals!

Morningstar Entertainment
1986
29 minutes
Directed by: David Moore
Starring: Johnie Chase, Carrie Loring

John and Carrie find out about pond animals and recycling. Polkaroo watches a film concerning the Space Shuttle and suffers from the delusion that he is an astronaut.

Look Up!

Morningstar Entertainment
1992
29 minutes
Directed by: David Moore
Starring: Johnie Chase, Carrie Loring

The PDD duo learns about birds, planes and kites. Polkaroo inexplicably develops flight capabilities.

CAUTION: Not for the squirmish. When my niece was three she said that Polkaroo scared her... but she watched him anyway.

GO: Uncomplicated, straight-forward, doesn't talk down to kids.

POSTMAN PAT

Strand Home Video
1990
30 minutes each
Directed by: Ivor Wood
Narrated by: Ken Barrie

Postman Pat's ABC. While delivering mail to the Greendale Farm, Pat discovers that young Tom Pottage is crying, because he has a cold and he can't learn his letters. Pat helps by making an A-B-C, a red notebook in which he puts a new letter each day. Tom's many friends help out and Tom soon learns his ABCs.

Postman Pat's 123. Tom Pottage has to learn to count before Easter. Pat helps, this time with a blue notebook, which he uses to help both Tom and Katie with their one-to-tens.

CAUTION: The British accents may be difficult for some children to understand.

GO: These charming, fully animated episodes are leisurely paced, and somewhat similar to Richard Scarry's learning videos in their approach.

■

Cluck, Cluck Red Hen
The Corner Grocery Store
Down by the Bay
He's Got the Whole World in His Han
I've Been Workin' on the Railroad
The More We Get Together
Mr. Sun
Peanut Butter Sandwich
Shake My Sillies Out
The Shoe Song
Six Little Ducks
Something in My Shoe
Sur le pont d'avignon
Thanks a Lot
There's a Rat
You Gotta Sing
  When the Spirit Says Sing
The Wheels on the Bus

CAUTION: This is a concert tape. There is no story woven between the songs.

GO: Although some adults find Raffi to be bland and his sound, monotonous, children adore him. His humor is genuine; he's never condescending; and he works at a pace well-suited to his young audiences. The audience participation in this tape is great.

RAFFI: A YOUNG PEOPLE'S CONCERT

A & M Video
1984
45 minutes
Directed by: David Devine
Starring: Raffi

Raffi performs to a sold-out crowd at a concert filmed in Toronto. Teacher/parent notes and song lyrics are included with the tape.

Songs featured are:
Baa, Baa Black Sheep
Baby Beluga
Brush Your Teeth
Bumpin' up and Down

RAFFI IN CONCERT WITH THE RISE AND SHINE BAND

A & M Video
1988
50 minutes
Directed by: David Devine
Starring: Raffi, Deenis Pendrith,
  Nancy Walker, Mitch Lewis,
  Bucky Berger

Favorite Canadian performer Raffi sings his best-loved songs to a lively and attentive audience. Backed by his four-person band, Raffi accompanies himself on an acoustic guitar.

Songs featured are:
All I Really Need
Apples and Bananas
Baa, Baa Black Sheep
Baby Beluga
Bathtime
Day-O
De Colores
Everything Grows
Five Little Ducks
Go to Sleep (Fait dort dort)
He's Got the Whole World in His Hands
I Gotta Shake My Sillies Out
If You're Happy and You Know It
Itsy Bitsy Spider
Knees up Mother Brown
Like Me and You
The More We Get Together
One Light, One Sun
Rise and Shine
This Little Light of Mine
Time to Sing
Tingalayo
Twinkle, Twinkle Little Star

CAUTION: This is a concert tape. There is no story woven between the songs.

GO: Raffi is a genuine favorite with young children.

RAFFI ON BROADWAY: A FAMILY CONCERT

MCA Music Video
1993
63 minutes
Directed by: Milton Lage
Starring: Raffi, Michael Creber,
    Connie Lebeau, Kids For Saving Earth

Raffi entertains the audience by asking them to make rain sounds, answers a banana phone, and sings with a group of children called Kids For Saving Earth. A pared-down back-up band consists only of synthesizer and bass. Raffi shows how the synthesizer can simulate drum sounds. Filmed at the Gershwin theater in New York City.

Songs featured are:
Overture
All I Really Need
Rise and Shine
Rainstorm
Big Beautiful Planet/Clean Rain
The Bowling Song
Like Me and You
Day-O
De Colores
Will I Ever Grow Up
Everything Grows
Baby Beluga
K.S.E. Promise Song
Evergreen Everblue
One Light, One Sun
This Little Light of Mine
Brush Your Teeth (rap)
Down By The Bay
(after the credits these songs are added)
Haru Ga Kira
May There Always Be Sunshine

SESAME STREET PRESENTS: FOLLOW THAT BIRD

Warner Home Video
1985
92 minutes
Directed by: Ken Kwapis
Starring: Carroll Spinney, Joe Flaherty,
    Dave Thomas, Chevy Chase, John Candy,
    Sandra Bernhard

When the children's aid society decides that Big Bird needs a better home environment, he's taken to live with a foster family in Illinois. But when his new parents forbid him to make friends with anyone other than birds, Big Bird decides to leave his foster family and go back to Sesame Street. As soon as it's discovered that he's run away, the whole Sesame Street gang goes looking for him, and comic incidents abound. The Sleaze Brothers plan to kidnap Big Bird, paint him blue and make a fortune by displaying him as the Blue Bird of Happiness; Bert and Ernie buzz Big Bird with a biplane in a hilarious send-up of the classic scene from Hitchcock's North By Northwest, and the Sesame Street gang samples the not-so-delicious offerings at the Grouch Restaurant. Only the timely intervention of a motorcycle policeman saves Big Bird from a fate worse than having to eat spinach for breakfast.

GO: *Follow that Bird* is one of the few full-length films that very young children will sit and watch. It's full of great songs and classic cameo performances and it even teaches a wonderful lesson on racism.

SESAME STREET VIDEOS

Random House Home Video
1987-1992
30 minutes each volume
Directed by: Jon Stone and others

What we find most people ask about when it comes to the Sesame Street series is if a particular favorite segment, either animated or live-action, is on a particular video since individual segments are not described on the boxes. Some favorites are Ernie singing Rubber Duckie, that little red ball that rolls down a roller coaster apparatus counting off 1-2-3, Kermit reporting

for Sesame Street news, and What's the Name of That Song Lyric song posters or activity bor are included.

Count It Higher: Great Music Videos from Sesame Street

Hip video jockey Count Von Count hosts this tape of eight songs between which he counts the number of things in the video. Ernie, Kermit, The Count, Oscar and Big Bird all make appearances.

Songs featured are:
Count It Higher
   (by Chris and the Alphabeats)
Counting to 10
   (to the tune of "Twist and Shout")
Do De Rubber Duck (a reggae tune)
Doo Wop Hop
   (a Doobie Brothers style song)
Letter B (by the Beetles)
Honk around the Clock (by the Honkers)
The Ten Commandments of Health (by
   Dr. Thad and the Medications)
Wet Paint (featuring the group How Now
   Brown Cow)
ZZ Blues (by Over the Top)

CAUTION: The video is a parody of adult music and MTV music videos.

Dance Along!

This tape, presented in the style of American TV dance shows, features the Sesame Street kids, demonstration dancers Gina and Mike, Big Bird and the Count all dancing to rock music. Some of the dances are performed in a studio, some on the Sesame Street set, and some are from old Sesame Street clips interspersed with shots of the children in the studio dancing along.

Dances featured are:
ABC Disco
Any Way You Feel Dance
The Batty Bat
The Birdcall Boogie
The Birdland Jump
Doin' the Pigeon
A New Way to Walk
Stop Dancing
A Very Simple Dance to Do

Elmo's Sing-Along Guessing Game

Elmo hosts a TV game show in which contestants must listen to a song, bounce on a trampoline, ring a bell and shout out answers. It might be easy if Elmo didn't keep enthusiastically shouting out the answers. Featuring Kermit, Ernie, Elmo, The Alligator King, Big Bird, Snuffy, Gordon, Olivia, Oscar and The Count.

Songs featured are:
Eight Balls of Fur
Elmo's Song
Get Along
I Love My Elbows
I Love Trash
The Lambaba!
My Best Friend
One Fine Face

Monster Hits

Herry Monster hosts The Fuzzy Awards in which the monster song hit of the year receives the Fuzzy Award. Elmo holds the envelope with the winner's name. Herry is kept busy trying to stop him from opening it before all the songs have been played and before Cookie can eat the envelope. Herry's mother receives a Lifetime Achievement Award.

Songs featured are:
C is For Cookie
Comb Your Face

Frazzle
Fur
Fuzzy and Blue
Healthy Food
Herry's Family Song
That Furry Blue Mommy of Mine
Two Heads Are Better Than One
We Are All Monsters
What Do I Do When I'm Alone

Sesame Songs: Rock and Roll

Deejay Jackman Wolf answers phone requests from Chrissy (a high energy real life teen), Bert, The Count, Officer Little Red Riding Hood, Maria, Gina and Grover. Animation and live-action footage are included. Other Sesame Street characters featured are Ernie and Bert, Oscar, The Cobble Stones, Jerry and the Monotones and Chrissy and the Alphabeats.

Songs featured are:
Count up to Nine
Forty Blocks from My Home
(I Can't Get No) Cooperation
Hand Talk
It's Hip to Be a Square
Monster in the Mirror
Rock 'n' Roll Readers
Telephone Rock
The Word Is No
You're Alive!

Sing, Hoot and Howl with the Sesame Street Animals

The Sing, Hoot and Howl Club is where Big Bird and the Sesame Street animals gather to sing their favorite animal songs. Some of the songs are sung by Sesame Street characters and some are dubbed over live-action footage of real animals. The menagerie includes a horse, a lion, an elephant, a cow, a wolf, a lamb, a pig and a goldfish.

Songs featured are:
Baa Baa Bamba
Hard Working Dog
I Love Being a Pig
I'm an Aardvark
I'm Proud to Be a Cow
The Insects in Your Neighborhood
Laying Eggs Around the Clock
Old MacDonald Had a Farm
Starfish
We Are All Earthlings
Which Came First, the Chicken
   or the Egg?

Sing Yourself Silly

Big Bird, the Count, Ernie and
Kermit introduce some really silly
songs performed by characters from
the Sesame Street programs. "Put
Down the Duckie" features cameos
by Jeremy Irons, Madeline Kahn,
Ladysmith Black Mombazo, Itzak
Perlman, Paul Simon, Danny
DeVito, Pete Seeger and Pee-Wee
Herman.

Songs featured are:
Calcutta Joe
The Everything in the Wrong Place Ball
The Honker Duckie Dinger Jamboree
Jellyman Kelly
I'm Wavin Goodbye to You with My Heart
The Ladybug Picnic
Old MacDonald Cantata
One Banana
Mary Had a Bicycle
Put Down the Duckie
Ten Turtles

Singalong

Bob, Maria, David, Luis, Big Bird,
Olivia, Linda and a group of kids
move a piano up to the apartment
building roof to sing songs together.
They are joined by Sully and Biff,
the construction workers. Some of
the songs are performed by the
group and some are clips from other
Sesame Street programs.

Songs featured are:
The Alphabet Song
Cheer Up
Doin' the Pigeon
John Jacob Jingleheimer Schmidt
Old MacDonald
Rubber Duckie
Sing a Song
   (Olivia and Linda sign this one)
Sing after Me
Stand Up and Pinch Your Nose
We All Sing with the Same Voice
What's the Name of That Song

GO: The songs on this tape are some of
the most popular ever performed on Sesame Street.

SESAME STREET SINGALONG EARTH SONGS

Random House Home Video
1993
30 minutes
Directed by: Emily Squires
Starring the voices of: Frank Oz,
   Carroll Spinney

The Sesame Street Muppets
discuss littering, emissions,
recycling, saving water, proper
disposal of trash, and other aspects
of responsible ecological behavior.
The centerpiece is Grover and his
hiking team, who cannot escape the
pervasive pollution created by
humans, both individually and
collectively.

Songs featured are:
Every Bit of Litter Hurts
Just Throw It My Way
Air!
If Every Kid Did It
On My Pond
I Have a Little Plant
Recycle!

Oscar's Junk Band
Keep the Park Clean
Are You a Wasteroo!
They're a Gift

We All Sing Together

Random House Home Video
1993
30 minutes
Directed by: Ted May

The Monster Report looks at kids. What do they look like? Herry Monster hosts and Elmo the Reporter scoops the big stories. Telly Monster is the on-the-spot newscaster, while Count Von Count counts kids. The monsters eventually learn that while every kid is different, they are also all in essence the same, regardless of race or skin color.

Songs featured are:
Skin
I'm Fixin My Hair
Faces
I'm Happy Bein' Me
Dance Away the Blues
A Family
We're the Same
No Matter Who, No Matter What
My Name is You

SESAME STREET'S 25th BIRTHDAY: A MUSICAL CELEBRATION

Random House Home Video
1993
60 minutes
Directed By: Mustapha Khan, Jon Stone

Outside in the park Big Bird, Telly and Prairie Dawn organize a show but they can't find any La La-ers. New sequences with video effects are added to old favorite segments.

Songs featured are:
Adventure (En Vogue)
Doo Wop Doo Wop
The Batty Bat
The Alligator King
I Love Trash
Count It Higher
Duckie medley (including Rubber Duckie, The Honker Duckie Dinger Jamboree, Put Down the Duckie, Do De Rubber Duck)
Jamaican drumming
C is For Cookie
Monster in The Mirror
I'm An Aardvark
Fuzzy and Blue
Skin
It's Not Easy Being Green
Dance medley (including Happy Tappin', Doin' The Pigeon, I Dance Myself to Sleep)
I Dont Want to Live On The Moon
We Are All Earthlings
Sing (Ladysmith Black Mambazo)

SHARON, LOIS AND BRAM SERIES

These videos are episodes of the highly successful television program, *Sharon, Lois and Bram's Elephant Show*. Each video contains two episodes; some have guest stars and they all have songs.

Animal Pals
(Volume 8)

C/FP Video
1987
60 minutes
Directed by: Wayne Moss (episode 1),
   Michael McNamara (episode 2)
Starring: Murray McLaughlin (episode 1),
   Max the Dog (episode 2)

Urban Cowboy Sharon, Lois and Bram and friends head out to Farmer John's for the weekend for a taste of life on the farm. They do chores, go for a hayride and, of course, sing songs.

Songs featured are:
Ferdinand
Goin' to the Country
Have a Banana, Hanna
Little Boy, Little Girl
The Muffin Man
Straw Hat and Old Dirty Hankies
Uncle Joe
When Other Friendships Be Forgot
   (Friendship)

Pet Fair Sharon, Lois and Bram decide to have a pet fair and everyone enters in hopes of winning big prizes. Elephant doesn't enter the contest until she finds a pet of her own — a friendly stray dog in the park. She's quickly introduced to the responsibility of pet ownership. In the end, everyone wins a prize, even Bram, whose pet rock garners the best-behaved pet award.

Songs featured are:
A Happy Disposition
The Animal Fair
I Had a Pet and My Pet Pleased Me
I Have a Dog and His Name Is Rags
Hercules, King of the Fleas
The Little Green Frog
Rock around the Clock
Three Little Fishes
Twinkle, Twinkle Little Star

Elephant Chef (Volume 11)

C/FP Video
1987
60 minutes
Directed by Eleanor Lindo (episode 1),
   Stan Swan (episode 2)
Starring: Sam Moses (episode 1),
   Circus Shmirkus (episode 2)

Cooking School. The gang hires a chef to teach them the culinary arts, but he turns out to be a complete flake. They then cook a big meal which ends in a pie fight. Elephant saves the day with a special desert, and earns a medal.

Songs featured are:
Among the Leaves So Green-oh
Hi ho hi ho hi ho
Turkey in the Straw
The Caligrow Soirée
Bippity Boppity Boo
Cooking Song
Wishy Washy We
Jelly

Food Show. The gang decides on a pot-luck supper. They gather together the ingredients and sing songs. At the end of the day they've worked so hard they're too tired to eat … except for Elephant.

Songs featured are:
Ha Ha Thisaway
My Little Rooster
Aiken Drum
Ain't it Great to be Crazy
Food Song
Turkey in the Straw
The Echo Song

Elephant Tales (Volume 10)

C/FP Video
1987
60 minutes
Directed by Stan Swan (episode 1)
   Richard Mortimer (episode 2)
Starring: The Shuffle Demons (episode 1),
   Toller Cranston (episode 2)

An Elephant Never Forgets. At a picnic, the trio haul out the photo album. Elephant, who isn't particularly interested in pictures, goes off and promptly gets herself conked by a tetherball, lapsing instantly into a state of amnesia. While Sharon, Lois and Bram go looking for her, Eric makes a replacement guitar for Bram.

Songs featured are:
Here We Go Round the Chingoring
The Seven Seas
A Ricka Bamboo
Number One I Dream of You
Gonna Find You
One Elephant Went Out to Play
Bananas in Pyjamas

Elephant Finds Its Game Lois is channel-switching, and tunes in to an exercise show. Sharon, who has just returned from shopping, gets the idea that they should all exercise. Elephant dreams of becoming a sports champion, but cannot find a sport in which she excels. She tries a variety, including golfing, hiking, and jogging, before finally discovering that she is a born figure skater.

Songs featured are:
Shimmy Shimmy
Golfing Song
All My Life
Flea Fly Mosquito
Lazybones
One Finger One Thumb
Keep Moving
I Am Slowly Going Crazy

Making News (Volume 6)

C/FP Video
1991
60 minutes
Directed by: Eleanor Lindo (episode 1),
    Richard Mortimer (episode 2)
Starring: The Beirdo Brothers and
    Sister Sheila (episode 1),
    Ron Rubin (episode 2)

Newspaper Sharon, Lois and Bram read the newspaper and decide to create a neighborhood paper of their own called *Elephant News*. But they soon discover that the newspaper business is more complicated than they'd expected. Elephant takes terrible pictures, and Bram is the butt of a series of practical jokes.

Songs featured are:
Bizet's Toreador Song
Dear Eric, Dear Eric
Reporting's Lots of Fun
Shoo-fly Pie
The Wheels on the Bus
When Are We Gonna Be Married?
Who Are the People in Your
    Neighborhood?
The Wee Cock Sparrow

Radio Show When the television blows up, Bram gets out the old-fashioned radio and he and the gang are whisked back to 1947 where they hear the old radio shows, *Jimmy Rock, Private Eye* and the zany *theater of the Imagination*.

Songs featured are:
Don't Poke Your Finger in Your Eye,
    Tommy Thumb
Fifteen Years on the Erie Canal
Samba Lalay
A Tisket a Tasket

Out and About
(Volume 9)

C/FP Video
1986
60 minutes
Directed by: Stan Swan
Starring: The Inter-Community Group
    (episode 1), The Leahy Family (episode 2)

Kensington Market Sharon, Lois and Bram and friends go to Kensington market for lunch, where they experience the rich diversity of a multicultural market.

Songs featured are:
Ché Ché
Five Brown Buns
Here We Go Cheerio
How Could Anything Be Wrong With
   Being Different
My Mother Did-A-Tell-Me (Mango Walk)
Portugese Dance Song
She'll be Coming 'Round the Mountain
Sitting Around Playing the Spoons
There Once was a Woman Who
   Gobbled Swiss Cheese
There Was a Little Man
There's a Brown Girl in the Ring

Pioneer Village Sharon, Lois and
Bram go to Black Creek Pioneer
Village during the apple harvest and
learn how pioneers baked, made
brooms and used a printing press.
Elephant makes an apple cake and
Eric eats "eleventy-seven" apples.

Songs featured are:
"A" You're Adorable
ABCDEFG
Hey, Ho, Makes You Feel So Fine
Hop Along Peter Where You Goin'?
Horsey, Horsey, on Your Way
Little Liza Jane
Six Men Went to Mow
Step-dancing by the Leahy Family
There Was an Old Woman
There's a Little Wheel A-turning
   in My Heart
Weevily Wheat

Summer Fun (Volume 7)

C/FP Video
1984
60 minutes
Directed by: Stan Swan
Starring: Denis Simpson (episode 1),
   Susan Mendelson (episode 2)

Amusement Park Sharon, Lois and
Bram go to the amusement park
and goof around with their pal,
Denis. Elephant drives a a train, an
antique car and a swan paddle boat.

Songs featured are:
We Have a Band
The Darby Ram

Hi Ho, Come to the Fair
It's a Small World
Oh, Dear, What Can the Matter Be
Well, Once I Saw Three Goats
When I See an Elephant Fly
Where's Thumbkin

Camp Sharon, Lois and Bram visit
Camp Elephant Walk where they
hike, sing songs and experiment
with different rhythms. Ms
Mendelson makes pita pocket
sandwiches for lunch and Eric
demonstrates some interesting
homemade instruments by the
campfire.

Songs featured are:
Do Si Do Means Dough
Flea Fly Mosquito
Frère Jacques (and R2D2)
Here We Go Looby-Loo
Home On the Range
I'm Going to Leave Ol' Texas Now
John Jacob Jingleheimer Schmidt
One More Hour
Piccolo Mine
Row, Row, Row Your Boat
Three Chants from Ghana, the West
   Indies and Mexico

SHARON, LOIS AND BRAM SING A TO Z

Elephant Records
1992
50 minutes
Directed by: Don Allan

In this live concert, Sharon, Lois and
Bram and Elephant sing a song for
every letter of the alphabet.

Songs featured are:
ABCDEFG
B-I-N-G-O
C-H-I-C-K-E-N
Come Ride with Me

Down in the Valley
Five Little Fishes
Grampa's Farm
Ham and Eggs
Hush Little Baby
Ice Cream
In the Land of the Pale Blue Snow
Jelly Man Kelly
Junior Birdsmen
Kitty Come Kimo
Little Sir Echo
The Lollipop Song
Mares Eat Oats (Mairzy Doats)
The Name Game
The Play Song
Skinamarink
S-M-I-L-E
There's a New World Coming
Tongue-Twisters
Tzena, Tzena
Up in the Air
W-a-l-k in the P-a-r-k

SHINING TIME STATION

Kid Vision
1993
35 minutes each
Directed by: Wayne Moss
Starring: George Carlin, Didi Conn,
    Tom Jackson, Erica Luttrell, Ari Magder,
    Danielle Marcotte

Each episode of Shining Time Station chronicles the happenings in the railroad station of the town of Shining Time (pop. 5008). The main characters are Mr. Conductor, a magical miniature storyteller; Becky, a young girl; Stacey, the ticket agent; her young nephew Dan; Billy Twofeathers the handyman; Mr. King, the manager of the railroad; and Schemer, the sleazy arcade manager. Mr. Conductor introduces and tells a "Thomas the Tank Engine" story in every episode.

Becky Makes a Wish (Vol. 4)

Becky is bored. Mr. Conductor tells her the story of Duck's fervent wish to sail away to far-off lands. Mr. Conductor's bag of wishes, with a wishing star in it, accidentally comes into the hands of Schemer, who promptly releases the star, and a flood of fulfilled wishes. Chaos ensues, until Becky manages to wish eveything back to normal.

CAUTION: There is a brief but bizarre image of a busybody with a zipper across her mouth.

Bully for Mr. Conductor (Vol. 3)

When Stacey has to go to Chubby Corners, Mr. King takes over. Dan and Becky have to play with Mr. King's horrible nephew Buster, who is a bully. Mr. Conductor tells the story of Bulgie, a nasty bus who tells lies about the railroad on the island of Sodor. Dan then learns that the only way to deal with bullies is to stand up to them.

CAUTION: Buster repeatedly threatens to beat Dan up.

Schemer's Alone (Vol. 2)

Schemer's mother goes away overnight, leaving him a list of chores. He gets everyone to do them for him with insincere promises of payment, a scheme which eventually backfires on him. Mr. Conductor tells the story of the bossy James, who badmouths Percy. Percy subsequently rescues James, but he himself gets into a jam with his holier-than-thou attitude.

Stacey Cleans Up (Vol. 1)

It's garbage day at Shining Time Station, and top reporter Ted Typo shows up with blockbuster news: the Shining Time Garbage Dump has closed. To make matters worse, a smelly "garbage train" run by crusty old engineer Rusty McRail camps out on a siding. Mr. Conductor tells the story of James and the Bees, and the Shining Time gang learns a lesson in the essentials of composting and recycling.

STORIES TO REMEMBER COLLECTION

This set of videotapes is an elaborately produced, award-winning collection of animated children's stories. Rich voice talent and continuous music accompany a variety of animation styles. Other titles in the series include: *Beauty and the Beast*, *Merlin and the Dragons*, *Noah's Ark* and *Pegasus*. See Ages 3-6 for more information.

Baby's Bedtime

Oak Street Music
1989
26 minutes
Directed by: Daniel Ivanick
Starring the voice of: Judy Collins

Adapted from *The Baby's Bedtime Book* by Kay Chorao into a fully-animated video, this tape has original songs by Ernest Troost and lullabies sung by Judy Collins. Winner of a Cine Golden Eagle Award for Outstanding Children's Films.

Songs and rhymes set to music are:
Hush Little Baby (Mockingbird)
The Land of Nod
Lullaby and Good Night

Baby's Morningtime

Oak Street Music1989
30 minutes
Directed by: Daniel Ivanick
Starring the voice of: Judy Collins

This fully-animated video, based on Kay Chorao's best-selling book *The Baby's Good Morning Book*, features Judy Collins singing and reciting the poems of Robert Browning, Emily Dickinson and Gertrude Stein. All designed to help parents and children greet the day. Set to music by award-winning composer Ernest Troost.

Baby's Nursery Rhymes

Oak Street Music
1991
26 minutes
Directed by: Russell Calabrese
  and Jeffrey Gatrall
Starring the voice of: Phylicia Rashad
Music By: Jason Miles

This award-winning fully animated video, based on *The Baby's Lap Book* by Kay Chorao, contains 36 nursery rhymes. An orchestra accompanies a little stage presentation of the rhymes with animated animals in the starring roles. Animation is similar to book illustrations with moving elements.

Rhymes featured are:
Sing A Song of Sixpence
Hickety Pickety My Black Hen
Humpty Dumpty
Mary Had A Little Lamb
There Was A Crooked Man

Little Miss Muffet
Little Jack Horner
It's Raining, It's Pouring
Doctor Foster Went to Gloucester
Rub A Dub Dub
This Little Pig Went To Market
Baa, Baa Black Sheep
Little Boy Blue
Jack and Jill
Old Mother Hubbard
Oh Where Has My Little Dog Gone?
Little Tom Tinker's Dog
Charlie Barley Butter and Eggs
Ding Dong Bell Pussy's In The Well
Pussy Cat, Pussy Cat,
   Where Have You Been?
Mary, Mary Quite Contrary
There Was a Little Girl
   Who Had A Little Curl
Little Bo-Peep
Old King Cole
Hey Diddle Diddle
Three Little Kittens
The North Wind Doth Blow
Little Poor Parrot Sat In His Garret
Jack Be Nimble
Wee Willy Winkie
Goosey Goosey Gander
Hickory Dickory Dock
Three Blind Mice
Rockabye Baby
There Was An Old Woman
Tossed Up In A Basket
Twinkle Twinkle Little Star

CAUTION: Rhymes sung to synthesized contemporary lounge music.

Baby's Storytime

Oak Street Music
1989
26 minutes
Directed by: Michael Sporn
Starring the voice of: Arlo Guthrie

Based on Kay Choao's book *The Baby's Story Book*, this animated video features the voice and storytelling of singer/songwriter Arlo Guthrie. Winner of a Cine Golden Eagle Award for Outstanding Children's Films.

Stories featured are:
The Ginger Bread Boy
The Hare and the Turtle
Henny Penny
The History of the Apple Pie
The Lion and the Mouse
The Little Red Hen
Little Red Riding Hood
The Princess and the Pea
The Three Billy Goats Gruff
The Three Little Pigs
The Wind and the Sun

CAUTION: All of the videos in the Stories to Remember collection are animated; there is no live action. Waltzes and folk-style tunes are used, making the videos low key and less stimulating than other videos at this level.

GO: These gentle videos are well-done and are edited to the rhythm of the music.

■

THE THOMAS THE TANK ENGINE AND FRIENDS COLLECTION

Britt Allcroft's production of *Thomas the Tank Engine and Friends* is based on The Reverend W. Awdry's books, *The Railway Series*. Each multi-episode video combines working model electric trains with still models to tell the stories produced for the popular PBS TV series, *Shining Time Station*. Each video contains about seven short stories about the Island of Sodor where station master Sir Topham-Hatt runs an efficient railway system with the mischievous engine, Thomas, and his friends. Because people frequently order these videos by the color of the box, we have included this information for each title.

Daisy and Other Stories
(pink)

Strand Home Video
37 minutes each
1992
Directed by: David Mitton
Voices by: George Carlin

Daisy When Thomas is in for repair, Sir Topham-Hatt sends Daisy, a brand new but lazy diesel engine, as a replacement.

Percy's Predicament When lazy Daisy leaves the milk car behind, Percy and Toby have more work, but they decide to switch duties: Toby takes the milk and Percy fetches Toby's freight cars. Percy has an accident, forcing Daisy to learn to work hard.

Whistles and Sneezes Gordon complains about Henry's new shape and tendency to whistle too much. Gordon's whistle sticks in place, and he is embarrassed about what he said. Some boys drop rocks on Henry's coaches, so Henry sneezes soot on them.

Saved From Scrap Edward asks the vicar to save Trevor, an old-fashioned traction engine, from being broken up at the scrapyard.

A New Friend For Thomas Edward introduces Trevor the traction engine to Thomas. Thomas, who is pulling metal pilings, takes Trevor to the harbor. The track is blocked and Trevor drags the piling into place.

Tender Engines Gordon feels he needs tender cars, but becomes worried when told that diesel engines do not need tenders and will therefore replace tank engines.

Henry, who also wants a tender, is tricked by Duck into pulling six old, dirty tenders.

Percy Takes the Plunge Percy disobeys a Danger sign and asks his freight cars to push him on. They push too much and Percy slides into the harbor.

James Goes Buzz Buzz
(navy)

Strand Home Video
37 minutes each
1993
Directed by: David Mitton
Voices by: George Carlin

James Goes Buzz Buzz James boasts that bees do not bother him. While being loaded, a beehive breaks, and the bees swarm around him. To get them off, James must take them to a new beehive.

One Good Turn Bill and Ben, the twin engines, are asked to help the other engines. They get in each other's way at the turntable and start to feud. Sir Topham-Hatt forces them to work together, settling their dispute.

Bertie's Chase When Thomas is late, Bertie the bus must take Thomas' passengers to Edward. Edward leaves and Bertie must catch up to deliver the passengers on time.

Heroes Bill and Ben are asked to help with Edward's cars, but are very late. When a rock slide occurs at the quarry, they save the workmen and are praised by Sir Topham-Hatt.

Bulgy Bulgy, a mean bus, tries to outrun Duck with the passengers. He gets stuck under a bridge, and Duck rescues the passengers.

Wrong Road A mishap at the station causes Edward to run on the main line, and Gordon, the bigger engine, to run on the smaller branch line.

Percy, James and the Fruitful Day James complains of Percy's tardiness. James' brakes jam while carrying fruit, and Percy is asked to help. Percy goes too fast, does not see a wrongly switched track, crashes, squashing the fruit everywhere.

James Learns a Lesson and Other Stories (red)

STRAND V.C.I. Entertainment
1985
40 minutes
Directed by: David Mitton
Voices by Ringo Starr

James Learns a Lesson James, a cocky special mixed traffic engine, talks back to Sir Topham-Hatt and gets into trouble.

Foolish Freight Cars After completing an extremely difficult trip, Sir Topham-Hatt congratulates James on his perseverance.

A Proud Day for James Gordon, an old double engine, teases James about his mishaps until the day Gordon is unable to pull the express and James is asked to fill in.

Thomas and the Conductor Thomas is impatient with Henry, the conductor, and leaves him behind. To make up for lost time Thomas runs the route faster than ever before.

Thomas Goes Fishing When the water station closes down, Thomas is filled with river water and his boiler almost bursts because it's full of fish.

Terence the Tractor When Terence helps Thomas out of a snow bank, Thomas is thankful for Terence's unique ability.

Thomas and Bertie's Great Race Thomas races Bertie the Bus.

Better Late Than Never and Other Stories (purple)

STRAND V.C.I. Entertainment
1986
40 minutes
Directed by: David Mitton
Voices by Ringo Starr

Better Late Than Never Bertie is angry with Thomas for always being late, but when Bertie breaks down, it's Thomas who arrives to take Bertie's passengers home.

Pop Goes the Weasel A boastful new diesel comes to work and causes a great deal of damage when he ignores instructions and tries to move the wrong cars.

Diesel's Devious Deed Diesel tells the cars nasty stories about Gordon, Henry and Thomas and says that Duck made them up. Furious, the engines send Duck away.

A Close Shave for Duck Mischievous cars try to run Duck off the rails, but he bravely manages to stop them from causing a serious accident.

Gordon Takes a Dip When Gordon is asked to pull a special train, he considers the job to be beneath him and in trying to jam the turntable gets himself stuck in a ditch.

Down the Mine Thomas gets stuck in the mine and Gordon must pull him out.

The Runaway When his newly repaired brake is not applied,

Thomas slides away without a driver and must be rescued by Harold the Helicopter and the Inspector.

helps to clean up the mess. Sir Topham-Hatt rewards Thomas by giving him his own branch line.

Thomas Gets Tricked and Other Stories (blue)

STRAND V.C.I. Entertainment
1986
40 minutes
Directed by: David Mitton
Voices by Ringo Starr

Thomas Gets Tricked Tired of hearing Thomas call him lazy, Gordon tricks Thomas into pulling his express route. In the end, an exhausted Thomas realizes that Gordon isn't lazy at all.

Edward Helps Out Rarely removed from the shed, Edward is excited when he's finally taken out to do some work. The other engines jealously belittle his contributions until Gordon gets stuck and Edward saves the day.

Come Out, Henry! Henry refuses to work in the rain for fear of spoiling his beautiful paint and takes refuge in a tunnel. In the end, the soot and dirt from the tunnel spoil his paint.

Henry to the Rescue Sir Topham-Hatt coaxes Henry out of the tunnel to help Edward pull Gordon's load to the end of the line.

A Big Day for Thomas When Henry is ill, Thomas is asked to pull the passenger cars. He's so excited he starts off before the coaches are hooked up, feeling very important and looking very silly.

Trouble for Thomas When he swaps jobs with Edward, the cars Thomas is pulling cause him to go so fast that he nearly crashes.

Thomas Saves the Day James is forced into an accident and Thomas

Tenders and Turntables and Other Stories (yellow)

STRAND V.C.I. Entertainment
1989
40 minutes
Directed by: David Mitton
Voices by Ringo Starr

Tenders and Turntables While Thomas is running his own branch line, the important tender engines are angered by the increased workload and decide to go on strike.

Trouble in the Shed Sir Topham-Hatt temporarily replaces the striking tender engines with Edward, Thomas and a new tank engine named Percy.

Percy Runs Away Percy is so frightened after Gordon almost runs into him that he runs away. He's finally stopped by a clever signal box operator.

Thomas Comes to Breakfast Thomas foolishly decides to run the line without his driver. The next morning when a careless cleaner fiddles with his controls, Thomas runs into the side of the Stationmaster's house and sees the value of having someone at the controls.

Henry's Special Coal It is discovered that Henry needs special coal because his firebox is too small to process regular coal properly.

The Flying Kipper Henry runs into another freight train during a blizzard.

Toby the Tram Sir Topham-Hatt has to shut Toby's line down because fewer people are buying tickets and trucks are taking over the shipping industry. This story continues in the *Thomas Breaks the Rules* video

Thomas Breaks the Rules and Other Stories (green)

> STRAND V.C.I. Entertainment
> 1989
> 40 minutes
> Directed by: David Mitton
> Voices by Ringo Starr

Thomas Breaks the Rules A policeman stops Thomas for not having a cow-catcher or wheel-covers.

A Cow on the Line Gordon and Henry boast that cows on the tracks would never stop them, until some do.

Old Iron Edward proves he's useful when he saves a runaway James.

Double Trouble Thomas and Percy make up after an argument.

James in a Mess James crashes into a tar wagon after making fun of Toby and Henrietta.

Duck Takes Charge A new engine named Duck stands up for Edward.

Percy Proves a Point Percy proves that he's not slow and out-of-date.

Thomas Gets Bumped and Other Stories (white)

> STRAND V.C.I. Entertainment
> 1991
> 37 minutes
> Directed by: David Mitton

Thomas Gets Bumped Bertie the Bus helps Thomas out with his passengers and returns a favor.

Edward, Trevor and the Really Useful Party Trevor the traction engine is the star of the vicar's garden party fund-raiser.

Diesel Does It Again When Percy and Duck are forced to work with the oily Diesel, they go on strike.

Gordon and the Famous Visitor A famous engine comes to visit Sodor. Pompous Gordon gets jealous and tries to match the famous engine's record but only succeeds in blowing his dome.

Donald's Duck Duck works hard and earns his own branch line. Donald gives him a hard time until Duck plays a joke on Donald, putting a duck in his water tank. Donald gets him back in fine fashion.

Percy and the Signal Percy loves playing jokes until Gordon and James pay him back with a joke of their own.

Thomas, Percy and the Mail Train Because mail service by rail permits delivery in all kinds of weather, plans to replace it with air mail service are abandoned.

Thomas, Percy and the Dragon and Other Stories (silver)

> STRAND Home Video
> 1991
> 37 minutes
> Directed by: David Mitton

Thomas, Percy and the Dragon Sometimes Percy teases Thomas about being frightened, but the tables are turned when Percy thinks he sees a dragon.

Donald and Douglas Twin engines from Scotland cause confusion. When a brake van takes a dislike to Douglas and Donald is involved in an accident, Douglas is left to push.

The Deputation Donald and Douglas, afraid Sir Topham-Hatt will send one of them back to Scotland, prove how valuable they are.

Time for Trouble James does Gordon's job and when Toby is stranded on the mainline James must push Toby.

A Scarf for Percy One cold winter Percy wants a scarf for his funnel. Instead he has a pair of trousers twisted around his funnel after an accident in which he gets covered with ham.

The Diseasel Bill and Ben are twin tank engine diesels who pull cars at the harbor.

Edward's Exploits When old Edward struggles to move a heavy train, he is derided by Gordon and James. Later, he breaks a crank pin, but still manages to get back to the station, battered but unbeaten.

Trust Thomas and Other Stories (orange)

> STRAND Home Video
> 1985
> 40 minutes
> Directed by: David Mitton

Trust Thomas Thomas recovers a missing load of tar to repair Bertie's rough road.

Mavis Mavis ignores Toby's advice and gets stuck crossing an icy portion of the line. Toby agrees to help only because Mavis was doing a job that he was supposed to do.

Toby's Tightrope When the bridge is falling apart, lazy Mavis redeems herself by preventing certain disaster.

No Joke for James To prove to Gordon that Sir Topham-Hatt has

great plans for him, James takes Gordon's passenger coaches and leaves Gordon with the freight cars.

Percy's Promise Even when bad weather floods the tracks, Percy and Harold manage to pull two coaches full of children home.

Henry's Forest When a strong wind destroys the trees in Henry's favorite forest, Toby helps him transport new trees to plant.

The Trouble with Mud When Gordon refuses to be cleaned, James is asked to pull the express instead.

CAUTION: The characters in the series are often jealous and insulting (often telling each other to shut up) and not every argument is completely resolved. At times, Ringo Starr's accent is difficult to understand and he frequently uses British words and expressions not familiar to North American audiences. There are only three female characters in the series. Although the creators of these videos recommend them for children ages two to seven, we recommend them only for children under five.

GO: Cleverly produced and gentle in tone, the stories move quickly, but without the manic tempo of some programs, and most are complete in themselves so it's easy to stop the video and save the rest for another time. *Shining Time Station* is one of the few videos featuring trains available for young children and has won an Emmy, an Action for Children's Television award and a Parents' Choice award.

■

WEE SING COLLECTION

(continued on next page)

The Wee Sing videos are based on the highly successful book and audio series created by mothers Susan Hagen Nipp and Pamela Conn Beall. They feature children and adults singing and dancing to up-tempo versions of favorite songs. Each tape has a simple story-line of songs interspersed with dialogue and includes finger-plays, fanciful creature costumes and puppets. Music arranged by Cal Scott. A song book is included with each tape.

The Best Christmas Ever

Price Stern Sloan Video
1990
60 minutes
Directed by: Claudia Sloan
Starring: Melanie Chang, R. Dee,
   Sam Howard, Vic McGraw,
   Robert Milam, Sarah Werle

Susie, Johnny, Nellie and Will go to Santa's workshop where they solve a problem for the elves.

Rhymes and finger plays featured are:
The Chimney
Chubby Little Snowman
Down through the Chimney
Here Are Mother's Knives and Forks
Star Light Star Bright
Tapping, Tapping Little Elf
'Twas the Night before Christmas
Two Little Christmas Trees
When Santa Comes

Songs featured are:
Angel Band
Christmas Is Coming
Christmas Wrap
Deck the Halls, Christmas Day
Gusty the Elf
Here We Come A-Caroling
Jolly Old St. Nicholas
Little Bells of Christmas
Oh Christmas Tree
Santa Claus Is Coming
Up on the Housetop
We Wish You a Merry Christmas

Grandpa's Magical Toys

Price Stern Sloan Video
1988
60 minutes
Directed by: Susan Shadburne
Starring: Kevin Hageman, Sharene Mackall,
   Francisco Reynders, Daniel Straugh

Peter, David and Sarah visit Grandpa's toy-making workshop where they shrink down to the size of toys and play singing and clapping games and jump rope.

Songs featured are:
A Sailor Went to Sea
Did You Ever See a Lassie?
The Farmer in the Dell
Hambone
The Hokey-Pokey
I Love Coffee
Long-Legged Sailor
Mabel, Mabel
The Merry-Go-Round
Miss, Miss
The Muffin Man
One Potato
One, Two, Buckle My Shoe
One, Two, Three A-Twirlsy
One, Two, Three O'Leary
Playmate
Pretty Little Dutch Girl
Punchinello
Roll That Red Ball
Who Stole the Cookies
   from the Cookie Jar?

In the Big Rock Candy Mountains

Price Stern Sloan Video
1991
60 minutes
Directed by: David Poulshock
Starring: Renee Davis, Lisa White

Lisa takes the Snoodle-Doodles (stuffed bears that come alive) to the magical land of the Big Rock Candy Mountains for a picnic where they sing, tell stories and play games.

Songs featured are:
Baby Bird
The Big Rock Candy Mountains
The Fly Has Married the Bumble Bee
Follow Me
For He's a Jolly Good Fellow
The Hammer Song
Howdy-Ho-Hiya
Jimmy Crack Corn
Little Bunny Foo Foo
Nobody Knows the Trouble I've Seen
Nobody Loves Me, Everybody Hates Me
Rillaby Rill
Ring Around the Rosey
Row, Row, Row Your Boat
S.M.I.L.E.
This Is the Way We Wash Our Hands
The Upward Trail

King Cole's Party: A Merry Musical Celebration

Price Stern Sloan Video
1987
60 minutes
Directed by: Susan Shadburne
Starring: Gary Basey, Zina Moreno,
    Joshua Taylor, Wendy
    Westerwelle

Everyone is invited to King Cole's castle to celebrate 100 years of peace. Jack and Jill, Mary and her lamb, Little Boy Blue, Humpty Dumpty and King Cole himself are all in attendance.

Nursery rhymes featured are:
Betty Botter
Humpty Dumpty Sat on a Wall
Jack and Jill
Jack, Be Nimble
Jack Sprat
Little Bo-Peep
Little Boy Blue
Little Jack Horner
Little Miss Muffet
Little Tommy Tucker
Mary Had a Little Lamb
Old King Cole
Pat-A-Cake
Pease Porridge Hot

Peter Piper
Polly Put the Kettle On
Rub-a-Dub-Dub
See-Saw Sac-Ra-Down
Sing a Song of Sixpence
Six Little Ducks
There Was a Crooked Man
This Old Man
Walking Chant
Wibbleton to Wobbleton

Wee Sing in Sillyville

Price Stern Sloan Video
1989
60 minutes
Directed by: David Poulshock
Starring: Joy Anderson,
    Renee Margolin, Ryan Willard

When no one is getting along in the coloring book land of Sillyville, Barney the basset hound and his owners, Laurie and Scott, magically pay a visit and help Sillywhim bring peace.

Songs featured are:
A Cold upon His Chest
An Austrian Went Yodelling
Boom, Boom, Ain't It Great to Be Crazy?
Do Your Ears Hang Low?
Down by the Bay
Fish and Chips and Vinegar
I'm A Nut
John Jacob Jingleheimer Schmidt
The Little Green Frog
Make New Friends
Michael Finnegan
Rillaby, Rallaby, Mauw, Mauw, Mauw
Roll Over
Sing Together a Joyous Song
We're Here Because We're Here

Wee Sing Together

Price Stern Sloan Video
1985
60 minutes
Directed by: John W. Mincey Jr.
Starring: Aaron Cooley,
    Marky Mason, Hollie Weikel

On the night of her sixth birthday, Sally's toys Melody Mouse and Hum Bear come to life and take her and her brother, Jonathan, to Wee Sing Park where they celebrate with Wee Rabbit Peter III and a real dog named Bingo.

Songs featured are:
The Alphabet Song
Bingo
The Finger Band
Head and Shoulders
Here We Go Looby Loo
I'm a Little Tea Pot
If You're Happy and You Know It Clap Your Hands
The Itsy Bitsy Spider
Knees and Toes
Little Peter Rabbit
    Had a Fly upon His Ear
Old MacDonald Had a Farm
Rain, Rain Go Away
Rickety Tickety Look at Me
Sally's Wearing a Red Dress
Skidamirink
Teddy Bear
Twinkle Twinkle Little Star
Walking, Running, Now Let's Stop

Wee Sing Train

Price, Stern, Sloan Video
1993
60 minutes
Directed by: Claudia Sloane
Starring: Kaci Garcia, Andrew Goodman

Casey and Carter play train in their room until Wee Sing magic shrinks the kids down into their own train set. Tusky, their toy elephant, takes them on the talking train where they meet singing cowboys and dancing paper dolls, save Tusky from a rooftop, watch broccoli sing opera, visit singing farm animals, talk to two little black birds and an enchanted frog-prince, meet a beautiful blonde princess, and cooperate in moving a tree from the rail-line.

Songs featured are:
Down By The Station
Train Is A-Comin'
Get On Board/Wee Sing Train
Home On The Range
Old Chisholm Trail
Chuggin' Along
Put Your Little Foot
Hey, Mr. Knickerbocker
Engine, Engine
The Vegetable Song
Had A Little Rooster
The Old Gray Mare
I Love the Mountains
The Train Went Over The Mountain
Keemo, Kymo
Jennie Jenkins
You Are Special
I've Been Working On The Railroad

GO: Elaborate sets and costumes, unaffected children, unusual traditional songs played by an actual band (*not* a synthesizer) and a thread of a story make this music video series a cut above the rest.

Coming soon: Wee Sing Under the Sea

Wee Sing in the Marvelous Musical Mansion

Price Stern Sloan Video
1992
60 minutes
Directed by: David Poulshock

Alex, Benji, Kelly and Auntie Annabella visit Great Uncle Rubato and his cat Cadenza in the Marvelous Musical Mansion.

Songs featured are:
The Ballerina's Waltz
Clap Your Hands
The Doodle-Det Quintet!
Hey Diddle Diddle
Hickory Dickory Dock
How Do You Do, My Friends
The Magic of Music
The Marching Song
The Melody Song
My Aunt Came Back

My Hat It Has Three Corners
Oh, When the Saints Go Marching In
Oh Where, Oh Where Has the Little
  Gong Gone
The Orchestra Game Song
Round the Clock
Rueben and Rachel
She'll Be Coming 'Round the Mountain
Tap-A-Capella
Vive La Compagnie

CAUTION: The sound track is over-dubbed and most of the music is synthesized. The producers recommend the series for children ages two to eight, but because the stories tend to be babyish, we recommend it only for children under five years of age.

GO: The Wee Sing videos have simple story lines and contain no violence, sarcasm or conflict; they have positive themes and demonstrate good relationships. This is a good series for young children who are just beginning to watch complete story videos.

■

WINNIE -THE-POOH CLASSICS SERIES

The following films are based on the characters and stories from the books by A. A. Milne, but include dialogue contributed by other writers.

Winnie-the-Pooh and a Day for Eeyore

Walt Disney Home Video
1983
25 minutes
Directed by: Rick Reinert
Starring the voice of: Paul Winchell

Pooh, Piglet, Rabbit and Roo are playing Pooh Sticks when they see Eeyore floating down the river on his back. After a daring rescue, Eeyore explains that Tigger had bounced him into the river (the latter claims that it was only a joke) and goes on to complain about the fact that no one has remembered his birthday. Christopher Robin saves the day when he throws Eeyore a party with cake and presents and everyone goes to play Pooh Sticks together.

■

Winnie-the-Pooh and the Blustery Day

Walt Disney Home Video
1968
25 minutes
Directed by: Wolfgang Reitherman
Starring the voices of:
  Sebastian Cabot, Sterling Holloway,
  Paul Winchell

On a windy day, Pooh visits Owl whose whole tree has been blown over by the gale. That night the wind rages on and Pooh hears strange sounds. It is Tigger (introduced in this story) who bounces in and out singing. Later Pooh falls asleep and dreams of strange elephant and weasel-like creatures he calls heffalumps and woozles. When he awakes, the Hundred Acre Wood is flooded and Piglet must send a message in a bottle. However, when everyone is rescued they have a Hero Party and Eeyore finds a new house for Owl. Songs are interspersed throughout the story.

Songs featured are:
Happy Windsday
Heffalumps and Woozles
The Wonderful Thing about Tiggers

61

CAUTION: Some children may be frightened by the storm and the dream-sequence in which plaid creatures continuously change shapes.

■

Winnie-the-Pooh and the Honey Tree

Walt Disney Home Video
1965
25 minutes
Directed by: Wolfgang Reitherman
Starring the voices of:
Sterling Holloway, Howard Morris,
Sebastian Cabot

After a failed attempt at disguising himself as a little black rain cloud to steal honey from the bees, Winnie-the-Pooh raids Rabbit's honey pantry instead. He eats so much honey and becomes so big that he gets stuck in the doorway when he tries to leave. Unable to remove the pudgy bear, Christopher Robin, Rabbit, Gopher and Owl decide to postpone their efforts for a few days until Pooh becomes thin again.

Songs featured are:
I'm Just a Little Black Rain Cloud
There's a Rumbly in My Tumbly

CAUTION: Some children may be frightened by the stinging bees.
■

Winnie-the-Pooh and Tigger Too

Walt Disney Home Video
1974
25 minutes
Directed by: John Lounsbery
Starring the voices of:
Sterling Holloway, Sebastian Cabot,
Paul Winchell

Rabbit is so bothered by Tigger's bouncing that he convinces the gang to help him with a plan to "take the bounce out of [Tigger]." One cold misty morning they all go for a walk and "lose" Tigger, but their plan backfires when Pooh, Piglet and Rabbit are the ones who really get lost. Tigger does learn to control his bouncing, however, when after one tremendous bounce he finds himself stuck in a tree. This tape also contains the sequence in which Pooh tracks a mysterious creature around a tree.

CAUTION: Very little ones are sometimes wound up or frightened by the high energy of Tigger's bounciness. Too, the thought of getting lost in the woods may frighten some children.

GO: At around twenty-five minutes each, the animated tapes in the Winnie-the-Pooh series are good first animated films for young viewers. True to the original stories, Christopher Robin has an English accent. For more Pooh stories see also *The New Adventures of Winnie-the-Pooh* (ages 3 to 6 section).
■

Chapter 4

VIDEOS FOR AGES THREE TO SIX

At a certain stage in any child's life, the stories he or she is told, reads or sees on the screen are going to become more sophisticated. With that increase in sophistication will come an increase in the intensity of the situations in which the story's characters find themselves. Where only a short time ago your child was watching the musical antics of the Sillyville characters and learning how to count with Richard Scarry's Busytown gang, he or she is now approaching the cannibal witch's house with Hansel and Gretel. And things just might get a tad unpleasant.

True, if your child were reading the story *Hansel and Gretel*, the experience probably wouldn't be very traumatic. But when the drama is acted out on the television screen, there is a quantum jump in the intensity of the experience. Your child no longer has the power to control the images that tell the story (with a book, a child can create a monster only as scary as his or her imagination will allow); adults have harnessed artistic talent and technology to create what is, for a child, the unimaginable.

But instead of simply saying book equals good, video equals bad, and putting the VCR in the yard sale, let's look at a few ways you can make video-watching a positive experience, by teaching your child to use the same control they use when reading a book. Video watching needn't be a passive experience.

When reading, children can:

▶ imagine the detail for themselves
▶ control the pace (reading as fast or as slowly as they want)
▶ pause to think about scenes they have not understood
▶ skim scary content, and linger on the rest
▶ skip graphic descriptions.

The same control is available when you and your child are watching a video. You can:

▶ Stop the action to discuss with your child how an image may have been created, stressing the fact that one doesn't have to accept the filmmaker's version of, for instance, the witch. (My witches' faces are always blue, but the filmmaker's are green. What color are your witches' faces?) This will help to demystify a character and possibly reduce a child's fear.
▶ Fast-forward over scary parts.
▶ Turn the sound down (or even off) to reduce the intensity of the experience, to reinforce pleasant images.
▶ Rewind and review parts your child likes.
▶ Freeze-frame or play in slow-motion parts your child likes, for extra fun.
▶ Demonstrate that it is your child who has control over the evil or frightening images on a video, and not the other way around.

One parent we know was watching *The Wizard of Oz* with his four-year-old daughter. When the Wicked Witch appeared, his child, like so many others, was terrified. But then he had a brilliant idea. He handed her the remote control, pointed out the Pause button and said: Make the witch stop.

When the child pressed the button indicated, the witch magically froze.

The child was amazed. And when she learned how to use the Fast-forward and Rewind buttons to make the witch go away, it was a different ball game. Terror was a thing of the past, and *The Wizard of Oz* became her favorite movie.

Try to establish your child's control over frightening images early because he or she will be bothered by things you can't possibly anticipate. A video which thrills your neighbor's four-year-old may terrify yours — and vice versa. We have, for instance, heard of children who were afraid of:

- Puff the Magic Dragon . . . but only when he sang
- the balloon in the film *The Red Balloon*
- fireworks, after seeing the scene in *Mary Poppins* in which Admiral Boom shoots fireworks at the dancing chimney-sweeps
- Sesame Street's The Count
- Polkaroo (Who could be less scary than Polkaroo?)

Inevitably, after a certain period of time, characters and situations will lose their power to frighten your little viewers.

MOVING FROM LIVE-ACTION TO ANIMATION

We created the ages three to six category when we first began our business; however, experience has since taught us that this is a tremendously wide age range, which spans many developmental periods in the viewing preferences of children.

People often associate very young children with animation, and literally hundreds of times parents have come into our store believing that their three-year-old is abnormal because he or she shows no interest whatsoever in Bugs Bunny. But the fact of the matter is that for most children, live-action (or real people) is the preferred entertainment from babyhood right through to the age of four. These productions (which are usually concert or song videos) rarely exceed one hour in length, which seems to be the outer limit of the average three-year-old's attention span.

But around the age of four this preference changes, and suddenly children become interested in cartoon images. There are some four-year-olds who want nothing but animation, and whose entire perception of fairy tales, folklore and legends is learned through that medium.

One day, in the children's theater in our store, we were showing the Errol Flynn version of *Robin Hood*. A four-year-old came in, plunked himself down, studied the morning's offering and asked: What's this?

When the answer came that it was Robin Hood, he gave us a skeptical look and said: That's not Robin Hood; Robin Hood's a fox!

(Incidentally, if you want to use videos to introduce your child to fairy tales in their traditional form, be careful. Fairy tales and nursery rhymes are easy targets for updating or satirizing. Not everything on video with a fairy tale or nursery rhyme in the title will be the version you expect.)

Watch out! Not all cartoons are made for children

Some animations are not created specifically for children and some are not for children's eyes at all. Older children may be able to watch some, though parental guidance (and maybe even previewing) will be in order.

Specific examples of animations for mature viewers (some with adult themes and terrifying representations of evil) are:

- ▶ *The Point*, a morality tale about self-sufficiency and the absurdity of prejudice
- ▶ *Watership Down*, a social comment on ecology
- ▶ Ralph Bakshi's *Lord of the Rings*
- ▶ *Who Framed Roger Rabbit?*

Animations that are definitely *not* for children are:

- ▶ Ralph Bakshi's *Wizards*, *Fritz the Cat*, *Heavy Traffic* and *Cool World*
- ▶ *When the Wind Blows*, which is about the aftermath of a nuclear explosion
- ▶ *Animal Farm*, a political satire
- ▶ *Heavy Metal*, a sexy collection of stories originally featured in the illustrated French magazine *Metal*

Hurlant and the American *Heavy Metal*.

▶ *Akira*, about government experiments on psychic children in a post-nuclear war Tokyo

Be careful. Often video personnel will put these films in the children's section simply because they believe that all animated films are for children. Read the box before you rent.

A wealth of animation choices

If you are looking for animations of high quality there are many on the market. Some are now out of print, but are still available for rental at some stores. Don't forget to read the box, because even though an animation can be of high quality, the story may not be to your taste.

Look for:

▶ the VidAmerica series called *Forever Fairy Tales*

▶ Michael Sporn's *Abel's Island*, *The Story of the Dancing Frog*, *The Marzipan Pig*, and *Nonsense and Lullabyes*, and Sony's *The Snowman*, *Granpa* and BMG's *The Angel and the Soldier Boy*

▶ the Children's Circle series, featuring animation styles derived from the illustrations of well-known books such as *Dr. De Soto*, *Really Rosie* and *The Maurice Sendak Library*.

▶ the National Film Board's *Fables and Fantasy* and *The Magic of Discovery* (though be careful, not all NFB animations are suitable for children).

▶ Babar movies and the Care Bears movies by Nelvana Studios

▶ the MCA series featuring *The Little Mermaid*, *The Selfish Giant*, *The Remarkable Rocket* and *The Happy Prince*

▶ British animations such as *Jimbo and the Jet Set*, *Ivor the Engine* and *Rupert*

▶ pixilations such as *The Wombles* and *The Wind in the Willows*

- Will Vinton's claymation films *The Star Child*, *Martin the Cobbler*, *The Little Prince*, and *Rip Van Winkle*
- all of Jim Henson's work, particularly the Muppet movies (just be careful with *The Dark Crystal* and *Labyrinth*)

OTHER INFORMATION FOR PARENTS
Tie-in merchandise

The problem with tie-in merchandise (movie-related paraphernalia which saturates the market before, during and after the release of certain mega-hits) is that it often interests very young children in movies that are not made specifically for them. What child with *Jurassic Park* T-shirts, lunchboxes and play figurines can possibly understand his parents' flat refusal to allow him to watch the movie that inspired it all?

What can a parent do? If your child is clamoring for a video featuring the latest object of fascination, look for tamer alternatives. Instead of Tim Burton's *Batman* or *Batman Returns*, try renting *Batman: The Movie* (which was the pilot for the mild-mannered TV show starring Adam West), or a Batman animation, such as *Batman Superpowers*.

There are also animations available of *Beetlejuice*, *Robocop* and even *Rambo*, but these are still primarily about fighting and may only serve to sustain your child's fascination with the characters.

What is the appeal of these toys, anyway? In many cases, it's possible that these characters simply represent the power to directly resist violence. For a small child, bombarded with frightening images of violence, the concept of meeting fire with fire must be attractive. But there are other film heroes who have the same power, whose primary response to any crisis is not to instigate a full-scale massacre, and who are much more suitable role models for young children. Try sharing some of these heroes with your child:

- Sinbad
- Jason and the Argonauts
- the *Star Wars* good guys, Luke Skywalker, Obi Wan Kenobi, Yoda and Han Solo
- Superman
- Wonderwoman
- even Nancy Drew and the Hardy Boys qualify

There are also real live heroes to consider, such as explorers, inventors and ordinary people who respond heroically in crises.

Play it again

Try to remember that it's better for your child to watch an old favorite with benign images over and over again than to be pushed into something different because your own tolerance level is dropping fast. Children, especially those under ten, are repeat viewers. They seem to want the same thing over and over again. (You have probably noticed the same phenomenon happening with favorite bedtime stories.)

One parent told us: I used to try to steer him toward new things in the hope of expanding his horizons, but I found that if I left him alone and just rented the same one again and again he was happy, and then one day, all of a sudden, he'd say he was finished with that one and wanted something new.

Our theory about all of this is that some children watch things over and over because movies are so loaded with content that they just can't take it all in in a single viewing — or even in several viewings. It's as if children have their own time frames. They move on to new material when they are good and ready.

✗ 101 DALMATIANS

Walt Disney Home Video
1961
79 minutes
Directed by: Clyde Geronimi,
    Hamilton S. Luske,
    Wolfgang Reitherman
Starring the voices of: Betty Lou Gerson,
    J. Pat O'Malley, Rod Taylor

When Dalmatians Pongo and Perdita are blessed with a litter of fifteen puppies, it doesn't take long for something to go wrong. The evil Cruella de Vil hears about the puppies, steals them away and adds them to her collection. (She and her henchmen have already collected eighty-four puppies which she intends to skin and make into a coat.) Pongo and Perdita use the night bark, a kind of dog telegraph, to call for help. And when Captain, Sergeant Tibbs and Colonel Tolboy (a horse, a cat and a sheepdog, respectively) hear the call, they begin an investigation that leads them right to the puppies. In the end, Pongo and Perdita rescue their children and then must escort all ninety-nine puppies back to safety. Based on a book by Dodie Smith.

✗STOP: Cruella de Vil is scary, vicious and unrepentant.

CAUTION: The climactic car chase and the puppies' long trudge through bitter winter winds may upset some children. One overweight puppy is chastised for impeding the progress of the group and another is thought to be stillborn. The animation is not as detailed as in some Disney films.

GO: This film has enchanted young viewers for generations.

A BUNCH OF MUNSCH COLLECTION

Sony
1991
25 minutes each
Directed by: Greg Bailey, Meinert Hansen,
    Steven Majaury, Richard T. Morrison,
    Bill Speers, Craig Wilson
Starring the voices of: Julian Bailey,
    Sonja Ball, Gary Jewell, Rick Jones,
    Tamar Kozlov, Michael O'Reilly,
    Jory Steinberg, Christian Tessier

This animated series, based on Robert Munsch's books and stories, is fully animated. Each episode has one song, about halfway through.

Tape 1. 50 Below Zero

A scary noise wakes Jason, who goes downstairs to find his sleep-walking Papa asleep on top of the fridge, snoring loudly. After he returns Papa to bed, the noises continue and things are "going crazy" all over the house. Finally Papa sleepwalks out into the 50-below-zero night. Jason retrieves Papa and thaws him out in a hot shower, but Papa is still asleep. Jason wants his Papa to stop the nonsense because he is tired of the responsibility, so he ties Papa to the bed. The next morning Mother finds Jason asleep on top of the fridge. He tries to tell her what happened in the night, but she thinks it was a dream. Jason believes her until Papa sleep-walks into the kitchen with the string still tied to his foot.

CAUTION: The opening sequence is scary, and scary music continues throughout. During the story, inanimate objects come to life, and some children have a particular terror associated with this. Just in case your little one isn't partial to music, this episode contains songs.

Thomas' Snowsuit

The children at school taunt Thomas because of his old, ugly brown snowsuit. Thomas swears he will never wear it again, so his mother buys him a new one — but to his horror it is exactly the same. No matter how much Thomas resists, his mother makes him wear it. Thomas imagines the suit is a spacesuit with super powers, but his friends overhear him and things are even worse than before. Thomas' refusal to put on his snowsuit at recess gets him into a lot of trouble. While being forced to wear the snowsuit, he gets the better of the principal and the custodian, On hearing this, the children cheer and invite him out to play. Now, when his mother buys him a fancy new suit, Thomas prefers to wear his ugly brown one. He arrives at school to find that all his friends are wearing ugly brown suits too.

CAUTION: Thomas has a point, but he is really rude and disrespectful about it.

Tape 2. The Paper Bag Princess

Princess Elizabeth is about to marry Prince Ronald. He is the perfect prince except for one small thing — he is arrogant and not very gallant. When a huge green dragon appears, Ronald runs. The dragon terrorizes Princess Elizabeth and burns everything she owns, leaving the princess to wear a paper bag she finds in the garbage. Meanwhile, the dragon has moved on to Ronald's castle, wreaking havoc and making off with the craven Ronald in the process. Elizabeth sets off to free her handsome prince, and in the process frees Hansel and Gretel from the Wicked Witch, outruns The Three Bears and saves Granny from the Big Bad Wolf. Finding the dragon's cave she outsmarts him and saves Ronald. But she sees Ronald's flaws and literally gives him the boot.

CAUTION: The dragon says he has already eaten a 1st Grade, a 2nd Grade and a Day Care Center.

Tape 3. Moira's Birthday

Moira is having problems with her birthday plans. She wants the whole school to come to her party but her parents say: only six kids! Unfortunately Moira has a little trouble saying no to everyone else. The party is a parent's nightmare, and Moira eventually gets what she wants.

Blackberry Subway Jam

After Jonathon's mother cleans up the house, she goes out shopping with one edict: Don't make a mess! But this is impossible for him to do, since a mysterious subway stop opens into his living room and empties out hundreds of passengers who trample through the house. Jonathon cleans up, but it happens over and over again. Something must be done! So he goes to City Hall to remedy the situation. He gets lost in the building, finds the computer and makes his request. After paying the computer with blackberry jam, he gets the subway rerouted through the mayor's office.

Tape 4. Pigs

Megan's father warns her not to open the pigpen gate when she goes to feed them. However, Megan has a low opinion of pig intelligence, and she goes ahead and opens the gate anyway. The pigs immediately invade the house and make a mess. Next they go to Megan's school and destroy the principal's office. In math class one little pig pulls the teacher's pants down and steals his toupée, then plays with the computer. Megan takes the pig home and calls him Einstein. At the zoo, Megan cannot resist opening the elephant cage, and oh no… not again!

David's Father

Julie meets David's father. He is a kindly giant who eats whole octopuses and chocolate-covered bricks. Julie tells her parents, but they attribute the tales to Julie's overactive imagination. When the kids are ignored at the candy store, David's father gets the shopkeeper to serve them. The giant also scares away bullies. After Julie introduces David's father to her parents, she meets David's grandmother. Now it all makes sense!

Tape 5. Something Good

When three children go to the Super supermarket with their father, they pull down displays, play bowling in the aisles and fill carts with junk food. Dad refuses to buy any candy he will only buy "something good." The children resist his dictum. Finally, Dad tells little Tyya to just stand still. She does, but a clerk puts a price tag on her and Dad is obliged to pay the money before he can take her from the store. He does admit, however, that Tyya is something good.

Mortimer

When a houseful of screaming, naughty, noisy children are sent out to a movie, Mom and Dad are able to get some peace and quiet until baby Mortimer finds a star in the kitchen and makes a terrible racket trying to catch it. Finally his mother sends him to bed saying: Be quiet. But Mortimer and the star make so much noise that the police are called. Eventually a huge crowd gathers and begins arguing and telling each other to be quiet until the din is heard even beyond the earth. So Mortimer shuts his bedroom window and goes to sleep in peace and quiet.

Tape 6. Murmel Murmel Murmel

Robin finds a baby in her sandbox and sets out to find someone to take care of him. But no one can see the advantage of having a baby, except a truck driver who exchanges the baby for his truck.

The Boy in the Drawer

Shelley finds a naughty imp-boy in her sock drawer. He throws socks all over her room, and her mother doesn't believe her story. The boy then pushes the cat down the stairs, grows a tomato plant in her bed, and paints the window black. Her parents are oblivious to all of this, and it is only when the boy floods the kitchen that they finally notice him; but as soon as everyone is nice to him, he shrinks and vanishes.

Tape 7. Angela's Airplane

Angela puts an ice cream sandwich in the VCR before she and her dad go to the aiport. She plays with every button she can find in the car, her father's orders notwithstanding. At the airport it's more of the same, until she wanders into an empty airplane and presses the button that makes the plane take off. She barely makes it back to earth, destroying the place in the process, and promises the airport staff that she won't fly an aircraft again. But she does when she grows up.

The Fire Station

Sheila and Michael enjoy imagining that they are driving a fire truck. They go to the fire station to ask if they can see a real one. After a tour they hide in a truck and are taken to a real fire, where they are chased by a menacing black smoke-being. A fireman saves them, but when they return home they are unrecognizeable under the soot. After their parents finally identify them and clean them up, they go to a police station, and the whole thing starts over again.

CAUTION (applies to all tapes in series): High energy Saturday morning cartoon-type music makes this series a little manic. Some concepts may frighten some children. Unfortunately, no video version could possibly compare to a live performance by this master story-teller.

GO: Fully animated. Familiar stories for Robert Munsch fans.

■

A CRICKET IN TIMES SQUARE

fhe
1973
30 minutes
Directed by: Chuck Jones
Starring the voice of: Mel Blanc

Chester, a little country cricket, hitches a ride in a picnic basket to a newsstand in Times Square. In New York City he meets Tucker the mouse and Harry the cat. As it turns out, Chester has an unusual talent: when he rubs his legs together he doesn't make ordinary chirping, he makes music that sounds like violins. And when the newsstand encounters financial problems, Chester helps out by bringing in crowds with his amazing music. Based on the book by George Selden.

GO: This fully-animated video is the winner of a Parents' Choice Award.

■

ADVENTURES IN WONDERLAND

Walt Disney Home Video
1992
57 minutes each volume
Directed by: Kam Anway, Annie Court
Starring: Elisabeth Harnois, Armelia McQueen

Music and video effects combining live-action and fantasy, tell the story of Alice (a contemporary little girl with a cat named Dinah) in Wonderland (a strange place full of fanciful characters where lessons are learned through misadventures).

Titles in the collection are:
Hare-Raising Magic (Vol. 1):
Off the Cuffs; For Better or Verse
Helping Hands (Vol. 2):
Pop Goes the Easel; Techno Bunny
The Missing Ring Mystery (Vol. 3):
Pretzelmania; Noses Off

GO: This program is an Emmy Award Winner and was recommended by the National Education Association.

THE ADVENTURES OF RAGGEDY ANN AND ANDY COLLECTION

CBS Video
1988
30 minutes each
Directed By: Jeff Hall
Starring the voices of: Ruth Buzzi, Dana Hill

The Ransom Of Sunny Bunny Adventure

Cracklen the Wizard and Mynx the Witch need dog hair for their recipes in order to win the Witches' Cook-Off. The Raggedys' animal friends are targeted and stolen, and the Raggedys are forced to rescue them. Things get complicated in a hurry, and Sunny Bunny ends up winning the cook-off.

CAUTION: Cracklen ties the Raggedys to a spit and plans to boil them into soup.

The Perriwonk Adventure

The Raggedys must go to the Land of Cranberry Knoll to find Marcella's locket, where they encounter a dragon who's working for the wizard Cracklen.

The Pirate Adventure

Raggedy Dog finds a treasure map to Mickey the Leprechaun's gold. The Raggedys must find the gold before the pirates and return it to the disappearing gnome.

The Mabbit Adventure

Trying to keep their Book of Spells away from Cracklen is not an easy task for the Mabbits. They must turn themselves into statues and rely on the Raggedys and Sunny Bunny's magic pen to save them.

CAUTION: Standard Saturday morning cartoon animation and story lines.

GO: A series with attempts at lesson learning and problem-solving with little violence.

ALICE IN WONDERLAND

Walt Disney Home Video
1951
75 minutes
Directed by: Clyde Geronimi,
Wilfred Jackson, Hamilton Luske
Starring the voices of: Kathryn Beaumont,
Richard Haydn, Sterling Holloway, Ed Wynn

One afternoon during Alice's lesson in the meadow, a white rabbit dressed in a waistcoat speeds by. Imprudently, Alice follows the rabbit down a hole and finds herself in a strange land where animals talk. There she meets the Cheshire Cat and Tweedle Dum and Tweedle Dee; attends the Mad Hatter's Tea Party; encounters a philosophically inclined Caterpillar; plays flamingo-hedgehog croquet with the Queen of Hearts; and goes on trial for her very life.

Songs featured are:
All in the Golden Afternoon
The Caucus Race
I'm Late
In a World of My Own
The Unbirthday Song
The Walrus and the Carpenter
Very Good Advice
We're Painting the Roses Red

CAUTION: Some children may find the strange world of Wonderland disorienting and inaccessible. The Queen of Hearts is savage and leering.

GO: Superior effort has gone into this classic Disney animation, full of fanciful characters and songs. Alice is a self-assured and mostly undaunted heroine.

■

ALL DOGS GO TO HEAVEN

MGM/UA
1989
87 minutes
Directed by: Don Bluth
Starring the voices of: Loni Anderson, Dom DeLuise, Burt Reynolds

When his evil partner has him killed, German shepherd and gambler Charlie B. Barkin gets into heaven on a technicality. But he finds it boring, and even though he knows that once he leaves he can never return, Charlie conspires to escape back to Earth. There he uses Anne-Marie, an unwitting orphan who can communicate with animals, to set up a betting scam. But Charlie soon realizes the error of his ways, and when the chips are down he sacrifices himself for his devoted friend Anne-Marie.

CAUTION: Charlie dies twice in this film, lies through most of it, and in one particularly frightening scene, dreams he goes to hell. The themes of damnation and redemption, and the big handkerchief ending, may be too much for young children.

GO: Former Disney animator Don Bluth did a superb job with the animation, voice-overs and characterization. This film is best suited to children over five.

ALLIGATOR PIE

C/FP
1991
47 minutes
Directed by: Christopher Sanderson
Starring: Alanna Budhoo, Heath Lamberts,
Lance Paton, Kate Trotter

Unaware that he's being followed by Mr. Hoobody, a frightening character who lives in the furnace and whose job it is to spread temptation (when you've eaten too much candy, he always brings some more), Nicholas sets off for the park with his best friend, Egg. Nicholas's friends Bigfoot, Hanna and McGonigle see the danger at once and try to warn Nicholas, but Mr.

Hoobody delays them, sets up an ambush and captures Egg. With nowhere to turn, Nicholas and his friends must overcome their fear of Mr. Hoobody to rescue Egg.

CAUTION: Mr. Hoobody is a bit scary, especially when he speaks from the furnace vents. There is a food-fight which might give your three-year-old some ideas.

GO: Based on the clever, quirky poems in Dennis Lee's books *Alligator Pie*, *Nicholas Knock* and *Garbage Delight*, this is a good video about kids overcoming their fears. The claymation interludes are excellent.

■

AN AMERICAN TAIL

MCA
1986
81 minutes
Directed by: Don Bluth
Starring the voices of: Dom DeLuise, Peter Falk, Madeline Kahn, Christopher Plummer

When they hear a rumor that there are no cats in America, Fievel Mousekewitz and his family decide to emigrate from Russia. During the voyage across the Atlantic, Fievel is swept overboard and instead of arriving with the rest of his family, reaches New York City in a bottle. He then spends the rest of the film searching for his family and encounters a number of honest and dishonest street characters along the way. Throughout the film there's an ongoing struggle between the forces of justice (the mice) and the forces of evil (a group of cats led by

Warren T. Rat, who just happens to be a cat in disguise).

Songs featured are:
Never Say Never
Somewhere Out There
There Are No Cats in America

CAUTION: A number of scenes may disturb young children, not the least of which is one in which cossack cats attack at the beginning of the film. As in most films produced by Steven Spielberg, the sound track is intense. This film is probably too complex for children under four, and may be too much for sensitive four-year-olds.

GO: This is an excellent animated film. The voice treatments are charming, and the songs are memorable.

●

AN AMERICAN TAIL: FIEVEL GOES WEST

MCA
1991
75 minutes
Directed by: Phil Nibbelink, Simon Wells
Starring the voices of: John Cleese, Dom DeLuise, Amy Irving, James Stewart

Young Fievel's fantasy about living in the wild west promises to become a reality when he and his family happen upon a cowboy mouse handing out train tickets to the western town of Green River. But when he and his family are aboard the train, Fievel learns that the whole western trip is nothing more than an elaborate plot, devised by Cat R. Wall, leader of a dastardly gang of cats, to turn the mice into mouseburgers. Forced off the train before he can warn the others,

Fievel must make the dangerous trip to Green River on foot. And when he arrives to discover that no one believes his story, Fievel turns to the legendary dog sheriff (now something of a laughing stock) Wiley Burp. In a dramatic showdown, with some help from Fievel's friend Tiger, Wiley saves the mice and the day.

CAUTION: The plot may be too complicated for very young children. Also, the bad-guy cats are pretty scary and in one scene Fievel encounters a terrifying scorpion in a dark hole.

THE ANGEL AND THE SOLDIER BOY

BMG Video
1989
25 minutes
Directed by: Alison de Vere

For her birthday, a little girl gets a new coin and the miniature figurines of an angel girl and a soldier boy. That night when the girl is asleep, two pirates from a picture in a book come to life and steal the coin. The soldier boy wakes up and tries to stop them, but his sword is no match for the Pirate Captain's revolver and the two thieves take him away as their prisoner. Soon after, the angel awakes. Certain that something is wrong, she ventures downstairs, climbs into a model pirate ship and is whisked away into a picture of a roaring sea. There she finds and frees the soldier and together they retrieve the coin and escape back to the little girl's room.

CAUTION: On her way downstairs, the angel has frightening encounters with a huge black spider and a cat. The pirates may be a bit threatening for some children. There is no dialogue in this video.

GO: This film is an exciting, exquisitely animated romp, perfect for small children. The musical score is by the popular Irish group Clannad.Because there is no dialogue, it can be understood by children of any language.

ANGELS IN THE OUTFIELD

Title: Angels in the Outfield
Studio: Walt Disney
Date: 1994
Running Time: 95 minutes
Directed By: William Dear
Starring: Danny Glover, Tony Danza, Brenda Fricker, Christopher Lloyd
MPAA Rating: G

Roger has been living in a foster home since the death of his mother. His father, a young drifter, has more or less abandoned him, and at their last farewell, when Roger asks if they will ever be a family again, his father replies: "when the Angels win the pennant." Roger prays for divine assistance, and at a California Angels game soon after, he alone witnesses the arrival of a "team" of ghostly, beatific beings led by their captain, who introduces himself as Al. Al explains that the angels have come to help answer his prayers. They promptly proceed to help the Angels win their first game in a long time. Right after the game, Roger and his friend J.P. win the chance to get their picture taken with the Angels' cantankerous and short-tempered manager, George Knox. During the photo session with the sullen George (who hates kids, along with just about everything else), Roger confides to him that he saw angels in the outfield. At first, Knox thinks Roger is psychotic, but an examination of some of the game's highlight replays leads him to suspect that something extraordinary did take place. Knox seeks out Roger and J.P. and invites them to the next game. Roger again reports angels and, based on what he sees, advises Knox to make some extremely unorthodox managerial moves. Knox, with nothing to lose, does so. The bizarre moves pay off in another win, and Knox decides that Roger and J.P. should come to *every* game, and the Angels promptly embark on a winning streak. The film then proceeds in the classic "sports comeback" form, as a bunch of last-place ne'er-do-wells take a legitimate shot at the championship. Of course, it all boils down to one game, and in the climax, Al explains to Roger that there is one major angel rule: no helping in a championship game. The bumbling baseball team must go up against the highly-skilled White Sox alone.

CAUTION: Roger's angst at having been abandoned may be upsetting for young children going through family upheaval. Al tells Roger that one of the team's hard-luck but gutsy players only has six months to live because "he smoked for years" (even though he has since quit). This is all very well as a non-smoking message, but think of all the children whose parents smoked for years and then quit.

GO: There are lots of sight gags and physical humor for the little ones (the theater was in an uproar during some scenes), empathetic kid heroes, and a great "only I know what's happening" plot reminiscent of such classics as *The Cat From Outer*

Space and *Son of Flubber*. We particularly enjoyed the fact that neither the opposing teams nor the owners were villified. And the adults *believed* the children (for once).

✗ ANNIE

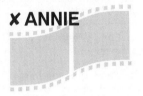

RCA/Columbia Pictures Home Video
1981
128 minutes
Directed by: John Huston
Starring: Carol Burnett, Albert Finney,
    Aileen Quinn, Ann Reinking
MPAA rating: PG

After living with orphan Annie for just one week, billionaire philanthropist Daddy Warbucks and his secretary Miss Farrell offer to adopt her. But Annie declines. Showing them half of a locket, she explains that one day her real parents will come to get her, bringing the other half of the locket with them. However, Miss Hannigan who runs the orphanage knows that Annie's parents are dead and has in her own possession the other half of the locket. And when Daddy Warbucks offers $50,000 as an incentive for Annie's parents to come forward, Miss Hannigan's con-artist brother Rooster and his girlfriend impersonate Annie's parents to claim the reward. After a dangerous chase, Annie is rescued and goes to live with Daddy Warbucks and Miss Farrell.

✗**STOP**: In the chase scene, Rooster punches Miss Hannigan in the face, knocking her unconscious. Annie is forced to climb to the top of a high railway drawbridge where she clings perilously.

CAUTION: Miss Hannigan is nasty to practically everyone and she drinks heavily.

GO: The dancing, singing and gymnastics are excellent. This film is extremely popular with girls ages four to eight. Featuring the hit song "Tomorrow."

✗ BABAR: THE JUNGLE TALES

Malofilm
1989
113 minutes
Directed by: Raymond Jafelice
Starring the voices of: Dawn Greenhalgh,
    Gavin McGrath, Gordon Pinsent
    Chris Wiggins

City Ways

Babar's eldest son has invited two schoolmates over. He is anxious to become more interesting, so as to impress them. Babar cautions his son trying to that change who he is is no way to impress people. He then tells his son about his first encounter with the big city, the nice old lady who befriended him, and a social occasion in which his attempts to impress people went terribly awry.

Babar Returns

Flora is suffering from a crisis of confidence. Babar tells her the tale of his reunion with his family, and his return to the jungle. We learn of the untimely death of the king, Babar's defeat of the evil hunter, and Babar's coronation.

✗**STOP**: The king eats poisoned mushrooms and dies. The hunter is malevolent.

City of Elephants

Flora is trying to prepare her kite for kite-flight Sunday, and is frustrated at her lack of progress. Babar explains the need for careful planning, telling her the story of how he designed and built Celesteville, and how he struggled with his own self-doubt.

Babar's Triumph

Babar's children learn about the origins of the Jungle Federation, which was originally created, despite serious differences among the members, to defeat the evil hunter and his minions.

✗**STOP:** The hunter shoots up the jungle and sets it on fire. He is then consumed by the flames, still snarling with rage and hatred.

GO: These are faithful to the spirit and tone of the original book, and replete with examples which stress a positive approach to life.

✗ BABAR: THE MOVIE

AGES 3 TO 6

Astral
1989
77 minutes
Directed by: Alan Bunce
Starring the voices of: Elizabeth Hanna,
Gavin McGrath, Gordon Pinsent,
Sarah Polley

When the film opens, a mature King Babar is telling his children a bedtime story. In the story, a young Babar receives word from Celeste that the rhinos are attacking villages and snatching elephants. Impatient with the bureaucracy involved in organizing an army, Babar and Celeste set out alone. They learn that the rhinos are forcing the kidnapped elephants to labor on a colossal building project and after a couple of daring escapes, Babar and Celeste participate in a final confrontation with the rhino horde.

✗**STOP:** A rhino raiding party attacks an elephant village, torching the houses and carrying the adult elephants away. Celeste's mother is bound, painfully, and Celeste is thrown into a well.

CAUTION: This is a film about war and viewers can expect to see a great deal of violence.

GO: An exciting and well animated adventure that stresses the values of courage, perseverance and inventiveness.

BABAR THE ELEPHANT COMES TO AMERICA

Vestron Video
1974
30 minutes
Directed by: Ed Levitt, Bill Melendez
Starring the voice of: Peter Ustinov

When Babar and his family are invited to tour America, he and Celeste decide to travel by balloon; they encounter rough weather and crash land on a beach. After an encounter with a friendly but forgetful whale, the ocean liner carrying Cornelius and Arthur happens by and rescues them, and all four arrive in New York City together. They tour New York, then move on to visit Washington, New Orleans and Chicago, and when they arrive in Hollywood, they all become big stars.

GO: The film's animation is similar to the illustrations in the book by Jean and Laurent de Brunhoff on which the film was based.

■

✗ BABAR'S FIRST STEP

---

f.h.e./Nelvana
1990
49 minutes
Directed by: Raymond Jafelice
Starring the voice of: Gordon Pinsent

Babar is born in the great forest, and immediately begins to display the courage and resourcefulness that will one day make him a good leader. When a strange monster with a voice like thunder (a hunter with a gun) comes to the forest, Babar's mother is killed and Babar must learn how to deal with his grief as well as with the terrible enemy.

✗ **STOP:** There are frightening close-ups of the hunter's face and of an elephant gun being loaded. The sequence in which Babar's wounded mother charges the hunter to save the herd may disturb some children.

GO: This is an environmentalist's film, albeit heavy-handed.

BABES IN TOYLAND

Walt Disney Home Video
1961
105 minutes
Directed by: Jack Donohue
Starring: Ray Bolger, Annette Funicello, Tommy Kirk, Tommy Sands, Ed Wynn

Based on an operetta by Victor Herbert and Glen McDonough, the story begins when Mother Goose invites viewers to celebrate the wedding of Mary Contrary and Tom Piper in Toyland. Aware of the fact that Mary will inherit a great deal of money when she weds, the villainous Barnaby will stop at nothing to make her marry him instead of Tom. To this end, he instructs his thugs to drown the young man. But they are unable to follow through with the terrible deed and instead sell Tom to a band of

gypsies. Unaware of the fact that her fiancé is still alive, Mary is inconsolable when, dressed as sailors, the thugs explain that Tom was lost at sea and that his dying wish was that she marry Barnaby (for her own good). She agrees to accept Barnaby's proposal, but before the marriage can take place an amazing army of toys led by Tom himself restores order in Toyland.

Songs featured are:
Castle in Spain
I Can't Do the Sum
Toyland, Toyland

CAUTION: Young children may be frightened by the Forest of No Return, where trees have faces and branches that move menacingly.

GO: Full of fantasy toys and effects, this was Disney's first live-action musical.

BAMBI

Walt Disney Home Video
1942
69 minutes
Directed by: David D. Hand

This film, based on the classic book by Felix Salten, tells the story of a fawn named Bambi and his friends Flower the skunk and Thumper the rabbit. As Bambi grows, he experiences the wonders and hardships of life in the forest. (His mother is shot by hunters; he matures and experiences the first awakenings of love.) And in the powerful climax, careless hunters set the forest on fire, and Bambi is shot and wounded.

CAUTION: Bambi's mother is shot by hunters (not shown). When Bambi is grown he fights an intense battle with a rival deer and later he and his new mate, Faline, are pursued by a terrifying pack of wild dogs

GO: This film features superior animation. Older children will benefit from its message.

BASIL HEARS A NOISE

CTW/CBC
1990
28 minutes
Directed by: Wayne Moss
Starring: Kevin Clash, Tim Gosley, Pier Kohl, Rob Mills

Big lovable bear muppet Basil is camping out in the backyard with muppets Dodi, Elmo and Louie. Basil is very nervous and can't fall asleep, so Dodi tells him a story about Basil the Shepherd, a handsome shepherd bear who has lost a lamb. Basil wanders into an enchanted forest, where the creatures complain that a mean trickster is terrorizing them. They send Basil into the spooky forest in search of the Fountain of Riddles. There, Basil meets the unhelpful Information Dragon, and eventually runs into the very brave Sir Louie. Basil eventually discovers the fountain, which tells him the identity of the trickster: a scary witch. Basil must then screw up his courage and confront the witch to get his lambs back, but he discovers, much to his surprise, that the witch isn't scary at all; in fact, she's a princess in disguise, who is just as frightened as everyone else.

CAUTION: The video is very mild in tone, but some of the youngest and most timid kids may be a little frightened.

GO: An entertaining little tale which stresses conquering fears. Includes some snappy Muppet musical numbers.

BEATRIX POTTER: THE WORLD OF PETER RABBIT AND FRIENDS

HGV
1993–1994
30 minutes each
Starring: Niamii Cusack

Each of the videos in this fully animated series opens with a live action segment in which Potter is painting outdoors. A flash rainfall sends her rushing home, where she talks with a lop-eared rabbit and gives a brief introduction to the story. The single exception is the beginning of the Tailor of Gloucester, in which Ms. Potter observes a group of children carolling.

GO: A highly-regarded series, faithful to the spirit of the books, the quality of animation keeping close to the original illustrations.

The Tale of Peter Rabbit and Benjamin Bunny

Naughty Peter Rabbit goes to Mr. McGregor's farm, eats so many carrots that he gets a tummy-ache, is discovered by Mr. McGregor, and barely makes his escape; however, he loses all his nice clothes in the process, which McGregor uses to make a scarecrow. The next day, his cousin Benjamin convinces him to make another raid on the McGregor farm to get the clothes back. The raid goes awry, and only the intervention of brave Mr. Bounce, a full-grown rabbit, saves the boys.

CAUTION: The naughty boys are spanked with a cane. Rabbits in peril.

The Tale of Tom Kitten and Jemima Puddleduck

Tabitha Twitchit is having friends over for tea, and her three unruly kittens, Moppet, Mittens and Tom, are none too pleased about having to dress up. Things get even more complicated when the kittens promptly lose their good clothes to a trio of passing geese. One of the geese is Jemima Puddleduck, a nervous sort who leaves the farm to find a dry nesting place away from a vexing neighbor. She encounters a crafty fox, who tricks her into laying a batch of eggs for him. He is preparing to eat Jemima herself when a group of dogs interrupt his dastardly plans; however, some of Jemima's rescuers promptly devour her eggs, leaving her quite distraught.

CAUTION: The fox-chasing and egg-eating scene may upset some little ones.

The Tale of Mrs. Tiggy-winkle and Mr. Jeremy Fisher

Lucie of Littletown Farm is always losing her handkerchiefs. In the course of her search for them, she meets Mrs. Tiggy-winkle, who does the laundry and mending for all the animals. Lucie and Mrs. Tiggy-winkle then go to see Mr. Jeremy Fisher, who tells them the harrowing tale of a fishing expedition which he barely survived.

CAUTION: Jeremy gets swallowed by a big fish and is underwater for quite some time.

The Tale of Pigling Bland

Aunt Pettitoes has eight piglets who eat like mad. She is forced to send some of them away. Two in particular, Alexander and Pigling Bland, are given licenses and sent off to market. Alexander loses his license and is forced to return, while Pigling must press on alone. He takes refuge in a farmhouse overnight, and is granted hospitality by the sinister Farmer Piperson. There Pigling discovers that another pig, Pigwig, is being held prisoner there. Pigling and his new friend make good their escape.

The Tailor of Gloucester

The aged, exhausted tailor has one chance left to make his fortune, and that is to craft a fine coat for the mayor's wedding. To this end he spends his last pence, sending his cat Simpkin out into the winter night to fetch the twist for the trim. However, the tailor releases some mice Simpkin has captured and the enraged cat hides the twist. The tailor collapses with a fever. The grateful mice then sew the coat while he recovers from his ailment, and Simpkin relents and gives the tailor back the twist necessary to finish the job.

The Tale of Mr. Samuel Whiskers (or the Roly Poly Pudding)

Tabitha Twitchit's three mischievious children are giving her such a hard time that she can't get on with her baking, so she tries to round them up and put them in a cupboard. Tom, fearing being shut in, flees up the chimney, and finds himself in the domain of two kitten-eating rats, the sombre, bloated Samuel Whiskers and his harsh wife Anna Maria. While his mother and his aunt Ribby are frantically searching the house for him, Samuel and Anna Maria industriously start turning Tom into a Roly Poly Pudding. Only with the help of the sharp-nosed terrier John Joiner saves Tom, and Samuel and Anna Maria flee, finding another place to live in a neighbouring barn.

CAUTION: This is the grimmest of all the Potter tales, with an eerie edge to it, particularly when Tom is bound and lies mewing helplessly while the rats prepare him for the oven.

■

BEAUTY AND THE BEAST

Walt Disney Home Video
1992
84 minutes
Directed by: Gary Trousdale and Kirk Wise
Starring the voices of:
Robby Benson, Angela Lansbury,
Paige O'Hara, Jerry Orbach

Long ago, an enchantress disguised as a hag offers a spoiled young prince an enchanted rose in exchange for lodging. But the prince, repulsed by the hag, refuses and is subsequently turned into a hideous, buffalo-like beast. The only way he can break the spell is to earn the love of a young woman. And as the years pass, he falls into despair, convinced that no one could love a beast. Enter Belle, the kind and bookish daughter of eccentric inventor Maurice. (Belle is being pursued by the handsome but arrogant Gaston, whose affections she absolutely rejects.) One day, when Maurice becomes lost in the woods, he tries to take refuge in the beast's castle and is thrown into the dungeon. Belle discovers her father's plight and agrees to change places with him and be the beast's captive forever. At first immovable, her heart softens as she grows to know the beast, and when he grants her request to go to her ailing father, she realizes that the beast loves her. But Gaston and his henchmen then learn of the beast's existence and lay siege to the castle, setting up a dramatic final confrontation, after which Belle declares her love for the dying beast and releases him from his curse.

CAUTION: The forest outside the beast's castle is home to a pack of vicious wolves that attack anyone who passes. In their final confrontation, Gaston stabs the beast in the back and falls from the castle tower, shrieking as he disappears into the abyss.

GO: The combination of photo-realistic, computer-generated backgrounds and hand-drawn character cels is pure state-of-the-art. (The ballroom scene is particularly stunning.) This film was nominated for six Academy Awards including Best Picture. Three songs from the team of Howard Ashman and Alan Menken were also nominated for Academy Awards. Winner of the Golden Globe Award for best picture.

■

BEDKNOBS AND BROOMSTICKS

Walt Disney Home Video
1971
117 minutes
Directed by: Robert Stevenson
Starring: Angela Lansbury, Roddy McDowall, David Tomlinson

The film opens in England in 1940 in a children's evacuation center, where Miss Eglantine Pryce, a motorcycle-riding apprentice witch (who has just received her first broom), is assigned three children: Carrie, Charles and Paul. She reluctantly agrees to take them in, on the understanding that they will stay with her only until a suitable home is found. But when the children accidentally witness her first solo flight, the jig is up and she's forced to take them into her confidence. In order to seal their pact, Miss Pryce gives the children a travelling spell which she conjures onto Paul's bedknob. When the war forces the closure of the college of witchcraft, Miss Pryce takes the children to London on the magic bed to get her final spell (which is used to give life to inanimate objects). But her professor turns out to be a huckster who got his spells out of some old book, so the crew has no choice but to set off in search of the now missing book and the final spell. Meanwhile, the German army is massing on the beaches of France and Belgium in preparation for the invasion of England. And when a German raiding party arrives, the group is ready with the last spell. Based on the book by Mary Norton.

CAUTION: The Professor makes some disparaging remarks about women. The climax of the film features a battle between the Germans and an army of animated armor; there is a great deal of combat, though no one gets killed.

GO: The resemblance in style of *Bedknobs and Broomsticks* to the earlier *Mary Poppins* is unmistakable and children who enjoyed one will likely enjoy the other. Winner of the 1971 Academy Award for best visual effects.
■

BEN AND ME

Walt Disney Home Video
1953
25 minutes
Directed by: Hamilton Luske
Starring the voice of: Sterling Holloway

Based on Bill Peet's charming book, this film tells the story of Amos Mouse, Benjamin Franklin's best friend and the real brains behind the famous inventor's insights and contributions to civilization.

GO: Children will get a glimpse into the origins and workings of such things as printing presses, bifocals and electricity. The animation isn't Disney's best, but the quirky story is very engaging.
■

THE BERENSTAIN BEARS FIRST TIME VIDEO SERIES

Random House Home Video
1982–1990
30 minutes each volume
Directed by: Buzz Potamkin
Starring the voices of: Ruth Buzzi,
   Brian Cummings, Christina Lange,
   David Mendenhall, Frank Welker

Based on the books by Stan and Jan Berenstain, these fully-animated videos chronicle the experiences of Mama Bear, Papa Bear, Sister Bear and Brother Bear, a kind and loving family who live in a split-level treehouse in the friendly community of Beartown and who face the typical problems of people everywhere. As the children grow they constantly encounter new aspects of growing up. Mama and Papa Bear do their best to be good parents and in turn learn valuable life-lessons from the children.

Titles in the series are:
The Berenstain Bears and the Messy
   Room plus The Terrible Termite
The Berenstain Bears and the Truth plus
   Save the Bees
The Berenstain Bears Get in a Fight plus
   The Bigpaw Problem
The Berenstain Bears and the Trouble
   with Friends plus The Coughing Catfish
The Berenstain Bears and Too Much
   Birthday plus To the Rescue
The Berenstain Bears No Girls Allowed
   plus The Missing Dinosaur Bone

■

THE BERENSTAIN BEARS AND THE MISSING DINOSAUR BONE

Random House Home Video
1990
20 minutes
Directed by: Ray Messecar
Starring the voices of: Fran Brill,
   Michael Fass, Alison Hashmall,
   Ron Marshall, Brandon Pamy

This video is iconographic with voice-over narration.

Stories featured are:
The Berenstain Bears and the Missing
   Dinosaur Bone
Bears in the Night
The Bear Detectives
■

THE BERENSTAIN BEARS SERIES

HGV
1980–1983
30 minutes each volume
Directed by: Mordecai Gerstein, Al Kouzel
Starring the voices of: Gabriela Glatzer,
   Knowl Johnson, Pat Lysinger, Ron McLarty

Titles in this fully-animated series are:
The Berenstain Bears Meet Big Paw
The Berenstain Bears Play Ball
The Berenstain Bears and Cupid's
   Surprise
■

BIG BIRD IN CHINA

Random House Home Video
1982
60 minutes
Directed by: Jon Stone
Starring: Brian Muehl,
    Quyang Lien-Tze, Caroll Spinney

Big Bird and Barkley the dog go on a "treasure-hunt" to find the magical Phoenix and are helped in their search by the Monkey King. Actually filmed in China, this video introduces the Chinese culture through stories, language and songs. Shown are: the Great Wall of China, little girls performing the "duck dance," tai-chi in the park and children playing games in a schoolyard.

CAUTION: The Monkey King, although familiar to most Chinese children, may frighten some North American viewers.

GO: Featured are Oscar the Grouch, Ernie and Bert, Cookie Monster and Grover. This is a charming, albeit simplistic, look at Chinese life.

BIG BIRD IN JAPAN

Random House Home Video
1991
60 minutes
Directed by: Jon Stone
Starring: Maiko Dawakami,
    Brian Muehl, Caroll Spinney

Big Bird and his dog Barkley embark on a whirlwind tour of Japan, where they visit Tokyo, Mt. Fuji, Naguya and Kyoto. Predictably, Big Bird gets lost right away and ends up touring Tokyo alone, unable to understand a single word anyone says. Then a young English-speaking Japanese woman comes to his rescue and promises to help him link up with his tour. She teaches him about Japanese culture and as he gets to know her, the air of mystery around her deepens. And it's only when Big Bird sees a play called "The Bamboo Princess" about a princess from the palace of the moon that he realizes his mysterious friend is one and the same.

CAUTION: In one scene, Barkley goes into a temple and sees some very frightening gargoyle-type statues. Children who cannot yet read will miss the subtitled dialogue.

GO: A good way to introduce children to Japanese culture, this video is warm and friendly.

BONGO: A MUSICAL STORY ABOUT A BEAR

Walt Disney Home Video
1947
36 minutes
Directed by: Hamilton Luske
Narrated by: Cliff Edwards

Bongo is a multi-talented, world-famous circus bear, who, when he's before the crowds, performs amazing feats of strength and agility. But when he's out of the limelight, he's treated as a prisoner, and more and more Bongo feels the call of the wild. One day, when the circus train is rumbling through some mountainous forestland, Bongo makes his escape. He immediately discovers the drawbacks of his decision, however (he can't find food and the night sounds keep him awake), and is beginning to regret his choice when he encounters a female bear named Lulubelle. It's love at first sight. Unfortunately, a huge and hostile bear named Lumpjaw also has his eye on Lulubelle. And to complicate matters, Bongo is unfamiliar with bear etiquette, so when Lulubelle reaches out to slap him (a bear custom, meaning she has chosen him), Bongo ducks and she accidentally smacks Lumpjaw instead. Believing himself to be chosen, the delighted Lumpjaw grabs Lullubelle. But when Bongo realizes what has happened, he uses his circus skills to take on Lumpjaw and rescue his true love. Based on the story by Sinclair Lewis.

CAUTION: The bears' method of communicating positive feelings is a little contrived and may confuse young viewers. The fight between Bongo and Lumpjaw is intense.

GO: This film is funny, charming and well-animated.

■

CHILDREN'S CIRCLE VIDEO SERIES

CC Home Video
1960–1992
30–50 minutes each volume

Producer/filmmaker Mort Schindel created Weston Woods studio to bring faithful adaptations of critically acclaimed children's books to film. On the Children's Circle label, these videos are presented in a variety of styles, from fully-animated to iconographic, and have won over one hundred prestigious awards. Recommended for children ages three to nine.

The Amazing Bone and Other Stories

Stories featured are:
A Picture for Harold's Room
The Amazing Bone
John Brown, Rose and the Midnight Cat
The Trip

Animal Stories

Stories featured are:
Andy and the Lion
Petunia
Why Mosquitoes Buzz in People's Ears

Christmas Stories

Stories featured are:
The Clown of God
The Little Drummer Boy
Morris's Disappearing Bag
The Twelve Days of Christmas

Corduroy and Other Bear Stories

Stories featured are:
Blueberries for Sal
Corduroy
Panama

Danny and the Dinosaur and Other Stories

Stories featured are:
The Camel Who Took a Walk
Danny and the Dinosaur
The Happy Lion
The Island of the Skog

Doctor Desoto and Other Stories

Stories featured are:
Curious George Rides a Bike
Doctor Desoto
The Hat
Patrick

The Emperor's New Clothes and Other Folktales

Stories featured are:
The Emperor's New Clothes
Suho and the White Horse
Why Mosquitoes Buzz in People's Ears

The Ezra Jack Keats Library

Stories featured are:
A Letter to Amy
Getting to Know Ezra Jack Keats
  (documentary)
Pet Show
Peter's Chair
The Snowy Day
The Trip
Whistle for Willie

Five Stories for the Very Young

Stories featured are:
Caps for Sale
Changes, Changes
Drummer Hoff

Harold's Fairy Tale
Whistle for Willie

Happy Birthday, Moon and Other Stories

Stories featured are:
Happy Birthday, Moon
The Napping House
The Owl and the Pussy-Cat
Peter's Chair
The Three Little Pigs

Homer Price Stories

Live-action stories featured are:
The Case of the Cosmic Comic
The Doughnuts

Joey Runs Away and Other Stories

Stories featured are:
The Bear and the Fly
The Cow Who Fell in the Canal
Joey Runs Away
The Most Wonderful Egg in the World

Madeline's Rescue and Other Stories About Madeline

Stories featured are:
Madeline and the Bad Hat
Madeline and the Gypsies
Madeline's Rescue

The Maurice Sendak Library

Stories featured are:
Getting to Know Maurice Sendak
  (documentary)
In the Night Kitchen
The Nutshell Kids
Where the Wild Things Are

Maurice Sendak's Really Rosie

Stories featured are:
Alligators All Around
Chicken Soup with Rice
One Was Johnny
Pierre

Mike Mulligan and His Steam Shovel and Other Stories

Stories featured are:
Burt Dow: Deep-Water Man
Mike Mulligan and His Steam Shovel
Moon Man

More Stories for the Very Young

Stories featured are:
The Little Red Hen
Max's Christmas
The Napping House
Not So Fast, Songololo
Petunia

The Mysterious Tadpole and Other Stories

Stories featured are:
The Five Chinese Brothers
Jonah and the Great Fish
The Mysterious Tadpole
The Wizard

Norman the Doorman and Other Stories

Stories featured are:
Brave Irene
Lentil
Norman the Doorman

Owl Moon and Other Stories

Stories featured are:
The Caterpillar and the Polliwog
Hot Hippo
Owl Moon
Time of Wonder

The Pig's Wedding and Other Stories

Stories featured are:
The Happy Owls
A Letter to Amy
The Owl and the Pussy-Cat
The Selkie Girl

Raymond Briggs' The Snowman

The Robert McCloskey Library

Stories featured are:
Lentil
Make Way for Ducklings
Blueberries for Sal
Time of Wonder
Burt Dow: Deep-Water Man
Getting to Know Robert McCloskey
  (documentary)

Rosie's Walk and Other Stories

Stories featured are:
Rosie's Walk
Charlie Needs a Cloak
The Story about Ping
The Beast of Monsieur Racine

Smile for Auntie and Other Stories

Stories featured are:
Make Way for Ducklings
Smile for Auntie
The Snowy Day
Wynken, Blinken and Nod

Stories from the Black Tradition

Stories featured are:
A Story, A Story
Goggles!
Mufaro's Beautiful Daughters
The Village of Round and Square
   Houses
Why Mosquitoes Buzz in Peoples Ears

Strega Nona and Other Stories

Stories featured are:
Strega Nona
Tikki Tikki Tembo
The Foolish Frog
A Story, A Story

Teeny-tiny and the Witch Woman and Other Scary Stories

Stories featured are:
A Dark, Dark Tale
King of the Cats
The Rainbow Serpent
Teeny-tiny and the Witch-Woman

The Three Robbers and Other Stories

Stories featured are:
Fourteen Rats and a Rat-Catcher
The Island of the Scog
Leopold and the See-Through
   Crumbpicker
The Three Robbers

The Ugly Duckling and Other Classic Fairy Tales

Stories featured are:
The Ugly Duckling
The Stonecutter
The Swineherd

What's Under My Bed and Other Creepy Stories

Stories featured are:
Georgie
Teeny-Tiny and the Witch-Woman
The Three Robbers

CINDERELLA

Walt Disney Home Video
1950
76 minutes
Directed by: Clyde Geronimi,
   Wilfred Jackson, Hamilton Luske

This beloved Disney classic is an expanded version of the famous fairy tale in which Cinderella, slave to her horrible stepmother and stepsisters, dreams of the day when a prince will come to take her away from her misery. That day's arrival is facilitated by the appearance of Cinderella's kindly fairy godmother who, with the help of a little magic, sends her off to the ball. There, Cinderella enchants the prince and, in her haste to be home before the magic wears off, loses a slipper. The king's servants try the slipper on every woman in the kingdom until they discover Cinderella. Then she and the prince are reunited and are married.

Songs featured are:
Bibbidi-Bobbidi-Boo
Cinderelly
The Work Song

CAUTION: The direct correlation of evil with unattractiveness may concern some parents.

GO: Cinderella is accompanied by a host of singing mice and birds, the antics of which make the story more accessible to young children. The songs are terrific.

CINDERELLA

Playhouse Home Video
1964
84 minutes
Directed by: Charles S. Dukin
Starring: Stuart Damon, Walter Pidgeon, Ginger Rogers, Lesley Ann Warren

Although produced for television some thirty years ago, this traditional telling of the classic fairy tale still works today.

Some of Rodgers and Hammerstein's songs are:
Do I Love You Because You're Beautiful?
In My Own Little Corner
Impossible

GO: Lesley Ann Warren has an average singing voice, but she portrays Cinderella sweetly.

CLASSIC FAIRY TALES

f.h.e./MCA
1982
62 minutes
Narrated by: George Cole,
    Sheila Hancock

Six well-known fairy tales are told via narration and illustrations.

Stories featured are:
The Emperor's New Clothes
The Four Magicians (The Bremen Town Musicians)
The Princess and the Pea
Puss in Boots
Rapunzel
The Ugly Duckling

CAUTION: The music doesn't vary very much and, despite what the box says, the stories are *not* animated. Some children may snicker to see the Emperor in *The Emperor's New Clothes*, who is shown in full frontal nudity.

GO: Often humorous, the traditional stories are faithfully and simply told. Don't be put off by the fact that this tape is not animated; there is plenty of movement and visual appeal to make it a superior fairy tale video.

CURIOUS GEORGE

SVS
1983
83 minutes
Directed by: Alan J. Shallock

Curious George, the mischievous little monkey, has been a popular literary character for over forty years. No matter what trouble he gets into, it always seems to work out in the end.

This tape is very simply animated with single moving elements in each scene. Sometimes the effect of animation is achieved by zooming in on a picture or by the rapid editing of still pictures. The stories are narrated and the music and sound effects are subtle. Based on the books by Margaret and H.A. Rey.

Stories featured are:
Curious George and the Dump Truck
Curious George and the Lost Letter
Curious George at the Greenhouse
Curious George at the Pet Shop
Curious George Gets a Pizza
Curious George Gets an X-Ray
Curious George Goes Hiking
Curious George Goes to a Wedding
Curious George Goes to the Amusement Park
Curious George Goes to an Ice Cream Shop
Curious George Goes to the Library
Curious George Meets the Balloon Man
Curious George Meets the Painter
Curious George Paints a Billboard
Curious George Rings the Bell
Curious George Takes a Ferry
Curious George Visits a Catsup Factory
Curious George Visits a Hotel
■●

CURIOUS GEORGE COLLECTION

Sony
1983
30 minutes each
Directed by: Alan J. Shallock

Curious George
(Vol. 1)

Stories featured are:
Curious George at the Ballet
Curious George Goes Sledding
Curious George Goes to an Art Show
Curious George Goes to the Aquarium
Curious George Plays Basketball
Curious George Walks the Pets

Curious George
(Vol. 2)

Stories featured are:
Curious George Goes to a Flower Show
Curious George Goes to a TV Station
Curious George Goes to the Circus
Curious George Goes to the Library
Curious George Visits the Railroad Station
Curious George Goes to the Tailor Shop

Curious George
(Vol. 3)

Stories featured are:
Curious George and the Costume Party
Curious George Goes Fishing
Curious George Goes Skiing
Curious George Goes to a Bowling Alley
Curious George Goes to a Restaurant
Curious George Goes to the Zoo

CAUTION: In every episode George disobeys an adult's instructions. Then, just as he is about to suffer punishment for his disobedience it's discovered that some inadvertent good has resulted and George is forgiven.

GO: These videos, despite their simple animation, still keep the attention of very young children.

CURIOUS GEORGE AND THE DINOSAUR

Fisher-Price
1979
45 minutes

This video consists of nine episodes in the partially animated style which characterizes the earlier, and very popular, original Curious George video adaptations.

Curious George and the Dinosaur

During a field trip to the local museum, George stimulates class interest in dinosaurs in very unorthodox fashion.

Curious George Goes to a Museum

George goes to a museum and, as usual, gets into trouble. This time his shenanigans result in the museum recovering a lost sword.

Curious George Wins a Race

The inquisitive simian inadvertently helps Jane win a soap-box derby, but throws the local community, particularly a tire dealership, into chaos.

Curious George Washes the Little Blue Car

He also washes a whole lot more, when he employs a fire hydrant to complete his chore.

Curious George Goes to a Gym

The Man in the Yellow Hat decides it's time to work out, and George promptly terrorizes the neighborhood gym, taking time out from dodging his furious pursuers to beat the district ping-pong champion.

Curious George Goes Tomato Picking

George throws a nearby farm into utter chaos with his accustomed gusto.

Curious George Wins a Contest

After alienating vendors at the local county fair, George helps two young friends win a corn-husking derby.

Curious George Goes to an Airshow

The featured sky divers fail to show at the local airshow, and George accidentally becomes the main parachuting attraction.

Curious George Goes Skiing

When trick skiers don't make it for their regularly-scheduled show, George inadvertently provides the entertainment.

■ ●

DANCE! WORKOUT WITH BARBIE

Buena Vista Home Video
1991
30 minutes

Exercise with Barbie and a group of nine energetic pre-teen girls. Computer animation brings Barbie to life in this well-produced, well-choreographed tape. Great exercises with lots of variety teach rhythm and coordination in a fun way. Approved by the Aerobics and Fitness Association of America. Songs performed by Love Hewitt.

CAUTION: No boys are shown working out.

GO: Wonderfully put together, this video features routines that are more fun and choreographically complex than some tapes for adults. Moms may want to work out with their daughters after seeing this video!

DARKWING DUCK — HIS FAVORITE ADVENTURES COLLECTION

Walt Disney Home Video
1991
48 minutes each
Starring the voices of: Christine Cavanaugh, Jim Cummings, Terry McGovern

In the crime-plagued metropolis of St. Canard, the intrepid and flamboyant Darkwing Duck battles evil-doers, aided by his adopted daughter Goslyn and his sidekick Launchpad McQuack.

Titles in this fully-animated collection are:
Birth of Negaduck (Vol. 4)
Comic Book Capers (Vol. 3)
Darkly Dawns the Duck (Vol. 1)
Justice Ducks Unite (Vol. 2)

DAVID COPPERFIELD

Astral
1993
92 minutes
Directed by: Don Arioli
Starring: Sheena Easton, Kelly LeBrock, Julian Lennon, Howie Mandel, Andrea Martin

This animated musical uses cartoon animals to tell this liberal adaptation of the famous Dicken's tale. The wealthy widow Clara Copperfield gives birth to a boy on Christmas Eve. Years go by, and David grows into a strapping teen. All seems well; however, the evil Edward Murdstone, who uses child slave laborers in his successful cheese factory, woos and marries Clara. Murdstone immediately conspires to acquire Clara's estate, embarking on a deliberate campaign to destroy his wife's health and get David permanently out of the picture. To this end, he sends David to work in his horrific factory. On the way, David encounters the Duke and his lovely daughter Agnes, and once in the factory he meets two loveable rascals, the kindly Micawber, who is the nominal overseer, and the mischievious Mealy, who becomes his best friend. David uses his intelligence and resourcefulness to revolutionize the cheese factory, which promptly earns him and Mealy a stay in the tower. Meanwhile, his mother is falling into worse and worse health, primarily because the evil Murdstone has been intercepting and destroying all of David's letters to her. In the climax, Agnes helps David escape, and after a number of wild chases and adventures they bring about Murdstone's downfall and save the day.

CAUTION: This film should not be used with the intention of introducing children to the original story. Rebels in the factory are shown as mold-covered denizens of a dank dungeon. The story has been completely bastardized and "modernized," except for one aspect: the authors have managed to retain nineteenth-century stereotypes of women. Curious.

GO: The animation is weak, but the story is reasonably paced and is practically devoid of scenes of real concern.

DIG AND DUG WITH DAISY

Alliance
1993
40 minutes each
Directed By: Terry Ward
Narrated by: George Layton

"Playmobil"-like pixilated figures Dig and Dug (two lovable, but not too bright fix-it men), Dug's niece Daisy and their boss Mr. Rubble are featured in this British series designed to teach children about machines.

On the Building Site
Mrs. Sparkle's Shed
Cement Pudding
Mr. Rubble's Wall
Daisy's Kite

On the Farm
The New Tractor
The Turnip Mountain
Farmer Stubble's Fence
The Haybarn
Other titles in the series: Dig and Dug With Daisy At The Factory, and Dig and Dug With Daisy On The Road

CAUTION: Some British words like spanner and lorry may confuse North Americans. The videos stereotype construction workers as not too bright.

GO: Gentle stories are told using excellent model animation. Racial and gender equality is shown.

DIRTY BEASTS

Strand HomeVideo/Tempo Video
1990
30 minutes
Starring the voices of: Prunella Scales,
  Timothy West

This is a collection of Roald Dahl verse. The video is described as an "animatic moving picture book." The animation is simple, but the narration is engaging.

Stories featured are:

The Pig

A pig puzzles about what life is all about. When he realizes his purpose is to be food for Farmer Bland, he eats the Farmer instead.

The Lion

The lion prefers to eat the waiter rather than the food he offers.

The Scorpion

A scorpion stings a little girl in her bed.

The Ant Eater

Plump, unattractive and spoiled Roy gets an anteater as a present. When he does not feed it, the anteater eats his aunt, then Roy.

The Porcupine

The dentist pulls quills from a little girl's bottom after she sits on a porcupine.

The Cow

Daisy the cow grows wings. While flying she is insulted by a rude man, so she drops a cow pie on him.

The Crocodile

The vile crocodile crunches six boys and six girls for lunch.

The Tummy Beast

A little boy claims that it's the beast in his tummy that makes him eat so much food. His mother doesn't believe him until she hears it for herself.

The Toad and the Snail

An egotistical, magic, giant toad takes a little boy for a ride all the way to France where frog's legs are a delicacy. But when the toad changes into a giant snail it is worse. A final transformation into a roly-poly bird restores the situation.

CAUTION: Humor is black and irreverent; practically everyone is eaten.

GO: The verse is clever and everyone gets his or her comeuppance.

■

DISNEY'S SING-ALONG SONGS SERIES

Walt Disney Home Video
1987–92
30 minutes each

This series has been extremely successful, particularly with children who are just becoming interested in animation. The lyrics run across the bottom of the screen and a bouncing ball indicates the words as they are sung. (This is especially useful when Donald Duck sings!) Each tape, with the exception of *Disneyland Fun*, features songs taken from a variety of Disney full-length features. The tapes in this series include songs from films that have gone into moratorium and songs from films which have not yet been (and may never be) released on video.

The Bare Necessities
(Vol. 4)

Songs featured are:
The Bare Necessities
Cinderella Work Song
Everybody Wants to Be a Cat
Figaro and Cleo
I Wanna Be Like You
Look out for Mr. Stork
Old Yeller
The Ugly Bug Ball
Winnie-the-Pooh
You Are a Human Animal

Be Our Guest
(Vol. 10)

Songs featured are:
Be Our Guest
Beauty and the Beast

Bella Notte
Heffalumps and Woozles
Little Wooden Head
Spoonful of Sugar
The World's Greatest Criminal Mind

Fun With Music
(Vol. 5)

Songs featured are:
All in the Golden Afternoon
Blue Danube Waltz
Boo Boo Boo
Fun with Music
Good Company
Green with Envy Blues
Let's All Sing Like the Birdies Sing
Old MacDonald Had a Farm
Scales and Arpeggios
While Strolling through the Park
Why Should I Worry?
With a Smile and a Song

Heigh-Ho
(Vol. 1)

Songs featured are:
A Cowboy Needs a Horse
The Dwarf's Yodel Song
Heigh-Ho
Hi Diddle Dee Dee
Let's Go Fly a Kite
The Siamese Cat Song
Theme From Zorro
The Three Caballeros
Up, Down and Touch the Ground
Yo-Ho

I Love to Laugh
(Vol. 9)

Songs featured are:
Bluddle-Uddle-Um-Dum
Everbody Has a Laughing Place
I Love to Laugh
Jolly Holidays
Oo-De-Lally
Pink Elephants on Parade
Quack, Quack, Quack Donald Duck
Supercalifragilisticexpialidocious
Who's Afraid of the Big Bad Wolf?
The Wonderful Thing about Tiggers

Under the Sea
(Vol. 6)

Songs featured are:
At the Codfish Ball
By the Beautiful Sea
Kiss the Girl
Never Smile at a Crocodile
Sailing, Sailing
Sailor's Hornpipe
Someone's Waiting for You
That's What Makes the World Go Round
Under the Sea
A Whale of a Tale

Very Merry Christmas Songs
(Vol. 8)

Featured are vintage Disney cartoons and the Disneyland Santa Claus Parade.

Songs featured are:
Deck the Halls
From All of Us to All of You
Here Comes Santa Claus
Jingle Bells
Joy to the World
Let It Snow! Let It Snow! Let It Snow!
Parade of the Wooden Soldiers
Rudolph, the Red-Nosed Reindeer
Silent Night
Sleigh Ride
Up on the Housetop
We Wish You a Merry Christmas
Winter Wonderland

You Can Fly!
(Vol. 3)

Songs featured are:
The Beautiful Briny
Colonel Hathi's March
He's a Tramp
I've Got No Strings
Little Black Rain Cloud
The Merrily Song
Step in Time
When I See an Elephant Fly
You Can Fly

Zip-A-Dee-Doo-Dah
(Vol. 2)

Songs featured are:
The Ballad of Davy Crockett
Bibbidi-Bobbidi-Boo
Casey Junior
Following the Leader
Give a Little Whistle
It's a Small World
The Mickey Mouse Club March
The Unbirthday Song
Whistle While You Work
Zip-A-Dee-Do-Dah

DON'T EAT THE PICTURES: SESAME STREET AT THE METROPOLITAN MUSEUM OF ART

Random House Home Video
1987
60 minutes
Directed by: Jon Stone
Starring: Linda Bove, Paul Dooley, Bob McGrath, James Mason, Carroll Spinney, Fritz Weaver

At closing time on a visit to The Metropolitan Museum of Art, Big Bird and friends go looking for Snuffy and everyone is accidentally locked in overnight. This gives the whole gang a chance to learn an awful lot about art from different cultures. Cookie Monster drools over the beautiful still lifes of food and is constrained only by an official looking sign which reads: Please Don't Eat the Pictures. Oscar is really in his element in the Greek and Roman galleries where he discovers broken statues. Meanwhile, Big Bird finds Snuffy and together they meet Sahu, the son of an Egyptian God. Sahu is under a spell and cannot depart this earth until he answers the riddle: Where does today meet yesterday? (which is posed by a demon who comes every night at midnight). In the end, Sahu answers the question correctly, and the love of his new friends sees him through the final trial.

CAUTION: Very young children may find the demon and Sahu's plight a little scary.

GO: This is a terrific way to introduce very young children to the art of the ages. (And the songs are there, just in case.)

AGES 3 TO 6

THE DRAGON THAT WASN'T (OR WAS HE?)

MCA
1983
83 minutes
Directed by: Bjorn Frank Jensen,
  Bob Maxfield, Ben Van Voorn

In this animated film produced in the Netherlands, baby dragon Dexter mistakenly thinks that Ollie the bear is his father. Which is fine, until Ollie finds that whenever anything upsets Dexter, he grows to gigantic proportions, often larger than the house. Ollie knows that it's best to take Dexter to the Dragon Realm beyond the Misty Mountains where he can live with others of his own kind. And after harrowing experiences with a couple of thieves and an unjust internment in jail, Ollie finally returns Dexter to the Dragon Realm.

CAUTION: This film has an overly complex plot and some children will be quite upset when Dexter leaves his adopted bear father.

DUCKTALES: THE MOVIE — TREASURE OF THE LOST LAMP

Walt Disney Home Video
1990
74 minutes
Directed by: Bob Hathcock
Starring the voices of: Terence McGovern,
  Russi Taylor, Alan Young

While exploring a pyramid on an archaeological expedition, Uncle Scrooge and friends find a lamp. They take it home and polish it up, and when a genie appears, promptly squander their first two wishes by wishing for an elephant, then wishing the elephant would go away. Meanwhile, the evil magician Merlock wants the lamp for himself, and Scrooge is only narrowly saved from the villain when the genie pulls him into the safety of the lamp. Then, as an appreciative Scrooge prepares to return the lamp to the pyramid, Merlock's sinister accomplice Dijon takes the lamp and wishes to be the rightful owner of Scrooge's fortune. And at the film's climax, Merlock returns, takes control and prepares to return to his desert home as ruler of the world.

CAUTION: There is a recurring theme of violence in the film. In one scene, Merlock changes himself into a frightening ferocious ape, and in another, huge crabs climb up onto a sinking platform and threaten the escaping ducks. One of Merlock's toadies is an unfortunate caricature of an Indo-Aryan.

GO: This fully-animated movie will not disappoint fans of the popular television series.

DUCKTALES SERIES

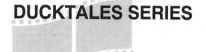

Walt Disney Home Video
1987
45 minutes (each two-episode volume)
Directed by: various
Starring the voices of: June Foray,
   Joan Gerber, Terry McGovern,
   Russi Taylor, Alan Young

Huey, Dewey and Louie live in a huge mansion with their Uncle Scrooge McDuck, a Scottish skinflint billionaire. In this fully-animated series the McDucks's good friends Gearloose and Launchpad McQuack help them thwart the evil villains Magica de Spell and the Beagle Boys.

Titles in the series are:
Accidental Adventurers:
   Jungle Duck; Maid of the Myth
Daredevil Ducks:
   Home Sweet Homer; The Money
   Vanishes
Duck to the Future:
   Duck to the Future; Sir Gyro de
   Gearloose
Fearless Fortune Hunter:
   Earth-Quack!; Masters of the Djinni
High-Flying Hero:
   Hero for Hire; Launchpads Civil War
Lost World Wanderers:
   The Curse of Castle McDuck; Dinosaur
   Ducks
Masked Marauders:
   Send in the Clones; The Time-Teasers
Raiders of the Lost Harp:
   The Pearl of Wisdom; Raiders of the
   Lost Harp

Seafaring Sailors:
   All Ducks on Deck; Sphinx for the
   Memories
Space Invaders:
   Micro Ducks from Outer Space; Where
   No Duck Has Gone Before

GO: With lots of action-adventure, these stories are lively and adequately animated.

DUMBO

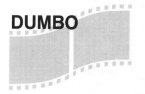

Walt Disney Home Video
1940
63 minutes
Directed by: Ben Sharpstein

A stork brings a baby elephant to the circus — a baby elephant with huge, outlandish ears who promptly gets the cruel nickname Dumbo. Enraged when nasty kids tease her son, Dumbo's mother is moved to physically defend him. Unjustly accused of dementia, she is carted off and put in solitary confinement, leaving baby Dumbo alone. His only friend is a tiny mouse named Timothy who tries everything in his power to find Dumbo a place in the circus. When the pair awake one morning in a tree, Timothy puts two and two together and realizes that Dumbo must have flown in his sleep. The nervous Dumbo refuses to try flying while he's awake until Timothy presents him with a "magic feather." But when Dumbo loses the feather in a high diving act, he realizes that his flying abilities depend on his skills alone.

CAUTION: The idea of being forcibly separated from one's mother can be very upsetting for young children. Also potentially frightening is the "Elephants on Parade" sequence. The black crows are un-pleasant caricatures of Black Americans.

GO: The song "When I See an Elephant Fly" is a favorite with children.

FAERIE TALE THEATER

Playhouse Home Video/CBS Fox
1982–1984
54–60 minutes each

This series of twenty-six live-action films produced by actress Shelley Duvall were directed by a host of accomplished directors and feature well-known film stars in the lead roles. Some stories are played more or less traditionally, while others are tongue-in-cheek portrayals with satirical elements, sexual innuendo and humor.

Films in this group are, for the most part, traditionally played:
Aladdin and His Wonderful Lamp
Beauty and the Beast
The Boy Who Left Home to Learn about the Shivers
Cinderella
The Dancing Princesses
The Emperor's New Clothes
Goldilocks and the Three Bears
Hansel and Gretel *
Jack and the Beanstalk *
The Little Mermaid
The Nightingale *
The Pied Piper of Hamelin
Pinocchio
Puss in Boots
Rapunzel
Rip Van Winkle *
Rumpelstiltskin *
The Snow Queen
Snow White and the Seven Dwarfs *
Thumbelina
(*contains frightening scenes)

Films in this group include sexual innuendo, coarse language and satire:
Little Red Riding Hood
The Princess and the Pea
The Princess Who Had Never Laughed
The Sleeping Beauty
The Tale of the Frog Prince
The Three Little Pigs

✗ FERNGULLY: THE LAST RAINFOREST

20th Century Fox
1992
76 minutes
Directed by: Bill Kroyer
Starring the voices of: Tim Curry,
    Samantha Mathis, Christian Slater,
    Robin Williams

The film begins in the ancient past when Hexxus, the spirit of pure destruction, escapes during a volcanic eruption. He causes havoc around the world until he is finally imprisoned in a tree by Magi, the leader of the Faeries. All humans are believed to have perished in the calamity. The story then returns to the present, where Magi is giving her young apprentice Crysta a history lesson. But Crysta is a reluctant pupil, and as soon as her lesson is over she sets out to investigate rumors that the humans have returned. Before long she comes across some humans herself, busy levelling the forest with an enormous tree-cutting machine. Believing that the machine is a monster, Crysta saves a young man named Zak from a falling tree by shrinking him to her own size. And while Zak comes to understand the beauty and sanctity of the forest, his friends inadvertently liberate the evil spirit Hexxus from his prision. Hexxus promptly possesses the levelling machine and prepares to exact his revenge on Ferngully, and only the combined efforts of every fairy in the forest can defeat the evil spirit and the humans. In the end, Zak is returned to his normal size and leaves the forest sadder and wiser. Based on the Ferngully stories by Diana Young.

✗STOP: Hexxus is a pretty scary character, especially when he transforms from his smoky form into a horrible skeletal figure.

CAUTION: The film's environmentalist message is timely, but clouded by the participation of the evil spirit in the destruction of the forest; the humans would have destroyed the forest all by themselves had Hexxus not appeared.

GO: Despite certain flaws this is an entertaining animation, featuring high production values and excellent voice-overs. The plants featured in the film are botanically correct (the animators spent time in the rain forest) and the music is by world-renowned musicians Johnny Clegg, The Bulgarian Women's Choir and L.L. Cool J. ∎

THE FROG PRINCE: A CANNON MOVIETALE

Warner Home Video/ Cannon Home Video
1988
86 minutes
Directed by: Jackson Hunsicker
Starring: Helen Hunt, John Paragon,
    Aileen Quinn

When the king announces that the throne will go only to the true princess, Princess Zora worries that she isn't one. After all, she doesn't have long hair, grace and a beautiful face like her sister. (Zora is a tomboy who likes to play ball and whose hair never seems to grow.) Then one day, when she drops a ball into a well, a frog retrieves it and makes her promise to be his friend. She honors her promise even when doing so jeopardizes her chance for the throne. It's through this commitment that Zora learns she is a true princess; and that her friend the frog is a handsome prince.

CAUTION: This film is not for fairy tale purists. Some little ones get upset when the evil sister throws the frog in a hole.

GO: Elaborate sets and costumes, a nonthreatening plot and no sexual overtones make this film suitable for young children. Actress Aileen Quinn performs a number of songs. ●

FUNHOUSE FITNESS: THE SWAMP STOMP

Warner Home Video
1991
40 minutes
Directed by: Anita Mann
Starring: Jane Fonda, J.D. Roth

J.D. Roth and costumed animal characters lead a group of girls and boys in simple, silly dance routines called "The Penguin Waddle," "The Spider Crawl" and "The Swamp Stomp." Recommended for children ages three to seven.

GO: Funhouse Fitness is a high-quality production designed to help children develop balance, co-ordination, agility, endurance and strength.

GOOF TROOP COLLECTION

Walt Disney Home Video
1992
47 minutes each
Starring the voices of: Jim Cummings,
Bill Farmer, Dana Hill, Rob Paulsen

Disney's legendary character Goofy is cast as the father of a very hip eleven-year-old named Max. Max's best friend is P.J., whose father is Pete (often cast as a Disney villain), and together they share some slaptstick adventures.

Titles in the fully-animated collection are:
Banding Together (Vol. 3.):
    Shake, Rattle and Goof; Close Encounters of the Weird Mime
Goin' Fishin' (Vol. 1):
    Slightly Dinghy; Wrecks, Lies and Videotape
The Race Is On! (Vol. 2):
    Meanwhile, Back at the Ramp; Tub Be or Not Tub Be

GRANPA

Sony
1992
30 minutes
Directed by: Dianne Jackson
Starring the voice of: Peter Ustinov

This fully-animated film tells the story of a young girl named Emily and her beloved grandfather who empowers her imagination every time he visits. When they're out skipping, he whisks her back to the days of his own youth; when it rains, it becomes the Great Flood of Noah and all the animal pairs swim aboard the house; when Granpa plays the piano, the dolls and the teddy bears come alive and sing along; a simple donkey ride at the beach turns into an elaborate parade; and a roller-coaster ride becomes high-speed maneuvering in a WWII Spitfire. Their days of imagining together end when Granpa passes away.

CAUTION: Granpa's death is tastefully handled; he falls asleep in his chair and when his granddaughter returns from playing outside his chair is empty. She is very sad, until the spirit of her grandfather in his youth, surrounded by the spirits of his childhood playmates, reaches out to take her hand.

GO: Description hardly does justice to this splendid effort. John Burningham's book is a testament to the human imagination and the film has captured it expertly. A marvelous musical score is featured. There is no dialogue ■

✗ THE GREAT MOUSE DETECTIVE

Walt Disney Home Video
1986
74 minutes
Directed by: Ron Clements, Burny Mattinson,
    Dave Michener, John Musker
Starring the voices of: Val Bettin,
    Barrie Ingham, Vincent Price, Alan Young

The Great Mouse Detective opens in London in 1897. When a toy shop owner is kidnapped by a fierce, peg-legged bat, his daughter manages to escape into the rain-drenched streets. There she meets Dr. Dawson, a military surgeon who has just returned from India. The pair seek out the famous detective Basil of Baker Street, who takes on the case. Basil soon determines that the toy shop owner is the prisoner of the evil criminal genius Professor Ratigan, who has forced the toy shop owner to create a mechanical duplicate of the mouse Queen of England; Ratigan plans to replace the real queen with his wind-up robot and thus gain control of the whole country. High adventure ensues as Basil thwarts the evil Ratigan's designs.

✗STOP: This film is too violent and too scary for most children under the age of five; it's replete with images of snarling faces illuminated by lightning flashes and saliva dripping from bared fangs. Of special concern may be the scenes in which one of the evil villain's incompetent henchmen is fed to a huge cat.

CAUTION: There is a real Saturday morning cartoon flavor to this film and the final chase scene goes on and on.

GO: Kids who like this film, *really* like it.

✗ THE HAPPY PRINCE

Random House Home Video
1987
30 minutes
Directed by: Michael Mills
Starring the voices of: Glynis Johns,
    Christopher Plummer

After his untimely death, the spirit of a happy young prince inhabits a beautiful, gold-plated statue, where he is forced to oversee the misery of his poverty-stricken city. Helped by a courageous young swallow, the Happy Prince distributes pieces of his gold covering throughout the city to alleviate the suffering of the masses. Based on the story by Oscar Wilde.

✗STOP: The swallow dies.

CAUTION: The story's ancient themes of enlightenment, suffering, repentance and redemption may be inaccessible to younger children, and its tragic ending upsetting for older ones.

■

HORTON HEARS A WHO!

MGM/UA
1970
26 minutes
Directed by: Chuck Jones
Narrated by: Hans Conreid

In the Jungle of Nool, Horton is taking refuge from the noon heat in a refreshing pool, when his super-acute hearing alerts him to the presence of a microscopic world called Whoville on a speck of dust on a poppy. No one else can hear the Whos, they ridicule him and, seeking to destroy the source of his madness, decide to boil Whoville, dust mote, poppy and all. Horton implores the Whos to make as much noise as they possibly can in order to prove that they really do exist. So every Who responds by whacking pots and blowing a horns, but it isn't until the last and tiniest Who makes his contribution to the din that Horton's fellow jungle-dwellers hear the Whos. And Horton helps them recognize the maxim: A person's a person, no matter how small. Based on the book by Dr. Seuss.

CAUTION: The original text guides this fully-animated production, but some small additions and changes have been made to the story. Songs were added, the lyrics written by Dr. Seuss.

GO: The story makes it clear that everyone's contribution is important in a group effort, and that size is not an indicator of worth.

I LOVE DINOSAURS SERIES

Fisher-Price
1987, 1989
30 minutes each
Directed by: Ernest Schultz
Narrated by: Harlan Rector

Each tape contains three short episodes which discuss various aspects of dinosaurs. The animation is rudimentary, but the subject is fascinating, and the writing and narration are generally excellent, with a few exceptions.

King of the Dinosaurs

King of the Dinosaurs Discusses Tyrannosaurus Rex: his weight, size and possible habits, his foes, and the discovery of fossil remains. Also discusses the end of the dinosaur era.

CAUTION: Casually mentions that most scientists consider the dinosaurs to be reptilian, a viewpoint which has since changed dramatically.

Flying Dinosaurs Discusses the various species and their characteristics, their similarities and differences with respect to modern birds and bats, their evolution and possible habits.

The Horned Dinosaur Discusses the appearance and possible habits of Triceratops, and the appearance of other cerataurs, as well as the first fossil findings.

The Biggest Dinosaurs

The Biggest Dinosaurs Features the Apatosaurs, their possible habits and physiology, the mechanics of their digestion, and the manner in which they cared for their young. It discusses the various sizes of each member of this monster family.

The Day of the Dinosaur This summary of the dinosaurs is delivered in poetic form, which is the likely reason for its two inherent inaccuracies.

CAUTION: Two glaring mistakes: says the Brontosaurus was the biggest dinosaur, and says the Pteranadon was the biggest flying dinosaur. Both these statements are inconsistent even within the framework of the series itself.

The Spike-tailed Dinosaur Chronicles the appearance, habits, and eventual dying out of Stegosaurus and its cousin species.

IRA SLEEPS OVER

f.h.e.
1993
27 minutes
Directed By: Michael Sporn
Starring the voices of: Danny Gerrard,
   Grace Johnston, Jarrod Spector

Ira is invited to sleep over at his friend Reggie's house. Should he take his teddy bear TaTa along? He knows it is silly, so he decides not to take the toy, mostly because of his sister's claim that Reggie will laugh at him. He has a wonderful time with Reggie until Reggie tells ghost stories in bed. Reggie scares himself so much that he has to get his teddy bear FooFoo. Ira runs to his house and gets TaTa. Reggie doesn't laugh and both boys sleep just fine. Based on the book by Bernard Waber.

CAUTION: Broadway-style songs will either appeal or annoy.

GO: The animation is unusual. Done simply with watercolour-like tones, it gives a gentle impression.

■

IT'S THE MUPPETS COLLECTION

Buena Vista Home Video
1993
35 minutes each
Directed by: Jim Henson

Both videos are compilations of *Muppet Show* highlights and have been put together in the same format as the original shows.

Titles in the collection are:
Meet the Muppets (Vol. 1)
More Muppets, Please! (Vol. 2)

IVOR THE ENGINE

BFS Video
1991
60 minutes each
Starring the voices of: Olwen Griffiths,
   Antony Jackson, Oliver Postgate

Together, a steam engine named Ivor and his driver, Jones, run a Welsh railway line. Ivor is a very human character; he communicates with Jones the Steam by blowing his horn, and even sings bass in the local choir. Created, written and produced by Oliver Postgate.

Ivor the Engine and the Dragons

When Ivor and Jones the Steam encounter Adrius the Dragon and his family, they discover that Welsh dragons are hardly the bold, ferocious monsters of classical mythology. On the contrary, they are small and mischievous and enjoy flitting around. Their only problem is that they require intense heat to survive, which Ivor's fire temporarily provides. But problems arise when the dragons make a nuisance of themselves and steps must be taken to find them a permanent home before the authoritarian Antiquarian Society locks them away.

Ivor the Engine and the Elephants

Ivor, Jones the Steam and choir director Eben Evans are riding the line when they discover an elephant sleeping on the tracks. After she's awake, they discover that the elephant has a nasty cut on her foot. They give her a ride, and while Jones the Steam gets the vet, discover both the elephant's name (Alice) and her owner (Banger's Famous Circus).

CAUTION: The heavily-accented narration of the films in this series is bound to cause some difficulties for North American viewers. The animation is limited and the stories are rather complex. In *Ivor the Engine and the Elephants* the depiction of a South Asian may offend some viewers.

GO: The *Ivor the Engine* films are charming and gentle.

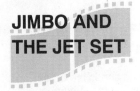

JIMBO AND THE JET SET

BFS Video
1987
50 minutes (Vol. 1),
    54 minutes (Vol. 2)
Directed by: Keith Learner
Starring the voices of:
    Peter Hawkins, Susan Sheridan

When one of the designers at the aircraft factory mistakes inches for centimetres, a small new jumbo jet is built. And when the Chief Controller of London Airport sees the unusual little plane and exclaims that he ordered a Jumbo, not a Jimbo, Jimbo gets his name. Both volumes describe the misadventures of this endearing character and his friends, Tommy Towtruck, Amanda Baggage and Chrissy the Catering Truck.

Jimbo and the Jet Set
(Vol. 1)

Stories featured are:
April Fool's Day
The Chief Gets a Rocket
Chinese Pandemonium
First Time Flyers
Jimbo and the Whale
Jimbo Down Under
Jinglebells Jimbo
Jungle Jimbo
The Little Big Problem
The Old Timer
Quiet Please
Trouble at Sea

Jimbo and the Jet Set
(Vol. 2)

Stories featured are:
Bermuda Triangle
The Computer Clanger
The Controller's Apprentice
Every Silver Lining Has a Cloud
The Great Air Race
Holiday Weather
Jet Lag
Jimbo and the Astronaut
The Little Red Devil
The Royal Visitors
The Penn and Inca Story
The UFO
Winter Wonderland

CAUTION: In the story *The UFO*, the Chief is beamed up by a friendly alien whose skeletal face may frighten very young children. There are a few simplistic representations of a number of cultures that may be considered offensive.

GO: Although somewhat stilted, these simple animated stories are ideal for young vehicle fans.

JOANIE BARTELS' SIMPLY MAGIC SERIES

The Rainy Day Adventure (Vol. 1)

BMG Kidz
1993
45 minutes
Directed by: Sidney J. Bartholomew
Starring: Joanie Bartels, Brandon Cook, Michelle Ingrid, Heather White

On a miserable rainy day, Jason, Allison and Rebecca come home to find a note from Mom saying that she is running some errands and will send a babysitter. To make things worse, their dog Ginger has run off. Magic Joanie finds Ginger and, since she can understand dog-speak, learns where Ginger lives. Meanwhile, back at the house, the electricity has gone out and the phone is dead. When Joanie arrives with Ginger, she fixes the phone and engages the children in a number of incredible singalong activities. By the time Mom returns Joanie has gone, but everything is perfectly in order, even though the babysitter never showed up.

Songs featured are:
Barefootin'
Limbo Rock
Happy Feet
Animal Crackers

Splish Splash
On the Road to Where We're Going
Somewhere Over the Rainbow
Twinkle Twinkle Little Star

CAUTION: There is a scary image of a wolf.

GO: Joanie Bartels' customary magic is enhanced with some clever special effects.

The Extra-Special Substitute Teacher (Vol. 2)

BMG Kidz
1994
45 minutes
Directed by: Sidney J. Bartholomew and Dominic Orlando
Starring: Joanie Bartels, Kenny Mirman, Cindy Warden

Principal Tudball hires Joanie to be the substitute teacher for Room 8. She can speak in sign language and has magical abilities. She can roar, write with lightning speed, and rapidly change costumes. She takes the children to a variety of locales, where they sing, dance, play pinata, and learn many useful things.

Songs include:
La Bamba
Dinosaur Rock and Roll
The Martian Hop
The Alphabet (Consonant) Song
The Loco-motion
The Name Game
Sillie Pie
Put On A Happy Face
Would You Like To Swing On A Star

GO: Well-produced, with a good choice of songs, and cast with personable children. Informative without being obnoxious.

THE JOHN MATTHEWS COLLECTION

Golden Book
Directed By: John Matthews
Rating: Not Rated

The Adventures of Curious George

1982, 1984
Starring the voices of: June Foray, Ruth Buell,
Corey Burton, Bobby Spiedel
Running time: 30 minutes each

This charming work of puppetmation (pixilation) chronicles two of the famous monkey's adventures. It opens with George and the Man with the Yellow Hat looking through a photo album. A flashback takes us to the jungle. The Man with the Yellow Hat — demonstrating a stunning lack of ecological consciousness — sets eyes on George and promptly decides that the monkey would be happier in a zoo. He captures George and takes him aboard a ship, where George immediately gets into trouble. Once in the big city, George gets in more hot water by accidentally summoning the fire department, is jailed, escapes and flies across the city, held airborne by a bunch of stolen balloons. The next picture reminds George and the Man about the time George ate a piece of a jigsaw puzzle and had to go to the hospital. Based on the books *Curious George* and *George Goes to the Hospital* by Margaret and H.A. Rey.

CAUTION: The idea that animals would be happier in a zoo belongs to another time period. When George is taken away from the jungle, and when he is put in prison, he cries. Little ones may be upset.

GO: Wonderfully animated. The hospital episode may be very helpful for little ones who are faced with the prospect of going into one.

Frog and Toad Are Friends

1985
Starring the voices of: Hal Smith, Will Ryan,
Jan Colmar
30 minutes
Includes the short *Frog and Toad: Behind the Scenes* (1986)

Frog is a quick, light-hearted fellow, while Toad is somewhat slower and more ponderous. After a long hibernation, Frog tricks his stick-in-the-mud friend into getting out of bed and enjoying the clear warm light of April. The two amphibious amigos have many subsequent gentle adventures.

Frog and Toad: Behind the Scenes (1986) is an exposition of John Matthews' claymation techniques and shows how the series was made. A great little featurette for everyone, large and small, who is interested in animation.

CAUTION: In the first story, Frog plays a slightly dishonest trick on Toad.

GO: This wonderful series is based on Arnold Lobel's book, and designed from the illustrations.

Frog and Toad Together

1987
Starring the voices of: Hal Smith,
Will Ryan
30 minutes

The Garden: Toad learns the value of patience.

Cookies: Frog and Toad explore the virtues of willpower and learn that it is a two-edged sword.

Dragons and Giants: Frog and Toad test their personal courage by climbing a mountain fraught with various perils.

The Dream: Toad has a vainglorious dream in which he appears on stage before Frog as the "greatest toad in the world," playing piano, walking a tightrope, etc. After each splendid performance he asks Frog if Frog can do the same, and each time Frog replies "no," and gets smaller, until finally, to Toad's horror, Frog disappears. Toad then awakens and is relieved to see his friend alive and well.

CAUTION: In *The Dream,* Toad tells the M.C. to "shut up."

GO: Superbly done

Mouse Soup

1992
Starring the voices of: Buddy Hackett, Will Ryan, Hal J. Rayle, Pat Musick
26 minutes

Based on Arnold Lobel's book of the same name. When a wise-cracking storytelling mouse gets captured by a dim-witted weasel, the little guy has to think fast to avoid becoming mouse soup. He explains to the weasel that the most important ingredient in mouse soup is stories. The gullible weasel buys it, and the mouse promptly spins a succession of yarns: the story of a mouse in a fix with some angry bees, the story of two stones, the story of a singing cricket and a mouse who can't sleep, and the story of a mouse with

a thorn bush in her chair. In accordance with the wily mouse's instructions, the weasel then stalks off to find the ingredients featured in the stories, a bee-hive, two stones, some crickets and a thorn bush. When he returns, the mouse has, of course, made good his escape.

GO: Amazing pixilation and a very funny storyline highlight this tale.

Stanley and the Dinosaurs

1989
Starring the voices of: Will Ryan, Corey Burton, Jim Cummings, Pat Musick, Rick Polizzi
26 minutes

Based on the book *Stanley,* by Sid Hoff, this award-winning claymation effort concerns a young boy, Stanley, who is obsessed with dinosaurs at the expense of his education and his social skills. During a trip to the Museum of Natural History, he falls asleep in the dinosaur exhibit and dreams the story of a caveman named Stanley who is a real innovator with the motto "work smarter, not harder." Stanley gets kicked out of the cave because of his progressive attitude, but makes his own house with the help of his dinosaur friends and eventually enlightens his beetle-browed clansmen. Stanley then wakes up inspired, and sets his own situation to rights.

CAUTION: In Stanley's dream, cavemen and dinosaurs appear in the same time period (not exactly educational by purist standards). The dinosaurs and even the style of animation, marvelous as it is, may frighten very little ones.

GO: Amazing claymation highlights this hilarious "brain versus brawn" tale.

Uncle Elephant

1991
Starring the voices of: Will Ryan, Pat Musick
30 minutes

Based on the book *Uncle Elephant,* by Arnold Lobel. Arnie, a young elephant, loves to tell jokes. The problem is, he's not funny. One day his parents go on a little sailing jaunt around the bay and inexplicably vanish. Arnie is in mourning, and "kind of sad," but his wonderful kindly — and very wrinkled — uncle comes to take him to live with him. Uncle Elephant turns out to be a master *cheerer-upper* and helps Arnie through the tough wait, until his parents come back home safe and sound.

CAUTION: Arnie is understandably and clearly devastated when his parents vanish. He sings a surrealistic song about it, the images in which may frighten the very small.

GO: Unbelievable animation highlights this charming story of never-say-die hope and friendship between the young and old.

THE JUNGLE BOOK

Walt Disney Home Video
1967
78 minutes
Directed by: Wolfgang Reitherman
Starring the voices of: Sebastian Cabot
    Phil Harris, George Sanders

This fully-animated film opens in the middle of the Indian Jungle where Bagheera, a black panther, has just discovered a basket containing an abandoned newborn. Realizing that the child will die before he can get it back to the "man-village," he elects to take it to a family of wolves that has just had a litter of cubs. Luckily, the child is accepted by the mother and raised with the other cubs. And he lives in this way for ten years, unaware of the civilized world. Then, in the tenth year, news spreads through the jungle that the great tiger Shere Khan has returned. Shere Khan hates all humans and Bagheera and the wolves know that the tiger will kill Mowgli as soon as he finds him. So they decide to return Mowgli to his own kind. But the journey to the "man-village" is a perilous trip of many days, which is complicated by Mowgli's unwillingness to go. On the way, they encounter the boa constrictor Kaa, a free-spirited bear named Baloo, a monkey named King Louie and finally the ferocious Bengal tiger, Shere Khan himself. In the end, Mowgli is saved by Baloo and a quartet of vultures (a hilarious send-up of the early Beatles), and eventually makes it to the "man-village."

Songs featured are:
The Bare Necessities
Colonel Hathi's March
I Wanna Be Like You

GO: There's little to worry about here. Even Shere Khan is so dignified that he's only marginally scary, and very young children routinely enjoy this film.

■

THE JUNGLE KING

Sony
1994
48 minutes
Directed by: Kamoon Song

Maximillian (Max) is a lion, and the ruler of the jungle kingdom. He is a narcissistic egomaniac, surrounded by fawning sycophants and hated by the common folk. His twin brother Irwin is a gentle recluse intent only on finishing an ambitious bird catalogue. The chancellor of the kingdom, Hyena, plans to usurp the throne; to this end, he is plotting with the tiger king of a neighbouring country to take control. Both Hyena and Max desire the beautiful Lionette, who is scheduled to be married to Max on Saturday. Hyena sets up Max to be captured by hunters; however, a loyal supporter recruits Irwin to take Max's place until Max can be rescued. In the meantime, Irwin and Lionette meet and fall in love. Irwin changes the whole kingdom as well, setting wrongs right. In the climax, the tigers attack, and Max returns just in time to help his brother repel the invaders and run off the evil Hyena. Irwin marries Lionette, and Max learns how to be a nice king.

CAUTION: B-level animation and obnoxious characters dominate this effort. Lionette is perceived by Max and Hyena as a slave to be married or not as they see fit. There is violent combat at the climax. The non-stop stock music obliterates half the dialogue.

GO: This film contains positive messages about reforming.

✗ THE LAND BEFORE TIME

MCA
1989
69 minutes
Directed by: Don Bluth
Starring the voices of: Judith Barsi,
Burke Byrnes, Gabriel Damon,
Pat Hingle, Candy Hutson, Helen Shaver

An earthquake separates four little dinosaurs from their families. Pursued by predators, they are forced to journey without their parents through fire and famine to the Great Valley, where happiness awaits.

✗STOP: Littlefoot's mother is killed. (Her death is tempered slightly by her appearance as a guiding force, and by the viewer's knowledge that Littlefoot also has grandparents.)

CAUTION: This is a visually beautiful, but often intense, full-length animation. After a great earthquake the four toddler dinosaurs are separated from their families and left to find their way alone and as they travel they encounter volcanoes and terrifying predators. (Some children we have talked to worry: Will we have an earthquake here?)

GO: The underdogs win, overcoming significant odds, and the film does show the benefits of positive working relationships, and of overcoming stereotyping. Breathtaking animation, adorable characterizations and an inspirational story make this film a classic.

AGES 3 TO 6

AGES 3 TO 6

LEARN THE ALPHABET WITH PROFESSOR PLAYTIME

DMS Ltd. Video
1990
40 minutes
Visual production and animation by
Toy Box Prod. Ltd.
Starring the voices of: Lisa Abbott,
Anthony Corriette, the Bolam Children
Rating: British rating of Universal. Particularily
suitable for children

Using rudimentary animation, continuous rhythmic music and frequent repetition this video moves along at a good tempo teaching the alphabet by means of an easily learned alphabet song (not the alphabet song familiar to North American children). Animated character voice-overs by Lisa and Anthony teach the letters phonetically and use an animal association, rhythmic visual images and rhyming phrases. Songs and images including Victor the viper, Garth the goat, Kenny the kangaroo, Alice the alligator, Y for yellowhammers (will North American children wonder what they are?) A little test at the end asks the child to repeat the letters phonetically by himself. Produced for Preschool and Primary age. From the Play and Learn series of videos and cassettes.

GO: Simple, straightforward, effective.

CAUTION: British accents. For non-American children the letter Z is pronounced zed not zee.

THE LION, THE WITCH AND THE WARDROBE

CTW/Republic
1979
95 minutes
Directed by: Bill Melendez
Starring the voices of: Beth Porter,
Stephen Thorne, Rachel Warren

When English children Lucy, Peter, Edmund and Susan discover that another world can be reached through the back of an old wardrobe in their guardian's house, their adventures in the land of Narnia begin. There, they learn that the evil White Witch keeps Narnia in an eternal winter and agree to help the magical lion Aslan restore spring to the land. But Edmund has become a traitor and informs the Witch of their plans. Aslan is forced to give himself to the Witch in exchange for the boy's freedom. (In Narnia, the law dictates that traitors belong to the Witch.) Aslan is killed, but in the end is restored to life by virtue of a higher law, and returns to conquer the Witch. Lucy, Peter, Edmund and Susan are made the rulers of Narnia where they live for a long time, eventually returning to England to discover that no time has passed. This is a fully-animated version of the first book of seven in the *Chronicles of Narnia* by C.S. Lewis.

CAUTION: The animation is very simple and seems to lack the depth necessary to sustain the scenes of long and faithful-to-the-book dialogue. Although the children are supposed to be English, their accents are American (or inconsistently English, or Australian) and the White Witch screams her lines throughout the film. The story's language may be too sophisticated for little ones and at 95 minutes is very long. The White Witch tries to kill Edmund and does kill Aslan with a sharp dagger; the battle is quite scary.

GO: Recommended by the National Education Association and funded by the Episcopal Radio/TV Foundation, the story is often considered to have religious overtones.

● ■

THE LITTLE CROOKED CHRISTMAS TREE

C/FP
1990
24 minutes
Directed by: Ron Broda,
    Michael Cutting
Starring the voices of:
    the Appleby College Choir,
    Christopher Plummer

When a dove lays her eggs in its branches, a little tree on Brown's Christmas Tree Farm protects the chicks by leaning into the sun. In so doing, he becomes crooked and learns that he is no longer desirable as a Christmas tree. Unsure about what this means, the little tree asks: What is Christmas and what is a Christmas tree? The dove tells him that Christmas is the celebration of the birth of Jesus Christ and the coming together of family. She also tells him that he has been spared the fate of being decorated for a day and then discarded after the celebrations. But after all of his friends are taken to be decorated, the tree becomes lonely. Then in the summer The tree is transplanted to a garden where the following Christmas he is decorated so

beautifully that people come from miles around to see him. Based on the book by Michael Cutting and Ron Broda.

CAUTION: This video is not fully-animated; the camera pans over the beautiful paper sculpture illustrations, zooming in and out on elements of the picture.

GO: A charming but somewhat melancholy story about sacrifice. A portion of the purchase price of this video is donated to the Hospital For Sick Children and to your local children's hospital.

THE LITTLE ENGINE THAT COULD

MCA
1991
30 minutes
Directed By: Dave Edwards
Starring the voices of: Bever-Leigh Banfield,
    Kath Soucie, Frank Welker

A little boy waits hopefully for Georgia the birthday train, loaded with toys, to come over the hill. Meanwhile at the train yard, little switch engine Tillie is eager for a real job. When Georgia breaks down on the way, the toys appeal to every train that comes by. Not one will help, so Tillie gets her chance. The hill is very steep, the going tough and scary. Just when she thinks it is impossible she intones, "I think I can, I think I can ... " over and over until she does! Based on the book by Watty Piper.

Song featured:
Nothing Can Stop Us Now

CAUTION: Chip the bird calls the nasty tower "You old blowhard."

GO: Excellent full animation of the old story about determination, and this time the engine is a girl.

■

THE LITTLE FOX

Celebrity Home Entertainment
1987
80 minutes
Directed by: Attila Dargay
Starring the voices of: John Bellucci,
    Anne Costelloe, Maia Danziger

A young fox named Vic isn't content to stay at home with the rest of the family when his father goes hunting, and sets out to help. His father sends him back, but Vic becomes lost, and that night a farmer (Chester) tracks his father back to the den and discovers the whole family. When Vic finally returns to the den hours later, his family is gone and his Uncle Karak is waiting. Karak explains that his family will not be returning and proceeds to teach Vic the essentials of being a fox. Seasons pass and Vic grows big and strong and very clever. And when Chester launchs an all-out foxhunt and Karak is forced to give his life to save Vic and his new mate Foxy, Vic vows revenge and steals all of Chester's chickens, roosters and geese.

CAUTION: Death is a relentless feature of this story. Though none of the deaths are graphic, characters are obviously killed. One young viewer we know told us she thought that the story was a bit depressing.

GO: Despite the stiff animation and the not-so-great score, this film does give viewers a glimpse at the life of a wild

creature living on the fringe of human civilization.

THE LITTLE MATCH GIRL

f.h.e.
1990
30 minutes
Directed by: Michael Sporn
Starring the voice of: F. Murray Abraham

The story takes place in New York City in the year 1999, where the city's poor find homes wherever they can. Angela's family lives in the 18th Street subway station where Angela sells matches to subsidize her family's income. On New Year's Eve, a cold and snowy night, Angela goes into an alley and finally strikes a match to try to get warm. It doesn't work. Instead though, an apparition of Angela's favorite aunt appears. Together they fly over the rooftops to the Botanical Gardens New Year's Eve Benefit for the Homeless, where she meets the Monkey Puzzle Tree and other plants with whom she has a swinging time. Then suddenly, she is back out in the cold again. She lights another match and from the street hears the saxophone of Louis, her favorite street musician. They go ice-skating and see fireworks. Back in Times Square once more, Angela strikes a third match and this time flies with her grandmother to their old home, which has long since been torn down. The storm grows worse and when it breaks early the next morning, a crowd has gathered around a bluish little girl lying on the pavement. But she comes back to life when she hears the promises of people to help the homeless. This contemporary version of the popular Hans Christian Andersen fairy tale features jazz music by Caleb Sampson and hip-hop New York talk.

GO: In its updated version, this little moral tale has now become a tale of social conscience dealing with the homeless, the rainforest and urban expansion.

■

THE LITTLE MERMAID

Random House Home Video
1986
26 minutes
Directed by: Peter Sander
Starring the voice of:
    Richard Chamberlain

This story is similar to the 1979 version, but when the little mermaid refuses to kill the prince and save her own life, she floats up into the skies and becomes a Daughter of the Air. We are told that if she strives for 300 years to help the children of the earth, she will receive a soul. (When a child is bad, a day is added to her sentence; when one is good, a year is removed.) The time passes quickly and the mermaid earns everlasting happiness.

CAUTION: This is a bizarre and depressing tale, and there are many references to death and life after death. The Enchantress is frightening.

GO: The animation and production are good and the narration is excellent.

■

THE LITTLE MERMAID

Walt Disney Home Video
1989
83 minutes
Directed by: Ron Clements,
    John Musker
Starring the voices of: Rene Auberjonois,
    Pat Carroll, Buddy Hackett

Concerned by his youngest daughter Ariel's fascination with all things human, King Triton assigns Sebastian (a crab and the royal court composer) the job of watching over her. Sure enough, Ariel goes to the surface where she sees Eric, a handsome prince. When a sudden storm causes a fire and explosion which sinks his ship, Ariel drags him safely to land. The prince awakens just in time to catch a glimpse of Ariel and hear her lovely voice before she disappears back into the water. When Sebastian informs Triton of Ariel's latest escapade, Triton is livid. He angrily destroys Ariel's prize possession (a statue of Eric she retrieved from the ship's wreckage), and in an act of defiance Ariel vows to find a way of being with the prince. She makes a deal with the sea-witch Ursula: Ariel will receive a human form, in return for her voice. And if the prince doesn't kiss her within three days, Ariel will be Ursula's forever. On the surface, Ariel and Eric get along splendidly, but the sea-witch puts a stop to that; using Ariel's stolen voice, she bewitches Eric and arranges to be married to him. Ariel and her friends do manage to stop the wedding and break the enchantment, but it's too late for Ariel. The sun has gone down on the third day and she now belongs to Ursula. Then the sea-witch's true plans are revealed. With Ariel as a hostage, Ursula blackmails Triton and replaces him as ruler of the oceans. But at the last minute, Eric steers the bowsprit of an old wreck through the witch's heart and the next morning Triton himself returns Ariel to human form.

CAUTION: A great many small children have been scared by Ursula who, when she grows huge at the end of the film, is a fairly terrifying figure.

GO: With splendid animation, lively characters and an engaging tale, this feature contains some of the best Disney songs ever, including "Under the Sea" and "Kiss the Girl."

●

THE LITTLE MERMAID: ARIEL'S UNDERSEA ADVENTURES

Walt Disney Home Video
1992
44 minutes each
Directed by: Jamie Mitchell
Starring the voices of: Jodie Benson, Jim Cummings, Sam Wright

The adventures of Ariel, Flounder and Sebastian continue in the undersea realm of Atlantica. (Ariel is in mermaid form throughout.) Ariel sings songs, outwits villains and has fun with her friends, some familiar and some new.

Titles in the collection are:
In Harmony (Vol. 4):
  In Harmony

Double Bubble (Vol. 3):
  Double Bubble; Message in a Bottle
Charmed Ariel's Gift (Vol. 5)
Stormy, the Wild Seahorse (Vol. 2):
  Stormy, the Wild Seahorse; The Great Sebastian
Whale of a Tale (Vol. 1):
  Whale of a Tale; Urchin

✗ LITTLE NEMO: ADVENTURES IN SLUMBERLAND

Astral
1992
86 minutes
Directed by: Masami Hata and William Hurtz
Starring: Rene Auberjonois, Gabriel Damon, Danny Mann, Mickey Rooney

After awakening from a nightmare, Nemo discovers that the circus is coming to town. To his disappointment, his father seems ambivalent about taking him. That next night, Nemo has another dream. He and his pet flying squirrel, Icarus, are visited by a delegation from the kingdom of Slumberland. The delegation consists of Professor Genius and his assistant, Bon Bon, who have been sent by King Morpheus (the protector of everyone's dreams), to bring Nemo back as a companion to his daughter, Princess Camille. Nemo agrees to go, and after a flight to Slumberland in a fancy dirigible and a number of amusing adventures, he meets Morpheus. Morpheus gives him a golden key which will open any door in Slumberland, with the caution that he is not to open one particular door. The king then decrees that Nemo should be trained as a prince.

During the course of Nemo's increasingly boring education, the mischievous hobo-type Flip persuades Nemo to open the forbidden door. A gruesome substance, the stuff of nightmares, engulfs Morpheus and takes him away to Nightmareland. Nemo, accompanied by Flip, the Professor and Camille, sets out on a quest to the evil domain to rescue the king. After a series of harrowing adventures, Nemo succeeds in restoring king and kingdom. He returns home to the real world just in time for the circus.

✗STOP: The opening nightmare is intense. The nightmare kingdom, and in particular its demonic ruler, are unsuitable for children under five.

CAUTION: A generally eerie atmosphere pervades this film. The excellent animation lends power to the darker scenes, in particular the opening of the forbidden door and the abduction of the king, not to mention the final combat with the demon lord.

GO: This effort features brilliant animation and a highly imaginative and unusual plot which will appeal to older children and many adults.

LITTLE RASCALS

Universal
1994
80 minutes (approx)
Directed By: Penelope Spheeris
Starring: Travis Tedland, Kevin Jamal Woods, Jordan Workol, Bug Hall
MPAA rating: G

The biggest event of all time, the Go-Kart Race, is looming and the Rascals' vehicle, "The Blur," is heavily favored. But all is not well. Dissension has wracked the Little Rascals' club (known by the politically-incorrect moniker: "He-Man Woman-Haters"), because Alfalfa is entertaining treacherously amorous thoughts concerning the fetching Darla. In the ensuing chaos, the He-Man Woman-Haters' clubhouse burns to the ground. The end result of this catastrophe is that Darla vows to hate Alfalfa for eternity, and Alfalfa is sentenced to death by the club (his sentence is commuted to being forced to guard The Blur until the big race). But after Alfalfa's attempts to reconcile himself to Darla go comically awry, he abandons his responsibility and makes one last stab at winning her back from a tycoon's oily son. The local bully/villains promptly steal The Blur, and it appears that Alfalfa and Spanky's friendship is irrevocably shattered. But the Gang gets back together and builds The Blur 2, and Spanky and Alfalfa race the bullies and the rich kid to a wild finish.

CAUTION: Bodily-function humor, moderate name-calling. Some people may find the portrayal of children acting like adults, especially in romantic situations, inappropriate given the current climate of child abuse. If the film wasn't based on a classic series, the filmmakers might not have gotten away with it.

GO: Our hats off to Ms. Spheeris. The performances of the children and animals were nothing short of amazing, and film was briskly paced. A faithful tribute to the vintage Little Rascals.

LYRIC LANGUAGE (FRENCH/ENGLISH) SERIES 2

Penton Overseas Inc.
1992
35 minutes
Directed by: Mike Sarain/Terramar Video
Starring: Olivia Haskell and Jean Haskell

This bilingual music program, winner of the 1992 California Children's Media Award, has 10 original songs in English and French, introduced by the animated characters from the Family Circus comic strip. Recommended for children of all ages, this video even works for adults trying to become more familiar with another language. Each song is dubbed over a live-action sequence based on a theme. Lyrics are clearly subtitled on the screen in English and French.

Songs featured are:
The Opposites Song
A Picnic
A Walk In The Forest
I'd Like To Read
The Spider
I Have Five Senses
There Is A River
The Clown
Clap Your Hands
Family
Also available in Spanish/English.

MADELINE COLLECTION

Sony
1988–1993
24–30 minutes each
Directed: Stephan Martiniere, Stan Phillips
Starring the voices of: Marsha Moreau,
Judith Orban, Christopher Plummer

Based on Ludwig Bemelmans' famous children's stories, with animation similar to the original book illustrations and with songs interspersed throughout.

Madeline

In this video we meet Madeline, the littlest of twelve girls who live with Miss Clavell at a boarding school in Paris, France. One day the usually cheerful, and much-loved Madeline cannot smile ... but everything is restored to normal after she has her appendix removed and impresses the other girls with her scar.

Madeline's Christmas

The girls visit their friend Madame Maria and tell her of their plans to go to their homes for the Christmas holidays. They wrap presents and bake goodies but on the night before Christmas everyone, except Madeline, comes down with a cold. Madeline nurses them all, but the girls are worried about not being able to get the gifts to their families. When Madame Maria is unable to travel because of a bad storm and seeks refuge at the school she makes a special porridge that cures everyone. Then the girls' families come to the school, and while they are having the best Christmas ever, Madame Maria disappears.

Madeline's Rescue

One day Madeline falls into the river. A stray dog saves her and

Miss Clavell allows the dog to stay, but Lord Cucuface sends the dog away. The girls (even though they argue over the dog) are miserable until she finds her way back. All arguments are settled however, when twelve puppies arrive.

Madeline and the Bad Hat

A bratty little boy named Pepito moves into the Spanish Embassy next door. Madeline says there is nothing worse than him except a bad hat. Pepito torments the girls by doing things like building a guillotine to do away with the chickens. But when one of his pranks backfires on him he learns his lesson.

Madeline and the Gypsies

During a rainstorm at the carnival, Madeline and Pepito are stranded on a ferris wheel. Circus performers save them and move on, unaware that Madeline and Pepito are following. The children earn their keep by performing. It is a great holiday until they get homesick. When Miss Clavell brings the girls to see a show, Madeline and Pepito are glad to go home with them.

Madeline in London

When a reluctant Pepito moves to London, he misses the girls so badly, they visit and bring him a birthday present of a horse! Picadilly, the horse, takes Madeline and Pepito on a ride. Madeline meets the Queen and on returning to the Embassy everyone has a birthday meal. But Picadilly is left with nothing to eat. After he eats Pepito's mother's entire vegetable garden, they find him lying in the street sick. Dr. Stone says they must feed him oats and hay. When they find that Pepito's mother is allergic to the horse, the girls take Picadilly home with them to Paris.

GO: Dr. Stone, the vet, is a woman.

Madeline and the Dog Show

The twelve little girls want to enter their talented dog, Genevieve, in a dog show but she has no pedigree. Madeline pleads her case and Genevieve is in. After an amazing display of super canine qualities, the dog wins, but a jealous owner accuses her of giving the other dogs fleas. Jumping into the fountain to escape the fleas, the dogs nearly drown, as they cannot swim. Genevieve comes to the rescue and is crowned Best of Show.

CAUTION: Anglophone actors speak with French accents instead of French actors speaking English with an accent.

GO: These are non-threatening stories, with charming songs and the occasional French word.

■

THE MAGIC VOYAGE

Hemdale
1994
82 minutes
Directed by: Michael Shoeman
Starring the voices of: Irene Cara,
    Dom DeLuise, Samantha Egar,
    Corey Feldman, Dan Haggerty
    Mickey Rooney

In this musical animation, Christopher Columbus has a problem. Everyone thinks the world is flat except him. He thinks it's square; that is, until Pico the woodworm shapes one of his models into a globe. Armed with this revolutionary thought, Chris goes to the royal court and meets the malevolent king and his wife, Queen Isabella. Meanwhile, Pico meets Marilyn, a moon-sprite, and instantly falls in love with her. His romance is short-lived, however, because Marilyn is a prisoner of the swarm king, an evil being who is trying to force her into revealing the secrets of her magic. Pico's rescue attempt fails, and the swarm king flees across the ocean with Marilyn. Pico must then go to the Indies with Chris. After numerous adventures on the high seas, climaxing in Chris' near-lynching, land is spotted. Chris, Pico, and various animal friends explore the New World, meeting natives and discovering the lair of the swarm king in a Mayan temple. They then rescue Marilyn and squish the swarm.

CAUTION: The swarm king may frighten some younger children. Just before land is spotted, the crew has a noose around Chris' neck. There is threatening language, and a rather strange representation of natives.

GO: Pico epitomizes perserverance.

MARY POPPINS

Walt Disney Home Video
1964
139 minutes
Directed by: Robert Stevenson
Starring: Julie Andrews, Karen Dotrice, Matthew Garber, Glynis Johns, David Tomlinson, Dick Van Dyke, Ed Wynn

When George and Winifred Banks put out an ad for a new nanny (none of them ever lasts long), their children, Jane and Michael, prepare an ad describing their own requirements, which George promptly tears up. The next morning, a grim crew of nannies assembles outside of the house, only to be blown away by a mysterious magical wind. A single young woman floats calmly to earth (by virtue of her unusual umbrella) and presents George with the children's note, mysteriously reconstituted. Before the dumbfounded George knows what has happened he hires Mary Poppins, and for the children, the most amazing adventures are about to begin. Under Mary's direction the nursery cleans itself, so there's plenty of time to explore the magical world in a sidewalk chalk illustration and to visit Uncle Albert who floats in the air when he laughs. When George tries to fire Mary for her unorthodox methods, he finds himself instead taking the children to his stodgy bank where he tells Michael to open an account. Michael, however, wants to use his money to feed the birds and screams to get it back, causing mass panic and a run on the bank. The children flee the scene and are rescued by Bert, the chimney sweep who, along with Mary Poppins, takes them up to the smoky roof tops of London for a dazzling song-and-dance. George, meanwhile, is summoned to the bank to be reprimanded, but during the process experiences a transformation, thumbs his nose at his superiors and returns home in good spirits to enjoy the company of his children. Her work done, Mary opens her umbrella and drifts back up into the sky. Based on the *Mary Poppins* books by P.L. Travers, the story is set in Victorian London and combines live-action with animation.

Songs featured are:
Chim, Chim Cher-ee
Feed the Birds
Let's Go Fly a Kite
Step in Time
Supercalifragilisticexpialidocious

CAUTION: Very young children may find the dancing chimney sweeps and the fireworks which drive them away scary. The acerbic Mary Poppins as portrayed in the books is changed instead into saccharine sweetness in the film.

GO: The film won five Academy Awards (best actress, editing, song, musical score and visual effects).

■

THE MARZIPAN PIG

f.h.e.
1990
30 minutes
Directed by: Michael Sporn
Narrated by: Tim Curry

Based on the story by Russell Hoban, this is the tale of a little candy pig that falls behind the sofa and is forgotten. One day he hears a mouse and hopes that he will be saved, but is instead eaten by the hungry mouse who all the while marvels at his sweetness. The

mouse, intoxicated by the sweetness, becomes enamored of a grandfather clock. And when one day the clock stops ticking the mouse is heartbroken and runs out into the street where she is eaten by an owl, who is also touched by the sweetness. "The sweetness" is then transferred from creature to creature in this beautiful but almost incomprehensible story which has something to do with the spreading of love and the unsuspected connections between apparently unrelated things.

CAUTION: As you may guess from our outline, this is a bizarre story.

GO: Beautifully animated by Tissa David and marvellously narrated by Tim Curry, this is certainly a quality animation. Recommended for children ages five and up.

■

MICKEY AND THE BEANSTALK

Walt Disney Home Video
1967
29 minutes
Directed by: Hamilton S. Luske

Professor Ludwig Von Drake tells his own version of *Jack and the Beanstalk* in which idyllic Happy Valley is kept prosperous by the presence of a singing harp. When a giant comes and steals the harp, Happy Valley is devastated, and three young peasants (Mickey, Donald and Goofy) find themselves on the brink of starvation. To make matters worse, Mickey trades their cow for a couple of magic beans

123

which an enraged Donald throws away. That very night, a magic beanstalk grows and takes the trio (and their house) up into the clouds where they find the giant's castle and the harp. And after a number of exciting Disney chases and escapes, everyone lives happily ever after.

CAUTION: At first, some children may be frightened of the giant, although he is soon revealed to be more of a simple-minded stumblebum than a ferocious monster.

GO: This short features some of the finest animation on record.

MIKE MULLIGAN AND HIS STEAM SHOVEL

Golden Book Video
1990
30 minutes
Directed by: Michael Sporn
Narrated by: Robert Klein

Animated with a combination of still drawings and simple movement, this is the story of Mike and his steam shovel Mary-Anne who can (according to Mike) move as much dirt in a day than 100 men in a week. They work even better in front of an audience. When the new gasoline, electric and diesel shovels take all the work Mike has a dilemma. He still believes in Mary-Anne's capabilities but he has no job with which to prove it. If he cannot, Mary-Anne will be disassembled. When he hears that Popperville needs a cellar dug for their new town hall he bets that he and Mary-Anne can do it in a day. If

not, then mayor Henry B. Swap doesn't have to pay him. As they begin to work a crowd gathers, and this is the incentive Mike needs. The job is completed but there is one problem-they were in such a hurry to dig, Mike and Mary-Anne failed to provide a way out of the hole. But everything works out for the best when a little boy suggests that Mary-Anne be converted into a steam furnace for the new building and Mike be the custodian. Adapted from the book by Virginia Lee Burton.

Songs featured are:
Working Together
No Steam Shovel Wanted
No One Wants Us Anymore
Do It Anyway

CAUTION: Numerous pop songs give this animation a Broadway-show feel that often doesn't hold children's attention. If your child doesn't like songs, don't even try this one.

GO: A wonderful story about creative thinking, adaptability and confidence.

MILO AND OTIS

Columbia Home Video
1989
76 minutes
Directed by: Masanori Hata
Starring the voice of: Dudley Moore

When a farm kitten named Milo meets a pug-nosed puppy named Otis, the two are best friends right from the start. One day disaster strikes when, during a game of hide-and-seek, the crate in which

Milo is hiding falls into the water and is swept downstream. Otis tries to save his friend, but when a bear cub threatens to interfere, Otis gives up the rescue in order to lead the bear away. Now separated and far from home, the two are caught up in a series of exciting adventures as they search for food, warmth and each other. In their travels they encounter a fox, a fawn, screech owls, racoons, ducks, pigs, seagulls, snakes and finally, when Milo falls into a pit, each other. But on their way home they are separated again when Milo meets and runs off with Joyce, a female cat. Otis soon finds a mate of his own in a pug-nosed pup named Sandra. And that winter, after Joyce and Sandra both have litters, Milo and Otis agree to meet again in the spring and travel back to the farm with their families.

CAUTION: In one scene, an owl pounces on a mouse and carries it away. There are close-ups of Joyce having kittens and of Sandra having puppies.

GO: Gentle, non-threatening and funny, this is a good film for viewers of all ages.

MOTHER NATURE TALES OF DISCOVERY

C/FP Video
1992
25 minutes each
Produced by: John Anthony, Ralph C. Ellis, David Smith
Narrated by: Su Ours

These are straight-ahead nature videos showing animals and birds in their environments, accompanied by informative narration and low-key guitar/synthesizer music.

Nursery Habitat
Bringing Up Baby (seals)
Babes In the Woods (koala bears)
Springtime Toddler Tales
(wild animal babies)

Mountain Habitats
Good Neighbor Ground Squirrel
Curious Cougar Kittens
When Goats Go Climbing

Coastal Habitats
Orca Whales and Mermaid Tales
Castaways of the Galapagos
Penguins In Paradise

Forest Habitats
When Bears Go Fishing
The Business of Beavers
Antlers Big and Small

CAUTION: In Springtime Toddler Tales, shots of newborn babies struggling to their feet may be worrying for young ones.

GO: For the true nature lover.

THE MUPPET BABIES SERIES

Jim Henson Video
1989
48 minutes
(each two-episode volume)
Directed by: various

The videos in this series are fully-animated and sometimes include segments of live black-and-white footage.

Titles in the series are:
Explore with Us (Vol. 2):

The New Adventures of Kermit Polo;
Transcontinental Whoo-Whoo
Let's Build (Vol. 1):
Eight Flags over the Nursery; Six to
Eight Weeks
Time to Play (Vol. 3):
Muppet Babies: The Next Generation;
Beauty and the Schnoz

MUPPET SING-ALONGS

Jim Henson Video
1993
30–37 minutes each
Directed By: David Gumpel
Starring: The Muppet Performers: Fran Brill,
Frank Oz, Steve Whitmire

Billy Bunny's Animal Songs

Billy Bunny's mother suggests he go
to the woods and learn some new
songs because he keeps singing
the same one over and over and
over. . . . So Kermit introduces new
Muppet characters: the gophers,
three polite bears, a teeny termite,
two raccoons, a porcupine and a
penguin, as well as frogs and a
turtle who teach him upbeat songs
(with creative on-screen lyrics).

Songs featured are:
Hoppity Boppity
We Are Different
Bear Rap
The Termite Chew
I Have A Secret
Please Don't Bump Into Me
Frog Talk
Swim Away, Hooray!

It's Not Easy Being Green

Kermit, along with Clifford and an
affectionate octopus, hosts a
selection of songs, with on-screen
lyrics, from programs that feature
the Muppets.

Songs featured are:
Kokomo
Splish, Splash
Octopus Garden
Pass It On
Movin' Right Along
Over The Rainbow Medley
Bein' Green
Eight Little Notes
BBQ
Frog Talk
In A Cabin In The Woods
Heat Wave
Sweet Vacation

CAUTION: Elaborate lettering may make
the words difficult for a new reader to read.

GO: In some numbers, different colors and
lettering styles are related to different characters. This may make it easier for hearing
impaired children to relate to the song's
action.

THE MUPPETS TAKE MANHATTAN

CBS Fox Home Video
1984
94 minutes
Directed by: Frank Oz
Starring: Art Carney, James Coco,
Dabney Coleman, Joan Rivers

After performing their variety show
Manhattan Melodies to a cheering
audience at Danhurst College, the
Muppets are so encouraged they
decide to take their show on

Broadway. In New York, they approach countless Broadway producers, but are completely unsuccessful. Finally, out of money, they decide to go their separate ways, find work and reunite when Kermit is able to sell the show. Kermit devises some pretty elaborate plans to get his scripts read and eventually sells the show. But Kermit's excitement is short-lived when he is promptly hit by a car and hospitalized with amnesia. And when the gang gathers in New York with opening day only two weeks away, they're forced to go into rehearsals without him. It isn't until opening night that his friends finally find Kermit, and after a sock to the head from Miss Piggy, he regains his memory just in time for the opening number.

GO: The film is another great in the Muppet tradition, full of funny sketches, catchy songs and cameos by notables.

THE MUSICAL LYLE, LYLE CROCODILE: THE HOUSE ON EAST 88TH STREET

Hi-Tops Video/HBO/Astral Video
1987
25 minutes
Directed by: Michael Sporn
Starring the voices of: Liz Callaway,
  Tony Randall, Arnold Stang

When the Primms move into a house on East 88th Street they are amazed to find a crocodile in the bathtub. They are even more surprised to learn that the crocodile (whose name is Lyle) eats only Turkish cavier and is an artist and a performer who wouldn't hurt a flea. The Primms come to see that Lyle is a dream come true — he cooks and helps their son Joshua with his homework — and they soon can't remember how they ever did without a crocodile. Then one day a brass band parades past the house and Lyle joins in, marching and twirling a baton. He becomes famous and receives great numbers of letters from his fans. He also, however, receives a letter from his former owner, Hecta P. Valenti, who plans to fetch him. When Hecta comes, Lyle hides. The Primms ask Hecta why he left Lyle behind in the first place and when Hecta explains that he couldn't afford the caviar any more, but that this has changed since Lyle has become famous, it's a tearful parting for everyone. Hecta, it turns out, has big plans for Lyle; they perform all over the world and stay in many hotels, but in the end the crocodile is not happy and returns to live with the Primms. The songs are by Charles Strouse. Based on Bernard Waber's book *The House On East 88th Street*.

GO: Up-tempo songs and unusual animation make this video a charmer for any age.

∎

MY SESAME STREET HOME VIDEOS

Random House Home Video
1986–1988
30 minutes each

These videos, compiled from the *Sesame Street* progams aired by

The Children's Television Workshop, are not song videos — although each does contain a couple of songs. Each video also comes with an activity book.

The Alphabet Game

Play "The Alphabet Treasure Hunt" with host Sunny Friendly. When the alphabet flashes on the board contestants have 30 seconds to find and bring back something that begins with that letter. Also on this tape are songs and animated segments featuring the letters D, H, J, Q and S.

Bedtime Stories and Songs

The Sesame Street characters prepare for bed in a series of segments (some sketches, some songs) devoted to: getting comfortable at bedtime, counting sheep, lullabies, sleep-overs and overcoming a fear of monsters and shadows.

Songs featured are:
Everybody Sleeps
Snuffleullaby

The Best of Ernie and Bert

Ernestine the baby looks at a photo album of Ernie and Bert and asks about the pictures. "Best-of" vignettes include those in which: a lady with a tall hat sits in front of Ernie at the movies; Bert tries to sleep on a camping trip, while Ernie identifies night sounds; a doctor visits Ernie but can't find anything

wrong with him; Ernie and Bert visit the pyramids of Giza where a statue talks to Ernie; the friends go to a meeting of the National Association of W Lovers; and Bert teaches Bernice (a live pigeon) to play chess.

Songs featured are:
I'd Like to Visit the Moon
That's What Friends Are For

Big Bird's Favorite Party Games

Songs and games featured are:
The Clap Your Hands Game
Head, Shoulders, Knees and Toes
I Have a Furry Shadow
In a Cabin in a Wood
Oscar (Simon) Says
The Remembering Game
The Stop Game
Wheels on the Bus

Big Bird's Storytime

Big Bird and Snuffy want Maria to read them stories, but they don't have a book. Then Gilbert and Sullivan sing to Oscar about the different kinds of books in the library with help from Maria, Olivia, Linda, Gordon, Bob, Luis and David dressed in fanciful costumes.

Stories featured or retold are:
Goldilocks and the Three Bears
Humpty Dumpty (Kermit reports)
Rapunzel (Kermit reports)
Snow White (Kermit reports)
The Three Little Pigs (Kermit reports)

Getting Ready for School

Big Bird admits that on the first day of school he was scared. But after he saw the alphabet on the wall he felt better (even though he did think it was all one word). Combinations of live-action and animation allay children's fears about what to expect at school. Featuring the Count counting to twenty, Snuffy, real children forming huge letters and David singing about how to tie your shoes.

Songs featured are:
Big Bird's Alphabet Song
Everyone Makes Mistakes
Raise your Hand

Getting Ready to Read

Animation segments and Muppet sketches demonstrate how words are formed. Suggestion for rhyming words, creating poems and sounding words out are included.

Songs featured are:
A Fat Cat Sat on a Mat, a Small Ball on a Tall Wall, See a Red Head Being Fed Bread on His Sled
Take an H That's … and an O P Op, Put 'Em All Together and They Spell Hop

I'm Glad I'm Me

Maria reads the story *I'm Glad I'm Me* while the Sesame Street Muppets act it out. Also featured are segments in which: Maria identifies Big Bird's eyes, ears, beak etc; an animated mountain climber climbs up a real boy identifying parts as he goes; Kermit talks about hands; four scarecrows (David, Maria, Luis and Bob) sing a song about the ankle, shoulder and knee; Kermit shows what is inside Herry Monster and Princess Grouchy talks about the other things inside people, like feelings and imaginings.

Songs and stories featured are:
It's Not Easy Being Green (Kermit)

Let's Make a Face (pictures of eyes, ears and noses are used to compose a picture of a face)
Me Got to Be Blue (Cookie Monster)

Learning about Letters

The Sesame Street characters perform in sequences (some songs, some sketches) about the letters B and M. There is one animated sequence about the villain in the Panama hat and another of the alphabet which is accompanied by Elizabethan music.

Songs and stories featured are:
The Alphabet Song (Lena Horne)
C is for Cookie (Cookie Monster)
The King Banishes the Letter P
La, La, La ,La, Lightbulb (Ernie and Bert)

Learning about Numbers

Big Bird and The Count introduce short segments (some animated) about numbers. Featured are: Chip and Dip meowing about the number two; animated chickens who dance 1-2-3; and The Count counting rings of the phone, honks of The Honkers and floors on a ride in the elevator; Grover counting to ten with John-John.

Songs featured are:
I Just Adore Four (Big Bird)
The Tucan Two-Step

Learning to Add and Subtract

Big Bird promises to teach Elmo how to add and subtract, only he doesn't know how himself. He asks Maria to help and, using animated segments and Sesame Street live segments, Big Bird adds cookies,

129

crayons, spoons and his fingers. Other animated segments feature Cookie Monster subtracting cupcakes from Ernie's plate and an animated King Minus touching his princess with disastrous results.

Song featured is:
Six Cookies (Cookie Monster)

Play Along Games and Songs

This is a collection of eleven games and songs in which children are invited to play along. Featured are segments in which: Herry Monster puts objects into a child's hand while his eyes are closed and asks him to identify them; a con man sells Ernie a picture that he says has four elephants in it, but only Bert can find them; Grover sings a song around a door, demonstrating the concepts around, under, through, near and far. At the end, Big Bird makes Forgetful Jones try to remember all the games they have seen in sixty seconds.

Songs and games featured are:
Beat the Time (Guy Smiley)
Follow That Penguin (an animated penguin makes rhythmic sounds and participants must repeat it)
One of These Things Is Not Like the Others
The Rhyme Game

NATIONAL GEOGRAPHIC REALLY WILD ANIMALS COLLECTION

Columbia/Tri-Star
1994
45 minutes each
Series Producer: Jonathan Grupper
Narrated by: Dudley Moore

A series of documentary-like videos full of fascinating live-action footage (some vintage black-and-white) showing creatures and their environments, accompanied by upbeat pop songs and narration by Dudley Moore as the animated planet named Spin.

Deep Sea Dive

Spin explains about the four oceans and shows film of Australia's Great Barrier Reef. Topics include coral, schools of fish, the mating and birthing of seahorses, dolphins, spiny sea creatures, snails, starfish, a cuttlefish eating its prey, octopus camouflage, jellyfish, sea otters, pollution, and a beautiful montage of clear ocean floors. A diver strokes a shark, a great white bites at divers in a cage, another consumes a large fish whole, whale sharks feed on plankton, a tiny horn shark escapes being eaten and hammerheads find fish hiding in sand. Then we take a trip to Antarctica where we see Emperor penguins, and finish with a look at the great whales.

Titles in the series are:
Swinging Safari
Wonders Down Under
Amazing North America
Totally Tropical Rain Forest
Adventures In Asia

GO: Extraordinary underwater photography. Educational, superior quality entertainment for everyone, not only children. A large cut above the rest.

THE NEW ADVENTURES OF PIPPI LONGSTOCKING

RCA/Columbia
1988
100 minutes
Directed by: Ken Annakin
Starring: Eileen Brennan, Dennis Dugan,
    Tami Erin, Dianne Hull

Pippi Longstocking and her father, a fierce but kindly pirate captain, are sailing to see the Kuri islanders (whose specialty is Little Girl Stew) when a storm blows Pippi out of the crow's nest and into the sea. The currents carry her away and wash her up near a small town where her father owns a house. There she lives with her friends Alphonso, a talking horse, and Mr. Nielsen, a monkey, but without any grown-ups. She befriends her next door neighbor's children, Annika and Tommy, who soon discover that Pippi's life is a kid's fantasy. When the floor needs cleaning, she straps brushes to her feet and skates around in a house full of soap bubbles. When she needs money she finds more than she needs in her father's treasure hoards which are buried in the basement. She doesn't see the purpose of going to school, so she doesn't go. And villainous treasure-hunters and child welfare workers hold no terror for Pippi. In one scene Pippi even walks a high-wire to rescue her friends from a flame-wrapped building. When adventure after adventure is complete, and even though Pippi's father comes back for her, Pippi decides to give up life at sea to attend school and to be with her friends.

CAUTION: The storm and the fire may frighten some children.

GO: Fearless Pippi is a good female role model and splendid fun for the young crowd (we even know a few boys in their early teens who like her). The film contains some songs. This is an American film company's version of the previously produced Swedish films of Astrid Lindgren's books.

■

THE NEW ADVENTURES OF WINNIE-THE-POOH SERIES

Walt Disney Home Video
1988–1993
45 minutes
    (each multi-episode volume)
Directed by: Karl Geurs
Starring the voices of: Jim Cummings,
    John Fiedler, Tim Hoskins, Ken Sanson,
    Hal Smith, Paul Winchell

Titles in this series feature the characters from the original series in new situations.

Titles in this fully-animated series are:
All's Well that Ends Well! (Vol. 6):
    All's Well that Ends Wishing Well!;
    Bubble Trouble; Where Oh Where Has
    My Piglet Gone?
Everything's Coming up Roses (Vol. 9):
    Eeyi, Eeyi, Eeyore; My Hero; Honey for
    a Bunny; Owl Feathers
The Great Honey Pot Robbery (Vol. 1):
    Stripes; Monkey See, Monkey Do Better
King of the Beasties (Vol. 7):
    King of the Beasties; Tigger's Shoes;
    Up, up and Awry; Luck Amok
Newfound Friends (Vol. 3):
    Find Her, Keep Her; Donkey for a Day;
    Friend in Deed
Pooh to the Rescue (Vol. 10):
    Oh Bottle; The Old Switcheroo; The
    "New" Eeyore; Goodbye, Mr. Pooh

131

The Sky's the Limit (Vol. 8):
    Pooh Skies!; Rabbit Takes a Holiday;
    Owl in the Family
There's No Camp Like Home (Vol. 4):
    There's No Camp Like Home;
    Balloonomatics; Paw and Order
Wind Some, Lose Some (Vol. 5):
    Gone with the Wind; How Much Is That
    Rabbit in the Window?; Nothing But the
    Tooth
The Wishing Bear (Vol. 2)
    The Piglet Who Would Be King; The
    Wishing Bear

CAUTION: Fans of the classic A.A. Milne stories, as presented in the original four Winnie-the-Pooh episodes, should be warned that these new episodes are not based on Milne stories.

GO: In relation to other TV fare available today, these episodes are benign and pleasant

NONSENSE AND LULLABIES COLLECTION

f.h.e./MCA
1991–1992
30 minutes each
Directed by: Michael Sporn
Starring the voices of: Karen Allen,
    Giana Cherkas, Linda Hunt, Grace Johnston,
    Donny Jones, Randy Kaplan, Sue Perrotto,
    Phillip Schopper, Heidi Stallings,
    Jessie Suma-Kusiak, Courtney Vance,
    Eli Wallach

Nursery Rhymes

The following fully-animated rhymes are told by a variety of people. Caleb Simpson provides the music and songs. The changing channels of a television set are used as a bridge between stories.

Rhymes featured are:
A Young Lady of Linn
Animal Fair
The Boy and the Wolf (The Boy Who
    Cried Wolf)
The Chivalrous Shark
The Crooked Man
Did You Ever Go Fishing?
Hey Diddle Diddle
The House That Jack Built
I See the Moon
Little Miss Muffet
Little Robin Red Breast
The Queen of Hearts
See a Pin and Pick It Up
Solomon Grundy
Star Light, Star Bright
Toot Toot (Peanut Butter)
Turtle Soup
Twinkle Twinkle Little Star
Wynken, Blinken and Nod

Poems for Children

This is a collection of fifteen poems, some fully-animated, some stills. Musical accompaniment and songs are featured throughout and the changing channels of a car radio are used as a bridge between stories.

Rhymes featured are:
Autumn Fires
The Bogeyman
Bugs in the Night
Creature in the Classroom
The Duel
Homework
Jigsaw Puzzle
Matilda
Mr. Nobody
The Owl and the Pussycat
The Story of Augustus Who Would Not
    Eat His Soup
The Tin Frog
Windy Nights
Wrimples

CAUTION: In *The Story of Augustus Who Would Not Eat His Soup*, Augustus dies of starvation. In *Matilda*, the fireman won't save her from a fire. *The Bogeyman* is about scary things in the basement.

THE NUTCRACKER PRINCE

MCA
1991
72 minutes
Directed by: Paul Schibli
Starring the voices of: Megan Follows,
    Peter O'Toole, Kiefer Sutherland

When Clara finds a nutcracker shaped like a toy soldier under the Christmas tree, Uncle Drosselmeier, the toymaker, tells her a story about the King's birthday, when mice got at the King's favorite blue cheese cake. In the story, the King orders the Mouse Queen executed, but she and her muscular son cannot be caught. And when the Queen's son scares the beautiful young princess so badly that she becomes hideous, the King learns that there is only one way to throw off the spell: a young man with certain characteristics (Hans) must crack a certain nut. This done, the enraged Mouse Queen turns Hans into a nutcracker, and when a pillar falls over and kills the Mouse Queen, her son becomes king. And so ends the tale. That night, Clara can't sleep. When she goes downstairs and introduces her nutcracker to her dolls, an apparition of Drosselmeier appears and throws magic dust over everything. A fierce battle is suddenly engaged between the Mouse King and the dolls, during which Clara falls and knocks herself unconscious. She wakes up Christmas day with her head bandaged and that night, the Mouse King returns and demands the Nutcracker, only to be defeated again. The dolls then shrink Clara to their size and take her to the land of the dolls. And although Clara would like to stay with the romantic Nutcracker Prince, her own world is where she belongs, and she decides to return. The Mouse King returns too, staggering back to kill Clara. But he expires after a tense chase and Clara springs out of bed and rushes to see the toymaker, demanding to know the truth.

CAUTION: There is a lot of fairly intense fighting in this movie, and the Mouse King is evil, rude and frightening.

GO: This is a convoluted tale, but the voice-overs are great.

PETE SEEGER'S FAMILY CONCERT

Sony Kids Video
1992
45 minutes
Directed by: Jim Brown

This video is live-action outdoor footage of families spending a day on the banks of the Hudson River in Kingston, New York. People play, swim, sail boats, skip rope while Pete Seeger performs to a large gathering.

Songs featured are:
Skip To My Lou
Sailin' Up, Sailin' Down
Seneca Canoe song
She'll Be Comin Round The Mountain

This Land Is Your Land
Abiyoyo
Somas El Barco
Guantanamera
The River That Flows Both Ways
Lonesome Valley
Freight Train
My Rainbow Race

CAUTION: A straight-ahead folk concert tape. No special effects, no other performers or musicians.

GO: Seeger gives heartfelt commentary on environmental concerns.

✗ STOP: After clamping a patient's mouth to a device that looks as if it came out of a medieval torture chamber, Doc abandons his victim, telling him to keep his foot on a certain pedal or the weight will rip his lips off and break his jaw. Viewers are left with a close-up of the poor wretch, his mouth painfully stretched open and his eyes wide with horror.

CAUTION: The film takes an unbelievably long time to tell its story and many young viewers may lose interest.

GO: This is a generally friendly, happy film with a warm message about love, friendship and the joys of belonging.

✗ PETE'S DRAGON

Walt Disney Home Video
1977
128 minutes
Directed by: Don Chaffey
Starring: Helen Reddy,
  Mickey Rooney, Shelley Winters

Young Pete escapes from a nasty family of unkempt hillbillies with the help of his dragon, Elliott (a large green cartoon who can disappear at will). The two make their way to the small coastal town of Passamaquitty where Elliott, though invisible, wreaks havoc. Pete is blamed. He's driven out of town and takes refuge in a cave on the seashore. There he is discovered and taken in by a lonely lighthouse keeper named Nora, who sings a *lot* of songs. Meanwhile Doc, a con man, and his accomplice arrive in Passamaquitty and, learning of the existence of the dragon, devise an evil plan to kidnap Pete and use Elliott to make a lot of money. This film combines live-action and animation.

PETER PAN

Walt Disney Home Video
1952
76 minutes
Directed by: Clyde Geronimi,
  Wilfred Jackson, Hamilton Luske
Starring the voices of: Bobby Driscoll,
  Kathryn Beaumont, Hans Conreid

On a quiet street in Bloomsbury, George and Mary Darling prepare for a night out, while their children, Peter, Michael and Wendy, get ready for bed. George is concerned that Wendy is stuffing the boys' heads full of nonsense about Peter Pan, and also informs her that this is her last night in the nursery. Children are people, he says, and sooner or later, people have to grow up. (So is established the central theme of *Peter Pan*.) And on that last, very important night, Peter returns to the Darling household to retrieve his shadow (lost on a previous visit) and transports the children through faith, trust, and

Tinkerbell's pixie dust, to Neverland. There they meet Tinkerbell, Captain Hook and his sidekick Mister Smee, The Lost Boys, the Indian braves and the famous alarm-clock crocodile. After fantastic adventures, the children leave the land where no one grows up and return home. Based on the book by J.M. Barrie.

Songs featured are:
Following the Leader
You Can Fly

CAUTION: The portrayal of the Indians in this film has caused some controversy and the crocodile may be too scary for some children. Slitting throats is mentioned twice.

GO: Considering the date of its production, this film is remarkable; particularly striking are the scenes in London, the natural look of the flying sequences and the terrific songs and score.

■

line: "Boy, why are you crying?" Peter tells Wendy all about his life in a kingdom far away (Never-Never Land) while Wendy sews his shadow back on. After some discussion and a sprinkling of fairy dust it's agreed that Wendy and her brothers will accompany Peter back to Never-Never Land. There they meet The Lost Boys, Captain Hook and Mr. Smee, the alarm-clock crocodile, and Tiger Lily and the Indians. After a number of adventures, the pirates are defeated and the children bring the Lost Boys home, where their parents adopt everyone. Only carefree Peter comes back to Earth decades later when Wendy is married and grown with a child of her own.

GO: This Broadway musical version of the play by Sir James M. Barrie is filmed entirely on stage, and represents an opportunity for young viewers to experience the theater. The songs are engaging and the production still entertains in spite of its age.

■

PETER PAN

✗ PINOCCHIO

HGV
1960
90 minutes
Directed by: Vincent J. Donehue
Starring: Margalo Gillmore, Sondra Lee, Mary Martin, Cyril Ritchard

Wendy, Michael and John are put to bed in the nursery as their parents prepare to go out. When they leave, Tinkerbell heralds the arrival of Pan who is looking for his shadow. When the shadow refuses to stick, Peter begins to weep, awakening Wendy who then utters the famous

Walt Disney Home Video
1940
87 minutes
Directed by: Hamilton Luske, Ben Sharpsteen

When a kindly toymaker named Geppetto wishes for a son, he fashions one out of wood and calls him Pinocchio. That night the Blue Fairy grants his wish and brings the marionette to life.But living is not that easy for Pinocchio who is so trusting that he finds himself in many dangerous predicaments.

AGES 3 TO 6

135

One day unsavory con men convince him to come with them to meet Stromboli where fame on the stage of his travelling sideshow is assured. But Stromboli keeps Pinocchio locked in a cage and the Blue Fairy must come to his rescue. She warns him that from now on every time he tells a lie his nose will grow (which it does — to ridiculous proportions). He runs home only to meet the two con men again and this time they convince him that he's ill and needs a vacation on Pleasure Island. They even give him a ticket to get there. On the island, Pinocchio finds himself in a boys' fantasy land where he can do whatever he wants (smoke, drink, fight or play pool). But it's a trap. That night the boys turn into donkeys and are taken away to be sold to the salt mines. Pinocchio witnesses the terrifying transformation of one of the boys, and manages to escape having only acquired donkey ears and a tail. He returns home to learn that Geppetto has gone looking for him and has been swallowed by a whale. So Pinocchio ties a rock to his body (the only way a wooden boy can sink) and throws himself into the sea where he is eventually swallowed by the same whale. Reunited with Geppetto, the two build a fire inside the whale. The whale expels them and Pinocchio (who floats) saves Geppetto from drowning, but doesn't recover himself until the Blue Fairy turns him into a real boy.

✗STOP: The boys' unnerving transformation into donkeys may frighten some children. The donkeys are threatened with a whip until the transformation is complete.

CAUTION: Other things to watch out for include Pinocchio's captivity with the travelling sideshow and the black shadowy demons with burning white eyes who are Stromboli's servants. The idea of being swallowed by Monstro the whale has given many a little one nightmares.

GO: This is an 1882 Italian story by Carlo Collodi, unusual in its creativity. A classic. And every child should know the origin of the saying "tell a lie and your nose will grow." Winner of two Academy Awards: Best Original Score and Best Song for "When You Wish Upon A Star." Also includes the terrific song "There Are No Strings on Me."

■

THE PIRATES OF DARK WATER

Hanna Barbera
1991
90 minutes
Directed by: Don Lusk
Starring the voices of: Jodi Benson, Barry Denmen, Frank Welker

"The alien world of Mir is being devoured by Dark Water. Only Ren, a young prince, can stop it by finding the lost treasures of Rule. At his side is an unlikely but loyal crew of misfits. At his back, the evil pirate Lord Bloth, who will stop at nothing to get the treasures for himself."

The preceding introduction pretty well tells it all, and if you can steer your way through the host of Tolkienesque names (Octopon, Lord Bloth, Alamar, King Primus, the Abbey of Guldobar, etc.) and hang in there through 90 minutes of non stop wisecracks, sword-fights and boat chases, you'll end up discovering that this is only the introduction to a continuing swashbucklerama.

CAUTION: If your child tends to behave aggressively after watching videos that feature combat, you'll probably want to avoid this video as it's pretty much nothing but fighting and posturing from start to finish; also, be warned, unlike a lot of efforts in this vein, people die.

THE PRINCESS AND THE GOBLIN

Hemdale
1994
82 minutes
Directed By: Jozsef Gémés
Starring: Joss Ackland, Claire Bloom,
  Ray Kinnear, Sally Ann Marsh
MPAA rating: G

One late afternoon, Princess Irene, her nanny Leutie and her cat Turnip are out walking in the forest, far from the safety of her father the king's castle. Leutie falls asleep, and Irene and Turnip discover some strange gravel mounds, which turn out to be breathing holes for goblins. The goblins' hideous pets then appear and close in on the terrified Irene. She is saved at the last moment by the singing of Curdie, a young boy whose father works in the mines, and who knows about goblins. He escorts the Princess safely to her home. The next day, Irene discovers a secret door in her bed chamber that leads her up to an unused and ruined tower. There she encounters the beatific spirit of her great, great grandmother who promises to guide her through the coming time of trial. Meanwhile, Curdie, while working in the mines, breaks through into the goblin kingdom and accidentally becomes privy to their evil plans to destroy the surface-dwelling "sun people." Most odious of the goblins is their prince, Froglip. Curdie has only heard half the plan when he is discovered, and barely escapes. Bravely, he returns to the subterranean kingdom, and overhears Froglip's plans to kidnap and marry Irene. Curdie is then discovered. Meanwhile, Irene has also bravely descended into the depths, guided by her guardian spirit. She rescues Curdie, and they return to the castle to warn everyone. Due to mischance, the warning fails to reach the king in time, and the goblins are upon them before the guard can be organized. Curdie's goblin-fighting experience proves invaluable, and thanks to this expertise the goblins are repulsed; however, the underworlders release a devastating torrent that floods the castle, and in the resulting chaos, Curdie and the princess meet Froglip in final combat.

CAUTION: Fans of the well-known book by George MacDonald may find that this adaptation is somewhat loose. Many young ones will certainly find elements of it scary, particularly the opening, in which a claw-like hand reaches up out of the breathing hole and grabs Turnip's tail, trying to pull him down. Froglip pets a bird in pseudo-affectionate fashion, then promptly throws it into the mouth of his waiting cat. A goblin driver lashes his beast mercilessly. There is violence and combat throughout.

GO: The voice-overs are good (at least they use children's voices to play children), and the film may serve to increase awareness of, and promote the reading of, a very popular children's book.

THE RELUCTANT DRAGON PLUS MORRIS THE MIDGET MOOSE

Walt Disney Home Video
1946 (episode 1), 1950 (episode 2)
28 minutes
Directed by: Hamilton Luske (episode 1),
    Charles Nichols (episode 2)

The Reluctant Dragon A young shepherd-boy's conceptions about dragons are altered when he meets a nonviolent dragon who recites poems and coaches the local birds in singing. So when Sir Giles, the famous dragon-slayer, arrives in town to take on the beast, the young shepherd explains that the dragon is a poet and he, Sir Giles and the beast devise a ruse. They stage a mock fight in which the dragon pretends to be defeated and reformed, after which he is accepted into the village society.

Morris the Midget Moose
"… Morris was four years old, and should have been full grown, but no matter how hard he tried, he couldn't grow an inch …" So begins the story of Morris, a small moose with big antlers and a host of problems, not the least of which is putting up with the way the other moose tease him. Then comes the big day when all of the bulls challenge an enormous moose named Thunderclap for the leadership of the group. Morris teams up with Balsam, a huge moose with tiny antlers, and together they take on the big boss and win.

CAUTION: There is some fighting.

GO: These are great stories about two friends who work together to overcome their difficulties.

THE REMARKABLE ROCKET

Random House Home Video
1986
26 minutes
Directed by: Gerald Potterton
Starring the voice of: David Niven

When the king's son marries a Russian princess, the delighted kingdom celebrates wildly. The last item on the wedding program is a grand display of fireworks, to be let off at midnight. The fireworks are set up on a great stand at the end of the royal gardens, and (excited themselves about the festivities) begin to converse. Each of the fireworks represents a certain sort of person, the most notable being the conceited title character, the infinitely self-important Rocket, who thinks the entire world revolves around him. He doesn't hesitate to let the others know just how absolutely superior he is, over and over again, until he drives himself into fits of affected weeping. But when midnight arrives, the rocket is so wet with his own tears that he can't go off. So he stands alone until the next morning. When the workmen come to tidy up, one of them contemptuously throws him over the wall into the moat. That doesn't stop the Rocket, however, who continues pontificating about his own glory, until two small peasant boys find him and stick him on top of their campfire. Eventually the Rocket dries out and goes off, but no one sees or hears him, not even the two small boys; they are asleep. Based on the story by Oscar Wilde.

CAUTION: During one of the Rocket's meandering soliloquies, he imagines that the prince's future son falls off a cliff into the river and drowns. Also, we question the back of the jacket which describes this video as a story in which "… a conceited rocket learns an important lesson about humility." But in fact, he doesn't, and that's the whole point.

GO: Good animation, terrific music and superb voice-overs highlight this strong effort.
■

RESCUE RANGERS SERIES

Walt Disney Home Video
1989
44 minutes
   (each two-episode volume)
Directed by: Alan Zaslove

Classic Disney trouble-makers Chip 'n' Dale are involved in a series of new adventures with their friends Gadget, a girl chipmunk; Zip, a superpowerful fly; and Monty, a large mustachioed English-type mouse.

Titles in the series are:
Crimebusters:
   Catteries Not Included; Pirates under the Sea
Danger Rangers:
   Kiwi's Big Adventure; Bearing up Baby
Double Trouble:
   Dale beside Himself; Flash, the Wonder Dog

Super Sleuths:
   The Pound of the Baskervilles; Out to Launch
Undercover Critters:
   Adventures in Squirrel-sitting; Three Men and a Booby

CAUTION: Those who remember the classic cartoons with Chip 'n' Dale vs. Donald Duck should be sure not to confuse them with the *Rescue Rangers*.

GO: The stories are lively and the animation is adequate, but the effort is very definitely of the Saturday morning variety.

THE RESCUERS

Walt Disney Home Video
1977
76 minutes
Directed by: John Lounsbery,
   Wolfgang Reitherman,
   Art Stevens
Starring the voices of: Eva Gabor,
   Bob Newhart, Geraldine Page

Penny, a ragamuffin orphan, sends out a distress note in a bottle. It is found by the animals of the Rescue Aid Society. Penny is being held captive in an old river boat in Devil's Bayou by the mean Medusa, who needs a small child to go down a narrow shaft in the ground and retrieve the largest diamond in the world. Brave little mice Bernard and Bianca join forces with Evinrude the dragonfly and Orville the Albatross to rescue Penny.

CAUTION: Medusa's two huge crocodiles carry out her evil wishes and there are three near-drownings (which young children find particularly scary). Alcohol is used to revive both Evinrude and Bernard, and the scene in which Penny is lowered into the shaft may be upsetting for some. Penny is told that she won't be adopted because she is too plain.

GO: Penny is a brave little girl who gets parents at the end of the film.

■

✗ THE RESCUERS DOWN UNDER

Walt Disney Home Video
1991
77 minutes
Directed by: Hendel Butou, Mike Gabriel
Starring the voices of: John Candy,
    Eva Gabor, Bob Newhart, George C. Scott

Cody is a young boy who lives in the Australian Outback. He learns that the giant golden eagle Marahuté is caught in a poacher's trap. To release her, he must scale a sheer cliff. After the daring rescue, Marahuté offers her thanks in the gift of a feather, and sets Cody down on solid ground. But Cody becomes caught in another of the traps, where he's found by McLeach, the vile poacher himself. McLeach notices the feather in Cody's pack and, determined to find the location of Marahuté's nest, abducts him. Then it's up to the Rescue Aid Society to speed to Cody's rescue and stop McLeach from getting Marahuté.

✗ STOP: Many children are frightened by McLeach, a sinister and threatening character.

CAUTION: Cody is in peril throughout this film. He plunges from a precipice (and is saved by the eagle) and, when McLeach

tries to make him reveal the location of Marahuté's nest, he is suspended over a river full of crocodiles and even has knives thrown at him.

GO: This is a brilliant state-of-the-art animation and the sequel to *The Rescuers*.

RIKKI-TIKKI-TAVI

f.h.e.
1974
30 minutes
Directed by: Chuck Jones
Starring the voices of: June Foray,
    Michael Le Clair, Shepard Menken,
    Les Tremayne, Orson Welles (narration)

A flash flood carries a young mongoose downriver. Taken in by a kindly British family, Rikki-Tikki-Tavi achieves the ultimate objective of his kind: he becomes a house mongoose. His mission is to protect the bungalow and its surrounding gardens from the incursion of snakes, and this he does with aplomb. His greatest test comes against the fearsome cobra couple Nag and Nagaina, who are plotting to kill the humans so Rikki-Tikki-Tavi will leave and they can again rule a garden safe for their young. But, aided by some of his wildlife friends, the resolute Rikki confronts the cobras one at a time and dispatches them. From the story by Rudyard Kipling.

CAUTION: Intense scenes of mongoose snake combat. Absurd Saturday-morning cartoon music almost wrecks a fine effort.

GO: This is a faithful and exciting adaptation of the original story.

ROAD CONSTRUCTION AHEAD

Focus Video
1991
30 minutes
Directed by: Fred Levine

Two little boys playing with trucks in the dirt wonder how roads are really built. Live-action footage shows the making of a road from site surveying to finished asphalt. Personable young construction worker George gives simple on-site explanations of the process. Close-up shots of bulldozers moving huge piles of earth as well as rock crushers, drills and blasting crews are edited in time to up-tempo rock music. Exciting shots of ground explosions, some in slow-motion and reverse, are filmed at fairly close range giving the viewer the feeling of being right in the action.
Bucket-loaders and front-shovels move the newly excavated rubble, George explains what is done when a 35-ton truck breaks down and how the job superintendent keeps things running smoothly. Rollers flatten the earth and the asphalt is made and laid, the lines are painted and a family tries out the new road.

CAUTION: This is an all-male film which doesn't show women in any aspect of the road realization. The only woman in the film is the mother who takes the boys for a car ride on the new road. She is shown putting on her seatbelt but not buckling up the children.

GO: Video effects are used to vary the presentation. Shots from inside the trucks and at four-year-old eye level, and rapid editing synchronized to rock music all combine to make this video highly effective, engaging and suitable for repeat viewing as well as being educational for all ages.

Titles in this series:
Fire And Rescue
Coming soon: Cleared For Takeoff

■

ROBIN HOOD

Walt Disney Home Video
1973
83 minutes
Directed by: Wolfgang Reitherman
Starring the voices of: Brian Bedford, Phil Harris, Terry Thomas, Peter Ustinov

This animation masterwork, featuring a star-studded voice-over cast, is a reasonably faithful retelling of the classic tale — only in this version the characters are animals. Robin and Marion are a pair of charming foxes, Prince John is a lion, Little John is a bear and Friar Tuck is a badger. Original songs are by Roger Miller.

GO: This cartoon (like Lady and the Tramp) is one of the few Disney features that is suitable for the very young. There is a decided absence of frightening characters and what little violence there is, is harmless. (Swords don't cut and arrows always miss.)

✗ ROCK-A-DOODLE

(continued on next page)

AGES 3 TO 6

HBO Video
1990
75 minutes
Directed by: Don Bluth
Starring the voices of: Glen Campbell,
  Phil Harris, Christopher Plummer,
  Charles Martin Smith

In the animated introduction, an old dog named Patou tells the story of Chanticleer, an Elvis-like rooster who believes that his crowing raises the sun each morning. Then one dawn, an evil owl called the Grand Duke sends a hired thug to prevent Chanticleer from performing his morning ritual, and when the sun rises anyway, Chanticleer leaves in shame. Then comes perpetual darkness and rain, and the Grand Duke and his band of owl henchmen terrorize the farm. The film then becomes live-action where Edmond's mother is reading him a bed-time story about Chanticleer. But the story is interrupted when torrential rains threaten to flood the farm. And when Edmund goes to the window to summon Chanticleer and end the storm, a lightning bolt promptly blasts him into the world of the story, and into an instant confrontation with the Grand Duke. In order to make Edmund more digestible, the owl turns him into a kitten, but Patou arrives just in time to save Edmund, who then assembles a band of adventurers. Leaving the rest of the farm animals behind and armed only with a failing flashlight to ward off the owls, they set out for the big city to find Chanticleer. But when they finally arrive in the city, Chanticleer has become such a big star that his former friends can't get near him, and to complicate matters, Chanticleer's millionaire manager is actually in cahoots with the Duke, and takes every opportunity to thwart their attempts to contact the rooster. High comedy/adventure

then ensues, climaxing in a long chase scene which brings everyone back to the farm for a final confrontation.

✗ **STOP:** Some scenes may be too frightening for young children. The Grand Duke's first confrontation with Edmund, the owls that come to eat the farm animals, and the Grand Duke's metamorphosis into an enormous creature are probably the ones of greatest concern.

CAUTION: The plot is meandering and convoluted. Violent scenes and images abound, and are magnified in power by Bluth's masterful animation.

GO: The animation, voice-overs and breath-taking mattes (background paintings) are first rate, and rock-and-roll fans will enjoy the songs.

SEBASTIAN'S CARIBBEAN JAMBOREE

Walt Disney Home Video
1991
30 minutes
Directed by: Steve Purcell
Starring: Sam Wright

Animated Sebastian the crab and live-action singer Sam Wright perform with a group of children at Walt Disney World.

Songs featured are:
Arise
Day-O
Hot, Hot, Hot
Jamaica Farewell
Music Sweet
Three Little Birds
Under the Sea
You Can Get It If You Really Want

SEBASTIAN'S PARTY GRAS

Walt Disney Home Video
1991
30 minutes
Directed by: Steve Purcell
Starring Sam Wright

Sebastian the crab and entertainer Sam Wright perform live at Walt Disney World. A thread of a story is woven through these songs.

Songs featured are:
Carousel
Give a Little Love
Iko, Iko
In the Conga Line
Life Is a Magic Thing
Limbo Rock
Octopus's Garden
Sing Along
Twist and Shout

✗ THE SECRET OF THE SEAL

Just for Kids Home Video
1992
90 minutes
Directed by: Norifumi Kiyozumi

When Antonio's mother dies of pollution-related diseases, he and his family return to his father's hometown on the island of Sardinia. While his father Cypriano restores the ancestral home, Antonio, called Tottoi by his cousin Bilia, has a

delightful summer. One day, while accompanying Bilia on Captain Marco's tour of the coastal caves, Tottoi goes for a swim and encounters a full-grown Mediterranean monk seal, a species thought to be extinct. At first no one believes Tottoi's story, but his father, convinced that his son would never lie, sends him to see the grizzled ecologist Noni Spanu. Noni takes Tottoi back to the cave, and sure enough, the seal is there, with a young pup. Now comes the hard part keeping the seal a secret. Before long, the secret is out, and a ruthless, evil aquarium owner from Florida finds out about the seal and prepares to take it by force. It is up to Tottoi, his cousin and friends, and the brave ecologist to thwart the man and his cutthroat crew. Based on the book *Tottoi* by Gianni Padoan.

✗**STOP:** In the first scene, Antonio sees his mother lying dead in a hospital bed. The evil-doers shoot at the seal, and even at children. The seal is shot and we only discover later that it is with a tranquillizer dart. There is also fist-fighting, with the realistic sound of blows landing.

CAUTION: The animation is stiff, and the voice used for Tottoi's young sister is that of a woman impersonating a young child.

GO: For older children, this is a relatively hard-hitting but honest portrayal of human-kind's needless destruction of other species.

■

THE SELFISH GIANT

(continued on next pgae)

Random House Home Video
1986
26 minutes
Directed by: Peter Sander
Narrated by: Paul Hecht

AGES 3 TO 6

Oscar Wilde's morality tale about the price of selfishness begins in a small town, where at three o'clock of every day, the children stream out of the local school to the abandoned giant's castle to play in his lovely garden. The giant is away, visiting his friend the Cornish Ogre. But after seven years — having said all that he had to say — the Selfish Giant returns to his own castle, scares the children away, and builds a great wall around the garden to keep everyone out. The seasons turn. But when spring comes, it does not come to the giant's garden. Spring has forgotten it. And so the castle and the grounds stay locked in ice, at the mercy of the cruel spirits Frost, Snow, North Wind and Hail. Then, one day, the children creep in through a hole in the wall, and the garden flowers again. The giant sees the error of his ways and is especially touched by one mysterious little boy. But the little boy is never seen again. Long years pass, and the giant grows old, then in the middle of one winter, the farthest tree in the garden flowers, and there stands the little boy. He has come back, to take the giant to paradise.

CAUTION: The conclusion of the tale has religious overtones that may leave some families uneasy.

SESAME STREET START-TO-READ VIDEOS

Random House Home Video
1987
30 minutes each

These videos are iconographic (slides with words running along the bottom of the picture). The story is narrated as the words go by. The aim is to enable beginning readers to follow along with the story.

Titles in the series are:
Don't Cry, Big Bird and Other Stories
Ernie's Big Mess and Other Stories
Ernie's Little Lie and Other Stories
I Want to Go Home! and Other Stories

SESAME STREET VISITS THE HOSPITAL

Random House Home Video
1990
30 minutes
Directed by: Ted May
Starring: Sonia Manzano, Robert Klein, the Sesame Street cast

When Big Bird has a sore throat and a cough, Maria decides to take him to the hospital. There they take his blood pressure, listen to his heart, take blood (it pinches), give him an X-ray and put him on intravenous. Learning that he has to stay for a few days, Big Bird is afraid and wants to go home. But Hootz the Owl sings him to sleep when he is feeling alone in the middle of the night. And in the morning when friends begin to arrive with gifts and good wishes, Big Bird is no longer angry with Maria for bringing him to the hospital. Of course, just when he's all better and it's time to leave, Big Bird wants to stay.

Songs featured are:
Busy Getting Better
You've Got to Be Patient to Be a Patient

CAUTION: This is an instructional tape and not purely for entertainment.

GO: Up to the middle of the tape it doesn't seem like this video would alleviate any child's fear of the hospital, and your child may want to turn it off when Big Bird seems to be in distress, but try to stick it out because the ending resolves itself nicely.

SESAME STREET VISITS THE FIREHALL

Random House Home Video
1990
30 minutes
Directed by: Ted May
Starring: Bob Gunton, Roscoe Orman

Big Bird, Elmo, Lisette and Gordon call the fire department when they think there's a fire in Oscar's trash can. But when it turns out that Oscar is only barbecuing, they go back to the firehouse with the firemen. There they learn that firemen take their own air and water to a fire; they see how a hose works and how a ladder extends; and they even get to try on fire-fighter's helmets, coats and boots. And when the bell rings they rush off to a real fire and watch as the fire department saves a gentle furry monster.

Song featured is:
Waiting for the Bell to Ring

GO: This film is one of the very few available for young children about fire engines.

SHALOM SESAME

CTW
1986
30 minutes each
Directed by: Moti Aviram

Sesame Street favorites Bert, Ernie, Grover, Cookie Monster, Elmo and Oscar sing, cavort and speak Hebrew. Each video features celebrities such as Itzak Perlman, Mary Tyler Moore, Sarah Jessica Parker, Joan Rivers and many more. Kippi ben Kippod, Israel's peppiest porcupine, hosts, and live-action segments show the people, places, traditions and culture of Israel in Sesame Street style.

Show 1: The Land of Israel

Featuring: Mary Tyler Moore and Bonnie Franklin.

A fun-filled journey through Israeli cities Metulea, Haifa, Jerusalem, Tel Aviv and Caesaria.

Show 2: Tel Aviv

Ernie and Bert tour the Carmel Market, Jaffa and Tel Aviv.

Show 3: Kibbutz

Featuring: Itzak Perlman and Bonnie Franklin.

Orchards, animals, kids; life on an Israel Kibbutz.

Show 4:
The People of Israel

Sweden, Russia, Egypt and America; being different is something everyone has in common.

Show 5: Jerusalem

A visit to the capital of Israel.

Show 6: Chanukah

Shalom Sesame celebrates the Festival of the lights.

Show 7:
Sing Around the Seasons

Featuring: Jeremy Miller

Sing along in Israel as the seasons are a little different from ours, with New Year in autumn and rain in winter.

Show 8:
Journey to Secret Places

Journey to far out places and exotic places.

Show 9:
Aleph-Bet Telethon

Featuring: Nell Carter, Tracey Gold.

Discover the Hebrew letters.

Show 10: Passover

Featuring: Sarah Jessica Parker, Anne Meara

Jerusalem Jones and the lost Afikomen: features Kippi the porcupine in ancient Egypt making a narrow escape from the world's largest matzoh ball.

Show 11: Kids Sing Israel (Grouches Don't)

Featuring: Paul Shaffer and B.B. King.

Kippi hosts an all-request musical trip through Israel.

CAUTION: Sesame Street characters have their voices dubbed. Some are not even close to the voices American kids are used to.

GO: A fun-filled and educational series.

SHARI LEWIS PRESENTS 101 THINGS FOR KIDS TO DO

Random House Home Video
1987
60 minutes
Directed by: Jack Regas
Starring: Charlie Horse, Lamb Chop, Shari Lewis

Creative PBS star, well-known ventriloquist and Emmy Award winner Shari Lewis leads kids through one hundred and one really neat things to do. Activities require only household objects like paper clips, old rubber balls and pens and include: making simple puppets and masks, telling riddles and doing tongue twisters, performing magic tricks, and learning trick questions — just to name a few.

CAUTION: This video is too full of information to be used all at once. You'll probably want to remember the number of the stunt you finished with, then begin the tape there on another day.

GO: A number of things can be done by children as young as five and the video is still entertaining for kids as old as ten. Great for rainy days.

Also available from Shari Lewis are eight 30-minute videos compiled from the PBS television series *Lamb Chop's Play Along* (A & M Video, 1992). These are interactive and theme-based and include:

Action Songs
Action Stories
Betchas, Tricks and Silly Stunts
Jokes, Riddles, Knock-Knocks
  and Funny Poems
Do as I Do
On Our Way to School
Jump into the Story
Let's Make Music

You may also find re-releases of Shari's older but still great tapes:
Kooky Classics (an introduction to music)
Have I Got A Story for You
You Can Do It (be a magician)

SHELLEY DUVALL'S BEDTIME STORIES

> MCA
> 1992
> 25 minutes
> Directed by: Arthur Leonardi,
>   Jeff Stein
> Narrated by: various (see below)

These videos based on books are partly animated.

Titles in the series are:

Blumpoe the Grumpoe Meets Arnold the Cat (John Candy); Millions of Cats (James Earl Jones)
Elbert's Bad Word (Ringo Starr); Weird Parents (Bette Midler)
Elizabeth and Larry (Jean Stapleton); Bill and Pete (Dudley Moore)
Little Toot and the Loch Ness Monster (Rick Moranis); Choo Choo: The Story of a Little Engine Who Ran Away (Bonnie Raitt)
Patrick's Dinosaurs; What's Happened to Patrick's Dinosaurs? (Martin Short)
There's a Nightmare in My Closet (Michael J. Fox); There's an Alligator under My Bed (Christian Slater); There's Something in My Attic (Sissy Spacek)

SIMPLY MAD ABOUT THE MOUSE

> Buena Vista Home Video
> 1991
> 35 minutes
> Directed by: Scot Garen
> Starring: Michael Bolton, Harry Connick Jr.,
>   The Gypsy Kings, Billy Joel, LL Cool J,
>   Bobby McFerrin, Ric Ocasek, Soul II Soul

Eight contemporary artists perform Disney's classic songs in music-video style.

Songs featured are:

A Dream Is a Wish Your Heart Makes
The Bare Necessities
I've Got No Strings
Kiss the Girl
The Siamese Cat Song
When You Wish upon a Star
Who's Afraid of the Big Bad Wolf?
Zip-A-Dee-Doo-Dah

SLEEPING BEAUTY

Walt Disney Home Video
1959
75 minutes
Directed by: Clyde Geronimi
Starring the voices of: Eleanor Audley,
  Mary Costa,
  Taylor Holmes, Barbara Luddy

When Princess Aurora is born, King Stefan and his queen invite everyone to a great feast. The most prestigious guests are Stefan's lifelong friend Hubert and his young son Phillip, who is that day betrothed to the infant princess. Also in attendance are the three good fairies, Flora, Fauna and Merriweather. Flora and Fauna each give their gifts, but before Merriweather has a chance to present hers, there is a sudden interruption. The evil sorceress Maleficent (who was not invited to the celebration) makes a sudden and frightening appearance, and as everyone looks on in horror, presents her gift: a dreadful curse, which promises that before the sun sets on Aurora's sixteenth birthday, she will prick her finger on the spindle of a spinning wheel and die. But Merriweather still has her gift to give, and although she cannot prevent the curse from coming true, she can soften it, which she does, ordaining that "The princess shall not die, but will merely sleep until the kiss of true love awakens her." Still, all of the spinning wheels in the kingdom are burned and Aurora is kept safely hidden in a secluded cabin until after her sixteenth birthday. But on that day, Aurora returns to the castle, where she is trapped by Maleficent, and the good fairies decide to put the whole place to sleep along with her. Meanwhile, Maleficent seizes Phillip, intending to keep him a prisoner until he is old and bent before releasing him to wake Aurora. But the three fairies rescue the prince, and he defeats Maleficent and awakens the slumbering castle.

CAUTION: Maleficent, who among other things turns into a fire-breathing dragon, has scared thousands of little kids. So be careful. If your little one is prone to being frightened, this film may *terrify*.

GO: Exquisite animation and wonderful songs make this a favorite Disney classic.

●

THE SNOWMAN

Sony and Children's Circle
1982
26 minutes
Directed by: Dianne Jackson

This is a charming story about a boy who spends a magical evening when the Snowman he builds somehow comes to life. The boy shows the Snowman the inside of his house where the Snowman tries on clothes and powders his cheeks. (His favorite place is the freezer.) Then the Snowman takes the boy on a breathtaking flight to the icelands where they meet the Snowman's friends and Santa Claus. After their return, however, the Snowman melts in the dawning sunrise and the boy is left with his memories. Based on the book by Raymond Briggs.

CAUTION: The Snowman melts (read: dies) at the end. There is no dialogue.

GO: This fully-animated film is a one-of-a-kind collector's item. Superbly animated in the same illustrative style as the book and without any dialogue (Briggs's books are known for not having text), it is accompanied only by an award-winning score.

■

SO DEAR
TO MY HEART

Walt Disney Home Video
1948
84 minutes
Directed by: Harold Schuster
Starring: Beulah Bondi, Bobby Driscoll,
    Burl Ives

"The greatest wealth a man may acquire is the wisdom he gains from living, and sometimes out of small beginnings come the forces that shape a whole life."

So begins the 1903 tale of young Jeremiah whose Granny allows him to keep a newborn black lamb. Jeremiah dreams of entering his lamb in the county fair even though it has no pedigree. And it's because he presents himself so earnestly that the judges are moved to award him (and his lamb) a special prize.

Song featured is:
Lavender Blue (Dilly Dilly)

CAUTION: Jeremiah and his friend appear to have no parents, although they do receive guidance and affection from caring adults. In one scene, the lamb runs away and is lost in the woods on a stormy night.

GO: A gentle story full of love and lessons (Granny warns Jeremiah that he is thinking of things that are vain, and has forgotten about things of the spirit), the film contains a number of gentle songs performed by Burl Ives. Animated sequences are interspersed throughout and add to the overall charming effect of the film.

SPORT GOOFY
(Cartoon Classics, Vol. 4)

Walt Disney Home Video
1942–1947
43 minutes

In this cartoon compilation, Goofy participates in and demonstrates a number of different sports.

Stories featured are:
Footracing
Goofy Gymnastics
Hockey Homicide
How To Play Baseball
How to Play Golf
The Olympic Champ
Tennis Racquet
Track

GO: A cartoon compilation truly for all ages.

STORIES TO
REMEMBER
COLLECTION

Sony/Oak Street Music
1992–1994
30 minutes each

(continued on next page)

This fully animated series uses well-known personalities to narrate fairy-tales, myths or verse. Music is often by a noted composer or performer. Animation techniques range from standard Saturday morning quality to camera panning of well-drawn illustrations.

Titles recommended for five- to twelve-year-olds include:

Noah's Ark, told by James Earl Jones

Pegasus, told by Mia Farrow

Merlin and the Dragons, told by Kevin Kline

Beauty and the Beast, told by Mia Farrow

The Snow Queen, told by Sigourney Weaver

See the Up to 3 section for the following titles:

Baby's Storytime, told by Arlo Guthrie

Baby's Morningtime, told by Judy Collins

Baby's Bedtime, told by Judy Collins

Baby's Nursery Rhymes, told by Phylicia Rashad

CAUTION: Although the attempt to bring quality entertainment to children is to be applauded, by the time children are old enough to appreciate these types of stories, they may have outgrown the format in which they are presented.

GO: A commendable attempt to produce a series of high-quality stories and entertainment for children.

THE STORY OF BABAR THE LITTLE ELEPHANT

MCA
1968
30 minutes
Directed by: Ed Levitt, Bill Melendez
Starring the voice of: Peter Ustinov

When his mother is killed by a hunter, Babar runs away to the city where he stays with a kindly old lady. Two years later his cousins, Arthur and Celeste, find Babar and take him back to the forest where he's promptly made king of the elephants. He begins his reign by building a city, thereby angering the rhinos who declare war on the elephants. Babar eventually defeats the rhinos, and the elephants rebuild their city and live happily ever after.

CAUTION: The story begins with the death of Babar's mother.

GO: This is a credible effort to bring the Babar books to life, with a few songs for the little folk.

■

THE SUPERPOWERS COLLECTION

Warner Home Video
1985
60 minutes (each multi-episode volume)

In each of these multi-episode volumes, superheroes go up against their perennial enemies to triumph in the end. *Batman* is by far the current favorite of *The Superpowers Collection*.

Titles in the collection are:
Aquaman
Batman

Superboy
Superman

CAUTION: The animation is simplistic and very stilted, although this is not necessarily a bad thing because it causes the violence (the odd punch or tackle) to lose its impact.

GO: Because this collection contains only minimal violence it's a great compromise for the parents of a young child with a Batman fixation (thanks to all of that dreaded tie-in merchandising).

THE SWORD IN THE STONE

Walt Disney Home Video
1968
79 minutes
Directed by: Wolfgang Reitherman
Starring the voices of: Sebastian Cabot, Rick Sorenson, Karl Swenson

Based on the first and best-known book of T.H. White's four-book novel *The Once and Future King*, *The Sword in the Stone* chronicles the early life of young Arthur (Wart), who has been hidden away by concerned parties, and who, unbeknownst to himself and his guardian, is destined to become a great king.Wart, as he is known to Sir Ector, his guardian, is forced to perform the menial castle chores; that is, until a search for an errant arrow leads him to the forest home of Merlin the Magician, who takes young Wart in as his student. Magical adventures follow as Merlin instructs his young friend by turning him in turn into a fish, a squirrel and a bird. Wart's tutelage reaches a climax when he falls into the hands of Merlin's evil rival, the sinister

Madame Mim, and Merlin is forced to fight a wizard's duel to save him. True to the book, the first part of Arthur's life comes to a close at a great tournament where, having left his knight's sword at the inn, Authur pulls Excalibur from the anvil and is chosen to be the next king.

CAUTION: Some little ones find Madame Mim's transformations pretty scary. Arthur is in peril in the animal scenes, particularly when, as a fish, he encounters a monster pike in the moat.

GO: A charming effort, featuring two of the most beloved characters in English literature. This is a good way to introduce young viewers to the Arthurian lore.

■

THE TALE OF THE BUNNY PICNIC

Jim Henson Video/Buena Vista Home Video
1986
51 minutes
Directed by: Jim Henson and David G. Hillier

When Lugsy and his sister Twitch are getting ready for the bunny picnic, their little brother Bean wants to help. When they send him away because he's too little, Bean goes for a walk through the farmer's lettuce patch. There he runs into a barking dog and when his siblings don't believe him (he's always playing pretend) the dog raids the picnic. (The mean farmer has ordered the dog to bring him rabbits for a stew.) Now aware that the dog exists, the bunnies are left to wait for the next attack. Bean suggests they give the dog a sleeping potion, but Lugsy gets caught. So the bunnies fashion a Trojan Horse-type rabbit and scare the dog into letting Lugsy go. Then, taking pity on the terrified dog, the bunnies use their knowledge of the farmer's allergy to rabbits to drive the farmer away.

CAUTION: Lugsy is nasty to Bean and is constantly making disparaging remarks; consequently Bean tells Lugsy he hates him. The farmer is ominous and his dog is afraid that the farmer will kill him when he sees that he didn't get any bunnies.

GO: This video contains songs and ingenious puppetry without anything really scary, making it suitable for little ones. This is a Henson Associates Production in association with BBC-TV.

CAUTION: The film may simply be too much, and too long, for very little children. There is no dialogue.

GO: The dexterity of the performers, considering the restraints imposed by their costumes, is astonishing, though those viewers who are looking for the acrobatics associated with some ballet may be disappointed. All in all, this is a terrific way to introduce young children to ballet, and will certainly be enjoyed by adult fans of the genre.

■

THE TALES OF BEATRIX POTTER

TALES OF BEATRIX POTTER

Thorn EMI
1971
86 minutes
Directed by: Reginald Mills
Starring: The Royal Ballet

Set to the music of John Lanchbery and choreographed by Sir Fredrick Ashton, various Beatrix Potter tales are brought to life with a dazzling array of incredible sets, and splendid masks and costumes, all portrayed as if through the imagination of Beatrix Potter. Characters featured are: Mrs. Tiggywinkle, Peter Rabbit, Mrs. Tittlemouse, Johnny Townmouse, Jemimah Puddleduck, the Fox, Pigling Bland, Alexander, Mrs. Pettitoes, the Black Berkshire Pig, Jeremy Fisher, Tom Thumb, Hunca Munca, Squirrel Nutkin, Owl, Tabitha Twitchit.

C V L
1986
43 minutes
Directed by: Brian McNamara
Starring the voice of: Sidney S. Walker

The illustrations in this video are from Potter's books and are accompanied by a musical score. The video also features rhymes by Cecily Parsley printed at the bottom of the screen.

Stories featured are:
The Story of Miss Moppet
The Tale of Benjamin Bunny
The Tale of Jeremy Fisher
The Tale of Peter Rabbit
The Tale of Tom Kitten
The Tale of Two Bad Mice

Rhymes featured are:
Cecily Parsley
Goosey, Goosey Gander
Little Garden
Ninny, Ninny Netticoat
Pussycat, Pussycat
Three Blind Mice
Three Little Pigs
Tom Tinker's Dog

CAUTION: This video is not animated; rather, it's similar to watching the pages of a book while the story is being read. There are some moving elements.

GO: These are gentle, classic stories.

■

TALESPIN SERIES

Walt Disney Home Video
1990
30–46 minutes each
Directed by: Ed Ghertner,
  Larry Latham, Jamie Mitchell, Robert Taylor
Starring the voices of: Jim Cummings,
  Ed Gilbert, Sally Struthers

The Talespin Series features some characters who originally appeared in the feature film *The Jungle Book*. Baloo the bear flies a pontoon plane for his own transport business, Higher for Hire. Along with him are new creations, his bear friends Rebecca, Kit and Molly. The orangutan Louie is also back as a club owner on his own island, and Shere Khan the tiger owns a huge corporation, Khan Industries. There is also the sporadic menace of air-pirates, led by the swashbuckling Don Karnage.

Titles in the series are:
Fearless Flyers (Vol. 4):
  Jumping the Guns; Mach One for the Gipper
Imagine That! (Vol. 6):
  Flight of the Snow Duck, Flight School Confidential
Jackpots and Crackpots (Vol. 3):
  A Touch of Class; Her Chance to Dream
Search for the Lost City (Vol. 8):
  For Whom the Bell Klangs
That's Show Biz! (Vol. 2):

Stormy Weather; Mommy for a Day
Treasure Trap (Vol. 5):
  Idol Rich; Polly Wants a Treasure
True Blue Baloo (Vol. 1):
  From Here to Machinery; The Balooest of Blue Bloods
Wise Up! (Vol. 7):
  Molly Coddled; The Sound and the Furry

CAUTION: Don't be confused by the presence of the *Jungle Book* characters. These stories are only based on the characters and are in no other way connected to the original feature film.

GO: The plots are fast-moving and engaging and the animation is better than the average Saturday-morning fare.

TEENAGE MUTANT NINJA TURTLES ANIMATIONS

fhe
1987–1991
47–72 minutes each

There are a number of Teenage Mutant Ninja Turtles animation series, but they all share the same basic points and so we have grouped them all here together. To understand the series you really need to know the characters. The Turtles are distinguishable by their colored half-masks and by the weapons they use. Leonardo is the leader and is the most mature of the group; he is in blue and he carries two katanas (swords). Michelangelo is the most juvenile and he's always watching TV and reading comic books; he is in orange and uses the nuchakus. Donatello has a technical bent; he wears purple and uses the bo or staff. And finally, Raphael is the rebel and the agitator; he wears

red and uses the sais (daggers).
And there is Splinter, a huge rat
who is the Turtles' spiritual mentor
and martial-arts master. The villains
are Krang (a disembodied brain
from Dimension X) and Shredder (a
mysterious, masked martial-arts
master who is constantly hatching
plots to rule the world).

Titles in the Bad Guys (Sewer Heroes Series 2) series are:

Turtles vs. The Fly
  Turtles vs. The Fly; Shredderville
Turtles vs. Leatherhead
  Turtles vs. Leatherhead; Leatherhead
  Meets the Rat King
Turtles vs. Rhinoman
  Turtles vs. Rhinoman; Blast from the
  Past
Turtles vs. The Turtle Terminator
  Turtles vs. The Turtle Terminator;
  Turtles, Turtles Everywhere

Titles in the Bodaciously Big Adventures series are:

The Big Blow Out
The Big Cuff Link Caper
The Big Rip Off
The Big Zipp Attack

Titles in the Hollywood Dudes series are:

Four Turtles and a Baby:
  Four Turtles and a Baby; Shredder's
  Mom
Planet of the Turtles:
  Planet of the Turtles; Plan Six from
  Outer Space
Rebel Without a Fin:
  Rebel without a Fin; Splinter Vanishes
Turtles of the Jungle:
  Turtles of the Jungle; Turtlemaniac

Titles in the Sewer Hero series are:

Donatello's Degree:
  Donatello's Degree; Donatello Makes
  Time
Leonardo Lightens Up:
  Leonardo Lightens Up; Leonardo vs.
  Tempestra
Michelangelo Meets Bugman:
  Michelangelo Meets Bugman; What's
  Michelangelo Good For?

Raphael Meets His Match
  Raphael Meets His Match; Raphael
  Knocks 'Em Dead

Titles in the Teenage Mutant Ninja Turtles series are:

Attack of the Big Macc
Case of the Killer Pizzas
Cowabunga, Shredhead
The Epic Begins
Heroes in a Half Shell
Hot Rodding Teenagers
The Incredible Shrinking Turtles
Pizza by the Shred
The Shredder Is Splintered
Super Rocksteady and Mighty Beebop
Turtles at the Earth's Core
The Turtles' Awesome Easter
Turtles Soup

CAUTION: Though the violence in the
Teenage Mutant Ninja Turtles animations
is nowhere near as graphic as it is in the
live-action Turtle movies, the Turtles do
solve all of their problems with force.
Granted, you don't discuss problems with
supervillains, but it is possible that this
distinction is lost on very young children.
We have received feedback from many
parents who have informed us that their
young children become more agressive
after exposure to the show.

TEX AVERY ANIMATIONS

MGM/UA
circa 1940–1955
44–60 minutes each
Directed by: Tex Avery
Starring the voices of: Tex Avery

Tex Avery is one of the great
pioneers of animation. His wild and
zany adventures have captured the
imaginations of generations of
viewers (much of the animation in
Who Framed Roger Rabbit? pays a

heavy tribute to Tex). And his jokes come from an age when it was still funny to have a character get shot a hundred times, say "Ha! You missed me!" then have a drink of water and have the water spurt out of all the holes. Depending on the period from which a particular cartoon comes, the animation can vary from classic Warner Bros. quality ('60s Bugs Bunny et al), to the "Saturday-morning" look. But no matter what the budget, Tex's genius shines through.

Titles in the collection are:
The Adventures of Droopy
Here Comes Droopy
Droopy and Company
Tex Avery's Screwball Classics (Vol. 1)
Tex Avery's Screwball Classics (Vol. 2)
Tex Avery's Screwball Classics (Vol. 3)
Tex Avery's Screwball Classics (Vol. 4)

CAUTION: Tex also made a few racier cartoons with some sexy women in them, like *Swing-shift Cinderella* and *The Lady Who's Known as Lou*. Also, be aware that Tex's stuff is primarily adversarial; that is, good guys conking bad guys on the head.

GO: The jokes may be old to us, but remember that it's all new to your six-year-old, and when it comes to kids, Tex sure knows how to crack 'em up.

This is a straightforward concert tape but features occasional video visuals and outdoor footage. Chapin is joined by two other musicians on electric bass and piano.

Original songs featured are:
The Nick of Time
Uh, Oh Accident
Alphabet Soup
Family Tree
Cousins
This Pretty Planet
Someone's Gonna Use It
The Wheel of the Water
Good Garbage
Sing A Whale Song
Happy Earth Day
Shovelling
Together Tomorrow

GO: Songs are singable, with intelligent lyrics. The combination of instruments gives the concert more of a folk feel than other concert videos aimed at children that feature larger bands. The songs that are environmentally oriented seem genuine and not at all preachy.

THIS PRETTY PLANET: TOM CHAPIN IN CONCERT

Sony Kids Video
1992
50 minutes
Directed by: Denver J. Collins
Starring: Tom Chapin, Jon Cobert, Michael Mark

THUMBELINA

Warner Home Video
1993
87 minutes
Directed by: Don Bluth and Gary Goldman
Starring the voices of: Jodi Benson, Carol Channing, Charo, Gino Conforti, Barbara Cook, Gilbert Gottfried, John Hurt, Gary Imhoff, Joe Lynch

In this version of Hans Christian Andersen's classic, a lonely woman gets a tiny barleycorn from a good witch. It grows into a flower containing a miniature young woman, Thumbelina. She lives

155

happily enough with her mother, but dreams of folk her own size. Then one day, Cornelius, prince of the fairies, happens to spy her through the window. He woos her successfully, but that same night, a family of show-biz toads kidnaps her, their intention being to make her a star and wed her to the loathsome eldest son. Thumbelina escapes, only to fall into the clutches of the odious Beetle. Thumbelina escapes him as well, but meanwhile the toad is on her trail, and joins forces with Beetle to track her down. Their first move is to try to kill Cornelius, and they half-succeed, freezing him in a block of ice. Meanwhile, Thumbelina has wandered the winter landscape until she comes into the not-so-friendly hospitality of Mrs. Fieldmouse, who tries to wed her to the sombre Mr. Mole. Thumbelina, thinking Cornelius dead, agrees to the wedding, but has a change of heart at the last minute. She then discovers to her joy that Cornelius is alive and well.

CAUTION: There is some hitting and punching. The entire toad family is portrayed as Hispanic caricatures. At one point, Cornelius is frozen. Jacquimo the swallow is found dead (he comes back to life).

GO: The animation is up to Mr. Bluth's usual high standards, and even quite young children can enjoy this one.

THE TIMELESS TALES SERIES

Hanna Barbera/Turner Home Entertainment
1990,1991
30 minutes each
Directed by: Don Lusk, Carl Urbano
Hosted by: Olivia Newton-John

Each 1990 episode begins with a short live-action introduction by Olivia Newton-John. Then the camera pans up to the attic, where a teddy bear comes alive and two children, Emily and Kevin, discover a fantastic book which opens and projects pictures right out of its pages. The animation is decent, and more importantly, the storylines more or less adhere to the classical versions of the fairy tales. There are also songs in the episodes, which may help keep the little ones interested. At the end of each of these episodes, Olivia Newton-John gives viewers some brief tips on how to help the environment.

Titles in the series are:
The Elves and the Shoemaker ●
The Emperor's New Clothes ●
Puss in Boots (not introduced by Olivia Newton-John) ●
Rapunzel
Rumpelstiltskin
The Steadfast Tin Soldier (not introduced by Olivia Newton-John)
Thumbelina
The Ugly Duckling

CAUTION: The two titles filmed in 1991, *Puss in Boots* and *The Steadfast Tin Soldier*, are not completely true to the classical versions; the ending of each has been softened, probably to make them more palatable for young viewers.

■

TINY TOON ADVENTURES: HOW I SPENT MY SUMMER VACATION

Warner Home Video
1991
80 minutes
Directed by: Rich Arons, Ken Boyer,
    Kent Butterworth, Barry Caldwell,
    Alfred Gimeno, Art Leonardi,
    Byron Vaughns
Starring the voices of: Edie McClurg,
    Jonathan Winters

Stephen Spielberg had a hand in this effort (as executive producer), which features junior versions of Bugs (Babs and Buster Bunny), Daffy (Plucky and Shirley), Porky (Hammy or Hampton), Sylvester, Pepe LePew, Wile E. Coyote, the Road Runner, the Tasmanian Devil (Dizzy), and totally original characters Elmira and Fowlmouth in musical adventures of their own. The film opens at ACME Looniversity, during the last minute of the last school-day before summer vacation. The kids get out, and Babs and Buster engage in the greatest water fight of all time, which ends up washing them through satires of *Deliverance*, *Superman*, and *The Little Mermaid*; meanwhile, Plucky contrives to be invited along with Hampton's family to Happy World Land (the ultimate new fun megalopolis on the other side of the country), and ends up on the cross-country ride from Hell. And young female skunk Fifi tries to get into a four-star hotel to see her idol, Johnny le Pew.

CAUTION: The kids in this film are rude and combative and may not provide the best behavioral role models for children too young to identify satire. Hampton's family (Uncle Stinky, in particular) is disgusting and on their trip to Happy World Land, Plucky must endure such things as car-sickness and saliva jokes. The Hamptons are also menaced by an insane axe-wielding mass-murderer who really is hideous.

GO: No one makes fun of the Californians like the Californians. This is a wild send-up of California culture and youth, with shots at such celebrities as Carson, Arsenio Hall, Roseanne Barr, and Letterman, and plenty of tongue-in-cheek humor. It really is designed more for adults than for children, but should provide an enjoyable viewing experience for the whole family. (See cautions!) Don't miss the credits at the end.

✗ TOM AND JERRY: THE MOVIE

f.h.e./MCA
1993
84 minutes
Directed by: Phil Roman
Starring the voices of: Dana Hill, Richard Kind,
    Anndi McAfee, Charlotte Rae

This effort features the famous duo in a full-length musical animation. Tom's family is moving, and when Jerry tries to come along, Tom does his best to get rid of him. In the process, both are left behind. Tom is then besieged in the house by a giant bulldog. To make matters worse, the house is scheduled for demolition, and Tom (who has a change of heart and saves Jerry's life), barely escapes with his diminutive buddy. The two wander the city, homeless, encountering Robyn, an orphan who has run away from her evil guardians, the two-faced Pristine Figg and her lawyer accomplice Lickboot. The sinister duo are managing Robyn's trust fund, and mistreating her into the bargain. However, there are rumors that Mr. Starling, Robyn's explorer father, has survived the avalanche that supposedly killed him and is about to return. This information is being withheld from Robyn, and when Tom and Jerry find out they are promptly shipped off to the evil Dr. Applecheek, who runs a pet shelter (in reality a prison for animals he is holding for ransom). Figg pays Applecheek to kill Tom and Jerry, but the duo wisely escape with all the other animals. Tom and Jerry then rescue Robyn, and the chase is on. In the climax, Robyn's father returns in time to rescue everyone.

✗STOP: An apparently kindly kids' amusement park owner, Cap'n Kidee, befriends Robyn and gives her shelter; however, the moment he hears about the reward, he promptly betrays her. In another scene, Dr. Applecheek appears to be nice, but turns into an ogre the moment Tom and Jerry are alone with him.

CAUTION: Animals are in peril throughout. More than once, people who appear nice turn out ot be evil. This film features yet another "fat equals evil" villain.

GO: Great animation and rapid pace.

TOO SMART FOR STRANGERS WITH WINNIE-THE-POOH

Walt Disney Home Video
1985
40 minutes
Directed by: Philip F. Messina,
    Ron Underwood

Winnie-the-Pooh, Tigger, Piglet, Owl, Eeyore, Rabbit and Roo explain what a stranger is and give kids sound advice about avoiding unsafe places, answering the phone when you're home alone and knowing when to say no. They talk about the tricks strangers use (your mother asked me to pick you up) and urge kids to tell a grown-up about strangers they encounter and about upsetting experiences. Also included is a song about not letting people "touch you in your private parts" in which Pooh explains the difference between "OK touching" and "not OK touching." The characters sing songs to emphasize each lesson. This is a live-action video with people in costumes.

GO: This is one of the best tapes available for young children on this subject and its entertaining presentation makes it more watchable. Professionals from the Child Welfare League and others contributed to the preparation of this video for children ages three and up.

THE VELVETEEN RABBIT

f.h.e./MCA
1985
30 minutes
Directed by: Pino Van Lamsweerde
Starring the voice of: Christopher Plummer

Because he's just an ordinary stuffed animal, the toy soldiers want to send the rabbit away. But they cannot find his wind-up parts, so they banish him instead to the farthest part of the nursery. There a skin horse reassures him by telling him that the soldiers are nothing but wind-up, and that they will never be real. He goes on to explain that real isn't how you are made, but something that happens to you after you have been loved for a very long time. One night during a thunderstorm, the rabbit is taken to comfort the boy, and from then on they are inseparable. But after the boy recovers from a serious illness, the doctor orders that everything the boy touched be destroyed and, the rabbit is thrown out. As night falls a magical transformation takes place and a fairy turns the Velveteen Rabbit into a really real rabbit. Based on the book by Margery Williams.

GO: This fully-animated effort, due to its weighty theme, is more suited to children five and up.

■

WALT DISNEY CARTOON CLASSICS

Walt Disney Home Video
1930s to 1950s
22–27 minutes each

This collection is made up of vintage cartoons and in some cases two or three short films are included on each video.

Titles in the collection are:
Donald's Scary Tales (Vol. 13)
Halloween Haunts (Vol. 14)
Here's Donald (Vol. 2)
Here's Goofy (Vol. 3)
Here's Mickey (Vol. 1)
Here's Pluto (Vol. 5)
Mickey and the Gang (Vol. 11)
Nuts About Chip and Dale (Vol. 12)

Silly Symphonies (Vol. 4)
Starring Animals 2 X 2 (Vol. 8)
Starring Chip and Dale (Vol. 9)
Starring Donald and Daisy (Vol. 7)
Starring Mickey and Minnie (Vol. 6)
Starring Pluto and Fifi (Vol. 10)

WALT DISNEY CARTOON CLASSICS SPECIAL EDITION

Walt Disney Home Video
1930s to 1950s
27–31 minutes each

Titles in the collection are:
Fun on the Job:
    Clock Cleaners; Baggage Buster; Mickey's Fire Brigade; The Big Wash
The Goofy World of Sports:
    Olympic Champ; Donald's Golf Game; The Art of Skiing; Aquamania
Happy Summer Days:
    Father's Lion; Tea for Two Hundred; The Simple Things; Two Weeks Vacation

WALT DISNEY MINI-CLASSICS: PETER AND THE WOLF PLUS TWO MORE CARTOONS

Walt Disney Home Video
1946
30 minutes
Directed by: Clyde Geronimi
Narrated by: Sterling Holloway

In this fairy tale, with music by Sergei Prokofieff, viewers are first introduced to the instruments of the orchestra as they will represent the characters in the story — Peter, by a string quartet; Sasha the bird, by a flute; Sonia the duck, by an oboe; Ivan the cat, by a clarinet; Grandpa, by a bassoon; the hunters, by the kettledrums, and of course the wolf, by the brass section.

One day, when his grandfather is asleep, Peter ventures out of his yard (with his popgun in hand) to catch the wolf. He is joined by Sasha, Sonia and Ivan. The wolf is soon upon them and appears to swallow the duck, Sonia. Sasha goes after the wolf but to no avail. Just as he is going to be eaten too, Peter lowers a rope down from a tree and catches the wolf by his tail. The hunters happen along just in time to help Peter with the wolf and Sonia reappears from the tree, none the worse for wear.

CAUTION: The wolf has scary yellow eyes and huge teeth and a drooling mouth. There are frightening close-ups.

GO: This video is a palatable version of the famous Russian tale and also contains two shorts: *Music Land* and *Symphony Hour.*

Other Mini-classics include:

Ben & Me
Bongo
Donald in Mathemagic land
Mickey & the Beanstalk
Mickey's Christmas Carol
Mickey's Magical World
The Reluctant Dragon
Wind in the Willows
The Prince and the Pauper
Willie the Operatic Whale

WARNER BROTHERS ANIMATIONS

Warner Home Video
1950–1965
38–91 minutes each
Directed by: Chuck Jones,
  Fritz Freleng, and other notables
Starring the voice of: Mel Blanc

We have to mention the Warner Brothers animations. It seems evident that these cartoons have always been made more with adults in mind; it may even be that the people who enjoy these cartoons most are the people who made them. The cartoons themselves have come under some criticism in recent years for the level of inherent violence; however, when compared to today's fare, this is something of an open question. Certainly, many of the Warner Brothers cartoons (of the sixties especially) are masterpieces. The zany characters are blistering send-ups of different personality types, and each has a particular identity which the creators have rigidly maintained through the years. Bugs is the Bronx trickster; Yosemite Sam is always angry to the point of idiocy; both Sylvester's and Wile E. Coyote's complicated gadgets never work; Foghorn is a loudmouth; Daffy is an egocentric; and Porky usually ends up with the short end of the stick until the final scene. Tied in with it all is Mel Blanc's genius. He's one of the greatest comics of the age. May kids and adults watch these characters forever.

Titles in the Warner Brothers collection are:

The Bugs Bunny Road Runner Movie
Bugs Bunny, Superstar
Bugs Bunny's Third Movie: 1001 Rabbit Tales
Bugs Bunny's Hare Raising Tales
Daffy Duck's Madcap Mania
Porky Pig Tales
Salute to Chuck Jones
Salute to Friz Freleng
Salute to Mel Blanc
Looney Tunes Video Show (Vol. 1)
Looney Tunes Video Show (Vol. 2)
Looney Tunes Video Show (Vol. 3)

Titles in the Warner Brothers Golden Jubilee collection are:

Bugs Bunny's Wacky Adventures
Daffy Duck: The Nutiness Continues
Elmer Fudd's Comedy Capers
Foghorn Leghorn's Fractured Funnies
Pepe LePew's Skunk Tales
Porky Pig's Screwball Comedies
Road Runner vs Wile E. Coyote
Speedy Gonzales Fast Funnies
Sylvester and Tweety's Crazy Capers

WE'RE BACK! A DINOSAUR'S STORY

MCA Universal
1993
101 minutes
Directed by: Phil Nibbelink, Simon Wells, Dick Zondag, Ralph Zondag
Starring the voices of: Walter Cronkite, John Goodman, Jay Leno, Martin Short, Yeardley Smith

Buster, the smallest bird in his nest, runs away and meets Rex, a gentle, golf-playing tyrannosaur. Rex recounts his past, beginning with his violent early life, in which he meets Captain NewEyes, a time-traveller who gives Rex Brain Grain, a food

which instantly turns Rex into a compassionate, sentient being. Rex meets three other such creatures. The evolved saurans discover that the children of the middle future (our time) desperately wish to see real live dinosaurs, and the four dinosaurs agree to accompany NewEyes in his time machine to that period. In New York City, the dinosaurs meet Louie, a young runaway who is off to join the circus, and Cecilia, the neglected daughter of socialites. The dinosaurs promptly cause mass panic in the city, and after the resulting confusion, they discover that both Louie and Cecilia have signed a contract with NewEyes' evil brother ScrewEyes. The dinosaurs arrive at ScrewEyes' dreadful circus too late to prevent this, and are forced to make a deal with the evil one to save the children. The crux of the deal is that the dinosaurs must must revert to their former savage selves to serve as the centerpiece of ScrewEyes' circus. But during the very first show, something goes terribly wrong. The reverted Rex is about to go on a rampage when the courageous Louie talks him back into his evolved self. The dinosaurs then go to work at the Museum of Natural History, fulfilling the wishes of children.

CAUTION: For very little children, the scary scenes may be a bit much; in particular, Dr. ScrewEyes' fright radio sequences, and many of the images in his demonic circus.

GO: Produced by Steven Spielberg, with great animation, lively pace and excellent voice-overs, this is the little ones' *Jurassic Park*.

THE WHITE SEAL

f.h.e.
1975
30 minutes
Directed by: Chuck Jones
Starring the voice of: Roddy McDowall

Kotik the seal is in search of the perfect island where he can go during the hunting season to be safe and free. His search for refuge takes him to the Galapagos, Georgia and the Orkneys. He seeks out the Great Whale who takes him to the sea-cow (a creature that has found a haven from hunters). And so Kotik leads a great migration to the mystical island where all the seals find safety. Based on Rudyard Kipling's story.

CAUTION: The story is about a seal hunt and is not all pleasant. Commercial blacks interrupt the story.

GO: This fully-animated video is targeted to children aged three to eight; however, the film's tone and its conservationalist message make it better suited to older children.

■

THE WILL VINTON COLLECTION

Golden Book Video
1977–1989
30 minutes each
Directed by: Will Vinton

Will Vinton's remarkable talents are showcased in these four claymation films. His figures move with a life-like quality that is absolutely magical, and their faces are extraordinarily expressive. The casting and direction of voice-overs is superb.

Martin the Cobbler

(Features a brief introduction by Alexandra Tolstoy.) This is a fine telling of Leo Tolstoy's wonderful story of a bitter, lonely man who sees the face of God. Martin the cobbler has lived a hard life. His beloved wife and son died when he was still young, and he gave way to despair, blaming God for taking his family from him. He only wishes to die as well, and his days have passed practically unnoticed. Now he is old and bitter, and when his jolly friend Vladimir comes to ask him to help with a festival, Martin rudely refuses him. Then a holy man comes to ask him to rebind his holy book and that night, Martin begins to read it. He is particularly moved by a passage about a rich merchant who invites the Lord into his house, but does not welcome him. When Martin falls asleep, a mysterious voice says: Martin, tomorrow I will come. But the next day only a raggedy old street-sweeper, a desperately cold woman and her baby, a street urchin and an old apple-woman come to the house. Because Martin is waiting for God, he notices their troubles and helps them. And that night, God appears to him in a vision, taking on the forms of all the people Martin helped, and Martin realizes the truth. Full of new life, he rushes off to join his friend at the festival.

■

The Little Prince

In Antoine de St. Exupéry's magnificent, haunting tale, a pilot stranded in the desert a thousand miles from the nearest human habitation encounters an explorer, the beautiful, child-like ruler of a distant, alien world. With drinking water in short supply, and while he desperately effects repairs to his damaged aircraft, the true nature of his inquisitive companion is revealed. And as their relationship evolves, and the Little Prince relates his discoveries (both external and internal), the pilot, who had long turned his attention to matters of consequence, experiences a reawakening of the heart.

■

Rip Van Winkle

Washington Irving's classic story concerns the man who meets the ghost of Henry Hudson and his crew, and subsequently sleeps for twenty years.

Rip Van Winkle, the laughingstock of the village, is a good-hearted but shiftless dreamer who spends his time flying kites, telling stories and singing songs. One day, Rip does what he does best: he ducks his responsibilities and goes squirrel hunting. But Fate has a surprise in store for Rip. He stops at a stream and as he bends to take a drink, his reflection becomes unfriendly. Rip runs away and stumbles upon Hudson and his boys, who are boozing it up and bowling (the source of thunder in New England). Rip has a drink and passes out, and when he wakes up he is an ancient, white-bearded man.

CAUTION: Rip has a psychedelic nightmare which contains a number of frightening images, and his return is fraught with anxiety and confusion.

■

The Star Child

Oscar Wilde's dark story of vanity, suffering and redemption is faithfully recreated. Two woodcutters out on a bitter winter's night witness a shooting star run to its landing site. There they discover a beautiful boy-child — the Star Child. One of the woodcutters keeps the child and raises him as his own. But despite his foster father's kindness, the Star Child grows to be a spoiled and heartless boy, an expert with the slingshot who delights in tormenting others. Then one day, an ugly old beggar woman comes to the village. And when she tells him that she is his mother, the Star Child ridicules her. She then rises up and announces that, as she has been forced to travel the roads of the earth under an evil spell, so too shall he. He is then instantly transformed into a misshapen, rag-clad hunchback, which is how he remains until at last he finds the true meaning of beauty.

CAUTION: There are some intense moments in the scene where the young boy is transformed, and again when he is forced into the service of a hideous magician.

GO: An excellent effort. This film has great songs and a timeless message that we can all afford to hear again.

■

WILLY WONKA AND THE CHOCOLATE FACTORY

Warner Home Video
1971
100 minutes
Directed by: Mel Stuart
Starring: Jack Albertson, Peter Ostrum,
Gene Wilder

Based on Roald Dahl's stories, this musical succeeds admirably in its own right. Charlie Bucket, a little boy from a destitute family, finds a Golden Ticket in a Willy Wonka chocolate bar, which entitles him and his grandfather to a lifetime supply of Willy Wonka's chocolate, and an invitation to a tour of the enigmatic Willy Wonka's legendary Chocolate Factory. Four other children (naughty, disrespectful, and spoiled) have found tickets as well, and are also along for the tour. Throughout the tour, the spoiled children each receive their due through Willy's magic in a variety of humorous ways. And in the end, Charlie's qualities of fairness, kindness and honesty earn him the greatest reward of all: Willy Wonka's legacy, the Chocolate Factory.

Songs featured are:
Candy Man
Pure Imagination

CAUTION: The scenes in which the bad children receive their just desserts may worry young viewers (for example, a girl turns into a blueberry and appears as if she will explode; although it is, of course, explained later in the film that this is just a way of teaching them a lesson and that they will all be all right later. Also, a boat ride down the chocolate river complete with flashing images and psychedelic effects and a menacing song sung by Willy

Wonka himself may disturb or confuse some young children.

GO: Charlie's relationship with his grandfather and his behavior in general are exemplary. Kids are sure to recognize and enjoy Anthony Newley's songs.

WINNIE-THE-POOH LEARNING SERIES

Walt Disney Home Video
1989
43–49 minutes each
Directed by: Karl Geurs, Terence Harrison,
Ken Kessel
Featuring the voices of: Jim Cummings,
Paul Winchell

Videos come with flash cards enclosed.

Sharing and Caring

Lights Out Rabbit borrows Gopher's helmet-lamp without asking. Without the light, Gopher is apprehensive about going down into his dark hole. Rabbit has trouble admitting he borrowed it because he can't recall where he put it. After everyone searches, Rabbit admits that he took it. Retracing his steps he finds the helmet but Gopher, now used to the dark, decides he doesn't need it anymore.

The Rats Come to Dinner A terrible rainstorm floods the packrats' den and they come to Pooh for help. But Pooh's house leaks badly and the packrats steal pots from Pooh's friends to hold the drips. Pooh tells the packrats a bedtime story about how it is better to give than to take. The rats understand the lesson enough to save everyone's furniture from the flood by moving it all up into Owl's house.

No Rabbit's A Fortress No one has any regard for Rabbit's "Keep Owt" signs in his garden. The last straw comes when Gopher dynamites the garden. In a last desperate attempt, Rabbit erects booby-traps and a wooden fortress around what's left of the garden. But he has neglected to build a door to get out and now he needs his friends' help to remedy the situation.

Helping Others

Owls Well That Ends Well Owl's off-key singing causes trouble, so Pooh and Piglet try to teach him. Meanwhile Tigger tries to help Rabbit keep the marauding crows out of his garden. Pooh appeals to the crows to teach Owl to sing but the crows can't stand Owl's singing and beat a hasty retreat much to Rabbit's delight.

A Very, Very Large Animal Christopher Robin's magnifying glass makes everything look very big, so when Piglet feels sad because of his size, his friends use the glass to make him feel bigger. But it is an awful lot of work maintaining the facade especially when Piglet, full of bravado, takes on the big crows. When Piglet discovers the truth he runs away, and on his trip he finds creatures much smaller than himself.

Caws and Effects It is finally Rabbit's harvest day. He tries to train Pooh, Tigger and Piglet to help him combat the black crows but when the birds paint themselves red Pooh' doesnt recognize them. He unwittingly helps the crows to

harvest the garden. When the crows are scared away Rabbit is left with the harvest all done.

To Dream the Impossible Scheme Rabbit is afraid a visit from Gopher's grandfather will cause more tunnelling under his garden so he asks his friends to keep Grandpappy busy doing nothing. But Gopher is determined not to have his Grandpappy's dream of winning the Pewter Pick Axe Award sabotaged and tries to help him win it. It turns out to be impossible, but that's what Grandpappy likes about it!

Making Friends

Cloud, Cloud Go Away Tigger's bouncing annoys a cloud, and it follows him around. Tigger is obliged to disguise himself and finally hides out in his house. But when the cloud finds him, Tigger needs Pooh and Piglet's help. They lasso the cloud, Tigger apologizes and all is well.

Tigger's House Guest Everyone's wooden things mysteriously disappear. No-one can figure it out until it is discovered that Tigger's new house guest is a termite.

The Bug Stops Here Kanga asks Pooh to babysit Roo and little owl Dexter while she and Owl go out. Pooh takes them to Christopher Robin's where they inadvertently let Christopher's science project out of its box. Now they must find him a new bug. They bring back a large outcast bug, and Christopher lets it go after showing it at school.

Tigger Is the Mother of Invention Tigger takes up the challenge to invent a machine to make snow-shovelling easier but he gets carried away and instead invents a machine that invents machines. It takes him all spring and summer and when winter rolls around again the machine does clear snow, quite inadvertently.

GO: Quality TV animation and inventive short story lines make these gentle life-lesson videos accessible to little ones.

WINNIE-THE-POOH PLAYTIME SERIES

Walt Disney Home Video
1989, 1990, 1991
47–55 minutes each
Directed By: Carole Beers, Karl Geurs,
 Terence Harrison, Ken Kessel,
 Charles A. Nichols
Featuring the voices of: Jim Cummings,
 Paul Winchell

Three titles have been released so far in this fully animated made-for-television series.

Pooh Party

Party Poohfer Rabbit is having a party for 500 relatives so he gets Pooh, Tigger and Piglet to help. But Rabbit is a terrible stickler for order, organization and schedules, and tries to make everyone do things his way. When all is ready, there are no bunnies and Rabbit realizes that he would rather have everyone come late than not at all.

A Bird in the Hand Rabbit's bird friend Kessy is coming to visit. She is grown-up, but Rabbit still treats her like a baby. When Stan the weasel and Heff the Heffalump want to kidnap the bird for ransom, Kessy pulls a trick on them that shows Rabbit she can take care of herself.

A Pooh Day Afternoon Tigger does disappearing magic tricks using Gopher's vacuum cleaner; Christopher Robin gets a job taking care of a dog with disastrous results.

Cowboy Pooh

The Good, the Bad and the Tigger Tigger plays with Christopher Robin's trains and imagines himself in the old west where he becomes a train-napper.

Rabbit Marks the Spot The friends play pirate and Rabbit makes a treasure map to teach them a lesson for messing up his garden. Then his conscience gets the better of him and he tries to stop them from opening the treasure chest full of rocks. When the plan fails, he finds to his amazement that the friends are delighted with the "treasure" anyway.

CAUTION: Rabbit's bad dream may be scary.

The Masked Offender When Christopher reads the animals a swashbuckling story they pretend they are "Masked Offenders" but they can't find anything to rescue.

Detective Tigger

Tigger, Private Ear Tigger fancies himself a private ear. When a honey jar disappears he has to solve the mystery. The problem is he stole it himself.

Sham Pooh Pooh has lost his appetite for honey. His friends think he must not be the real Pooh until they find his appetite in the honey tree.

Invasion of the Pooh Snatcher Tigger says the Springing Jagular likes to snatch animals, so everyone tries to rescue everyone else from being snatched.

Eeyore's Tail Tale Eeyore parts company with his tail and the friends each find a good use for it.

CAUTION: Rabbit is always anxious, bossy, critical and negative. Note: There are no songs although there is musical accompaniment.

GO: Non-threatening stories and good animation make these excellent videos for little people.

■

THE WIZARD OF OZ

MGM/UA
1939
101 minutes
Directed by: Victor Fleming
Starring: Judy Garland, Margaret Hamilton, Bert Lahr, Frank Morgan, Ray Bolger

Dorothy is more or less content living with her aunt and uncle on their farm in Kansas, until a nasty neighbor, Miss Gulch, threatens to take away her beloved dog, Toto. Dorothy runs away with her pet, but she doesn't get very far. A kindly travelling magician, recognizing that she's a runaway, contrives to send her back. Even as she returns, a tornado strikes the farm and, after a board hits her on the head, Dorothy dreams that the house is whisked up into the air. The house lands in a strange place (Oz) directly on top of the Wicked Witch of the East, and Dorothy immediately finds herself on the bad side of the dead witch's sister (the Wicked Witch of the West, who bears a startling

resemblence to Miss Gulch). But before tragedy strikes, Glinda the Good Witch of the North gives Dorothy the Witch of the East's ruby slippers, and frightens the Witch of the West away. Glinda tells Dorothy that in order to get back to Kansas, she must find the Wizard of Oz by following the yellow-brick road. So, Dorothy sets off, and on the way she meets the Scarecrow, the Tin Woodsman and the Cowardly Lion. Together they travel through peril to the Emerald City, all the while threatened by the Wicked Witch of the West. And when they do finally meet the Wizard, he demands one token of them—the broomstick of the Wicked Witch of the West. After perilous adventures the quartet destroys the evil witch and returns to the Emerald City. But they soon discover that the wizard is a fraud who cannot help. Glinda then returns and tells Dorothy that the ruby slippers, coupled with her own desire to return home, are all she needs to get back to Kansas.

CAUTION: Dorothy is separated from her family during the tornado and as the house is flying, Miss Gulch appears on her bicycle outside of Dorothy's window where she turns into the Wicked Witch of the West, on a broom and cackling hideously. In Oz, the dead witch's feet are shown sticking out from under the house (most children are disturbed by this) and the Wicked Witch of the West appears suddenly, in a ball of fire, and threatens to kill Dorothy and Toto. The witch's henchmen are flying monkeys (winged creatures resembling bats) and they fill the whole screen in one scene. The witch throws fire onto the scarecrow and his arm burns before Dorothy can extinguish it.

GO: This film won an Oscar for the musical score and a special miniature Oscar went to Judy Garland for her performance. A family classic for the past fifty years.

■

Chapter 5

VIDEOS FOR AGES SIX TO TEN

Try to remember what you were like when you were six, or eight or ten years old. How did you perceive the world? What did you like and what kinds of things frightened you? Did particular situations, characters and monsters (not just in movies) cause you anxiety? Now add to that memory the high-powered impact and realism of the modern media (compare *Lost in Space* to *Star Wars*, or *Godzilla* to *Jurassic Park*), and this can help to give you a frame of reference for understanding what children are up against today.

In this introductory section we will look at two ways you can make your visits to the video store as positive as possible: by becoming knowledgeable about suitable films and by giving your child the power to say "no."

KNOW WHAT'S OUT THERE
Using the rating system

When a film receives a PG rating, this means that young viewers require some guidance from a responsible adult. To better prepare yourself to provide that guidance, you should know something more about the PG rating itself. (See chapter 2 for more on ratings.)

Gender and racial stereotyping still abound, providing generally poor role models for young viewers. And there is more violence in PG films than ever before.

And to compound the problem, it is reaching the point where no self-respecting teen will see a "baby PG film." And the peer pressure is filtering all the way down to younger friends and siblings.

HELPING YOUR CHILD BECOME A RESPONSIBLE VIEWER
The demon: peer pressure

Right from their earliest social interactions, children have to cope with the pressure to belong. Today, belonging also means seeing the "coolest" movies — movies which are usually totally inappropriate for young children. But that doesn't prevent some children from seeing these films, and then putting pressure on others to do so as well.

The following examples of peer pressure at work have been overheard in our full-line video store.

▶ Why won't your mother let you watch this?
▶ How is she going to know if we watch it at my house?
▶ What can she do after you've already seen it?
▶ All the movies you want to see are stupid baby movies.
▶ I've seen everything you pick.
▶ If that's all you want then I don't want anything.
▶ You're such a suck.
▶ I've already seen it. There's no bad stuff in it. It's really good.

We even heard one weary seven-year-old sigh and mutter to himself: I guess I *should* see *Raiders of the Lost Ark* ... I'm the only one in my class who hasn't; and a ten-year-old who was using most of the phrases above to convince his buddy to rent *The Hand that Rocks the Cradle*.

The situation quickly reaches a point where it must become the child's responsibility to resist the peer pressure and become a self-moderating viewer.

Becoming a self-moderating viewer

When Fiona's daughter Natasha was ten, she went to a
birthday party where they showed the film *The Watcher in the
Woods*. It's not *The Silence of the Lambs*, but it's scary
enough, with lots of terrifying, supernatural imagery. And for
Natasha, it was simply too much. Finally, she got up, said:
I'm sorry, but this movie's too scary for me, and left the room.
Before very long, one of the other girls joined her, and then
another, and another, and so on, until fully half the party
had walked out on the film. The girls later confessed to
Natasha that they were glad that someone had been the first
to leave.

It takes real self-assurance to risk the ridicule of peers by
walking away from frightening, disturbing or disgusting films.
We should do everything in our power to cultivate that
self-assurance in our children.

Doug recalls an incident from his own childhood: "I vividly
remember watching a Bob Hope movie with my mother when
I was eight. It was, of course, a comedy, but it had a
supernatural element in it, and I can still feel the cold,
electric dread I experienced when the ghost appeared. My
mother noticed my obvious discomfort and quietly said: You
know, you don't have to watch this if you don't want to. With
relief, I replied that I'd rather not, and she turned the movie
off."

What your child really thinks about a film

There will be times when your child will see a frightening
film — with or without your permission. But because children
often have trouble expressing complicated emotions, they will
not be able to tell you how they feel.

They're scared all right, but they'll deny it under oath. And
instead of admitting their true feelings, frightened children
often say things like:

- That wasn't scary, that was stupid.
- It's just a movie.
- It doesn't scare *me*.
- It was really cool. (Remember: we're talking about things like torture, murder and extreme sadism here.)

Even before you rent, your child may give you clues that he or she is leery about seeing a particular film, by saying things like:

- That's too confusing.
- That's boring.
- It sounds stupid.
- I don't like it. (Even before your child has seen it.)

Some children will avert their eyes when the box is moved closer to them, while others know their own limits and will come right out and ask: Will this give me nightmares?

Altered states

Renting movies for children aged six to ten isn't all hard work, though. The reviews in the section that follows will get you off to a start, and we have included plenty of tips and suggestions in chapters 1 and 2 of this book to help you along. Beyond that you might want to try one of the following:

- Introduce your child to a number of more obscure feature films that his or her friends have probably never heard of, films that the child will want to turn his or her friends on to, that still provide the excitement young viewers crave without containing negative images and nightmare-inducing elements. (This will help get past some of the peer pressure.)
- Try renting different types of films — branch out if you are stuck in action-adventure or comedy.
- Look for a theme that might pique your child's interest in a subject, inspiring him or her to explore the subject further. (These don't necessarily have to be educational films, but could be feature films or made-for-TV

specials with subjects that can lead to more exploration.)

▶ Rent films that are based on books; you might even encourage reading in an otherwise reluctant reader.

Hosting a video party

If you're planning to show a film to a group of kids, there are some things you can do to empower your guests:

▶ Make other activities available simultaneously, and make it clear to your young guests that they do not have to watch the film if they don't want to.

▶ Select films according to tried-and-true criteria (either your own criteria, built up through experience, or those we have suggested in this book).

▶ Keep in mind that you don't have to show a feature film. Why not try one of the following:
— a film that documents the making of a popular feature film
— cartoon compilations
— a documentary or how-to video that complements your party's theme.

3-2-1 CONTACT "EXTRA" SERIES

Children's Television Workshop
1990–1991
30 minutes each; *Bottom of the Barrel*
  is 60 minutes)
Directed by: Ozzie Alfonso
Starring: Stephanie Yu, Z Wright

Full of facts that will amaze even adults, this quality program (shown on PBS television) offers children information simply but without condescension.

Bottom of the Barrel

Stephanie Yu and Z Wright host this program which examines oil — where it comes from and how we drill for it, refine it and make use of it. Also included are animated illustrations, location visits and hands-on demonstrations.

CAUTION: There are shots of animals killed by oil spills.

Down the Drain

Engaging teen host Stephanie Yu investigates the water cycle — how we get water, how we clean it and how we save it — and makes viewers aware of the large role water plays in our lives.

The Rotten Truth

Viewers learn the rotten truth about garbage when Stephanie Yu visits a landfill mountain and a recycling facility. Amazing facts and colorful animation make this informative video fascinating.

You Can't Grow Home Again

Stephanie visits the Costa Rican rainforest to see the diversity of its wildlife, and to witness its destruction. Accompanied by a twenty-four page booklet, the video also talks about ways the rainforests can be saved.

GO: This is an educational series without the flavor of "those films you see in school."

20,000 LEAGUES UNDER THE SEA

Walt Disney Home Video
1954
127 minutes
Directed by: Richard Fleischer
Starring: Kirk Douglas, Peter Lorre,
  Paul Lukas, James Mason
MPAA rating: G

Rumors of a terrible sea monster are sweeping the western coast of the United States to the point where it's almost impossible to collect a crew for a sailing vessel. There are, however, a few brave souls: Ned Lands, skeptical of the rumors, signs on with a warship to harpoon the beast. A marine biologist named Professor Aronnax and his faithful apprentice, Conseille, also join the crew and the search. After a long voyage, the monster finally makes its appearance and sinks the ship. Only the Professor, Conseille and Ned survive the terrible collision, and in the mist they find that the monster is in fact a bizarre nuclear-powered submarine called The Nautilus. The ship seems abandoned at first, but the trio are soon captured by the twisted genius, Captain Nemo, and become witnesses to the most incredible marine adventure in human history. Based on the book by Jules Verne.

CAUTION: Nemo is initially cruel, and rough scenes include a fairly tough fist-fight and a harrowing battle with a giant squid. At the climax of the film, Nemo is mortally wounded and dies.

GO: The cinematography is extraordinary. Winner of two Academy Awards (Best Special Effects and Best Art Direction/Set Decoration). Young viewers may be inspired to read the prophetic book.

■

idea in his parents' subconscious. For school, he writes an impassioned theme on the virtues of owning a Red Ryder rifle and gets a C+ accompanied by the warning: You'll shoot your eye out. He goes before the grouchiest department-store Santa of all time, who warns him of the same and when the Big Day finally arrives (and it doesn't look good), we see that the excitement has only just begun. Based on the novel *In God We Trust: All Others Pay Cash* by Jean Shepherd.

GO: One of the greatest Christmas films of all time, *A Christmas Story* can be enjoyed by viewers of any age, anytime—even in July.

■

A CHRISTMAS STORY

MGM/UA
1984
95 minutes
Directed by: Bob Clark
Starring: Peter Billingsley, Darren McGavin, Melinda Dillon
MPAA rating: PG

In Holman Indiana, in 1947, nine-year-old Ralphie Parker is looking forward to Christmas. And there's only one thing on his mind: a Genuine Red Ryder Carbine Action Two Hundred Shot Lightning Loader Range Model Air Rifle (with a compass in the stock). But it isn't going to be easy to convince his mother of the worthiness of the gift. (Her automatic block is: You'll shoot your eye out.) So, Ralph conspires and schemes daily to embed the

A SUMMER TO REMEMBER

MCA
1989
93 minutes
Directed by: Robert Lewis
Starring: James Farentino, Louise Fletcher, Sean Gerlis, Tess Harper, Burt Young
MPAA rating: NR

When a highly intelligent orangutan who understands sign language is being transferred back to her home facility, a mishap with a drunk driver causes a serious accident and the terrified creature flees the scene. Meanwhile, on a nearby farm, a deaf boy named Toby Wyler has completely withdrawn from the world — only his sister Jill can communicate with him through sign language. When Toby is the only one to see the orangutan, his parents don't believe him, since there has been no mention of its escape in the media (the authorities have suppressed all news reports to protect the ape from trigger-happy locals). But when the kids leave fruit out and it vanishes, they know that the ape exists and they camp out in their treehouse where they discover that the orangutan is living above them. When the creature rescues Jill from a potentially nasty fall, not only do they realize that the ape is friendly, they also learn that she can sign! The children decide to keep the orangutan a secret; that is, until a circus moves into the area — a circus featuring a giant gorilla named Mighty Max. In the end, Toby finally speaks when he must call out to the orangutan to save her.

CAUTION: Some people may be a little concerned about the emphasis placed on the importance of Toby's speaking aloud. There is a scene in which some local children are cruel to both Toby and the orangutan.

THE ABSENT-MINDED PROFESSOR

Walt Disney Home Video
1961
96 minutes
Directed by: Robert Stevenson
Starring: Tommy Kirk, Fred MacMurray,
   Nancy Olson, Keenan Wynn
MPAA rating: G

Ned Brainard, a chemistry professor at Medfield College of Technology, is so forgetful that he leaves himself reminder notes about his impending marriage. But even they don't help, since on the day of his third attempt to marry he invents a miraculous gravity nullifying substance, flubber (flying rubber), and again misses the big event. Meanwhile, tycoon Alonzo Hawke is angry with the college (and Brainard in particular) for flunking his lazy son Biff. He plans to pull the plug on the college, which owes him a great deal of money. As if that weren't enough, the big basketball game against rival Rutland College is scheduled for that night, and Biff had been Medfield's star player. After a dreadful first half they are behind 46-3, so Ned sneaks into the Medfield locker room and flubberizes the players' shoes; Medfield then annihilates Rutland. And after more exciting episodes (Alonzo tries to steal the flubber), Ned flies his flubberized Model T to Washington where he makes sure that the military gets his invention. Ned becomes a celebrity, and he and Betsy finally get married. Black and white. Based on the story by Samuel W. Taylor.

CAUTION: The film is dated where women are concerned. Betsy, a full-grown woman, is referred to as a girl, and her main aspiration is to get married.

GO: Despite its age, this film still stands up as a good fantasy film for kids under ten.

◼

✗ ADVENTURES IN DINOSAUR CITY

Malofilm Video
1991
90 minutes
Directed by: Brett Thompson
Starring: Shawn Hoffman,
    Omri Katz, Tiffanie Poston
MPAA rating: not rated

Walt Disney Home Video
1993
108 minutes
Directed by: Stephen Sommers
Starring: Robbie Coltrane, Jason Robards,
    Courtney B. Vance, Elijah Wood
MPAA rating: PG

Timmy and his friends, Mick and Jamie, decide to watch a new dinosaur cartoon on the huge screen in his physicist parents' lab. Unaware that Timmy's parents have set up an experiment involving the transference of living beings in time and space, they inadvertently activate the device and are transferred into the fantasy world of their dinosaur video. There, they discover themselves in a place co-inhabited by dinosaurs and Cro-Magnons. The three are quickly drawn into an adventure in which they must enlist the aid of Rex, a tyrannosaur private eye, and his styracosaur sidekick, Tops, to foil the plans of a nasty allosaur.

✘STOP: The movie is violent, full of martial arts and fistfights, and probably isn't a great choice for children who are prone to emulating aggressive behavior.

CAUTION: Rex's imprisoned father sacrifices himself. One of the Cro-Magnon women isn't exactly a positive female role model. This film isn't going to impress young viewers who are keen on scientific accuracy.

GO: Despite the low-budget effects, the film manages to be entertaining.

✘ THE ADVENTURES OF HUCK FINN

Unruly ten-year-old Huck Finn is taken in by two kindly widows, but all he can think about is acquiring his freedom from the privileged but strait-laced life they provide. One night his drunken father brutally kidnaps him, but Huck fakes his own death and escapes to Jackson's Island where he runs into runaway slave Jim, an old friend. The police are after Jim, who has disappeared at the same time as Huck and is wanted for Huck's supposed murder. After a harrowing adventure on a riverboat during which they nearly drown, Huck is taken in by wealthy landowners. Jim works in the fields like all the other slaves. Huck finds Jim's predicament intolerable. After the family is wiped out in a feud, Huck and Jim move on, going down the Mississippi on a raft. They are obliged to take aboard two snake-oil salesmen whose names change according to the situation. The thieves recognize Jim as having a price on his head and use this knowledge to blackmail the two heroes into participating in their scheme to bilk a huge fortune from the daughters of the late Peter Wilks by posing as Wilks' British brothers. The scam works nearly too well, but Jim and Huck like the daughters and feel guilty for taking their money. The two con artists turn Jim in for the reward and with Jim in jail, continue their plans to scam the rest of the fortune. Huck steals the Wilks gold but inadvertently leaves it in Wilks' coffin. The gold is buried along with the corpse. Things begin to unravel when Wilks' *real brothers* arrive from Britain and during a contest to prove their authenticity, Huck steals the jailor's keys and frees Jim. They high tail it to the river with the whole town in hot pursuit. Huck is shot in the back and Jim turns back to save his friend. The townspeople catch Jim and prepare to lynch him but Wilks' daughter Mary-Jane stops them. Huck recovers and Jim is set free. Based on the novel *The Adventures of Huckleberry Finn* by Mark Twain.

✗**STOP:** Huck witnesses the outcome of a family feud in which a whole family is ambushed and his friend Billy is shot. There are intense slow-motion effects, and Billy's dead body is shown. Huck's mother is dead and he learns that his father has just died.

CAUTION: This movie contains realistic fistfights, drownings, rifle-fire, point-blank shooting, knifings, stealing, a description of tarring and feathering, frightening images and visual surprises. White plantation owners whip slaves. We recommend this film for viewers on the older end of the 6-10 age group.

GO: High-quality production makes this a truly exciting and entertaining rendition of a classic story replete with social messages.

■

AFRICAN STORY MAGIC

A young African-American boy named Kwaku lives in an unfriendly inner-city neighborhood. One day, as he's searching for mirrors in abandoned buildings, he is visited by a round hovering light which introduces itself as Sam and tells him that it brings magic words from far away. But Kwaku doesn't want any stupid stories and Sam makes an equally mysterious exit. Then Kwaku becomes aware that he's being followed by a green man; he hides, and Sam reappears telling Kwaku to use the mirror he has found to enter the world of imagination. Kwaku (and the green man) pass through a magic door into the Africa of his ancestors, where they hear the stories of the magic story people. One storyteller tells about an eagle that thought he was a chicken, while another uses sign language to tell about a mouse who saved a lion king. They learn why mosquitoes buzz in people's ears and how the lion got his roar. And, in the end, when the story people tell Kwaku to take courage from the drumming, he faces the green man and has a wonderful encounter. The stories are accompanied by African drumming, singing and dancing, and either tell life-lessons or encourage self-esteem.

CAUTION: The green man who stalks Kwaku is supposed to represent Kwaku's fear, and he is scary.

GO: This is an unusual but effective sort of storytelling.

f.h.e.
1992
27 minutes
Directed by: Peter Thurling
Narrated by: Brock Peters
Starring: Ricky O'Shon Collins,
   Diane Ferlatte, Tejumola Ologboni
MPAA rating: not rated

ALADDIN

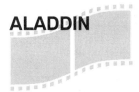

Walt Disney Home Video
1992
90 minutes
Directed by: John Masker, Ron Clements
Starring the voices of:
    Robin Williams, Gilbert Gottfried
MPAA rating: G

Hoping to steal the magic lamp, Jafar, advisor to the Sultan, summons the entrance to the legendary Cave of Wonders from the desert sands, only to learn that the only one who can set foot inside is a young street thief named Aladdin. Disguising himself as an old soothsayer, Jafar visits Aladdin and tells him about the cave of wonderous riches and about the lamp, which Jafar hopes to steal from Aladdin when he leaves the cave. Aladdin is warned not to touch anything except the lamp (those who do, forfeit their lives). Jafar then follows the boy out into the desert. Inside the cave, Aladdin finds the lamp, but when his pet monkey touches one of the jewels the cave immediately begins to collapse, and Aladdin is trapped inside with his monkey and their new-found friend, a courteous but mute flying carpet. Aladdin rubs the lamp while examining it, and out pops a genie, who releases them from the cave and transforms Aladdin into a prince in order that he may better woo the princess Jasmine. (The law decrees that Jasmine must marry a prince.) But not recognizing him in his princely disguise, and determined to marry the young thief she knows as Aladdin, Jasmine turns the "prince" away. It's only when Jafar tells Jasmine that Aladdin has been beheaded that she finally agrees to marry Jafar instead. In the end, Aladdin reveals himself and with the genie's help, tricks Jafar into imprisonment in the lamp; the Sultan changes the law so the lovers can marry and they live happily ever after (or at least until the sequel, *The Return of Jafar*).

CAUTION: The tempo of this film is intense (the genie's rapid-fire transformations, in particular) and may be too much for children under five. There are also some pretty tense moments when, in one scene, Jafar ties Aladdin to a ball and chain and throws him in the ocean, and in another, Jasmine is imprisoned in an hourglass with the sand running onto her. The climax includes a very scary Jafar transforming himself into increasingly threatening entities.

GO: Where the film really succeeds is in its animation. Robin Williams's wacky genie provided animators with virtually unlimited possibilities for creative invention. There are just enough songs to appeal to the little ones, but not too many to turn older ones off. And popular Disney characters like Pinocchio and Sebastian the crab turn up in the corners of the frame.

AMERICAN HEROES AND LEGENDS

Rabbit Ears Productions
1992
30 minutes each
Directed by: various

These quality efforts are iconographic; that is, they feature still pictures, moving mats, and lots of camera motion. The illustrations are uniformly excellent, as are the music and the narration.

Titles in the collection are:
Annie Oakley (told by Keith Carradine, music by Los Lobos)
Brer Rabbit and Boss Lion (told by Danny Glover, music by Dr. John)
Davy Crockett (told by Nicolas Cage, music by David Bromberg)
Follow the Drinking Gourd (told by Morgan Freeman, music by Taj Mahal)
John Henry (told by Denzel Washington, music by B.B. King)
Johnny Appleseed (told by Garrison Keillor, music by Mark O'Connor)
Princess Scargo and the Birthday Pumpkin (told by Geena Davis, music by Michael Hedges)
Rip Van Winkle (told by Anjelica Huston, music by Jay Ungar and Molly Mason)
The Song of Sacajawea (told by Laura Dern, music by David Lindley)
Squanto and the First Thanksgiving (told by Graham Greene, music by Paul McCandless)
Stormalong (told by John Candy, music by NRBQ)

AND YOU THOUGHT *YOUR* PARENTS WERE WEIRD!

Malofilm/Vidmark Entertainment
1991
92 minutes
Directed by: Tony Cookson
Starring: Edan Gross, Joshua Miller, John Quade, Marcia Strassman, Eric Walker
Starring the voice of: Alan Thicke
MPAA rating: PG

Josh Carson and his younger brother Max are technical wizards, intent on designing and building a fully functional robot. The boys win the Junior Inventor Award with their prototype for a garbage removal robot and invest half their prize money in Newman, their most advanced effort. That same night, Josh goes to a Halloween party, and during some Ouija board fun, his dead father (whom Josh believes commited suicide) tries to contact him. Josh thinks the whole thing is a bad joke, until a mysterious entity flashes down from the heavens and enters Newman. Newman instantly begins to exhibit some very sophisticated behavior and informs the boys that he is, in fact, their father, returned from heaven. Meanwhile, as Newman renews acquaintance with the boys' mother, a nosy reporter starts snooping around, and the evil Cottswinkles (the Carsons' arch-rivals) form a pact with a sinister industrialist to steal Josh's invention.

CAUTION: The villains are fat and ugly and it's a shame that fat equals bad. The film deals with the problems of grief, and may raise some questions about Ouija boards, the hereafter, and so on.

GO: At the climax of the film, the truth about Josh's father's death is revealed—his death was an accident, not a suicide—and Josh and his father are reconciled. This film won an Award of Excellence from Film Advisory Board, Inc.

ANNE OF GREEN GABLES

Wonderworks
1985
196 minutes
Directed by: Kevin Sullivan
Starring: Colleen Dewhurst, Richard Farnsworth, Megan Follows
MPAA rating: not rated

Elderly brother and sister Matthew and Marilla Cuthbert run a farm near the town of Avonlea on Prince Edward Island. Matthew is getting too old to do the heavy labor, so he and Marilla send for a boy from the orphanage to help out. But the orphanage makes a mistake and sends a girl instead, and Matthew, at a loss for what to do, takes her home. Marilla insists that the girl must go back, and plans are made to return her the next day. But Anne so bewitches the pair with her enthusiasm and charm that she ends up staying for a "try-out." That try-out turns into a permanent relationship, and Anne, brilliant, talented and wildly imaginative, turns the Cuthberts' staid life utterly upside down. Anne's escapades are outrageous: she gets her best friend Diana Barry drunk (by serving her what she thinks is raspberry cordial, but is in fact wine), and accidentally dyes her hair green (in an attempt to achieve an auburn tint). But her capers are counterbalanced by her love of life and learning. And as Anne grows up, the Cuthberts come to see her as their own child. When Matthew dies suddenly; Anne's entire life is dramatically changed, and she discovers compassion and friendship from an unexpected source. Based on the book by Lucy Maud Montgomery.

CAUTION: Matthew dies of a heart attack.

GO: Absolutely terrific, this is a uniformly excellent production.
■ ●

ANNE OF AVONLEA: THE SEQUEL

Wonderworks
1987
232 minutes
Directed by: Kevin Sullivan
Starring Frank Converse, Jonathan Crombie, Colleen Dewhurst, Megan Follows
MPAA rating: not rated

Anne, as romantic and dreamy as ever, is now a teacher, and an aspiring writer of romantic fiction. Her former arch-rival and now fast friend Gilbert Blythe is going to medical school and has fallen in love with her, but Anne rejects him — her own notions of romance are much more flowery. When Anne's former teacher Miss Stacy becomes head of the school board, she recommends Anne for a teaching job at an exclusive ladies' college in Kingsport. However, Kingsport is ruled by the snobbish Pringle family, who aren't fond of Anne and do everything in their power to sabotage her career. But Anne prevails. She charms almost everyone she meets and even wins the admiration of the handsome Michael Harris. In the end, though, Anne discovers that despite his charm, Michael is not for her, and when she returns to Green Gables and learns that Gilbert Blythe is very ill, Anne realizes the true depth of her feelings for her childhood friend. This sequel to *Anne of Green Gables* is based on Lucy Maud Montgomery's novels *Anne of Avonlea*, *Anne of the Island* and *Anne of Windy Poplars*.

GO: Warm-hearted and witty, this is a positive film about persistence and recognizing the worth of a true heart.
■ ●

AGES 6 TO 10

THE APPLE DUMPLING GANG

Walt Disney Home Video
1975
100 minutes
Directed by: Norman Tokar
Starring: Bill Bixby, Tim Conway,
   Don Knotts, Henry Morgan, Slim Pickens
MPAA rating: no rating given

When travelling gambler and conman Russel Donavan drifts into town, he makes a deal to pick up some valuables for an old acquaintance. Thinking he has made an easy score, Donavan meets the stage (driven by an attractive woman named Dusty) and discovers that the "valuables" are three children. With the kids in tow, Donavan tries to find a family in town that will take them; of course, no one will, and Donavan is stuck. The kids are no end of trouble, and they single-handedly annihilate the town, leaving Donavan stuck with the tab. But when the kids discover a huge gold nugget (worth $87,425), there is suddenly no shortage of people willing to take the children in. Meanwhile, the villainous bank-robber Stillwell and his evil gang of desperados come to town and plot to rob the bank, while the kids form The Apple Dumpling Gang with stumblebums Theodore and Amos (who used to ride with the Stillwell Gang until Amos accidentally shot Stillwell in the leg). The climax of the film is a collection of shoot-outs and good old-fashioned chases, during the course of which the kids' gold nugget is destroyed. Then, once again, no one wants the kids — except Donavan and Dusty.

CAUTION: There is some comic violence in this film and, of course, some very physical slapstick involving Knotts and Conway.

GO: For young fans of action and comedy, this is the film.

BABES IN TOYLAND

Orion
1986
96 minutes
Directed by: Clive Donner
Starring: Drew Barrymore,
   Eileen Brennan, Googy Gress,
   Richard Mulligan, Keanu Reeves,
   Jill Schoelen
MPAA rating: G

On a stormy Christmas Eve in Cincinnati, Lisa Piper, her older sister Mary and their friends Jack and George quit their jobs working for obnoxious store owner Mr. Barney. While driving the others home through a blizzard, Jack swerves to avoid a falling tree and Lisa is thrown out of the jeep, hits her head and is promptly projected into Toyland, a magical kingdom surrounded by the Forest of the Night. There she discovers that the evil Barnaby Barnacle is forcing his nephew Jack Nimble's sweetheart, Mary Contrary, to marry him instead. Lisa arrives just in time to break up the wedding and learns the whole story. Jack was supposed to have become keeper of the cookie factory when his father died, but Barnaby had a law passed saying that Jack must be married by his twenty-first birthday before he can assume control. If he isn't married in time, then Barnaby gets the factory for life. But Barnaby's ambitions are even higher than that; he intends to unleash a dreadful army of forest trolls upon Toyland, and take over. And it's only Lisa's rekindled belief in toys that enables an army of toy soldiers to drive away the monsters.

CAUTION: Young children may be frightened by the army of spooky, misshapen trolls. There is a rough fistfight between Jack and Barnaby at the climax of the film.

THE BABY-SITTERS CLUB COLLECTION

Goodtimes Video/HGV Video
1990–1991
30 minutes each
Directed by: Abbie H. Fink,
    Carol S. Fink, Lynn Hamrick
Starring: Meghan Andrews, Melissa Chase,
    Avriel Hillman, Meghan Lahey, Nicole Leach,
    Jessica Prunell, Jeni F. Winslow
MPAA rating: NR

Seven enterprising teenage girls form a club in order to deal with baby-sitting jobs. They earn money through fund-raisers to put together "kid kits" which they then use to occupy their young charges. The girls are Claudia, Stacey, Mary Anne, Kristy, Dawn, Mallory and Jessica. Based on Ann M. Martin's popular series of books.

The Baby-sitters Club Christmas Special (Vol. 5)

When Stacey's diabetes lands her in the hospital, Kristy finds the true spirit of Christmas and gives her hard-earned baseball glove to a boy convalescing there.

Claudia and the Missing Jewels (Vol. 6)

At a craft show, Claudia displays the jewelry she has made. And when a local merchant places an order everything seems great, until one pair of earrings mysteriously disappears.

Dawn and the Dream Boy (Vol.7)

Dawn loves Jamie Anderson, but a misunderstanding about him causes a rift between her and Mary Anne.

Dawn and the Haunted House (Vol. 2)

Dawn believes Mrs. Slade is a witch, and when she learns the truth she feels pretty silly.

Kristy and the Great Campaign (Vol. 4)

Kristy tries to help Courtney win the Grade Three student council election, but soon realizes that she is trying to live Courtney's life for her.

Mary Anne and the Brunettes (Vol. 1)

Marcey, the most popular girl in school, invites Logan, the boy Mary Anne likes, to a costume party.

There is rivalry until Mary Anne works it out with Logan.

Stacey's Big Break (Vol. 3)

Stacey gets a chance to see what life is like for a fashion model, but prefers to spend her time baby-sitting.

CAUTION: The girls spend a great deal of time talking about boys, putting on make-up and shopping for clothes.

GO: The girls are responsible, innocent, loyal and caring.

Titles also available are:

Kid Vision
1992
30 minutes each
Directed By: Lynn Hamrick

Dawn Saves the Trees

Dawn is outraged when she hears that a new road is being constructed through the park. She sets out to lobby against it, only to learn a valuable lesson about constructive listening and compromise.

Babysitters and the Boy-sitters

When the girls need more babysitters in the club, Alan and Pete volunteer. Kristy is vehemently opposed, as she says they have no skills. The girls try to teach Alan and Pete some rudiments but the boys have their own method, which, predictably, leads to chaos.

Claudia and the Mystery of the Secret Passage

When a note from the past is discovered in a secret passage at Mary Anne and Dawn's house, the Babysitters are plunged into a strange adventure. An ancient feud needs to be settled but the adventure is more dangerous than the girls had bargained for.

✗ BATMAN: MASK OF THE PHANTASM

Warner Home Video
1994
77 minutes
Directed by: Eric Radomski and Bruce W. Timm
Featuring the voices of: Kevin Conroy, Mark Hamill, Hart Bochner, Abe Vigoda
MPAA Rating: PG

In this fully animated film, an evil-looking being called the Phantasm is bumping off the powerful gangsters of Gotham City. Before each murder, the Phantasm, caped in black and wearing a mask that resembles a skull, tells its gangster prey that their angel of death awaits. Batman, vowed to stop crime, is seen at the first murder site and is blamed for the deed. To effect justice and clear his name, Batman must stop the Phantasm.

As the plot unfolds, Bruce (Batman) Waynes past is revealed. Bruce had vowed to fight crime before he met his true love Andrea Beaumont, the daughter of prosperous lawyer Carl Beaumont, but this turned sour during one of his crime-fighting stunts. Beaumont created money laundering corporations for the cities mafia bosses but in order to provide a better life for his daughter he borrowed some of the start-up money. In the midst of Bruce and Andrea's romance, Carl is threatened by the gangsters and is forced, with his daughter in tow, to flee Gotham City all the way to Europe. Bruce is crushed by the sudden disappearance and throws himself into the personna of Batman in order to carry out his original intentions.

In the present, the last gangster, Salvatore Valestra, goes to the maniacal criminal, the Joker, and pleads for protection. His actions make sense when Batman realizes that, years ago, a young Joker was the crime boss's hitman. Since that time, however, the Joker has become far more malicious than when Valestra knew him. The Joker simply kills Valestra, takes his money, and sets a trap for both Batman and the Phantasm. Andrea confesses that she suspects her father of being the Phantasm, but when Batman learns that her father was, in fact, murdered by the gangsters, he forms his own theory. As the climactic battle approaches between Batman, the Phantasm, and the Joker, Batman must face the fact that the identity of the Phantasm is someone much closer to him than he expected.

✗STOP: The gangster killings are graphic: Chuckie Sol is forced to drive through the side of a building and is killed when he crashes into the building across the street; Buzz Bronski is pushed into a fresh grave and crushed by a tombstone (his bodyguards show visible disgust at the sight); the Joker kills Salvatore Valestra with a lethal laughing toxin, leaving his face in a hideous grin. Batman is bloodily wounded in an encounter with the police; his appear-

ance distressing. There are other images of blood and gunshots throughout the film. In the final battle, Andrea is nearly sucked through a giant fan.

CAUTION: This is a film with a plot line more suited to adults, but because it is animated it inevitably holds appeal for the youngsters. The story is even less action-packed than the animated television series and consequently may bore young children. The Batman mythology is frequently referred to but not fully explained. Viewers who are unfamiliar with the murder of Bruce Waynes parents and subsequent crime-fighting career might find the plot confusing.

GO: The story, filled with subplots, gives the history of Batman a unique twist. The film attempts to show the consequences of leading a life directed by vengeance.

■

BATMAN: THE MOVIE

Playhouse
1966
104 minutes
Directed by: Leslie H. Martinson
Starring: Frank Gorshin, Burgess Meredith,
    Lee Meriwether, Cesar Romero,
    Burt Ward, Adam West
MPAA rating: no rating given

In this made-for-TV, tongue-in-cheek send-up of the Caped Crusader, all of Batman's supervillain foes (The Penguin, The Joker, The Riddler and Catwoman) team up against him. Sure that Batman will attempt to rescue a prominent citizen, the evil quartet plot to kidnap Bruce Wayne. Catwoman's alter-ego, a sophisticated Soviet reporter, lures Bruce to her pad where the rest of the gang arrive on giant flying umbrellas, knock him out and take him to their secret wharf-side hideout. But Bruce makes a daring escape and returns as Batman, even as the Penguin is testing out a new weapon which will freeze-dry people, allowing him to reconstitute them at will. (He plans to ambush a conference of world leaders, freeze-dry them and hold the world hostage.) Only the Dynamic Duo can save the day, which they do in a final punch-out. And when Catwoman trips and her mask falls off to reveal herself as Batman's sweetheart, Robin sums up the whole film with the words: Holy heartbreak!

CAUTION: The violence is so utterly spoofed and comic that it should be of little concern; however, parents should know that fighting (wimpy fighting, but fighting nonetheless) is a central element of this film.

GO: If you have a little person who's Batman crazy, this film is the perfect solution. Like all great family films, this movie can be appreciated on two levels: as an action film for little kids and as a zany send-up of the Dark Knight.

BEETHOVEN

MCA
1991
87 minutes
Directed by: Brian Levant
Starring: Charles Grodin, Bonny Hunt,
    Dean Jones, Alice Newton
MPAA rating: PG

Beethoven is an adorable St. Bernard puppy, but he's already big, and he's having trouble getting

himself sold to the right family for just that reason. Then, to complicate his young life even further, he's kidnapped by the henchman of an evil vet who uses dogs to test ammunition. But, thanks to a resourceful little terrier, Beethoven makes his escape, and the next morning sneaks into the family home of uptight businessman and dog-hater George Newton. When he is discovered in the bed of George's youngest daughter, George's wife quickly points out that you can't just show a child a puppy and then take it away, so George is stuck with a lovable monster who tears up his home and drools on everything in sight. But Beethoven isn't just your average slobbering St. Bernard; he's a very special dog who helps the family in some extraordinary ways. Still, George is determined to get rid of the mess-maker, until the evil vet Dr. Yarnick kidnaps Beethoven for a particularly gruesome test. Only then does George understand how much he's come to love the big dog, and sets out to rescue him.

CAUTION: For young dog-lovers, a number of scenes may be a bit intense. For instance, it is revealed in dialogue that the evil vet is using dogs for ammunition testing, and needs Beethoven because he requires a full-sized skull for a particularly powerful type of bullet. Also, in one scene the evil vet strikes Beethoven repeatedly.

GO: Grodin is wonderful as the finicky, harried father, Dean Jones is perfect as the sinister veterinarian and the canine lead is the best of all. This is a great film for the family.

BEETHOVEN LIVES UPSTAIRS

filmed in both Port Hope and Prague. The score comprises well-known selections of Beethoven's music, which is bound to attract the interest of many a budding musician.

■

The Children's Group
1991
60 minutes
Directed By: David Devine
Starring: Sheila McCarthy, Neil Munro, Fiona Reid, Illya Woloshyn
MPAA rating: no rating given

In Vienna, 1827, nine-year-old Christoph is shattered by the unexpected death of his father. The family is now in dire straits, and Christoph's mother is forced to rent out the upper room to a lodger, who turns out to be none other than the great composer Ludwig van Beethoven. Beethoven promptly terrorizes the poor family with his eccentricities and tyrannical behavior, and Christoph instantly loathes him, cheered only by the knowledge that the mad genius is famous for never staying in one place for very long. But as time passes, Christoph comes to appreciate the great heart which lies beneath the composer's rough exterior, and the tremendous will with which Beethoven battles his failing hearing. As he himself says: Great men like Beethoven don't conform to other people's standards, they make their own. Based on the story by Barbara Nichol.

CAUTION: Although related to the highly successful book and audio-cassette of the same name, this is a feature film set in period costume and may not be too sophisticated for children who enjoyed the audio-cassette.

GO: This is a refreshing film, beautifully

BEETHOVEN'S 2nd

MCA/Universal
1994
89 minutes
Directed By: Rod Daniel
Starring: Charles Grodin, Bonnie Hunt, Nicholle Tom, Christopher Castille, Chris Penn
MPAA rating: PG

The colossal canine has made a permanent home for himself in the Newton household, but life is not perfect. Beethoven is a lonely guy. Out in the park one afternoon, he spots a fetching lady St. Bernard named Missy, and the pair immediately hit if off. Unfortunately, Missy's kindly owner Cliff is in the middle of a custody dispute with his estranged wife Sebrina. Sebrina has legal custody of Missy and is using Cliff's love of Missy to blackmail him into a huge divorce settlement. Meanwhile, George Newton, as uptight and finicky as ever, is obsessed with his new business idea, a freshener for sports bags. While George tries to score a bank loan to finance his idea, Beethoven tracks down his lady-love and manages to establish a secret relationship with her. The result, ten weeks later, is a litter of four puppies. The Newton kids, curious as to Beethoven's mysterious comings and goings, track the big dog to Missy's secret den in the basement of Sebrina's condo building, getting there just in time to save the puppies from Sebrina herself. Beethoven and the kids are unable to help Missy, but they do manage to smuggle the puppies back to the basement of their own house, and unbeknownst to the obsessed George, nurse the puppies until the little dogs can eat by themselves. Finally, a horrified George learns the dreadful truth. Five dogs! However, after his family's assurances that everything will work out fine, George, family, and canines head up north for the Fourth of July weekend. In a coincidence of towering proportions, Sebrina, her hulking boyfriend Floyd, and Missy are staying in the same resort area. Beethoven rescues Missy at the county fair, but Sebrina steals the puppies from George's children and tries to use them to find Beethoven and Missy. George and his family must then pursue the villains and the dogs.

CAUTION: At a loud cottage party, drunken youths pour beer on Beethoven's head. One of their ring-leaders lures George's attractive older daughter into a bedroom and locks the door, clearly indicating that a rape is imminent. While picking teams for a sandlot softball game, Ted, George's small and bookish son, is the last to be chosen; at that point, the team captains ask a girl in the crowd of bystanders if she's like to play — instead of Ted. This subtle dig at women (Ted is so bad that even a *girl* is better) is perhaps unintentional; nonetheless, it sends out a distinct message.

GO: A light-hearted dog-lover's film, with lots of shots of huge cute puppies. George's children are honest and responsible, and his wife is capable, confident, calm, and intelligent.

✗ BENJI THE HUNTED

Walt Disney Home Video
1987
89 minutes
Directed by: Joe Camp
Starring: Benji
MPAA rating: G

While filming in Oregon, Benji and his trainer are out in a small, open fishing boat, when the boat capsizes. His trainer is rescued, but Benji is stranded in the coastal forestlands of Oregon, and is forced to fend for himself. To complicate matters, he witnesses the shooting of a cougar, and foregoes rescue to stay and care for the cougar's orphaned kittens. Benji tries his best to feed his charges, but he doesn't have the heart to kill anything for them. Then he discovers a woodsman's cabin and steals one of the dead birds the woodsman has left out to cure. The kittens get their meal, but when Benji goes back to the cabin the next day, the woodsman captures him and ties him up. Benji manages to escape and returns to take care of the kittens, but it's an uphill battle as he's forced to face the threatening advances of a wolf, a bear, a fox and a hawk. In the climax, Benji lures the wolf to its death, and when another cougar appears and is willing to assume responsibility for the kittens, Benji is free to be rescued.

✗STOP: The female cougar is shot dead near the beginning of the film and later, a hawk swoops down and carries one of the kittens away — the kitten doesn't come back. Benji tricks the wolf into leaping to its death.

CAUTION: Benji and the kittens are in peril right from the start, and the relentless tension, combined with the animal casualties, may be too much for some young viewers.

GO: Spectacular scenery, great editing and solid animal training highlight this faced-paced animal adventure.

THE BEVERLY HILLBILLIES

20th Century Fox
1994
93 minutes
Directed by: Penelope Spheeris
Starring: Diedrich Bader, Dabney Coleman,
    Erika Eleniak, Cloris Leachman,
    Lea Thompson, Lily Tomlin, Jim Varney
MPAA rating: PG

The hillbillies become instant billionaires when Jed Clampett accidentally makes the largest single oil strike in human history on his modest Arkansas farm. Beverly Hills banker Drysdale is waiting with open, fawning arms to receive Jed and his money, and to get him set up in the mansion next door. Together with his assistant, Miss Hathaway, they desperately try to cope with the backwoods family, who promptly set Beverly Hills on its collective ear. Jed makes it public knowledge, by virtue of an incredibly tacky commercial, that he's in the market for a new wife, someone who can feminize his tomboy daughter Ellie May. Tyler, one of Drysdale's assistants, is an evil embezzler with an unscrupulous gold-digging girlfriend who promptly worms her way into Jed's affections, posing as a French tutor and setting up an elaborate scam to wed Jed

and get his bankroll. When Granny finds out about the plot, the conspirators have her secretly committed to a sanitorium with a staff of doctors who prefer electro-shock therapy. It is then up to the loyal Miss Hathaway to rescue Granny and prevent the wedding from taking place.

CAUTION: There is a certain amount of coarse humor. Women are also poorly represented, tackily dressed and flocking to Jed and Jethro simply for their fortune.

GO: Children who have little or no associations with the original series will probably find this effort entertaining enough.

BIG TOP PEE-WEE

Paramount Home Video
1988
86 minutes
Directed by: Randal Kleiser
Starring: Valeria Golino, Kris Kristofferson,
    Penelope Anne Miller, Paul Reubens
MPAA rating: PG

Pee-Wee runs an unusual farm where, with the help of his friend Vance the Pig, he makes concoctions to stimulate the growth of vegetables. When a terrible storm blows the Cabrini Circus onto his farm, Pee-Wee suggests they stay and have a vacation. But the crabby townspeople reject the circus, and the disheartened ring master, Mace, decides that he needs a new theme to liven up the show. Pee-Wee tries to find an act for himself and falls for a trapeze artist named Gina Piccolapupola. And when Pee-Wee's fiancée Winnie catches them together she breaks off the engagement and joins the Piccolapupola brothers' act. Even when the circus performers are ready to do their show, the townsfolk still won't have anything to do with it. But Pee-Wee has a great idea: he uses one of his experiments gone wrong to turn the crabby old townspeople into children, who are only too delighted to attend. So the circus has an audience, Mace has his barnyard theme, and Pee-Wee and Gina, Winnie and the Piccolapupola Brothers are together for good.

CAUTION: There is some sexual parody in this film and Winnie's comment after catching Pee-Wee and Gina together (I'm not surprised, you're a man, she's Italian) may be offensive to some.

GO: *Big Top Pee-Wee* is a fun, silly film for the kids and a plethora of parody for adults. This film features the longest screen kiss in history.

THE BLACK STALLION

MGM/UA
1979
117 minutes
Directed by: Carroll Ballard
Starring: Hoyt Axton, Teri Garr, Kelly Reno, Mickey Rooney
MPAA rating: G

In 1946, on a voyage with his father, Alec Ramsey sees a group of Arab trainers struggling to control a wild Arabian stallion. He tries to befriend the horse, but is sent away by the horse's handlers. Then one night, a fierce storm rises and the ship begins to sink. Alec and his father are separated and the boy follows the black stallion overboard. The pair save each other and the next morning Alec finds himself washed up on an unknown shore. He finds the stallion, completely tangled in ropes, and cuts it free. The stallion runs off, but later saves Alec from a cobra and eventually lets the boy ride him. Then fishermen arrive, and the two are saved. At home, Alec is hailed as a boy celebrity, but his happiness is short-lived when the black stallion escapes. Alec finds him in the care of a horse trainer named Henry Dailey and together they decide to run the stallion in a head-to-head competition against the two greatest horses in America. (Alec will ride.) And at the film's climax, viewers are treated to one great horse race. Based on the novel by Walter Farley.

CAUTION: During the panic aboard the sinking ship, a frightened adult tries to cut Alec's life-jacket off to use it himself; Alec's father and the man vanish, struggling into the chaos. The horse, panic-stricken, is pulled underwater. Alec shows an eerie lack of emotion over his father's death.

GO: This classic adventure story is renowned for its breathtaking images.
■

THE BLACK STALLION RETURNS

CBS/Fox
1983
103 minutes
Directed by: Robert Dalva
Starring: Teri Garr, Alan Goorwitz, Ferdinand Mayne, Kelly Reno, Vincent Spano
MPAA rating: PG

One year after their victory, Alec Ramsey and the Black Stallion are living an idyllic existence together. However, two Arabic factions are conspiring to take the stallion back to the Sahara — the first, the stallion's original owners, hope to retrieve property they feel is rightly theirs; the second, the evil Kurr, leader of the Uruk, hope simply to stop the stallion from taking part in the great race in the Sahara. When Berbers from the first faction take the horse back, Alec hides in the trailer and rides undiscovered as far as the seaport. There the Berbers find Alec, tie him up and leave him behind to watch as they load the black stallion onto a ship bound for the Sahara. Undaunted, Alec escapes and stows away on an airplane bound for Casablanca. There, Alec soon becomes embroiled in the tribal politics which are gripping the region, all the while guided by the unshaken belief that the horse belongs with him. He locates the stallion, and it becomes apparent to everyone that no one can ride the great horse but Alec. The day of the great race arrives, pitting the rival horsemen against each other. Alec wins, but in the end comes to realize that the great horse is where he belongs. This film is the sequel to *The Black Stallion*.

CAUTION: Alec bids a tearful farewell to his horse at the end of the film.

GO: *The Black Stallion Returns* is a delightful, basically nonviolent adventure about persistence and love.

BLACKBEARD'S GHOST

Walt Disney Home Video
1968
107 minutes
Directed by: Robert Stevenson
Starring: Dean Jones, Suzanne Pleshette, Peter Ustinov
MPAA rating: G

When coach Steve Walker arrives in the small New England town of Godolphin to help the track and field team, he encounters a number of problems: the team is utterly and completely hopeless; Blackbeard's Inn, where he's staying, is about to be repossessed by local gangster-cum-businessman Silky Seymour, and on his first night there Steve accidentally resurrects the ghost of Blackbeard. The only person who can see or hear Blackbeard is Steve, so everyone thinks he's crazy. Comic adventures ensue as Steve's invisible companion raises heck, helps him win the track and field meet, saves the inn and defeats the evil Seymour.

CAUTION: There is some comic violence, and a scene in front of the old a-kiss-for-a-dollar booth could be considered sexist. When Blackbeard's ghost is summoned, it is mildly spooky.

GO: One of Disney's best, this film can be appreciated by the whole family.

✘ THE CALL OF THE WILD

RHI Entertainment Inc.
1992
97 minutes
Directed by: Alan Smithee
Starring: Duncan Fraser, Mia Sara,
   Rick Schroder, Gordon Tootoosis
MPAA rating: Not Rated

Rumors of a gold strike are flooding Seattle. John Thornton, the son of a wealthy mill owner, decides to head north to seek his own fortune in the Klondike. Concurrently, Buck, a pampered German shepherd in Santa Clara, California, is smuggled off to unscrupulous dog peddlers, who sell the desperately needed animals at inflated prices in the gold fields. Buck and John end up on the same boat headed to Skagway. There John meets and befriends Charlie, a tough white-hating Indian, and sees Buck sold to a Frenchman running a mail sled. Meanwhile, John is confronted with the challenge of White Pass. He makes a deal to help Charlie build a cabin. Charlie then leaves to get his family, and John must cope with the Northern winter alone. By chance, Buck has now been sold to some inexperienced prospectors, who have been driving their team too hard and who stop at John's cabin hoping to get some supplies. John rescues Buck from them, and he and the dog develop a lasting friendship. In the spring, John takes Buck to the Klondike. There, he wins a bet that Buck can break a sled loaded with one thousand pounds. Then he learns about a fabled abandoned gold mine

beyond the Klondike. The mine, unfortunately, is on an Indian burial ground. Charlie reunites with John and they work the mine, while Buck wanders more and more with a pack of wolves. Finally, John and Charlie, their fortunes secure, leave the mine, but are attacked by Indians. John is killed. Buck returns to rescue Charlie. He then vanishes with the wolf pack and becomes an Indian legend, the Ghost Dog. Based on the book by Jack London.

✘ **STOP:** John dies at the end. His body is seen floating in the river, an arrow in the chest. Buck kills three Indians, ripping out their throats (non-graphic but evident). Buck is beaten with an axe handle. Dogs are whipped (off-camera). John confronts a mean-spirited prospector, hits him with a stick and then dashes a gun from the man's hand.

CAUTION: John is forced to shoot a horse. Animals are generally mistreated. Sensitive children will most likely find this very upsetting.

GO: A fairly accurate rendition of the classic tale. ■

CANDLESHOE

Walt Disney Home Video
1977
101 minutes
Directed by: Norman Tokar
Starring: Jodie Foster, Helen Hayes,
   David Niven
MPAA rating: G

Casey Brown, an orphan and a perennial escapee from Juvenile Hall, is selected by master con artist

Harry Bundage for the ultimate scam. Casey happens to bear an uncanny resemblance to the long-lost granddaughter of Lady St. Edmond, the aged mistress of Candleshoe Manor. And as it is rumored that pirate-captain Joshua St. Edmond hid his vast treasure somewhere in the manor, Harry intends to insert Casey into the family as the miraculously found granddaughter so that she can search for the lost loot. But in the course of her stay, Casey swiftly grows to appreciate the family, especially the wonderful butler, who impersonates other servants in order to hide the truth about the family's plummeting fortunes from Lady St. Edmond. In the end, Casey must chose between gaining wealth and protecting those she has come to love.

CAUTION: There is a little slapstick violence in the finale, but no one is seriously injured.

GO: This is a wonderful film with a positive message.

✗ THE CANTERVILLE GHOST

Columbia
1986
96 minutes
Directed by: Paul Bogart
Starring: Sir John Gielgud, Alyssa Milano
MPAA rating: no rating given

When Harry Canterville loses his job, he decides to move with his second wife Lucy and his daughter Jennifer to the English castle he stands to inherit. To gain ownership of the property, the family must occupy Canterville Castle for three months. But no one has ever stayed even three weeks in the spooky place, which is rumored to be haunted by the ghost of Sir Simon de Canterville. Sure enough, on the very first night, the chain-wrapped spirit appears; however, Harry and Lucy are unimpressed, suspecting that the ghost is really the result of special effects created by someone who is trying to frighten them away. Their lack of terror leaves the ghost powerless. Meanwhile, Jennifer, who intensely dislikes her stepmother, tries to strike a deal with the ghost to scare Lucy off. In the course of negotiations, the two become friends and Jennifer learns about the ghost's plight. (He murdered his wife in 1635 and is now forced to walk the earth in perpetuity.) Life begins to run smoothly for all of the Cantervilles; that is until the ghost learns that they plan to sell the castle to a hotel chain. Then his antics get so outrageous that Harry brings in a paranormal specialist. But when the doctor's equipment succeeds in briefly bringing back the spirit of Sir Simon's wife, the ghost falls into a depression. Only Jennifer can save the day by appealing to the Angel of Death to give Sir Simon rest. Based on a story by Oscar Wilde.

✗STOP: Look out! There are plenty of scares in this one, including a scene in which Lucy looks into the mirror and sees her own reflection, hideously aged.

CAUTION: The ghost is scary, and his wife-killing past is grim. The final scene in which Jennifer prays to the Angel of Death is full of spooky atmospherics and ghostly light.

GO: This is a good ghost story with enough frights to keep kids interested. If they like this one, your gang may even want to see

Margaret O'Brien's black and white version, filmed in 1944.

CHARLOTTE'S WEB

Paramount Home Video
1972
85 minutes
Directed by: Charles A. Nichols,
  Iwao Takamoto
Starring the voices of: Henry Gibson,
  Paul Lynde, Debbie Reynolds
MPAA rating: G

Wilbur, the runt of a litter of pigs, is saved from certain death by the farmer's daughter, Fern, who takes him in as a pet. Wilbur grows up strong and healthy and pampered and, after six weeks, Fern's father decides it's time Wilbur stopped being a pet and started being a pig. So Wilbur is moved down the road to Fern's uncle's farm where he soon learns he will be slaughtered when the weather gets cold. Understandably distraught, Wilbur finds consolation from a literate spider named Charlotte, who assures him that she will take care of him when the time comes. Sure enough, when the snow falls, Charlotte does indeed save Wilbur from the chopping block. She writes "Some Pig" in her web above Wilbur's pen. People come from miles around to see the amazing pig and Charlotte spins new messages in her webs again and again until Wilbur becomes a star attraction. All the while, Charlotte is teaching Wilbur all about the cycles of life and death and about the coming

and going of the seasons. The following year, Wilbur is taken to the county fair as a show pig where he wins a special award. His safe future assured, the film ends as Charlotte dies. But she leaves behind an egg-sack which releases hundreds and hundreds of children, three of which stay with Wilbur. This animated musical version of E.B. White's famous children's book is a perennial favorite of both children and adults.

CAUTION: Charlotte dies. Questions may arise about the mechanics of farm life and animal husbandry in general. (Why does Fern's daddy want to kill the runt?)

GO: The animation isn't the greatest and the musical interludes seem imposed, but the story is so strong that it doesn't matter. This is a solid film and a good way to introduce kids to the book.

COOL RUNNINGS

Walt Disney Home Video
1993
98 minutes
Directed by: John Turtletaub
Starring: Raymond J. Barry, John Candy,
  Doug E. Doug, Leon, Rowl D. Lewis,
  Malik Yoba
MPAA rating: G

Jamaica, 1987: Sanka has won six push-cart derbies in a row. Star is a top runner, but an accidental stumble in the 100 meter Olympic try-outs ruins his chances of making the sprinting team. Star then gets the idea to form a Jamaican bobsledding team, and seeks out his late father's best friend, Irving Blitzer, a former gold-medalist in the bobsled who now lives on the island and has become a decrepit bookie. Star persuades Blitzer to coach him and Sanka and, ironically, the other two men who were involved in the try-out accident: Yul Brynner, Star's hulking, shaven-headed monster of a rival, and Junior, the rich mama's-boy who tripped them both. Hilarity ensues as Blitzer coaches his inexperienced charges in the rudiments of bobsledding. They must also overcome other obstacles, most notably financial, to get to Canada. There they encounter the greatest barrier of all: *cold.* Meanwhile, Blitzer wangles and barters to get his team equipped, and must face the facts of his own dark past.

CAUTION: Minimal course language. There is a fistfight in a bar, and veiled references to racism when the Jamaicans are arbitrarily disqualified. There is also a mild parody of the Lord's Prayer, and a scary accident near the end (although no one is hurt).

GO: This is a wonderful underdog film, comic without being patronizing. There is a strong message about the importance of participation versus winning. Based on a true story.

■

✗ CRYSTALSTONE

MCA
1987
90 minutes
Directed by: Antonio Pelaez
Starring: Laura Jane Goodwin, Frank Grimes,
　　Kamlesh Gupta, Edward Kelsey
MPAA rating: PG

It is 1908. Deserted by their father and orphaned by their mother, Pablo and Maria avoid being separated by their mean-spirited aunt by running away and jumping a train, where they meet a mysterious white-bearded man. He tells them the story of Alonzo d'Alba, a sixteenth century caballero, who came into the possession of the Aztecs' sacred gem, the Crystalstone. The story goes that Alonzo set sail for Spain, but was shipwrecked near an ancient monastery and ended his days in a French prison. The only clue as to the location of the Crystalstone is to be found when three wooden crosses are reunited. After the story, the three go to sleep, and when the children awake in the morning, the old man is gone, and in his place they find the first wooden cross. Pablo and Maria then leave the train. The next day, while walking through a village, they witness a one-armed man murdering another man, whom they quickly realize is wearing the second wooden cross around his neck. (Only the chance passing of a drunken Captain saves them from a similar fate.) Pablo and Maria begin their search in earnest. They discover d'Alba's diary in an antique shop, and after narrowly escaping the one-armed man (who falls into the sea) and rescuing the Captain (who has taken the rap for the murder) the three sail to d'Alba's monastery where they discover vital clues in its dusty, abandoned library. That night, the Captain puts the children to bed, then begins to play the flute. Pablo realizes that the Captain is their father and, after a stormy argument, runs away. The Captain goes after him and when Pablo slips and falls over a waterfall, he discovers a secret subterranean chamber containing the gem.

✗ STOP: There is a very scary scene in which Pablo and Maria dig up a grave and are terrified by a close-up of a dead man's maggot-ridden face.

CAUTION: The children see the silhouette of a murder taking place as a hook rises and falls and a man screams in pain. The one-armed man who pursues the children is scary.

GO: This is an exciting mystery, probably most suitable for children over nine, with stirring themes of physical and spiritual rehabilitation.

D2:
THE MIGHTY DUCKS

Walt Disney
1994
107 minutes
Directed By: Sam Weisman
Starring: Emelio Estevez, Jan Rubes,
    Michael Tucker, Carsten Norgaard
MPAA rating: PG

Gordon Bombay's attempt to reach the NHL has been put on indefinite hold, thanks to a serious knee injury. While he's recuperating at his friend Jan's sports store, he receives an offer from the senior VP of a large corporation to coach the Mighty Ducks at the Junior Goodwill Games. Lured by a hefty signing bonus and lucrative endorsements, Gordon goes for the green. The Ducks, bolstered by an improbable group of "ringers" from around the country, begin their quest for the championship, but they have one serious obstacle — a team of monsters from Iceland who are coached by a former NHL goon. The Ducks' morale further deteriorates as Gordon becomes more and more seduced by the business side of his deal and begins fraternizing with an attractive woman on the Icelandic staff. Meanwhile, his team barely squeaks past the squads from some non-hockey nations, and in the first meeting with Iceland, the get routed. The Ducks are then in complete disarray, and only a return to their own roots and a revitalized and focused Gordon can save the day. Thus invigorated, they march to the finals for a showdown with the Icelandic villains.

CAUTION: Some coarse language. There is a certain amount of violence and crude behavior. The rough-house tactics of a couple of the Ducks are glorified. The scripted exclusion of the star female goaltender until the final play of the tournament was unfortunate. The neo-nazi Teutonic portrayal of the Icelanders is a bad xenophobic, and the vilifying of one opposing team has become a cliché, to say the least. Some of the on-ice antics are so improbable that young hockey purists may be turned off.

GO: Positive messages about learning to work together, playing fair, and being yourself.

✗ DARBY O'GILL AND THE LITTLE PEOPLE

Walt Disney Home Video
1959
90 minutes
Directed by: Robert Stevenson
Starring: Sean Connery, Janet Munro,
    Jimmy O'Dea
MPAA rating: G

The film takes place in turn-of-the-century Ireland, where Katie O'Gill and her father Darby run the manor house for Lord Fitzpatrick. Katie works hard, but her shiftless father has been distracted for years — ever since he caught the leprechaun king and was tricked out of his three wishes. So, when Lord Fitzpatrick hires a new groundskeeper, and a crestfallen Darby is retired on half-pay, Darby doesn't dare tell Katie. Meanwhile, to complicate matters, Darby falls into the leprechaun kingdom, where they plan to keep him forever. But the sly Darby has his own agenda. He makes his escape and recaptures the leprechaun king. And this time, he won't be outwitted.

✗**STOP:** At one point, when Katie is on her deathbed, Darby hears a mournful wailing outside. He goes to the door and encounters the truly terrifying apparition of Death. Darby takes his daughter's place in the Death Coach and viewers see things from his point-of-view as he is carried away. (You may want to fast-forward over this.)

CAUTION: Darby "bends the truth" every now and again and there is one fairly intense fistfight.

GO: Decent special effects (for the time) and fine performances mark this fanciful tale of a man who sacrifices everything for those he loves.

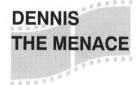

DENNIS THE MENACE

Warner Home Video
1993
96 minutes
Directed by: Nick Castle
Starring: Christopher Lloyd, Walter Matthau, Lea Thompson
MPAA rating: PG

Dennis Mitchell is up to his usual antics, terrorizing everyone in the community, in particular curmudgeon George Wilson. Dennis fires aspirin down Wilson's throat with a slingshot and accidentally drops paintbombs on Wilson's barbeque. Meanwhile, a super-sinister thief hits Dennis' idyllic small town and promptly goes on a robbing spree. At the same time, Dennis's parents have to go out of town, and the Wilsons agree to babysit him. Not suprisingly, life with Dennis proves to be living hell for George, especially when Dennis spoils the crowning achievement of his horticultural life. George upbraids Dennis, who runs off in utter distress and is then taken prisoner by the thief. The thief quickly finds out that he has a lot more than he can handle, as Dennis accidentally conks him on the head (and other vulnerable parts of the body), sets him on fire more than once, and more or less reduces him to a quivering shell of a villain.

CAUTION: Dennis inflicts unbelievable damage on the thief. Some children may find the thief a little scary, and he does shout "Shut up!" Dennis, in *Home Alone* style, sets the thief on fire.

GO: Despite its obvious debt to the *Home Alone* movies, this is a faithful attempt to bring Hank Ketcham's famous hellion to life. Dennis is a real five-year-old, and he never hurts anyone intentionally.

THE DIRT BIKE KID

Charter Entertainment
1985
91 minutes
Directed by: Hoite C. Caston
Starring: Peter Billingsley, Anne Bloom,
  Patrick Collins, Stuart Pankin
MPAA rating: PG

When Jack's mother Janet finally gets a job interview, she gives him her last fifty dollars to buy groceries. On his way, Jack stops at the track to watch his friend Max in a dirt bike race. During the race, Max's bike starts doing strange things, and an elderly man turns to Jack and says that Max doesn't deserve the bike. When Jack looks around again, the old man is gone, and a disgusted Max agrees to sell the dirt bike to his friend … for fifty dollars. Jack's mom is in no way thrilled. He is exiled to his room, but manages to sneak away to try his bike out. Well, it's soon obvious to Jack that this is no ordinary bike; it proves to be supernaturally fast *and* it can fly. It even seems to have a kind of personality, which becomes evident the next day when Jack's mother tries to take it out and sell it, and it refuses to go with her. Meanwhile, Mike, manager of the local favorite burger and fries hang-out, is up against the sinister Mr. Hodgkins of Hodgkins bank, which has selected Mike's restaurant as the perfect location for its next bank site. The magic bike takes Jack right into the bank just as Hodgkins is making a sleazy come-on to Janet (her interview was for a position with the bank) and Jack is able to get Hodgkins's assurance that he won't appropriate Mike's restaurant. But when Hodgkins immediately goes back on his word and forecloses, Jack and his bike must take on the bank any way they can.

CAUTION: One of Jack's friends leers at a well-endowed young woman, and remarks, "… more bounce to the ounce." Hodgkins's attitude towards women is despicable; he even uses a guard dog to keep them in the house while he's making his sleazy come-ons.

GO: *The Dirt Bike Kid* is a fun, inoffensive fantasy.

DIVORCE CAN HAPPEN TO THE NICEST PEOPLE

LCA
1987
30 minutes
Directed by: Andrea Bresciani

This fully-animated video answers questions children have about divorce, explaining such things as how nice people like mom and dad can fall into and out of love, and what might be involved when a new parent comes into the picture. Based on the book by Peter Mayle and Arthur Robins.

GO: Humorous yet informative, this video is caring and honest.
■ ●

DRAGONWORLD

Paramount Home Video
1994
84 minutes
Directed by: Ted Nicolaou
Starring: John Calvin, Lila Kaye,
 Sam Mackenzie, Brittney Powell,
 John Woodvine
MPAA rating: pending

Recently orphaned Johnny McGowan is sent to Scotland to live with his grandfather Angus in McGowan Castle. The castle is in tax arrears, but stands on magic land. Johnny, despite his youth, is put to work tending the sheep, and hears strange sounds. He also greatly admires his grandfather's bagpipe playing, and soon becomes a good little piper himself. His piping and his wish summon a baby dragon from the elven kingdom. He makes a vow to protect it from the outside world, and he and the dragon become best friends. Fifteen years pass. Angus has died, and Johnny is now the lord of McGowan Castle. Bob Armstrong, a sleazy documentary filmmaker, sees the dragon. He and a ruthless businessman, Macintyre, join forces to trick Johnny. They get him to agree to place the dragon in a medieval theme park, Dragonworld. But when Johnny sees that his dragon is being mistreated, he and Beth, Bob's daughter, try to rescue it. Finally, Bob repents, and helps Johnny and Beth rescue the dragon. Johnny is forced to send the dragon back to the elven kingdom to save it from its pursuers, then he and Beth get married. When Johnny and Beth have a child, the dragon returns.

CAUTION: Some children may be disturbed by the incarcerated dragon's distress. Guards shoot it with tranquilizer darts. Bob punches Macintyre in the face. Two guards get their heads conked together. Younger children may find the dragon, in its various stages, scary.

GO: There is a message about drinking and driving in the beginning of the film. The animated dragon is remarkably good considering the film's modest budget.

✗ E.T.: THE EXTRA-TERRESTRIAL

MCA
1982
115 minutes
Directed by: Steven Spielberg
Starring: Drew Barrymore, Peter Coyote,
 Henry Thomas
MPAA rating: PG

While on a sample-gathering expedition, an explorer from another solar system is stranded when his ship is forced to take off without him to avoid detection by the "natives." The "natives" are a group of human scientists, intent on obtaining clear-cut evidence of extra-terrestrials. The little alien evades them and finds refuge in a suburban backyard. There, he is discovered by a young boy named Elliott who lures the alien into the open with candy. Soon Elliott and the extra-terrestrial (which he names E.T.) become fast friends. They form a deep telepathic bond, which plays havoc with Elliott's classroom life, and E.T. has an opportunity to learn more about how humans live in North America. But the conditions on Earth are not good for E.T., who is slowly dying, and he builds a device from everyday implements with which to "phone home." And as E.T. grows weaker and weaker, an army of scientists descends on Elliott's house, placing the neighborhood under quarantine and encasing the whole house in a huge plastic bubble. Nothing seems able to save E.T., but just as he seems to have died, E.T.'s distress call is answered. The alien miraculously revives and Elliott, his brother and his friends help E.T. return to his ship and to safety.

✗STOP: Certain images in this film have terrified children too young to understand that the alien, despite his bizarre appearance, is kind and friendly. This is an emotionally intense film especially during the scene in which doctors try to "jump start" E.T.'s heart, and at the end when E.T. leaves and Elliott must stay.

CAUTION: Many young children are frightened when, at their first meeting, Elliott and E.T. scream; the scene in which scientists take over Elliott's house may be upsetting, too. There is some coarse language in this film and at nearly two hours it may be too long and too much for young viewers.

GO: A heart-warming story full of magic, *E.T.* is one of the biggest box-office hits ever.

✗ THE ELECTRIC GRANDMOTHER

LCA
1981
50 minutes
Directed by: Noel Black
Starring: Charlie Fields, Edward Herrmann,
    Tara Kennedy, Robert MacNaughton,
    Maureen Stapleton
MPAA rating: no rating given

After the premature death of his wife, Henry and his three children, Tom, Timothy and Agatha, visit the Fantoccini Company, which specializes in made-to-order robotic humans. There, they choose the characteristics they would most like to have in a caregiver and, in a short time, receive a wonderful electric grandmother. She is a marvel. She makes their favorite meals, pours drinks from her index finger and runs the household splendidly, retreating to her basement rocker at night to recharge her batteries. There's only one problem. Agatha has still not recovered from the death of her mother, and she utterly rejects the grandmother, until the grandmother can prove to her that she will never leave. The grandmother proves that she cannot die when she pushes Agatha out of the way of an oncoming car and is struck herself, but remains unharmed. She stays until the children go off to college, then returns to care for them in their old age. Based on Ray Bradbury's story "I Sing the Body Electric."

✗STOP: The film opens immediately after the death of the children's mother. Any child who has suffered a recent loss should not see this film.

CAUTION: The Fantoccini Company is dark and scary and the car accident scene is very traumatic. Viewers may find the whole concept of the film a little bizarre.

GO: Despite its melancholy feeling, has heartfelt sentiments.
■ ●

EMIL AND THE DETECTIVES

Walt Disney Home Video
1964
92 minutes
Directed by: Peter Tewkesbury
Starring: Roger Mobley, Bryan Russell,
    Walter Slezak
MPAA rating: no rating given

Ten-year-old Emil Tischbein boards the morning bus in Neustadt for post-World War II Berlin, carrying a large sum of money for his grandmother. Little does he know that The Mole, a small-time crook, spotted the money changing hands and has arranged to sit beside Emil on the bus. Hypnotizing Emil with a pocket watch, The Mole lifts the money and makes off with it. Emil dashes off the bus and into the street, but when the police ignore him, Emil is alone and penniless in the shattered city. Soon though, a multi-talented street urchin named Gustav Fleischman and his comrades, The Detectives, come to his aid. The crew fans out through the streets of Berlin and in so doing, stumble upon a greater crime than just petty theft. A conspiracy to rob a major bank is afoot and someone plans to tunnel into the vault from the ruins down the street. But as The Detectives uncover more evidence, they have more trouble convincing the police to do anything about it. There's another problem, too. The time is near when Emil will have to confront his grandmother and admit that he doesn't have the money. On Emil's last night in Berlin, the boys stake out the ruins and sure enough, the conspirators

arrive. But when Emil is captured, things get tense, especially when the crooks force him to help them finish the tunnel, then leave him and The Mole to be blown up by a bomb. In the end, it's up to Gustav and The Detectives to rescue Emil before it's too late. Based on the novel by Erich Kastner.

CAUTION: During the climax, as The Mole and Emil are frantically trying to dig their way out, The Mole's claustrophobic panic is evident.

GO: For young mystery fans, this is the movie. It's also a great film about kids making a difference.

■ ●

✗ THE EMPIRE STRIKES BACK

CBS/Fox
1980
124 minutes
Directed by: Irvin Kershner
Starring: Carrie Fisher, Harrison Ford,
    Mark Hamill, Billy Dee Williams
MPAA rating: PG

Despite their success in destroying the Death Star, the rebels have fallen on dark times and they are hidden in a secret base on an ice-world in the Hoth system. Vader has been searching the galaxy for them, and as the film opens Imperial probes have landed on the planet and identified the rebel base. Sure enough, the Empire launches a massive assault, but an incompetent Imperial admiral brings the huge armada out of warp too close to the system, and the element of surprise is lost. As the rebels get set to flee, Vader orders another sinister general to prepare his troops for a surface assault. The Imperial forces must attack on the ground to knock out the force field generators which protect the rebel base. This sets the stage for one of the most memorable battle scenes in sci-fi history, as the Imperial troops advance in giant elephantine walking machines. A handful of rebels escape — Han Solo and Princess Leia in the Millenium Falcon and Luke Skywalker in a single-seat fighter. As Han and Leia run from the agents of the Empire, Luke travels to the Dagobah system to study under the ultimate Jedi master, the eight-hundred-year old Yoda. But before Luke's training is complete, Vader captures Han and Leia and sets a fiendish trap, luring Luke into a duel he does not yet have the strength to fight. At the height of the confrontation, Vader reveals the awful truth about his identity. This film is the second in the Star Wars trilogy; the first is *Star Wars* and the third is *Return of the Jedi*.

✗STOP: Vader absently dispatches an incompetent subordinate who gargles and chokes before falling dead. The duel between Luke and Vader is extremely intense and Vader cuts off Luke's hand. Han Solo is lowered into a huge machine and carbon-frozen, a look of anguish on his face.

CAUTION: The film is replete with combat and frightening images. If comparisons are to be made, this is probably the darkest film of the trilogy.

GO: Cautions aside, this is also the most exciting film in the trilogy.

●

ENCINO MAN

Hollywood Pictures Home Video
1992
98 minutes
Directed by: Les Mayfield
Starring: Sean Astin, Brendan Fraser, Marriette Hartley, Pauly Shore, Megan Ward
MPAA rating: PG

When Dave Morgan is digging a swimming pool by hand in his backyard, an earthquake reveals an underground glacier in which a Cro-Magnon man is frozen. Dave and his friend Stoney decide to thaw the iceman out, thereby gaining fame, fortune and popularity. They clean him up and introduce him to Dave's parents as Linkavitch Chomofsky, an exchange student who has come to help dig the pool. The next day they take "Link" to school where the girls begin to vie for his attention and where, during a class trip to the museum, Link realizes the truth of his dilemma. He is understandably upset but, after a series of crazy incidents, finds his place in high school society, and when Link's true identity is finally revealed to the other students, no one minds a bit.

CAUTION: Some coarse language and sexual gestures. The "defrosting" scene frightens some children as Link's rastafarian hair looks like exposed brains.

GO: *Encino Man* is a fun, if completely improbable, yarn. At the end of the film it is suggested viewers read *Encino High: Stoney's Notebook.*

✗ ERNEST GOES TO CAMP

Touchstone Home Video
1987
92 minutes
Directed by: John R. Cherry
Starring: Victoria Racimo, Jim Varney,
John Vernon
MPAA rating: PG

At Camp Kikakee, blundering camp handyman Ernest P. Worrell dreams of one day becoming a camp counselor. He eventually gets his wish, when the Governor (as part of a state program) delivers a group of disadvantaged youngsters to the camp and a full-scale war errupts. The "second-chancers" dispose of their regular counselor in short order, and are handed over to Ernest. Meanwhile, Krader Industries, run by ruthless mining executive Sherman Krader, has targeted Camp Kikakee as the site of a huge deposit of the mineral petricide and is trying to get the owners, Miss St. Cloud and her grandfather, to sell. When this fails, Sherman resorts to trickery and force, and it's up to Ernest and his young charges to stand up to Sherman's thugs.

✗STOP: There is one particularly violent fight, after which Ernest is kicked while lying on the ground bleeding.

CAUTION: A lot of the humor is violent. At the climax of the film, Krader fires a rifle at an unarmed Ernest, clearly attempting to kill him in cold blood.

GO: If you like slapstick comedy, this is the film for you. The kitchen features such delicacies as eggs erroneous and Varney's Ernest is the classic stumblebum.

✗ ERNEST GOES TO JAIL

Touchstone Home Video
1990
81 minutes
Directed by: John R. Cherry
Starring: Barbara Rush, Gailard Sartain,
Jim Varney
MPAA rating: PG

Know-it-all Ernest P. Worrell (now a night cleaner at a bank) is a dead ringer for Felix Nash, a notorious crime czar who rules Dracop Prison from the inside. And when Ernest is assigned to jury duty, and the defendant is one of Nash's fellow-prisoners, the cons arrange a switch and Ernest is incarcerated. Felix then takes over Ernest's bank job and his life, changing his gadget-filled house into a tacky seduction parlor and completely alienating his prospective girlfriend. Meanwhile, Ernest is forced to impersonate the crime czar in his daily prison routine. Unbeknownst to our mutton-headed hero, he is only days away from the electric chair, and as the days turn to hours Ernest must break out and foil Nash's plans to rob the bank.

✗STOP: One scene involves the electric chair, so be prepared to answer your child's questions about capital punishment.

CAUTION: Ernest is electrocuted three times in the film, once in the electric chair. As in other Ernest films, a lot of the humor revolves around violent slapstick comedy, with a great deal of punching.

GO: For older kids and adults — particularly fans of slapstick — Ernest is hilarious. The disaster sequences always have a cartoon flavor to them.

ERNEST SAVES CHRISTMAS

ESCAPE TO WITCH MOUNTAIN

Touchstone Home Video
1988
91 minutes
Directed by: John Cherry
Starring: Oliver Clark, Noelle Parker,
    Jim Varney
MPAA rating: PG

Walt Disney Home Video
1975
94 minutes
Directed by: John Hough
Starring: Eddie Albert, Ike Eisenmann,
    Ray Milland, Donald Pleasance, Kim Richards
MPAA rating: G

AGES 6 TO 10

Stumblebum cab driver Ernest P. Worrell drops an elderly white-bearded man at the Children's Museum to meet with Joe Carruthers, a man who has dedicated his life to entertaining children. Although Joe doesn't know it yet, the elderly man is the current incarnation of Santa Claus, who is about to retire and who has chosen Joe as his replacement. But things begin to go wrong. Ernest leaves with Santa's sack still in his cab and Joe thinks that Santa's merely a confused, ordinary elderly man. Santa ends up being arrested for vagrancy, and it isn't until Ernest happens to glance in the sack and realizes, "He's him," that Santa manages to get out of jail. Together they find Joe, and try to convince him to carry on the tradition. Still unconvinced (Santa's bag has been stolen and there is no other tangible proof of his identity), Joe sets off to pursue a movie career instead. It's up to Ernest to save the day, driving Santa's sled across town from the airport, just in time to pick up Joe, who has come to realize that he is, indeed, the "new him."

GO: Jim Varney does his Ernest shtick, the usual gallery of funny impersonations.

Orphans eleven-year-old Tony and his nine-year-old sister Tia are psychics, capable of telekinesis, telepathy and clairvoyance. One day, Tia uses her powers to save the life of a man named Lucas Deranian, a sinister servant of the unscrupulous billionaire Aristotle Bolt. After hearing about the gifted children and seeing the opportunity for increased wealth, Bolt adopts Tony and Tia under false pretenses and brings them to his coastal mansion. There, he lavishes gifts upon the children, but they soon see through him, and telepathically overhear his plans to ship them to an inaccessible island. That night the children escape, sneaking into the back of tourist Jason O'Day's camper. The bitter and reclusive Jason grudgingly helps the children, and as they drive towards Witch Mountain, Tia and Tony begin to remember their origins. They belong to a race of aliens from a dying world who migrated to earth, and who have been living secretly and peacefully among humans. But when their particular starship arrived, it crashed in the ocean and Tony and Tia are afraid that they may be the only survivors. Meanwhile, Bolt and Deranian are in hot pursuit and the children narrowly escape capture, time after time. They follow a mysterious voice and the directions on a map (which they've always had, but which only now begins to make sense) and reach Witch Mountain, where they are greeted by their guardian Bené. Bené informs Jason that there are many others like Tony and Tia lost in the world, and Jason vows to help them get to Witch Mountain as well.

GO: This is an entertaining effort without violence, but sophisticated enough for the older crowd.

EWOK ADVENTURE

MGM/UA
1984
96 minutes
Directed by: John Korty
Starring: Warwick Davis, Aubree Miller, Eric Walker, with narration by Burl Ives
MPAA rating: not rated

After a crash landing on the forest moon of Endor, humans Catazine and Jezemitt are captured by the giant Gorax. Their children Mace and Cindel befriend the denizens of an Ewok village (Ewoks are, of course, the chubby little teddy-bear people from the film *Return of the Jedi*). When the Ewoks rescue the children from a huge carnivore, the children find, tied to the animal's harness, a signal-bracelet owned by their parents. The children then seek out Logray, the Ewoks' village mystic, who shows them a vision of their imprisoned parents. The children and their new friend Wicket (Warwick Davis) set out with an

expedition of Ewoks to rescue their folks. There are many perils, including a sinister pool which entraps its victims below its glassy surface, the odd runaway pony, the searing crossing of a scorched desert, spiders the size of cars, and the hazard-filled mountain citadel of the giant troll, Gorax.

CAUTION: In the first scene, a giant axe-wielding hominid with a skeletal face looms out of the mist, roaring ferociously. The children get chased through the forest by a huge, snarling rat-like monster, cornering them in a hollowed-out stump. There is an anxious scene when Mace is trapped, struggling and screaming, below the surface of the pool, and another when the giant spiders attack the company. And finally, the huge, hideous troll terrorizes the parents, and chases the pesky Ewoks around his huge cavern. The brave Ewok Kiroto dies standing off the troll.

GO: This is a great kids-making-a-difference film, and for Ewok fans it has lots of the little guys running around just being themselves.

EWOKS: THE BATTLE FOR ENDOR

MGM/UA
1985
98 minutes
Directed By: Jim and Ken Wheat
Starring: Wilford Brimley, Warwick Davis, Sian Phillips
MPAA rating: not rated

While on a brief stopover for repairs on the forest moon of Endor, a family befriends an Ewok village. However, the village is attacked by the Marauders of Lord Terak, big mean ugly guys with bad complexions and poor social skills who are looking for the power cylinder from the family's starship. Only young Cindel, the daughter of the family, and her Ewok friend Wicket survive, as prisoners of Lord Terak. Thanks to the resourceful Wicket, he and Cindel escape. After a near-miss with a pterodactyl-like creature, they encounter Teek, a furry little biped who moves at super-speed. This character leads them to the house of a gruff and reclusive galactic castaway named Noa. At first Noa wants the pair out, but in time he comes to love them, and when the evil Lord Terak kidnaps Cindel, Noa sets out to rescue her, instigating the final showdown.

CAUTION: Cindel's mother, father and brother are killed right at the beginning. There is fighting throughout: hand-to-hand, shooting and swordplay. There are chase scenes and Cindel is constantly in peril. The bad guys are ugly and scary and cruel.

GO: This is a Lucasfilm production, and the special effects and makeup are far and above most films on this scale.

AGES 6 TO 10

EXPLORERS

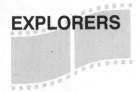

Paramount Home Video
1985
107 minutes
Directed by: Joe Dante
Starring: Ethan Hawke, River Phoenix, Mary Kay Place, Jason Presson
MPAA rating: PG

Explorers concerns the adventures of three boys: Ben, a visionary;

Wolfgang, a scientific prodigy; and Darren, a social rebel whose father owns a junkyard. Ben has been having strange dreams in which he feels he is being "called" (he hopes by some alien force, so he can learn from them the secrets of the universe). He draws sketches of machinery from the dreams and Wolfgang enters them as three-dimensional drawings into his computer. Then, quite unexpectedly, Wolfgang hits upon a spherical object called an "electrically generated point of force" which escapes from the computer and actually comes to exist. They find that this sphere can travel at unimaginable speeds with no inertia or resistance; so, using Darren's father's junkyard for parts, they fabricate a vehicle to fit inside it and christen this space ship the Thunder Road. Then they launch themselves into space and are beamed aboard an alien ship, where they encounter two friendly, insect-like creatures who know all about Earth's civilizations from television programs. Ben is disappointed that they cannot tell him the secrets of the universe, but after a crash landing in which the Thunder Road is destroyed, the boys learn that things are not always as they seem and that dreams and aspirations can sometimes be of real value.

CAUTION: The boys are trapped inside the spacecraft and are chased by a huge iron insect-like creature. Later they are photographed, smelled, frisked and inspected by the creature. The aliens project a blue beam of light into Darren's head. He is unperturbed, saying "they put pictures into your head." The aliens show the boys — via old movies — that earthlings kill aliens, and there is a bit of swearing, but usually in the context of exclamations.

GO: Light, humorous and (by today's standards) nonviolent, this is a film for the whole family. Parents, in particular, will appreciate parodies the aliens make on television shows of the '50s and '60s.

FANTASIA

Walt Disney Home Video
1940
120 minutes
Directed by: Walt Disney
MPAA rating: G

Arguably the most famous assembly of animation in the history of film, *Fantasia*'s timeless appeal has enthralled generation after generation of film-goers. Working in conjunction with the composer Leopold Stokowski and the Philadelphia Orchestra, Walt Disney and an imaginative group of artists took several favorite pieces of music and expressed their impressions of them in the form of brilliantly conceived fantasies. No words can do justice to the impact of this work.

Animated sequences were created for:

A jazzy musical interlude
A Night on Bald Mountain (Modeste Mussorgsky)
Ave Maria (Franz Schubert)
Dance of the Hours (Amicare Ponchielli)
The Nutcracker Suite (Tchaikovsky)
The Pastoral Symphony (Ludwig von Beethoven)
The Rite of Spring (Igor Stravinsky)
The Sorcerer's Apprentice (Paul Dukas)
Toccata and Fugue in D Minor (Johann Sebastian Bach)

CAUTION: There is a prevailing misconception that *Fantasia* is a children's film; it is not, although older children may indeed enjoy it. And there are some frightening images, particularly in *The Sorcerer's Apprentice* and *Night on Bald Mountain*.

GO: The plan for *Fantasia* is an interesting one. Following Disney's original concept that this film would be the first in a series, Disney studios will no longer release this version of *Fantasia* but will drop one of the sequences and add a new one, releasing the new combination as *Fantasia II*. The plan is to continue to drop and add sequences so each combination is unique. One of the great achievements in animation, this film has more than survived the test of time.

●

FLIGHT OF THE NAVIGATOR

Walt Disney Home Video
1986
89 minutes
Directed by: Randal Kleiser
Starring: Mark Adler, Veronica Cartwright, Joey Cramer, Cliff De Young, Howard Hesseman, Sarah Jessica Parker, Paul Reubens
MPAA rating: PG

One night, twelve-year-old David Freeman falls into a ravine and is knocked unconscious. And when he awakes and struggles home, he finds that his parents don't live there anymore — in fact, they haven't lived there for eight years. He himself has not changed, but his parents have aged, and his once "younger" brother is now twice his size. David's traumatic reappearance is investigated, and it's discovered that an alien spacecraft crashed at the same time that David returned home. So, David is taken to a research center for an examination, where the scientists find that his mind is absolutely full of star charts. They plan to keep him until the mystery is unravelled, but David sneaks out and is drawn psychically to the spacecraft. And when its previously impenetrable hull opens to admit David, the frantic security forces rush to prevent him from going aboard ... too late. David finds that the spacecraft is intelligent, that it responds to his verbal commands and that he has already been the ship's navigator for an eight-year interstellar trip. Frightened by the commotion he has caused, and afraid that he's in trouble, David wishes out loud that he could get away, and the ship complies, taking him twenty miles straight up into the atmosphere. David shortly realizes that the ship will do anything he asks and when he also learns that the star charts were transferred to his mind as a means of safeguarding them in the landing accident, he transfers them back to the ship's memory banks. But in so doing he also transfers many of his human characteristics, and the ship begins talking suspiciously like Pee-Wee Herman and takes David on a wild joy-ride, during which the pair get lost. Then it's up to David to find his way back home, and eventually, to his own time eight years in the past.

CAUTION: Young ones may find the time paradox confusing and frightening. David is obviously alone and afraid, and finding his family again provides little initial comfort. In one scene, when they stop at a roadside filling station, the talking spaceship insults the overweight attendant.

GO: This film features brilliant special effects and an entertaining and nonviolent plot.

AGES 6 TO 10

✗ THE FOX AND THE HOUND

Walt Disney Home Video
1981
83 minutes
Directed by: Ted Berman, Richard Rich, Art Stevens
Starring the voices of: Jack Albertson, Pearl Bailey, Sandy Duncan, Jeanette Nolan, Mickey Rooney, Kurt Russell
MPAA rating: G

As the credits roll, an adult fox (presumably the mother) is running from braying hounds, carrying a fox kitten as she flees. She leaves the kitten in a safe place, runs over a hill and is killed off-camera. An owl, Big Mama, finds the kitten and, with Dinky and Boomer (two feathered friends), arranges to bring him to the farm of the kindly Widow Tweed. The widow takes the kitten in and names him Tod. At about the same time her nearest neighbor, crusty curmudgeon and big-time hunting fanatic Amos Slade, brings home a new hound pup. The pup, Copper, is destined to help him further deplete the wildlife he so despises. The hound pup and the fox kitten meet one day and become fast friends, but Tod's presence on Slade's farm sends the old coot into a foxicidal frenzy. Then Copper is taken away for hound-dog indoctrination. Seasons pass. The fox and the hound grow up, and when they meet again, Copper explains to Tod that their friendship is over, and consequently the hunt is on. Tod is cornered, but Copper lets him escape; shortly thereafter, Copper's mentor, Chief, is badly injured, and Copper vows to get

Tod. The widow, fearing for the fox's life, sends him out to a game preserve to fend for himself, where he meets a vixen and falls in love. Slade and Copper enter the game preserve illegally and lay a succession of murderous traps, leading to a violent confrontation between the hunters and the foxes, during which Slade sets the entire forest on fire. Slade and Copper then encounter a huge and justifiably angry bear. In the harrowing climax, Tod returns to save both Copper and Slade. Based on the book by Daniel P. Mannix.

✗STOP: This film is replete with violence and frightening images.

CAUTION: As an allegory for racial intolerance, this film may be instructional for older children; however, from the middle onward it is dominated by angst, the heartbreak of irredeemably lost friendship, and the bizarre character of Slade, a man so full of venom and unfeeling hatred for wild creatures that he is almost a monster. After Tod saves Slade's life, Slade *still* wants to kill him!

■

FLINTSTONES

MCA/Universal
1994
85 minutes (approx)
Directed By: Brian Levant
Starring: John Goodman, Rick Moranis,
   Elizabeth Perkins, Rosie O'Donnell
MPAA rating: PG

The Flintstones opens at a critical juncture. Barney and Betty Rubble are arranging to adopt Bam-Bam,

thanks to a timely and incredibly generous loan from their big-hearted friend Fred Flintstone. Barney vows to repay his friend somehow, and his chance comes during the Junior Vice-President Aptitude Tests at the quarry, where he and Fred work. Barney scores sky-high on the tests, but Fred is hopeless, so Barney selflessly switches their test results. As a result, Fred is promoted to VP, but Barney is fired (thanks to Fred's horrible test results). While Fred rises to the social elite and lives a lavish life-style, enjoying huge bonuses, fancy new cars, a flirtatious and curvaceous secretary named (ouch) Sharon Stone, and all the other amenities, Barney moves into lower and lower social echelons. Then the roof caves in on Fred. He has been the stooge of evil senior VP Cliff Vandercave, who has conspired to pin the embezzlement of the plant funds, and the firing of all the quarry workers on the hapless Fred. At the climax of the film, Fred must reconcile himself to his loved ones, prove his innocence and, with the help of Barney, rescue Pebbles and Bam-Bam from Vandercave.

CAUTION: Some disturbing images for very *very* little ones. Pebbles and Bam-Bam are shown sitting in a cart on a factory line (right out of Perils of Pauline) bound and in danger at the climax. One young movie-goer (4 1/2 years old) wondered during the film when "Fred was going to turn good again."

GO: In the end, Fred turns down an offer of wealth and a higher social station, content with job satisfaction and secure in the love of his family and friends. Almost every kid has seen the Flintstones on TV, so they will have a frame of reference for the characters and antics in the film. The sets are astonishing, and the special effects are great.

FREAKY FRIDAY

FREE WILLY

Walt Disney Home Video
1977
95 minutes
Directed by: Gary Nelson
Starring: John Astin, Kaye Ballard, Ruth Buzzi, Jodie Foster, Barbara Harris
MPAA rating: G

Warner Home Video
1993
112 minutes
Directed by: Simon Wincer
Starring: Jayne Atkinson, Michael Madsen, Lori Petty, James Jason Richter, August Schellenberg
MPAA rating: PG

On Friday the thirteenth, teenage baseball and field-hockey star Annabel fervently wishes for the easy life her mother enjoys; conversely, her mother Ellen longs for the bygone days of high school. And as their powerful wishes are made on this particularly spooky day, their consciousnesses switch bodies. Annabel must stay home and cook and clean (with disastrous results) while her mother goes back to school. In her mother's body, Annabel plays a mean baseball game and everyone is astounded to see "Ellen" whacking home runs, making diving catches and stealing home. Ellen is not so lucky as she encounters the usual teen traumas, making such gaffes as scoring on her own net in a critical field-hockey match. At the end of this slapstick farce, both individuals are relieved to return to their own lives. Based on the book by Mary Rogers.

CAUTION: The portrayal of the female situation is a little dated.

GO: The end degenerates into pure slapstick, but the film is loads of fun for kids under ten. Children who enjoy *Freaky Friday* may also enjoy films with similar situations, *Big* and *Vice Versa*. (Check the ratings to make sure that these films are suitable for your child before you rent.)

Jesse is a troubled ten-year-old. His mother dropped him off with youth services when he was four, and no one's heard from her since. Jesse, however, still harbors the fantasy that she will return for him one day; in the meantime, he's been in and out of a string of foster homes and is on the verge of being sent to juvenile hall. His latest stunt was defacing an adventure park, and his last chance is Glen and Annie Greenwood, a wonderful young couple who only want to make a home for him. But Jesse is bitter, withdrawn and afraid, and nothing but trouble. Jesse's probation is to clean up the mess he made at the park, during the course of which he meets Randolph the custodian, Rae the trainer, and Willy, a foul-tempered orca who was captured too old and is resisting every effort to train him. Willy and Jesse become friends, and this proves to be the best therapy for both of them. Willy, who is extremely intelligent, learns a number of tricks, and the adventure park's coldhearted owner prepares to showcase him. Then everyone discovers — belatedly — that Willy will only perform for Jesse; in other words, he's a bust. Jesse decides that he has had it with everyone, and makes plans to run away to California. That same night the unscrupulous owner decides to cash in the orca's huge insurance policy. He arranges a midnight "accident" during which Willy's tank will rupture and drain. Jesse discovers the plot and enlists Randolph and Rae's aid in rescuing Willy. But in the effort to avoid their pursuers, their trailer runs off the road, and they must enlist Glen Greenwood to save Willy.

CAUTION: At the beginning of the film Jesse is tackled and handcuffed by the police. Jesse is bitter and rude and devoid of charm. His deplorable attitude toward his kindly foster parents is relentless.

GO: This is a compelling tale of a young boy's rehabilitation through his friendship with another intelligent being. It also addresses environmental concerns without being preachy.

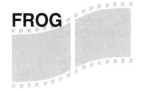

FROG

Orion
1988
55 minutes
Directed by: David Grossman
Starring: Shelley Duvall, Elliott Gould,
  Scott Grimes, Amy Lynne, Paul Williams
MPAA rating: no rating given

Arlo Anderson is a nerd who's fascinated with reptiles and amphibians. And when the latest addition to his collection, a huge bullfrog, suddenly starts talking to him, Arlo has trouble convincing himself that he hasn't lost his mind. The frog introduces himself as

Italian prince Guiseppi Buono Duno, and goes on to explain that he is under a six-hundred-year-old curse that can only be broken if he is kissed by a pretty young woman. Arlo, now convinced that the frog really is talking to him, is at a loss as to how to help. None of the girls in his class will even talk to him, let alone kiss his hideous bullfrog. But then an attractive girl named Suzy cynically tries to raise her grades by becoming Arlo's partner in the science fair, and the strangest thing happens: Suzy gets to really like Arlo, enough even to kiss his frog or, as it turns out, a lot of frogs, because right at the critial moment Gus accidentally falls into a pool full of thousands of them. Still, Suzy gamely kisses away, frog after frog, but nothing seems to happen, and although Arlo *does* win the respect of the scientific community for his work on frog communication, he's upset that the prince's best chance to achieve human form seems to have been lost. As it turns out, though, all is well. And in an Italian restaurant, the prince — complete with polyester leisure suit — shows up to serenade his friends.

CAUTION: The prince sings "That's Amore" right at the end of the film, and it isn't pretty.

GO: At one hour in length, this is a great party video that will appeal to kids of all ages.

FUNHOUSE FITNESS: THE FUNHOUSE FUNK

Warner Home Video
1991
45 minutes
Directed by: Anita Mann
Starring: Jane Fonda, J.D. Roth

The MTV-style dancing and exercise routines in this video will help kids develop balance, co-ordination, agility, endurance and strength. With a mixed group of boys and girls, J.D. Roth shows that boys can do aerobics too! Recommended for children ages seven and up.

CAUTION: Included are scenes from the show *Fun House* where kids get covered with paint and whipped cream.

GO: An effective aerobic video, Funhouse Fitness has great music and high energy.

GEORGE'S ISLAND

Astral
1991
90 minutes
Directed by: Paul Donovan
Starring: Ian Bannen, Maury Chaykin,
   Sheila McCarthy, Nathaniel Moreau
   Gary Reineke, Vicki Ridler
MPAA rating: no rating given

Strict teacher Miss Cloitha Birdwood is making life miserable for George Waters, a young orphan who lives with his salty, wheelchair-bound grandfather. She sends Bonnie, a despised over-achieving classmate, to befriend George and spy on his home life, and once (what she believes is) sufficient damning evidence has been collected, Miss Birdwood goes to a deranged childcare worker named Mr. Droonfield and manages to have George removed from his grandfather's care and sent to live with evil foster parents Roger and Buelah Beane. But the Beanes keep George in a cell, and he makes a hasty escape (accompanied by foster child number one who is, oddly enough, Bonnie). George's grandfather rescues the kids, and with Miss Birdwood and Mr. Droonfield in close pursuit, they race to George's Island (an island on which a treasure has been buried and which is guarded by the ghosts of Captain Kidd and an assortment of pirates). In the end, everyone ends up on George's Island where Kidd orders the ghosts to kill everyone. But after some discussion, the ghastly crew is persuaded to haunt the Beanes' residence, instead. George and his grandfather are reunited, and Bonnie is adopted by the newly married Droonfield and Birdwood.

CAUTION: At the beginning of the film, Kidd and his henchman kill the other members of the treasure-burying party, and heads literally roll (no blood, though). Some children have been frightened by the opening sequence. The pirate ghosts are scary, and one young Halloween prankster is shot in the behind with rock salt. Some viewers — both children and adults — may find the treatment of George and his grandfather upsetting.

GO: Spooky and packed with adventure, this excellent film is full of great kid performances.

GIRLS JUST WANT TO HAVE FUN

✗ GNOME NAMED GNORM, THE ADVENTURES OF A

New World Video
1985
90 minutes
Directed by: Alan Metter
Starring: Helen Hunt, Lee Montgomery,
Sarah Jessica Parker, Jonathan Silverman
MPAA rating: PG

Polygram
1993
85 minutes
Directed by: Stan Winston
Starring: Claudia Christian,
Anthony Michael Hall, Jerry Orbach
MPAA rating: PG

Janey Glenn is a terrific dancer, and when a show called *Dance TV* holds auditions for two new dancers, she and her outrageous friend Lynne Stone enter the competition. Sure enough, the talented Janey makes the finals, but she is to be paired with a stranger, Jeff Malene, and in order to do their routines they need to practice. But there are three problems: first, Janey and Jeff just can't seem to get along (one of the promoters calls them *Rebel Without a Cause* meets *The Sound of Music*); second, Janey's hopelessly spoiled rival Natalie Sands schemes constantly to ruin her chances, and third, Janey's father Colonel Glenn will have none of it, so Janey has to sneak out after everyone thinks she has gone to bed. And Jeff has his own problem: it turns out that Natalie's dad owns the factory where Jeff's father works, and Mr. Sands puts pressure on Jeff to drop out, or else. But through all of this, Janey and Jeff begin to develop a relationship and eventually win the contest.

CAUTION: This film has a lot of coarse language and characters make quite a few sexual references.

GO: Despite the above, this is a fun, relatively inoffensive film.

Casey is an eccentric young cop who doesn't like guns and incurs the ire of most of his associates. Only his partner, the attractive Samantha, sticks up for him. Casey has been given a prime assignment, to bust the evil diamond smuggler Zidar. But during the exchange Casey is knocked out and robbed, and Zidar's runner is killed and robbed. Casey is blamed for blowing it. He then goes for a walk and finds the missing diamonds. He also discovers a real live gnome. The gnome, Gnorm, is in search of his missing lumen, a stone of magical properties, without which his people will die. Casey captures the gnome and takes him home in a cage. Realizing that the gnome is the only witness to the crime he promptly enlists its aid in solving the case. But things go instantly awry. Casey is framed for murder, and both Casey and Gnorm are arrested. Eventually, of course, Casey and Gnorm track down the killer, and Gnorm gets back his all-important gem.

✗**STOP:** A bad guy slugs Casey and knocks him out. A man opens a bomb disguised as a briefcase right in his lap, and it goes off. The gnome bites Zidar on the behind and squeezes his groin. There are numerous violent fistfights, a shooting death, and someone gets a meat hook in the posterior.

CAUTION: The gnome checks out Samantha's figure and makes lude gestures of appreciation. Samantha "uses her feminine wiles" to distract an obnoxious fellow cop while Casey makes a getaway. This is yet another example of depressingly ordinary, cliché-driven writing.

GO: The puppetmation is good, and Gnorm is very believable.

GODZILLA VS. MOTHRA

Paramount Home Video
1966
93 minutes
Directed by: Inoshiro Honda
Starring: Yu Fujiki, Yuriko Hoshi,
Akira Takarada
MPAA rating: not rated

AGES 6 TO 10

After a cataclysmic storm a huge egg washes up on Japanese shores. It is Mothra's egg and her emissaries, mysterious tiny twin girls, come to Japan to beg for its return. But they are too late; the egg has been purchased by unscrupulous entrepreneurs who plan to become wealthy by selling tickets to the hatching. Greater trouble strikes when Godzilla makes an appearance, destroying highways, dams and entire apartment blocks. The people of Tokyo need Mothra's help, but the Polynesian people who inhabit Mothra Island refuse to intervene (they've suffered much at the hands of the Japanese, the most recent imposition being a series of atomic tests conducted on their island that nearly destroyed all life there).

Luckily, the tiny twin girls intervene, wake Mothra up (by singing!) and send her off to fight Godzilla. Mothra is old and tired, though, and she dies in battle. The safety of Japan now depends on the as yet unhatched Mothra. And at the thrilling climax, by an amazingly good stroke of luck, the egg hatches and a pair of larval Mothra twins emerge! They make quick work of Godzilla, restore peace to the Japanese countryside and swim home with the tiny twin girls in tow.

CAUTION: Godzilla loses. This can be a terrible shock to young fans who are accustomed to seeing Godzilla in the hero's role. The film is racist; the Polynesians seem to have the same kind of role as tribal Africans did in the old Johnny Weissmuller Tarzan flicks (except that when the Polynesians sing and dance there is a decidedly ·Broadway flavor to their choreography). There is some hand-to-hand combat with blood (not graphic).

GO: There are some great shots of Godzilla, who is unusually naturalistic.

GODZILLA VS. THE SMOG MONSTER

Orion Home Video
1971
86 minutes
Original Japanese version directed by:
Yoshimitu Banno; additional segments directed by: Lee Kresel for North American release
MPAA rating: G

Off the coast of Japan, an unknown monster is sinking ships. A fisherman takes what appears to be an unnaturally big tadpole to a local scientist who deduces that it was formed from a mineral (although later the monster is characterized as being born of sludge). He is able to generate more such tadpoles, and when he puts two together they join and grow larger, thus creating Hedora, a new and terrifying monster. Hedora develops the ability to fly and emits a sulphuric acid mist which makes him particularly dangerous. The death toll mounts, and the entire coastline is placed under a military alert. Meanwhile, the doctor, despite his deteriorating condition, has discovered that the monster can be destroyed by passing an electrical current through it. Godzilla has also come out of the ocean to battle this new opponent, and together with the help of the military, he defeats Hedora at the last possible moment as the powerlines are broken.

CAUTION: A young boy is shown playing with a very large knife, and people are dissolved instantly, leaving only their skeletons behind. This movie features the worst theme song of all time.

GODZILLA'S REVENGE

Simitar Entertainment
1969
70 minutes
Directed by: Inoshiro Honda
Starring: Machiko Naka, Kenji Sahara
   Tomori Yazaki
MPAA rating: not rated

A lonely victim of neighborhood bullies, Ichiro goes to Monster Island through the power of his imagination, where he meets Minia, the young son of Godzilla. Minia is a self-proclaimed coward who knows he must learn to fight his own battles, and at the insistence of Godzilla — whose anger Minia greatly fears — Minia gamely takes on a variety of monsters with varying degrees of success. (On Monster Island the chief entertainment seems to be fighting other monsters!) Encouraged by the lessons in self-defense, Ichiro returns home fully capable of dealing not only with the neighborhood bullies, but with the evil thieves who kidnap him as well.

CAUTION: Much fuss is made about the fact that both of Ichiro's parents must go to work and Ichiro's social problems are all presented as stemming from this. Ichiro's mother even weeps from the guilt she experiences over neglecting her son. In one scene, possibly meant to depict the normal behavior of a child, Ichiro talks with his mouth full of half-chewed food. A masterpiece of offensive dubbing, this film features both Ichiro and his young girl friend (possibly dubbed by the same person!) speak in irritating broken English. The voice characterization for Minia is especially frightful.

GO: *Godzilla's Revenge* is basically a showcase for scads of monsters, with some out-of-date social commentary that kids will love and parents will run screaming from.

✗ THE GOLDEN VOYAGE OF SINBAD

(continued on next page)

Columbia Home Video
1973
105 minutes
Directed by: Gordon Hessler
Starring: Tom Baker, John Phillip Law,
     Caroline Munro
MPAA rating: G

When a strange bat-like gremlin flies over Sinbad's ship and one of his men fires an arrow at it, the creature drops a golden amulet on the deck. This, Sinbad recovers, and in so doing earns the everlasting enmity of Prince Koora, who is versed in every black art. Pursued by the evil prince, Sinbad comes under the protection of the masked vizier of a great city, a man who was terribly burned by the dark magic of that same evil prince. The vizier too, possesses an amulet and it turns out that if it and Sinbad's amulet are placed before a great spiritual power in the Temple of Many Faces, absolute power will be granted. And so, Sinbad begins his voyage to the islands of the Temple, accompanied by a drunk named Haroon and a beautiful slave-girl named Marianna, and followed by Prince Koora. After a host of adventures (including a battle with a six-armed Kali and a fight between a centaur and a huge griffin), Sinbad confronts Koora in the Temple. But Koora has arrived first and now possesses the power.

✗STOP: At one point, a sinister witch invokes an incarnation of the devil with a frightening face and a malevolent voice.

CAUTION: The prince makes the figurehead of Sinbad's ship come alive and this may be too much for young viewers.

GO: Sinbad makes a distinctive statement about slavery and respect for others. He tells the slave girl that no human being has the right to own another.

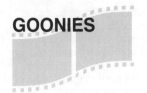

GOONIES

Warner Home Video
1985
114 minutes
Directed by: Richard Donner
Starring: Sean Astin, Corey Feldman,
     Kerri Green, Anne Ramsey
MPAA rating: PG

A group of young outcasts called the Goonies is being forced to disband because their neighborhood is being torn down by developers. (There has been a foreclosure on mortgages and none of their families has the money to buy their homes.) On the last day they are together, the Goonies happen upon an authentic seventeenth-century treasure map in the attic of one of the boy's homes. Hoping to find the treasure and help their parents out (so the Goonies can stay together) they follow the map and encounter a counterfeiting gang, newly escaped from prison. They are chased through subterranean tunnels, lagoons and caverns, and they encounter a dead man in a freezer, lots of gruesome skeletons, booby traps and a deformed man with piglet ears who turns out to be a good friend. They, of course, find the treasure, save their parents' homes from the developers and catch the counterfeiters. They even discover the value of paying attention during your piano lessons.

CAUTION: The film is very loud, with aggressive music, lots of screaming and noise from things blowing up and falling apart. In one scene, a boy is locked in a freezer with a dead man who is quite white and green, and in another, the counterfeiters threaten to put a boy's hand in a blender in an effort to make him "talk." There is some fighting and there are lots of skeletons with creatures crawling out of their mouths. Also two teenagers in the gang even in dangerous situations manage to sneak long kisses.

GO: With extraordinary special effects, the film is generally good clean fun — an exciting adventure in true Spielberg style.

CAUTION: This film is replete with sexual vocabulary, most of which is in the lyrics to songs. Rizzo has sex with one of Danny's friends in a car; he has a condom, but it breaks and they go ahead anyway.

GO: In spite of its overt sexuality this film is popular with girls, mainly because the clothes, cars, hairdos and songs of the '50s are depicted in a fun way. There are fabulous song and dance numbers throughout the film and plenty of sight-gags.

GREASE

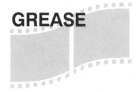

Paramount Home Video
1977
110 minutes
Directed by: Randal Kleiser
Starring: John Travolta, Olivia Newton-John, Stockard Channing
MPAA rating: PG

High school students Danny and Sandy have a wonderfully innocent, romance-filled summer at the beach before Sandy has to go back to Australia. School starts again at Rydell High where Danny is the leader of a group of over-sexed, unruly and immature young men who call themselves the T-Birds. (Their girlfriends, the Pink Ladies, are their ideal counterparts.) Danny brags to his friends about his outrageous summer when he "scored" and is horrified to see goody two-shoes Sandy at school (her plans changed). Danny's jealous ex-girlfriend wastes no time in telling Sandy all about his reputation. Meanwhile Danny tries his best to reform in order to win Sandy's respect. But it doesn't quite work and it's up to Sandy to find a way to bring them together.

GREASE II

Paramount Home Video
1982
114 minutes
Directed by: Patricia Birch
Starring: Maxwell Caulfield, Lorna Luft, Michelle Pfeiffer, Adrian Zmed
MPAA rating: PG

Stephanie Zinnoni, suffering from boredom, is fed up with being someone's "chick" and longs for something more exciting that the Pink Ladies. Excitement comes in the form of a mysterious and handsome motorcycle rider who appears out of nowhere whenever she is in need of help. She pines for this romantic vision, completely unaware that he is really the academic exchange student who is tutoring her.

CAUTION: The video includes the song "Reproduction" which is often edited out when the film is aired on television. There is some coarse language.

GO: With its silly sight gags and terrific song-and-dance routines, and with far less sexual innuendo than *Grease*, *Grease II* is a big favorite with this age group.

THE GREAT MUPPET CAPER

CBS/Fox
1981
98 minutes
Directed by: Jim Henson
Starring: John Cleese, Charles Grodin,
  Diana Rigg, Jack Warden

When investigative reporters Kermit the Frog and Fozzie Bear completely miss the scoop on the robbery of fashion designer Lady Holiday's jewels, they are fired from the newspaper and vow to travel to England to interview Lady Holiday and catch the thieves themselves. Meanwhile, Miss Piggy arrives in London hoping to become a fashion model for Lady Holiday, but is hired as her secretary instead. And when Kermit arrives for his interview and mistakes Miss Piggy for Lady Holiday, Miss Piggy keeps up the charade until the real Lady Holiday is robbed again. Gonzo gets a shot of Lady Holiday's parasitic brother Nicky stealing her diamond necklace, but the picture is destroyed. And when Miss Piggy goes on the runway as a last-minute replacement, Nicky plants the jewels on her and she is thrown in jail. In the end, Gonzo overhears Nicky and the models planning their next heist, and the Muppets (including Miss Piggy, who has broken out of jail) save the day.

CAUTION: The odd scene may be upsetting for small children. Miss Piggy is in jail with a group of snarly, scary-looking women and in the end she beats up Nicky and the thieves. In one scene, a man admits that he's out with another woman while his wife is at home.

GO: In the great Muppet tradition, the music is lively. This is a film that can be enjoyed by young and old alike.

GRYPHON

Public Media Video
1988
58 minutes
Directed by: Mark Cullingham
Starring: Amanda Plummer, Alexis Cruz,
  Nico Hughes
MPAA rating: not rated

Ricky Carreros is a tough kid who's continually getting into trouble both at school and at home because of his maliciously satirical drawings. But his life is transformed the day that the utterly bizarre Miss Ferenczi comes to his class as a substitute teacher, enthralling some students and repulsing others with her unorthodox lecture material. She teaches the class about magical things — mythical creatures, her family's royal ancestry, and angels that walk the earth in formal evening wear, listening to the sounds of humans singing — and Ricky is enthralled. He even researches these things when he's at home and, inspired by her description of a gryphon, makes a beautiful drawing of one and gives it to her. However, his new-found love of lore and learning causes a rift between himself and his former gang. Despite this falling out, Ricky finds that Miss Ferenczi's influence has somehow had a positive effect on his life. He develops a close friendship with another classmate, and also grows closer to his mother and his once-despised stepfather. In the end, a group art project initiated by Ricky brings him and his friend and gang leader Hector back together again. Based on a short story by Charles Baxter.

CAUTION: There is one non-graphic fist-fight between Ricky and Hector, but there are no bruises or broken bones.

GO: This is a wonderful story about the transformative power of trust, beauty and imagination.

✗ HAPPILY EVER AFTER

World Vision Home Video
1993
74 minutes
Directed by: John Howley
Starring the voices of: Edward Asner, Irene Cara, Carol Channing, Dom DeLuise, Phyllis Diller, Zsa Zsa Gabor, Sally Kellerman, Tracey Ullman

This is the continuing story of the Prince and Snow White. The happy couple are now pledged to be married, and the wicked queen's a goner. Then the late queen's brother, the powerful sorcerer Lord Maliss, makes an appearance. Learning of his sister's fate, he vows revenge on Snow White and her fiancée, changes himself into a dragon-like creature, and falls upon the happy couple. Maliss captures the Prince but Snow White escapes into the enchanted forest, only to find herself at the cottage of her old friends the seven dwarfs. She then discovers that the seven dwarves have opened up a new mine somewhere else, and that their

cousins, seven female dwarfs, have moved into their old digs. Snow White and the new dwarfs, who have powers over various elements of creation (sunlight, earth, water, animals, night, etc.) then join forces and embark on a quest to the Realm of Doom to learn what dreadful fate has befallen the Prince. During their journey, the group is aided by a mysterious, hunched shadowy figure who is tortured by the sight of his own reflection. After a series of adventures, everything works out all right.

✗ STOP: Beware the commercials right at the end of the video.

CAUTION: Lord Maliss' dragon incarnation is threatening enough to frighten young children. The evil lord also sends a pack of hideous horned wolf-like creatures to attack the protagonists, whose peril is clearly depicted.

GO: The figure animation is inconsistent, but the backgrounds are absolutely first-rate, and the story features good voice-overs from a star-studded cast. ∎

THE HARDY BOYS: ACAPULCO SPIES (Vol. 8)

MCA
1977
47 minutes
Directed by: Keith Atkinson
Starring: Shaun Cassidy, Parker Stevenson
MPAA rating: not rated

Fenton Hardy, the boys' famous detective father, desperately summons his sons to Mexico to bring him an important file. Upon arriving, they are to register at their

219

hotel under false names and await a contact who will use a prearranged code. But when two American girls, Jackie and Sue, accidentally use the code phrase, Frank and Joe think they've met the contacts and there is some confusion. Then the boys receive a dinner invitation from a professed friend of their father's, Cartell, and they accept, only to become involved in a cat and mouse game with the evil enemy agent who holds their father prisoner. When that agent kidnaps Jackie, the boys go after him.

CAUTION: A thug kidnaps Fenton, and his jailers try to starve him. There is some mild innuendo when the boys think the girls are the contacts; the girls misunderstand what the boys are talking about (let's get down to business, etc.).

GO: These made-for-TV adventures are harmless.

Other titles in the series are:
The Flickering Torch Mystery (Vol. 2)
The Mystery of King Tut's Tomb (Vol. 6)
The Mystery of the African Safari (Vol. 7)
The Mystery of the Flying Courier (Vol. 4)
The Mystery of Witches Hollow (Vol. 1)
The Secret of Jade Kwan Yin (Vol. 3)
Wipe-Out (Vol. 5)

AGES 6 TO 10

HARRY AND THE HENDERSONS

MCA
1987
101 minutes
Directed by: William Dear
Starring: Don Ameche, Melinda Dillon,
    John Lithgow, Lainie Kazan
MPAA rating: PG

An "average American family" meets a Sasquatch when they are on vacation. They accidentally hit "Harry" with the car, and figuring they've killed him, take him home on the roof-rack. But that night Harry regains consciousness. He creates havoc, and as he's trashing the Hendersons' house, hunting enthusiast George points his rifle at Harry. Their eyes meet, and George withdraws when he realizes that Harry is a sentient being. And even though they quickly grow to love him, it soon becomes obvious to the Hendersons that they must return Harry to his home — but not without difficulty, and not before he changes their and other people's attitudes toward creatures of the wild.

CAUTION: Startling scenes include those in which Harry pops his head into the car and surprises George while he is driving. Harry is shot at by an obsessed hunter, but he doesn't get hit. The Hendersons own a sports store that features guns. Minimal swearing.

GO: This is the film from which the television show originated. It is a comedy so none of the conflicts are particularly violent. Sympathy for creatures of the wild and the idea that ignorance can cause fear are explored. The family is a happy, solid one, and the ending is magical.

HOMEWARD BOUND: THE INCREDIBLE JOURNEY

Walt Disney Home Video
1992
84 minutes
Directed by: Duwayne Dunham
Starring the voices of: Don Ameche,
    Sally Field, Michael J. Fox
MPAA rating: G

This is a remake of the 1963 classic *The Incredible Journey*, after Sheila Burnford's book of the same name. Unlike the original, this effort features narration from the point of view of Chance, a young adopted dog who is always getting into trouble. He lives with Shadow, a faithful elderly dog, the pristine and haughty feline Sassy, and their human family. When circumstances force their family to leave them with other people in the country, the animals believe they've been abandoned. They set out on the most perilous journey of their lives, to return home. At first, they believe that their home is just over the next hill. They soon discover the immensity of the journey ahead of them, but resolve to press on anyway. In the course of their adventures they are chased by a grizzly bear and a mountain lion, and Sassy is swept away trying to ford a roaring river. They are reunited, but Chance gets stuck by a porcupine. They also find a lost little girl, and help her parents and the rangers to recover her. The animals are taken to a shelter to await their family, but this time they mistakenly believe that they will be put down, and make a daring escape. They are almost home when Shadow falls through some rotten boards into a hole and is badly hurt, but thanks to a pep talk from Chance he regains his strength, and all three make it home safe and sound.

CAUTION: The animals are in peril throughout. Mild language.

GO: Chance learns a lesson about sacrifice, friendship and love.

■

HONEY, I BLEW UP THE KID

Walt Disney Home Video
1992
100 minutes
Directed by: Randal Kleiser
Starring: Lloyd Bridges, Rick Moranis, Daniel and Joshua Shalikar, John Shea, Marcia Strassman
MPAA rating: PG

In the sequel to *Honey, I Shrunk the Kids*, Wayne Szalinski is up to his old inventing tricks, but this time, due to his previous successes, he has the backing of billionaire military-industrialist Clifford Sterling. However, things aren't going too well. A combination of the brightest minds in the country can't replicate Szalinski's original experiments, and when Szalinski puts in a little Saturday overtime (and sons come along) an experiment gone awry turns his two-year-old son, Adam, into a rapidly-growing mutant baby. Szalinski is then forced on a quest after his 100-foot son, to Las Vegas, of all places. But in the end, only Adam's mother can save him.

GO: Some of the effects are mind-boggling. This is a fun adventure film with tension but no violence.

HONEY, I SHRUNK THE KIDS

Walt Disney Home Video
1989
101 minutes
Directed by: Joe Johnston
Starring: Matt Frewer, Rick Moranis,
    Jared Rushton, Marsha Strassman
MPAA rating: PG

Wayne Szalinski is working on a device which will alter the size of objects, but despite his genius and dedication, the machine refuses to function. Then a neighbor's son, Ron, hits a ball through the Szalinski's upstairs window, striking the machine and accidentally making it fully functional. When Ron and his older brother, Russ, show up to get the ball and to apologize for the breakage, they and Wayne's children, Amy and Nick, go upstairs to the room and are instantly targeted by the machine and shrunk to the size of insects. Wayne returns to see the broken window and inadvertently sweeps up the children with the debris and puts them out with the garbage. The children emerge unscathed, but their only hope is to get back to the house, and to do this they must march through what has now become miles of backyard, a dangerous jungle full of unknown terrors. Meanwhile, Wayne finds the couch shrunk to miniature size, and when he sees that the kids are missing, realizes the terrible truth. While he and his wife conduct a frantic search in the backyard, the children, who couldn't get along at normal size, quickly unite and brave a succession of threats in their

voyage to the house. After a full night in the yard, they grab onto the Szalinski's dog and ride him into the house, where Wayne sees Nick in his cereal just before he puts the spoon in his mouth. Wayne repairs the machine and restores the children to their normal size.

Tummy Trouble, the Maroon Cartoon that precedes this feature, is a madcap, slapstick send-up of the medical profession starring Roger Rabbit and Baby Herman.

CAUTION: On their trek the children narrowly survive often-terrifying encounters with giant bees, ants, scorpions, sprinklers, lawn mowers, dogs and cigarette butts. In one scene, Amy almost drowns (Russ saves her with CPR) and in another Ron's gigantic pet ant is killed defending the kids against a scorpion-like creature; the children's grief is evident.

GO: A good kids-working-together film, this movie features stunning special effects. All of the negative relationships become positive in response to the crisis.

✗ HOOK

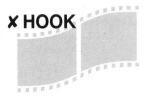

Columbia/Tri-Star
1991
142 minutes
Directed by: Steven Spielberg
Starring: Dustin Hoffman, Bob Hoskins,
    Julia Roberts, Robin Williams
MPAA rating: PG

Peter Banning, a successful acquisitions lawyer, takes his family to England where his philanthropist adoptive grandmother Wendy is dedicating a new wing for an orphans' hospital. While the

Bannings are at the ceremony, their children are kidnapped, and a note from none other than Captain Hook is left, daring Peter to retrieve them. Granny Wendy faces the difficult task of convincing Peter that he is the real Peter Pan — the boy who would never grow up, but did — and that his children really have been taken by Captain Hook. Peter is highly skeptical, until he himself is forceably spirited to Never Land by his old friend Tinkerbell. Once there, he finds that his children are indeed in Hook's clutches, and a deal is struck: Peter has three days to get back into Pan-type shape and fight Hook for his children. And this means that Peter must rediscover the wonderful ageless qualities of the child he once was, and learn, once more, how to fly. Based on characters by J.M. Barrie.

✗ STOP: Many small children are terrified by the abduction scene, which in true Spielberg style is filled with amazing special effects; it has moments that are truly intense and sinister. Other potentially upsetting scenes include one in which a mutinous pirate is put into a box with a scorpion, and another in which the child-hero Rufio is killed by Hook.

GO: Staggering visuals and inventive plot twists add to this family adventure film that was nominated for five Academy Awards.

I CAN DANCE

Kultur Video
1989
30 minutes
Directed by: Ron Kanter
Starring: Diana Kettler

Professional dancer Deborah Maxwell designed this video specifically for boys and girls ages seven and up. It follows a ballet lesson featuring five girls and a boy through a series of progressive levels of ballet. Pliés, center work, the five basic positions and more are covered to familiarize children with the facts (and fun) of ballet.

GO: This video shows exactly what a real ballet class is like.

IN SEARCH OF THE CASTAWAYS

Walt Disney Home Video
1962
98 minutes
Directed by: Robert Stevenson
Starring: Maurice Chevalier,
    Wilfrid Hyde-White, Hayley Mills
MPAA rating: G

In 1858, indomitable Mary Grant arrives with her brother Robert and their friend Professor Paganelle in Glasgow, Scotland. There they petition Lord Glenarbin and his dashing young son John (director of the ship line), to outfit an expedition to track down and rescue the children's father, Captain Grant, who has been shipwrecked and is presumed dead. At first His Lordship doesn't believe them, but soon Mary befriends John who wears his father down until at last he agrees to finance the search for Captain Grant. Thus begins an epic quest which takes them (among other places) to the southern latitudes of South America, up into the highlands of the Andes, through an earthquake, down a glacier, across the Indian Ocean and through a volcanic eruption.

GO: This is an improbable but exciting yarn for action fans of all ages. There is some platonic romance.

THE INCREDIBLE JOURNEY

Walt Disney Home Video
1963
80 minutes
Directed by: Fletcher Markle
Starring: Emile Genest, John Drainie,
　Tommy Tweed, Jan Rubes
MPAA rating: no rating given

Deep in the Canadian wilderness, John Longridge is caring for his godchildren's pets (Luath, a labrador retriever; Tao, a siamese cat; and Bodger, a bull terrier). One day when Longridge leaves on a duck hunting trip, the animals mistakenly think that he will not come back, and decide to make the long trek home alone—little knowing that home is 200 miles away. Luath leads the way, Bodger follows and Tao brings up the rear (when he feels like it). But Bodger finds the going rough and after the second day, the old dog is slowing down. Luath encourages him, and as the group struggles on they encounter a large black bear, dangerous rapids, a lynx, a porcupine and a hunter. And when Longridge returns, he realizes that the animals are on their way home, and begins to search for people who have sighted them. Sure that the animals have survived 100 miles at least, Longridge tells his godchildren what has happened, and they are devastated. But the family soon hears the barks of a dog and are delighted to see all of the animals come running home together, safe and sound after an incredible journey.

CAUTION: It is upsetting to some that the animals are hungry on their voyage and children may also be disturbed when the cat seems to be drowned in the river. This film may give some children the unrealistic hope that animals that run away will return home safely, even if they must travel great distances to do it.

GO: A wonderfully hopeful and fascinating story for animal lovers, *The Incredible Journey* shows the bond between animals and the bond between animals and their human caregivers. This film was remade in 1992 as *Homeward Bound: The Incredible Journey.*

■

THE INCREDIBLE MR. LIMPET

Warner Home Video
1963
99 minutes
Directed by: Arthur Lubin
Starring: Carole Cook, Andrew Duggan,
　Don Knotts, Jack Weston
MPAA rating: PG

Bookkeeper Henry Limpet has one dream — to live as a fish. And after being rejected by the U.S. navy, a magical fall into the waters off Coney Island brings about some amazing circumstances. Henry is transformed into a fish and upon the discovery that he can detect Nazi

U-boats with his underwater abilities, he becomes the navy's secret weapon. He finds fulfilment, success (in the form of a military decoration) and the love of a good fish in his new life under the sea.

CAUTION: A little dated, this film includes some female stereotyping and may be too slow for today's young audiences.

GO: The combination of live-action and animation makes this film accessible to young children.

✗ INTO THE WEST

C/FP
1992
97 minutes
Directed By: Mike Newell
Starring: Ellen Barkin, Gabriel Byrne,
   Ruaidhri Conroy, Ciaran Fitzgerald
MPAA rating: PG

In present-day Ireland, a mysterious wild horse follows an old man from a ruined gravesite near the sea back to Dublin. There, severely-depressed gypsy widower John Riley is struggling to provide for his two sons, asthmatic seven-year-old Ossie and his older brother Tito. When their grandfather (the old man) appears with the white horse, Ossie demonstrates his "gift" to pacify the horse. Ossie calls the horse Tirnanoke, and the boys ride him home to their run-down tenement building where they use the elevator to take the horse right into their apartment. After a few days the neighbors call the Board of Health, and John is powerless to save the horse. When Tirnanoke becomes extremely distressed Ossie calms him and agrees to let the officers take the horse away. The next day John goes to the police station to retrieve the horse, only to find it has been sold to a show-jumping syndicate. One day, on a video store TV, the boys see Tirnanoke competing in a show-jumping event and set out hitch-hiking across country to save their horse. They steal the horse right in the middle of a show and the chase is on. They elude the police, and end up with a price on their heads. They are elated, as this fits in very nicely with their image of themselves as cowboys. John and his gypsy friends track the boys back to the old ruined gravesite at the beach. When the police and gypsies converge on the beach, an altercation takes place that drives Ossie and the horse into the sea. As he is sinking into the water, Ossie has a vision of a beautiful lady's hand reaching for him. The next thing he knows he is carried from the water by his father but Tirnanoke has vanished. The gypsies burn the family's old caravan to put their mother's soul to rest and the image of Tirnanoke appears, suggesting that the horse is the spirit of the mother.

✗ **STOP:** The horse disappears into the sea (read: dies).

CAUTION: The father is on two occasions unable to help his distressed son. The boys are acutely aware of their father's drinking problem, and Ossie longs for his mother. John whacks a policeman on the face with a branch (drawing blood), trying to save Ossie. Because there is a magical quality to the story and the horse itself, little ones may not understand the supernatural connection between the horse and the mother. Thick Irish accents make the dialogue sometimes difficult to understand.

Note: the video starts with trailers for *Benefit of the Doubt* (a horror film) and *Strictly Ballroom* (a dance movie).

GO: An exciting and heart-warming story with moments of charm and virtually no violence. Horses are featured throughout.

✗ JASON AND THE ARGONAUTS

RCA/Columbia
1963
104 minutes approx.
Directed by: Don Chaffey
Starring: Todd Armstrong, Nancy Kovack
MPAA rating: G

When the warlord Polias overthrows King Aristo, Polias is enraged to learn that he will, in turn, lose his throne to Aristo's son, Jason. (It is ordained by Zeus.) So when Jason appears, speaking of a golden fleece which hangs on a tree at the end of the world — a fleece that has the power to heal, bring peace and rid the world of plague and famine — Polias encourages Jason to go on a suicidal mission to retrieve it. And so, Jason holds games to determine the greatest champions in Greece (one of whom is Hercules), and he has the strongest ship built (the Argo). With the powerful ship and the mighty crew, he sets out into unknown waters. In the course of their adventures they encounter the living gargantuan statue of Talos; Phineas, a blind sage who is tormented by harpies; Medea, a high priestess of Caucus; the seven-headed Hydra and an army of skeleton warriors.

✗ **STOP:** Polias stabs a woman (off-camera), and there is a blood-curdling scream and a realistic cleaving sound. This moment is totally out of character with the rest of the film.

CAUTION: The giant Talos, the hydra and the harpies may frighten young viewers.

GO: This is a more serious effort than the Sinbad movies, but with many of the same exciting characteristics and animation. Splendid sound effects add to the realism of the mythical characters.

JAZZ TIME TALE

f.h.e.
1992
29 minutes
Directed by: Michael Sporn
Narrated by: Ruby Dee
MPAA rating: not rated

Rose (whose father is a talent scout) is always left at home when her father goes out. Feeling lonely one night, she hides in the back of his car when he goes to the Lincoln theater. She doesn't go in, but instead takes a walk down the street for some air. And as she walks she hears the "jumpiest" music she has ever heard coming from one of the houses. She goes to the house where she meets a girl named Lucinda and learns that the music is that of a neighbor, Thomas Fats Waller. The girls become fast friends and when, at the Lincoln theater, the organist is unable to play, Fats takes over and Lucinda's family takes Rose along to hear him. Meanwhile, Rose's father has discovered that she is missing and after searching the streets finds her in the theater. She introduces him to Lucinda's family who draws his attention to Fats on the organ. His jazz playing brings down the house, and the rest is history.

GO: Beautifully animated by Bridget Thorne, this film provides a terrific glimpse of New York City in 1919. There is even a cartoon movie within the cartoon!

THE JOURNEY OF NATTY GANN

Walt Disney Home Video
1985
101 minutes
Directed by: Jeremy Kagan
Starring: John Cusack, Lainie Kazan, Meredith Salenger, Ray Wise
MPAA rating: PG

During the Great Depression, Sol Gann is forced to travel west to the timberlands of Washington State to find work, leaving his young daughter, Natty, in the care of a sleazy hotel manager. But when life becomes unbearable, Natty strikes out west alone to find her father. Thus begins an incredible journey. On her way, Natty happens on a gruesome pit fight between a wolf and another dog. When the wolf wins, it escapes with a spectacular leap over the drunken spectators. Later that night, a chance encounter brings Natty face to face with the wolf; she shows it kindness, and it begins to follow her, even bringing her a rabbit when she is starving. Then Natty falls in with a group of thieving tramps, gets arrested and is sent to an orphanage (which is

more like a prison camp). She makes her escape, finds her wolf and (after a considerable trek accompanied by a tough young drifter she meets on the way) is finally reunited with her father.

CAUTION: People are generally portrayed as being rude and hard (it is, after all, a hard time). Also of concern may be the pit fight and a scene in which Natty is molested by a truck driver when she accepts a ride.

GO: This is an exciting adventure film with a terrific musical score.

✗ KIDNAPPED

Walt Disney Home Video
1960
94 minutes
Directed by: Robert Stevenson
Starring: Peter Finch, James MacArthur, Peter O'Toole
MPAA rating: not rated

After his father's death, David Balfour, an honest, high-spirited young man, sets out across the highlands of Scotland. On the strength of a letter delivered to him after his father's death, David goes to his mysterious uncle Ebenezer's half-finished castle, the House of Shaws (cursed twelve hundred and nineteen times by a witch), and stays with the suspicious skinflint. But when Ebenezer arranges an "accident" for David, David begins to suspect the worst. Sure enough, Ebenezer conspires with the sinister Captain Hosesan to trick David aboard Hosesan's ship, intending to send him to the Carolinas and sell

AGES 6 TO 10

him off as an indentured servant. Enroute, an accident brings rebel fighter Alan Breck Stewart aboard, and when Hosesan and his evil first mate Mister Shawn plot to kill him, David stands with Stewart against the entire crew. They triumph, but Stewart himself is a vainglorious, quarrelsome handful, and David is subsequently drawn into a harrowing series of events which lead him into the maelstrom of Scottish clan feuding and, eventually, back to the House of Shaws and a confrontation with his miserly uncle.

✗STOP: During the voyage, the cabin boy is abused and killed by Mister Shawn. There is a bloodcurdling scream, and then the boy's body is carried out of the deckhouse.

CAUTION: There is heroic violence. Alan and David hold off an entire crew of sailors at half-sword and the fighting is intense. In one scene, David dangles from the highest parapet of the castle.

GO: This is a stirring, action-packed adventure replete with colorful characters (including a debut cameo by Peter O'Toole). ∎

THE KNIGHTS OF THE ROUND TABLE

MGM/UA
1953
116 minutes
Directed by: Richard Thorpe
Starring: Felix Aylmer,
    Stanley Baker, Anne Crawford, Mel Ferrer,
    Ava Gardner, Rod Taylor
MPAA rating: not rated

In feudal England, Morgan le Fey and her champion Mordred meet Arthur and Merlin to contest the right of kingship of Britain. (Arthur is the illegitimate son of the last king, while Morgan is the king's legitimate daughter.) They put their claims to the test against Excalibur, a sword embedded in a stone, and Arthur prevails by pulling the sword clear. Knights from all over flock to Arthur's standard, including Lancelot and his companions. Soon thereafter, Arthur and Lancelot journey to Stonehenge for a conference of rival barons, which breaks down and turns into a skirmish. War rages between the rival factions, but Arthur wins the climactic battle and pardons his foes, including Mordred. Arthur then creates the famous round table and, as time passes, he and his knights survive campaigns and adventures. All the while, though, Lancelot wrestles with his love for Arthur's bride, Guinevere. When Morgan and Mordred become suspicious of his desires, they spring on the lovers, leaving them no option but to flee. Lancelot returns and tries to explain to Arthur, but the king sends Guinevere to a convent and has Lancelot banished. Then Mordred and Arthur war on each other, and Lancelot returns again, too late; Arthur lies dying. It is up to Lancelot to seek out Mordred and settle the issue in a combat to the death.

CAUTION: There is minimal heroic violence.

GO: This not very accurate rendition of Malory's *Morte d'Arthur* should at least get children interested in the legend. And certainly, it's got enough good clean knights-in-armor action for young fans of chivalry. ∎

✗ LABYRINTH

Nelson
1986
102 minutes
Directed by: Jim Henson
Starring: David Bowie, Jennifer Connelly
MPAA rating: PG

Teenager Sarah lives in a fantasy world. She is constantly acting out the part of heroic princesses from books. And when she must baby-sit her baby half-brother, Toby, and he wails and cries interminably, Sarah's fury knows no bounds. She grabs her little brother and screams a poetic entreaty to the Goblin King to come and take the baby away. Nothing happens, of course, but as Sarah pauses in the doorway of her brother's room, she turns back and quietly adds that she really *does* wish that the goblins would come. And sure enough, seconds later, Toby's crying abruptly stops. Sarah rushes back into the room and Toby is gone; there are goblins all over the house. Then the sinister Goblin King appears and informs her that her wish has been granted. Sarah tries to explain that she didn't really mean it, at which point the Goblin King lays down the law. In the land of the goblins, she will have thirteen hours to solve the Labyrinth, reach the Goblin King's castle and rescue her brother. If she is unable to complete the test in the time allotted, Toby will become one of the goblins. Sarah has no choice; she sets out through the enormous maze, encountering a host of bizarre characters (some of which she befriends) and resisting the Goblin King's crafty intrigues along the way. In the end, Sarah makes it through the Labyrinth in time, besieges the goblin castle with her brave friends and confronts the Goblin King in his eerie sanctuary. There, she pronounces the words which will send the King to oblivion, and return her and her brother to safety.

✗ **STOP:** The scene in which the goblins come into Sarah's house is definitely too scary for little ones.

CAUTION: Certain images in this film may disturb or frighten the young crowd. In one scene, Sarah, in a daze, encounters Muppet witches who resemble bag ladies and who burden her down with toys and stuffed animals in a replica of her room. In another, Sarah takes a bite of a poisoned apple and, in the grip of a trance, dances with the Goblin King at a strange party.

GO: This is a terrific film about shedding selfishness and growing up, without losing the essential joy of youth. A plethora of Henson creatures and visual ideas make this a top favorite film with kids six to ten.

THE LAST UNICORN

f.h.e/ITC
1982
84 minutes
Directed by: Jules Bass,
   Arthur Rankin
Starring the voices of: Alan Arkin, Jeff Bridges,
   Mia Farrow, Angela Lansbury,
   Christopher Lee, Keenan Wynn
MPAA rating: G

The Last Unicorn, having become lonely in her solitude, bids farewell to her beautiful forest and sets out

229

on an epic journey to look for other unicorns. Her journey spans many seasons, and on the way she encounters Mommy Fortune's Midnight Carnival and is imprisoned. There she learns of the Red Bull, a huge magic-spawned monster who (at the bidding of King Haggard) has been hunting down all of the unicorns and pushing them to the ends of the earth. And so, after escaping the carnival with the help of a not-very-good magician named Shmendrick, the Last Unicorn, Shmendrick and a hardened outlaw named Molly Grue venture into the desolate domain of King Haggard. That very night the monster is released, and as it is closing on the Unicorn, Shmendrick in desperation yells out the spell: "Magic! Do as you will!" And the Unicorn is mysteriously transformed into a young woman, whom they name the Lady Amalthea. The trio go to the fortress, where they meet King Haggard and his son, Prince Leer, and where they learn more about the destruction of the unicorns. It turns out that a prophecy has foretold that a unicorn will bring about Haggard's doom, so he has been getting rid of the unicorns by throwing them into the sea where they become the surging white crests of the waves. When King Haggard realizes who Amalthea really is, he unleashes the Red Bull again. But Prince Leer (who has fallen in love with Amalthea) comes to her aid, and when he is struck down, the Unicorn finally fights back, driving the Red Bull into the sea, freeing all of the unicorns and sending King Haggard plunging amidst his crumbling castle to his doom.

CAUTION: This animated film has scared a lot of kids, and the Red Bull is really terrifying. A huge harpy kills Mommy Fortune, and we see from the back the vulture-like form hunched over her body, obviously feeding. A tree turns into a lascivious creature and hugs the young wizard suggestively. Some children are upset at the loneliness of the unicorn.

GO: The children who like this film really like it m— possibly because of its overwhelming romanticism.

LET'S DRAW!

Random House Home Video
1992
35 minutes
Directed by: Malcolm Hossick
Narrated by: Brett Ambler

Based on the books by Colin Caket and Leon Baxter, this guide shows even the youngest artists how to find a way to draw by using basic principles and familiar shapes and figures.

■

LET'S GET A MOVE ON! A KID'S VIDEO GUIDE TO A FAMILY MOVE

KidVidz
1990
30 minutes
Directed by: Jane Murphy, Karen Tucker

This is a well-paced live-action video about moving house. Using songs, animation and recreated situations the video deals with the concerns children will have about such things as prospective buyers who visit the home, watching a room being taken apart and saying good-bye. Children are reminded that home is where the family is. Recommended for children aged four to ten, this tape includes an activity guide.

LIFE WITH MIKEY

Touchstone Home Video
1993
91 minutes
Directed by: James Lapine
Starring: Michael J. Fox, Nathan Lane, Cyndi Lauper
MPAA rating: PG

Michael Chapman is a has-been. Once he was the child star of the popular sitcom *Life With Mikey*. Now he's thirty-one years old, partners with his brother in Chapman and Chapman, a two-bit talent agency which has one star client, Barry Corman, a horrible, egomaniacal, eleven-year-old cereal commercial veteran. One day Michael gets his pocket picked by Angie, a wise-cracking street kid, and when he subsequently witnesses her talking her way out of a jam he realizes that her acting ability is without parallel. He lands her an audition for a commercial at a huge cookie company, and Angie scores big. There's one catch: the cookie commercial is a few weeks away, and Angie, who's living with her sister and her sister's bonehead boyfriend, finds it impossible to concentrate on her lines. She

literally forces her way in to Michael's life, moving into his apartment. Michael in turn reluctantly takes her under his wing, making sure she attends school and becoming more sensitive to her needs. But as the two grow closer and closer, Michael understands that Angie's most important need is to be reconciled with her real father, a recovering substance abuser.

CAUTION: In order to win the repulsive child star Barry back to the agency, Angie meets him in a swank restaurant, in a femme-fatale parody. The parody may well be lost on the younger viewers, leaving a rather dreary "feminine wiles" message.

GO: A decent film about love, trust and understanding, with excellent performances from the children and some truly funny moments.

✗ LION KING

Walt Disney Home Video
1994
85 minutes (approx)
Directed By: Roger Allers, Ron Minkoff
Starring the voices of: Matthew Broderick, James Earl Jones, Moira Kelly, Whoopi Goldberg, Jeremy Irons, Robert Guillaume
MPAA rating: G

NOTE: At the time of publication, the Lion King is not available on video; however, due to its high profile, its continuing theatrical release, and the controversial nature of its content, we have included it in this book.

Simba, a young cub, is born to the lion king Mufasa and his queen Sarabi. With the coming of the Heir, there is great joy at Pride Rock and in the surrounding lands; however, not everyone rejoices. The king's evil brother Scar lusts for the throne and sees Simba's arrival as yet another obstacle in his path to power. To achieve his dream of becoming ruler, Scar enlists the aid of three odious hyenas, who are chafing under Mufasa's rule. Scar then tricks Simba and his best friend Nala, a young lioness cub, into going to an elephant graveyard, where the three hyenas are lying in wait. Mufasa arrives just in time to save the cubs. The resourceful Scar then concocts another nefarious scheme. This time he tricks Simba into a canyon, then has his hyena henchmen stampede a herd of wildebeests into the gorge. At the same time, in feigned terror, Scar summons Mufasa to save Simba. Mufasa succeeds in getting his son to safety, but as he himself clings desperately to the cliff above the rampaging herd, Scar appears above him and claws Mufasa's paws. Mufasa falls to his death. Scar then suggests to Simba that his mother will hate him when she hears he is responsible for his father's death. Simba flees. Scar sends his hyenas to kill Simba, but the cub escapes through a thorn patch and races out into the desert to almost certain death. Scar then returns to Pride Rock and proclaims himself king, backed up by an army of hyenas. Meanwhile, Simba is rescued from the wastes by a warthog and a meercat, two outcasts. In their freewheeling company, he grows into a young lion. Then one day Nala is out hunting far from Pride Rock, and she and Simba meet. Nala insists that Simba return and reclaim his rightful place, as he is needed desperately. At first Simba is unwilling to accept the

responsibility, but then Rafiki, a mystic ape-shaman, conjures up a vision of Simba's father, which convinces him to return and set things right. Simba goes back to Pride Rock, rallies the lionesses, and defeats Scar and his army of hyenas. In the end, Simba and Nala give birth to yet another Heir, and the circle of life continues.

✗**STOP:** The incredible effects and stylish camera work only reinforce the tremendous impact of the state-of-the-art animation. It's almost impossible to calculate the impression this can have on the very young. Given the film's mature story and content, we're surprised the film got a family rating. In Mufasa's death scene, the sneering Scar places his paws on his brother's, as if to assist. The camera then closes in on Mufasa's horror-filled eyes as he gauges Scar's real intentions, and he screams in pain as Scar lacerates his paws, causing him to fall to his death. Simba witnesses his father's terrible death, and his reaction, during and after, is authentic. Late in the film, when Sarabi defies Scar, he brutally backhands her across the face, knocking her unconscious. (This is *totally* gratuitous. By now, we already *know* Scar is evil.) In the final combat, Scar is torn to pieces by his rebelling hyena army.

CAUTION: Scar convinces Simba that the cub is responsible for his father's death, and Simba lives with guilt for *years.* The fight between Scar and Simba is intense, played in slow-motion, and the blows of paw on face, clearly depicted, are accompanied by imposing sound effects. As the wildebeest herd thunders down upon Simba, the camera zooms in on the cub's terror-filled face. During the confrontation with Scar, Simba is hanging from a cliff, and Scar places his paws on Simba in exactly the same way he did with his father.

GO: This is not really a children's film, and adults should exercise caution before they take their little ones to see it. It is in fact an animated film for adults, and viewed from this perspective it is a refreshing change from the usual adult animated fare, which is mostly hyper-violent, ultra-sexist, and immature. The Lion King's story line is sophisticated (the time-honored plot of the usurper and the Heir in hiding), the voice-overs are superb, and the animation — especially the far away shots and backgrounds — is stunningly beautiful.

LITTLE HEROES

Select Home Video
1991
78 minutes
Directed by: Craig Clyde
Starring: Raeanin Simpson, Katherine Willis
MPAA rating: G

Ten-year-old Charley Wilson's family is poor, and she worries because, although her parents love each other, they fight about the situation. At school Charley is taunted by the other more affluent girls and her only real friends are her dog, Fuzz, and Alonzo, the elderly farmer who lives next door. One day, Charley is invited to Carol Evans's birthday party, and Charley's mother uses her mad money to buy fabric and make Charley a dress. But Carol's mother uninvites her, and Charley, humiliated and unable to tell her mother what has happened, dresses up anyway and pretends to go to the party. A few days later, Charley finds Alonzo in the field; he has just cut his thumb off in a farm machine. Charley runs to get help and is later surprised to see Mrs. Evans at the hospital. It turns out that Alonzo is Mrs. Evans's father. She explains to Charley that she was mean to her because Charley's poverty reminded her of her own

tough childhood. And in the end, when Fuzz is found dead (poisoned by a piece of meat Alonzo left out to catch a fox), Alonzo and Mrs. Evans find a way to thank Charley for her kindness by buying her a new puppy. This film is based on a true story.

✗**STOP:** The dog dies! There is a sentimental montage with music reminiscing about the good times Charley and Fuzz had together. The box cover gives the impression through photos and words that this is more of an action film.

GO: This is a relationship film about tolerance and prejudice.

LITTLE WOMEN

MGM/UA
1949
122 minutes
Directed by: Mervyn LeRoy
Starring: June Allyson, Mary Astor,
    Rossano Brazzi, Peter Lawford,
    Janet Leigh, Margaret O'Brien,
    Elizabeth Taylor, Lucile Watson
MPAA rating: no rating given

The plot of the 1949 version of *Little Women* follows almost exactly the plot of the 1933 version.

CAUTION: Beth dies. The death is not overtly depicted, but anyone over five is going to get the idea.

GO: *Little Women* is an American paean to innocence, independence, and the true heart.

∎

LOOK WHAT I FOUND: MAKING CODES AND SOLVING PROBLEMS

Pacific Arts Video/MCA Home Video
1992
45 minutes
Starring: Amy Purcell

Host Amy Purcell shows kids how to become junior detectives with fingerprint games, secret codes, tin can telephones, code wheels and treasure hunts. Recommended for children aged five to twelve.

●

LOOK WHAT I GREW: WINDOWSILL GARDENS

Pacific Arts Video/MCA Home Video
1992
45 minutes
Starring: Amy Purcell

Amy Purcell's easy-to-do gardening experiments include seed viewers, sprouting vegetable tops, apple finger puppets, terrariums and garden journals. Suitable for children aged five to twelve, this film is recommended by the National Gardening Association.

LOOK WHAT I MADE: PAPER PLAYTHINGS AND GIFTS

Pacific Arts Video/MCA Home Video
1990
45 minutes
Starring: Amy Purcell

Amy Purcell teaches children to make piñatas, origami, paper hats, flower bouquets, newspaper hammocks and more. Winner of the Parent's Choice Award and the 1990 Action for Children's Television award, this video is recommended for children aged five to twelve.

THE LORD OF THE RINGS

HBO
1978
133 minutes
Directed by: Ralph Bakshi
MPAA rating: PG

In an indeterminate, ancient age, man shares the world, Middle Earth, with a variety of other intelligent bipeds — elves, dwarves, orcs (goblins) and hobbits (little furry-footed folk). In the story, a hobbit named Frodo Baggins unwittingly comes into the possession of the Ruling Ring (a plain gold ring which is a token of enormous power). The Ring is being sought by its owner, the dreadful

234

Sauron, who has already sent his ghastly servants, the Ringwraiths, out into Middle Earth to look for it. With this horrible crew closing in on him, Frodo takes to the road, and thus begins an epic journey through peril and war, as the film chronicles the adventures of Frodo and the companions he gathers with him on his quest to destroy the Ring.

CAUTION: This animated film based on the popular book is a remarkable effort, but it's incomplete, telling the story approximately until the halfway point, to the first stage of Frodo and Sam's journey into the dreadful realm of Mordor, and the seige of Helm's Deep. There are elements in this story which are likely to frighten small children; the ringwraiths, for example, are blood-curdling, red-eyed incarnations of evil. The sequel is *The Return of the King*.

GO: The look of the animation in this film is both unique and striking. (Frodo's ride to the river near Rivendell, with the dreadful Ringwraiths in swift pursuit is especially breathtaking.) Of course, when an animator takes on a masterpiece, read by millions, that animator risks coming under some criticism. But certainly this is a worthy effort, and perhaps a way to introduce young people to the epic.

■

THE LOVE BUG

Walt Disney Home Video
1969
108 minutes
Directed by: Robert Stevenson
Starring: Buddy Hackett, Dean Jones, Michele Lee, David Tomlinson
MPAA rating: G

Down-on-his-luck racecar driver Jim Douglas has cracked up so many cars that his sponsor is dumping

him. And his best friend and roommate Tennessee Steinmetz (a modern sculptor who uses the pieces of Jim's wrecks to create art), is trying to convince him to quit before he destroys himself on the track. But Jim is immovable and as he is drooling over a Jaguar at a local import dealership a little Volkswagen nuzzles up to him; in fact, the car won't leave him alone. It follows him home, and as a result he is arrested for grand theft the next morning, and forced to purchase the car. It soon becomes obvious that the "Love Bug" (Herbie) has a life of its own. And when they race, Herbie leaves the opposition in his dust. But Jim begins to attribute his new-found success solely to his own abilities, and it's up to his friends, and Herbie, to set him straight.

Other Herbie movies to try are:
Herbie Goes Bananas
Herbie Goes to Monte Carlo
Herbie Rides Again

CAUTION: One of the characters, Mr. Wu, is not portrayed in a particularly favorable light (he will not speak English until the subject of money is broached); in fact, there are a number of rather unfortunate depictions of Chinese-Americans in the film.

GO: This is a wonderful comic effort in the Disney tradition.

●

MAC AND ME

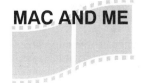

(continued on next page)

Orion
1988
99 minutes
Directed by: Stewart Raffill
Starring: Christine Ebersole, Jonathan Ward,
  Katrina Caspary, Lauren Stanley
MPAA rating: PG

The film opens in a distant solar system, where a family of aliens is scratching out a meager existence on an arid world. There a United States spacecraft lands, evidently taking samples, and inadvertently sucks up the curious family. And when the craft is recovered, the terrified aliens burst out of the compartment and escape from the scientific facility. One of the younger aliens hides in a van belonging to Janet and her sons Michael and Eric. The family is moving from Illinois to Sacramento, and they inadvertently take the alien with them. When they arrive at their new home, the alien moves in with them, causing havoc (for which Eric, who uses a wheelchair, is usually blamed). But Eric is suspicious and he and his new friend Debbie finally see the strange little alien, whom they call MAC (Mysterious Alien Creature). MAC's hijinks soon begin to attract attention, however, and a govern- ment capture group shows up when the teens go to a local burger joint. Eric is forced to flee with MAC on his lap and his older brother, Michael, shows up just in the nick of time with the van. They follow MAC's directions to the desert, where they find MAC's family hiding in an abandoned mine. The kids bring the alien family back, but when frightened police officers open fire on them in a parking lot and several cars are blown up, the massive explosion apparently kills them, and Eric as well. But, the aliens miraculously walk out of the fireball, revive Eric and stay to become American citizens.

CAUTION: The scene in which MAC is stuck to the windshield of a car may upset young viewers and the fire at the end of the film is also scary. *MAC and Me* is a blatant commercial for a certain fast-food chain.

GO: Not much reference is made to Eric's disadvantage; he is simply treated like any hero. Nor does the film fall into the soppy trap of having the aliens cure Eric of his disability.

THE MAGNIFICENT SIX-AND-A-HALF

MCA
1987
91 minutes
Starring: Michael Audreson, Ian Ellis,
  Brinsley Forde, Lionel Hawkes, Len Jones,
  Kim Tallmadge, Suzanne Togni
MPAA rating: no rating given

When Toby, Steve, Liz, Dumbo and Stodger are walking beside the river one afternoon, they spot two other children, Whizz and Pee Wee, on the bank. A dog is in trouble in the water, and Dumbo clumsily falls in to save it. It turns out that the dog belongs to a junkyard owner, so the children return it to its master and ask permission to use an old van in the junkyard as their gang's hideout. And when Whizz and Pee Wee want to join the gang, Pee Wee is turned away (she's too young) and Whizz is told that he must spend the night in a local haunted house to prove his worth. The rest of the gang, of course, decides to give him a good scare, but it backfires when they discover that there is a someone — or something — in the house. That someone turns out to be Pee Wee who snuck in by herself. This is just one of the many adventures included in this film.

CAUTION: There is a lot of slapstick humor in this film.

GO: *The Magnificent Six-and-a-Half* is curiously reminiscent of the famous *Our Gang* series of early film history.

●

THE MAN FROM SNOWY RIVER

CBS/Fox
1982
115 minutes
Directed by: George Miller
Starring: Tom Burlinson,
   Kirk Douglas, Sigrid Thornton
MPAA rating: PG

When a great wild stallion causes a stampede, killing Jim Craig's father, Jim leaves their small mountain ranch to learn about ranching in the lowlands. There, he seeks employment with a rich rancher named Harrison who has just purchased a colt worth a thousand pounds. And when the dangerously unruly colt nearly tramples Harrison's headstrong daughter, Jessica, Jim comes to her aid and Harrison hires him. Eventually, Jim tames the colt, and he and Jessica become close. Then one day, Harrison slaps Jessica during a heated discussion, and she rides off into the high country and falls from a cliff. Jim saves her, and on their way back to the ranch introduces her to Spur, a friend of Jim's who also happens to be her uncle and Harrison's twin brother. At home, Jessica's aunt tells her the

long-guarded family secret. Twenty years ago, Jessica's father and her uncle quarreled over a spirited young woman named Matilda. Harrison won her hand, but she still cared enough for Spur that Harrison wasn't sure that Jessica was his daughter and, in a jealous rage, he shot off his brother's leg. For bringing the long-buried story to life, Jim is told to leave the ranch. After Jim beats up two other hands who picked a fight with him, the hands set the colt loose and Jim is blamed. Jim retrieves the colt, captures the great wild stallion and, vowing to return for Jessica, rides off to reclaim his ranch.

CAUTION: There is some coarse language and during a fight in the bunkhouse Jim thumps a couple of bullies (no blood). Harrison slaps his daughter's face.

GO: This is an exciting adventure with a minimum of violence, incredible riding and spectacular scenery.

THE MIGHTY DUCKS

Touchstone Home Video
1992
104 minutes
Directed by: Emilio Estevez
Starring: Joss Ackland,
   Emilio Estevez, Joshua Jackson,
   Heidi Kling, Lane Smith,
   Josef Sommer
MPAA rating: PG

Gordon Bombay is a ruthless young Minnesota trial lawyer who lives his life on the edge. And when he is arrested for drunk driving and reckless endangerment, his powerful boss Gerald Duckworth gets him off relatively lightly...with community service. This service turns out to be time spent coaching the local hockey team, District Five. The team is pathetic and, once a pee-wee superstar himself, the competitive Bombay believes he's been consigned to his own personal hell; worse, Gordon's old team, the Hawks, is still coached by Coach Reilly, a success-oriented ogre who ruined Gordon's own youthful hockey experience. At first, Gordon is determined to beat him with his own win-by-any-means attitude. But when young Charlie Conroy refuses to cheat and quits the team, Gordon has second thoughts. He apologizes to his young charges, then proceeds to drill them in the fundamentals of good hockey. He gets them properly outfitted with the Duckworth firm's financial backing and District Five becomes the Ducks. The Ducks soon become the terror of the league, and despite pressure from his boss and friends Gordon sticks with his new-found principles. He and his team sneak into the playoffs, resulting in a final confrontation with Reilly and the Hawks.

CAUTION: There is minimal sport violence (body-checks, pucks in the head) and at the film's climax, two of the Hawks are ordered to knock the Ducks' star player out of the game. (He is viciously cross-checked into the goal post and taken out on a stretcher.) In one scene the boys ogle some discarded *Sports Illustrated* swimsuit issues and make generally rude comments.

GO: In an interview, Estevez indicated that he wanted to make a film that his own children could see, and he has succeeded. This is a rousing Cinderella sports epic, in which the sad-sack team effects a miraculous turnaround and rises to become champions. There are few suprises, but this a welcome entry for the six and up crowd.

AGES 6 TO 10

✗ MIGHTY MORPHIN POWER RANGERS

PolyGram Video
1993
25 minutes
Starring: Amy Jo Johnson, Walter Jones, Austin St. John, Thuy Trang, David Yost

This live-action television series has become wildly popular. The central characters are a group of teenagers from Angel Grove City who have been granted superpowers by Zordon, an interdimensional being trapped in a time warp that was created by his archenemy, the evil space sorceress Rita Repulsa. Zordon and his helpful automaton pal Alpha 5 have given the teenagers Power-Morphers, badges which transform their bearers into Power Rangers. Each Ranger has a special color and weapon, and each takes on the powers of a unique prehistoric creature when they morph into Dinozords, giant exoskeletal combat suits. The Dinozords in turn can combine forces to become the Megazord. Jason, the Red Ranger, uses a sword and has the power of the Tyrannosaurus Rex; Trini, the Yellow Ranger, uses daggers and has the power of the Sabertooth Tiger; Billy, the Blue Ranger, uses lances (actually sais) and has the power of the Triceratops; Zack, the Black Ranger, uses an axe and has the power of the Mastodon; and Kimberly, the Pink Ranger, uses a bow and has the power of the Pterodactyl. Many viewers of the TV show will be familiar with a sixth Ranger, Tommy; he was added later and does not appear in these episodes. Rita Repulsa, the villain of the series, is always determined to conquer Earth from her palace on the moon. She has a gallery of monster servants. Goldar looks like a blue wolf in gold samurai armor, Finster creates monster models out of putty and brings them to life, and comic relief is provided by Squatt (a blue troll) and Baboo (an ape-like creature with a Bullwinkle-like voice). Rita spies on the Power Rangers' activities with a telescopic device and can beam her monsters down to Earth to create havoc. In addition to Rita's destructive schemes, the Rangers also have to suffer the juvenile taunts of schoolyard bullies Bulk and Skull.

Vol. 1:
Day of the Dumpster

Written by: Tony Oliver and Shuki Levy
Directed by: Adrian Carr

Astronauts open a space dumpster on the moon and accidentally release Rita and her monsters. The teenagers fight off Rita's Putty Patrollers and force Goldar back to the moon.

Vol. 2: High Five

Written by: Steve Kramer
Directed by: Adrian Carr

Trini overcomes her fear of heights and Jason fights Bones.

Vol. 3: Food Fight

Written by: Cheryl Saban
Directed by: Robert Hughes

At a school food fair, Rita creates a new pig monster to menace Earth (the pig costume is dumb-looking but really disgusting: its forearms come out of its mouth). The pig eats all the Rangers weapons but when Trini and Billy feed it a spicy dish, it vomits up all the weapons. The Rangers combine their weapons into a single gun which fries the pig permanently.

Vol. 4:
Happy Birthday, Zack

Written by: Stewart St. John
Directed by: Jeff Reiner

Zack is upset when the other Rangers apparently forget his birthday. The day gets worse when Rita sends down the Knasty Knight to confront Zack, hoping the predicament will lure the other Rangers into danger.

Vol. 5:
No Clowning Around

Written by: Mark Hoffmeier
Directed by: Adrian Carr

Rita has set a trap at a local carnival, where the clowns are all Putty Patrollers in disguise and the head clown turns into Pineoctopus (he looks like an octopus crossed with a pineapple). He zaps little cousin Sylvia into a cardboard cutout, using her as bait for the Rangers.

Other titles in this series: The Green Ranger Mini-Series, Vols. 1-5.

✗STOP: The production values of this series are terrible and it is difficult for anyone over the age of about ten to watch without being distracted by the incredibly poor dubbing (virtually all the monster scenes are shot in Japan). It is worth paying some attention, though, in order to be aware of how sexist, racist, and violent the show is. Pink Ranger Kimberly in particular is an awful stereotype; her dialogue seems to consist solely of jokes about how much she likes shopping and how much fighting musses up her hair. It is also offensive that Asian-American Trini is the Yellow Ranger and that African-American Zack is the Black Ranger; one wonders why the Red Ranger isn't a native American. Bulk and another character, Ernie, perpetuate the idea that fat people are amusing and stupid. The monsters often have revolting characteristics: Bones can take off his own head and chuck it around, for example.

CAUTION: There is a great deal of fighting, consisting of martial arts moves, characters getting blasted by energy beams, people being hurled off cliffs and into walls, and generally excessive comic-book violence. This is probably of the greatest concern when it involves the Rangers out of costume as human teenagers, slugging it out with the Putty Patrollers. There are commercials for the tie-in toys at the beginning of the tapes.

GO: There's not much to recommend the series except that young viewers' minds must be stretched at least a little by all of its bizarre elements.

MOM AND DAD SAVE THE WORLD

Warner Home Video
1992
88 minutes
Directed by: Greg Beeman
Starring: Teri Garr, Eric Idle, Kathy Ireland, Jeffrey Jones, Jon Lovitz, Wallace Shawn
MPAA rating: PG

Tod, Emperor of Spengo, planet of idiots, has plans to destroy the planet Earth. But even as their visual detectors zero in on Woodland Hills, California (Earth's most vulnerable spot), Tod sees what he believes to be the most beautiful woman he has ever seen, frumpy Marge Nelson exercising beside the pool in her sweats. The nefarious Tod decides to delay the destruction of Earth for a single day, while he kidnaps the object of his affections. Meanwhile, Marge and her chronic complainer of a husband, Dick, are preparing for a fun anniversary weekend, but before they get very far, Tod has beamed the Nelsons across the galaxy. Marge is taken to a gilded tower and pampered in preparation for her upcoming wedding, while Dick is tossed in the dungeon. Thanks to Marge, Dick eventually escapes in a weird little aircraft. When he is shot down in the desert, he meets some not-very-intelligent tribesmen with whom he organizes a resistance. Using subterfuge only a moron would fall for, Dick and his followers enter Tod's fortress, rescue Marge and save the world; or rather, they would have saved the world, if it had ever really been in danger in the first place. And they have some great photos of their trip.

CAUTION: In one scene, Dick, bound and gagged, is jolted with electric current, and in another, guards surround him and punch him.

GO: Despite the few above-mentioned concerns, this is a mostly inoffensive, funny film suitable for children.

THE MOON STALLION

BBC
1985
95 minutes
Directed by: Dorothea Brooking
Starring: James Green, David Haig,
    Sarah Sutton
MPAA rating: no rating given

While accompanying her father on an archaeological dig in northern England, young blind Diana Purwell encounters the Moon Stallion, a magnificent wild white horse with whom she shares a strange, almost psychic relationship. The horse, it turns out, is the servant of the lunar goddess Diana, and it's being hunted down by Professor Purwell's patron, Sir George Mortenhurze, who wishes to exploit its tremendous power. The Moon Stallion engages Diana in a dangerous and mysterious adventure with mythological repercussions.

CAUTION: Sir George Mortenhurze dies, leaving behind his teenage daughter (Diana's friend) who is very upset. At the film's climax, an evil antagonist is stomped to death by the Stallion.

■

MONKEY TROUBLE

When gangsters hire a larcenous organ-grinder and his accomplice monkey to perform a big heist, they make him prove the monkey's skill by stealing from a test house. The house happens to belong to Eva, her mother, her police lieutenant stepfather and younger half-brother. Eva wants a pet desperately, but she is hopelessly disorganized and failing at school. After being threatened by the evil organ grinder, the monkey flees and seeks Eva out, intercepting her after school. She smuggles him home in her knapsack, names him Dodger, and then goes through the standard convolutions of attempting to keep the monkey's presence a secret. Eva's life gets complicated fast, especially since the monkey is a trained thief. The climax comes when Eva conspires to spend a weekend alone with the monkey at her absent father's house. Inevitably, Dodger's evil former master tracks her down, and her monkey's kleptomaniacal habits get her in dutch with just about everyone.

CAUTION: The organ grinder raises his hand to his son, and he grabs the monkey's throat at one point. The gangsters call an elderly woman an "old broad." They also grab the organ grinder and threaten him. The organ grinder chases Eva through her father's house. Her parents don't believe her when she tries to tell them the truth.

GO: Eva learns the value of responsibility.

Alliance
1994
97 minutes
Directed By: Franco Amurri
Starring: Thora Birch, Mimi Rogers,
Christopher McDonald, Victor Argo, Harvey
Keitel
MPAA rating: PG

AGES 6 TO 10

THE MOUSE AND
THE MOTORCYCLE

Strand VCI
1986
42 minutes
Directed by: Ron Underwood
Starring: Mimi Kennedy, Thom Sharp,
   Phillip Walker, Ray Walston
MPAA rating: no rating given

When the Gridleys arrive at the Mountainview Inn, eight-year-old Keith discovers that he has no one to play with. He does, however, have a couple of great toys, the best of which is a snazzy model motorcycle. The moment Keith leaves the room Ralph, a mouse who lives at the inn, tries it on for size and almost immediately becomes trapped in a garbage can. Sure he'll be thrown out with the trash, Ralph is relieved to be discovered by Keith, and the two become friends. With Keith's blessing, Ralph races around the inn and, despite his friend's warnings, loses the bike. Keith is upset; however, even though he is ill, he forgives Ralph for his carelessness. Then Keith becomes progressively sicker, and the required medicine is not available. But Ralph remembers having seen some in a cubbyhole in the inn, and after an epic search, finds the medicine and borrows Keith's toy ambulance to pick it up. And in a last happy scene, the motorcycle is discovered in a bin full of dirty laundry, and Keith generously gives it to Ralph for keeps. See our review for the sequel, *Runaway Ralph*. Based on a novel by Beverly Cleary.

GO: This film features a lively, humorous story and absolutely superb pixilation.

MRS. DOUBTFIRE

Fox
1993
125 minutes
Directed by: Chris Columbus
Starring: Pierce Brosnan, Sally Field,
   Harvey Fierstein, Robin Williams
MPAA rating: PG-13

Daniel Hillard, a hyperactive and often unemployed voice-over actor, is having continued marital problems with his interior designer wife Miranda. The relationship has been breaking down over the past 14 years and finally Miranda asks for a divorce. Their three children, Chris, Lydia and Natty, adore their father and are naturally upset at the unravelling of their lives. They do the best they can to adjust. Custody is awarded to Miranda with limited visitation rights for Daniel until he can keep a steady job. He is devastated and tells the judge he must see his children they are like food and air to him. Miranda places an ad for a housekeeper and through some subterfuge and a lot of help from his special effects make-up artist brother, Daniel (disguised as a mild-mannered British nanny) gets the job. He turns out to be a better man as a woman than he ever was as a man and brings long overdue order and harmony to the family. The only fly in the ointment is the courtship of Miranda by a very rich, handsome and wonderful ex-beau. The

AGES 6 TO 10

242

situation becomes more tense when Chris and Lydia discover the ruse. Then Daniel has two important appointments in his two different personas scheduled for the same time and place. After a lot of slapstick quick changes the truth is out. Miranda and Natty are shocked and Daniel is ostracized. But things work out in the end when Daniel lands the job of host on a children's television show as Mrs. Doubtfire and, with the court's conditions met, is able to see his children whenever he wishes. Based on *Alias Madame Doubtfire* by Anne Fine.

CAUTION: The film contains mild language and sexual innuendo. Stereotyping is present in the portrayal of Daniel's make-up artist brother as gay.

GO: The children are charming, well-behaved dreams. It is refreshing to see no one portrayed as the bad guy. The ending gives a thoughtful message about divorce without being preachy.

■

MYSTERIOUS ISLAND

Columbia Tristar Home Video
1961
101 minutes
Directed by: Cy Endfield
Starring: Michael Callan, Michael Craig,
   Joan Greenwood, Herbert Lom
MPAA rating: not rated

In 1865 five men escape from a Confederate prison in a hot air balloon and are wrecked over a supposedly deserted volcanic island. They are soon joined by two woman who survive a shipwreck and together they must battle some bizarre creatures, including a giant crab, a giant bee and a chick large enough to ride on. They find that these animal anomalies are the product of the infamous Captain Nemo's experimentation. And they must make an agreement with Nemo in order to escape the island before the volcano erupts. Special effects by Ray Harryhausen.

CAUTION: Pirates are shot and some people are lost at sea. There are skeletons. Nemo is crushed by a falling beam and dies with his eyes open. And for the most part the women in this film wear scanty clothes and run around being helpless.

GO: It's a great adventure film that holds up well for young viewers who are interested in an exciting movie that isn't too scary.

■

THE MYSTERY OF THE MILLION DOLLAR HOCKEY PUCK

Dal Productions
1975
89 minutes
Directed by: Jean Lafleur, Peter Svatek
Starring: Angele Knight, Michael Macdonald,
   Jean-Louis Millette
MPAA rating: not rated

Pierre, a promising young hockey player who adores the Montreal Canadiens, lives with his sister, Catou, at the Chicoutimi Orphanage. One day, he is sent to the florist's to pick up some daffodils, but he forgets his wallet in the shop and returns to overhear the details of a sinister plot.

Gangsters, operating out of the back of the shop, plan to smuggle a fortune in stolen diamonds into the United States inside one of the Canadiens' team hockey pucks. Startled, Pierre knocks over a flowerpot, and in his haste to get away, leaves his wallet behind again. Unable to convince the nuns of the trouble afoot and with the gangsters hot on his trail, Pierre collects his sister and gets ready to run. The gangsters arrive at the same moment, and the resourceful children wait until the gangsters have gone inside then climb into the back of their truck. And so, as stowaways, they begin their trek to Quebec City where they beat the gangsters to the jewels. Finally, during the confusion of a narrow escape at a Canadiens-Detroit Red Wings hockey game, the million dollar puck ends up on the ice in the middle of the action.

GO: This is a sweet film, exciting without violence, and great for young mystery fans. Pierre, initially worried about bringing his sister along, learns to appreciate her foresight and courage.

●

NANCY DREW: THE MYSTERY OF THE DIAMOND TRIANGLE (Vol. 2)

MCA
1977
47 minutes
Directed by: Noel Black
Starring: Pamela Sue Martin,
   George O'Hanlon, Jean Rasey
MPAA rating: no rating given

When trying for the coveted Diamond Triangle Award for airplane pilot excellence, Nancy Drew and her friend George see an automobile run off the road. But in their resulting investigation they find no trace of the car, and they learn that the road has been closed for a long time. Determined to unravel the mystery, Nancy finds the owner of the car — a car that he thought was locked up in his garage, but which now appears to have been stolen. Unfortunately, Morgan's car was a restored antique and the book value of the insurance is nowhere near the value of the car. And while Nancy's father, a lawyer, works out the insurance claim, the sheriff suspects Morgan of trying to swindle the insurance company (particularly when parts that were supposedly used to improve the vehicle are found still in the garage). In the end, when Nancy sets out to prove that Morgan has been framed, she discovers that a ring of car thieves have been operating in cahoots with an upstanding member of the community.

CAUTION: The music is a bit intense, and there is pushing and shoving.

GO: Nancy is shown as an intelligent, capable young woman.

Titles in the series are:
The Mystery of Pirate's Cove (Vol. 1)
A-Haunting We Will Go (Vol. 3)
Secret of the Whispering Walls (Vol. 4)
The Mystery of the Fallen Angels (Vol. 5)
The Mystery of the Ghostwriters' Cruise (Vol. 6)
The Mystery of the Solid Gold Kicker (Vol. 7)
Nancy Drew's Love Match (Vol. 8)

GO: The Nancy Drew series is, from a violence standpoint, quite mild. Some episodes contain moderately intense scenes of Nancy being held captive, and the viewer can generally count on a chase scene or two per episode.

THE NEVERENDING STORY

Warner Home Video
1984
94 minutes
Directed by: Wolfgang Petersen
Starring: Noah Hathaway, Patricia Hayes,
    Barrett Oliver, Tami Stronach
MPAA rating: PG

When a bookseller in a queer little bookshop warns Bastian not to read *The Neverending Story* (for those who read it become strangely intertwined with the destiny of the characters in the story), Bastian is intrigued and steals the book away to read in the school attic. Sure enough, as he reads, Bastian is drawn into the world of Fantasia, a land that is slowly being destroyed by an evil force called The Nothing. Fantasia's only hope is the Empress, who is dying with her world and who chooses a boy named Atreyu to be the last great warrior. As Bastian reads, he and Atreyu become one, and together they discover that the reason Fantasia is dying is that people no longer use their imaginations. And they also discover that the only way to save Fantasia is for Bastian (a human boy) to give the Empress a new name; which, at the last possible moment, Bastian does, and Fantasia rises again. Based on the book by Michael Ende.

CAUTION: There is an intense scene when a storm rages against the attic. Atreyu's horse drowns in a bog of quicksand and Atreyu cannot save him. (Although the horse does reappear at the end of the film when Fantasia is recreated.) Atreyu stabs a creature and when he with-

draws his hand there is blood. Creatures of Fantasia at first appear grotesque although they become more endearing as the film progresses. In one scene, rays from the Southern Oracle's eyes pierce a knight and his visor flips up revealing a charred and bloody face. Bastian's mother is dead and he reads in order to escape the reality of his relationship with his father. Fans of the book be warned: the film is based only on one third of the original text.

GO: One of the best films available in the fantasy film genre, this is the story of courage and the power of imagination.

■

THE NEVERENDING STORY II: THE NEXT CHAPTER

Warner Home Video
1989
90 minutes
Directed by: George Miller
Starring: Clarissa Burt, Jonathan Brandis,
    John Wesley Shipp
MPAA rating: PG

At the advent of his second adventure into Fantasia, Bastian is suffering from a crisis of courage. He's desperate to make the school swim team, but the very first test is a dive from the tower, and when he gets up to the top, he finds he's looking out over a huge waterfall, thundering into an abyss. So, the next day he goes into K. Koreander's shop, looking for a book on how to jump from very great heights. But when he sees *The Neverending Story* he changes his mind and decides to take that instead. Bastian finds a safe place and begins to read. And he enters Fantasia again, this time on a mission to save the childlike

Empress. He finds that he has the power to wish for anything he chooses. But he is unaware that every time he makes a wish, Xayide, the sorceress of emptiness, will steal one of his memories until he has forgotten his world, and his mission. In the end, through the love he bears for his friend Atreyu, Bastian breaks Xayide's spell and triumphs. But a final test of courage remains: the giant waterfall of his vision. (This video also contains the G-rated Bugs Bunny cartoon *Box-office Bunny*.)

CAUTION: Xayide's minions are hostile beetle-like giants and they may be too intense for small children. Also, the sophisticated nature of the plot may leave young viewers baffled. This sequel to *The Never-ending Story* is loosely based on more of the book by Michael Ende, but it still doesn't tell the complete story.

GO: All in all, this is an engaging fantasy film with strong themes of courage, resistance to temptation and reconciliation. ■

NEWSIES

Walt Disney Home Video
1992
121 minutes
Directed by: Kenny Ortega
Staring: Christian Bale, Max Cansella,
   Robert Duvall, David Moscow, Bill Pullman
MPAA rating: PG

Newsies is a full-scale big-budget musical, set in New York City in the early part of this century. During a newspaper war between Joseph Pulitzer and William Randolph

Hearst, Pulitzer decides to beef up his profits by increasing the wholesale cost of the paper to the newsies (the disadvantaged youngsters who peddle his papers on the street). This triggers a full-scale revolt among the boys, who, led by Jack Kelly and Dave Jacobs, and aided by reporter Bryan Denton, stand up to the newspaper baron and his henchmen, no matter how tough the going gets.

CAUTION: There is one close-up of a face being punched, and there are fistfights between goons and newsies, in which noses and lips bleed.

GO: This is a terrific film about kids making a difference and can also serve as an introduction to the historical reality of child labor. The song-and-dance sequences are spectacularly staged.

THE NIGHT TRAIN TO KATHMANDU

Paramount Home Video
1988
102 minutes
Directed by: Robert Wiemer
Starring: Eddie Castrodad, Milla Jovovich,
   Pernell Roberts
MPAA rating: No rating given

Fourteen-year-old Lily McLeod's parents are Princeton archaeology professors, and when they agree to spend a year in Kathmandu in Nepal, Lily and her nine-year-old brother Andrew must go with them. Lily is unhappy to be leaving her school and her friends, but on the last leg of their journey (on the night train to Kathmandu) she meets a handsome, mysterious young man named Johar, who is aboard without a ticket. Lily saves him from being thrown off the train by telling the guard that he is her servant — much to Johar's indignation. Lily and Andrew then persuade their parents to allow Johar to accopany them to Nepal, where he agrees to work for them. But Johar is more than he seems; in fact, he is a prince of the mythical Invisible City (a city in the remote Himalayas which appears periodically for a single moon, allowing one of royal birth to leave and experience our world). In Kathmandu, the City is regarded as legend, but two academics, Hadley-Smithe and Dewan, both suspect that the city is very real.With the arrival of Johar they quickly deduce his true identity. At the film's climax, Johar must find his way back to the Invisible City before the new moon appears. In the end, it's up to Lily alone to help her friend return before he perishes.

CAUTION: Lily's parents won't listen to her when she goes to them for help.

GO: The film is a little slow moving in the middle, but it's an excellent attempt to make an interesting family film in an exotic location. There is no violence or swearing.

In the 1860s, a Texas pioneer leaves his wife and sons, Travis and Arliss, for four months while he goes to bring in a herd of cattle. While he is away, a stranger comes to the homestead searching for his "big yeller dog." He finds the dog, but recognizing Arliss's affection for Yeller, allows the family to keep it. The dog proves to be a protector and a playmate to both boys. However, after saving Travis from an attack by a rabid wolf, the dog develops "hydrophobia" and must be shot. The dog is replaced by one of its pups, but the boys know it will never grow to be like Old Yeller.

✗STOP: In spite of the G rating, this is a tough film for animal lovers. Old Yeller has vicious fights with wild pigs and a wolf; he gets covered with blood and in one scene has to be sewn up. Travis shoots a buck for dinner (the deer is shown falling) and he carries the dead animal home. And Travis also has to shoot Old Yeller because he contracts rabies, which makes for a very sad but realistic ending.

GO: Featuring a stable household and loving and sensitive relationships, this film shows just how hard the pioneers worked. The children are encouraged to "look for something good to replace the bad" when Old Yeller dies.

✗ OLD YELLER

✗ ONCE UPON A FOREST

Walt Disney Home Video
1957
84 minutes
Directed by: Robert Stevenson
Starring: Chuck Connors, Tommy Kirk, Dorothy McGuire, Fess Parker
MPAA rating: G

Fox
1993
71 minutes
Directed by: Charles Grosvenor
Starring the voices of: Ellen Blain, Paige Gosney, Ben Gregory, Elizabeth Moss
MPAA rating: G

The land of Dapplewood is a forest paradise, and four good friends, Abigail the mouse, Edgar the mole, Russell the hedgehog, and Michelle the badger are Furlings (students) under Michelle's uncle, Cornelius. But a tanker truck carrying toxic cargo goes off the road, spewing deadly gas, and most of Dapplewood is destroyed. Michelle is stricken by the fumes, and Abigail, Edgar, and Russell must go to a meadow to find the special plants Cornelius needs to cure his niece. They travel through a desolate landscape filled with the threat of predators and man-made machines until they reach Oakdale, obtain the necessary plants by virtue of a marvelous invention, and return in time to save Michelle.

✗STOP: Abigail goes into Michelle's den and sees Michelle's parents lying there, dead. Edgar, blind without his glasses, is trapped by sinister figures wearing protective suits.

CAUTION: This film deals with a tough topic: the senseless destruction of the environment and the indiscriminate slaughter of wildlife.

GO: The animation is excellent. At the end of the film, good-guy humans are shown cleaning up the environment.

■

PADDLE-TO-THE-SEA

NFB
1966
28 minutes
Directed by: Bill Mason
MPAA rating: no rating given

An Indian boy, who lives in a small village north of Lake Superior, has a vision during the long winter nights, and painstakingly begins to carve and paint the small wooden figure of a man in a canoe. On the bottom of the hull, he inscribes the request: I am Paddle-to-the-Sea, please put me back in the water. Then the boy leaves Paddle-to-the-Sea on the ice of a frozen river. With the spring, the ice melts, and the little wooden figure's epic journey through the great lakes begins. Paddle-to-the-Sea has many adventures, and though it occasionally seems that his journey will not be completed, he reaches the sea at last. There he is found by a lighthouse keeper, who respectfully touches up the wooden man's faded paint, and sends him out into the Atlantic on a new journey to unknown shores.

GO: Holling C. Holling's children's story is beautifully interpreted in this Oscar-nominated short, a travelogue which has charmed and educated generations of young children.

■

THE PARENT TRAP

Walt Disney Home Video
1961
127 minutes
Directed by: David Swift
Starring: Brian Keith, Hayley Mills,
    Maureen O'Hara
MPAA rating: not rated

Susan, a rough-and-tumble girl, lives with her father on a ranch in California, while Sharon, who is more of an artist, lives with her upper-class mother in Boston. When the two meet at an exclusive summer camp for girls, they instantly loathe each other, which is ironic … because they look exactly alike. But this doesn't stop them from playing tricks on each other, and one prank leads to another, escalating in severity until a war is raging. Finally, the exasperated camp directors sentence the pair to the ultimate punishment: bunking together until they sort out their differences. Before very long, the two discover that they actually like one another, and as their friendship deepens and they learn more about each other's pasts, they come to a startling revelation: they are twins, the children of estranged parents who separated while the girls were infants, each parent raising one child. The girls vow to reconcile their parents, and to this end, switch identities and set in motion their grand conspiracy to ruin their father's upcoming marriage to a super-sophisticated social climber, and get their parents together again.

CAUTION: This film can be a problem for children of separated parents who are clinging to the fantasy that their parents will reconcile.

GO: *The Parent Trap* is one of the all-time great Disney classics, a consumate blend of slapstick humor, childhood antics and rekindled romance suitable for everyone from the age of five and up.

✗ PEE-WEE'S BIG ADVENTURE

Warner Home Video
1985
92 minutes
Directed by: Tim Burton
Starring: Elizabeth Daly, Mark Holton,
Paul Reubens
MPAA rating: PG

Pee-Wee Herman lives a kid's fantasy. He has his own house, jam-packed with amazing toys. And his prize possession is his bicycle. Francis Buxton, a rich spoiled brat, wants it for his own, but Pee-Wee won't sell at any price. Then, horror of horrors, Pee-Wee's bike disappears! Of course, Francis is the prime suspect, but breaking into the Buxton mansion and threatening Francis doesn't get Pee-Wee anywhere. And after a huge unsuccessful search, Pee-Wee trudges through the rain to a bogus fortune teller, who tells him that his bike is in the basement of the Alamo. So Pee-Wee hitchhikes to Texas, accepting rides from a convict and a ghostly truck driver. After befriending a waitress at a truck stop and repeatedly dodging her jealous boy friend, he finally finds his bike on a set at Warner Brothers Studios. Pee-Wee steals the bike and leads his pursuers on a wild chase, stopping only to rescue pets from a burning pet store. Impressed by his heroism, the studio executives reward Pee-Wee by giving him back his bike and making a movie out of his story. And all of the friends he made along the way come to the drive-in to see it.

✗STOP: Large Marge, the ghostly truck driver, suddenly transforms into a horrible bug-eyed apparition right at the climax of her story. This is done in claymation.

CAUTION: There are a couple of incidents of innuendo, subtle enough that most little children will not pick up on them, and in one scene, Pee-Wee has a nightmare in which dark, evil clowns tear apart his bike — one even pulls down his surgical mask to reveal a leering face.

GO: This film has become a cult classic, and kids generally love it. The more you watch it, the funnier it gets.

THE PHANTOM TOLLBOOTH

MGM
1969
90 minutes
Directed by: Chuck Jones,
   Abe Levitow (animation),
   David Monahan (live action)
Starring: Butch Patrick
Starring the voices of: Mel Blanc,
   Hans Conreid, June Foray
MPAA rating: G

Nine-year-old Milo is always bored. When he's in school, all he wants is to get out, and when he's not in school, he just wants to be somewhere else. Then one afternoon he hears the sound of something heavy drop, and turns to see that a large striped package has appeared in his bedroom. There is a label on the package which says: If bored, pull tab marked tab and step back! Milo does, and in so doing becomes the proud owner of one Turnpike Tollbooth, which comes equipped with a galvanized automobile, a map and a gramophone horn which instructs him to select a destination. skeptical, Milo picks "The Castle in the Air," and upon entering the gate turns immediately into a cartoon. He proceeds forward and finds himself in an animated world on the road to Dictionopolis. There he has a number of exciting adventures, encountering a host of eccentric characters along the way (including a watchdog with a real watch in his stomach, named Tock). He discovers that in this world, you have to *think* your way out of difficulties, and he discovers that, in spite of the fact that he hasn't had much practice thinking, he actually has a flair for it. Based on a book by Norton Juster.

GO: This is an excellent production of a clever story that emphasizes the necessity (and fun) of education.

THE POLAR BEAR KING

Hemdale
1994
87 minutes
Directed by: Ola Solem
Starring: Maria Bonnevie, Jack Fieldstad,
   Tobias Hoesl, Anna-Lotta Larsson,
   Monica Nordquist
MPAA rating: PG

Winterland is rugged, beautiful and ruled by a beloved king. He has three daughters, one of whom will be queen; in particular, he adores his youngest, a seventeen-year-old who has the gift of communicating with animals. In Summerland, the neighboring southern kingdom, the recently deceased king is succeeded by young Prince Valemon, who is aided by his mother, a white magician. A powerful and evil witch with an agenda for world domination demands that the prince marry her. When the prince refuses, the witch wills him to become a bear by day and a man by night for seven years, with an added condition: if anyone sees him in his human form, he will be in the witch's power forever. The bear prince wanders in his misery up to Winterland, where he meets the king's youngest daughter and tells her of his curse. She falls in love with him. They return to Summerland and are married. At night the prince comes to see her as a man, but conceals his face so that she may not look on it. In a year, they have a baby girl. Valemon's mother, the Queen, makes herself permanently invisible and spirits the child away for protection against the witch. The princess is devastated at her loss, but soon gives birth to twins; the Queen takes them away as well. The princess is inconsolable and goes to her family for comfort. The prince lets her go but warns her not to take any presents from her sisters. Her sisters give her a tinder-box and candle with which to see the prince's face, and when she does, the witch comes to take him. The princess journeys to the witch's castle, along a way magically provided for her by Valemon's mother, who also gives all manner of magic tools to help her to save the prince. The princess disguises herself as a boy. She plots with the prince to trick the witch and makes a concoction of super evil with which to destroy the witch and her cronies. All are invited to the wedding of the witch and Prince Valemon, where the princess serves the potion. When the witch dies, the prisoners held by her are freed, and the princess and her newly crowned King are united with their children.

Note: This is a partially dubbed production, made in Norway. This story is a variation of the Scandinavian legend "East of the Sun, West of the Moon," based on the Cupid and Psyche myth.

CAUTION: The Witch's master is the devil, and she calls upon him on a number of occasions; he is more of a wicked imp than a terrifying figure. Dogs and wolves in the forest are staved off by fire sticks. The princess's sisters are jealous and unsympathetic.

GO: Although the princess makes a mistake, she makes up for it in her efforts to save her prince. She has the hero role, and is a very strong yet feminine heroine. The movie features interesting messages about good and evil, and the necessity of both.

■

POLLYANNA

Walt Disney Home Video
1960
134 minutes
Directed by: David Swift
Starring: Richard Egan, Hayley Mills,
  Agnes Moorehead, Jane Wyman
MPAA rating: G

Pollyanna Whittier is the irrepressibly cheerful orphan of a church missionary, who is sent to live with her stern aunt, Polly Harrington. The matriarch and virtual dictator of the small mid western town of Harrington, Aunt Polly's control is so complete that she even shapes the content of the Reverend Ford's sermons. But before very long, Pollyanna's sheer joy of living begins to rub off on everybody, breaking the spell of habitual misery which has fallen over the town. Coinciding with Pollyanna's arrival is the reappearance of her aunt's old suitor, Dr. Chilton. (Their long-lost love, as it turns out, is the source of Aunt Polly's bitterness.) And when the doctor learns that the town badly needs a new orphanage, and that Aunt Polly refuses to allow one to be built, the issue becomes a symbol of her control over the community, and he urges the people of Harrington to stand up to her. The townsfolk plan a fund-raising affair, which Aunt Polly fights tooth and nail. But it's Pollyanna's inadvertent influence on the Reverend Ford that turns the tide, and with him on their side, the townsfolk go ahead with their celebration. Aunt Polly angrily forbids Pollyanna to attend the party, but the child climbs out the window and down a tree. On her return, Pollyanna falls and is seriously hurt, and it's only then that Aunt Polly realizes how much she has come to love the child. After the accident, Pollyanna is paralyzed; worse, she has lost the will to live. But the entire town comes to wish her well, and return the love she has instilled in them; thus encouraged, Pollyanna's recovery is assured. Based on the novel by Eleanor H. Porter.

CAUTION: Pollyanna's fall from the third floor eaves is agonizingly realistic, and her subsequent black depression may be very upsetting for some children.

GO: A wonderful film for any age. Mills won an Honorary Academy Award for the Most Outstanding Juvenile Performance of the Year.

■

PRANCER

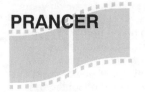

Orion
1990
103 minutes
Directed by: John Hancock
Starring: Sam Elliott, Rebecca Harrell,
    Cloris Leachman
MPAA rating: G

Nine-year-old Jessica, daughter of an embittered, down-on-his-luck farmer, takes a short-cut through the woods where she sees a great reindeer that allows her to go up and pet it. But no one believes her story until the next night, when she and her father are driving through the snowy forest and their truck hits the reindeer. Realizing that the animal is wounded, Jessica's father takes out his rifle to mercifully kill the deer. But Jessica begins to scream, momentarily distracting him, and when he looks around again, the creature is gone. At home, Jessica dreams of the reindeer falling from the sky, and when she looks out her window, she sees that the barn door is open, and soon discovers that Prancer (who is indeed one of Santa's reindeer) has taken refuge inside. She keeps him hidden, bringing him feed, and even gets a vet to come over and look at him. And all the while, Jessica plans to take the lost reindeer up to the ridge on Christmas Eve, where Santa can come and get him. But word gets out, and one day Jessica returns home to find an army of people gawking at Prancer. Her father sells the deer, and Prancer is taken away and caged as a Christmas exhibit. Jessica and her brother try to set Prancer free, but during the attempt Jessica falls and is badly hurt. Instead of escaping, Prancer stays by her side, and saves her life. In an emotional final scene, Jessica's father expresses his love for her, and when he buys Prancer back, they go together to the ridge and release him.

CAUTION: The scene in the woods is lonely and scary, and many young viewers will be upset when the truck strikes the reindeer.

GO: *Prancer* features a stirring theme of hope despite poverty and adversity.

✘ PREHYSTERIA

Paramount Home Video
1993
84 minutes
Directed by: Albert and Charles Band
Starring: Brett Cullen, Samantha Mills,
  Colleen Moris, Austin O'Brien
MPAA rating: PG

In a jungle in the Southern hemisphere, obnoxious museum owner/tomb robber Rico Sarno steals dinosaur eggs from a cave. Meanwhile, back in North America, Frank Taylor has his hands full. His daughter Monica is a beautiful fourteen-year-old with a tendency to sneak out of the house at night. His son, ten-year-old Jerry, is fixated on Elvis. Frank makes money collecting rare fossils and selling them to Rico's museum. There, he meets Rico's archaeology student

assistant, Vicky. He is striking a deal for some fossils with her when Rico shows up, carrying the dinosaur eggs in a cooler. The Taylor family also has a cooler, and a switch results in the Taylor family going home with the eggs. The eggs promptly hatch, releasing a collection of baby dinosaurs, who wreak havoc in the Taylor household despite the kids' best efforts to keep them a secret from Frank. Vicky shows up, having been threatened by Rico, and she and Frank begin a romance. Then Rico makes an appearance, gun in hand, and demands the return of the eggs. Frank runs him off, but he returns again with two thugs, and abducts Vicky and the dinosaurs. Frank must rescue Vicky and get the baby dinosaurs back before Rico goes before the media to announce his discovery.

✘STOP: Despite the director's claim that he is trying to make fantasy films without a hard edge, guns are waved around throughout the last third of the movie. In one scene, Frank disarms Rico, tells him to bend over, and then kicks him in the backside.

CAUTION: There is nongraphic fistfighting and head butting, mild language and some sexist dialogue. This effort suffers from a paradox common to many so-called children's movies. It has material which isn't really suitable for very young children, yet it's not likely to be of much interest to teens.

THE PRINCE AND THE PAUPER

(continued on next page)

Walt Disney Home Video
1962
120 minutes
Directed by: Don Chaffey
Starring: Donald Houston, Laurence Naismith,
    Sean Scully, Guy Williams
MPAA rating: G

Based on Mark Twain's classic novel of social injustice, *The Prince and the Pauper* is the story of two boys who look exactly alike. One, Edward Tudor, is born into kingly wealth and privilege, while the other, Tom Canty, is born into the most abject poverty sixteenth century London could offer. One day, when Tom goes to the palace to try to catch a glimpse of the prince, and the guards rough him up, the outraged prince orders that Tom be brought in to his apartments for a sumptuous meal. While he is there, the boys realize how much alike they look, and devise a clever plan: they will switch clothes and get a taste of each other's life. But Tom, subjected to an endless succession of state duties, hasn't been in the prince's shoes for an hour before he's ready to trade back. And worse, no one will believe him when he tells them he isn't the prince; they simply think he's mad. Meanwhile, Edward has disappeared into the streets of London, only to end up in Tom's evil home, where he soon knows that he too has had enough of the charade. But it isn't until a gallant knight, Sir Miles, becomes convinced that Edward really is the king that each boy is returned to his rightful place.

Versions of this story are also available from:
Media Home Entertainment
Storytime Video
Walt Disney Home Video (starring Mickey Mouse)
Warner Home Video

CAUTION: Tom's father bludgeons a priest and the abuse in his slovenly home is frightful. There are a number of sword-fights.

GO: Probably the most accessible of all the versions of this tale, this film presents a fascinating look at the times, with a lot of action thrown in.

◼

PRINCE CASPIAN AND THE VOYAGE OF THE DAWNTREADER

Public Media Video
1988
165 minutes
Directed by: Alex Kirby
Starring: Warwick Davi, John Hallam,
    Jonathan R. Scott, David Thwaite,
    Sophie Wilcox
MPAA rating: no rating given

Prince Caspian begins in the Land of Narnia, where Caspian, nephew of King Miraz, is the heir to the throne; however, when the Queen gives birth to a baby, Caspian is informed by a loyal friend that his life is in danger. He flees the castle, and in the forest encounters a multitude of talking animals (both familiar and mythological), all bent on recovering their kingdom from the nasty King Miraz (who, as it turns out, also murdered Caspian's father). The forest creatures rally around Prince Caspian, but a surprise attack by Miraz's army puts their entire cause in jeopardy. They are forced to hide in a cavern, and there Caspian blows the horn which will summon help. Sure enough, Lucy, Susan, Peter and Edmund are whisked from an English train station into the land of Narnia.

There the children encounter Aslan, and join up with Caspian in time to triumph in battle over the evil Miraz. And after establishing the Prince as King Caspian X of Narnia, Aslan returns Lucy, Susan, Peter and Edmund to the train station.

The Voyage of the Dawntreader begins with the arrival of Lucy and Edmund at the country house of their unpleasant cousin Eustace. Soon all three are transported through the beautiful picture of a ship and plunked into an ocean in Narnia. They are taken aboard the ship and are greeted by Caspian himself, now a number of years older. The young king is on a mission to find the seven lost lords of Narnia, who were banished by evil king Miraz, and to do it he plans to sail to the Lone Islands, and after that into uncharted waters. After a series of fantastic adventures, they find five of the seven lords. The last two, however, can only be awakened if one brave traveller will journey beyond the end of the earth to Aslan's country. And after much debate, it is agreed that the brave mouse Reepicheep will make the fateful trip. He sets out in a small boat, and Lucy, Edmund and Eustace are returned home.

CAUTION: Like the first film in the series, *The Lion, the Witch and the Wardrobe, Prince Caspian and the Dawntreader* is leisurely paced, and may leave the little ones far behind. It doggedly follows the narrative, lending credence to the notion that the best film adaptations of books are not those which stick religiously to the text. Also, the fighting scenes in the Narnia series are surprisingly violent (particularly considering the understated nature of the rest of the production).

GO: These videos succeed in capturing the spirit of the C.S. Lewis books and are richly produced. This is a BBC Television production in association with Wonderworks.

■

THE PRINCESS BRIDE

Nelson Home Entertainment
1987
98 minutes
Directed by: Rob Reiner
Starring: André the Giant, Cary Elwes,
    Christopher Guest, Mandy Patinkin,
    Chris Sarandon, Wallace Shawn,
    Robin Wright
MPAA rating: PG

When a young boy is sick in bed, his grandfather reads him a story called *The Princess Bride*. And as he reads, the action unfolds as if through the child's mind's eye. The story begins on a farm in a far away place where Buttercup and her desperately poor attendant Wesley grow to love each other. But before they marry, Wesley decides to go to sea to seek his fortune. And when his ship is captured by the dread Pirate Roberts (who takes no prisoners), the word is that Wesley is dead and the grief-stricken Buttercup is subsequently betrothed to not-so-nice Prince Humperdinck. While she is out on a ride one day, Buttercup encounters three strange characters, the diminutive Vizzini, the giant Fezzik, and the master swordsman Inigo Montoya. It turns out that the three are agents, intent on starting a war with Gilder, the country across the sea, and they kidnap Buttercup, sailing away in a small ship. But they are pursued across eel-infested waters and even up the Cliffs of Insanity by a mysterious masked man in black, who defeats Inigo in a sword fight, Fezzik in a duel of strength, and finally Vizzini in a battle of wits. The masked man is revealed as none other than Wesley, back from the dead and with an amazing (and hilarious) tale to tell. But the adventure is not over yet as the evil Prince pursues them. Westley and Buttercup must brave the Fire-forest and the Rodents of Unusual Size. And finally, Wesley must come back from the dead, join new allies and take Prince Humperdinck's castle. Based on the book by William Goldman.

CAUTION: Some images may frighten small children. Hideous Screaming Eels rush at Buttercup to devour her and Westley is tortured with a strange machine and writhes in pain as the life is sucked out of him. In an intense battle Wesley stabs a huge rat repeatedly with a sword. And the final confrontation between Inigo and his arch-foe Count Rugen is violent and bloody (swords pierce arms and legs, and slash faces with blood).

GO: Despite the cautions, this is full of wry humor and wit and splendid performances including a vignette with Billy Crystal and Carol Kane. An enchanting tale which can be enjoyed by viewers of a wide range of ages over and over again.

■

THE QUEST

MCA
1986
93 minutes
Directed by: Brian Trenchard-Smith
Starring: Henry Thomas, Tamsin West
MPAA rating: PG

In a bog in Australia, fourteen-year-old Cody and his friend Wendy witness some mysterious occurrences which, according to an old Aboriginal folk legend, are caused by the spirit of "Donkegin." Cody is compelled to uncover the mystery and his inquisitiveness gets him into dangerous trouble when he's trapped underwater in the bog. Then it's up to Wendy to unravel the mystery and save him.

CAUTION: The children come upon a gruesome skeleton of Cody's old friend, and when Cody disappears underwater, he is gone so long that everyone presumes that he has drowned (this is not a movie for children who are afraid of water). There is one instance of coarse language.

GO: The children in this film are intelligent, inventive, resourceful and courageous.

RAGS TO RICHES

Starmaker
1986
96 minutes
Directed by: Bruce Seth Green
Starring: Joseph Bologna, Tisha Campbell, Blanca DeGarr, Kimiko Gelman, Bridget Michele, Douglas Seale, Heidi Zeigler
MPAA rating: no rating given

Nick Foley is a self-made millionaire. He has a mansion, a beautiful fiancée and a devoted butler. Now he's ready for that last move which will take him to the top of the heap — the Big Merger. But his prospective partner, billionaire Baldwin, has problems with Nick's image. Meanwhile, across town at the orphanage, the six girls in Room 204 have gained a reputation for trouble, and since the orphanage is about to go down the tubes, things don't look good for the girls. But they vow to stick together, and when their leader, Rose, calls the papers to advertise their plight, Nick's right-hand man, Freddy, sees an opportunity to turn Nick into a family man by acquiring an instant family. And so he does. But the girls — feisty Rose, appearance-oriented Diane, Nina (with a biker boyfriend), Patty (with reading problems), financial wizard Marva and tiny Nicky — prove more than a handful. The girls don't exactly fit in, and Nick cynically plans to send them off to a boarding school as soon as they've served their purpose. But despite himself, Nick grows to care deeply for them. He starts to look forward to Saturday outings with the girls. And when Nina takes off with her biker boyfriend, Nick goes halfway across the country to get her back. But when Nick's scheming, jealous fiancée decides to implement Nick's original plan to send the girls away, the girls revolt and destroy Nick's deal-signing party, even ripping off Baldwin's toupée. The girls are promptly shipped back to the orphanage; that is, until Nick suddenly realizes where his priorities, and his heart, lie.

CAUTION: There is one fight scene, in which Nick takes on the bikers, but it's brief and not too violent.

GO: This made-for-TV movie is a popular little film, featuring the music of the girls and their band.

THE RAILWAY CHILDREN

Thorn EMI
1970
104 minutes
Directed by: Lionel Jeffries
Starring: Jenny Agutter, Bernard Cribbins,
    Iain Cuthbertson, Dinah Sheridan,
    Sally Thomsett, Gary Warren
MPAA rating: not rated

The Waterbury children, Roberta, Phyllis and Peter, live in rural Edgecombe Villa at the turn of the century with their wonderful mother and their father, who is simply perfect. But when Christmas comes and mysterious circumstances lead to Mr. Waterbury's arrest by Scotland Yard, things go from perfect to horrid. The family moves to a country house in Yorkshire, and the house proves to be a drafty affair, especially in the cold season. And despite Peter's best efforts (he steals coal from the local railway yard), their mother falls ill with influenza. The children must provide for themselves, and somehow get money for their mother's medication. Then salvation arrives, when the ingenious children befriend an elderly gentleman they have seen regularly, on a passing train. (He sends them a basket of food.) And when the children help avert a catastrophe by reporting a landslide on the tracks, they receive commendations for their efforts. Later, by accident, Bobbi discovers the truth about their father: he has been falsely arrested for selling state secrets and sentenced to five years in prison. In the end, the elderly gentleman works tirelessly to clear Mr.Waterbury's name, and the children's father is returned to them. Based on the story by E. Nesbit.

GO: This is an utterly delightful, charming and gentle film.

■ ●

THE RED BALLOON

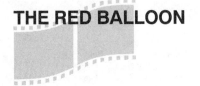

Embassy Home Entertainment
   (Children's Treasures)
1956
34 minutes
Directed by: Albert Lamorisse
Starring: Pascal Lamorisse

This is the story of Pascal, a young French boy who, on his way to school, saves a red balloon from certain death by untangling its string from a lamppost. It soon becomes obvious that this is no ordinary balloon; it comes when he calls and Pascal doesn't even have to hold its string — it just follows him! But no one else seems to appreciate the balloon (he's not permitted to take it on the bus, to school or even into his house). And when, after a chase through the narrow streets of Paris, a gang of bullies uses slingshots to take turns shooting at the balloon, Pascal urges the balloon to go, but it will not leave him at the mercy of the bullies. After a well-aimed shot the balloon is done for. The air slowly leaves the beautiful red balloon and a bully delivers the final blow by stepping on it. Then something strange and magical happens: suddenly, all of the balloons in Paris fly from their owners' hands, passing over the

rooftops in multicolored splendor to converge around a delighted Pascal. He holds as many strings as he can in his little hands, and the balloons lift him up into the air for the ride of his life.

CAUTION: Because it had such a personality and the outcome is so unfair, the balloon's death will disturb some viewers.

GO: The film has no dialogue and can be followed purely as the story unfolds. The film also provides a delightful glimpse of Paris in the '50s.

THE RETURN OF JAFAR

Walt Disney Home Video
1994
66 minutes
Directed by: Toby Shelton, Tad Stones and
   Alan Zaslove
Featuring the voices of: Dan Castellaneta,
   Jonathan Freeman, Gilbert Gottfried
MPAA rating: Not Rated

In this fully-animated sequel to the film *Aladdin*, the rotten parrot Iago wants to get back in power. Since his relationship with the evil Jafar is wearing thin, he plots to win Aladdin's sympathy and friendship. Meanwhile, Jafar is inadvertently released from his lamp prison by the bumbling, greedy, ambitious Abismal whom he blackmails into helping him exact revenge on Aladdin, Jasmine and the Sultan. Iago begins to gain Aladdin's confidence by saving him from a bunch of thugs in the market, but being nice is *really* hard. Jafar terrorizes Iago into cooperating with his evil plan and when Aladdin and the Sultan fall for their ruse to leave the palace, Jafar takes Genie, Abu and Jasmine prisoner. Aladdin and the Sultan are no match for Jafar and his magical flying horsemen but, strangely enough, Jafar allows Aladdin to escape and takes the Sultan prisoner. Now he weaves his twisted plot. When the unwitting Aladdin returns to the palace, Jafar pretends that Aladdin has murdered the Sultan. He disguises himself as an outraged Jasmine and sentences Aladdin to death. Moments before the execution Iago has a change of heart and helps Genie, Jasmine, Abu and the carpet escape to save Aladdin. Jafar is furious. The final confrontation has Aladdin trying to outrun fire, earthquakes and the wrath of Jafar. At the final moment Iago pushes the lamp into volcanic lava, destroying it and Jafar forever.

CAUTION: The songs are nowhere near as good as the ones in *Aladdin*. Robin Williams has been replaced as the voice of Genie. Jafar's demise is portrayed using scary skeletal images. Commercial blacks appear at the end of cliff-hanger scenes.

GO: The genie tells Aladdin, "the problem with doing the right thing is that sometimes you do it by yourself." The animation and voice treatments are still miles ahead of most other productions.

✘ RETURN OF THE JEDI

CBS/Fox
1983
132 minutes
Directed by: Richard Marquand
Starring: Harrison Ford, Mark Hamill,
   Carrie Fisher, Billy Dee Williams
MPAA rating: PG

After liberating his friend Han Solo from his frozen state in the fortress of Jabba the Hutt, Luke Skywalker returns alone to the Dagobah system to resume his studies with Yoda. But Yoda informs Luke that his training is now complete and tells him that it's time for him to return to face Darth Vader. Meanwhile, the Imperial Forces under Vader's command race to complete the new Death Star near the forest moon of Endor. Luke joins his friends with the rebel fleet to prepare for a surprise attack. Their first priority is to travel to the surface of Endor and knock out the force field generator which guards the half-completed Death Star. But when they arrive on the forest moon, Luke and company lose the element of suprise when they encounter an Imperial patrol on rocket-sleds. Realizing that his presence (which Vader can sense) is jeopardizing the mission, Luke gives himself up in hopes of turning Vader from the Dark Side. And while the fighting reaches a frenzied climax, Luke is brought into the presence of the awful Emperor, where he must duel with Vader and avoid being brought over to the Dark Side himself.

✘**STOP:** Jabba the Hutt and his cronies delight as a girl is thrown into a pit to be eaten by a hideous, drooling monster—in fact, a number of bad guys fall to their deaths in similar fashion. Luke removes Vader's helmet to reveal his face (scarier in its anticipation than in its reality). And at the climax of the film, Vader's hand is cut off, and the evil Emperor repeatedly zaps Luke as he lies writhing on the ground in agony.

GO: A great finish to a now-classic trilogy, this is the one that features the teddy bear-like creatures, the Ewoks, and the chase scene through the forest, which is, without question, a special-effects landmark.

THE RETURN OF THE KING

Morningstar
1991
96 minutes
Directed by: Jules Bass
Starring the voices of: Orson Bean,
   William Conrad, Hans Conreid, John Huston,
   Roddy McDowall
MPAA rating: not rated

This effort, named after the third part of J.R.R. Tolkien's famous epic, begins with the Companions, Gandalf and the hobbits, Merry, Pippin, Samwise and Frodo, returning to Rivendell, home of the northern elves. There they meet Bilbo Baggins, who asks about the Companions' adventures and what has befallen his magic ring. Gandalf and the minstrel of Gondor then tell the tale, giving the viewer a brief synopsis of the first half of the original tale, and beginning it in earnest during the scene in the tower of Cirith Ungol. The Orcs have captured Frodo, but Sam holds the Ring of Power, and he proceeds gamely into the grim fortress to rescue his friend. But first, he puts on the Ring, and wanders through a psychological morass of bombastic, megalomaniacal ravings and stinky songs. Meanwhile, Gandalf directs the defense of the city of Minas Tirith, which is besieged by hordes of Orcs and eastern warriors under the terrifying King of the Ringwraiths. While the Riders of Rohan and Aragorn's forces relieve the siege of the city, Sam rescues Frodo and the pair proceed into the dreary land of Mordor. From there,

the plot is straightforward. Frodo and Sam strike for smouldering Mount Doom, where the Ring is to be destroyed, while Gandalf, Aragorn and the Companions lead a host into certain death to distract the Dark Lord's omnipresent attention.

CAUTION: This is, as Tolkien himself described, a history of the War of the Ring, and it is filled with violent combat and images which may be frightening to young children. Also, it is probably necessary to have either read *The Lord of the Rings*, or have watched Ralph Bakshi's film of the same name, to make any real sense of this effort, synopsis notwithstanding. The songs, and there are lots of them, are the worst.

✗ RETURN TO OZ

Walt Disney Home Video
1985
109 minutes
Directed by: Walter Murch
Starring: Fairuza Balk, Mott Clark, Jean Marsh,
   Nicol Williamson
MPAA rating: PG

Six months after her legendary visit to Oz, Dorothy Gayle is still going on about ruby slippers and scarecrows, and still no one believes her; moreover, she's having difficulty sleeping and her worried aunt finally takes her to the sanitorium of Dr. J.B. Worley, who is convinced that shock therapy is the answer. But Dorothy is terrified in the creepy mental institution, and escapes to the nearby river, where she (along with her pet chicken, Billina) is swept away in the torrent, and carried to Oz. There, Dorothy returns to the Emerald City, but finds it in ruins and soon realizes that everyone there has been turned to stone. She learns that the Gnome King has conquered the Emerald City, and that only the sinister Princess Mombi knows where the Scarecrow is. When Dorothy approaches the Princess she is thrown into the tower prison. (Mombi, who changes her heads as it pleases her, intends to lock Dorothy in a tower for a few years until the girl's head is ready to be taken.) There, Dorothy meets a living Jack O'Lantern named Jack. Together they escape and make their way to the Gnome King's castle. But the evil king (who's terrified of eggs) has foreseen their coming, and draws them into the bowels of the mountain. Dorothy saves the Scarecrow and in the nick of time, Billina literally lays an egg, and Oz is saved. Based on characters and situations from *The Marvelous Land of Oz* and *Ozma of Oz* by L. Frank Baum.

✗**STOP:** The sanitorium is terrifing; thunder rattles in the distance as the lunatics shriek and wail. Mombi's head-changing scene is bizarre and even when she isn't wearing them they all have the ability to move and speak. And when the Wheelers, army of the Gnome King, reach the deadly desert, they turn to stone and crumble into sand. The final confrontation with the Gnome King is intensely frightening; gnomes grow out of every nook and cranny and threaten the fleeing companions.

CAUTION: Not to be compared with the musical feature *The Wizard of Oz*, The Disney Corporation printed a warning on the box: Portions of this material may not be suitable for small children. Parental discretion advised.

GO: This film is somber, but the special effects are dazzling, with claymation by Will Vinton.

■

✗ RING OF BRIGHT WATER

CBS/Fox
1969
109 minutes
Directed by: Jack Couffer
Starring: Virginia McKenna, Bill Travers
MPAA rating: G

When London resident Graham Merrill notices an otter in a pet shop window, it seems to him that the otter has singled him out. So he buys the creature and names it Mij. Graham and the otter get along well, but Mij proves to be more than a handful. He tears around Graham's place, getting into and upsetting everything, and soon Graham is forced to customize his entire home to accommodate the animal. But this very reorganization brings Graham to the realization that both he and Mij are prisoners in London, and he decides to move to the west coast of Scotland to complete his life's dream of writing a book. The hijinks begin before he even gets there, as Mij gets away during the train ride and causes mass panic. And so otter and owner are put off the train, and forced to travel the rest of the way by bus. When they finally do arrive, Graham sees a young woman freeing a trapped swan, and later discovers that she is Mary, the town doctor. She and Graham soon become fast friends, and their lives become more and more intertwined, while Mij seizes the opportunity to find a mate of his own. Then, Mij is killed by a roadside worker and Graham is devastated by the news. Still, he begins to write, and one magical day, sees Mij's mate and three baby otters that he knows belong to Mij. And while watching the otters at play in Mij's pool, Graham receives the inspiration for a book.

✗STOP: Mij is killed.

GO: This is a gentle, leisurely paced film with quiet, thoughtful characters and a poignant envrionmental message.

■

ROAD TO AVONLEA

Astral Video
1989
45–57 minutes each
Starring: Jackie Burroughs,
    Sarah Polley, Gema Zamprogna

This television series is based on the Lucy Maud Montgomery stories of *The Story Girl*. In nineteenth century Prince Edward Island, little Sarah Stanley must go to live with her deceased mother's family while waiting for the outcome of her father's embezzlement scandal. Things do not start off well, but slowly Sarah makes friends and finds a new life in the lovely rural town of Avonlea.

Titles in the series are:

Aunt Abigail's Beau; Malcolm and the Baby (Vol. 4)
The Blue Chest of Arabella King; The Witch of Avonlea (Vol. 6)
Conversions; Felicity's Challenge (Vol. 5)
■●

The Journey Begins: The Story Girl Earns Her Name (Vol. 1)
Nothing Endures But Change (Vol. 7)

Old Lady Lloyd; Proof of the Pudding (Vol. 3)
Quarantine at Alexander Abrahams; The Materialization of Duncan McTavish (Vol. 2)

ROOKIE OF THE YEAR

Fox
1993
103 minutes
Directed by: Daniel Stern
Starring: Gary Busey, Thomas Ian Nicholas, Daniel Stern
MPAA rating: PG

Henry Rowangartner is an average twelve-year-old boy growing up in suburban Chicago. He lives with his wonderful single mother, plays baseball poorly, and is beginning to be interested in girls. The day after a particularly humiliating outing with his baseball team, Henry tries to prove himself by catching a fly ball in the schoolyard. While running for it, he steps on another ball and lands heavily on his shoulder, dislocating it. This puts him in a cast until August. When the cast is removed, Henry discovers that his tendons have healed too tightly, and that he now has the greatest throwing arm in the history of baseball. The Chicago Cubs' management, tired of perpetual losing seasons and desperate for a draw at the gate, sign Henry immediately. Befriended and coached by a grouchy aging veteran, "Rocket" Chet Stedman, Henry turns into a phenomenon, helping the Cubs into a red-hot pennant race. But the pressures of being a superstar force Henry ever further into the adult world of endorsements and fan idolatry, alienating him from his real friends. Eventually, he must make a choice between being a baseball hero and being a kid. Along the way, he must also help the Cubs nail down a World Series berth.

CAUTION: Minor language. When Henry accidentally hits the doctor in the nose with his powerful new arm, the doctor snarls: Butt-loving! and the kids, their eyes huge, say to each other: Did he say "butt-loving"? so there's no way young viewers can miss this. During an angry confrontation with his mother's boyfriend Jack, Jack makes some very unflattering references to the probable identity of Henry's biological father.

GO: This film is a nonviolent, funny, true family film.

RUDYARD KIPLING'S JUST SO STORIES

f.h.e./MCA
1991
30 minutes each
Narrated by: Geoffrey Matthews

Each video contains three stories.

Volume 1:

The first story, "How the Whale Got His Throat" explains why whales only eat tiny fish. The second tale, "How the Camel Got His Hump" is about a camel who refuses to do any work. In the last story, "How the Rhinoceros Got His Skin," a Parsi pays back the ill-mannered rhino.

Volume 2:

In "How the Alphabet Was Made," a neolithic man and his daughter invent picture-sounds. The second story is "The Beginning of Armadillos," about how a hedgehog and a tortoise both become armadillos. In "How The First Letter Was Written," a neolithic human draws pictures on bark in order to explain to a wandering stranger from a far-off tribe that she needs him to fetch a spear from the cave.

Volume 3:

In "The Crab That Played With The Sea," the oldest magician calls the first animals to play on the earth and to be obedient to the first Man. All obey, except the King Crab who hides in the sea and causes havoc. "The Cat That Walked By Himself" is a tale about how the wild horse, cow, and dog are domesticated and do favors for Man and Woman in exchange for treats. The cat, however, still walks alone and accepts no-one's dominance. "The Butterfly That Stamped" is a story about how the very wise Suleyman Bin-Da-Oud's wife is able to help him indirectly silence his horrid, quarreling other 999 wives, through the boasting of a little butterfly.

Volume 4:

In "How The Leopard Got His Spots," the zebra and the giraffe are terrorized by the leopard and the Ethiopian, and as they go into the jungle, they seem to disappear. In "The Elephant's Child," the insatiably curious and short-nosed elephant's child travels to the great gray, green, greasy Limpopo River to find out that the crocodile's favorite dinner is him. In "The Sing Song of Old Man Kangaroo," the kangaroo goes from a four-short-legged, gray, woolly animal to the kangaroo we now know.

CAUTION: The box says "fully animated," which is true, but the animation is very simple for example, none of the characters have moving mouths when they talk.

GO: Kipling's stories are loved the world over for their lyric language, humor and whimsical explanations of how things in the world came to be.

RUNAWAY RALPH

Strand VCI
1986
42 minutes
Directed by: Ron Underwood
Starring: Conchata Ferrell, Sara Gilbert,
    Kellie Martin, Summer Phoenix,
    Fred Savage, Ray Walston
MPAA rating: no rating given

In this combined live-action and pixilated sequel to *The Mouse and the Motorcycle*, a boy named Garfield and his parents arrive to spend the night at the Mountainview Inn. (Garfield will be heading to Happy Acres summer camp the next day and he isn't exactly thrilled.) Meanwhile, Ralph, a motorcycle-riding mouse who lives with his family at the inn, is grounded for refusing to give rides to the smaller mouse kids and decides to run away. Eventually Ralph ends up at Happy Acres camp himself. And after a

frightening run-in with a ferocious cat, Ralph is rescued by Garfield and put in a cage. Ralph loathes the green pellets Garfield brings him, and realizes at once that he was much better off at the inn. He introduces himself to the surprised Garfield, and though the two become friends (Ralph outwits a cat to clear Garfield's name when a watch goes missing at the camp), it isn't until Ralph is back at home that he is truly happy.

CAUTION: Ralph is caught by the cat.

✗ RUSSKIES

Lorimar
1987
100 minutes
Directed by: Rick Rosenthal
Starring: Peter Billingsley, Whip Hubley,
    Leaf Phoenix
MPAA rating: PG

Three young Florida boys, Danny, Adam and Jason, are fans of Sergeant Slammer, a jingoistic commie-bashing comic-book hero. They have a secret clubhouse in an abandoned bunker on the coast, where they read Sergeant Slammer with great relish, and fantasize about a Communist invasion. Then one day, after a storm, the boys discover a ruined Russian raft and a Russian code book. They also discover an injured Soviet sailor named Misha, hiding in their bunker. When the boys try to warn their parents about what they believe is a Russian invasion, no one believes them. So they return to the clubhouse and try to decide what to do with their real live Russian. Danny and Jason leave Adam with their prisoner, and while they go off to assemble their "gear," Adam befriends the sailor. And by the time the others get back, Adam and Misha are playing cards. Jason, too, quickly becomes friends with Misha, but Danny, whose grandfather was killed by Russians in the Hungarian revolution of 1956, is immovable. Meanwhile, two Russian agents, who also survived the wreck, turn up in town and rendezvous with a traitor, who is supposed to deliver them a device. And at the same time, the boys' parents finally begin to believe the boys' story. Soon the entire U.S. military is after Misha, and the boys must find a way to get Misha back to the rendezvous point before he is captured for real.

✗ STOP: Some copies of *Russkies* include a trailer for *Return of the Living Dead II* at the beginning. (Go figure.)

CAUTION: Many of the characters are rough marine types who use some coarse language and there is one punch-up, in which Misha and the boys take on an obnoxious off-duty soldier and his buddies. Shots are fired near the end of the film.

GO: This is an excellent film which explains that, although people may be perceived as evil enemies, they are simply human beings.

THE SANDLOT

Fox
1993
101 minutes
Directed by: David Mickey Evans
Starring: Karen Allen, Tom Guiry,
   James Earl Jones, Dennis Leary
MPAA rating: PG

In the halcyon days of the early sixties, eleven year-old Scott Smalls moves to Vista Valley. It is the end of the school year, and Scott is worried that he won't have the opportunity to make any friends. As it happens, the local boys play baseball all day, every day, on a nearby sandlot, but they are a ragtag, tough-talking bunch, and Scott can't throw, catch, or hit. He tries to coax his stepfather into teaching him, but that doesn't work out too well. Then the boy's leader, the charismatic Benjamin Franklin Rodriguez, takes Scott under his wing and teaches him the fundamentals of baseball, as well as the game's primary rule: have fun. Scott and his new friends cruise through a great summer, until Scott takes his stepfather's prize possession without asking, a baseball signed by Babe Ruth, and promptly hits his first home run. The ball flies into the backyard of the meanest man in the world and his killer dog, The Beast. The boys then engage in a comic and wildly improbable series of misadventures in their attempt to retrieve the ball from the dreaded monsters' lair, but all their efforts come to naught. Then Rodriguez has a dream in which the Babe inspires him to retrieve the lost ball. This Rodriguez does, but to everyone's horror, the killer dog pursues him out of the backyard, right over the fence, and through the whole town, leading the boys to a meeting with the dog's owner who, to their surprise, isn't at all what they expected.

CAUTION: For very small children, the killer dog might be a little scary. Wendy Peppercorn, the local belle, is the object of the boys' pre-teen lust, and does nothing to discourage said reaction.

GO: This is a charming, funny tale of innocence and belonging in heartland America, sure to appeal to viewers of all ages.

THE SEA GYPSIES

Warner Home Video
1978
102 minutes
Directed by: Stewart Raffill
Starring: Mikki Jamison-Olsen, Robert Logan,
    Heather Rattray
MPAA rating: G

In order to bring himself and his daughters closer together, Travis McClean takes them on a voyage around the world in a large schooner (accompanied by an attractive female reporter named Kelly). They are well underway when the youngest daughter, Samantha, discovers a stowaway, Jesse, and agrees to keep mum about it. But when Jesse falls overboard, Sam is forced to reveal the truth to get her family to go back for him. And then a tremendous gale blows up and dashes them onto the coast of a remote part of Alaska. Shipwrecked, they have lost almost everything in the storm and the going is tough at first. But gradually they begin to eke out an existence, and as the weeks pass, the group survives attacks by grizzlies and a killer whale. And finally, with the Arctic winter coming on, and knowing that they could

never survive it, they work feverishly to build a boat that will take them to civilization. In the end, the lucky group is picked up by the Coast Guard.

CAUTION: Some of the animal attacks may be a little much for young viewers.

GO: This is an excellent adventure story without combat.

SEARCHING FOR BOBBY FISCHER

Paramount Home Video
1994
110 minutes
Directed by: Steven Zaillian
Starring: Joan Allen, Laurence Fishburne,
    Ben Kingsley, Joe Mantegna,
    Max Pomerance
MPAA rating: PG

Josh Waitzkin has just turned seven. At his outdoor birthday party, he sees the men in the park playing chess, and is instantly captivated. Josh is a prodigy who has learned the fundamentals simply by watching others play, particularly Vinni, a street-wise hustler with a fierce love of the game. When Josh's formidable abilities manifest themselves, his father takes him to see Bruce Pandolfini, a retired master who has a real aversion to the cutthroat nature of organized chess. Bruce takes Josh on as his student, and expresses his reservations when Josh's father enrolls him into the high-pressure junior tour. Josh wins tournament after tournament, and his father begins to drive him relentlessly. The pressure becomes intense, and

Josh begins to lose, primarily because he cannot learn to cultivate hatred and disdain for his opponents. He then meets his future archrival Jonathan Poe, who has done nothing but play chess since he was four years old, and the stage is set. On Bruce's advice Josh is forbidden to play his beloved speed chess in Washington Square, which Bruce claims is ruining his game, and all love of chess is finally driven out of him. At last his mother intervenes, threatening to take Josh away if the others won't ease up. Josh's father then relents. He brings Josh back to the park and lets him play speed chess with Vinni, and then, instead of an intensive training period before the nationals… he takes him fishing for two weeks. Finally, at the final hour, Bruce returns and gives Josh the inspiration he needs to face the formidable Jonathan in the championships.

CAUTION: Josh's anxiety, and his parents' conflict over his chess destiny, may be of some concern. Although this film features a young child, it has a sophisticated story line and treatment, making it of less interest to young children than the rating indicates.

GO: A film about decency, love and courage.

✗ THE SECRET GARDEN

Warner Home Video
1993
102 minutes
Directed by: Agnieszka Holland
Starring: Andrew Knott, Kate Maberly,
   Heydon Prowse, Maggie Smith
MPAA rating: G

Mary Lennox lives in British-ruled India with her indifferent, socialite parents. She is an angry, tearless child, and even when her parents are killed suddenly in an earthquake, Mary does not weep. She is sent to England to live with her brooding uncle, Lord Archibald Craven, Mistlethwaite Manor in the desolate moors. There Mary comes under the dominion of the sharp-tongued housekeeper, Mrs. Medlock, and makes friends with the good-natured maid-servant Martha and her noble brother Dickon, who has a magical way with animals. Mary herself is bitter and haughty, a miniature aristocrat who is not to be trifled with. She is instructed not to go poking about, but goes exploring anyway, and discovers that half of the dreary, sprawling manor has fallen into utter neglect. It also rings regularly with the distant cries of a person in distress. In the course of her explorations, and thanks to a friendly robin, Mary discovers a secret garden, hidden behind an overgrown wall. Mary's metamorphosis begins. She then meets the source of the strange cries, her bed-ridden cousin Colin, who has been utterly abandoned by his grieving father. Together with Dickon, and despite all the efforts of the tyrannical housekeeper to prevent it, Mary rehabilitates Colin. Father and son are then reconciled. Based on the novel by Frances Hodgson Burnett.

✗**STOP:** Colin's eerie cries may frighten little ones. In one scene, Dickon and Mary pull down the shutters which have kept Colin in the dark for years. When the light of day strikes him he flies into an absolute frenzy, a scene which may also frighten some.

CAUTION: This film is slightly dark and ominous in tone. There is a great deal of dread, particularly in the opening earthquake scene. Mary has a disturbing night-mare in which she is very young and loses her mother in a wood. The video includes a scary animated Batman trailer!

GO: Staggeringly beautiful visuals and solid performances lend a haunting, bitter-sweet atmosphere to this classic tale.

✗ THE SECRET OF N.I.M.H.

MGM/UA
1982
84 minutes
Directed by: Don Bluth
Starring the voices of:
  John Carradine, Dom DeLuise,
  Elizabeth Hartman, Derek Jacobi,
  Arthur Malet, Paul Shenar, Peter Strauss
MPAA rating: G

The rats of N.I.M.H. (The National Institute of Mental Health) were once ordinary animals, but a laboratory experiment has given them intellects comparable to humans. The story begins four years after their escape from the lab, as Nicodemus, an elder rat, recounts that a mouse named Jonathan Frisby has been killed while helping with the Plan. (The Plan revolves around the rats' preparations to become a self-sufficient farming community in the isolation of a nearby valley.) Meanwhile, Moving Day is also at hand for the widow, Mrs. Frisby, who is left alone with her children. (Every spring when the farmer begins to till the field the creatures who live there are forced to move.) But this year, grief for her lost husband is compounded by the fact that one of her sons is too sick to be moved. So, Mrs. Frisby braves a visit to the great owl for advice. The great owl tells her that in order to keep her son safe, her entire house must be moved, and that only the rats of N.I.M.H can do it. And when the rats learn that Mrs. Frisby is Jonathan Frisby's wife, they devise an ingenious plan to help. Meanwhile, the scientists have located the rats, and are planning to exterminate them. In the end, only Mrs. Frisby's courage of the heart, and the legacy of her departed husband, can save them. Based on Robert C. O'Brien's book *Mrs. Frisby and the Rats of N.I.M.H.*

✗STOP: In the climactic swordfight between one of the friendly rats and a dissident rat the struggle is extremely intense, and the blades leave visible cuts in the bodies of the victims. In the scene in the laboratory, the animals are in obvious distress, and the rats are given injections in their abdomens; it is scary.

CAUTION: The farmer's cat is frightening and when the tractor starts up, the creatures of the field panic. At one point, the Frisby house begins to sink into the mud, and the terrified children are suffocating.

GO: This film features brilliant animation, great voice-overs, and an important theme.

THE SEVENTH VOYAGE OF SINBAD

RCA/Columbia
1958
94 minutes
Directed by: Nathan Juran
Starring: Kathryn Grant, Kerwin Matthews
MPPA rating: G

On the island of Colossa, Sinbad encounters the evil black-robed magician, Sikura, who is pursued by a huge cyclops. And while Sinbad and friends hold off the cyclops, the magician produces a lamp and rubs it. Out comes a genie in the form of a small boy who protects the group. But in the chaos that follows, the magician drops the lamp and it is recovered by the cyclops. Sikura wants to go back to retrieve it, but Sinbad adamantly refuses. (He is on a critical mission to deliver the princess Parisa to the Caliph of Bagdad, in order that the two should marry, thereby ensuring peace between their two kingdoms.) Once in Bagdad, the evil Sikura shrinks Parisa, then bargains with Sinbad. A secret potion will restore the princess to her normal size, but the critical ingredient (made from the shell of a Roc's egg) can only be found on the island of Colossa. With little choice, Sinbad sets sail for Colossa again, where he and a few of his men are promptly caught and locked up by the hungry cyclops. But the tiny princess picks the lock on their cage, and Sinbad escapes to find the desired ingredient. At this point Sikura betrays Sinbad, forcing a final confrontation in which, among other things, Sikura unleashes a huge dragon upon Sinbad and his men.

See reviews for these Sinbad movies:
The Golden Voyage of Sinbad
Sinbad and the Eye of the Tiger

SHIPWRECKED

Walt Disney Home Video
1991
93 minutes
Directed by: Nils Gaup
Starring: Gabriel Byrne, Stian Smestad
MPAA rating: PG

In 1859 in Norway, young Haakon Haakonsen goes to sea to pay his family's debts and save their homestead. As Haakon's ship goes through pirate territory, a villain named John Merrick gains entry onto the ship by impersonating an officer. Merrick poisons the Captain and takes over the ship, crewing it with his own men. Before long, though, a great storm wrecks the ship on an island where Haakon finds a treasure and evidence of Merrick's treachery. Haakon is soon reunited with his friends (Jens, a shipmate, and Mary, a stowaway who taught him how to read), and together they scuttle the bad guys, escape with the treasure and return to Norway to pay the family debts and reclaim the homestead. Based on the Book *Haakon Haakonsen* by O.V. Falck-Ytter.

CAUTION: Gabriel Byrne's character may be too frightening (or too threatening) for young children.

GO: Featuring excellent cinematography, this is a pirate movie with plenty of adventure but no gratuitous violence. Potentially threatening situations are treated with humor, and there is an excellent role model in the character of Mary.

■

THE SILVER CHAIR

Public Media Video
1988
165 minutes
Directed by: Alex Kirby
Starring: Tom Baker, Richard Henders,
    Camilla Power, David Thwaites
MPAA rating: no rating given

Eustace and his friend Jill return to a rather nasty boarding school, where they are pursued by a gang of bullies. The pair escapes through a previously locked garden door, on the far side of which, they find themselves in the magical land of Narnia. But they soon become separated and Jill meets the great lion, Aslan, alone. Aslan explains that they have been called to perform a difficult task — to find a long-lost prince, or die trying. Aslan then gives Jill four signs to guide her in her quest; the first of which is that Eustace must greet an old and dear friend as soon as he sets foot in Narnia, in order to get the help they will need. But it's too late. Without the benefit of Aslan's instructions Eustace has already failed to recognize his friend (the now-aged King Caspian) and the old man has boarded a ship and set sail. The pair, having missed the first sign, are forced to spend the night at King Caspian's city of Cair Paravel. Their luck does improve, however, and they set out to find Caspian's long-lost son, Prince Rilian. As each of the signs is revealed, the children survive encounters with cannibal giants, and a treacherous witch, who rules a grim underground domain. The

children free Rilian from the witch's spell and return home.

CAUTION: The film is slow and long and will probably leave little ones far behind. Eustace and Jill provide a less than positive example as they are rude to each other during most of their stay in Narnia.

GO: The locations and the sets, while obviously created on a limited budget, are magnificent, and the special effects are decent enough. It has been remarked that the cast of the Narnia series isn't particularly charismatic, but they are generally true to C.S. Lewis's protagonists. This is a BBC Television Production in association with Wonderworks.

SINBAD AND THE EYE OF THE TIGER

Columbia
1977
113 minutes
Directed by: Sam Wanamaker
Starring: Kurt Christian,
    Taryn Power, Jane Seymour,
    Damien Thomas, Patrick Troughton,
    Patrick Wayne, Margaret Whiting
MPAA rating: G

Sinbad and his men arrive in port only to discover (to their disgust) that the city is closed. And after fighting off an assortment of evil creatures, Sinbad saves the Princess Farah and together they swim to Sinbad's ship. The princess tearfully explains that her brother, Crown Prince Kassim, has been turned into a baboon by the evil witch, Xenobia. And so, Sinbad sails to find the great sage Melanthias, a man of mythical wisdom, who will help Sinbad restore Kassim to his human shape. It's an exciting adventure from that point on, as Sinbad encounters giant wasps, bronze minotaurs and friendly troglodytes (all made wonderfully real by Ray Harryhausen's amazing effects). And when Sinbad and his friends find the sage and get the advice they need, they sail to the ice-locked land of Hyperborea, where Kassim is restored and the showdown with Xenobia, who turns into a giant sabre-toothed tiger, takes place.

Other titles in this series are:
The Golden Voyage of Sinbad
The Seventh Voyage of Sinbad

CAUTION: Young children may find some situations too intense, and the fight at the end of the film between the giant tiger and a troglodyte is particularly realistic.

GO: Once again, Sinbad is an excellent adventure from the Ray Harryhausen school of special effects.

THE SNOW QUEEN

BFS Video
1992
56 minutes
Directed by: Andrew Gosling
Starring: Linda Slater, Joshua Le Touzel
MPAA rating: not rated

When demons decide to take the devil's mirror (which makes beautiful things ugly, and hearts turn to ice) up to reflect the face of God, they laugh so hard that they drop it on the way and it shatters into thousands of pieces and falls to Earth. There, a small piece becomes lodged in the heart of Kay,

a young boy who is out walking with his good friend Gerda. One night as Gerda's grandmother tells the children about the Snow Queen on Christmas Eve, Kay becomes unusually belligerent and runs off into the snowy night. There the Snow Queen finds him and whisks him away to her ice palace, where she tells him that if he solves a puzzle he will gain a new pair of skates. Meanwhile, Gerda searches for her friend and eventually becomes hostage to some gypsies. The gypsies finally give Gerda a reindeer that she can ride to the Snow Queen's palace. When she arrives she melts the ice fragment in Kay's heart and the spell is broken. On Christmas morning Kay receives his new skates. Based on a story by Hans Christian Andersen.

CAUTION: This film is probably too scary for young children — the faceless witch, in particular. In one scene a robber is shown with a blood-covered knife, and in another a coachman is shown dead with a knife sticking out of his stomach. The sound track is ominous.

GO: An effective combination of animation and live-action, in this production the people are superimposed against painted backgrounds.

■

THE SOUND OF MUSIC

CBS/Fox
1965
174 minutes
Directed by: Robert Wise
Starring: Julie Andrews, Christopher Plummer
MPAA rating: G

When a young nun named Maria has trouble fitting in at the convent, she tries her luck at being a governess, taking an assignment with the von Trapp family. Baron von Trapp is an Austrian aristocrat and a captain in the Austrian navy, and his children are notorious for making short work of governesses. But the children soon learn that Maria is as tough as they are, and as she is by far the most entertaining nanny they have ever had, they befriend her. And when the Baron sternly expresses his reservations about Maria's casual style, she even stands up to him, and he is both dumbfounded and much-impressed by her strength of character. But as soon as Maria realizes that she is falling in love with the Baron (who is engaged to someone else), she returns to the convent, and the whole von Trapp family is crestfallen. But Maria can't stay away long and returns to confess her feelings for the baron (feelings which are mutual) just as the baron is being forced to command a ship in the German navy. The baron makes plans for the family's escape to Switzerland. And after nearly being captured by Nazi soldiers (alerted by the boyfriend of the eldest von Trapp girl), they receive help from Maria's friends at the convent, and escape Austria over the alps. This film is based on a true story.

CAUTION: You may have to do a little explaining about Nazis. The film is very long, so you may want to spread it over two nights.

GO: One of the great musicals of this era, its list of hit songs includes: "The Sound of Music," "My Favorite Things," "Sixteen Going on Seventeen."

STAR WARS

CBS/Fox
1977
121 minutes
Directed by: George Lucas
Starring: Carrie Fisher, Harrison Ford,
  Alec Guinness, Mark Hamill
MPAA rating: PG

In another galaxy, in the distant past, the democratic Republic has been undermined from within, by evil men using the enormous power of the dark side of the Force. To cement control of their Empire, the evil rulers design and build the Death Star, an enormous battlestation capable of destroying an entire world. Then, by chance, two droids, R2-D2 and C-3P0, carrying stolen schematics of the Death Star, come into the hands of a farm boy named Luke Skywalker; this attracts the attention of the evil Lord Vader whose minions will stop at nothing to track the droids down and retrieve the plans. And when R2-D2 goes to the desert home of Obi Wan Kenobi (one of the few remaining members of the nearly extinct mystical order of Jedi Knights), Luke follows and learns that his own father was once a Jedi, but was betrayed and killed by the evil Vader. He also learns that the droid contains critical schematics of the Death Star (sent by princess Leia, who's being held at the battlestation). Luke returns home, where he finds that the agents of the Empire have destroyed the farm and murdered his aunt and uncle. Luke vows to become a Jedi like his father. He and Obi Wan enlist the services of swashbuckling smuggler, Han Solo, to help them cross the galaxy, rescue Princess Leia and get the plans to the rebels.

Other titles in the Star Wars trilogy:
The Empire Strikes Back
Return of the Jedi

CAUTION: This is a film about the struggle between good and evil and consequently features a lot of combat. Darth Vader is certain to be a figure of terror for very young viewers and Obi Wan, a beloved central character, is killed in a duel with Darth Vader.

GO: This ground-breaking space opus is already considered to be a classic and a visionary effort. Its incredible effects (made on a modest budget, compared to today's standards) are still as vital and fantastic as they were in 1977.

THE SWISS FAMILY ROBINSON

Walt Disney Home Video
1960
128 minutes
Directed by: Ken Annakin
Starring: James MacArthur, Dorothy McGuire, John Mills, Tommy Kirk
MPAA rating: G

In the nineteenth century, a family headed for a colony in New Guinea is shipwrecked on a tropical island. Salvaging items from the ship, the father, mother and two teenage boys build a tree house complete with running water. The addition of a young woman from another ship (saved by the boys during a reconnaissance trip) causes some conflict between them, but this pales in comparison to the battle the family faces when an invading ship of sabre-wielding oriental pirates arrives on the island. Based on the book by Johann Wyss.

CAUTION: Some young animal lovers may be upset by scenes in which animals from the ship are attacked by sharks; large dogs attack a tiger, and a zebra in quicksand is surrounded by hyenas. Also, pirates with saber-like swords converge on one of their own with hacking motions, and the family is obliged to defend itself by shooting pirates (no blood).

GO: Baby monkeys, tigers, a baby elephant, dogs, sea turtles, ostriches, parrots and lizards are all featured in this exciting family adventure. Kids are sure to like the family's clever inventions, too.

■

TALES FOR ALL SERIES

Cinéma Plus/HBO Cannon Video/
Astral Home Video
1984–1993
90–100 minutes each

Produced by Québecois filmmaker Rock Demers and Les productions la fête, the *Tales for All* series of 14 films (with more to come) has garnered more than 135 international awards. The films feature many different writers and directors; many have magical or mystical elements, and all are generally geared for family viewing. In the majority of the films, there is no coarse language and almost no violence. (See our section for children aged ten to thirteen for more reviews in this series.)

The Case of the Witch That Wasn't (Tale #10)

Penpals Melanie and Florence spend the summer together, befriend an eccentric old woman and solve a mystery in what turns out to be a season of great change for everyone. Winner of the Most Popular Film Prize at the Beauvais Festival in France. (Astral Home Video, 1990)

✗ The Dog Who Stopped the War (Tale #1)

In a small Quebec town, school has just let out for the Christmas holidays. Mark and Luke and the rest of the kids arrange war games and divide into two armies, the main rule being that hostilities end at sundown. Luke is overbearing, bossy and generally a tyrant, while Mark is quieter and devoted to his beautiful St. Bernard, Cleo. Mark has the smaller force, but his intellectual friend Warren designs a massive snow-fort, and newcomer Sophie lends courage and tenacity. And so the great war begins, set to last for the entire Christmas holidays. After Mark's force builds the biggest snowfort of all time, Luke's swelling army besieges it. Meanwhile, Luke and Sophie begin to grow fonder of each other, to the point of after-dark meetings, when hostilities are suspended. But the war goes on, and assault after assault is repelled by the great fort, until the climactic attack.

✗STOP: Mark's dog dies, smothered by the fort as it collapses on her, and Mark is absolutely crushed by grief — as will many young viewers be who are caught unprepared for this shocker.

GO: Winner of Golden Reel Award in 1984 and the 1986 Grand Prize at France's Festival of Films.

✗ The Great Land of Small (Tale #5)

A little man named Fritz, from the Great Land of Small, comes to the woods of northern Quebec, with mystic gold which can bring great good to the world. He gives the gold to a rough pub owner, Flannigan, warning him: Use it wisely for the good of all, or it will cause your own downfall. But Flannigan is greedy, and when his daughter Sarah also receives a gold nugget he steals it from her. Convinced that Sarah and her friends, Jenny and David, are connected in some way to the little man, Flannigan chases them. Jenny and David escape in a canoe with Fritz, and are caught in the rapids and presumed drowned. In truth, the kids have travelled, for a time, to the Great Land of Small. Their return provokes a final confrontation with Flannigan, who, in the end, comes to realize that he cares more for his daughter than anything else.

✗STOP: Flannigan enters his daughter's room, paws through her things, and takes her gold nugget.

CAUTION: Some of the characters in the Great Land of Small are pretty strange, and Fritz, who is rather gross, has a propensity to burp. At the end of the film, Fritz, now out of magic, is stranded on Earth, where he must wait under every rainbow for his brother the king to save him.

Reach for the Sky (Tale #12)

Corina is a ten-year-old who dreams of winning an Olympic gold in gymnastics, so she begs her coach to allow her to apply to the prestigious school in Deva, Romania. It takes her two years to gain acceptance into the school and even then the tough Romanian coach disapproves of her. Soon the pressures of maintaining her marks and improving her skills as a gymnast become almost impossible to bear. But when the time for the world championship competition arrives, Corina finally realizes her dream.

CAUTION: In one emotional scene, a budding gymnast breaks her wrist and her career is over. This film was made with actors from the country of its origin and was dubbed into English. (Children find this technique less irksome than adults.)

GO: This is a true-to-life account of the hard-working and unglamorous world of gymnastics, which is not at all romanticized. Excellent for the budding athlete.

Tadpole and the Whale
(Tale #6)

Daphne, known as Tadpole, is a twelve-year-old girl with extraordinary powers. She is completely comfortable underwater; moreover, she can hear and understand the songs of whales. Her best friends are Grandpa Thomas, a salty old seadog, and a dolphin, Elvar, with whom she can communicate. She keeps busy recording the enchanting songs of humpback whales from Grandpa Hector's home, Old Manor. But when Grandpa Hector decides to sell the manor to a consortium which is planning to put in a resort, Daphne is inconsolable. Then the trouble is compounded when a young couple are stranded at sea. Daphne rushes to their aid only to hit her head and sink into the water. Then it's up to Elvar to save Daphne.

GO: Beautiful underwater photography highlights this exciting and informative adventure, which appeals to a very broad age range. (For young viewers this is a nonviolent film, featuring lots of dolphins and whales at play, and for older children, it's an entertaining way to learn about marine mammals, their origins, senses and behavioral patterns.)

Tommy Tricker and the Stamp Traveller (Tale #7)

Tommy Tricker is a young scamp who helps support his huge fatherless family with stamp-related scams. When he tricks fellow stamp enthusiast Ralph James into giving up Ralph's father's prize Bluenose stamp, "The Man in the Mast," a strange chain of events is set into motion. Ralph and his sister discover a cryptic letter hidden in the cover of an old stamp album, they learn of the existence of another stamp album which is hidden in Australia and which contains a fabulous fortune in rare stamps. The children also find an incantation which, when spoken, will cause the speaker to shrink onto a stamp. The "stamp traveller" can then be mailed anywhere in the world, and upon reaching his or her destination, will be restored to normal size. But there is a danger: If the stamp traveller does *not* reach the address on the letter, he or she must remain on the stamp forever. Tommy Tricker also learns the incantation, and he and Ralph engage in a race for the Sidney Stamp and Coin Shop, where the fortune is allegedly hidden. And after an exciting (and thoroughly informative) trip, the boys retrieve the valuable album and return home on a letter bound for Canada.

GO: Besides being a unique adventure which appeals to children of all ages, *Tommy Tricker and the Stamp Traveller* has inspired many a youngster to take up stamp collecting. Winner of the 1989 Parents' Choice Award for Best Children's Film of the Year, this film features original music by Kate, Anna and Jane McGarrigle.

The Young Magician
(Tale #4)

Pierrot, a devotee of the art of magic, discovers, to his infinite surprise, that he possesses real telekinetic powers. At first, this proves a major problem for him, as he is completely alienated from his peers and from society in general. But when a military weapon of enormous destructive power is accidentally dropped from an aircraft and ends up lodged in a factory roof, Pierrot is called upon to save the day.

✘ TEENAGE MUTANT NINJA TURTLES: THE MOVIE

Alliance
1990
95 minutes
Directed by: Steve Barron
Starring: David Forman, Judith Hoag, Elias Koteas, Josh Pais, James Saito, Michelan Sisti, Leif Tilden
Starring the voices of: Kevin Clash, Corey Feldman, David McCharen, Robbie Rist, Brian Tochi
MPAA rating: PG

When a highly organized gang of masked martial artists is recruiting young men and terrorizing New York City, only TV reporter April O'Neill has the courage to publicly identify the scourge. And in so doing she earns the attention of the evil head of the gang, Shredder. But Shredder's plans are thwarted when, as his gang ambushes April in a subway station, Raphael, a Teenage Mutant Ninja Turtle, intervenes and rescues her. She is taken to the Turtles' secret hideout where she meets the rest of the company (Leonardo, Donatello and Michelangelo, and their mentor, a mutant rat named Splinter), and learns about their radioactive origins. Then things get tense when Splinter is kidnapped and a troubled teenage boy Danny runs away to join the gang. But with the help of April and a fellow martial-artist, Casey Jones, the Turtles still manage to save the day.

✘ STOP: There is fighting throughout, and it's often accompanied by realistic sound effects. April is slapped and punched senseless by a group of masked thugs: twice. Casey refers to April as Broadzilla.

CAUTION: One complaint we have is that the Turtles, despite the efforts of their mystic teacher, are relentlessly low-brow. Also, the bad guys are hardly original: they've been stolen from every martial arts movie of the past twenty years, and the endlessly derivative evil folks do tend to get a bit tiring.

GO: It's action packed, good and evil are clearly defined, and Danny learns a valuable lesson about family values and hanging around with the right sort of people.

THAT DARN CAT

Walt Disney Home Video
1965
115 minutes
Directed by: Robert Stevenson
Starring: Dean Jones, Roddy McDowall,
  Hayley Mills, Dorothy Provine
MPAA rating: G

Two daring bank robbers kidnap a teller during a heist, and hide out a mere block and a half from where they pulled the job. When one of them stops off at the local fishmonger's, ultra-intelligent and ever-mooching feline D.C. (Darn Cat) tags along in hopes of a freebie. He gets into the robbers' hide-out where the resourceful teller scratches a message on her watch and slips it around D.C.'s neck. And that night, when D.C.'s owner sees the message "Hel …" she realizes what has happened, and goes to the FBI. Then a high-powered team of agents are instructed to tail D.C. And inevitably, shenanigans and hijinks galore follow, as D.C. leads the FBI to the bad guys. Based on the book *Undercover Cat* by the Gordons.

CAUTION: The bank robbers are a little scary, and at one point one of them raises his fist to strike the helpless teller. There is a fairly rough fistfight at the climax.

GO: This is an entertaining comedy-mystery in the classic Disney tradition.

■

THE THREE CABALLEROS

Walt Disney Home Video
1945
71 minutes
Directed by: Norman Ferguson
Starring: Donald Duck, Jose Carioca,
  Panchito
MPAA rating: G

It's Friday the thirteenth, Donald's birthday, and his Latin American friends send him a huge present which includes, among other things, a projector and a reel of film containing an assortment of stories. The first is the story of Pablo, a little penguin whose burning desire is to move to tropical shores, but who freezes whenever he moves away from his stove. The second is a film in which viewers learn all about a variety of South American birds. And the third tells the tale of an old gaucho from Uruguay who, as a little gauchito, found the most amazing bird in history, a small burro with a functional pair of wings. Donald is then joined by his friend Jose Carioca, a parrot who teaches him about Brazil, and by the Mexican bird, Panchito, who sings the legendary hit "We're Three Caballeros" and who takes Donald and friends on a tour of Mexican tradition and culture.

CAUTION: Some of the animation is downright psychedelic, representing a real exploratory phase in the company's history.

GO: *The Three Caballeros* was one of the first full-scale films to combine animation and live-action, and is a great way (if a tad dated) to introduce young viewers to the Latin cultures. The music is fantastic, too.

✗ THE THREE LIVES OF THOMASINA

Walt Disney Home Video
1964
97 minutes
Directed by: Don Chaffey
Starring: Susan Hampshire,
  Patrick McGoohan
MPAA rating: not rated

A new vet has moved into the small town of Inveragh, Scotland, in 1912. He is Dr. Andrew MacDhui, a most difficult man, full of newfangled medical ideas. He is also a widower and the father of young Mary MacDhui. Mary's pride and joy is a self-satisfied orange tabby named Thomasina, the narrator of the tale. And when a chance encounter with an otherwise gentle guide-dog named Bruce leaves Thomasina at death's door, MacDhui decides to put her to sleep. Thomasina travels into another world — to the dark, cat-filled domain of the goddess Bast. But Bast sends Thomasina back, and the cat finds herself in the care of Laurie MacGregor, a beautiful, mysterious young woman who lives in the glen and has a way with animals. Laurie nurses Thomasina back to health, but the cat has lost all knowledge of her former life. Mary, meanwhile, is crushed by grief, and won't even speak to her father. Desperate to reach his daughter, MacDhui breaks out of his cold shell, and, as Mary is failing, turns to Laurie for help. But in the end, it's all up to Thomasina.

✗STOP: Thomasina dies and Mary reacts violently to the cat's death.

CAUTION: Thomasina's mystical voyage to the domain of Bast is a little eerie, and may provoke some questions about the hereafter. In one scene a badger is shown with his bloody paw caught in a leg-hold trap and in another MacDhui fights with thugs at the circus. Also, some viewers are irritated by the way Mary treats her father.

GO: This is a magical tale in the Disney tradition.

TREASURE ISLAND

Walt Disney Home Video
1950
96 minutes
Directed by: Byron Haskin
Starring: Bobby Driscoll, Robert Newton,
  Basil Sydney
MPAA rating: G

When a former shipmate of the blood-thirsty pirate captain John Flint shows up at the Admiral Benbow Inn and promptly dies, Jim Hawkins, the son of a tavern mistress, comes into possession of a map which reveals the location of Flint's immense treasure. Local gentlemen outfit a ship to sail to Treasure Island but manage to hire a crew composed almost entirely of the late Flint's former shipmates. These knaves are led by the one-legged Long John Silver, and wherever Silver is, murder, treachery and savage combat are never far behind. Yet despite Silver's horrific past and intemperate nature, he has a soft spot in his heart for the brave and honest Jim.

CAUTION: The most intense moment is the famous scene in which Jim is pursued up into the rigging of the ship by the knife-wielding, homicidal Israel Hands, and in which Jim is forced to shoot the other, taking a dagger in the shoulder in the process.

GO: In this version of the classic tale, Robert Newton so popularized the character of Long John Silver that a television series was created featuring him and his scurvy mates. The violence is tame by today's standards, but represents a perfect example of exciting action contained within the boundaries of good taste.

■

THE TROUBLE WITH ANGELS

RCA/Columbia
1966
110 minutes
Directed by: Ida Lupino
Starring: June Harding, Hayley Mills,
    Rosalind Russel, Camilla Sparv
MPAA rating: no rating given

Two teenage girls from wealthy families are sent to St. Francis convent school. Rachel Devery comes from a loving family, but Mary Clancy is an orphan, cast away by her playboy uncle. The two become fast friends, and the film follows their three-year career at St. Francis, where their various spectacular pranks serve to infuriate the convent's Mother Superior, earning them constant kitchen duty and penance in the chapel. Finally, when the pair smoke a couple of left-over cigars in the basement and cause a full-scale fire alert, the Mother Superior is ready to expel the girls. But when she meets Mary's uncle, she decides to grit her teeth and hang on. The course of Mary's life begins to change when,

deserted at Christmas, she stays over at the convent for the holidays and experiences the simple beauty of the nuns' celebration; then, she discovers that her ideal, the radiantly-beautiful Sister Constance, is leaving to teach in a leper colony. Mary is profoundly touched by Sister Constance's selfless courage. Finally, after much agonized soul-searching, Mary makes the difficult decision to stay on and become a novice after graduation. At first, Rachel is devastated. She feels so betrayed that she won't even talk to Mary. But finally, the two are reconciled, and Rachel departs for the world with Mary harboring the hope that one day Rachel will return for good. If that should happen, the Mother Superior warns her: I quit!

CAUTION: One of the Sisters dies, and there is a scene of mourning.

GO: This is a gentle, humorous and touching tale for anyone over six. Mary's transformation from a hellion to a sensitive young woman is straightforward enough to be understood even by younger children.

THE UNDERCOVER GANG

MCA
1986
73 minutes
Directed by: Peter Sharp
Starring: Darryl Beattie, Alix Chapman,
    Peter Hayden, Miles Murphy, Jon Trimmer,
    Emma Vere-Jones
MPAA rating: no rating given

During World War I, in the small town of Jessop, New Zealand, a mysterious figure is sabotaging buildings. And while inspiring teacher Clippy Hedges is trying to give the children of Jessop a decent education, and Miss Bolton is busy directing a patriotic play, children Noel and Kitty Wix, Phil Miller and Irene, are doing their best to track down the perpetrator. While on a school swimming outing, Noel and Miller discover an incriminating oil-can at the bottom of the river. Meanwhile Edgar Marwick, the suspected firebug, is preparing another arson, and when the boys follow him, they prevent a destructive fire; however, nothing can be proven to the satisfaction of the law, and the sergeant even begins to suspect the boys. So Miller and Noel team up with Irene and Kitty to scout out the Marwick place. But things get hot quickly, and Kitty is captured. The gang does get the police out quickly enough to save her, but not quickly enough to incriminate the evil Marwick. Then the Undercover Gang really goes to work, keeping Marwick under surveillance until they can catch him red-handed. But catching a madman red-handed is not without perils of its own.

CAUTION: The Marwicks consistently accuse the children of lying and Hedges and Marwick duke it out, with bloody noses as the result.

GO: This is an intriguing period mystery for young fans of the genre, and a good example of kids making a difference.

●

Walt Disney Home Video
1981
84 minutes
Directed by: John Hough
Starring: Carroll Baker, Bette Davis,
    Lynn-Holly Johnson, David McCallum
MPAA rating: PG

From the novel *A Watcher in the Woods* by Florence Engel Randall. When the Curtis family rents a beautiful, secluded manor house in the country, everything seems a bit strange. Mr. Curtis, a pianist, and Mrs. Curtis, a writer of children's books, like it very much, but their older daughter, Jan, is uneasy. Immediately she feels that someone is watching her. Mrs. Aylwood, the eccentric lady of the manor, lives in a secluded cottage on the property and communicates with unseen entities. Jan sees a terrifying apparition in a mirror (a blindfolded girl reaching out to her); her younger sister Ellie hears voices and writes the name Karen backwards in the dust on a window. Jan learns that Karen was Mrs. Aylwood's daughter, who disappeared in a terrible fire in an old chapel. After a series of terrifying supernatural events, Jan begins an investigation to find out exactly what happened to Karen. She begins to put pressure on the three people who last saw the young woman, and learns that Karen was going through an initiation rite at the chapel, and vanished. The paranormal phenomena become more and more intense until, during a total

AGES 6 TO 10

eclipse of the sun, the dreadful mystery is revealed. Karen and a mysterious being from another dimension exchanged places during the strange rite, and now the three original participants must be assembled, and the rite reenacted, in order to bring Karen back.

✗STOP: Don't be deceived by the Disney label. This is a horror movie. Frightening events are introduced with sudden shock value and accompanied by loud bursts of spooky music. An apparition beckons and gestures from the wrong side of mirrors on several occasions, a blindfolded maiden lies in an ancient coffin, windows suddenly break. And there are lots of cheap false alarm moments. Ellie is possessed by a spirit and the final transformation is fraught with terror and peril. There is also a near-drowning sequence which is grotesque and extremely frightening for young children.

CAUTION: Even for grown-ups, this is a pretty intense effort.

■

WE ALL HAVE TALES

Rabbit Ears Productions Inc./Sony
1988–1992
30 minutes each
Directed by: C.W. Rogers

These videos are productions of fairy tales and legends and are not fully-animated. Motion is simulated by the camera moving over the quality illustrations. Top film stars provide the narration while the music is played by noted musicians.

Titles in the collection are:
Anansi (told by Denzel Washington, music by UB40)

The Boy Who Drew Cats (told by William Hurt, music by Mark Isham)

Brementown Musicians (told by Bob Hoskins)

Brer Rabbit and the Wonderful Tar Baby (told by Danny Glover, music by Taj Mahal)

East of the Sun, West of the Moon (told by Max Von Sydow, music by Lyle Mays)

The Emperor and the Nightingale (told by Glenn Close, music by Mark Isham)

The Emperor's New Clothes (told by Sir John Gielgud, music by Mark Isham)

Finn McCoul (told by Catherine O'Hara, music by Boys of the Lough)

The Fisherman and His Wife (told by Jodie Foster, music by Van Dyke Parks)

The Fool and the Flying Ship (told by Robin Williams, music by The Klezmer Conservatory Band)

The Gingham Dog and the Calico Cat (told by Amy Grant, music by Chet Atkins)

How the Leopard Got His Spots (told by Danny Glover, music by Ladysmith Black Mambazo)

How the Rhinoceros Got His Skin (told by Jack Nicholson, music by Bobby McFerrin)

Jack and the Beanstalk (told by Michael Palin, music by David A. Stewart)

King Midas and the Golden Touch (told by Michael Caine, music by Ellis Marsalis & Yo-Yo Ma)

Koi and the Kola Nuts (told by Whoopi Goldberg, music by Herbie Hancock)

The Legend of Sleepy Hollow (told By Glenn Close, music by Tim Story)

The Monkey People (told by Raul Julia, music by Lee Ritenour)

Mose the Fireman (told by Michael Keaton)

The Night Before Christmas; Best-Loved Yuletide Carols (told by Meryl Streep, music by The Edwin Hawkins Singers and others)

Paul Bunyan (told by Jonathon Winters, music by Leo Kottke with Duck Baker)

Peachboy (told by Sigourney Weaver, music by Ryuichi Sakamoto)

Pecos Bill (told by Robin Williams, music by Ry Cooder)

Puss in Boots (told by Tracey Ullman, music by Jean-Luc Ponty)

Rumplestiltskin (told by Kathleen Turner, music by Tangerine Dream)

The Three Billygoats Gruff; The Three

Little Pigs (told by Holly Hunter, music by Art Lande)

Thumbelina (told by Kelly McGillis, music by Mark Isham)

The Tiger and the Brahmin (told by Ben Kingsley, music by Ravi Shankar)

CAUTION: These are beautifully produced videos. However, they are not fully-animated and may be too slow for some children.

GO: Between them these videos have won sixteen Parents' Choice Awards, two Grammy Awards and seven Action for Children's Television Awards.

WILLIE THE OPERATIC WHALE
(with Ferdinand the Bull and Lambert, the Sheepish Lion)

Willie the Operatic Whale When news of a singing whale reaches the scientific community, they react by proposing the theory that the whale has somehow swallowed an opera singer, and send out an expedition, led by the impressario Tetti-Tatti, to kill him. Willie, under the mistaken impression that he has finally been discovered, races to his audition and is harpooned, but continues his career in heaven.

Ferdinand the Bull While all the other bulls run and jump and bang heads, Ferdinand sits quietly in the shade, smelling the flowers. But when the men in the funny hats

come to pick the bulls for the bullfight in Madrid, Ferdinand accidentally sits on a bumblebee. The men erroneously think that Ferdinand is the monster they've been looking for and put him into a bullfight. The result is a pacifistic fiasco, and Ferdinand is summarily retired to his flower garden.

Lambert, the Sheepish Lion It's the old stork mix-up routine in the pasture, as Lambert the Lion accidentally gets delivered to a flock of sheep, and has to adapt to a life as a herbivore. Lambert can't do anything right, and he is the butt of many pasture pranks. But as time goes by, and everyone grows up, and a wolf threatens the flock, Lambert recalls his heredity and saves the day.

CAUTION: *Willie the Operatic Whale* is billed as a Wagnerian-style tragedy and the ending is desperately sad.

THE WIZARD

Jimmy Woods is a traumatized little boy who is more than a handful for his mother, and she and her new husband intend to put him in a home. While his father Sam and his older brother Nick are screaming at each other, Jimmy's brother Corey slips out to collect Jimmy and together, armed only with Corey's skateboard, they stow away aboard an ice-cream truck heading for California. Jimmy's mother and stepfather then hire Putnam, a cold-hearted hunter who specializes in tracking down runaways, and Sam and Nick set off after the boys as well. At a stopover in a little midwestern town, Corey gives Jimmy a quarter for a video game to keep him amused. Jimmy racks up a huge score. It turns out that Jimmy is a video game wizard. And when he beats their new friend Haley, she and Corey realize that Jimmy has one hope: to get to Video Armageddon, the video championships in L.A., and win the big prize. So off they go, chased across the country by Putnam, and financing their trip by setting up video suckers on their way. In the course of their adventures, the reason for Jimmy's condition is revealed. Finally, the kids reach the championship, chased by everyone, and Jimmy takes on the best players in the country with his future at stake. In the end he prevails, the family is reconciled, and the central mystery of Jimmy's life, his constant urge to return to California, is solved.

CAUTION: The reason Jimmy has withdrawn from life is that he witnessed his twin sister drowning; certain unflattering references are made to Jimmy's state. At one point, to delay Putnam, Haley points at him and yells: He touched my breast! — a little unsettling as it gives kids the idea that they can use a false accusation of sexual abuse as a form of power.

GO: Haley is a good role model for girls. She is tough and resourceful and smart. And Corey must be the best brother in the history of the world.

WIZARDS OF THE LOST KINGDOM

Astral
1986
78 minutes
Directed by: Hector Olivera
Starring: Bo Svenson
MPAA rating: PG

It was an age of magic, an age of sorcery, an age of chaos, an age of cheesy special effects; it was an age of poorly choreographed swordfights and pompous musical accompaniment, when wizard fought wizard, warrior fought warrior, for yet another great sword of power, and yet one more ring of … yes, power. They lost the sword, but they kept tabs on the ring, and for a time, King Tyler ruled in peace. Simon is the son of a court magician. When the castle comes under attack from evil wizard-type Shirka, both the king and Simon's dad are killed, and Simon's girlfriend Laura is imprisoned. Simon escapes with the ring and his servant Gofax, and promptly falls into one of Shirka's traps. But he is rescued by the warrior Kor the Conqueror (Bo Svenson visibly reads cue cards in this appearance). And together he and Simon wander around for awhile, kick a few butts, and reclaim the castle and the girl. Hooray!

CAUTION: Humans over the age of twelve should not watch this film. Shirka turns people into mice, and his midget pet monster pounces on them.

GO: One eight-year old boy we know solemnly informed us that this is the greatest film ever made.

✘ X-MEN

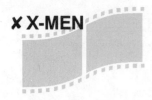

Based on the hugely popular comic books, this animated series features a group of mutant superheroes who have banded together to fight their evil counterparts. Many humans are frightened of the mutants' superpowers but the X-Men have pledged to uphold justice for all.

Pryde of the X-Men

New World Video
1988
23 minutes
Directed by: Rudy Cataldi, Charlie Downs, Eileen Dunn, Ray Lee, Margaret Nichols, Stan Phillips, Tom Ray, Neal Warner
Written by: Larry Parr
Narrated by: Stan Lee
Unrated made for television.

Featured X-Men: Colossus, the Dazzler, Nightcrawler, Kitty Pryde; Villains: Magneto, White Queen, Juggernaut, Blob, Pyro, Toad and Beast (not to be confused with "The Beast," an X-Man)

This stand-alone story features a slightly different group of X-Men.

Vol. 1: Night of the Sentinels

PolyGram Video
1992
44 minutes
Directed by: Graham Morris, Karen Peterson
Written by: Mark Edward Edens

Featured X-Men: Storm, Cyclops, Morph, The Beast, Rogue, Gambit, Jubilee

Prof. X discovers that the Mutant Control Agency's files are being used to hunt down mutants, so Storm and Cyclops lead a mission to destroy the files. Morph, one of the X-Men, is killed. Wolverine blames Cyclops for Morph's death.

Vol. 2: Enter Magneto!

PolyGram Video
1993
25 minutes
Directed by: Graham Morris, Karen Peterson
Written by: Jim Carlson, Terrence McDonnell

Featured X-Men The Beast, Wolverine, Storm.
Villains: Magneto, Sabertooth

Magneto sets in motion a plan to fire and detonate nuclear missles; foiled, he vows to make the X-Men his enemies, along with all humanity.

Vol. 3: Deadly Reunions

PolyGram Video
1993
25 minutes
Directed by: Graham Morris, Karen Peterson
Written by: Don Glutt

Featured X-Men: Jubilee, Storm, Cyclops, Rogue, Wolverine.
Villains: Magneto, Sabertooth

Magneto attacks a chemical factory and the X-Men respond.

Vol. 4: Captive Hearts

PolyGram Video
1993
25 minutes
Directed by: Graham Morris, Karen Peterson
Written by: Martin Isenberg, Robert Skir

Featured X-Men: Storm, Wolverine, Cyclops, Jean;
Villains: Callisto

A group of mutants called Morlocks live beneath the city. Eventually all

AGES 6 TO 10

the X-Men are either wounded or taken prisoner by them. Storm challenges the Morlocks' leader to a duel and wins.

Vol. 5: Cold Vengeance

PolyGram Video
1993
25 minutes
Directed by: Graham Morris, Karen Peterson
Written by: Michael Edens

Featured X-Men: Wolverine, Storm, Gambit, Jubilee.
Villains: Sabertooth

Wolverine goes to Alaska to be alone, and the evil Sabertooth follows him. The other X-Men check out an allegedly mutant-friendly country named Genosha. Genosha is not everything it seems: three X-Men are captured after a surprise attack by a Sentinel...

Also available: Vol. 6–12

✗**STOP:** The action and violence in these stories is virtually non-stop. The X-Men never kill humans but they do knock them out a lot, and the bad guys have no such moral qualms. And frankly, the animation is terrible.

CAUTION: Because the major characters are superhuman mutants, either superheroes or supervillains, they all experience a lot of physical abuse in their numerous battles. Characters get punched and kicked, shot at, threatened with mutilation, blown up, and zapped by energy beams. The male and female characters take equal part in this activity and suffer equal amounts of violence. There is a constant exchange of tough, aggressive talk which sometimes has sexual undertones; Rogue in particular tends to deliver lines like "Don't you know you're supposed to be polite on a first date, boys?" while tackling a bunch of troops. There are many characters and the newer series has fairly complex, interconnected plots which may be hard for younger children to follow. For instance, in Vol. 3 Storm has an attack of claustrophobia which is not explained until Vol. 4.

GO: Every episode deals with the prejudice of human society against the mutant outcasts. The anti-racist allegory is obvious to begin with and it is frequently reemphasized. The X-Men's team is almost evenly divided between the sexes, and the women play very strong, aggressive roles (the U.S. President is a woman, too). It's equality of a sort, but maybe not what Gloria Steinem had in mind.

ZORRO: THE LEGEND CONTINUES

Malofilm
1989
92 minutes
Directed by: Ray Austin
Starring: Patrice Camhi, Duncan Regehr, Efrem Zimbalist Jr.
MPAA rating: no rating given

In this remake of the traditional story, Zorro is thrown from his horse during a clash with the colonial soldiers, and lands in a rocky pit, hitting his head. When Felipe, his young deaf-mute servant, clambers down to rescue him, Zorro recalls his origins. Once known as Don Diego, the son of wealthy landowner Don Alejandro, Zorro was sent to Spain for four years to study with the greatest swordsman in Europe, in order to prepare him to lead the resistance against the oppressors of California. We then follow Don Diego's return to California, where he immediately earns the enmity of the evil governor, the Acalde, and, as the man in black, takes on the government troops single-handedly.

CAUTION: Certain scenes may be a little intense for young children.

GO: This film is a bit bland, but will entertain young swashbucklers.

Chapter 6

VIDEOS FOR AGES TEN TO THIRTEEN

If your child is between the ages of ten and thirteen, you are probably now in the area of quasi-adult films. So, for the purposes of this chapter, we are primarily concerned with films which fall under the PG heading, although we will include a handful of PG-13–rated films.

As we've already mentioned, the PG category is extremely broad and you can expect to find vastly different content from one film to the next. So you can't simply judge a film's suitability by its rating. (See chapter 2 for more information on ratings.)

WHAT WE'RE UP AGAINST
Peer pressure

Your child is now in social situations every bit as stressful as your own. He or she doesn't want to be perceived to be a loser. And having to hide the fact that mom and dad have disallowed *Terminator 2*, when it seems that everyone else has seen it, makes things tough. Visits to the video store often turn into battles. You want your child to watch *Treasure Island* because it's a great movie and you loved it when you were ten. But now he or she is ten, and in the nineties, Arnold Schwarzenegger is cool.

Star attraction

Preteens sometimes become attracted to an actor or actress and wish to watch everything that star appears in. However, often the films in which these teen stars play aren't even *remotely* suitable for your ten-year-old. So be careful. Check the ratings. Child star does not necessarily equal child viewing (a good example of this is *My Own Private Idaho*, an R-rated film featuring Keanu Reeves and River Phoenix).

The shrinking screen and other misconceptions

When the movies we've seen in the theater are transferred to video and shown on our television screens, we often succumb to the mistaken impression that the movies have been somehow magically transformed, losing their impact. And suddenly it seems all right to allow children to see a film that we wouldn't have considered taking them to in the theater.

But think again. Whether it's shown on the big screen or on your TV, it is *exactly* the same movie; the content is still the same. In fact, certain scenes of graphic or suggestive footage that were removed to lower the film's rating in the theater may, at the director's request, have been put back in in the video version, in effect making it even *more* unsuitable for child viewers!

THE CARE-GIVER'S LAMENT
Someone's not playing by the rules

If a family member or a baby-sitter is renting unsuitable films for your child, then while you are working hard at guiding your child's viewing, it is being undermined. (Sometimes even to score points with the child.)

Lay down the law and stick to it. (We have included a blank

page at the back of this book for you to list forbidden films, so that your baby-sitter can refer to it.)

Heading off the "can we get a horror movie?" request

Often when preteens get together they want to watch films that have the allure of the forbidden. Here are a few ways you can handle the situation:

You might prefer to settle for a comedy with a slightly racy theme, one which is obvious enough to make the older kids feel grown-up, but subtle enough that the younger ones simply won't get it. After all, children really like comedies and while they tend to associate horror films with being more mature, there are many lighthearted films that will serve the same purpose.

Empower your child to battle peer pressure by finding some more obscure films in different genres that your child can then introduce to his or her friends. It gives a child prestige to be able to say, "You mean you've never heard of this movie? It's great! Where have *you* been?"

Most stores have a VCR and a television out front. And generally, even a stubborn ten-year-old will agree to take a film after seeing a few minutes of it. (Especially if you don't recommend it too strongly!)

I give up

A lot of parents just give up and let their children see anything they want, wearily resigned to the fact that "if they don't see it at home, they'll see it somewhere else." But there are two very good reasons for maintaining your own standards in your own home. The first is that, if your children are watching grossly unsuitable material in your home as well as elsewhere, they are certainly going to be seeing a lot more of it. Research has given every indication that there is a direct correlation betweeen the amount of inappropriate viewing and the damage it can do. The second reason is that, without wishing to seem overly moralistic, it's one thing to acknowledge the inevitability of your child being exposed to unsuitable material, and it's quite another to be a contributor, especially in your child's eyes. And finally, while you're wrestling with this dilemma, keep in mind that you're not alone, and that consciousness of this problem is growing rapidly, spearheaded by the efforts of such celebrities as Arnold Schwarzenegger, Chuck Norris, and Emilio Estevez. Even now, plans are in effect to provide violence warnings on U.S. television programming.

When the genie is out of the bottle

There is a big jump in intensity from PG to PG-13 and then again from PG-13 to R. And once you've seen the next grade up, the previous rating does seem tame. So what do you do when your twelve-year-old has seen an R-rated action film and now everything in the PG category bores him? Following are a few suggestions:

> Choose PG films with an R feeling; that is, action-packed, fast moving and exciting films.
> Choose PG-13 films or PG–Warning films, and agree to compromise in one area. (It may be language.)
> Steer your child toward comedies, even cartoons. kids love comedies and are usually satisfied with a good laugh.
> Ask your retailer to suggest a title (within your specifications, of course).

One inventive fifteen-year-old we know puts the onus on herself. When she doesn't want her nine-year-old brother to see a film that's too advanced for him, she says it frightens her. He then feels very grown-up and, wanting to protect her, agrees to rent something else.

✗ ACE VENTURA: PET DETECTIVE

Warner Brothers
1993
85 minutes
Directed by: Tom Shadyac
Starring: Jim Carrey, Courtney Fox, Tone Loc,
    Sean Young
MPAA rating: PG-13

As his moniker indicates, Ace Ventura: Pet Detective specializes in locating and returning missing animals. In Miami, during the week leading up to the Superbowl, villains steal the Miami football team's mascot, Snowflake the dolphin. Ace Ventura is called in on the job. While relentlessly pursuing the investigation, rubber-faced Ace engages in various madcap hijinks, including antagonizing the local police, in particular their formidable lieutenant. He also engages in an unlikely romance with a beautiful Miami Dolphins executive. As the case takes its zany course, Ace nails down the culprit, a disgraced place-kicker who lost the 1984 Superbowl by missing a routine field goal and went mad. Now he has escaped from the sanitarium and is seeking revenge. Ace puts together the final pieces of the puzzle and saves the day.

✗ STOP: At the beginning of the film, a curvaceous client of Ace's offers him payment either in cash or, she says, "Shall I take your pants off?". She then drops to her knees and we see Ace from the waist up going through contortions. In another scene, Ace and his girlfriend tumble around suggestively under the covers with familiar sound effects. At the climax, Ace strips the evil transvestite lieutenant, and we are treated to a close-up outline of male genitalia. There is a vicious fistfight between the police lieutenant and Ace.

CAUTION: Coarse humor pervades this film, and there are a few scenes which may frighten very little ones, one involving the kidnapping of the dolphin, the other a nasty suprise in a shark tank.

GO: This is not a children's film; rather, it is a hilarious romp suitable for teens.

THE ADDAMS FAMILY

Paramount Home Video
1991
102 minutes
Directed by: Barry Sonnenfeld
Starring: Angelica Huston, Raul Julia,
    Christopher Lloyd
MPAA rating: PG-13

The Addams family is a macabre inversion of the normal North American family; immensely rich, they dwell in a sprawling run-down mansion straight out of a horror movie. The movie begins when Gomez Addams and his wife, Morticia, receive a visit from their crooked lawyer, Tully. Tully has been trying for years to swindle the wealthy eccentrics (without success), and when he is confronted by the evil Abigail Craven and her hulking son Gordon — who just happens to bear an uncanny resemblance to Gomez's long-lost brother Fester — a sinister plot is hatched: Gordon will impersonate Fester in order to gain access to the family's vault and its immense wealth. The delighted Addams family (although slightly suspicious) accepts the bogus Fester instantly, and the hijinks begin as Gordon must endure life with the Addamses. Oddly, he comes to cherish his new family, and a final showdown puts his loyalties to the test.

CAUTION: Overt sadism coupled with off-beat humor make this film unsuitable for some children. And the constant abuse in the Addams family's home — however satirical — leads one to speculate just how funny a child from a truly abusive household would find this film.

GO: This film is a big-budget extravaganza with superb casting. Connoisseurs will be struck by the uncanny resemblances of Julia, Huston and Lloyd to Charles Addams's original comic-strip characters.

✗ ADDAMS FAMILY VALUES

Paramount Home Video
1993
89 minutes
Directed by: Barry Sonnenfeld
Starring: Joan Cusack, Angelica Huston, Raul Julia, Christopher Lloyd
MPAA rating: PG-13

AGES 10 TO 13

Life is proceeding as usual for the Addams family when Morticia announces that she's going to have a baby: *now*. When the baby, Pubert, arrives, Wednesday and Pugsley promptly try to kill him. Chaos reigns. A succession of nannies cannot solve the problem, until the agency sends the irrepressible Debbie Dellinsky, who is absolutely unfazed by the Addams' grotesque lifestyle. Fester

falls for her like a ton of bricks; however, unbeknownst to the Addams family, Debbie is an evil "black widow" who identifies wealthy bachelors, marries them and then disposes of them. When Wednesday begins to suspect the truth, Debbie has her and Pugsley shipped off to Camp Chippewa, an exclusive and sickeningly cheerful summer camp for over-privileged children. In rapid succession, Debbie ensnares Fester, the children try in vain to bust out of the camp, the wedding takes place, and Debbie tries to electrocute Fester. When this fails, she makes Fester agree never to see his family again, and makes plans to blow him up. Meanwhile, Wednesday and Pugsley burn down Camp Chippewa. Finally, Debbie takes the entire Addams family prisoner and prepares to electrocute them. But deliverance comes from an unlikely source.

✗ STOP: The scenes of abuse, albeit in the style of black humor, are sure to frighten little ones. In the opening scene, the children are burying a live cat. In their efforts to kill their baby brother, they drop him off a roof, try to guillotine him, attempt to crush him with an anvil, and so on. Lurch gets a dart right in the mouth. Debbie sexually manipulates Fester, particularly on their wedding night, when she says, "After we make love, you can never see your family again, otherwise I could never achieve — you know …"

CAUTION: Faced with the reality of summer camp, Pugsley tries to hang himself. Wednesday drinks poison. Like the original, this is a relentlessly grim social satire, and the satirical intent may be entirely lost on the young. There is suggestive dialogue and sexual situations and Fester resembles a child in his response to them. Debbie calls Wednesday a tramp.

GO: You can't help liking the Addams family. This is one of the few sequels that holds up to the original.

ADVENTURES IN BABYSITTING

✗ THE ADVENTURES OF BARON MUNCHAUSEN

Touchstone Home Video
1987
102 minutes
Directed by: Chris Columbus
Starring: Maia Brewton, Keith Coogan,
   Anthony Rapp, Elizabeth Shue
MPAA rating: PG-13

RCA/Columbia
1988
126 minutes
Directed by: Terry Gilliam
Starring: Winston Dennis, Eric Idle,
   Charles McKeown, John Neville,
   Sarah Polley, Jonathan Pryce, Jack Purvis,
   Oliver Reed, Uma Thurman, Robin Williams
MPAA rating: PG

Chris Parker's easy baby-sitting job becomes complicated when a flaky friend calls and pursuades Chris to pick her up at the bus depot, taking the kids with her. On the way, the family station wagon blows a tire, and when the spooky one-armed truck driver who gives them a lift makes a detour to take pot-shots at his wife's lover, Chris and the kids become mixed up in all kinds of trouble. In short order, they make a daring escape from stolen-car dealers, sing the blues, battle street gangs, negotiate an inner city hospital, attend a wild university party, meet the living embodiment of Thor, confront the bad guys and get home before their parents do. It's all in a night's work for the greatest baby-sitter in history.

CAUTION: The children are frequently in peril. There is some racial stereotyping. Minimal swearing.

GO: This is a charming adventure that's low on swearing and violence (by today's standards), and high on excitement and fun. In one scene there is a significant message about the dangers of street life.

In the late eighteenth century, as the Sultan's army beseiges a European city, the play "The Adventures of Baron Munchausen" is being performed by a travelling theater group. Suddenly, the play is interrupted by the real Baron Munchausen, who (accompanied by a young stowaway named Sally) sets out in a hot air balloon in hopes of finding his lost companions with whom he will raise the siege. Those companions are: Berthold, who can run faster than a bullet; Albrecht, the strongest man on earth; Adolphus, who can see and shoot farther than a telescope; and Gustavus, who can hear over impossible distances and exhale harder than a hurricane. In the course of their search, the Baron and Sally visit the moon, where a jealous King is holding Berthold captive; they fall into a volcano and find themselves in the domain of Vulcan and his slinky wife Aphrodite; and they are swallowed by a sea-monster and expelled back to the city just in time to defeat the Sultan's forces and save the day.

✗**STOP**: In one scene, the Sultan plays an organ which produces screams instead of music as the victims trapped inside are tortured. Death is a frightening, skull-faced black angel and the eyes of the Sultan's executioner have been sewn shut.

CAUTION: The scene in Vulcan's domain has some very racy moments and the king of the Moon (when body and head aren't attached) is very carnal. There are noisy combat scenes throughout.

GO: A dazzling effort, *Baron Munchausen* has some incredible visual effects.

THE AIR UP THERE

Hollywood Pictures
1993
90 minutes
Directed by: Paul M. Glaser
Starring: Kevin Bacon, Charles Gitonga Maina, Yolanda Vasquez
MPAA rating: PG

Jimmy Dolan is a hotheaded assistant basketball coach at St. Joe's College. A former star player, his career was cut tragically short by a knee injury. His superior, Coach Fox, has been trying to groom Jimmy to succeed him when he retires, but Jimmy is still not enough of a team player to be ready for the job. The crunch comes when Jimmy alienates a potential star player that St. Joe's has been spending thousands to try to recruit. But Jimmy has seen footage of a potential superstar at the Winabi Parish School in northern Kenya. He undertakes the rigorous journey at his own expense and travels to Winabi, making a stopover in the larger town of Mingori where he encounters an odious landowner, Nyaga, who not only owns the whole town, but has his sights set on neighboring Winabi as well. Jimmy spurns Nyaga and proceeds to Winabi, where he meets the object of his quest, the boy Saleh, a natural player with the talent to become an NBA hall-of-famer. There Jimmy encounters hostility and suspicion, in particular from Saleh's chieftain father and from a selfless nun, Sister Susan. Saleh is the next in line to rule the Winabi, and everyone is suspicious (and rightly so) that Jimmy means to take Saleh away forever. But in the course of his attempts to wrest Saleh from his people, Jimmy himself undergoes a transformation. Meanwhile, the evil Nyaga is putting tremendous pressure on the Winabi to give up their land, and the climax comes in the form of a winner-take-all basketball showdown between the Winabi and the Mingori.

CAUTION: There is minimal language, including a rather crude joke in subtitles.

GO: Some of the plot subtleties may escape younger children; nonetheless, this is a great film which stresses courage, compassion, and working together.

∎

✗ ANGEL SQUARE

C/FP
1990
104 minutes
Directed by: Anne Wheeler
Starring: Ned Beatty, Marie Gaudry, Jeremy Radick, Guillaume Thivierge
MPAA rating: not rated

Christmas, 1945. Sammy Rosenberg's father, the railway

watchman, is knocked unconscious and taken to the hospital in a coma. When the police investigation goes nowhere, Sammy and his friend Tommy conduct their own investigation. They discover that two boys who were on the railroad grounds the night of the assault saw a comic book fall to the ground. Tommy locates the comic, but when he fingers the wrong man even his policeman friend Ozzy tells him to drop it. Then on Christmas Eve, Tommy solves the case. Based on the book by Brian Doyle.

✗ STOP: In one scene, Tommy's boy-crazy friend Florette gives him an elementary lesson in the biological differences between males and females with some drawings in the snow and in another, he asks a girl if she has ever French-kissed.

CAUTION: The film talks about anti-semitism and opens with a realistic war dream, involving boy soldiers who suffer realistic bullet wounds. The boys' evil teacher's head swivels right around and Tommy comments on the difficulties of having a sister with Down Syndrome. (He says, "… it's like having a younger sister for life.")

GO: This is an entertaining Canadian film.

■

✗ BABY: SECRET OF THE LOST LEGEND

Touchstone Home Video
1985
92 minutes
Directed by: B. W. L. Norton
Starring: Wiliam Katt, Patrick McGoohan, Sean Young
MPAA rating: PG

When Dr. Eric Kiviat learns that giant apatosaurs still inhabit the African rainforest, he will stop at nothing (murder included) to get credit for the greatest scientific discovery of all time. So when his assistant, Susan, discovers an apatosaurus skull, he convinces her that she's actually found the skull of a giraffe. But Susan suspects that Kiviat is concealing something, and that night she charters a helicopter into the interior. Her husband George follows, and finds Susan helping neolithic villagers who are dying after having eaten the flesh of what is apparently a dead apatosaurus. Meanwhile, Kiviat hires a boat of trigger-happy government soldiers, and the next day, when George and Susan come into close proximity with a family of apatosaurs, Kiviat and his party arrive, tranquilizing one of the adults and killing the other. George and Susan decide to take the baby apatosaurus back to the civilized world, but it gets away from them and after numerous adventures George and Susan trail Kiviat and his soldiers to their military base for a final violent confrontation.

✗ STOP: Automatic weapons fire, grenades explode and an arrow pierces a soldier's neck. Kiviat brutally murders the soldiers' commander with a tranquilizer gun and a apatosaurus kills Kiviat, who dies screaming horribly—considerable violence for a film associated with the Disney studios.

CAUTION: There is one love-making scene (partial nudity) and some coarse language.

GO: This film is amazingly popular with young children who seem to be able to overlook the carnage and concentrate on the antics of the cute baby dinosaur.

BACK TO THE FUTURE

MCA
1986
116 minutes
Directed by: Robert Zemeckis
Starring: Michael J. Fox, Crispin Glover,
    Christopher Lloyd, Lea Thompson,
    Thomas F. Wilson
MPAA rating: PG

When lunatic inventor "Doc" Emmett Brown creates a plutonium-powered time machine in the body of a DeLorean, he invites his friend, high school student Marty McFly, to help him test it. The testing is going well until terrorists, looking for the plutonium, interrupt at the critical point; Doc is gunned down and Marty flees in the DeLorean with the terrorists in hot pursuit. When Marty hits eighty-eight miles an hour, the machine is activated and he's zapped into the year 1955. There he meets his parents as teenagers and, through a series of fluke accidents, alters the future when his own mother falls in love with him. Dumbfounded, Marty does the only thing he can think of. He tracks down Doc, thirty years younger, and after finally convincing the scientist that he really is from the future, explains that the DeLorean is out of fuel. Doc devises a plan to power the DeLorean back to 1985 with a bolt of lightning. But first, Marty must attend the high school dance to make sure his mother and father get together or his very existence will be in jeopardy.

CAUTION: Doc is shot. There is the odd fight and some coarse language.

GO: Impressive art direction and a complex story line make this film watchable many times over.

BACK TO THE FUTURE II

MCA
1989
108 minutes
Directed by: Robert Zemeckis
Starring: Michael J. Fox, Christopher Lloyd,
    Lea Thompson, Thomas F. Wilson
MPAA rating: PG

Marty has only just returned to his own time when Doc reappears in the DeLorean. He's come from the year 2015 to take Marty and his girlfriend Jennifer back to the future where there are serious problems with their children. When they arrive, Doc puts Jennifer to sleep to prevent her from seeing more than she should. Then, Marty impersonates his own son to foil the criminal designs of Griff, his present-day nemesis Biff's psychotic grandson. His mission complete, Marty buys a sports almanac, intending to make a fortune on betting when he gets back to his own time. Meanwhile, the police discover Jennifer's unconscious body, identify her and take her to her 2015 home. While Marty and Doc frantically try to rescue her, Biff discovers the time machine and uses it to take Marty's almanac back to his own younger self in 1955. Marty and Doc retrieve Jennifer and return to 1985 to find that the world has been horribly altered and that the man in charge is millionaire Biff, the Luckiest Man

Alive. They return to 1955 to steal the almanac back from young Biff and at the climax of the film, the DeLorean is struck by lightning and Doc is blasted into 1885, leaving Marty stranded in 1955.

CAUTION: You may have to wrestle with a plot explanation for young viewers. There is some fighting and some coarse language.

BACK TO THE FUTURE III

MCA
1990
118 minutes
Directed by: Robert Zemeckis
Starring: Michael J. Fox, Christopher Lloyd,
Mary Steenburgen, Lea Thompson,
Thomas F. Wilson
MPAA rating: PG

Marty and the young Doc of 1955 receive a letter from the Doc of 1855 describing the location of the DeLorean. They find and repair the car, then Marty races to the Old West. But when he arrives, he ruptures a fuel line and he and the Doc of 1855 realize that the only way to get the DeLorean up to the critical eighty-eight miles an hour is to hijack a locomotive and push the car. Barroom brawls and gunfights at sunrise aren't enough to keep them from their work. But when Doc falls in love with a young teacher named Clara Clayton, things get horribly off-schedule. And when Clara shows up unexpectedly, Doc must stay behind to save her, and Marty returns to 1985 alone where even more surprises are in store.

CAUTION: There is some coarse language.

GO: The special effects are incredible, and the dazzling, madcap story features terrific performances by Fox, Lloyd, Steenburgen and Wilson. There is something for everyone.

✘ BATMAN

Warner Home Video
1989
126 minutes
Directed by: Tim Burton
Starring: Kim Basinger, Michael Keaton,
Jack Nicholson, Jack Palance
MPAA rating: PG-13

The futuristic metropolis of Gotham City is ravaged by crime and virtually run by criminal gangs, most notably that led by the evil Grissom and his chief henchman Jack Napier. But help comes in the form of the mysterious caped crusader Batman, alias Bruce Wayne, a troubled multi-millionaire whose parents were killed by a thug when he was just a child, and who is now exacting his revenge on the criminal community of Gotham. Wayne is indeed a tortured soul, but a little sunshine enters his life when he begins a relationship with the lovely photographer Vicki Vale. The plot thickens as Grissom discovers that Napier is having an affair with his own mistress, Alicia, and arranges to set Napier up to be busted. Napier escapes the trap but falls into a vat of toxic waste and is transformed into the Joker, a hideously deformed psychotic hellbent on avenging himself on just about everybody. The Joker knocks off Grissom, consolidates the forces of evil and prepares to take over Gotham City. Only Batman stands in his way.

✗STOP: People are killed in violent fashion. The Joker is grotesque and homicidal. In one scene, the Joker repeatedly pumps bullets into Grissom. In another, Alicia has obviously been tortured and disfigured. There are extended scenes of peril. At the climax, Batman and Vicki are suspended from the lofty heights of a cathedral steeple as the Joker tries to kill them. The Joker falls to his own death.

CAUTION: The mood of this film is relentlessly haunted, dark and brooding, like much of the work of Tim Burton who seems obsessed with deformity and alienation. And while this is a genuine tribute to the original Dark Knight, it will very likely be far too intense for the younger viewers. As an alternative, try *Batman: The Movie.*

GO: An exciting, action-packed adult fantasy.

✗ BATMAN RETURNS

Warner Home Video
1992
126 minutes
Directed by: Tim Burton
Starring: Danny DeVito, Michael Keaton, Michelle Pfeiffer, Christopher Walken
MPAA rating: PG-13

Batman Returns opens three decades before the present, where the Christmas season heralds the birth of a hideously deformed infant. After the infant eats the family's pet cat, his desperate parents dump him into the sewer, where he sails into a subterranean cavern beneath the Gotham City Zoo and is met by a flock of penguins. The film then returns to Christmas present, and the office tower of city big-shot Max Shreck. Shreck, who routinely abuses his mousy secretary Selina Kyle, is just about to give his annual holiday address when an army of heavily armed clowns machine-guns the city center, driving Shreck into the catacombs below. There he meets the Penguin (the once-abandoned infant who has grown to become the loathsome ruler of the sewers), and the pair forms an unholy alliance to rule Gotham. As their plot unfolds, Shreck pushes Selina Kyle out a window of his skyscraper. On the ground, she is resurrected by a swarm of alley cats to become the Catwoman; she then proceeds to terrorize the streets of Gotham and exact her revenge on Shreck. She also cuts a deal with The Penguin to destroy Batman. The Penguin then double-crosses Catwoman, is subsequently double-crossed by Shreck and undertakes to wreak vengeance on all of Gotham. Amidst this maelstrom of shifting alliances, Batman does violent battle with just about everyone, while his alter-ego Bruce Wayne has a neurotic romance with Selina Kyle.

✗STOP: This is not a film for children. De Vito's superb Penguin is a grotesque sociopath who eats raw fish, drools black blood and bites off the noses of people who annoy him. The violence level is extreme and the special effect of falling from great heights appears absolutely real, especially the impalings. The sexual dialogue between the villains is *highly* offensive.

CAUTION: The sets are magnificent, the effects are spectacular; unfortunately, all of this only contributes to the menacing impact of the film. Previewing by a parent is strongly advised. You might want to consider renting *Batman: The Movie* instead if you have young children who are Batman-crazy. (See the 6-10 section.)

✗ THE BEAR

Columbia/Tri-Star
1989
92 minutes
Directed by: Jean-Jacques Annaud
Starring: Tcheky Karyo, Jack Wallace
MPAA rating: PG

After his mother is killed in a rock slide, a little bear cub befriends an adult male grizzly and together they try to outrun hunters.

✗STOP: This is a social comment film and *not* a cute animal movie for young children. Concern has been raised about the manipulation of animals to tell this story of man against beast.

CAUTION: The male grizzly mates while the baby watches, and the baby bear has hallucinations after eating poisonous mushrooms.

GO: The film has a worthwhile message.

BEBE'S KIDS

Paramount Home Video
1992
74 minutes
Directed by: Bruce Smith
Starring the voices of: Nell Carter, Rich Little, Tone Loc
MPAA rating: PG-13

Based on characters created by the late comedian Robin Harris, this is a full-length animation about a man who meets an attractive woman named Jamika at a friend's funeral. He pursues her until she agrees to go out with him, but she insists that it be someplace appropriate for her and her young son. Her son is nice enough, but when Robin goes to pick Jamika up she has custody of three more children, her friend Bébé's kids. Robin and Jamika end up taking the whole gang to Funland, where Bébé's uncontrollable children set the amusement park on its ear. When Robin finally gets Bébé's children home, he finds that they live in a crack-infested dump and that their mother doesn't care about them.

CAUTION: The opening scene takes place in a bar with hookers where the main character is trying to drink away his troubles. This is a social comment film with gross humor and some coarse language.

GO: This video also contains the seven minute featurette cartoon, *Itsy Bitsy Spider*, which is a funny, well-animated look at the battle between an exterminator and a very resourceful spider.

✗ BEETLEJUICE

Warner Home Video
1988
92 minutes
Directed by: Tim Burton
Starring: Alec Baldwin, Geena Davis, Jeffrey Jones, Catherine O'Hara, Winona Ryder
MPAA rating: PG

(continued on next page)

Adam and Barbara Maitland are spending their vacation fixing up their home in Winsome River, Connecticut. When on a quick errand to the general store, they accidentally run their car into the river, and it isn't until they return home, soaking wet, that they discover they are dead. But the hereafter is totally unexpected. The Maitlands can't leave the house and the house's new owners are intent on customizing it to their own excessive tastes. Desperate, the Maitland's consult a copy of *The Handbook for the Recently Deceased* which tells them how to find their case-worker, Juno. But when they meet with Juno and she refuses to help, they turn to Beetlejuice, a free-lance bio-exorcist, and an expert at driving unwanted living people out of houses. Beetlejuice, however, has his own sinister agenda.

✗**STOP:** This film is full of potentially disturbing images. In the waiting room of the afterlife, people appear as they did when they died (for example, an explorer has a shrunken head), and while this is quite amusing for adults, it may terrify some young children. Beetlejuice also takes on some fairly frightening manifestations in the film.

CAUTION: In our experience, any film which is based in its entirety on a depiction of the afterlife — satirical or not — is bound to raise many questions for young people. Even teenagers have come to us with questions prompted by this film.

GO: This quality production features a stellar cast and plenty of Tim Burton's characteristic incredible special effects. Best suited to kids in their mid-teens and up; we recommend young children stick with the animated version.

BETTER OFF DEAD

Key Video
1985
97 minutes
Directed by: Steve Holland
Starring: John Cusack, Kim Darby,
    Diane Franklin, Anne Ramsey
MPAA rating: PG

Things aren't going well for sixteen-year-old Lane. His family (and everyone else in his hometown) is decidedly strange, and he's just lost the girl of his dreams because his popularity is sliding. After a series of wacky attempts at suicide, which fail miserably, he manages to get his life together with the help of a female foreign exchange student. And he soon comes to realize that the girl who cares about him enough to help him impress another girl is the *real* girl of his dreams.

CAUTION: The main characters are high school students, so expect gross behavior and some sexual innuendo.

GO: Despite its title, this is a comedy. The female foreign exchange student is intelligent, capable and sensitive and she demonstrates positive values.

BEYOND THE STARS

IVE
1989
94 minutes
Directed by: David Saperstein
Starring: F. Murray Abraham, Olivia D'Abo,
    Martin Sheen, Christian Slater
MPAA rating: PG

Suspended from high school for smashing a window with a model rocket, astronaut hopeful Erik Nichols goes to visit his father in Cedar Bay. There, he meets Mara who introduces him to her friend (and Erik's hero) Col. Paul Andrews, a retired astronaut who's been on the moon. Andrews is a bitter alchoholic, unable to reconcile something in his past. At first rude to Erik, Andrews is eventually won over by Erik's ideology and youthful enthusiasm. Erik's father, however, dislikes Andrews and what he represents (he harbors much bitterness about his own experiences with NASA) and refuses to allow Erik to continue visiting. Soon the men see how their animosity is hurting Erik and, after a violent verbal exchange, apologize to each other and to Erik. It turns out that Andrews is suffering from leukemia (contacted from exposure to radiation during the moon mission), but before he dies he reveals to Erik the secret of what he found on the moon and asks Erik to return the object when he becomes an astronaut himself.

CAUTION: In spite of the title this is not a film about space exploration, but rather about a rocky father-and-son relationship.There is some coarse language.

GO: The relationship between Erik's divorced parents is civilized. Messages about earth conservation are included in the film.

BIG MAN ON CAMPUS

Vestron Home Video
1989
102 minutes
Directed by: Jeremy Paul Kagan
Starring: Melora Hardin, Allan Katz,
    Corey Parker, Tom Skerritt, Cindy Williams
MPAA rating: PG-13

When an uncivilized hunchback swings down from the clock tower to save a beautiful university student named Cathy Adams, he is captured and taken into custody. At his hearing, psychologist Dr. Fisk claims that the creature is unable to fit into society, but the university's Dr. Webster disagrees, insisting that it's necessary to study him further before making such a conclusion. The university wins custody on the condition that if the creature exhibits any signs of hostility he's to be institutionalized. At the university, Cathy's boyfriend, Alex, is enlisted to baby-sit and civilize the creature and Dr. Diane Girard is brought in to teach him speech. Together they agree to call him Bob and lessons progress so well that when Dr. Webster is invited to bring Bob onto a talk show meant to discredit him, he accepts the offer as an opportunity to show the world how Bob has evolved. The show will, of course, make Dr. Fisk look like a total fool, so in order to save her reputation she calls Bob and tells

AGES 10 TO 13

him that Cathy is in trouble. He rushes to the dormitory to save her, causing a commotion and resisting arrest on the way. And it seems to many that Dr. Fisk was correct after all. But Bob manages to make it to the studio in time and during the outrageous live show discredits Dr. Fisk and finds true love.

CAUTION: The creature chants Cathy's name repeatedly and the doctor explains that this is "another form of masturbation." Also of concern may be a scene in which Bob gets a demonstration of French-kissing from Dr. Girard. Bob makes reference to his sexual experiences with appliances.

GO: Alex has continual one-liners and there are a lot of sight gags. In spite of the sexual references this is a very funny film, suitable for viewers of a great range of ages.

BILL & TED'S EXCELLENT ADVENTURE

Orion
1989
90 minutes
Directed by: Stephen Herek
Starring: George Carlin, Keanu Reeves, Alex Winter
MPAA rating: PG

San Dimas, California, the 27th century: A powerful utopian civilization is threatened because, in the past, the two Great Ones, whose music is destined to change the entire world, are flunking history. In order to preserve their civilization, the 27th century San Dimans send Agent Rufus back to the 20th century to help the two boys. The two Great Ones in question are Bill

S. Preston Esq. and Theodore Ted Logan, high school students and the founders and only members of the utterly horrible rock band Wyld Stallynz. Bill and Ted are, in fact, hopeless — not only as musicians but as students. Unfortunately, they have to make an oral history presentation the next day, and if they don't get an A they will flunk. This in turn means that Ted will be sent to a military academy in Alaska and the music of Wyld Stallynz will never exist. The boys are studying for their presentation outside the Circle K when a telephone booth drops out of the sky and Rufus steps out. He takes the boys back into the past, to a European battlefield, where they see Napoleon Bonaparte and accidentally bring him back to the present. Rufus then gives the boys the time machine and sends them off to prepare the most memorable history presentation ever, then leaves them to their own devices. Then follows manic chaos (and plenty of time-travel paradox) as the boys try to round up various historical figures and get to their presentation on time.

CAUTION: There is one unbelievably bizarre scene in which Bill's father and his young second wife Missy usher the boys out of Bill's bedroom so that the two adults can "make out."

GO: A fun-filled adventure with a little history thrown in and an oral history presentation that will be the envy of every student.

✗ BILL & TED'S BOGUS JOURNEY

Orion
1991
98 minutes
Directed by: Pete Hewitt
Starring: George Carlin, Keanu Reeves, Alex Winter
MPAA rating: PG - Frightening Scenes

Two years later, the boys are down and out. They're working at horrible jobs and their band still stinks. To make matters worse, an evil genius in the future has taken over the time portal in 27th century San Dimas. He sends back two evil robots, exact duplicates of Bill and Ted who have been programmed to kill the originals, replace them and ruin their lives. This the evil robots do with relish, taking Bill and Ted out into the desert and pushing them off a cliff. The spirits of Bill and Ted then encounter Death (an Ingmar Bergman rip-off complete with heavy hooded robes and scythe), whom they foil with a quick Melvin (don't ask). The boys then head back to town and try to thwart the evil robots, but are shortly sent to Hell by a seance gone wrong. Fortunately, they are too dumb to be really scared, but they quickly discover that Hell is a drag and the only way out is to play Death at a game of one's own choosing; in this case, Death turns out to be a lousy sport, and the boys are forced to keep beating him at parlor game after parlor until he agrees to return them to life. Bill and Ted decide to make a quick stop in Heaven to enlist some aid against the robots. The film gets even crazier after that.

✗STOP: The images in Hell will more than likely frighten some children, especially younger ones.

CAUTION: Some of the after-life scenes are quite eerie. The movie's focus on dying and returning may generate some questions. Evil Bill and evil Ted are incredibly dumb and mean, and heads literally fly.

GO: This effort is not considered as strong as the first film; nonetheless, fans of ridiculous fun will love it.

BINGO

RCA/Columbia
1991
90 minutes
Directed by: Matthew Robbins
Starring: David Rasche, Robert J. Steinmiller Jr., Cindy Williams
MPAA rating: PG

When Bingo, the world's smartest dog, runs away from the circus, he saves the life of a young boy named Chuckie and the two promptly become best friends. But Chuckie's mom won't have a dog in the house, so Chuckie is forced to conceal the dog's presence. And as if this weren't bad enough, Chuckie's dad, a place-kicker for the Denver Broncos, gets himself traded to Green Bay. Still, the intrepid boy and his dog have the move all worked out and even design a secret compartment in which Bingo will travel. But Bingo thwarts the plan when, after spending the night wining and dining the friendly lady dog next door, he sleeps in and misses the departure. Then follows one hilarious adventure after another as Bingo pursues his beloved master thousands of miles across America. He meets evil kidnappers, escapes a food stand featuring hot dogs made from real dogs and even ends up in jail.

CAUTION: This is a spoof on all of the dog movies in which dogs are shown to be smarter than humans, and its satirical humor may be lost on young children. There are some frightening scenes and there is some coarse language. There may be some moderately frightening scenes.

GO: A silly but fun movie, this is a nice attempt by a director to try something new.

✗ BLANKMAN

Columbia
1994
90 minutes (approx)
Directed By: Mike Binder
Starring: Damon Wayans, David Allan Grier, Robin Givens
MPAA Rating: PG

Kevin and Darryl Walker are two devoted brothers in the low-income district of a large city. Kevin is a decent cameraman with a tabloid-style news agency. He is also a karate expert. His younger brother Darryl is a geek, a brilliant but eccentric inventor who inadvertently discovers the secret to making fabric bullet-proof. When the boys' grandmother is murdered by the gunmen of a local mobster,

Darryl "snaps," dons a ludicrous outfit, and begins his crimefighting career. He is so inept that his brother is forced to bail him out of more than one jam; however, Darryl persists despite Kevin's objections, and ends up becoming a celebrity when he and Kevin aid a birth in a stuck elevator. Darryl then earns the moniker "Blankman," and despite his continued ineptness, he captures the imagination of the city, so much so that the once-intimidated mayor stands up to the mobsters. When the mayor's stand results in his death and Blankman's disgrace, Darryl retires to the ingnominity of crew chief at a local McDonald's. However, the mobsters are intent on pursuing their vendetta against Blankman, and to this end they kidnap his lady-love, anchorwoman Kimberly Jonz, and instigate a final showdown. During the climax, Kevin finally dons the superhero suit Darryl has made for him, becoming "the other guy."

✗STOP: This is really a borderline PG-13 film. Sexual innuendo is rampant, as is blatant language. At one point a pimp is preparing to beat an abject prostitute, then turns to Blankman and threatens to "slap" him like one of his "bitches." When Kimberly kisses Darryl, he goes through orgasmic convulsions. Non-graphic violence is standard fare.

CAUTION: The bad guy is sinister, the grandmother gets machine-gunned (off-camera), there are a million sex jokes.

GO: The film is a very witty tribute to the old Adam West/Burt Ward Batman and suitable for mid-teens and up.

✗ THE BOY WHO COULD FLY

Karl-Lorimar
1986
108 minutes
Directed by: Nick Castle
Starring: Bonnie Bedelia, Lucy Deakins,
    Colleen Dewhurst, Fred Savage,
    Jay Underwood
MPAA rating: PG

After her father's suicide, fourteen-year-old Millie moves with her mother and brother into a new neighborhood. There she meets Eric, who is strangely mute and rumored to be able to fly. Millie shows him some kindly interest and each day discovers something new about Eric. Then she has an accident that puts her in hospital, and is convinced that Eric's "magical qualities" saved her life. She begins to escape from the pain and grief of her father's death only to learn when she returns that Eric has been taken to the State Institution. Eric escapes and Millie runs away with him, and when they are cornered by state troopers it's discovered that Eric really can fly as he rises above the startled spectators with Millie in tow. In the end, Eric realizes that he cannot stay now that his secret has been revealed, so he flies off into the sunset, never to be seen again.

✗STOP: This is not a film for young children. It's emotionally disturbing and includes a confusing blend of fantasy and reality. Millie's father committed suicide (because he had cancer), and the family has trouble coming to grips with the situation. Eric's problems are a reaction to losing his parents in a plane crash and his resulting confinement in the mental institution is upsetting to watch. There is some swearing.

GO: Millie and her brother have a good relationship and their family is strong in spite of its difficulties. This is a movie about "magic" possibilities.

✗ BUFFY THE VAMPIRE SLAYER

20th Century Fox
1992
86 minutes
Directed by: Fran Rubel Kuzui
Starring: Rutger Hauer, Luke Perry,
    Paul Reubens, Donald Sutherland,
    Kristy Swanson
MPAA rating: PG-13

According to ancient tradition, only the Slayer, a young woman trained by the Watcher, can stem a plague of vampires. And sure enough, when Los Angeles is rocked by a series of bizarre murders (not only are the bodies drained of blood, but they're also vanishing from the morgue), Buffy, a California airhead, is approached by a man who tells her that she is the chosen one. Buffy thinks he's crazy. But he is, in fact, the next Watcher, and he knows that she is to be the Slayer. Reluctantly, she agrees to hear him out and accompanies him to the graveyard; after killing a couple of vampires, she is eventually convinced of her birthright and begins rigorous training. Then, night after night she's on the streets, secretly knocking off the undead, all the while undergoing a complete personality change. And in the final confrontation, at the big high school dance, Buffy battles a horde of vampires, led by their evil leader, Lothos.

✗STOP: The rating is appropriate. This is not a film for young children; it's full of frightening images and violent murders and combat. Spikes are plunged into vampire chests with realistic crunching noises, and growling vampires claw from fresh graves.

CAUTION: There are spooky white vampire faces with fangs and bloodshot eyes, and a lot of bloody neck-biting. There is some coarse language.

GO: For teens and adults this is a camp-a-thon, Paul Reubens' death scene in particular.

discover — nothing. But things aren't over yet, as this zany farce lurches to its madcap conclusion.

✗STOP: This is a black comedy, and the morbid elements are probably too frightening for anyone under the age of nine. In the end, it's revealed that Ray's suspicions were right all along as Professor Klopek tries to kill him with an injection in a frantic fight in an ambulance. Other scenes that may upset viewers are one in which Professor Klopek comes up from the basement covered in blood and another in which Ray has a nightmare about a satanic ritual.

GO: For kids thirteen and up, this film is definitely among the ranks of the great dark comedies.

✗ THE BURBS

CALENDAR GIRL

MCA
1989
101 minutes
Directed by: Joe Dante
Starring: Bruce Dern, Rick Ducommun, Carrie Fisher, Henry Gibson, Tom Hanks
MPAA rating: PG

Ray Peterson's quiet vacation at home is disrupted when the Klopeks, creepy, mad-scientist types, move into the dilapidated house next door. Bolstered by his suburbanite buddies, a neighborhood busybody and a crazed Vietnam vet, Ray does some major league snooping and becomes more and more convinced that the Klopeks are committing unspeakable atrocities in their basement. Ray's wife thinks he's gone crazy, but Ray persists, and he and his friends sneak into the Klopek's scary mansion and

Columbia
1993
91 minutes
Directed by: John Whitesell
Starring: Jerry O'Connell, Gabriel Olds, Jason Priestley
MPAA rating: PG-13

Ned is a nice young guy living in small-town America in the summer of 1962. Like many young men he has harbored a life-long fascination with Marilyn Monroe. He and his two best friends, the dorky Dude and the wild Roy, have led a relatively idyllic life, but this all comes to an end when Roy makes the announcement that he is joining the armed forces. Roy has planned one last sensational weekend. He will borrow his father's car and the thousand dollars he has saved up, travel to L.A. and secure a date with the screen legend herself. After much soul-searching, Ned and Dude agree to accompany him. They reach the big city and bunk down with Roy's cousin. Then the truth comes out. Roy didn't exactly "borrow" his father's car, and the thousand dollars was stolen from two very nasty gangster brothers who are now intent on mashing Roy to a pulp. The boys manage to avoid these goons, then go about trying to see Miss Monroe. But getting past her formidable housekeeper proves a daunting task. They go so far as to follow Monroe to a nude beach, without success. Then they steal a cow and put it on her front lawn. While the housekeeper is busy with this diversion, Roy enters in stealth and asks Marilyn out. She tells him to get lost. Their mission an utter failure, the boys eventually rekindle their spirits. Late that night, the phone rings. Marilyn wants to go out for a drive with Roy. But in a supreme gesture of friendship, Roy sends Ned instead, because, as Roy himself puts it: "You love her. I only want to—" So Ned makes the fateful trip to the Calendar Girl's house, takes her for a ride, and discovers that she is very much like himself.

CAUTION: This is actually a much milder film than one might expect; however, there is a certain amount of innuendo, coarse language and discussion of sex. The gangsters rough up Roy's cousin. The boys smoke a joint together. There is rear-view nudity during the beach scene.

GO: A suprisingly sweet coming-of-age film which affirms the inherent decency of human beings.

✘ CAN'T BUY ME LOVE

Touchstone Home Video
1987
94 minutes
Directed by: Steve Rash
Starring: Patrick Dempsey, Dennis Dugan,
  Amanda Peterson
MPAA rating PG-13

When Cindy Mancini, the most popular girl in school, accidently ruins her mother's best dress and needs $1000 to replace it, "nowhere-man" Ronny Miller comes to her rescue on one condition: that she pretend to be his girlfriend, thereby helping him achieve popular status. Reluctantly she agrees, and in the time they spend together Ronny opens her eyes to things that are much more important than money and clothes. Conversely, Cindy introduces him to all of her friends and soon Ronny becomes so popular himself that he no longer needs her. But that's not the end of it. Rejected by her own friends and now by Ronny, Cindy makes it known that Ronny bought his way into popularity by buying her, and every single person Ronny knows instantly loses respect for him. It's in this way that Ronny makes everyone else understand that money can't really buy popularity — it's being yourself that makes you loved.

✘STOP: Keep in mind that this film is about senior high school students so there's a fair amount of sexual activity, that pushes the PG limits. Also expect coarse language and some offensive behavior.

GO: The entire film is a message about the teenage struggle for popularity. There is a poignant portrayal of the stupidity of peer pressure.

✗ CHRISTOPHER COLUMBUS: THE DISCOVERY

Warner Home Video
1992
121 minutes
Directed by: John Glen
Starring: Marlon Brando,
   George Corraface, Tom Selleck,
   Rachel Ward
MPAA rating: PG-13

Genovese mapmaker Christopher Columbus is a proud, half-crazy visionary. Inspired by the tale of Marco Polo and tempted by maps of India, he is convinced there must be a way to reach Asia by sailing west. He finally secures financing from Queen Isabella herself, but Columbus's biggest challenge is convincing anyone to man his three ships (no one believes they will ever make it back) and he's eventually forced to hire criminals. His preparations made, Columbus sets off due west with favorable winds and a grumbling crew. But thirty-two days and twenty-four hundred miles later, the crew is ready to mutiny. And even as his men prepare to do him in, a heavenly wind arises, and land is sighted. The explorers go ashore and are soon greeted by the natives. Columbus then establishes Natividad, and the oppression of the new world begins.

✗ STOP: In the citadel of the Inquisition, it's clear that someone is being tortured as screams sound in the background. On the voyage, a traitor is hung out in the sun to make him talk, and is found one morning with a knife in his side. And at the end of the film, the murderous Spaniards are killed by the natives. (Spaniards are shown hanging and butchered.)

CAUTION: One of the ship's officers makes advances to a cabin boy. The natives are scantily clad (women are bare-breasted).

GO: A good way to introduce older children to the history of this cataclysmic episode in human history. The Spaniards are certainly not glorified in this film.

✗ CLASH OF THE TITANS

MGM/UA
1981
118 minutes
Directed by: Desmond Davis
Starring: Harry Hamlin, Laurence Olivier,
   Maggie Smith
MPAA rating: PG

King Acletius of Argos, jealous of his daughter Danae's beauty, keeps her locked away from the sight of men; however, this is no protection from the amorous attentions of the mighty god Zeus. And when Danae bears Zeus a son (Perseus), the furious king casts her and the boy adrift on the ocean. Zeus exacts terrible revenge on Acletius, killing him and unleashing the monstrous Titan Kraken upon his kingdom. Thus begins this epic, which chronicles the adventures of Perseus whose quest for the hand of his beloved Andromeda pits him against the sea-goddess Thetis, her deformed son Caballos, Medusa the Gorgon and the huge Titan Kraken.

✗ STOP: This film is likely to terrify little ones right from the first scene, when Danae and her child are locked in a chest and cast onto the waters. Many of the mythological creatures featured are grotesque and one battle is extremely graphic.

CAUTION: The story is so long and complex that anyone under the age of eight will probably fade out.

GO: Some of Ray Harryhausen's finest special-effects are featured in this film. (The scene in which Perseus battles the Medusa is a masterpiece of stop-animation.) *Clash of the Titans* will appeal to young people with a taste for fantasy and will serve to provide a loose introduction to Greek mythology.

✗ CLOAK AND DAGGER

MCA
1984
101 minutes
Directed by: Richard Franklin
Starring: Dabney Coleman, Michael Murphy,
   Henry Thomas
MPAA Rating: PG

Davey copes with his mother's death by immersing himself in fantasy role-playing. He substitutes an imaginary hero named Jack Flack for his practical air force colonel father (played by Dabney Coleman in a dual role). But the fantasy suddenly becomes real when Davey witnesses a murder and is forced to handle the situation only with the help of a younger girl as the hit men close in. The climax of the film brings with it the realization that life is no game, that Jack Flack is by no means the hero Davey had imagined and that the true hero is Davey's down-to-earth real father.

✗ STOP: Davey is thrown into the trunk of the car along with a dead friend (killed off-camera) and is later forced to shoot a villain in self-defense. Some children are disturbed by a scene in which the villain tells Davey in lurid, terrifying detail how he is going to kill him.

GO: The film is a great good guy vs. bad guy yarn, extremely suspenseful—great for boys and girls.

✗ CONEHEADS

Paramount Home Video
1993
87 minutes
Directed by: Steve Barron
Starring: Dan Aykroyd, Jane Curtin,
   Michelle Burke, Dave Thomas
MPAA rating: PG

Beldar and Prymatt Conehead are on a mission, testing Earth's planetary defenses in anticipation of a full-scale invasion from the highly advanced planet Remulak. Unfortunately, Beldar forgets to turn on the cloaking device (much to the ire of his nagging wife) and the pointy-headed couple are shot down by a trigger-happy jet pilot. The aliens are stranded on Earth, and it looks bad for them; however, Beldar is determined to blend in with the "blunt-skulls." Whenever anyone notices anything odd about them (for instance, that Beldar can drink a six-pack of beer in two seconds), they explain that they are from France. Beldar excels in a succession of jobs, and the Coneheads always stay one step ahead of a determined and obsessed immigration agent. They achieve contentment and middle-class suburban status, even bear and raise a young daughter, Connie, who is, like the children of many immigrants, totally American-ized. The rescue ship finally arrives from Remulak, just as the immigration agents finally catch up to them. The Coneheads escape into space, accidentally taking the agents with them, and return to Remulak where Beldar is condemned (for the crime of getting his teeth capped) to "snarfle the garthog." In a hilarious send-up of *Return of the Jedi*, Beldar prevails over a huge monster. He then foils the Remulakian invasion plans, gets a green card, and tothey all take up residence with his family in America.

✗ **STOP:** Young children who do not pick up on the parodies may find certain scenes distressing, for example, the garthog, Beldar's trip to the dentist.

CAUTION: There is a certain amount of mild sexual innuendo (for example, Pry-matt and Connie discuss Remulakian mating rituals), and certain antics that may offend some, but overall this is a safe film.

GO: For fans of off-the-wall comedies, this is a must-see.

AGES 10 TO 13

✗ CROCODILE DUNDEE

Paramount Home Video
1986
98 minutes
Directed by: Peter Faiman
Starring: Mark Blum, Paul Hogan, Linda Kozlowski
MPAA rating: PG-13

Sue Charlton, a glamorous and adventurous reporter, travels to the wilds of northern Australia to get the big scoop on famed croc-hunter Mick Dundee. In the process she learns how to survive in the "outback", and she discovers the truth behind the legend of "Crocodile Dundee." Sue then brings Mick back to New York City, where he in turn discovers a different kind of wilderness, one for which he too must learn new rules of survival.

✗ **STOP:** Although this is a comedy there are fistfights and much sexual innuendo. The New York scenes show drug use, trans-vestites, prostitutes and muggers.

CAUTION: Sue 's bottom is exposed in one scene, and many of the kids we know hooted and howled when they saw it. Blacks are given limited on-camera time in the city scenes, and are represented primarily as pimps and muggers.

GO: The film shows our own urban culture in a fresh light.

✗ CROCODILE DUNDEE II

Paramount Home Video
1988
110 minutes
Directed By: John Cornell
Starring: Paul Hogan, Linda Kozlowski
MPAA rating: PG

In this sequel to *Crocodile Dundee*, Mick saves his abducted girlfriend, Sue, from Columbian drug lords.

✗ **STOP:** In one of the many violent scenes, an informer is shot in the head, execution style.

CAUTION: Sue attends a party in a revealing dress. Although the MPAA rating of this film is lower than that of the first Crocodile Dundee film, the violence is more serious.

CURLY SUE

Warner Home Video
1991
102 minutes
Directed by: John Hughes
Starring: Jim Belushi, John Getz,
  Kelly Lynch, Alison Porter
MPAA rating: PG

Shiftless Bill Dancer and his young friend Curly Sue are a down and out con-artist team, who figure they have it made when they spot a rich lawyer named Grey Ellison and set her up for the old car-hits-pedestrian scam. They manage to score a meal and that's all, but the next evening Grey hits Bill again, and this time it's for real. So Bill and Curly Sue become fixtures in Grey's life; they stay at her apartment and take advantage of the benefits of her largesse. But charity has its limits and when Grey's jealous boyfriend calls the Children's Aid Society, Bill is thrown in jail and Curly Sue is taken to a children's hostel. By this time, Grey realizes that she loves the child and takes the necessary steps to become her legal guardian. Thus relieved of his responsibility, everyone expects Bill to leave, but he doesn't, and in the end Bill, Grey and Sue live happily ever after.

CAUTION: The film may raise some questions for children about derelicts and street people. There is some coarse language.

THE CUTTING EDGE

MGM/UA
1992
102 minutes
Directed by: Paul Michael Glaser
Starring: Moira Kelly, D.B. Sweeney
MPAA rating: PG

At the 1988 Olympics, amateur hockey superstar Doug Dorsey is crushed on the boards and his injuries knock him out of hockey forever. At the same time, star pairs figure skater Kate Mosley is dropped by her partner forty-five seconds from the end of a gold-medal performance. Doug returns to his brother's bar in Minnesota and plays hockey in a bar league; Kate, meanwhile, goes through eight partners in two years, and the only qualified skater left vows never to skate with her again. In desperation, Kate's Russian coach invites Doug to try figure skating. Reluctantly, Doug agrees and he and Kate fight from the first moment they meet. But neither has a choice: Doug's hockey career is over and no one else will skate with Kate. They must work together. And as their relationship evolves, Doug proves his intense dedication to his new endeavor and Kate manages to overcome the bitterness which has dogged her since her childhood. The climax of the film comes when Kate and Doug go to the 1992 Olympics in Albertville, France.

CAUTION: In the first scene Doug wakes up in bed with a young woman and can't remember her name. There is some coarse language and some sexual innuendo.

GO: Moira Kelly proves herself to be a fine comedian in places, and the overall story is a positive one for teens and preteens.

GO: The film shows that some scientists (a much-maligned profession in films) are concerned with "things of the heart."

D.A.R.Y.L.

DARK HORSE

Paramount Home Video
1985
100 minutes
Directed by: Simon Wincer
Starring: Mary Beth Hurt, Michael McKean, Barrett Oliver
MPAA rating: PG

Live Home Video
1992
98 minutes
Directed by: David Hemmings
Starring: Ed Begley Jr., Samantha Eggar, Tab Hunter, Ari Meyers, Mimi Rogers
MPAA rating: PG

D.A.R.Y.L. is a "Data Analyzing Robot Youth Lifeform" that looks like a human being. After a memory loss, he becomes disoriented and is taken in by Andy and Joan, a kind couple who desperately want a child of their own. Soon, though, D.A.R.Y.L.'s "real" parents (the scientists who created him) find him and take him to a military base where they discover that he is now more human than they realized. Disturbed when the military orders them to destroy the "experiment," they contact Andy and Joan and ask them if they still want to raise D.A.R.Y.L. Then they fake the robot's death, and using his remarkable brain D.A.R.Y.L. escapes to live with the foster parents who have learned to love him for his human qualities.

CAUTION: D.A.R.Y.L. looks human but isn't, so it's a little disconcerting when the military performs tests on him. D.A.R.Y.L.'s "father" (the scientist who created D.A.R.Y.L.) is killed by police while trying to help his "son" escape. He dies with his eyes open; there is blood.

Following the death of her mother, Allie moves with her father and brother to a small town, where in an attempt to fit in with her peer group she gets into trouble and is arrested. The sentence is ten weekends of community work at local veterinarian Susan Hadley's ranch. There, Allie feels a kinship with a dark horse named Jet and asks Susan to teach her to ride. As the weeks go by, Allie not only learns to ride but is happier about herself. Inevitably, though, the horse must go back to its owner and on the way Susan and Allie are involved in a serious accident. Allie and Jet fall down a steep cliff and Allie is left with severe damage to her spinal cord. The horse, too, is seriously injured, but Susan refuses to destroy it, preferring instead to rehabilitate it for Allie's sake. And with Jet to motivate her, Allie finds the strength to stand again. Based on a story by Tab Hunter.

CAUTION: Jet is involved in two accidents which may be hard on horse lovers. There is some fighting.

GO: Actress Ari Meyers gives the best fifteen-year-old-with-an-attitude looks. This film about overcoming difficulties has a happy ending.

DATE WITH AN ANGEL

HBO
1987
114 minutes
Directed by: Tom McLoughlin
Starring: Emmanuelle Beart,
  Phoebe Cates, Michael E. Knight
MPAA rating: PG

Jim Saunders and Patty Winston are about to get married, but at their engagement party Jim is having trouble mixing with her socialite friends. Then *his* friends arrive (disguised as terrorists) and take him away for a night of wild fun. The next morning, a blinding flash of light and an explosion of water wake Jim up, and he's surprised to find a beautiful mute woman floating in the pool. Even more surprising is the fact that she has wings (one of which was broken in her fall, rendering her incapable of leaving). His friends immediately begin planning ways of capitalizing on the angel's misfortune. Patty's psychotic father, meanwhile, is after Jim and the whole time Patty is drinking herself into a stupor. Chase scene follows chase scene, then at the film's climax Jim realizes that the angel is an angel of death and that she has come for him. He has one hope, though: through the course of their misadventures, the angel has fallen in love with him.

CAUTION: The morning after his stag, Jim is shown asleep holding a Love Doll. The film also includes an extremely negative representation of a Roman Catholic priest. Jim's friends are revolting and there is coarse language.

GO: Not bad, but it's rude.

DEFENSE PLAY

Trans World Entertainment
1988
95 minutes
Directed by: Monte Markham
Starring: Monte Markham, David Oliver,
  Susan Ursitti
MPAA rating: PG

When Scott Denton is joy-riding near the U.S. military base, he watches as a miniature helicopter (a Dart) explodes in midair. Scott then learns more about the Dart when he meets Karen, daughter of Professor Vandemeer who's heading the helicopter development project. That night, while the professor is analyzing data from the explosion, somebody activates one of the Dart prototypes and Professor Vandemeer is killed. Scott, who was on the phone with the professor at the time of his murder, is stunned to hear that the death is recorded as an accident. So, he and Karen break into the physics lab, uncover the mystery, and race to identify a Russian spy and destroy the rocket before it's launched.

CAUTION: Professor Vandemeer is cornered and killed by one of the Darts. The film is somewhat jingoistic in tone and there is some coarse language.

GO: Especially for young video-game fans, this is an exciting spy mystery with a minimum of violence.

DON'T TELL MOM THE BABYSITTER'S DEAD

Warner/HBO
1991
142 minutes
Directed by: Stephen Herek
Starring: Christina Applegate,
    Joanna Cassidy, Keith Coogan
MPAA rating: PG

When their mother decides to take a much-needed vacation, Sue Ellen and the rest of the kids are left in the care of what appears to be a very nice old lady. But the baby-sitter turns out to be a tyrant who makes the kids wear weird clothes and muster for roll call. And when she sees Sue Ellen's brother's rock-and-roll posters, she promptly dies from shock. Afraid of spoiling their mother's vacation and seeing the possibilities of the situation, the kids put the baby-sitter in a box and leave her outside a funeral home. All well and good, except for one thing: the baby-sitter just happened to have the money for the entire summer in her pocket. With no other alternatives, Sue Ellen and her brother toss to see who will get a summer job. Sue Ellen loses, and hits the work force armed with her mother's slightly altered resumé. By a series of comic misunderstandings she lands a job as an executive assistant in a svelte fashion house, and her dream career skyrockets. But success brings with it a heaping helping of adult stress, and while Sue Ellen copes with burnout her brother is undergoing a conversion of his own (from rock-and-roll animal to dedicated homemaker). The charade can't go on forever, though; Sue Ellen's company launches its new line of teen clothes at a party in her house, and the whole thing comes to an abrupt end when mom returns home.

CAUTION: There is some coarse language, and at the beginning of the film Sue Ellen's brother smokes a joint with his friends.

GO: This is a terrific little movie featuring teenage characters who display surprisingly good values. They learn to take responsibilty for themselves and for their younger siblings and there is a nice reversal of roles when Sue Ellen becomes the breadwinner and her brother stays home to run the household. We can't understand why this film would receive a "mature theme" warning when other, more extreme films don't.

✗ EDWARD SCISSORHANDS

CBS/Fox
1990
100 minutes
Directed by: Tim Burton
Starring: Alan Arkin, Johnny Depp,
    Anthony Michael Hall, Vincent Price,
    Winona Ryder, Dianne Wiest
MPAA rating: PG-13

Kim, now an old woman, tells her grandchildren the story of a kind old inventor who lived in the mansion at the top of the hill. In her story the inventor makes many wonderful things, including a man (Edward).

But the inventor dies before Edward is complete, and the poor creature is left alone with scissors instead of hands. Then one day, an Avon lady named Peg goes to the mansion on a whim. There she finds Edward and, sorry for his situation, takes him home with her. Peg, her husband Bill and their daughter Kim soon grow to appreciate their house guest. And Edward, meanwhile, proves himself to be the master hedgeclipper of all time, crafting stunning likenesses of dinosaurs and people out of the local trees and bushes. When one of the ladies asks him to trim her hair, Edward's place in the community as a master hairdresser seems assured. But then things begin to go wrong. When Kim's evil boyfriend, Jim, tricks Edward into using his marvelous hands to help him rob his father, Edward is arrested. And as the town turns against him, he's forced back to his mansion and into a final confrontation with Jim which ends in Jim's death.

✗STOP: In one sense this is a Frankenstein movie about deformity and alienation. There is a close-up of Jim's horrified face as he is impaled by one of Edward's blades and falls from a window.

CAUTION: Edward is highly unusual and may cause some unease for young viewers. (His scissor hands are very sharp and he is always cutting himself.) The inventor's death scene is intense and in the end, Edward is forced back into seclusion.

GO: This film is a surreal fairy tale. Imaginative and brilliantly crafted.

✗ ERNEST SCARED STUPID

Touchstone Home Video
1991
92 minutes
Directed by: John Cherry
Starring: Jim Varney
MPAA rating: PG

Long ago in Briarville, Missouri, a demonic, child-stealing monster is captured by a group of outraged pioneers (led by Phineas Worrell), who bury the creature alive under a young oak tree. But just before they begin to shovel the creature in, it utters this chilling prophecy: When the face of death covers the moon, one with your blood will release me. Sure enough, years later, that descendant arrives in the form of Ernest P. Worrell, Briarville's outrageous garbageman. Ernest is sent to clean up the Hackmore place, a spooky, run-down mansion inhabited by a pyromaniac witch. There, Ernest stops his work to help two young friends build a tree house and in so doing, unleashes the monster. Then only Ernest (and the witch) can stop it.

✗STOP: Many of the images at the beginning of the film will frighten young viewers. A terrified child is pursued through the woods by a nameless horror, and there's a really scary look-around-and-see-a-monster-in-your-bed scene.

CAUTION: The hideously misshapen, child-stealing monster turns its victims into dolls and new trolls are shown growing up out of the ground and dragging adults away.

GO: Though probably the weakest of the Ernest films, *Scared Stupid* still features

Jim Varney's great shtick, and its ending (in which the kids save the day) is a positive one for children.

FAR AND AWAY

MCA
1992
140 minutes
Directed by: Ron Howard
Starring: Tom Cruise, Nicole Kidman, Colm Meany
MPAA rating: PG-13

In Ireland at the turn of the century, Joseph Donnelly's father dies, and during the funeral, agents of the family's landlord, Mr. Christie, burn the family farm for want of unpaid rent. Joseph decides to exact his revenge by killing Christie himself. But his plan goes awry when his gun misfires, and Joseph ends up a prisoner recuperating in the Christie household. There he meets Christie's willful daugher Shannon, who hopes to make her way to Oklahoma, where one hundred and sixty acres of free land is being offered to each and every able-bodied man and woman who wants it. The two decide to go together and, after a narrow escape from Shannon's family, make their way to Boston. There they work in a chicken-plucking factory until Joseph's skill as a fighter earns him the favor of local kingpin Mike Kelly. Joseph's renown grows as he wins fight after fight, but his concern for Shannon proves his undoing and he loses the greatest fight of all. The two are then ostracized, forced to wander the streets of the city in the frigid winter. And when Shannon is shot and wounded by an angry homeowner, Joseph returns her to her family (now in Boston) and goes to work on the railroad. Unable to forget the land, Joseph eventually makes his way to Oklahoma where he's reunited with Shannon and the two stake a claim together.

CAUTION: Shannon stabs Joseph in the thigh with a pitchfork and Joseph is involved in numerous bloody fights with the realistic impact of fists on faces, stomachs and backs. Shannon is felled by a rifle-shot in the back and at the film's climax, a horse rolls over Joseph. There are some sexual situations as Shannon and Joseph, posing as brother and sister, share a room in a brothel.

GO: Based on an actual event in American history, this is a visually stunning epic, full of romance and adventure and featuring strong performances. One thirteen-year-old viewer we know remarked, "We studied the Oklahoma Land Rush in school but it wasn't anywhere near as exciting as this!"

✗ A FAR OFF PLACE

Walt Disney Home Video
1993
117 minutes
Directed by: Mikael Salomon
Starring: Sarel Bok, Ethan Randall, Maximilian Schell, Jack Thompson, Reese Witherspoon
MPAA rating: PG

This film is based on two Laurens van der Post novels, *A Story Like the Wind* and *A Far Off Place*. Harry Winslow, an American teenager, goes to a ranch in the poacher-plagued Kalahari desert to visit the

Parkers, friends of his late mother. Paul Parker has begun an investigation which has led him to believe that a huge corporation is behind the recent wholesale slaughter of elephants. He is planning to bring his evidence to the Minister of the Interior. That night, his adventurous daughter Nonnie sneaks off to join her bushman friend Xhabbo, whom she finds wounded by a leopard. Harry follows her out of the ranch and the three spend the night in a cave, only to be awakened by machine-gun fire. Nonnie runs back, to find that her parents and Harry's father have been killed by assassins. She exacts her revenge by dynamiting the place around the assassin's cars, then flees back into the bush with the remaining killers in pursuit. Nonnie, Harry and Xhabbo resolve to cross the great desert to escape their pursuers. On the way, Xhabbo enlists the help of a herd of elephants, with whom he can communicate. Then begins the trek across the enormous Kalahari. During the long and desperate journey, Harry undergoes a dramatic transformation, and in the final confrontation with the evil poachers, he and Nonnie overcome.

✗**STOP:** In the opening scene, a tranquil African waterhole is ambushed by poachers, who machine-gun a herd of elephants and then chop off the tusks with chainsaws. A ranger then guns down two of the poachers. Nonnie discovers her parents bloodily murdered in her house, and has an authentic reaction to the discovery.

CAUTION: The children are in peril practically throughout the film. A major concern is the macabre evil of the poachers, ruthless men who would even hunt down children to achieve their nefarious ends.

GO: Nonnie is a strong, independent young woman, a terrific role model. Harry is generous and intelligent.

■

✗ FATHERHOOD

Hollywood Pictures
1993
105 minutes
Directed by: Darrell James Roodt
Starring: Halle Berry, Brian Bonsall, Michael Ironside, Sabrina Lloyd, Patrick Swayze
MPAA rating: PG-13

Jack Charles has a strange job. He robs drug dealers for a living. As he puts it, the only thing he ever did that was any good at all was that he stayed *out* of his kids' lives, leaving his son in a foster home and his daughter in the care of the Bigelow reformatory. Unbeknownst to Jack, Bigelow is a hell-hole of abuse, controlled by thugs and headed by the odious bureaucrat Lazarro, who has been running a lucrative scam. But then Jack's daughter Kelly breaks out of Bigelow and tracks Jack down to his motel room. She informs Jack that his seven-year-old son, Eddy, is being taken to Bigelow in handcuffs. Grumbling, Jack goes to court and demands to see his son. One look at the boy confirms Jack's worst fears the boy is desperately unhappy. Later on, he and Kelly keep watch on the detention center and see the children being led into the bus in handcuffs. Enraged, Jack sticks up the bus and busts out his son. Now the chase is on in earnest. Thanks to wildly exaggerated media reports, every law enforcement agency in the country is looking for them. Jack and the kids lead them a merry chase across the country, punctuated by Jack's communication with newspaper reporter Kathleen Mercer, who's breaking a story on the corrupt reformatory. Finally Jack is forced to make a decision between assuming his responsibilities as a parent or scoring one last lucrative job and saying goodbye to his children forever.

✗**STOP:** There is obvious implied sexual abuse at Bigelow, hence the PG-13 rating. In one scene, we get a strong indication that a staff member is regularly assaulting a very upset young girl. One of Jack's robber buddies dies in a hail of gunfire during a shoot-out with drug thugs.

CAUTION: Coarse language. The characters are relentlessly low-brow. Jack and a buddy get drunk and talk "guns" in the presence of the children.

GO: There is a certain charm to Jack's reluctant reformation.

FATHER OF THE BRIDE

Touchstone Home Video
1992
105 minutes
Directed by: Charles Shyer
Starring: Diane Keaton, Steve Martin, Martin Short, Kimberly Williams, B.D. Wong
MPAA rating: PG

When George's daughter, Annie, returns home after a summer in Rome and announces that she's engaged, George doesn't handle the news very gracefully — even when "Mr. Right" also appears to be "Mr. Perfect." (Annie's fiancé is a sincere, handsome computer whiz who's so successful that no single firm can afford to keep him on staff.) And while George's wife and daughter plan an extravagant wedding with the help of two ultra-campy wedding coordinators, George marches steadily to the brink of madness. The climax comes when George is arrested in a grocery store because of a dispute over hotdog buns. Then it's up to his good-humored, sensible wife to set him straight. On the surface, the film appears to be an almost scene-for-scene remake of the 1950 effort starring Spencer Tracy and Elizabeth Taylor. The plot unfolds in nearly identical fashion, and many scenes are presented as virtual replicas. However, the grating sexism of the original has been eradicated and Martin's George Banks (unlike that of his 1950 counterpart) is something of a neurotic flake.

CAUTION: Some people who have been through the same grotesque wedding expenditure fail to find the film amusing. As a parent of a young child, you may end up having to explain what a condom is.

GO: *Father of the Bride* is a family film; that is, adults will want to see it and many children will end up watching it simply because it's not grossly unsuitable.

FERRIS BUELLER'S DAY OFF

Paramount Home Video
1986
103 minutes
Directed by: John Hughes
Starring: Matthew Broderick, Alan Ruck, Mia Sara
MPAA rating: PG-13

Easy-going high school senior Ferris Bueller devises an elaborate plan to play hookey, and he takes his girlfriend Sloane and his best friend Cameron along. Ferris bullies Cameron into borrowing his father's prized Ferrari and the three make their way to downtown Chicago where they attend a ballgame, have lunch in an expensive restaurant, visit a museum and even take part in a parade. And after a day of adventure and self-discovery, they return the Ferrari only to discover, to their horror, that they cannot reset the odometer to its original reading. Instead, in a fit of rage against a father who pays more attention to a car than to him, Cameron pushes the Ferrari through the window and into the ravine. His courage mustered after a day of risk-taking, Cameron is now prepared to face his father and discuss their problems.

CAUTION: Ferris takes advantage of his parents' kindness and gullibility without a second thought. There is a *lot* of coarse language in this film.

GO: In spite of the language, *Ferris Bueller's Day Off* is a funny, light-hearted movie. Don't forget to watch the film to the very end of the credits!

FORBIDDEN PLANET

Commanded by J.J. Adams, United Planets Cruiser C57D is headed for the planet Altair IV, where a group of scientists landed twenty years before. It is the ship's mission to search for survivors, and when they arrive they're relieved to make contact with Edward Morbius, the only surviving scientist. But Morbius is suprisingly irritated by the rescue team's appearance, and only reluctantly agrees to meet with the ship's officers (Adams and Ostrow) before sending them back. As Adams' unease with the situation grows, he decides to contact Earth Base; this, however, will require dismantling part of their own ship to create a transmitter, and before that can be done, the ship is sabotaged by a mysterious entity. When Adams and Ostrow press Morbius for an explanation, they learn about the Krell, ancient inhabitants of the planet who designed a machine that uses sheer intellectual power to transport matter. In the end, Ostrow sacrifices his life to learn the terrible truth: when they built their machine, the Krell failed to consider the power of the Id, and now Morbius's subconscious has become a monster.

CAUTION: The attack scenes are frightening and one of our nine-year-old friends had many serious questions about the nature of the invisible entity, and why it attacked and killed people.

GO: The film is moody and atmospheric, with a great score. An all-round great effort, one can only wonder what would have been created with a modern budget.

MGM/UA
1956
99 minutes
Directed by: Fred McLeod Wilcox
Starring: Anne Francis, Leslie Nielsen,
    Walter Pidgeon, Warren Stevens
MPAA rating: G

✗ FRANKENWEENIE

Walt Disney Home Video
1984
27 minutes
Directed by: Tim Burton
Starring: Shelley Duvall, Barrett Oliver,
    Daniel Stern
MPAA rating: PG

When Victor Frankenstein's beloved
dog, Sparky, is hit by a car, the boy
cannot contain his grief and his
parents don't know what to do.
Then, in science class, Victor sees
a demonstration of electricity
moving a dead frog's legs, and
decides to try the same thing on
Sparky. He goes to the graveyard
and digs the dog up, and after fitting
him with some electrodes, jolts him
back to life. Victor tries to keep
Sparky a secret, but soon the
rambunctious dog gets outside, and
he isn't exactly a hit with the
neighbors. (He's covered with large
stitches from the accident.) In an
effort to restore the peace, Victor's
parents invite everyone over to
introduce them all to the
newly-resurrected dog. But the
whole thing goes terribly wrong
when Sparky panics and runs off.
The villagers pursue him to an
abandoned mini-golf course where
Victor is trapped inside a windmill.
When the windmill catches fire, and
Sparky rescues his friend at the cost
of his own life, the townspeople help
to reanimate the dog again. This
film is black and white.

✗ STOP: Sparky is killed twice in this film.

CAUTION: Adults will find this is a brilliantly witty spoof on all of the great horror
films, but young children may be upset by
the scary music, gloomy images and frightening scenes.

✗ A FRIENDSHIP IN VIENNA

Walt Disney Home Video
94 minutes
Directed by: Arthur Allan Seidelman
Starring: Edward Asner, Kamie Harper,
    Jenny Lewis, Stephen Macht
MPAA rating: not rated

Based on the book *Devil in Vienna*
by Doris Orgel, this film opens in
Vienna in 1938. Inge, a young
Jewish girl, is best friends with Lise,
the daughter of a high-ranking Nazi
S.S. officer. Austria is torn into two
camps, one opting for independence, the other desiring to join Nazi
Germany. A plebiscite to determine
the country's fate is fast approaching, and the persecution of Jews is
becoming publicly acceptable. As a
result, Inge and Lise find their
friendship coming under increasing
strain. Both sets of parents have
forbidden the girls to see each
other; nonetheless, they maintain
their friendship in secret, until Lise's
family moves back to Munich. Social
unrest grows. The plebiscite goes in
the Nazis' favor, and the New Order
is imposed on Austria. Inge's father
and grandfather are publicly
humiliated in a calculated program
against all male Jews in the city.
Then Lise returns to Vienna with her
family. She has resisted the efforts
of her Nazi parents to indoctrinate
her, and goes so far as to sit with
the Jewish children when the

classes are ominously separated. By then Inge's parents realize that the writing is on the wall. It is time to leave the country. But this proves very difficult, and they must do the unthinkable — disguise themselves as Christians by getting themselves baptized. But only the faithful Lise can make this possible.

✘STOP: This film is billed as family fare, yet it is set during one of the most monstrous periods in human history, and chronicles, through the eyes of a *child*, the disenfranchisement, dehumanization, isolation and impending extermination of a whole race of people. The viewer is forced to witness the humiliation of innocents young and old, the segregation of children in a classroom, and a violent mob battle in which Nazi thugs crush skulls with cudgels. But perhaps the most disturbing aspect of all is the depiction of evil reflected in some of the young children.

CAUTION: It is essential to keep the memory of the Holocaust as vivid as possible. However, parents must consider how old children should be before they are confronted with its terrible reality.

GO: For older children and adults, this is a moving tale of human decency and courage in a horrific setting.

■

✘ GHOST DAD

MCA
1990
104 minutes
Directed by: Sidney Poitier
Starring: Ian Bannen, Bill Cosby,
    Brooke Fontaine, Salim Grant,
    Denise Nicholas, Kimberly Russell,
    Raynor Scheine
MPAA rating: PG

Widower Elliot Hopper must balance a high-pressure career with the job of raising his children, Diane, Danny and Amanda. With a critical deal coming up, Elliot stands to take a giant step up the corporate ladder. But his plans are short-circuited when he gets into a cab piloted by a madman cab driver who crashes on a bridge, causing them to plunge into the watery depths. Elliot climbs back up to the road and makes his way home where he discovers that his kids can only see him in the dark and that they can't hear him or touch him. He communicates his situation to them (first through charades, and then through the sheer will to talk to them), but in the middle of the conversation is sucked away by the actions of a British medium. The medium tells Elliot that he won't last long in his current state and that it will be a miracle if he makes it to the big meeting on Thursday. Determined to get his promotion, Elliot bluffs his way through meetings and appointments and even discovers a few advantages of his ghostly state. (He can frighten away his daughter Diane's obnoxious would-be boyfriend.) Then when Diane falls and suffers a life-threatening concussion, Elliot encounters her spirit in the hospital and after a reconciliation they both return to their respective bodies.

✘STOP: The film presents negative depictions of the afterlife and Elliott's use of his ghostly form to frighten people may frighten little ones.

CAUTION: There is coarse language.

✗ GHOSTBUSTERS

GO: *Ghostbusters* is a wild and wacky, fast-paced comic-fantasy.

✗ GHOSTBUSTERS II

RCA/Columbia
1985
105 minutes
Directed by: Ivan Reitman
Starring: Dan Aykroyd, Rick Moranis,
   Bill Murray, Harold Ramis,
   Sigourney Weaver
MPAA rating: PG

RCA/Columbia
1989
102 minutes
Directed by: Ivan Reitman
Starring: Dan Aykroyd, Peter McNichol,
   Rick Moranis, Bill Murray, Harold Ramis,
   Sigourney Weaver
MPAA rating: PG

When paranormal experts Doctors Peter Venkman, Egon Spengler and Ray Stantz lose their research grant at a large New York university, they open Ghostbusters, an agency for the removal of unwanted phenomena. Unfortunately, no one seems to need their services, and Ghostbusters lurches towards bankruptcy. But just when all seems lost, Dana Barrett, a violinist with a strangely behaving fridge, seeks their help, and the Ghostbusters are flooded with calls as paranormal activity in New York takes a sudden upsurge. They locate the source of the paranormal emanations (Dana Barrett's apartment building) and with time running out, and both Dana and her ultra-nerd neighbor possessed, the Ghostbusters do battle with an ancient entity in the form of a hundred-foot marshmallow man, and save the world.

✗**STOP:** In the opening scene, the ghost of a librarian becomes a hideous, demonic apparition. There is coarse language and sexual innuendo as in one scene Dana, possessed by a demon, tells Peter, "I want you inside me."

CAUTION: A number of the ghost scenes, funny for adults and older children, may be too intense for young viewers.

Five years after their first success, the down-and-out Ghostbusters reunite when they discover a river of psychically active slime running through an abandoned subway tunnel. Meanwhile, a gigantic eerie portrait of Vigo the Carpathian (also known as Vigo the Impaler) has been moved into the Metropolitan Museum. It turns out that the sorcerer Vigo is preparing to come back and rule the twentieth century. He sends his toady to kidnap Dana's baby as the chosen vessel for his return, and encases the entire Museum, with the baby inside, in an impenetrable slime mold. To break through, the Ghostbusters need a living symbol of goodness and purity. So they animate the Statue of Liberty, and crash through the roof to save the day.

✗**STOP:** When the boys are advancing on Vigo's stronghold, they find themselves surrounded by severed heads on stakes.

CAUTION: Some of the ghosts are pretty scary and there is some coarse language.

A GIRL OF THE LIMBERLOST

Wonderworks
1990
105 minutes
Directed by: Burt Brinckerhoff
Starring: Joanna Cassidy, Heather Fairfield,
Annette O'Toole
MPAA rating: no rating given

Embittered widow Kate Comstock struggles to run a farm with only her teenage daughter Elnora to help. Despite her mother's misgivings that she won't fit in with those frilly town girls, Elnora is resolved to attend high school. And with her mother's grudging permission, Elnora goes. She's a good student with the heart of a poet, but Elnora can't even afford books, and the rigorous demands of the farm are a massive obstacle. Then Elnora meets Mrs. Gene Stratton Porter, a naturalist photographer who requires butterflies and moths for her studies, and hires Elnora to catch some. Elnora is delighted to have found a way to earn some money. But suddenly, the taxes on the farm skyrocket. Then a miracle saves the day: Elnora finds the rarest of butterflies and sells it to make the taxes.

CAUTION: Grief, pain and anger are central elements in this story, and they are intensely portrayed. Elnora's stormy relationship with her mother is reconciled only after Elnora learns that her father died in an accident the night she was born.

GO: A moving story about self-discovery, reconciliation and emotional healing, this film has an environmentalist undercurrent.

THE GIRL WHO SPELLED FREEDOM

Walt Disney Home Video
1985
90 minutes
Directed by: Simon Wincer
Starring: Jade Chinn, Mary Kay Place,
Wayne Rogers
MPAA rating: not rated

In September of 1979, Cambodian refugees Fann Yann and her six children are taken in by an American family. Then comes the long process of forgetting the atrocities of war and adapting to a new culture. This film is a dramatization based on events in the life of Cambodian refugee Linn Yann; facts were obtained from newspaper articles and personal interviews.

CAUTION: This is an intense film. Scenes of Fann Yann's family struggling in Cambodia are juxtaposed with scenes of their American host family's idyllic life. No one is shot or killed (on screen).

GO: The film serves to enlighten North American audiences to the plight of southeast Asian refugees and offers positive solutions.

AGES 10 TO 13

323

THE GODS MUST BE CRAZY

20th Century Fox
1980
109 minutes
Directed by: James Uys
Starring: N!xau, Sandra Prinsloo,
  Louw Verwey, Marius Weyers
MPAA rating: PG

In the deep Kalahari, Xi and his tribal family of Bushmen have never seen, or even heard of civilization. Then one day, a pilot throws a Coke bottle out of the window of his plane, and Xi sees it land and takes it back to his people. The bottle is the most beautiful thing they've ever seen — and the most useful. (It can be used to grind food *and* carry water.) And it soon becomes apparent to everyone in the tribe that the gods have made a mistake in sending only one of the object. They become angry and jealous (once foreign emotions) and Xi decides that the only way to restore peace is to take the thing to the end of the world and throw it off. And after countless encounters (some comical, some nail-biting) with all kinds of people from "civilization," Xi reaches the end of the world (Angel Falls) and throws the bottle away.

CAUTION: A rather bloody assassination attempt is portrayed in slow motion, and is shockingly out-of-character with the rest of the film.

GO: This film is a splendid, light-hearted compassionate look at nomadic (and civilized) life.

THE GODS MUST BE CRAZY 2

RCA/Columbia
1990
98 minutes
Directed by: James Uys
Starring: Lena Faruga, N!xau, Hans Strom
MPAA rating: PG

When Xixo's young children happen on a poacher's vehicle and clamber aboard (they assume it's some strange kind of animal), it unexpectedly starts up and carries them away. Xixo realizes the children have been stolen by a mysterious thing and gives chase. Meanwhile, Dr. Anne Taylor arrives in Africa to give a seminar on corporate law and accepts an offer to go on an aerial sight-seeing jaunt with a zoologist named Stephen. But a freak storm forces them out of the sky, and not only is Anne unable to give her seminar, but she's forced to rough it in the deep Kalahari with the rugged Stephen. Improbable adventures occur, and after a brief encounter with Xixo and his children (who by this point have finally managed to get away from the poacher's truck), everyone goes home.

GO: A splendid film, *The Gods Must Be Crazy II* is far less violent than its predecessor, with lots of great jokes for old and young.

AGES 10 TO 13

✗ THE GOOD SON

20th Century Fox
1993
88 minutes
Directed by: Joseph Ruben
Starring: Wendy Crewson, Macaulay Culkin,
Elijah Wood
MPAA rating: R

This Is Not A Children's Film. We have included it only because it stars two very young stars and may be mistaken for material suitable for the *Home Alone crowd.*

Mark's mother has just died of cancer, and his father is on the verge of completing a business deal which will make sure he never has to leave Mark again. To complete the deal he must go to Tokyo for two weeks, so Mark is taken to spend winter break with his aunt and uncle and their children. The eldest is a boy Mark's age: Henry. At first Henry seems nice enough, but his dark side is revealed all too soon: Henry is a master at maintaining a facade of innocence, and no one believes Mark, who is dismissed as disturbed. Henry continues with his macabre plans to destroy his family (we learn that he is already responsible for the death of his younger brother). First he arranges for his sister to plunge through thin ice while skating (she survives). Then he pushes his mother off a cliff. (In a coincidence reminiscent of Warner Brothers cartoons, her coat catches on a branch and she is saved.) Henry, ever resourceful, decides to drop a sizable rock on her head, but Mark arrives in the nick of time. During the ensuing struggle, Henry's mother climbs back up just as both boys tumble over the precipice. She grabs an arm of each and grimly holds on; however, she can only save one of them. She chooses Mark, letting the little psychopath Henry plunge to a gory death.

✗**STOP:** An unpleasant little tale about an evil child (and not that original, either). Henry swears, shoots a dog, and acts convincingly menacing, particularly when he tries to dust his mom.

CAUTION: The whole film is relentlessly sombre. Wendy Crewson's fine talents are utterly wasted here.

■

✗ GREMLINS

Warner Home Video
1984
106 minutes
Directed by: Joe Dante
Starring: Hoyt Axton, Phoebe Cates,
Corey Feldman, Zach Galligan,
Judge Reinhold
MPAA rating: PG

When Billy's dad gives him a tiny creature called a mowgway, Billy is delighted. His dad explains that this is an unusual kind of pet and warns him to remember three important things: Billy must keep the mowgway away from bright lights and from water, and most important of all, he must never feed his mowgway after midnight. Of course, it isn't long before Billy's younger friend Pete spills water on the creature, and out pop five new mowgway. But these aren't like the original; they're mischievious. And when Billy's clock stops and he inadvertently feeds them after midnight, they go through a strange and terrible metamorphosis, turning into a nasty crew of mean-spirited little gremlins. Led by a particularly horrible gremlin named Stripes, an army of the creatures terrorizes the town — even the local law enforcement officers are helpless — and in the end it's up to Billy and his girlriend Kate to stop the dreadful little monsters.

✗ **STOP:** This is a horror movie, albeit a darkly funny one, and not a film for children. The gremlins kill a lot of people and many of the gremlins themselves meet a horrible end. (One is ground to bits in a blender while another blows up in the microwave.) *Gremlins II* is more of the same and was rated PG-frightening scenes.

THE HIDEAWAYS

Warner Home Video
1972
105 minutes
Directed by: Fielder Cook
Starring: Ingrid Bergman, Johnny Doran,
   Sally Prager, George Rose
MPAA rating: G

Based on the book *From the Mixed-Up Files of Mrs. Basil E. Frankweiler* by E. L. Konigsburg, *The Hideaways* follows the adventures of Claudia and her younger brother Jamie. Claudia is a bright, sensitive young girl who feels overworked, under-appreciated and distinctly unspecial at home. Her mother has little time for her, and her father tramples her imaginative inclinations. Then an accidentally discarded train ticket provides her with the opportunity for adventure she has been seeking, and she runs away from home, taking Jamie with her. Following Claudia's careful plan, the two go and live in the Metropolitan Museum of Fine Art. There they have a wonderful time, wandering around the galleries and joining school tours by day, sleeping in the Louis XIV beds at night, and taking baths in the museum fountains (which are also their source of finances). Shortly after their arrival Claudia becomes enthralled by a magnificent statue of an angel. The angel, which is attributed to Michelangelo himself, has been recently acquired by the museum for the paltry sum of two hundred dollars from the eccentric millionaire Mrs. Basil E. Frankweiler. Claudia's original plan was simply to make a point with her parents about being appreciated; however, fascinated by the statue, Claudia decides that she cannot return home until she has solved the mystery of its origins. Library research turns up nothing, so Claudia decides to contact the original owner, the strange and reclusive Mrs. Frankweiler. In Claudia, Mrs. F finds a kindred spirit. She is extremely reluctant to help the children in any other way than to simply send them home; however, she understands that Claudia cannot return until she has had an extraordinary experience. And so, Mrs. Frankweiler reveals to Claudia one of her great secrets, the identity of the statue's sculptor.

CAUTION: This is a movie about two children who run away from home and successfully establish themselves elsewhere, having a wonderful time in the process.

GO: Mrs. Frankweiler gives stern admonitions to the children about causing their parents grief. The film is a terrific adventure story, suitable for children with a slightly literary bent.

■

✗ HOCUS POCUS

Walt Disney Home video
1993
106 minutes
Directed by: Kenny Ortega
Starring: Thora Birch, Bette Midler,
  Kathy Najimy, Sarah Jessica Parker
MPAA rating: PG

Salem, 1693: three witches, the Sanderson sisters, have stolen a little girl and are in the process of literally sucking out her life energy to rejuvenate themselves. Her older brother Zachary tries *unsuccessfully* to save her, but the witches condemn him to eternal life as a cat. The witches are then caught and hanged, but according to a final spell, they will return when a virgin lights their black-flame candle on some future Halloween night. Exactly three hundred years later, California native Max Denison has just moved to Salem. He is forced to take his eight-year-old sister Dani out trick-or-treating. They meet Allison, the girl of Max's dreams, and together the three go up to the old Sanderson place. But when Max lights the black-flame candle the witches immediately appear and try to take Dani's life-force. The kids escape with the aid of Zachary the cat, taking with them the witches' book of magic spells, and flee to the graveyard, which is hallowed ground. The witches only have until

sunrise to get their book back and cast the spell that will grant them eternal life. A night of mayhem ensues as the witches search for the kids, raise the dead, make zombies of Salem's inhabitants, get burned up and reconstituted, catch and lose Dani again, and finally confront the kids in the graveyard just before dawn.

✗ STOP: Many parents who saw the film in the theater expressed surprise that it was so intense. The witches catch a little girl and suck out her life. They are hung and we see their feet dangling. A corpse with its mouth sewn shut claws itself out of a grave and chases the kids around. The witches' spells are hyper-realistic.

CAUTION: The tone of this film is quite dark: it's a spoof, but it's still basically a horror movie. The witches are quirky and evil. It is mentioned that they have killed hundreds of children. Zachary the cat dies at the end. His human soul returns with his sister and the two of them walk away out of the graveyard into the hereafter.

GO: The special effects are excellent, the pacing is good, and the story is better than that of your average supernatural spooky flick.

✗ HOME ALONE

20th Century Fox
1990
103 miuntes
Directed by: Chris Columbus
Starring: Macaulay Culkin, John Heard,
  Catherine O'Hara, Joe Pesci, Daniel Stern
MPAA rating: PG

A few days before Christmas, as his family prepares for a clan visit to relatives in Paris, eight-year-old Kevin is feeling ignored. That night before bed he wishes out loud that he didn't have a family, and the next morning when he's all alone in the house he believes that his wish has come true. (In truth, a severed power line prevents the alarms from going off, and in the chaos that ensues, Kevin is missed in the head count as his family leaves for the airport. It isn't until they're over the Atlantic that Kevin's mother realizes he's not with them.) For a while at least, Kevin is in kid heaven, playing with his older brother's stuff, tobogganing inside the house and so on. He even learns to do the laundry and goes shopping. Then burglers target the house and it's up to Kevin to outsmart them.

✗**STOP:** Some of Kevin's booby-traps — although hilarious in the film — could be extremely dangerous and children have been known to imitate them. (He sets off firecrackers in a kitchen pot, shoots one of the burglars with an air gun, heats a door-knob with a barbeque starter, etc.)

CAUTION: Kevin's siblings treat him miserably, and when he acts in self-defense he is punished. (His uncle angrily calls him a jerk.) Some children are upset because they get the impression Kevin is being locked in the attic for being bad; however, he is, in fact, sleeping there because all of the bedrooms are full of house guests. There is some coarse language.

GO: Kevin has a charming, realistic and insightful conversation with his next door neighbor. This is a comedy with some attention given to the value of family.

AGES 10 TO 13

✗ HOME ALONE II: LOST IN NEW YORK

20th Century Fox
1992
90 minutes
Directed by: Chris Columbus
Starring: Macaulay Culkin, Tim Curry,
  Brenda Fricker, John Heard,
  Catherine O'Hara, Joe Pesci, Daniel Stern
MPAA rating: PG

One year after his traumatic Christmas home alone, Kevin McCallister and his family wake up late on the morning of their vacation — again. And this time, the resulting chaos leaves Kevin alone on a plane to New York City (his family goes to Florida). However, he is armed with his father's flight bag, money and credit cards and Kevin soon cons his way into the swanky Plaza Hotel, where he proceeds to run up huge bills. Finally, the grown-ups catch on and Kevin is forced to flee into the unfriendly streets of the Big Apple. Meanwhile, the Wet Bandits (his adversaries from the first film) have escaped from jail and are planning to rob a toy store on Christmas Eve. They encounter Kevin, who lures them to his uncle's empty house which is loaded with booby traps.

✗**STOP:** Kevin's booby traps, while hilariously cartoonish, have been known to occasionally generate copy-cat pranks by children too young to know better.

CAUTION: Kevin makes no effort to contact his family once he's lost; rather, he cheerfully goes into New York City alone. The burglars are partially electrocuted, smashed with a steel bar, shot in the face with a staple gun, etc.

GO: This is a straight-ahead box-office comedy smash that's too similar to its predecessor to have any surprises.

HOT SHOTS!

20th Century Fox
1991
83 minutes
Directed by: Jim Abrahams
Starring: Lloyd Bridges, Jon Cryer,
    Kevin Dunn, Cary Elwes, Valeria Golino,
    Charlie Sheen
MPAA rating: PG-13

When former navy pilot Topper Harley is asked to return to the service for a secret mission (Operation Sleepy Weasel), Harley agrees, and finds himself with the weirdest flight group ever assembled. It becomes immediately obvious that the group's lead pilot, Kent Gregory, despises Harley. (Harley's father allegedly caused Gregory's father's death.) And Harley becomes so crippled by his family's shameful history that the mere mention of his father's name is enough to induce a psychotic episode. Navy psychiatrist Ramada Thompson plans to have Topper grounded, but his commander keeps him in the air. (He hopes the unpredictable pilot will contribute to the failure of Operation Sleepy Weasel, so the navy will buy more sophisticated fighters.) In the end, Harley learns the truth about his father and after some more than incredible flying, saves the day. But don't let this seemingly normal plot description fool you; this movie is a joke-every-five-seconds send-up.

CAUTION: The movie includes a spoof of a scene from the film *Nine-and-a-Half Weeks*, in which Harley puts food on Ramada's naked stomach. (She is in her underwear.) There is some coarse language.

GO: Suitable for the older crowd, this film includes hilarious send-ups of such films as *Top Gun*, *Dances With Wolves*, *Superman*, *Marathon Man* and *The Fabulous Baker Boys*. The jokes are literally nonstop.

✗ INDIANA JONES AND THE LAST CRUSADE

Paramount Home Video
1989
126 minutes
Directed by: Steven Spielberg
Starring: Sean Connery, Denholm Elliott,
    Harrison Ford, John Rhys-Davies
MPAA rating: PG-13

Philanthropist Walter Donovan has uncovered a twelfth-century tablet which indicates a possible location of the Holy Grail in the catacombs of Venice. But when Donovan's project leader, Dr. Jones Sr., is abducted, he hires Dr. Jones Jr. (Indiana Jones) to take up the search. In Venice, Indiana meets his father's associate, Dr. Elsa Schneider, who takes him to the place where his father vanished. There, Jones and Elsa are attacked by a group of fanatics who have defended the secret location of the Grail for a thousand years. They manage to assure the group that they are interested only in finding Dr. Jones Sr., and learn that he's being held by the Nazis in an Austrian castle. Indiana rescues his father, and after several narrow escapes and wild chases involving motorcycles, dirigibles and a Nazi tank, the Joneses ends up in a secret temple where they face the three deadly traps protecting the Grail's sanctuary. And with his father's life now on the line, Indiana must avoid the traps and face the terrible secret of the Grail. This is the last film in the Indiana Jones trilogy.

✗STOP: When Donovan chooses the wrong chalice (in one of the tests of the Grail), he ages in seconds and decomposes while still alive.

CAUTION: This film has the violence you would expect from an Indiana Jones movie (punching, shooting, killing, people being run over with tanks). There are many, many rats.

GO: Once again, Indiana Jones is a big-budget action adventure.

✗ INDIANA JONES AND THE TEMPLE OF DOOM

Paramount Home Video
1984
118 minutes
Directed by: Steven Sielberg
Starring: Harrison Ford, Kate Capshaw, Ke Huy Quan
MPAA rating: PG

In this "pre-quel" to *Raiders of the Lost Ark*, daredevil archeologist Indiana Jones embarks on a journey to India. There he hopes to find the Ankara Stone and bring it back to a museum. But a mysterious cult has enslaved all of the children of the village and, after numerous harrowing experiences, "Indy" saves the children and returns them and the stone to the village where they belong.

✗STOP: This film is not for young children and is the most violent of the trilogy. The violence is frequent and often gratuitous. One of the more disturbing scenes features a horrible cult ceremony, during which a beating heart is ripped out of a live victim. Also watch for gruesome skeletons, dead bodies, a banquet at which eyeball soup and fried beetles are served, and a fight scene in which two children try to kill each other.

CAUTION: Indiana's female companion is a poor role model and is more of a problem than a help.

GO: The violence is so extreme and situations are so impossible that the fact that Indiana always come out unscathed gives the film a comic book-like atmosphere.

✗ IRON WILL

Walt Disney
1993
119 minutes
Directed by: Charles Haid
Starring: Mackenzie Austin, August Schellenberg, Kevin Spacey, David Ogden Stiers
MPAA rating: PG

South Dakota, 1917: Will Stoneman is a tough but fair-minded young man of high aspirations, and his wonderful father is doing everything in his power to make sure that Will achieves his dreams. Then his father dies in a tragic dogsled accident, and Will and his mother are hard-pressed just to make ends meet. Will, an excellent dogsledder

330

himself, decides to enter the biggest race in the world, the Derby from Winnipeg, Manitoba to St. Paul, Minnesota, a gruelling event which even the greatest racers in the world are thankful just to finish. Will must overcome great odds even to enter. Given no chance to last, let alone win, Will is backed by an unscrupulous newpaper reporter who sees him only as a ticket to a few headlines. Then comes the rigorous race, the cold and the exhaustion. The greatest obstacle is a rival racer, a grim and vicious Swede who will do anything to win. But Will endures, and his resilience inspires his countrymen while drawing the ire of a powerful man who has big money on the race. The pressure mounts from every corner, until the last tension-filled day of the contest.

✗**STOP:** Will's father suffers an agonizing, albeit heroic death, saving Will and the dogs before drowning in ice-cold water. The evil Swede makes sneering reference to frostbite, and holds up a terribly ravaged hand to prove his point.

CAUTION: Will's grief after the death of his father is heart-rending. There are fist-fights, drawn knives and pointed guns. The Swede sabotages his fellow racers. He sics his lead dog on Will's, resulting in a bloody fight. The Swede mercilessly whips his own dogs. At the climax they turn on him, snarling and ripping at him.

GO: All in all, a great underdog film, beautifully shot and very exciting.

✗ JURASSIC PARK

Universal
1993
125 minutes
Directed by: Stephen Spielberg
Starring: Richard Attenborough, Laura Dern,
    Jeff Goldblum, Sam Neill
MPAA rating: PG-13

Previewing is recommended.

Jurassic Park is a prehistoric wildlife sanctuary-cum-theme park featuring an array of genetically engineered dinosaurs. The park is financed by philanthropist John Hammond. After an accident resulting in a worker's death, Hammond must convince his nervous investors of the park's safety, and to this end he invites a trio of scientists to take a tour. Paleontologist Dr. Alan Grant, paleobotanist Dr. Ellen Sattler and "chaotician" Ian Malcolm are joined by Hammond's grandchildren, Tim and Alexis, and his anxious lawyer. Things soon go awry. The group becomes separated, and glitches in the electrical systems are compounded by a raging tropical storm; then the park's computer programmer, Dennis Nedry, turns off the defense systems in order to smuggle some dinosaur embryos off the island. A tyrannosaur quickly breaks out of its enclosure and attacks the tour, wounding Malcolm, devouring the lawyer and tossing the car around with the children trapped inside. Grant saves the children in the nick of time, and as they struggle back through the park toward the central control center,

Sattler and the park's chief ranger Muldoon take a jeep and go out in search of the tour, finding only Malcolm and bringing him back with them to the center. Meanwhile, Nedry has been killed, leaving all the computers locked; Hammond orders them shut down, but when Sattler and Muldoon venture out to restore power and restart the systems, they discover that the vicious predatorial velociraptors have escaped. In the climax, the survivors find themselves hunted by the intelligent raptors.

✗**STOP:** This film is not for children under ten! The dinosaurs appear real and they may terrify even older kids. One character is eaten by a dilophosaur which spits a deadly venom all over his face, while a second is horribly killed by raptors. The lawyer is swallowed by a tyrannosaurus, and in a startling scene, Dr. Sattler grabs onto a severed human arm. In its intensity, this film rivals any other Spielberg production (eg. *Poltergeist*).

CAUTION: The scene in which Tim and Alexis are trapped in their car by the tyrannosaurus is particulaly unnerving, as is the scene in which Tim is electrocuted on a high-voltage electric fence, and Alexis is terrorized in the kitchen by predatory raptors. Hammond is not even remotely remorseful that his dinosaurs have killed people.

GO: The effects are remarkable, employing highly realistic computer-generated imagery. The film draws on much of the latest scientific information about dinosaurs. There's even a quick remedial science lesson to remind viewers what DNA is. The film contains strong female role models; Doctors Sattler and Grant are clearly on equal footing and Alexis is the computer hacker who eventually brings the defense systems back online.

■

✗ K-9

MCA
1990
111 minutes
Directed by: Rod Daniel
Starring: James Belushi, James Handy,
 Mel Harris, Ed O'Neill, Kevin Tighe
MPAA rating: PG-13

When narcotics cop Mike Dooley needs a dog to help him bust powerful drug lord Kent Lyman, he acquires Jerry Lee, a fierce and incredibly intelligent German Shepherd. Not only does Jerry Lee sniff out the drugs, he takes on a pool hall full of thugs, runs down the bad guys and saves Dooley's life more than once. But Lyman proves to be harder to nail than Dooley had expected. When Dooley's girlfriend Tracy is kidnapped, Dooley and his dog must intercept a drug shipment to rescue her. In the final confrontation, Jerry Lee is shot while trying to save Dooley.

✗**STOP:** This film is not for young children. In one disturbing scene, a villain describes a Columbian neck-tie (which involves cutting a victim's throat and pulling his tongue out through the wound), and in another, Lyman cruelly teases an intended victim, then coldly executes him.

CAUTION: The dog gets shot, and while he pulls through in the end, for a time viewers are made to think he has died. In an opening shot of a parking lot, sexual activity is implied through rain-drenched car windows.

GO: *K-9* is exciting, but definitely not for kids under twelve.

THE KARATE KID

CAUTION: Many of the fight scenes are brutal. There is some coarse language.

GO: This is an inspiring tale of an underdog, graced by a spiritually sensitive teacher, who earns self-respect and wins the day.

RCA/Columbia
1984
126 minutes
Directed by: John G.Alvlidsen
Starring: Martin Kove, Ralph Macchio,
   Pat Morita, Elisabeth Shue, William Zarka
MPAA rating: PG

Teenager Daniel LaRusso moves to Los Angeles with his mother, who is looking for a new start in life. But things aren't so good for Daniel. Soon after his arrival, he meets a charming girl at a beach party and is promptly beaten up by her jealous ex-boyfriend, Johnny. And this is only the beginning of a campaign of terror against him, as Johnny and his friends pound Daniel mercilessly at every opportunity. When Daniel goes to the local karate school to seek some training to defend himself, he discovers that his tormentors are already students there, under the tutelage of a merciless sensei, John Kreese. The bullies finally catch him, and are in the process of beating him within an inch of his life when Daniel is rescued by the building's mysterious caretaker, Mr. Miyagi, who also turns out to be a master of karate. After convincing Kreese and his students to leave Daniel alone until the All-Valley karate tournament, Miyagi himself trains Daniel in the fundamentals of karate. Against nearly impossible odds, Daniel enters the tournament and defeats opponent after opponent until in the final match he must face Johnny himself.

THE KARATE KID PART II

RCA/Columbia
1986
113 minutes
Directed by: John G. Avildsen
Starring: Daniel Kamekona, Ralph Macchio,
   Nobu McCarthy, Pat Morita
MPAA rating: PG

When Miyagi's father is dying, he returns home to Okinawa with considerable trepidation. When last he was there, he broke with tradition and announced to the whole village his intention to marry Yuki, who was already promised to his best friend Sato. This brought shame and dishonor to Sato who had no option but to challenge Miyagi to a fight. But because he did not believe in fighting, Miyagi left the island (and his great love) behind and moved to the United States. Now Miyagi must return to face a dying father, Sato (who has not forgotten) and Yuki (who has never married). Daniel accompanies his mentor on his trip and he, too, runs into problems. Sato's cruel nephew takes an instant dislike to him and begins a feud with him. And in a brutal climactic fight Daniel realizes that this time the fight is not a competition for points, but for his life. This is the sequel to *The Karate Kid*.

CAUTION: There is a lot of fighting in this film. Daniel's delicate girlfriend is savagely punched in the face by Sato's cruel nephew and the climax is brutal and bloody.

GO: Alongside all of the violence are the poignant and tasteful love stories of Miyagi and Yuki and Daniel and Komiko. The importance of "true honor" is demonstrated and hate and revenge are shown to be wrong. Japanese culture is treated with sensitivity and respect.

THE KARATE KID PART III

RCA/Columbia
1989
Directed by: John G. Avildsen
Starring: Thomas Ian Griffith,
    Daniel Kamekona, Sean Kanan,
    Ralph Macchio, Pat Morita
MPAA rating: PG

After losing to Miyagi and Daniel at the All-Valley karate tournament, John Kreese has lost all of his students and his school. So when his old army buddy and fellow karateka, Terry Silver, bails Kreese out, together they plot his revenge against Miyagi and Daniel: Daniel will be invited to defend his All-Valley title against killer karateka Mike Barnes. But when Miyagi refuses to allow Daniel to enter the tournament, Mike and Silver's thugs literally force Daniel to sign the entrance form. Still, Miyagi refuses to participate, prompting Silver to pose as a well-meaning sensei who agrees to take over Daniel's training. In reality, this is just a ruse designed to ruin all of Miyagi's hard work with Daniel. But Daniel's inner

strength allows him to resist Silver, and he eventually breaks off the relationship. Only then does Miyagi agree to conduct the training. And again, we return to the karate championships, where Daniel faces the fierce Mike in a final showdown.

CAUTION: There is violent fighting throughout. At one point, Mike coldly kicks a female friend of Daniel's in the stomach.

✗ LADY JANE

Paramount Home Video
1985
140 minutes
Directed by: Trevor Nunn
Starring: Helena Bonham Carter, Carey Elwes,
    Warren Saire, Patrick Stewart, John Wood
MPAA rating: PG-13

During the reign of the frail teenage king Edward the Sixth, powerful barons, looking beyond the young king's imminent death, maneuver for power. They plot to install Lady Jane Grey as the next ruler, hoping to marry her off to Guilford Dudley, thereby uniting their two houses. But Gilford is wild and Jane is quiet and studious, and at first the two can barely get along. Then they discover that they do have much in common, in particular a thirst to see a just and equitable government over England. But when the idealistic Jane finally becomes Queen of England, the coalition which keeps her on the throne crumbles, and her reign is over in nine days. She and Gilford are arrested, and like so many others before them, eventually go to the headsman.

✗ STOP: In one disturbing scene, Jane's mother forces her to lift her skirts and bend over a chair, where her mother gives her a savage and prolonged beating.

CAUTION: When they are married, Jane and Gilford are shown sitting up in bed, naked and facing each other. (They can be seen from the hips up.) The Machiavellian plottings of the barons may be too confusing for young viewers and the film's ending, too traumatic.

GO: A skilfully crafted love story about two people who put their lives on the line when they get a chance to really make a difference, this is a splendid depiction of a rich period in English history.

✗ LADYHAWKE

Warner Home Video
1985
121 minutes
Directed by: Richard Donner
Starring: Matthew Broderick, Rutger Hauer,
    Leo McKern, Michelle Pfeiffer, John Wood
MPAA rating: PG-13

When a beatiful woman named Isabeau rejects the advances of the corrupt Bishop of Aquila, she and her true-love Navarre are placed under a terrible curse: she is transformed into a hawk by day and he, into a wolf by night. And so they are always together, but eternally apart. Navarre and the hawk have been travelling for two years when they encounter Phillipe "The Mouse" Gaston (a petty thief, whom Navarre believes is his guiding angel). Sure that the curse cannot be broken, Navarre plans to kill the Bishop, and convinces Phillipe to join him in seeking his revenge. But their plans

are delayed when the hawk is wounded, and Phillipe is forced to take her to the old priest, who had originally betrayed their trust and who is the only one who knows how to heal her. In a moment of remorse, the priest tells Phillipe that the lovers' curse can be broken when "day is in night and night is in day," and the Bishop casts his eyes on both Isabeau and Navarre in human form. This seems impossible, but Phillipe goes along with Navarre to the castle hoping to dissuade him from his plan to kill the Bishop, just in case. There, to his amazement the moon covers the sun in a solar eclipse and Isabeau changes into human form to stand beside Navarre in full view of the Bishop. The lovers are reunited.

✗ STOP: There are some rough battle scenes in this film. Navarre impales the Bishop and the Captain of the Guard. (There is blood, and it is violent and graphic.) A wolf trapper dies a horrible death when his head is caught in one of his own traps.

GO: Adventurous and romantic, this story is based on a thirteenth century legend and features a modern but impressive musical score. There is no coarse language.

LAMBADA

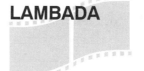

Warner Home Video
1990
104 minutes
Directed by: Joel Silberg
Starring: Shabba Doo, Melora Hardin,
    J. Eddie Peck
MPAA rating: PG

(continued on next page)

AGES 10 TO 13

When high school student Sandy Thomas goes to a new dance club in East L.A., she makes two shocking discoveries: the first is a new dance craze called the Lambada, and the second is that the strait-laced teacher she knows as Kevin Laird is leading a double life. By day, he's her math teacher at a posh high school in a privileged neighborhood, and at night he teaches at Galaxy High, where classes are held in the sleazy night-club after hours. Suddenly seeing him as sexy, Sandy incurs the ire of her jealous boyfriend by making advances toward Kevin. And in the end, in an effort to prove that he really is teaching math at the dance club, Kevin pits his Galaxy High students in a math contest against his students from Stonewood High.

CAUTION: There is a fistfight between the kids from the rival schools in which both boys and girls throw punches, and there is some coarse language.

GO: Don't be fooled by the sexy cover and the title; this film is not a dance movie. It's about a sympathetic teacher who puts his career on the line for his students, and it's about appreciating an education. Watch right through the credits!

✗ LANTERN HILL

Astral
1989
111 minutes
Directed by: Kevin Sullivan
Starring: Mairon Bennett, Zoe Caldwell,
    Colleen Dewhurst, Sarah Polley,
    Sam Waterston
MPAA rating: not rated

During the Great Depression, while her mother is recovering from polio, twelve-year-old Victoria Jane Stuart lives with her domineering grandmother. She hears nothing but negative stories about her absent father (he was involved with a woman named Evelyn, who mysteriously disappeared). Then one day her father sends a letter, asking Jane to come and visit him on Prince Edward Island. There, Jane learns the truth about her parents, and when she finds a letter from Evelyn explaining what really happened, she goes about reconciling her parents. Based on the book *Jane of Lantern Hill* by Lucy Maud Montgomery.

✗STOP: Jane's friend, a grandmother figure, dies in a heart-wrenching scene.

CAUTION: This ghost story/romance is too sophisticated for little ones. Jane's situation is not a happy one and there are some spooky elements.

GO: This is a sensitive film about family relationships.

✗ THE LAST ACTION HERO

Columbia
1993
130 minutes
Directed by: John Tiernan
Starring: Charles Dance, Anthony Quinn,
    Mercedes Ruehl, Arnold Schwarzenegger
MPAA rating: PG-13

Danny lives with his hard-working mother in a small apartment in a crime-plagued district of the big city. His favorite activity is to go to a local rundown theater and watch action movies featuring his hero, Jack Slater. The owner gives Danny a preview of the very latest Slater film. He also gives Danny a bizarre metal ticket which blurs the boundary between the screen and the real world. During a chase scene in the movie, Danny is literally blown through the screen by dynamite, landing right in the middle of the movie. He quickly discovers that his knowledge of film clichés, and his status as a former observer, stand him in good stead, and villains and good-guys alike are mystified by Danny's powers. Slater takes him on as a partner, while the evil Benedict, a one-eyed assassin with an assortment of weird prosthetic eyes, is out to get him. Eventually the magic ticket falls into Benedict's hands and he escapes into the real world, where he sets about to take over. But first he must destroy Slater, who has followed him. The climax takes place at a movie awards night, where Slater comes face to face with his alter-ego, the real Arnold Schwarzenegger.

✗STOP: This movie has correctly been billed as a toned-down action film for younger fans, but it is fairly intense. People get beaten up, blown up, electrocuted, shot repeatedly and bloodily killed in a variety of other ways. The assassin is shot through his glass eye at the end and a mad ax-wielding psychotic threatens children.

CAUTION: This is a surreal movie, and its bizarre treatment of alternate realities is sure to leave some viewers puzzled.

GO: Parts of this movie are good fun, and it might be the least violent selection for older kids who are eager to see a Schwarzenegger action movie.

■

✗ THE LAST STARFIGHTER

MCA
1984
100 minutes
Directed by: Nick Castle
Starring: Lance Guest, Dan O'Herlihy, Robert Preston, Catherine Mary Stewart
MPAA rating: PG

Alex Rogan is an expert at the videogame "Starfighter." Unbeknownst to him, the game has been installed by aliens who are seeking recruits for their interstellar forces, and when Alex breaks the game record, one of the aliens arrives and takes him to the planet Rylos. There, because of his talent, Alex is recruited to be a Starfighter, where he will battle the black terror of the Kodan, which is threatening the rapidly collapsing frontier. But Alex has no desire to become a Starfighter for real, and when he pleads to be returned home he is given two choices: return to Earth and live like everyone else until the Kodan's evil forces arrive and destroy the planet, or stay and become the last Starfighter, the only man who can save the galaxy.

✗STOP: The action is intense and often gruesome. In one scene, a clone of Alex develops a deformed head and bulging eyes and in another, the Star League's greatest spy, his neck bound to the wall, has his face disintegrated. There is some sexual suggestion and a little swearing.

GO: Ron Cobb (Alien, Star Wars, Conan the Barbarian) did an amazing job with the production design, and the computer-generated special effects are superb. The story will be especially appealing to science fiction and video-game buffs.

✘ LEAN ON ME

Warner Home Video
1989
109 minutes
Directed by: John G. Avildsen
Starring: Morgan Freeman,
 Robert Guillaume, Beverly Todd
MPAA rating: PG-13

Once considered one of the finest schools in America, Eastside High has fallen into ruin. Teachers are brutally beaten, guns are carried and drugs are dealt openly. Faced with the prospect of losing the school to the state, the Superintendant of Schools hires a gifted, arrogant teacher named Joe Clark to clean it up and raise the students' basic skills level; he gives Clark 110 school days in which to do it. Clark begins by expelling all of the trouble-makers and chaining the school doors shut to keep the remaining students safe. Convinced that the students will live up to what is expected of them, Clark bullies the staff into raising their expectations and reminds them that if they don't like his methods they can quit. After much work, the school is cleaned up, the students gain some self-respect and the Basic Skills test is written. But before the marks even come in, the parents of the expelled students have Clark arrested for disobeying the fire chief's order to unchain the doors. The entire student body demonstrates outside the jail where the glowing Basic Skills test scores finally arrive. This film is based on a true story.

✘STOP: During the opening credits a teacher is repeatedly kicked and his head is slammed into the floor; it is bloody. Even girls terrorize each otherThere is some coarse language.

GO: Most of the violence in the film is shown during the opening credits. (There is only one other fight.) This is an inspiring feel-good movie.

✘ LEGEND

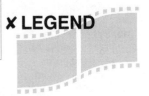

MCA
1986
89 minutes
Directed by: Ridley Scott
Starring: Tom Cruise, Tim Curry, Mia Sara
MPAA rating: PG

In a magical place, in another time, the Dark Lord plots his return to dominion over the world of light. However, standing in his way are a pair of unicorns, in whose souls the light is harbored, and who are beyond his evil grasp because they can only be found by pure-hearted mortals. One of the pure-hearted is Jack, who lives in a marvelous forest along with his lady-love Lily. When Jack shows Lily the unicorns, the young woman is so enchanted that she touches one, enabling the Dark Lord's servants enough time to *kill* the unicorn stallion. The world of light is immediately locked in a terrible winter; the goblins capture Lily and the mare unicorn, and Jack and his fairy friends are forced to follow the goblins into the dreadful realm of the Dark Lord. There, they pass through all the perils of hell, rescue Lily from the clutches of the demon ruler and use the power of the remaining unicorn and the sun itself to restore order to the universe.

✗**STOP:** *Legend* is not for most children. The film opens in hell, where writhing figures strapped to tables are beaten with whips. Later, a huge ogre carries away a shrieking dwarf and a swamp troll is beheaded.

CAUTION: The Dark Lord and his goblin servants are hideous. The plot is relentlessly grim, and the landscape, desolate.

GO: The performances are excellent; the costumes and sets are stunning, and the atmosphere, soundly established. An interesting attempt at a filmic fairytale.

LEGEND OF THE WHITE HORSE

CBS/Fox
1985
91 minutes
Directed by: Jerzy Domaradzki,
    Janusz Morgenstern
Starring: Allison Balson, Christopher Lloyd,
    Dee Wallace Stone
MPAA rating: no rating given

When environmental impact consultant Jim Martin is hired by a developer to survey a property in remote Karistan, he and his son move there and stay with the local witch and her blind adopted daughter, Jewel. Jim soon hears of the existence of a mysterious cave on the property, and learns that Jewel is the only person who can enter it safely past the watchful eye of the white horse/dragon that guards it. (The horse/dragon turns all others who try to enter into stone.) It turns out that the witch and her evil partner need Jewel to get into the cave where precious jewels and the secrets of youth and immortality await. In the end, the witch and her partner meet a grisly death when they turn on Jewel inside the cave. Then it's discovered that the mysterious horse/dragon is none other than Jewel's biological mother transformed. Jim exposes the developer's unscrupulous plans to the government in order to preserve the mystery of the white horse and the integrity of the land. Based on the book *Dark Horse, Dark Dragon* by Robert C. Fleet

CAUTION: The actors' accents are inconsistent and the music is invasive and inappropriate. In order to gain immortality, Jewel must die, so the witch kills Jewel with a knife. (Jewel comes back to life.) People are machine-gunned and die with their eyes open and blood coming from their mouths, and bad guys are vaporized by the dragon. Also of concern may be the fact that Steve's mother dies before the film begins.

■

LICENSE TO DRIVE

CBS
1988
90 minutes
Directed by: Greg Beeman
Starring: Corey Feldman, Heather Graham,
    Corey Haim, Carol Kane, Richard Masur
MPAA rating: PG-13

When sixteen-year-old Les Anderson meets Mercedes, he knows he's found the perfect girl. Now all he needs is the perfect car — and his driver's license — to make his dream complete. But the second half of his dream is slow in coming when, after sleeping through every one of his driver's education classes, Les fails the written portion of his test. Upset by his failure, and doubly mortified by his twin sister's success at *her* test, Les is further disgraced when his pregnant mother discovers his results and grounds him. Determined to see his dream girl, Les takes his grandfather's prize Cadillac and sneaks out. Almost immediately things begin to go wrong. Mercedes gets drunk and dances on the hood of the car, causing significant damage, before passing out. Friends help Les repair the damage then convince him to take *them* for a ride. They put Mercedes in the trunk and from there on in it's just one disaster after another until they finally manage to get what's left of the Cadillac home. Soon after, Les's mother goes into labor and Les has one final chance to prove his driving ability by getting his excited family to the hospital.

CAUTION: The boys try to decide in what kind of car a girl would be willing to lose her virginity; one of the boys lifts Mercedes's dress while she is passed out and takes photos; and a drunk vomits in the car. The teens in this film are out all night and there is coarse language.

GO: Despite the language and some sexual innuendo, this film is basically inoffensive.

✗ LIONHEART

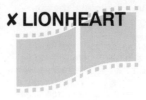

Warner Home Video
1986
104 minutes
Directed by: Franklin J. Schaffner
Starring: Gabriel Byrne, Nicola Cowper, Dexter Fletcher, Eric Stolz
MPAA rating: PG

In late twelfth century France, during a pitched battle with a rival fiefdom, a young knight named Robert Nera loses his nerve and flees. Haunted by his shame, he sets off to join the crusade of Richard I and encounters two young circus runaways on the way. The trio set out for Paris together, stopping at an abbey for shelter during a storm. There Robert first sees the Black Prince, a shadowy black-garbed warrior who prowls the roads looking for wayward children. Robert gathers many of these children under his protection as he travels. Once they reach Paris, he discovers a society of orphans hiding in a catacomb under the protection of a good but sickly knight. The knight convinces Robert to take the children south to the warmth of the sun and the sanctuary of Richard's armies. And so, tracked by the Black Prince and accompanied by his friends, Robert shepherds his charges through plague and peril, until a final confrontation with his enemy tests his skills and courage to the limit.

✗STOP: Robert wrenches open a confessional door, and the body of a priest tumbles out, his throat slit.

CAUTION: This film has some intense battle scenes. The Black Prince is a fearsome man who kills his own unarmed brother and commits sacrilege by throwing a knife into the statue of Christ.

GO: This film features two very positive role models for young women—one has a strange gift with animals and the other is a fierce, independent knight.

✗ LITTLE MAN TATE

Orion
1991
99 minutes
Directed by: Jodie Foster
Starring: Jodie Foster, Adam Hann-Byrd,
  Dianne Wiest
MPAA rating: PG

Fred Tate is a seven-year-old supergenius who paints like Raphael, plays advanced piano, writes opera and instantly visualizes the solutions to higher-order math problems. Alienated from his peers — and even from his own loving but uneducated mother, Deedee — all Fred really wants is someone to eat lunch with. Then he is interviewed by Dr. Jane Grierson of the Grierson Institute, a school specialized in meeting the educational needs of extremely gifted children, and things begin to change. The doctor instantly recognizes Fred's enormous potential, and invites him to attend a summer seminar course where he finally meets kids who are just like him. Upon his return, Fred's relationship with his mother is strained, and when she lands a job in Florida it's agreed that he will stay behind to attend university and live with Dr. Grierson. But Fred finds the university to be an achingly lonely place and Dr. Grierson isn't good with children. The crisis builds to a climax in which everyone comes to realize that no matter how immensely powerful his intellect, Fred is still a little boy who needs his mother.

✗STOP: While there are no particular scenes of concern, this film is unlikely to interest anyone under the age of nine.

CAUTION: In one scene, Fred walks in on a college friend in bed with a young woman. And throughout the film, Fred is afflicted with nightmares, one of which is depicted.

GO: The film is light, realistic and unsentimental. The performances are excellent, and there's a refreshing absence of villains. Altogether, an amazing effort from first-time director Jodie Foster.

✗ LITTLE MONSTERS

MGM/UA
1989
103 minutes
Directed by: Richard Allen Greenberg
Starring: Howie Mandel, Ben Savage,
  Fred Savage, Daniel Stern, Frank Whaley,
  Margaret Whitton
MPAA rating: PG

Brian Stevenson has a major problem: his parents are separating. So when his little brother Eric complains about monsters under his bed, Brian assumes it's a reaction to the family turmoil and gallantly offers to trade rooms with him. However, he soon discovers that there really are monsters under his brother's bed and sets a trap to catch one. Brian and his prisoner monster, Maurice, quickly become friends and embark on a nightly spree of mischievous capers until Brian notices that he's turning into a monster himself. Then, to make matters worse, Eric is kidnapped and Brian must go into the heart of the monsters' lair to rescue his brother and turn himself back into a boy.

✗ STOP: This movie is not for young children or for children who suffer from night terrors. In the final confrontation, the monster leader's face falls off, revealing a ghastly visage beneath.

CAUTION: Brian's parents are having marital problems throughout. This movie may give younger children some not-so-nice prank ideas, so be sure to debrief them afterwards.

GO: This film has helped some children deal with the "monster under the bed" problem.

LOST IN THE BARRENS

AGES 10 TO 13

C/FP
1991
94 minutes
Directed by: Michael Scott
Starring: Evan Adams, Lee J. Campbell, Graham Greene, Nicholas Shields
MPAA rating: NR

When Jamie McNair's trust fund runs out, he's forced to move from the boarding school at St. George's College to live with his uncle, a gruff woodsman named Angus Stewart who makes his living crafting canoes in Stewart's Landing, Manitoba. Jamie soon finds that he isn't suited to rustic living and is frustrated by the fact that his three-year stay will probably ruin his plans for a higher education. Angered by his predicament, he carelessly throws down a rifle and accidentally shoots Angus in the leg. With no choice but to do Angus's work for him, Jamie goes on a hunting expedition with Angus's native friend Menwanis, Menwanis's son, Awasis, and other members of their tribe. Their travels take them north into the Barrens where Jamie and Awasis separate from the group to go exploring. They happen on an ancient grave-site and, true to Awasis's fears of invoking a curse, emerge to find that their canoes have drifted away. Their only hope of rejoining the rest of the group is to cross the Barrens, a desolate wasteland reputedly populated with cannibals and made treacherous by the approaching winter. Still, they are plucky and resourceful, and in the end, they receive aid from their perceived enemy, the Inuit.

CAUTION: Angus is shot and, on the expedition, Awasis kills a caribou with a knife.

GO: *Lost in the Barrens* is a great adventure story about two young men who overcome vast cultural differences to help each other.

■

LUCAS

MAID-TO-ORDER

CBS/Fox
1986
100 minutes
Directed by: David Seltzer
Starring: Kerri Green, Corey Haim,
  Winona Ryder, Charlie Sheen
MPAA rating: PG-13

I.V.E.
1987
92 minutes
Directed by: Amy Jones
Starring: Beverley D'Angelo, Michael Ontkean,
  Valerie Perrine, Dick Shawn, Ally Sheedy,
  Tom Skerritt
MPAA rating: PG

When Maggie, the new sixteen-year-old girl in town, falls for the captain of the football team instead of for him, Lucas, a small fourteen-year-old with a keen interest in science, decides to prove his worth by trying out for the football team himself. He makes the team and steps in during a big game, hoping to be a hero. Instead, Lucas ends up under a pile of football players twice his size, embarrassed and seriously injured. In the end, Maggie, the captain of the football team and the rest of the school admire Lucas for his courage, and Lucas realizes the importance of just being himself.

CAUTION: In the locker room, when the boys are taking showers there is full nudity from the back. There is coarse language during one key scene.

GO: The film talks about peer pressure and the value of friendship, provides an alternate view to typical teenage stereotypes and has a stand-up-and-cheer ending.

Jessie is a rich, spoiled brat who's used to getting whatever she wants, whenever she wants it. Her philanthropist father is fed up with her expensive, irresponsible habits and absently remarks that sometimes he wishes he never had a daughter. A star flashes outside the window and his wish comes true; all record of Jessie's existence is erased. Stella, a cigarette-smoking jogger claiming to be Jessie's fairy godmother, explains to Jessie what's happened and cynically remarks that some princesses deserve to be maids. Jessie thinks the woman is crazy until, when she tries to go home, she's chased away by the outraged staff — even her father doesn't recognize her. Starving and filthy, she wanders into an employment agency and lands a job as a maid in the mansion of a bizarre Hollywood agent. Jessie is, of course, the worst maid in the world and she drives her co-workers crazy. But as time passes their kindness and generosity rub off on her and she becomes compassionate and respectful of both them and herself. She even develops a romance with the chauffeur — who's also an aspiring composer. And when her father organizes a charity benefit and the lead singer is knocked out by a coconut, Jessie inserts her friends into the musical program and they're a smash hit. In the end, Jessie's new-found selflessness wins her back her life.

CAUTION: There is some (nonsexual) nudity when Jessie goes skinny-dipping. Jessie is arrested with a vial of cocaine. Minimal coarse language.

GO: Jessie learns to appreciate what she has, and to love and respect others.

THE MAN WHO WOULD BE KING

CBS/Fox
1975
128 minutes
Directed by: John Huston
Starring: Michael Caine, Sean Connery, Christopher Plummer
MPAA rating: PG

In Colonial India, yet another caper by adventurers Peachy Carnehan and Daniel Dravot goes awry. Only the influence of their friend and fellow Freemason (an ancient order dedicated to the brotherhood of man) Rudyard Kipling can save them both. The three — now fast friends — return to Kipling's where Peachy and Danny reveal the details of their next scheme. They will enter Kafiristan, go into the service of one of the leaders of its warring tribes, use their military knowledge to make that tribe ascendent and take over the whole country. To do this they'll have to go over the Khyber Pass and cross the Hindu Kush — a trek no white man

has managed since Alexander the Great. They endure the hardships of the inhospitable mountains, waging nonstop tribal warfare until the natives believe that Danny is a god. Thanks to his Freemason's amulet (the symbol of Alexander the Great), Danny comes to be worshipped as Alexander's son, and the vast treasures of Alexander are handed over to him. Peachy and Danny plan to sit out the winter and make off with the treasure in the spring, but Danny comes to prefer governing to wealth and marries one of the natives. This proves to be Danny's undoing, and he and Peachy must fight their way out of the city and journey home through a bitter, hostile land.

CAUTION: Danny is killed by being thrown from a cliff. In one scene, Peachy reveals Danny's severed, rotting head and in another, the troops play polo with the head of a defeated enemy in a canvas bag. There is some combat violence.

GO: This is a splendid, sprawling epic which may encourage young people to learn more about colonial history and the Indian subcontinent.

✗ THE MAN WITHOUT A FACE

Warner Home Video
1993
113 minutes
Directed by: Mel Gibson
Starring: Mel Gibson, Fay Masterson, Nick Stahl, Margaret Whitton
MPAA rating: PG Mature Subject Matter

Chuck Norstadt's family is troubled. His mother isn't exactly the nurturing type, and the domestic turmoil is accentuated by the fact that Chuck and his two sisters are the product of three separate failed marriages. Chuck himself is a troubled slow-learner with one goal in life: to get away from his all-girl hell and into an elite military boarding school, a school which will give him the preparatory training to become a fighter pilot like his late father. But Chuck has already failed the entrance exams, and his mother is reluctant to allow him to try them again. Then, the family sets out for a summer vacation on a New England coastal island. While on the ferry, Chuck sees a man with disfiguring burns to one side of his face. He learns that this man is the mysterious McLeod, the man without a face, who lives alone in his big house in the shadows of his dark and painful past. Chuck is strangely compelled to seek him out, and asks McLeod to tutor him for his upcoming exams persisting, despite McLeod's reluctance, until the older man agrees to take him on. The two become friends. Then, when Chuck's vindictive older sister reveals to him that his father was not a hero test-pilot, but rather an abusive drunk who died in a sanitorium, he flees to McLeod's place. A terrible furor results, and it is then revealed that McLeod received his terrible injuries in a car crash which killed a student, and that McLeod was suspected of having abused the student. McLeod is forced to promise never to see Chuck again or have any contact with him. In the end, though, McLeod's influence has a positive effect on Chuck's life.

✗STOP: The film deals with *very* serious themes: wrongful accusations of child abuse, the total alienation caused by gross disfigurement, the inability of human beings to accept someone different or to see beneath surface ugliness, and basic injustice. McLeod's face is terribly burned, the kind of image that may haunt younger viewers for a long time.

CAUTION: Regardless of the rating, this really isn't a children's film.

GO: This is a compelling and topical tale for older teens and young adults — if you can stand the angst.

MANNEQUIN

Warner Home Video
1987
90 minutes
Directed by: Michael Gottlieb
Starring: G.W. Bailey, Kim Cattrall, Carole Davis, Estelle Getty, Andrew McCarthy, James Spader, Meshach Taylor
MPAA rating: PG

Mannequin opens in ancient Egypt, where a young Egyptian woman, refusing to marry a camel-dung dealer, prays for help from the gods. Her prayers are answered and she's transported into a twentieth century department store in the United States, where she inhabits the form of a newly made mannequin. In that very same department store, Jonathan Switcher, assistant to the outrageous window dresser Hollywood Montrose, makes a startling discovery: the mannequin, who comes alive and introduces herself as Emmie. Emmie, it turns out, has a real flair for window design, and she and Jonathan spend their nights creating dazzling displays. The only problem seems to be that whenever anyone other than Jonathan looks at Emmie she turns back into a mannequin. And, as the department store windows attract more and more customers, vice-president Richards and his manic security guards do their best to find out what Jonathan is up to. They finally decide that the mannequin must be connected to Jonathan's success, and kidnap her. This precipitates a wild chase, in which Emmie regains her human form when Jonathan risks his life to rescue her.

CAUTION: In one scene, Emmie opens her coat to reveal that she's wearing only lingerie underneath, and in another, Jonathan's former girlfriend is shown doing up her blouse after what was obviously a sexual encounter with a business associate. Hollywood Montrose is a stereotype of the gay window-dresser.

GO: Values of love, loyalty and persistence are highlighted. There is a sequel, *Mannequin II*.

✗ MASK

1994
100 minutes (approx)
Directed By: Charles Russell
Starring: Jim Carrey, Cameron Diaz,
    Peter Green, Peter Riegert
MPAA Rating: PG-13

Lowly milquetoast Stanley Ipkiss lives in the mythical metropolis of Edge City. There, he toils as a minion in a large bank, and has utterly failed at love. Every night, he goes straight home to his tiny bachelor apartment in a grungy building on the wrong side of town.

One day, a beautiful young woman enters the bank and opens an account with Stanley. She is, in fact, the moll of an ambitious young gangster who is planning to rob the bank, and she is there is case the bank. That night, Stanley's friend Charles invites him to check out the hottest new spot, the Cocobongo Club, which features the same young woman, sizzling night club singer Tina Carlyle. But everything goes wrong. A crooked car repair shop has Stanley's car on the blocks for a host of unnecessary repairs, Stanley gets separated from his friends, and his loaner car breaks down in the middle of a bridge. There, the disgusted Stanley spots the Mask, floating in some seaweed. He retrieves it, and in short order makes an astonishing discovery. Whoever puts on the Mask (after dark) receives enormous super-powers. Stanley personally finds this out when he puts it on and literally turns into a living cartoon. In the next few days he terrifies some local thugs, exacts revenge on the repair shop guys, robs a bank, ("you can't make the scene if you don't have the green"), and woos Tina. Thanks to his outrageous exploits, he also antagonizes the gangsters and the local police, both of whom are intent on tracking him down. Things get intense when Stanley, increasingly exhausted by his frenetic double life, is betrayed by an apparently-honest and trustworthy reporter, who hands him over to the gangsters. The chief villain then tries on the Mask, and turns into a horrific demon (the Mask amplifies people's most basic qualities). In the climax of the film, Stanley must escape from jail, somehow get the Mask back, and rescue Tina from the gangsters.

✗STOP: Lots of gunfire. The main villain puts on the Mask and becomes a hideous, basso-voiced monster. In one scene, the villain is taken before his sinister superior, who drives golf balls off his mouth.

CAUTION: The wild images are certain to haunt or frighten many children under the age of eight. We see the auto repair guys being wheeled from their shop, pinned down to trolleys with mufflers protruding obliquely from their behinds. The heroine is a depressingly-typical sexual stereotype. One viewer pointed out that Stanley in effect gets away with robbing a bank.

GO: This wacky and hilarious underdog-makes-good tale showcases the elastic-faced Carrey's considerable talent and features some of the most amazing special effects ever put on celluloid. Stanley literally becomes a living cartoon.

MORGAN STEWART'S COMING HOME

HBO
1987
92 minutes
Directed by: Alan Smithee
Starring: John Cryer, Viveka Davis,
    Paul Gleason, Nicholas Pryor,
    Lynn Redgrave
MPAA rating: PG-13

Morgan Stewart, a self-declared "orphan with parents," has been shunted from boarding school to boarding school since he was ten. Now, at seventeen, he learns that his parents, a prominent Republican Senator and a cold, ambitious socialite, suddenly want him to come back and live with them in their sprawling Washington mansion. But Morgan soon learns that the decision was purely political

and was prompted by Jay, a new assistant who's orchestrating the Senator's family-oriented campaign. Things seem to improve when Morgan meets Emily, a fellow horror fan, at an autograph appearance, and he steals his parents' car to take her out. But when Morgan's parents find out, he's grounded, and worse, his mother has closed-circuit cameras installed in his bedroom. The last straw comes when Morgan and Emily defy the grounding and Jay plans to have Morgan sent to military school. Morgan runs away, but returns when, after going to the bank to clear out his account, he discovers that Jay has been embezzling campaign funds.

CAUTION: Most of the adults in this film are portrayed as stupid, insensitive people. There is some mild language.

GO: Morgan remains loyal to his parents despite the neglect he has suffered and his relationship with Emily is based on mutual interest and respect. Emily is also a good role model.

MY BODYGUARD

20th Century Fox
1980
97 minutes
Directed by: Tony Bill
Starring: Matt Dillon, Ruth Gordon,
    John Houseman, Chris Makepeace,
    Martin Mull
MPAA rating: PG

On the first day at his new school, Cliff Peache is approached by bully Big M Moody. (He's collecting money in return for protection.) Cliff is not easily conned or intimidated, but when his father calls the school and Big M is given a week of detentions, things get much worse. The intimidation continues until Cliff convinces the hulking Ricky Linderman (who is rumored to have committed murder) to be *his* bodyguard. Intrigued by his new protector, Cliff follows him to an auto shop where Linderman shows him the motorcycle he's lovingly been rebuilding and the two become friends. Meanwhile, Big M has hired a bodyguard of his own, a thug named Mike who roughs up Linderman and his motorcycle. Cliff, unable to understand why Linderman wouldn't fight back, confronts him and learns the real story of his new friend's past. The next day at a chance meeting in the park, Mike and Linderman fight it out. And when Cliff and Big M get mixed up in the brawl, Cliff fights his own battle.

CAUTION: Linderman's emotional problems are caused by an accident in which his brother is shot while they are playing with their father's gun. Linderman describes "the blood pouring out of the side of his head." The fistfight at the end is realistic and there is blood when Cliff breaks Big M's nose. Mild language.

GO: This is a warm film with heart-quality about a problem some kids face at school, and is a cautionary tale about the perils of keeping a firearm in the house. Look for a young Jennifer Beals and Joan Cusack.

MY FATHER THE HERO

Touchstone Pictures
1994
90 minutes
Directed by: Steve Miner
Starring: Gerard Depardieu, Katherine Heigl, Lauren Hutton, Dalton James, Emma Thompson
MPAA rating: PG

Divorced Parisian father André hasn't seen his fourteen-year-old daughter Niki, who lives with her mother in New York, for five years. He takes her to the Bahamas for a vacation. Niki's mad at André for his absence. She's also going through the worst of the teenage phase, and she's generally rude. In order to impress an attractive seventeen-year-old named Ben, Niki tells him that she's eighteen and that she is vacationing with her "friend" André. This lie quickly evolves and poor André is implicated as her lover. As the scandal spreads, the unwitting André is reviled by the other tourists. When his daughter finally confesses to him, André is horrified, but vows to save Niki from her terrible predicament. He goes along with the scam, spinning wild tales of his heroic exploits in combat and so on, completely intimidating Ben. Then Niki goes out too far on a sailboard, and both André and Ben go after her. The truth comes out in the crisis, and Ben, furious with Niki for having lied to him, refuses to have anything more to do with her. It is then up to André to help Niki win Ben back, and this is accomplished in a reverse send-up of the famous window scene from *Cyrano de Bergerac.*

CAUTION: The whole movie is a double-entendre, with the implication being that a fifty-year-old man is having a grossly inappropriate (let alone illegal) relationship with a young girl. Niki wears a revealing bathing suit in one scene. There is minimal language.

GO: The film is genuinely funny, and has a gentle and charming quality. The ending depicts a functional, loving relationship between a divorced father and his daughter, one which promises to last.

✗ MY GIRL

Coumbial/Tri-Star
1992
102 minutes
Directed by: Howard Zieff
Starring: Dan Aykroyd, Anna Chlumsky,
  Macaulay Culkin, Jamie Lee Curtis
MPAA rating: PG

Vada, eleven-year-old daughter of the town funeral director, Harry Sultenfuss, is a hypochondriac obsessed with death (a condition stemming directly from the premature death of her mother). She imagines she's developing the symptoms of the dead people who are brought to the funeral parlor where she and her father live. Her best friend, Thomas Jay, is allergic to practically everything and, despite the mild abuse she directs his way, is devoted to Vada. When make-up artist Shelley Devoto answers Harry's want ad for a cosmetician, the Sultenfusses go through a period of upheaval. Harry

and Shelley start a relationship, and Vada must resolve her feelings of jealously and guilt. Then tragedy strikes: Thomas Jay dies after being repeatedly stung by a horde of wasps, and during his funeral Vada completely breaks down. It's only through Shelley's healing influence and Harry's new-found courage that Vada is able to reconcile her grief and overcome her preoccupation with death.

✗ STOP: For any child who has recently had to deal with the death of a loved one, this film is a definite NO. Thomas Jay is stung to death by a horde of wasps, and in a wrenching scene, Vada learns of the tragedy and is subsequently crushed by grief.

CAUTION: This film is about coming to grips with the passing of a loved one, and about the changes that time and life inevitably bring — pretty weighty stuff for young children. In one scene Shelley talks to Vada about menstruation and there are scenes in the mortuary, where Harry and his assistant are working on bodies. Thomas Jay is shown in his coffin.

GO: This film contains one of the great last lines of all time. (Too bad the kids won't get it!)

✗ MY SCIENCE PROJECT

Touchstone Home Video
1985
94 minutes
Directed by: Jonathan Betuel
Starring: Dennis Hopper, Fisher Stevens,
  John Stockwell, Danielle Von Zerneck
MPAA rating: PG

The film begins in the 1950s when the military discovers a crashed flying saucer, the burned-out hulk of which they cut into pieces and store away. The scene then shifts to the present, where Mike Harlan, a high school senior, interested only in cars and Bruce Springsteen, has learned that he will not graduate if he doesn't have a science project ready before the end of term. He visits a graveyard for outdated military equipment, hoping to chance upon something he can use for the much-despised project, and finds a bizarre machine in a container marked "top secret." After a number of strange incidents occur, he takes the machine to his science teacher, who identifies it as a time warp generator, and is promptly sucked into another dimension. General chaos ensues as Mike and his friends race against time, the authorities and a collection of teenage villains, to stop the gizmo from destroying the universe. The film comes to a climax when a time warp envelopes the entire school, bringing together past, present and future in a violent final confrontation.

✗ **STOP:** This film is definitely not for young children. The climax of the film is nothing more than one graphic killing after another, which comes as something of a shock because up to this point the film isn't violent at all. Viewers will see a gladiator die a gory death, Viet Cong machine-gunned, futuristic mutants annihilated by blasters and a dinosaur's stomach blown open.

CAUTION: Mike's father's girlfriend is portrayed as a sleazy, gold-digging floozie, the police are represented as idiotic Nazis, and all of the women (except the heroine) are interested only in chewing gum and sex. There is extreme coarse language and some of Vinnie's chauvinistic "girl advice" could be construed as offensive.

GO: The main characters display sensitivity, tolerance and understanding and there are reconciliations between enemies in the finale. The plot is well-paced, the special effects are dazzling and the story line is interesting.

NATIONAL GEOGRAPHIC VIDEO SERIES

Columbia
1980–1990
60 minutes each

National Geographic videos are a treasure-trove of information, and are a terrific way to educate kids and inspire a continued interest in various topics.

Titles in the series are:
Africa's Stolen River
African Wildlife
Amazon: Land of the Flooded Forest
Among the Wild Chimpanzees
Antarctic Wildlife Adventure
Atocha: Quest for Treasure
Australia's Aborigines
Australia's Improbable Animals
Baka: People of the Forest
Ballad of the Irish Horse
Born of Fire
Cameramen Who Dared
Creatures of the Mangrove
Creatures of the Namib Desert
Crocodiles: Here Be Dragons
Egypt: Quest for Eternity
Elephant
Explorers: Century of Discovery
For All Mankind
Gorilla
The Great Whales
The Grizzlies
Hawaii: Strangers in Paradise
Himalayan River Run
Hong Kong: A Family Portrait
Iceland River Challenge
In the Shadow of Vesuvius

AGES 10 TO 13

The Incredible Human Machine
The Invisible World
Jerusalem: Within These Walls
Killer Whales: Wolves of the Sea
Land of the Tiger
Last Voyage of the Lusitania
Lions of the African Night
Living Treasures of Japan
Lost Fleet of Guadalcanal
Lost Kingdoms of the Maya
Love Those Trains
Man-eaters of India
Miniature Miracle: The Computer Chip
Mysteries of Mankind
Polar Bear Alert
Rain Forest
Realm of the Alligator
Reptiles and Amphibians
Return to Everest
The Rhino War
Rocky Mountain Beaver Pond
Save the Panda
The Search for the Battleship Bismarck
Search for the Great Apes
Season of the Cheetah
The Secret Leopard
Secrets of the Titanic
Serengeti Diary
The Sharks
The Soviet Circus
Strange Creatures of the Night
Superliners: Twilight of an Era
Survivors of the Skeleton Court
Those Wonderful Dogs
The Tropical Kingdom of Belize
Volcano!
Wild Survivors: Camouflage and Mimicry
White Wolf
The Wilds of Madagascar
Yukon Passage
Zebra: Patterns in the Grass

✗**STOP:** As many of the videos in this series contain graphic live footage or mature topics, prescreening is highly recommended.

NECESSARY ROUGHNESS

Paramount Home Video
1991
108 minutes
Directed by: Stan Dragoti
Starring: Scott Bakula, Hector Elizondo, Harley Jane Kozak, Robert Loggia, Larry Miller, Sinbad
MPAA rating: PG-13

A massive corruption scandal has virtually destroyed the Texas State Fighting Armadillos; the coaches have been fired and the players, suspended. Ed "Straight Arrow" Ginero has been hired to take over as head coach and brings his friend Wally Riggendorf onto the team. And what a team it isn't. They have so few decent prospects they have to play Iron Man football (players play both offense and defense). And they recruit thirty-four-year-old former high school quarterback star Paul Blake, who for personal reasons never enrolled in college. Blake meets journalism teacher Dr. Suzanne Carter and gets off on the wrong foot right away. Things go even worse on the field as the Armadillos lose every game. But Blake and Suzanne eventually develop a relationship, and the Armadillos get better until finally, in the last game of the season, they have a chance to win.

CAUTION: There's some fairly graphic fighting, and Suzanne and Blake are shown naked in bed (under the covers). In one scene, a player's face mask is knocked off and blood pours from his mouth. There is coarse language.

GO: The central theme, that fair play is

AGES 10 TO 13

more important than winning, is strongly stressed. Unfortunately titled, this is not a negative movie.

NEVER CRY WOLF

Walt Disney Home Video
1983
105 minutes
Directed by: Carroll Ballard
Starring: Brian Dennehy, Charles Martin Smith
MPAA rating: PG

Tyler, a biologist, goes to the Arctic alone where he hopes to disprove the theory that wolves are a threat to people. He studies them for months before discovering that the wolves are catching and eating mice to survive. He even cooks and eats some mice himself (as an experiment, at first) and soon develops a taste for them. After many months of study, Tyler concludes that the wolves are more charitable and interesting than most humans. Based on the book *Never Cry Wolf* by Farley Mowat.

CAUTION: Wolves attack, kill and eat a caribou, and Tyler has nightmares about being attacked himself. In one scene, Tyler goes skinny-dipping, and in another he falls through the ice and is trapped underneath.There isn't a great deal of action in this film — it's more a story about a man's growing understanding of and appreciation for nature — so young children may not be engaged.

GO: This gentle story gives a new view of the much-maligned wolf.

THE NIGHTMARE BEFORE CHRISTMAS

Touchstone Home Video
1993
76 minutes
Directed by: Henry Selick
Starring the voices of Danny Elfman, Catherine O'Hara, Paul Reubens, Chris Sarandon
MPAA Rating: PG

This black musical was brought to life entirely by stop-motion animation/pixiliation techniques, and is based on a story and characters by Tim Burton.

It is the end of another wildly successful Halloween and the inhabitants of eerie Halloweentown are congratulating their leader, Jack Skellington, for his genius at creating the "scariest" Halloween ever. But Jack is strangely dissatisfied by his latest success — somehow it no longer fulfills him, and he longs to experience something new. One day by accident Jack ends up in Christmastown where he sees Santa Claus and his elves making their preparations for Christmas. He is enchanted and feels that he has found the answer to the void in his life. He immediately resolves that he and the inhabitants of Halloweentown will create the next Christmas. Another unhappy inhabitant of Halloweentown is Sally. She is slave to a revolting scientist, an inventor whom she attempts to lethally poison on a regular basis. She is his creation, a straw-filled ragdoll sewn together and made living for the express purpose of keeping him company and waiting on him. But she too abhors her life and sees in a Jack a kinship. After many unsuccessful attempts to be rid of her master she finally effects a daring escape. Meanwhile, Jack sets the townspeople to work making Christmas trees, decorations and presents. But he is incapable of transferring to them the innocence and sweetness of his experience in Christmastown and consequently their creations are extremely macabre. Jack himself fails to recognize that he too is attempting something beyond his limitations. The only dissenting voice is that of Sally, who reluctantly makes Jack proper Santa attire. Jack sternly assigns the vital task of kidnapping Santa to the three nastiest children of the town: Lock, Shock and Barrel. They live with Mr. Oogie-Boogie, a huge, fluorescent, gambling, bug-filled bag of a boogeyman, the one truly erratic and powerful, and therefore frightening, inhabitant of the town. After the kids successfully kidnap Santa, they leave him to the cruel whims of Oogie-Boogie. When Christmas Eve finally arrives, Jack goes out to make Christmas, but the presents are so horrifying that the world is quickly alerted to the ersatz Saint Nick and he is shot from the skies. In the end, Jack and Sally have to battle Oogie-Boogie to get Santa back and manage to return him, relatively unscathed, to Christmastown, but not before Jack is severely reprimanded. He then recognizes his feelings of kinship and love for Sally. After having faced his failure, Jack is happy to go back to creating Halloween, because he realizes it is the one thing that he does incredibly well.

CAUTION: Even though this film was advertised as a "fun-filled delight for the *whole* family", we wouldn't recommend this film for children under 8, but it depends very much on what scares your particular child. Oogie-Boogie is the stuff of nightmares, as is his torturing of Santa. Children need to understand the story in order not to be frightened. Jack's Halloween is very humorous if the irony is understood; when one child's parents ask what Santa brought, the child obediently holds up a severed head; other presents actually attack their recipients. The songs may be somewhat complex lyrically for younger children.

GO: Sally is a good female role-model; she is resourceful and courageous. The stop-motion animation is the best that has ever been produced, and it was awarded Academy Award nominations for Best Visual Effects. Grammy nominations for Best Musical Album For Children.

∎

✘ NOT QUITE HUMAN

Walt Disney Home Video
1987
97 minutes
Directed by: Stephen H. Stern
Starring: Joseph Bologna, Alan Thicke,
      Jay Underwood
MPAA rating: G

Eccentric cyberneticist Dr. Jonas Carson has created his ultimate scientific triumph, a fully functioning, incredibly sophisticated android which resembles a teenage boy. Carson's flesh-and-blood daughter Becky is a little apprehensive about her new brother, especially when Carson announces his intention to send Chip to high school. However, evil military toy distributor Colonel Gordon C. "Bang Bang" Vogel is anxious to get his hands on Carson's android, which he knows will revolutionize the military toy business, and Carson believes that it is in Chip's best interest to fully integrate with human society. So Chip goes to school. He does famously, except for the odd close call (someone slaps him in the wrong place and he starts talking in high speed; his battery pack runs down and he is forced to plug in at an obnoxious schoolmate's house). The climax comes when Vogel tries to kidnap Chip, leaving Carson and Becky to be crushed to death in an auto wrecking yard. Chip outwits his captor and saves his father and sister in the nick of time, but he is forced to sacrifice himself, and as Carson desperately works to rebuild his son, Becky realizes that she has come to love Chip as if he really *were* human.

CAUTION: Minimal rude behavior and violence (punching). Carson and Becky are in grave peril at the climax.

GO: This is a very entertaining little story, even for younger children. This is the first in a series of three movies which chronicle the adventures of the likeable Chip. The other two titles are: *Still Not Quite Human* and *Not Quite Human Two*.

■

✗ ONE MAGIC CHRISTMAS

Walt Disney Home Video
1985
88 minutes
Directed by: Phillip Borsos
Starring: Harry Dean Stanton,
    Mary Steenburgen, Jan Rubes
MPAA rating: G

Every year, a Christmas angel named Gideon is assigned the task of helping someone get into the Christmas spirit; this year that person is Ginnie Granger. Work is hard at the supermarket where she is employed; her husband's been laid off and they're being forced out of their home. Gideon reveals his assignment to Ginnie's daughter, Abbie, and tells her not to be afraid, no matter what happens. The next day, Ginnie's husband, Jack, is shot trying to foil a robbery and the thief makes a getaway in Jack's car, taking Abbie and her brother Cal with him. Desperate, Ginnie follows in the robber's car just in time to see the car with the children inside plunge into the river. Returning to an empty house, Ginnie realizes the most important thing in her life was her family. When her children are returned to her unharmed, she is grateful but must tell them that their dad is dead. Abbie goes to Gideon for help, but Gideon sends her to Santa Claus who tells her that only her mom can "make [Jack] not dead." Santa gives her something to take to her mother that causes a transformation in Ginnie and restores the family.

✗**STOP**: In spite of its innocent title, this is not a film for children. The film is emotionally trying. Jack is shot violently and the children's plunge into an icy river is shocking.

GO: A wonderful, magical film for everyone who feels overworked and has lost the sense of childhood wonder.

OPPORTUNITY KNOCKS

✗ PROJECT X

MCA
1990
103 minutes
Directed by: Donald Petrie
Starring: Julia Campbell, Dana Carvey,
Todd Graf, Robert Loggia, Milo O'Shea,
James Tolkan
MPAA rating: PG-13

CBS/Fox
1987
101 minutes
Directed by: Jonathan Kaplan
Starring: Matthew Broderick, Helen Hunt
MPAA rating: PG

On the run from the mob, small-time con man Eddie Farrell hides in a deserted suburban house until the owners, Milt and Mona Malkin, come home and mistake him for a friend of their son, David. They lend him five hundred dollars, give him a fancy car and clothes, and even introduce him to their gorgeous doctor daughter, Annie. Before Eddie knows it, he's been offered a vice-presidency in Milt's company, and Annie is beginning to fall in love with him. He has the perfect opportunity to work the ultimate con, settle things with the mob and set himself up for life. But as he begins to care more and more for the Malkins, he's compelled to change his ways and save Milt and his company instead. In the end, when his true identity is revealed, the Malkins come to love Eddie for the person he is.

CAUTION: There is minimal violence and some coarse language, but the PG-13 rating was most likely earned by the mature theme. Carvey's South Asian and Chinese impersonations may be considered offensive.

GO: The film has a decent redemption theme.

Jimmy Garret is an ambitious pilot who, after a disciplinary action, is relegated to assisting in a top-secret military project involving chimpanzees. At first he's reluctant to participate in the project, considering it to be a waste of time, but changes his mind when he realizes that it has extremely serious implications. He discovers that one of the chimps, Virgil, can communicate in sign language (a skill acquired from a young psychologist named Terry MacDonald in a previous training project) and is horrified to learn that the chimp is doomed to annihilation. Jimmy calls Terry to help him free Virgil and the other chimps in the lab (who have already devised an escape plan of their own). Jimmy and Terry are caught, but the chimps make use of their simulated flight training and escape for good to the Everglades.

✗**STOP:** The whole issue of experimenting on animals is very complex and may upset some children. In one scene a chimp is exposed to an enormous dose of radiation, wears an agonized expression and eventually dies. The U.S. air force use the word "Russian" as synonymous with "enemy."

CAUTION: The film is based on U.S. military tests of human endurance in the event of nuclear war. A chimp is shot and there is some swearing.

AGES 10 TO 13

355

GO: This film caused some controversy about experimenting on animals when it was released. The musical score is excellent.

✗ RAIDERS OF THE LOST ARK

Paramount Home Video
1981
115 minutes
Directed by: Steven Spielberg
Starring: Karen Allen, Harrison Ford, John Rhys-Davies
MPAA rating: PG

Indiana Jones, Ivy League professor, archaeologist and adventurer, is contacted by the U.S. government about a mission of extraordinary importance. A possible site of the Ark of the Covenant has been located in the lost city of Tanis, and the government is racing to find it before the Nazis do. However, the Ark is hidden in the Well of Souls and can only be located with the help of another artifact, an amulet called the Staff of Ra. Jones finds the amulet with archaeologist's daughter Marion Ravenwood, and together they race to Egypt where the Nazis already have a huge excavation underway (supervised by Jones' nemeis, Belloq). Jones and Marion infiltrate the digging site, sneak into the map room and find their way to the Well of Souls; however, Belloq and the Nazis discover them, take the Ark and imprison them in the Well. Jones and Marion escape, and after a number of spine-tingling fights, chases and more escapes, find

themselves prisoners again on a remote Mediterranean island. There they are present when the Nazis test the Ark and meet a grisly end.

✗ STOP: A man is shown impaled on spikes. When the Ark is opened, the faces of the evil melt like wax, and apparitions with angelic faces turn hideous and impale the Nazi soldiers. In one fight a mechanic is chopped up by a whirling propeller (blood splatters), and throughout people die with their eyes open, blood dribbling from their mouths.

GO: Blood and gore aside, this is surely one of the greatest action films of all time.

REAL GENIUS

RCA/Columbia
1985
106 minutes
Directed by: Martha Coolidge
Starring: William Atherton, Gabe Jarret, Val Kilmer, Michelle Meyrink
MPAA rating: PG

Mitch, a brilliant fifteen-year-old scientist, is accepted into the prestigious National Science Institute where he joins a team of the best minds on campus to work on a top-secret laser project. Professor Hathaway, who's heading the project, has given the team four months in which to complete their work, and as the deadline approaches he becomes increasingly more nervous. He forces the team to spend every spare moment in the lab, but despite their efforts, the laser will not work. Then Chris, supergenius and party animal of the the group, has a moment of brilliant inspiration and finds a way to make the necessary adjustments. They test the laser — it punches a hole through half the town — and the question comes up: Why does Hathaway need so much power? The team realizes it's been duped into building a weapon and, with Hathaway's unwitting help, sabotages the military test turning the weapon's demonstration into the biggest practical joke of all time.

CAUTION: There is coarse language, and sexual remarks are made.

GO: Ingenuity reigns supreme in this genuinely funny film. There is no violence and there are no disturbing scenes.

✗ RETURN TO SNOWY RIVER

Walt Disney Home Video
1988
99 minutes
Directed by: Geoff Burrows
Starring: Tom Burlinson, Brian Dennehy, Sigrid Thornton
MPAA rating: PG

Jim Craig returns to Snowy River with a stake of beautiful horses, where he intends to find his true love Jessica Harrison, marry her and set up a ranch. (He lets the great stallion run free, in hopes that it will recover his new mares.) To that end, Jim attends a horse race on the Harrison property, where he not only sees Jessica, but upperclassman Alistair Pattan and Jessica's father as well, who promptly informs him that he is not welcome on his ranch. Jim and

Jessica continue their relationship nonetheless, while Alistair's banker father pressures Harrison to help him drive the local land-owners out of the prime Snowy River grazing area. Alistair hires a gang of thugs to rob Jim. And when Jim goes after Alistair and his goons, Alistair shoots Jim's horse out from under him, knocking Jim out. When Jim comes to, the great stallion appears; Jim mounts him and renews the chase, encountering Harrison, Jessica, the mountain folk and the lowlanders on the way — all of them willing to help him recover his stock. Jim then catches up with Alistair, and with the help of the great stallion, beats him in a fight. In the end, Jim lets the great stallion go free once more. This is the sequel to *The Man from Snowy River*.

✗ STOP: Jim's horse is shot and dies.

CAUTION: During a fight at the end of the movie, Jim is cut with a saber and hit in the face with a branch. There are realistic punches and bloody faces.

GO: The riding and scenery are spectacular.

✗ THE ROCKETEER

Walt Disney Home Video
1991
109 minutes
Directed by: Joe Johnston
Starring: Alan Arkin, Bill Campbell, Jennifer Connelly, Timothy Dalton
MPAA rating: PG

In Los Angeles, in 1938, Clifford Secord, a daring young stunt pilot, is racing his Piper over California farmland when he accidentally becomes a target in a shoot-out between federal agents and the crooks who've just stolen Howard Hughes' latest aviation miracle, a rocket pack. When a fleeing crook dumps the pack on Cliff's airfield, Cliff and his partner Peevy test the pack by strapping it to a statue—it flies! Peevy then designs a helmet for Cliff, and when an aviation stunt goes wrong and Cliff dons the rocket pack to save the day, the Rocketeer is born. Neville Sinclair, a Nazi agent masquerading as a Hollywood celebrity, learns about Cliff's discovery and is intent on securing the rocket pack for himself. (He and his henchmen plan to rule the world with an army of Nazi rocketeers.) They kidnap Cliff's girlfriend in a huge dirigible and, after a nail-biting confrontation, are defeated by the Rocketeer. Based on the novel by Dave Stevens.

✗**STOP:** A huge Nazi assassin with a grotesque, disfigured face murders a wounded gangster in his hospital room.

CAUTION: Shoot-outs, death threats and punch-ups abound. One nine-year-old boy we know remarked, "Too much kissing, not enough flying."

GO: The special effects are great and the flying sequences are spectacular.

SHAKESPEARE, THE ANIMATED TALES

Random House Home Video
1992
30 minutes each
MPAA Rating: not rated

In this series, six of William Shakespeare's best-known plays are brought to life through various styles of animation, featuring the voices of well-known Shakespearian actors. The stories have been pared down to thirty minutes, and while some of the plays don't suffer too badly, others do. Overall, this series provides an accessible introduction to the great writer's work.

The Tempest

Directed by: Stanislav Sokolov

Prospero, the Duke of Milan, and his young daughter have been exiled to a small island. During his banishment the Duke studies magic and becomes a great sorcerer, eventually bringing his enemies within his reach.

GO: Breathtakingly beautiful pixilation highlights this wonderful adaptation.

Twelfth Night

Directed by: Maria Muat

The lovely Lady Olivia is in mourning after the death of her brother, and has vowed to entertain no thought of love for seven long years, much to the chagrin of the bachelors of Illyria. But when a shipwreck casts a set of twins upon the Illyrian shores, everything changes.

GO: This pixilated effort rivals The Tempest.

A Midsummer Night's Dream

Directed by: Robert Saakiants

Comedy operates on many levels in this, one of Shakespeare's most accessible and beloved plays. A quarrel between Oberon and Titania, the king and queen of the faeries, results in a cruel joke being played on four high-born lovers. At the same time, a crew of blockheads prepares the worst performance of the worst play of all time, hoping to impress the noble Duke Theseus on his wedding night.

CAUTION: Some of the female attire is transparent.

GO: Charming, succinct, and fully animated, characterized by terrific narration.

Romeo and Juliet

Directed by: Efrim Gambourg

Two young people from feuding families meet and fall in love. Their attempts to marry and flee the city have tragic consequences.

GO: The tragic romance is dutifully outlined and competently animated in this functional adaptation.

Hamlet

Directed by: Natalia Orlova

This dark tale of ghosts and regicide, royal incest and brooding revenge is condensed in this haunting little effort.

CAUTION: Without the pacing necessary to alleviate the torment-filled aspects of the tragedy, the condensed version is sombre.

GO: The animation is effective and unique.

✗ Macbeth

Directed by: Nikolai Serebriakov

It doesn't get any bloodier than this, as weak-willed strongman Macbeth slices and dices his way to the top of the Scottish heap.

✗STOP: The viewer sees severed heads, bleeding from the mouth, and so on. Lady Macbeth is astonishingly curvaceous and, in one scene, revealingly clad, which some viewers may find offensive.

CAUTION: This effort concentrates on the external events of the tragedy at the expense of examining the forces which drive Macbeth's tortured psychology. The animation is dark and sombre from start to finish, and the result is a horror movie.

SIDEKICKS

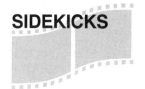

Alliance
1993
66 minutes
Directed by: Aaron Norris
Starring: Johnathan Brandis, Chuck Norris, Joe Piscopo
MPAA rating: PG

Barry Gabrewski is a young boy with severe asthma who lives with his hard-working single father Jerry. Barry drifts in and out of a fantasy world in which he is Chuck Norris' skillful sidekick and the two of them engage in many exciting adventures. But Barry is also a ninety-eight-pound weakling, who provides more or less continuous sport for the local bully, a karate student of an evil lout, Stone. Then Barry's kindly teacher, Miss Chan, introduces Barry to her relative, Mr. Lee, who is a master of martial arts. Barry becomes Mr. Lee's student, and soon the teaching begins to take effect. Barry becomes less dependent on his inhaler and able to handle himself against the bully, generating a showdown at the local karate championships. Barry's team consists of himself, Miss Chan and Mr. Lee; however, four are needed to make a team. Then Barry's dream comes true. The real Chuck Norris is there to preside over the tournament, and when he finds out that Barry's team may be disqualified, he becomes the fourth man. Barry, Miss Chan, Mr. Lee and Chuck go out and win one for the home team, then Norris mysteriously vanishes.

CAUTION: Minimal heroic and comic violence; for example, there is a fight in a restaurant in which Mr. Lee "accidentally" beats up bikers, and the bouts in the tournament are a bit rough, although Chuck Norris' fight with Stone is so hilarious as to resemble a cartoon.

GO: A charming underdog film with a storybook ending.

■

SISTER ACT

Touchstone Home Video
1992
100 minutes
Directed by: Emile Ardolino
Starring: Whoopi Goldberg, Harvey Keitel, Maggie Smith
MPAA rating: PG

When two-bit night-club singer Deloris Van Cartier goes to break off her affair with her gangster boss Vince, she inadvertently bursts into his office while he is having his driver "eliminated." Unconvinced that she will not spill the beans, Vince sends his thugs to kill her, but Deloris escapes to the police and tells all. Placed in protective custody until the hearing, Deloris is disguised as Sister Mary Clarence and sent to the San Francisco convent of St. Catherine. The Mother Superior will have none of it at first, but her small convent is in danger of closing, and the police promise a generous donation. So Deloris is admitted and she and convent life meet in a head-on clash, during the course of which Deloris is forced to come to grips with her own shortcomings. But those shortcomings are nothing compared to those of the deplorable convent choir which Deloris rebuilds and turns into a spiffy, jazzy musical ensemble that entices the local populace into the church. Deloris incurs the ire of the Mother Superior, but also attracts huge crowds to the convent — even the Pope decides to stop by during his North American tour. The climax comes when the gangsters find and kidnap Deloris, taking her back to Reno to finish her off. The nuns then spiritually blackmail a helicopter pilot into flying them to Reno, and as Deloris escapes her captors, everyone converges in the casino.

CAUTION: Staunch Roman Catholics may be a bit put off by some of the film's antics. One gangster is shot.

GO: This is a wildly-popular and generally inoffensive film.

SISTER ACT 2: BACK IN THE HABIT

THE SKATEBOARD KID

Touchstone Home Video
1993
117 minutes
Directed by: Bill Duke
Starring: James Coburn, Whoopi Goldberg,
 Kathy Najimy, Maggie Smith
MPAA rating: PG

C/FP
1993
93 minutes
Directed by: Larry Swerdlove
Starring: Bess Armstrong, Timothy Busfield,
 Rick Dean
MPAA rating: PG

Deloris Van Cartier is now a Las Vegas headliner. Her nun friends, conversely, have been appointed teachers in a San Francisco slum school, St. Francis. The sisters are in way over their heads. They desperately need some of the magic provided by Deloris as Sister Mary Clarence, and seek her out. After a little guilt-tripping from the Mother Superior, Deloris agrees to become the St. Francis music teacher. But she quickly discovers that her music class is a den of troublemakers. The kids are instantly hostile, and decide to be rid of her as quickly as possible. Their ringleader is Rita, a talented but troubled teen whose no-nonsense mother has forbidden her to sing. To complicate matters, Deloris accidentally discovers that St. Francis is to be closed immediately following the semester. Deloris decides to lay down the law. Rita angrily leaves the school, but the other teens quickly learn to love music. Deloris begins to mold them into an excellent choir, and even persuades Rita to return. She then begins preparing the choir for the State Championships; if they win, the school will be saved.

CAUTION: Very minimal language.

GO: Harmless.

Teenage skateboard thrasher Zach moves to Mill Creek, where his father Frank has been hired as the new TV station manager. He quickly discovers that a gang of skateboarding creeps is terrorizing the neighborhood. In the course of events Zach's skateboard is broken. When Zach helps local antique dealer Maggie out of a jam, she gives him a replacement skateboard that used to belong to The Amazing Verinni, an old magic store proprietor. That night, after Zach adds some custom fittings to the skateboard, lightning strikes it and it takes on a life of its own. The skateboard begins to talk, among other things, and helps Zach take on the creeps. Meanwhile, romance blossoms between Zach's father and Maggie; however, used car dealer Big Dan has other plans for Maggie. Knowing that Maggie is in desperate financial shape, and that her daughter Jenny needs a life-saving heart operation, Big Dan demands that Maggie marry him in exchange for his monetary support. Zach discovers the truth: Big Dan doesn't care as much about Maggie as he does about her property, within which is buried Big Dan's outlaw grandfather's huge treasure. Zach then steals Big Dan's treasure map, and as the day of the wedding dawns, he and the magic skateboard effect a daring plan to foil Big Dan's plans.

CAUTION: The soundtrack is a little on the heavy-metal side, somewhat incongruous in a film designed primarily for younger children, and one might wish to skip the rock video by the fringe rock group Trashkittens, which appears during the closing credits.

GO: A decent, low-budget effort with clear delineations between good and evil, and a lot of great skateboarding sequences.

✗ SO I MARRIED AN AX MURDERER

Columbia/Tri-Star
1993
93 minutes
Directed by: Thomas Schlamme
Starring: Anthony LaPaglia, Mike Myers,
   Amanda Plummer, Nancy Travis
MPAA rating: PG-13

Charlie MacKenzie is a coffeehouse poet who has had no luck in love. Charlie's Scottish-born parents give the term eccentric a whole new meaning, and his best friend is an easygoing undercover cop. Then he meets an attractive butcher, Harriet Michaels, and falls in love with her; however, his new lover is a woman of mystery. A series of eerie and improbable clues, mainly fuelled by stories in the Weekly World News, lead Charlie to suspect that Harriet may be a deranged psychotic, Mrs. X, who marries men and kills them on the honeymoon. Charlie eventually overcomes his paranoia, weds a reluctant Harriet, and takes

her to Poets' Corner, an ultra-spooky, sprawling old countryside mansion resort. Meanwhile, Charlie's cop-buddy makes the terrifying discovery that Harriet may very well *be* Mrs. X, and races through the storm-wracked night to try to save Charlie.

✗STOP: This movie is a spoof of the psycho-thriller genre and therefore not particularly suitable for anyone under the age of ten.

CAUTION: There is sexual innuendo, particularly in the butcher's shop. Mild language.

GO: Okay for older teens. Myers is great as his own Scottish dad. It's meant to be both scary *and* funny, and it succeeds.

✗ SOMETHING WICKED THIS WAY COMES

Walt Disney Home Video
1983
94 minutes
Directed by: Jack Clayton
Starring: Diane Ladd, Jonathan Price,
   Jason Robards
MPAA rating: PG

Fall comes to a small town in the mid-west, and with it comes Mr. Dark's Pandemonium Carnival. Mr. Dark isn't just an impresario; he can also see and grant one's heart's desire. However, each wish is fulfilled with a terrible price and one by one the townspeople fall victim to his temptations. A plain spinster who wishes to be beautiful is granted beauty, but made blind. A war amputee and former football star who wants to be whole again is granted his wish, but turned into an evil child. And so on. The town librarian's son and his best friend spy on the carnival and discover the dreadful truth — that Mr. Dark and his infernal accomplices intend to destroy the whole town. The agents of hell try to kill the boys with a plague of spiders and when that doesn't work, Mr. Dark himself comes for the boys. They hide in the library, and during a confrontation with Mr. Dark, the courageous librarian resists the ultimate Faustian temptation, setting up a violent climax which releases a long-awaited rainstorm, destroying the satanic carnival. Based on the book by Ray Bradbury.

✗ STOP: Frankly, this is not a children's film. One of Mr. Dark's henchmen is turned into an evil child and Mr. Dark crushes the librarian's hand to a pulp while demanding to know the location of the boys. During the assault on the house, the boys are trapped by hundreds of huge spiders.

CAUTION: This tale of a modern Mephistopheles, who grants wishes for souls is replete with haunting images. There is a rift in the relationship between father and son, a key element in the film.

✗ SON-IN-LAW

Hollywood Pictures
1993
96 minutes
Directed by: Steve Rash
Starring: Carla Gugino, Pauly Shore, Lane Smith
MPAA Rating: PG-13

Becky Warner graduates from high school and abandons the midwest for college on the west coast, leaving behind her burned-out, stuck-in-a-rut family, her farm, and her possessive boyfriend Travis. But things don't go well at school. Becky has difficulty relating to the ultra-chic chaos of residence life, and she is in the process of contacting her parents to come home when Crawl, a fun-loving valley-boy airhead, pleads with Becky to stay just long enough to give school a chance. Under his tutelage, Becky is transformed. When Thanksgiving break rolls around, Becky invites the eccentric Crawl back to the farm. Things get complicated fast. Becky's now-unwanted boyfriend is getting set to propose to her at a dinner, and Crawl's response is to stand up and blurt that he and Becky are already engaged. Becky's family comes under Crawl's bizarre yet rejuvenating influence, and Crawl struggles to perform routine chores. Before very long they all come to like him, except of course for Becky's jealous ex. As Becky's parents become more pleased about the engagement, Becky and Crawl are forced to deal with the fact that their relationship *is* in fact growing less platonic every day. The climax comes when Becky's boyfriend devises a mean ruse to drive Becky and Crawl apart forever.

✗ STOP: At the beach, Crawl ogles a girl's bottom through binoculars. There is a tasteless mud-wrestling scene. When Becky arrives at school, she and her parents see two female lovers embraced in a lengthy, passionate kiss.

CAUTION: Crawl has some strange ways to describe some elements of female anatomy. There is innuendo. Crawl and a local beauty are drugged and left in the barn in a compromising position.

GO: Crawl is in every sense a person of goodwill. The movie sends a positive message about learning to appreciate people of different appearance, dress and manners.

■

GO: Based on a real NASA summer camp, this is a terrific film for young fans of adventure and science fiction. Positive female role models highlight this film.

SPACE CAMP

Vestron
1986
116 minutes
Directed by: Harry Winer
Starring: Kate Capshaw, Tate Donovan, Leaf Phoenix, Kelly Preston, Larry B. Scott, Lea Thompson
MPAA rating: PG

Andy is an astronaut assigned to teach kids at a space camp, simulating NASA flights and training them to be astronauts. She has four special students: Katherine, who dreams of becoming the first female shuttle commander; Tish, who has an incredible memory and who wants to contact alien life-forms in the universe; Rudy, who's fiercely detemined even though he's of average intelligence; and Kevin, whose father has forced him to go to the camp and who doesn't take anything seriously. It's up to Andy to teach her students to work together as a team on a spacecraft. At first, the team works badly together and it's only when Andy and her group are accidentally sent up into space, and the kids are forced to handle reentry by themselves, that they finally learn to work together as a team.

CAUTION: Andy's injuries in the accidental launch are traumatic. There is some mild language.

SPACEBALLS

MGM/UA
1988
97 minutes
Directed by: Mel Brooks
Starring: Mel Brooks, John Candy, Rick Moranis, Bill Pullman, Joan Rivers, Daphne Zuniga
MPAA rating: PG

This spoof on the *Star Wars* trilogy manages to poke fun at a few other epics as well, including a hilarious final vignette based on *The Planet of the Apes*. Under the command of the fiendish Darth Vader clone Dark Helmet, the evil Spaceballs of the Planet Spaceball have a clever plan: They will kidnap the Druish Princess Vespa and force her father, King Rolland, to give them the combination to the air-shield of Planet Druidia (which protects the precious atmosphere the Spaceballs desire). But their plans are thwarted by the renegade Lone Star and his sidekick Barf, who rescue Vespa and her robot Dot Matrix. With the stumblebum Spaceballs in hot pursuit, the four flee across the galaxy in search of the mystic Yogurt, master of the Schwartz. After numerous chases, duels and corny jokes (when they comb the desert for the fugitives, the Spaceballs use a real comb), everyone lives happily ever after — except the Spaceballs, of course.

CAUTION: Sexual innuendo, double entendres, crude jokes and coarse language permeate this film. President Scroob is obnoxious and leering, and his female chief in command is a real dominatrix. There is a send-up of a grotesque death scene from the movie Alien that will almost certainly terrify young children.

GO: Young kids don't seem to get many of the mature jokes. This is one of those films that's perfect at sleep-overs for kids eight and up; it gives them that racy, forbidden feeling without going to extremes.

SPACED INVADERS

Touchstone Home Video
1990
100 minutes
Directed by: Patrick Read Johnson
Starring: Douglas Barr, Royal Dano,
    Ariana Richards, Gregg Berger
MPAA rating: PG

In Big Bean, Illinois, new sherrif Sam Hocksley takes his daughter Kathy to a Halloween party to help her adjust to her new home town. Meanwhile, The Martian Imperial Atomic Space Navy has programmed new Enforcer Drones to oversee all of its starships, and launches an ill-fated attack on the Arcturus system. The Space Navy is completely destroyed, and its last forlorn distress signal is picked up by a lone Martian patrol ship. The crew scans for the source of the distress signal and picks up a Halloween broadcast of Orson Welles' "War of the Worlds" instead. They come to the mistaken conclusion that the attack on Arcturus was just a feint, and that the real assault is on the insignificant planet Earth. So the Martians land in Big Bean, Illinois on Halloween night, where they intend to join up with their armada, which they assume is taking over Earth. There, some of the Martians join Kathy's group of trick-or-treaters and it doesn't take long for Kathy to determine the truth ("these kids aren't from around here"). She follows the Martians as they head off to destroy what they believe is one of Earth's missile defense systems (a granary). And from that point on, the film careens from one wild episode to another as the mixed-up Martians are chased by practically everyone, including their own Enforcer Drone. Eventually, the town manages to defeat the Enforcer Drone, saving both the Martians and Earth, and they send the little green guys home.

CAUTION: The Martians are kind of rude, and their Enforcer Drone might be a little spooky for some kids. The Martian captain is hit by a truck (he survives).

GO: All in all, a fun flick for kids over six.

STAND AND DELIVER

Warner Home Video
1988
103 minutes
Directed by: Ramon Menendez
Starring: Andy Garcia, Edward James Olmos,
    Lou Diamond Phillips
MPAA rating: PG

Jaime Escalante quits his upscale job to teach calculus at a high school in East Los Angeles only to find that the senior students can't even do basic arithmetic. Determined to teach his students what they need to know, Jaime tells them that if they pass the Advanced Placement Calculus Exam they will all be assured of college entrance. He threatens, wheedles, begs and cajoles; he encourages them to believe they can accomplish anything. When the exam day arrives they write the test and they all pass. But the results are so revolutionary that the Board of Education suspects Jaime and his students have cheated. An inquiry is made and Jaime convinces the class that the only way to prove their innocence is to write the exam again. Apprehensive, they undergo the ordeal a second time and achieve even better results. This film is based on a true story.

CAUTION: The film contains a little coarse language and Jaime has a heart attack (he survives).

GO: This is an inspiring film for teachers, students and anyone with a math phobia.

✗ STAND BY ME

RCA/Columbia
1987
87 minutes
Directed by: Rob Reiner
Starring: Richard Dreyfuss, Corey Feldman, River Phoenix, Kiefer Sutherland* Wil Wheaton
MPAA rating: R

Four twelve-year-old friends: sensitive Gordie, tough-guy Chris, joker Teddy and conservative Vern, hear about the accidental death of a boy their age, killed by a train while walking on the tracks. This is a big event in their small town and they think that if they can discover the body and report it, they will be famous. They undertake an epic two-day journey across the countryside to the rumored site of the body, sharing anecdotes and adventures. They endure some close calls: one on a railroad bridge, one with an allegedly tough dog, and another with a leech-filled swamp. A gang of teenagers, including Chris's and Vern's brothers and the town bully, have the same idea; they close in on the body via the main highway. The climax comes at the site of the body, when the older and younger boys square off. It is only then that Gordie finds a strength he never knew he possessed.

✗ STOP: Pervasive coarse language, hence the "R" rating. This film is a retrospective of an adult's life. Although it features twelve-year-olds (all popular teen stars), it is not a film for children in general. In the climactic scene the face of the dead boy is shown. This is the most difficult scene for children, although the corpse is not particularly gruesome, and the boys in the movie are not especially disturbed, just amazed at the reality of someone being dead.

CAUTION: The boys go swimming and encounter leeches, so they strip to their underwear. There is a great deal of swearing and coarse language and a vomiting scene. The boys want to prove how "cool" they are so they sneak smokes, swear every second word, tell tales and bait each other.

GO: This is a touching coming-of-age film about friendships that are never forgotten.

✗ STAR TREK II: THE WRATH OF KHAN

Paramount Home Video
1982
113 minutes
Directed by: Nicholas Meyer
Starring: Kirstie Alley, Ricardo Montalban,
Leonard Nimoy, William Shatner
MPAA rating: PG

A Federation starship is conducting a survey to find a suitable test-world for the top-secret Genesis Project, when its landing party inadvertently stumbles upon a group of sinister genetic mutants (marooned by Kirk fifteen years before). The mutants, led by the vengeful Khan, take over the Federation Starship and the Genesis Orbital Station. From there they send out a distress call, which is picked up by Admiral Kirk and the Enterprise. Khan then ambushes the Enterprise and a harrowing game of cat and mouse ensues. In the final confrontation, Khan sets the Genesis device to explode, planning to destroy both his own vessel and the Enterprise. The crew's fate appears sealed until Spock enters a lethally irradiated chamber and repairs the starship's drive. The crew escapes, but Spock dies in the process. However, the movie does end with a message of hope.

✗ **STOP:** There are a great many scenes in which people are tortured, burned, crushed and disintegrated. Kirk is reunited with his son—a son from a relationship with a woman to whom he was obviously never married. And Spock, a universally popular character, dies as he is slowly disfigured by radiation poisoning.

GO: The film is replete with positive messages and features a number of women in positions of authority. The special effects are spectacular.

✗ STAR TREK III: THE SEARCH FOR SPOCK

Paramount Home Video
1984
105 minutes
Directed by: Leonard Nimoy
Starring: DeForest Kelley, Christopher Lloyd,
Leonard Nimoy, William Shatner,
George Takei
MPAA rating: PG

Kirk and his companions have paid a heavy price for the defeat of Khan and the creation of the Genesis planet; Spock is dead and McCoy is inexplicably being driven insane. Then an unexpected visit from Spock's father, Ambassador Sarek, provides a startling revelation: McCoy is harboring Spock's living essence, placed in his mind by Spock himself just before his death. However, in order to release that essence they must retrieve Spock's body. Kirk and his crew have no choice but to steal the Enterprise, defy Starfleet's quarantine and go to the Genesis planet. There they unexpectedly encounter a resourceful group of Klingons who are determined to seize the secret of the Genesis torpedo to use it as a weapon. A desperate struggle follows in which the Enterprise is destroyed and the rapidly regenerating body of Spock, now a small boy, is discovered. Subsequently, Kirk's son is killed and the battle culminates in a brutal

AGES 10 TO 13

hand-to-hand fight between Kirk and the Klingon commander. Kirk triumphs and he and his companions take Spock's new body and his essence to the planet Vulcan, where the two are reunited.

✗**STOP:** In one tense scene, the Klingons prepare to kill a hostage—and do.

CAUTION: The battle scenes and hand-to-hand combat are brutal (often the innocent are victimized) and there is some coarse language.

GO: Friendship and loyalty are positively portrayed.

✗ STAR TREK VI: THE UNDISCOVERED COUNTRY

Paramount Home Video
1991
110 minutes
Directed by: Nicholas Meyer
Starring: Kim Cattrall, Iman, Leonard Nimoy, Christopher Plummer, William Shatner, David Warner
MPAA rating: PG

When an explosion on a Klingon moon, caused by overmining and insufficient safety precautions, critically pollutes the atmosphere of the Klingon homeworld, the desperate Klingons have no option but to sue for peace. Klingon Chancellor Gorkon is summoned to discuss the terms, and the Enterprise is chosen to escort his battlecruiser into Federation space. Soon after the rendezvous, the Enterprise inexplicably fires photon torpedoes at the Klingon ship. The craft is badly damaged, though no order was given and the Enterprise

still retains its full complement of torpedoes. Then two masked commandos board the Klingon vessel and kill the ambassador. To prevent an incident, Kirk and McCoy surrender themselves and are taken to the Klingon world where they are tried and sentenced to a frozen prison planetoid. But Kirk and McCoy soon make some unusual allies and plan an escape with Martia, a bizarre shape-changing being. The arrangements turn out to be a set-up, but Kirk and McCoy are rescued by the Enterprise. Now aware of the conspiracy afoot, they race to the site of a major peace conference where they defeat General Chang, a Romulan conspirator who is lurking in a cloaked warship near the planet.

✗**STOP:** This film features relatively graphic violence. The commandos shoot Klingons with beam weapons which sever arms and punch holes in bodies, leaving globules of blood floating in a weightless environment.

CAUTION: A hapless wretch is tossed out into the snow on the prison planetoid and left to die. Spock interrogates a fellow-Vulcan with a brutal telepathic method that causes her obvious trauma. During the assassination attempt, an assassin lies dead in a pool of blood.

STAY TUNED

Warner Home Video
1992
89 minutes
Directed by: Peter Hyams
Starring: Pam Dawber, Jeffrey Jones, Eugene Levy, John Ritter
MPAA rating: PG

Roy Knable isn't exactly a success story — he sells plumbing supplies door-to-door. Threatened by his wife Helen's success (she's a big-time advertising executive), Roy lives in front of the television in order to escape. Helen has had enough, and the night comes when she decides to leave him. But that same night, a shadowy figure named Spike shows up and gives Roy a huge home entertainment center, complete with a satellite dish guaranteed to bring in six hundred and sixty-six channels. But the television only seems to pick up grotesque shows with names like *Three Men and Rosemary's Baby*. And when Roy goes out to adjust the dish to fine-tune the reception, he and Helen are sucked into a satanic television nightmare called Hell Vision (run by Spike) in which the acquisition of lost souls is turned into high entertainment for The Boss Down Below. Roy and Helen must survive twenty-four hours in Hell Vision, living through a succession of macabre send-ups, gruesome game-shows and even a Bugs Bunny/Tom and Jerry style cartoon. Meanwhile, their children Darryl and Diane discover the enormous new set, and gradually begin to catch on: Their parents are trapped in the television. As Roy and Helen travel through the infernal world, Roy gains strength and confidence in his resourcefulness and, with the help of the children, they draw ever closer to the twenty-four hour deadline. But when a technicality sends Roy home without Helen, he has to prove himself by returning voluntarily to rescue his wife, setting up the final confrontation with Spike.

CAUTION: While the tone is mild, the satirical humor in this film may be lost on young children. There are numerous grotesque images, and the lead characters are in peril throughout. The film is bound to raise questions about the hereafter in the minds of some young viewers and there is some coarse language.

GO: For teens and adults this is a light-hearted romp through send-ups of many familiar shows and movies. The theme is hopeful and the special effects are great.

STRANGE BREW

MGM/UA
1983
91 minutes
Directed by: Rick Moranis, Dave Thomas
Starring: Rick Moranis, Dave Thomas,
    Max Von Sydow, Paul Dooley,
    Angus MacInnes
MPAA rating: PG

When their irritated father orders them to get more Elsinore beer, Doug and Bob Mackenzie plan to trick the store into giving them some free; they will use the old "mouse in the bottle" ruse. They take their complaint right to the brewery, a huge castle located next to the Royal Canadian Institute for the Criminally Insane. There, by a stroke of luck, they save the life of Pamela, daughter of the company's late president, and promptly land jobs at the brewery. It turns out that only one day after the president's recent passing, his brother Claude married his wife and took over the whole brewery. (Holy Hamlet!) Meanwhile, Brewmeister Smith, an evil genius, is conducting experiments on the patients in the asylum next door and has laced Elsinore Beer with a powerful drug, which will enable him to rule the world. When the boys unwittingly

AGES 10 TO 13

expose his plans, Smith sets the boys up as Pamela's kidnappers, hoping to get rid of all three of them. He arranges for the boys' van, with Pamela inside, to crash into the river. Pamela is left totally traumatized, the boys are blamed and all three end up in the Institute for the Insane. But Bob and Doug manage to escape, save Pamela and defeat the evil doctor before his beer drug completely ruins Oktoberfest.

CAUTION: Beer-drinking, burping and generally gross behavior are all part of this film.

GO: It's a silly film, but it's funny.

✗ SUPER MARIO BROS.

Hollywood Pictures
1993
114 minutes
Directed by: Rocky Morton and Annabel Jankel
Starring: Dennis Hopper, Bob Hoskins, John Leguizamo, Samantha Mathis, Fiona Shaw
MPAA rating: PG

The two Mario brothers, Mario and Luigi, are out-of-work plumbers. By misadventure, Luigi meets Daisy, a young archaeologist who is studying a strange dinosaur bone discovery at a construction site in downtown New York City. When an evil construction boss tries to flood the dig site, Daisy calls upon Luigi and Mario to help her save it; however, it turns out that the dig site is also a portal to a parallel dimension, one ruled by dinosaurs who were blasted out of our universe by a meteor impact sixty-five million years ago. These dino-exiles subsequently evolved into intelligent bipeds, and their leader, the sinister Koopa, is plotting to return with his army, deevolve all humans into apes, and rule Earth. To this end, he kidnaps Daisy, who is in fact a princess and who wears as an amulet the last shard of the meteor. Once the shard is placed in the meteor, the two dimensions will merge, and Earth will be doomed. Koopa gets Daisy, but the Mario brothers get the amulet and go into the other world to rescue their friend. They promptly lose the amulet, have many adventures requiring a ton of special effects, restore Daisy's deevolved father to his natural form, and return her to her rightful place as a princess of the realm. Koopa gets transmogrified into primordial slime.

✗ STOP: Koopa's evil henchwoman Lena is turned into a skeleton when she tries to insert the shard into the meteorite. For one gruesome moment, we see her transfixed by agony.

CAUTION: An otherwise decent effort is marred by the same old dreary female stereotypes. Most of the women in the dinosaur dimension are gum-chewing floozies with twenty-inch waists, heaving bosoms, big hair, spike heels and skin-tight miniskirts.

GO: Tremendous special effects and huge, lavish sets highlight this picture. The stars, particularly Shaw as Koopa's campy, creepy second-in-command, obviously had a lot of fun with their roles.

SUPERMAN

Warner Home Video
1978
127 minutes
Directed by: Richard Donner
Starring: Marlon Brando, Gene Hackman,
  Margot Kidder, Christopher Reeve
MPAA rating: PG

On the advanced planet Krypton, Jor-El has discovered that his home world will be destroyed within 30 days. When the ruling council of the planet refuses to believe him and commands him to keep silent, he arranges to send his son to the primitive planet Earth, where the child will have extraordinary powers and an excellent chance of survival. The tiny spaceship carrying the toddler escapes just before the planet is destroyed. It lands in the mid-western United States and is discovered by Martha and Jonathan Kent, who name the baby Clark. When the baby saves Jonathan by holding up a toppling pickup truck, Jonathan realizes that Clark is here for a reason. Later, Clark suffers over having to hide his special gifts when he is a teenager. After Jonathan dies, Clark is woken in the middle of the night by some strange static. An artifact from his spaceship, long hidden, has come to life. Clark travels up into the arctic, flings the crystal into the white wastes and watches it explode, creating the Fortress of Solitude. Clark remains there and discovers the nature of his origin.

Then he moves to the city of Metropolis, gets a job as a reporter at the *Daily Planet,* and, masquerading as an ineffectual wimp, hangs around star reporter Lois Lane. As Superman rescues Lois from certain death and performs other heroic acts (rescuing cats, saving airplanes) he attracts the attention of the evil super-villain Lex Luthor. Luthor deduces that meteorite fragments of the exploded planet Krypton will be lethal to Superman, and takes steps to obtain some. Then he arranges to divert the flight path of two nuclear missiles during a test, his master plan being to nuke the San Andreas fault, drop California into the sea, and become the owner of thousands of miles of new waterfront property. When Superman arrives to stop him, Luthor tricks him into exposure to Kryptonite; but Luthor has made a fatal error in judgment and Superman has an unexpected ally, allowing him to race to the aid of the country. But in the end he is forced to violate one of his father's decrees in order to save Lois.

CAUTION: Lex Luthor has an FBI agent pushed in front of a subway train. Lois is smothered to death in a car which is trapped in a cave-in. During the earthquake resulting from the missiles, many people are shown in peril.

GO: This film is faithful to the spirit of the original comic book, and its dazzling special effects, innovative for their time, still hold up well today.

AGES 10 TO 13

✘ SUPERMAN II

Warner Home Video
1980
127 minutes
Directed by: Richard Lester
Starring: Gene Hackman, Margot Kidder,
    Christopher Reeve, Terence Stamp
MPAA rating: PG

When an explosion in space shatters The Phantom Zone (a floating exile chamber created by the leaders of Krypton to imprison their worst criminals), General Zod, Ursa and Non are released and make their way to Earth. And when Superman's old foe, Lex Luthor, encounters them, he enlists their help to battle Superman. (He tells them that Superman is their jailor's son, and together they vow to destroy him.) Unaware of the trouble afoot, Lois finally comes to the realization that Clark Kent and Superman are one and the same, and she and Superman fall in love. He takes her to the Fortress of solitude where a holographic image of his deceased mother tells him that in order to be with the woman he loves, he must become an ordinary mortal. He undergoes the change and, now unable to fly, drives Lois back to the city. On the way, after stopping at a diner, he sees the President on TV submitting to Zod and pleading for Superman's help. Recognizing his responsibility to mankind, Superman returns to the Fortress of Solitude and regains his powers. Then the four super-beings battle it out above the streets of New York. Eventually, Superman renders the villains powerless and, when order is restored, gives Lois a kiss of forgetfulness so that his true identity will remain a secret. This is a sequel to the very successful *Superman* film.

✘**STOP:** Because this is a movie about battling super-beings, the violence is on a grandiose scale. The speical effects are so believable that they will frighten some children. People are crushed, shot and hurled through windows.

CAUTION: Clark and Lois are shown sleeping naked together, covered by sheets. It may be disturbing to some that earthlings are totally helpless against the super-beings.

GO: The film has great special effects and the plot is exciting and clever. There are the usual in-the-nick-of-time rescues and some fun stuff as Lois gradually figures out Clark's true identity.

SUPERMAN IV: THE QUEST FOR PEACE

Warner Home Video
1987
90 minutes
Directed by: Sidney J. Furie
Starring: Jon Cryer, Gene Hackman,
    Mariel Hemingway, Margot Kidder,
    Christopher Reeve
MPAA rating: PG

When the *Daily Planet* is purchased by a press tycoon with a reputation for turning his papers into money-making tabloids, the staff anticipates trouble. Sure enough, trouble comes in spades, especially for Clark Kent. The tycoon's daughter develops an inexplicable crush on the bumbling Kent, and to make matters worse, she and Lois arrange for a double date with him and Superman. This, needless to say, necessitates some very quick changes for the Man of Steel. Meanwhile, there's trouble of a much more serious nature brewing as Lex Luthor, Superman's arch enemy, sets in motion an ingenious plan to prevent Superman from ridding the world of nuclear weapons. He and his nephew clone Superman's genetic material and fire it along with a nuclear missile into the sun; the evil Nuclear Man is born. Nuclear Man is as powerful as Superman and serves Lex Luthor as a devoted servant. His only weakness is a total dependence on light for power. In their first fight, Nuclear Man scratches Superman on the back of the neck, and Superman is forced into hiding, where he grows progressively weaker from radiation sickness. But Superman receives aid from a surprising source and returns to defeat Nuclear Man by creating an eclipse and dropping the hapless villain down the exhaust vent of a reactor.

CAUTION: There is violence throughout the film, including punching and smashing and so on. When Superman is ill, the scenes of his sickness may cause concern among very young children.

GO: The story ends on a hopeful note.

✗ SWING KIDS

Hollywood Pictures
1993
114 minutes
Directed by: Thomas Carter
Starring: Christian Bale, Kenneth Branagh, Barbara Hershey, Robert Sean Leonard
MPAA rating: PG-13

In 1939 Hamburg, as the Nazis exert a growing control, a group of young rebels called Swing Kids cling to their love of freedom, dancing the nights away at local clubs. Two of the young rebels, Peter and Thomas, are best friends. Thomas comes from a wealthy, influential family, but Peter's family is impoverished because his father, a famous violinist, was put to death for speaking on behalf of the Jews. To make matters worse, the Gestapo continues to keep an eye on Peter and his mother, and when Peter steals back a radio that an SS thug has taken from the scene of an arrest, only the intervention of a favorably disposed high-ranking Gestapo officer saves him. Peter is forced to join the Hitler Youth to keep his family safe. Thomas joins simply to support him, but he breaks under the intense propaganda. Peter feels the pressure, too, and the situation gets worse until the Nazis finally order Peter to deliver three strange packages to the families of individuals who have been taken away by the Gestapo. Peter discovers to his horror that the boxes contain human ashes. He then decides to follow in his father's footsteps and makes a suicidal public protest against the Nazis.

✗**STOP:** There are numerous violent moments in this film. At one point a group of Hitler Youth thugs beats a young musician and crushes his hand so he can never play again. In the climax of the film Thomas and Peter have a violent fight. When Peter makes his gruesome deliveries, one of the wives starts to scream in horror. In the end, Peter is taken away by the Gestapo after having been beaten up.

CAUTION: This is a social commentary based on the events leading up to the Holocaust. There is an atmosphere of dreary hopelessness around the inevitability of Peter's sacrifice. One teenager commented, "Too many Nazis, not enough dancing."

GO: Peter summons the courage to do what is right, even at the cost of his own life.

TALES FOR ALL SERIES

Cinema Plus/Astral
1985–1992
90–100 minutes each

Produced by Québecois filmmaker Rock Demers, the *Tales for All* series has garnered more than 135 international awards. The films feature many different writers and directors; many have magical or mystical elements, and all are generally geared for family viewing. There is no coarse language and almost no violence. (See our section for children aged six to ten for more reviews in this series.)

Bach and Broccoli
(Tale #3)

A young orphan named Fanny is sent to live with her eccentric Uncle Jonathan. (Jonathan was in love with Fanny's mother, who married his brother instead.) An organist practicing almost single-mindedly for a music festival, Jonathan finds Fanny's resemblance to his lost love almost too much to bear, but agrees to take her in until a proper foster family can be found. Despite his unwillingness to change his ways, Jonathan comes to appreciate Fanny more and more. Then comes the day when a foster family is found, and Jonathan realizes he · must chose between the solitude he once prized so highly, and the little girl he has come to love.

CAUTION: This might not be a good choice for a child who has recently lost a loved one.

GO: This is a good story about appreciating the important things in life.

Bye Bye Red Riding Hood (Tale #9)

Fanny lives in the forest with her meteorologist mother where she meets an apparently kind wolf, a city boy named Nicholas and an ornithologist who bears a striking resemblance to the father who abandoned her long ago. This is a modern retelling of the Red Riding Hood story. (Astral Home Video, 1989).

CAUTION: There are some frightening and disturbing scenes. The wolf is shot and the great-grandmother dies.

✘ The Peanut Butter Solution (Tale #2)

One morning, eleven-year-old soccer star Michael Baskin wakes to learn that there has been a fire in the neighborhood's spooky old house, and that two street people were killed inside. He dares to enter the burned-out house and sees something so terrible that his hair falls out. Hoods, hats, wigs and all the efforts of medical science do not help. Then one night, the ghosts of the street people come to see Michael. Sorry for his condition they give him the Peanut Butter Solution (a disgusting recipe that includes dead flies, rotten eggs and peanut butter) to make his hair grow back. He's warned not to use more than a spoonful of peanut butter, but when the mixture won't stick Michael ignores the warning and adds more. The tonic works too well; in fact, his hair won't stop growing. Strangley, his creepy art teacher, decides that Michael's hair will make perfect paint brushes and kidnaps him, taking him to a sweatshop where other students are also being held. It's up to Michael's sister, Suzy, and his friend, Connie, to find him and rescue him. Also available in French under the title

✘ **STOP:** Young viewers may be disturbed by the creepy art teacher who kidnaps his own students and by some of the ghost scenes.

GO: This is a rather strange film, but it *is* a ghost story without the elements of horror.

·The Summer of the Colt (Tale #8)

When Laura, Daniel and Phillipe visit their grandfather Don Federico's horse ranch in South America, Laura notices at once that her grandfather is avoiding her. (It turns out that Laura, having grown, now bears an uncanny resemblance to her grandmother, Don Federicos's long-lost love, and Don Federico can hardly stand to look at the girl.) There is more promise of a happy summer for Daniel, however, when Martin, the ranch foreman's son, shows him a new stallion named Fiero. Stunned by its beauty, Daniel asks his grandfather if he can have the horse. His grandfather agrees on the condition that Daniel break the horse himself. But Martin has already broken the stallion in secret, and when Daniel tries to ride it, he's thrown off and hits his head on a fence. He tells his grandfather he doesn't want to ride the horse anymore, but thinking that his grandson is a coward, Don Federico demands that Daniel continue to ride. Angrily, Laura intervenes, and when her infuriated grandfather banishes her to her room, Laura takes a horse, and rides off into the wild. Then it's up to Daniel and Martin and Don Federico to find her.

CAUTION: There is a great deal of angst in the relationship between Don Federico and his grandchildren. Laura tells her aunt that she has had her period.

GO: This is a moving tale of people learning to understand one another, with plenty of stuff to interest horse lovers.

Vincent and Me (Tale #11)

Thirteen-year-old Jo's work bears such a striking resemblence to that of Van Gogh that unscrupulous people plan to use her talents to help them pull off the art con of the century. But Jo goes back in time to the nineteenth century, and Van

Gogh himself helps her thwart the criminals. The paintings of the master are prominently featured in the film. (Astral Video, 1991)

GO: Winner of the 1991 Parents' Choice Award for Best Children's Film of the Year and of the 1992 Emmy Award for Best Children's Special.

TEEN WOLF

Paramount Home Video
1985
92 minutes
Directed by: Rod Daniel
Starring: Michael J. Fox, James Hampton, Scott Paulin, Susan Ursitti
MPAA rating: PG

Scott, a player on his high school's losing basketball team, is alarmed by the way his body is changing. Wolf-like hair has begun to sprout on his chest; he develops a growl that sends chills through the toughest bully; and he can even hear a dog whistle. Desperate, he turns to his father for help, only to learn that his condition runs in the family — his father is a werewolf, too. Scott finds little comfort in his father's words until he discovers that his new-found werewolf strength makes him a great basketball player. His teammates, however, soon come to resent his abilities (they hardly ever get to play) and it isn't until Scott begins to work with the rest of the team that they are victorious.

CAUTION: A game of dares is played in which losers must perform tasteless acts, and partying teens are shown smoking and drinking. Scott's transformation may upset young children. The film includes mild innuendo, some fighting and coarse language.

GO: Scott rejects superficial rewards and develops confidence and self-respect.

TEEN WOLF TOO

Paramount Home Video
1987
95 minutes
Directed by: Christopher Leitch
Starring: John Astin, Jason Bateman, Kim Darby
MPAA rating: PG

In the *Teen Wolf* sequel, Scott's cousin, Todd Howard, is forced to accept a boxing scholarship to get into university. There, shocked by his own transformation into a werewolf (a condition that runs in the family), he finds the extraordinary strength that makes him the regional boxing champion. Success, however, makes Todd unpopular with his friends, as he becomes obnoxious, coasting on the strength of his athletic abilities. Todd's Uncle Harold talks to him about responsibility. When his boxing team makes it to the championships, Todd apologizes to his friends and, using only his human strength, is victorious.

CAUTION: There are boxing matches throughout the film, with plenty of punching. Todd fondles a girl's behind.

GO: This film emphasizes the importance of being yourself. There is no swearing.

THE THREE AMIGOS

Orion
1986
105 minutes
Directed by: John Landis
Starring: Alfonso Arau, Chevy Chase,
    Steve Martin, Patrice Martinez, Martin Short
MPAA rating: PG

In 1916, a little Mexican village is easy prey for the villainous El Guapo and his murderous banditos. In a direct send-up of *The Magnificent Seven* the desperate villagers gather what money they can and send the beautiful Carmen to seek out and hire The Three Amigos — Lucky, Dusty and Ned — gunfighters famous for helping the downtrodden. The villagers don't know that The Three Amigos are just actors who, among other things, have just been dropped by their studio. The Amigos, happy for the work and thinking that they've been hired to act in a movie, head south, hilariously unaware that the offer was real; that is, until one of El Guapo's henchman grazes Lucky with a real bullet. Then the truth dawns on the terrified thespians and they beg for mercy. El Guapo scornfully lets them live and rides off with the beautiful Carmen as his captive. Much shamed, the heroes recover their nerve and vow to become The Three Amigos for real. They follow a bizarre set of instructions and sneak into the fortress of El Guapo during his birthday party. There they save Carmen, make a narrow escape and use some good old-fashioned

trickery to finally defeat the bandit leader and his men.

CAUTION: There is the odd off-color joke and people do get shot, although nothing is graphic.

GO: This movie contains some first-rate comedy, and is sophisticated enough for adults while retaining enough physical humor for the eight to twelve set.

THREE MEN AND A LITTLE LADY

Touchstone Home Video
1990
103 minutes
Directed by: Emile Ardolino
Starring: Christopher Cazenove,
    Ted Danson, Steve Guttenberg,
    Tom Selleck, Nancy Travis,
    Robin Weisman
MPAA rating: PG

In this film (sequel to *Three Men and a Baby*), Peter, Michael and Jack are still living with Sylvia Bennington and her daughter Mary. They're the three best fathers any little girl ever had and everybody's happy; that is, until Sylvia, who has fallen in love with Peter, begins to demand a more passionate, conventional family life. Worried that Mary is confused by her extended family, and confused herself by the situation, Sylvia accepts her director friend Edward's proposal of marriage and moves to England. Soon after the big move, Michael talks to Mary on the phone and, realizing that she's desperately unhappy, the men decide to go to England. When they get there, Peter is horrified by Edward's attitude towards Mary, especially when he begins to suspect that Edward plans to shunt her off to a boarding school. But more importantly, he discovers that he's always loved Sylvia and goes to extraordinary lengths to get her (and Mary) back.

CAUTION: Mary mentions the word penis, and an embarrassed Peter mumbles an inadequate biological explanation. There is some sexual innuendo.

GO: This is a light, comical film about how an unconventional family can be just as happy as a more conventional one, and about how the weight of responsibility can sometimes cloud the expression of love.

✗ THE THREE MUSKETEERS

Walt Disney Home Video
1993
115 minutes
Directed by: Stephen Herek
Starring: Tim Curry, Rebecca de Mornay,
   Chris O'Donnell, Oliver Platt, Charlie Sheen,
   Kiefer Sutherland
MPAA rating: PG

A foul conspiracy is afoot in 17th century France. The musketeers, the king's personal guard, have been disbanded and the young king and his new bride left at the mercy of the ruthless Cardinal Richelieu and his henchman Rochefort. Only three musketeers have refused to disband: Athos, Porthos and Aramis, and they are now wanted men. Into this mess rides the headstrong D'Artagnan, swashing a few buckles on his way. He immediately becomes the fly in the

Cardinal's ointment, joining forces with the musketeers, getting captured, overhearing the details of the Cardinal's plot to take the throne, and then escaping to foil the plans. The musketeers finally discover the heart of the conspiracy, a plot to assassinate the king on his birthday. They rally their fellows, storm the palace, save the king and avenge D'Artagnan's father.

✗STOP: A fairly high level of violence characterizes this wild departure from the original tale. There are also some frightening images and characters in the Cardinal's spooky dungeon.

CAUTION: Realistic special effects, in particular aural ones, heighten the impact of the violence. There's a morbid quality to Rebecca de Mornay's sexy Countess de Winter, who thwarts the executioner by jumping off a cliff.

GO: If you want to introduce a child to the famous classic, this is *not* the movie; however, it overflows with enthusiasm and spirit, and it's nice to see such a clear differentiation between good and evil.

✗ THREE NINJAS

Touchstone Home Video
1992
85 minutes
Directed by: John Turteltaub
Starring: Rand Kingsley, Alan McRae,
   Chad Power, Max Elliott Slade,
   Michael Treanor, Victor Wong
MPAA rating: PG

The Douglas brothers spend their summers with their Japanese grandfather, Mori Tanaka, who trains them in the positive aspects of the ancient ninja arts. The boys' father, Sam Douglas, is an FBI agent who hates martial arts. (He's trying to track down arms dealer and expert ninja Hugo Snyder.) After a close call with the Feds, Snyder threatens Tanaka in an attempt to force Sam off the case. When that fails, Snyder hires three thugs to kidnap the boys. The Douglas boys easily defeat the comic villains in a style reminiscent of *Home Alone*, but more formidable goons soon arrive and take the kids to Snyder's ship in the harbor. Tanaka follows and sneaks onboard, and in the mayhem that ensues, Tanaka and Snyder face each other in a final showdown.

✘**STOP:** At one point, Snyder turns to an associate and says: "I'm going to crush your head until a slimey ooze comes out of your eyeballs."

CAUTION: There is violence throughout, though most of it is slapstick. Punches and kicks don't draw blood, and are accompanied by absurd sound effects. (When a villain is knocked out, we hear tweety-bird noises.)

GO: This fun, action-packed film stresses the positive aspects of martial arts.

✘ TREASURE ISLAND

Malofilm/Turner Home
   Entertainment
1990
132 minutes
Directed by: Fraser C. Heston
Starring: Christian Bale, Julian Glover,
   Charlton Heston, Richard Johnson,
   Christopher Lee, Oliver Reed, Clive Wood
MPAA rating: not rated

A grog-swilling seaman armed with a treasure map arrives at the Admiral Bensbow Inn and after he meets a grisly end the map comes into the possession of Jim, the innkeeper's son. Jim shows the map (which reveals the location and geography of Treasure Island) to Squire Trelawney, who resolves to outfit a ship and set sail for the Spanish Main. But the squire cannot hold his tongue, and news of the treasure attracts a scurvy crew of pirates led by Long John Silver. Despite the crew, the voyage proceeds uneventfully until Jim overhears Silver plotting to take over the ship and the treasure. He informs the officers of the planned mutiny and when they reach the island, they are prepared for the pirates' assault. Jim then sneaks back aboard the lightly guarded ship, and, to prevent the pirates from escaping, runs her aground on another part of the island. In the end, the pirates follow the map only to find that the treasure has been moved to safety, and after a final battle, Jim lets Silver escape.

✘**STOP:** A blind pirate's blindfold is ripped off, and his terrible, disfigured features are revealed; he is later run over in the road as he pathetically calls for his mates to help him. There is a graphic close-up of a pirate lying dead with his throat brutally cut.

CAUTION: The violence is more extreme than in previous versions; musket balls thud into chests and produce exit wounds and swords and knives cut into flesh.

GO: Jim is honorable to a fault. All in all, an exciting adventure.

■

✗ TRON

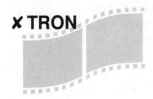

Walt Disney Home Video
1982
95 minutes
Directed by: Steven Lisberger
Starring: Bruce Boxleitner, Jeff Bridges,
Cindy Morgan,David Warner
MPAA rating: PG

In the world of virtual reality, sinister Master Control has established a totalitarian state. There, all programs must have permission just to travel around their own microcircuits, and belief in the Users (the humans in the physical world) is considered to be a false belief subscribed to only by religious lunatics. As Master Control dominates more and more programs, he sends those who defy him to The Game Grid, where they're forced to play an evil program called Sark and are destroyed. But one human is trying to break in from the outside. Determined to retrieve the innovative game programs he designed, video game wizard Flynn is intent on getting into his former employer Encom's system. Flynn's old rival at Encom, Allan Bradley, has also noticed something strange going on in the system. He creates a security program called Tron which will operate independently of Master Control. And when Encom shuts Allan down too, Flynn and Allan go to the company at night to confirm their suspicions. Master Control manipulates a laser matter transmission device, and Flynn is sucked into the computer world of virtual reality, taken prisoner and

sent to the Games Grid to be destroyed. There he meets Tron and, during a team game, the two escape. After a chase of epic proportions, Flynn and Tron finally reach the sanctuary of the master program where, with the fate of the world at stake, Tron goes up against Sark and Flynn pits his will against Master Control.

✗**STOP:** Master Control tortures one of Flynn's programs to try to make him reveal his User; the program's death is protracted and obviously painful.

CAUTION: Violent combat is a central element of this film. There are intense battle scenes.

GO: This is a staggering achievement with an interesting story and concept. The animation is superb and the theme of courageous resistance to tyranny is inspiring.

TROOP BEVERLY HILLS

RCA/Columbia
1989
105 minutes
Directed by: Jeff Kanew
Starring: Mary Gross, Shelley Long,
Craig T. Nelson, Betty Thomas
MPAA rating: PG

On the verge of a divorce, wealthy Beverly Hills socialite Phyllis Nefler is chosen to lead her daughter's Wilderness Girl troop. There are two obstacles standing in her way, however: One, the wealthy and pampered girls aren't typical Wilderness Girl recruits, and two, local Red Feather leader and reverse-snob Velda Plender intends to have the Beverly Hills troop disbanded. To this end, Vera sends her assistant to spy on the troop's unorthodox activities (which include a stay in a luxury hotel after a camping trip is rained out, and badges for gem identification and shopping instead of knot-tying). But when it comes to seeing which troop can sell the most Wilderness Girl cookies, Phyllis refuses to bend the rules and allow the girls' parents to buy the whole lot, and the girls are forced to come up with some original ideas to sell more than their share of cookies. The real test comes during the wilderness trek when the girls in Troop Beverly Hills must prove they have all the qualities necessary to be real Wilderness Girls.

CAUTION: Some references are made to the size of one woman's bust. Phyllis and her husband are divorcing, and he is going out with a younger woman. There is some mild swearing.

GO: The family reconciles. This is a great sleep-over movie for girls.

his house, Scott doesn't take him seriously. Then hoods operating out of the plant murder Amos. Scott is left with an unsolved case, few leads and Hooch, Amos's gigantic mastiff-type dog, who proceeds to destroy Scott's home. Hooch's one saving grace is that he brings home an attractive collie belonging to Emily Carson, a vet with whom Scott becomes involved. In time, destruction aside, Turner comes to love Hooch and Hooch, as it happens, is the only one who can I.D. the bad guys. He turns out to be a pretty good cop too, giving his own life to save Scott's. Scott is devastated to lose his new friend. But there are puppies on the way.

✗STOP: Hooch dies at the end.

CAUTION: A hood's leg and throat are cut. (The camera pans away, but we hear him gag horribly.) Amos is stabbed in the back.

GO: An excellent film, with a lot of warm-hearted humor. Some events may be too intense for young children.

✗ TURNER AND HOOCH

TWINS

Touchstone Home Video
1989
99 minutes
Directed by: Roger Spottiswoode
Starring: Tom Hanks, Mare Winningham
MPAA rating: PG

Scott Turner is a healthy living neatness freak and a cop in a small town. When his elderly friend, Amos, complains about strange noises at the seafood plant next to

MCA
1989
107 minutes
Directed by: Ivan Reitman
Starring: Danny DeVito, Kelly Preston, Arnold Schwarzenegger
MPAA rating: PG

When a group of scientists conducts a test-tube research experiment to produce the perfect human, things don't go quite as expected. Instead of one perfect baby, twins are born:

Julius is perfect and Vincent is anything but. It's decided that the twins must be separated. Julius is taken to a remote, tropical island where he learns to speak twelve languages, develops physically and spiritually and helps his foster-father with his scientific experiments. Vincent is abandoned as an orphan. But when the cloistered Julius is thirty-five, his foster father reveals to him the secret of his birth and tells him that he has a twin brother. Julius instinctively senses that his brother is in trouble and sets out to find him in jail for unpaid parking tickets and on the lam for a debt of $20,000. Julius bails him out and after failing to convince Vincent of his true identity, naively becomes involved in Vincent's illicit business ventures. Pursued by angry loan sharks and a vengeful assassin and accompanied by their girlfriends, Julius and Vincent visit the scientist who headed the test-tube experiment. He verifies Julius's story and Vincent is finally convinced of the truth. In the end, Julius puts his life on the line for his brother, and Vincent sacrifices a fortune for Julius. They find their mother and, now heirs to immense wealth, marry their respective girlfriends and have twins of their own.

CAUTION: There are fistfights and shootings and a brief sexual situation between Julius and his girlfriend.

GO: A cynical, selfish man comes to love his brother.

✗ UHF

Orion
1989
97 minutes
Directed By: Jay Levey
Starring: Victoria Jackson, Kevin McCarthy, Weird Al Yankovic
MPAA rating: PG-13

When George Newman's uncle wins a television station in a poker game, George is hired as the manager. Channel 69 is teetering on the verge of bankruptcy and all of George's efforts to turn the station around (which include a host of bizarre programs like a do-it-yourself show on which the guest star accidentally cuts off his own thumb) only result in lower ratings. And after inadvertently angering a psychotic competitor and losing his long-suffering girlfriend, George gives up and turns his children's program, *The Uncle Nutsy Show*, over to the station janitor. Incredibly, the bizarre Spadowski turns out to be a kids' show genius, and *Stanley Spadowski's Playhouse* rockets to number one, taking channel 69 with it. George's network enemies then plot his demise, and hilarious chaos follows.

✗STOP: Elements of the dark humor in this film are certain to be too extreme for young children; for instance, on a show called *Raoul's Wild Kingdom,* poodles are "taught" to fly by throwing them out the window.

CAUTION: A depiction of an Oriental karate school teacher might be considered stereotyping. Weird Al's off-the-wall satire is definitely not for little ones.

GO: This is a great comedy for preteens and young teens.

UNCLE BUCK

MCA
1989
100 minutes
Directed by: John Hughes
Starring: John Candy, Macaulay Culkin, Amy Madigan, Jay Underwood
MPAA rating: PG

When Cindy Russell's father has a heart attack and she and her husband Bob are forced to go to her parents, the only person available to baby-sit their three children is Bob's brother Buck. Buck is a notorious ne'er-do-well who's been making his living on fixed races at the track. He's also a classic stumblebum, and when he shows up at the Russell house with his smoke-belching old car, the children are stunned. Maisy and Miles quickly come to like him, but a real battle of wills develops between Buck and fifteen-year-old Tia. Tia rejects Buck's assessment of her odious boyfriend Bug until, in a final act of defiance, she sneaks out with him to a party where she discovers that Buck was right all along, and leaves in disgust. Buck, meanwhile, gives up his old ways to search for her and they meet on the street and reconcile.

CAUTION: There is some coarse language and Bug has a hard time taking no for an answer.

GO: Buck is persistent and patient with Tia, and the fact that he cares about her trans-

forms her. The film features a very positive message about accepting responsibility.

VICE VERSA

RCA/Columbia
1988
97 minutes
Directed by: Brian Gilbert
Starring: Swoosie Kurtz, Judge Reinhold, Fred Savage
MPAA rating: PG

Somewhere in Thailand, a thief steals a skull from a mountain temple. The priceless artifact is eventually brought into the United States by unwitting businessman Marshall Seymour, who, after discovering it in his luggage, decides to keep it in his apartment until the rightful owner comes to claim it. Meanwhile, Marshall's ex-wife goes on vacation and leaves his eleven-year-old son Charlie with Marshall. But Marshall is so busy that he doesn't have time for Charlie and the two just can't seem to get along. During one argument, while holding the skull, Charlie wishes he could change places with his father. And when Marshall replies that he wishes he could change places too, a magical transformation takes place: Charlie changes into Marshall, and Marshall changes into Charlie. Unable to change each other back, Charlie must impersonate his father in his high-pressure job and Marshall is forced to return to the terrors of sixth grade. All the while, the smugglers are after the skull. In time, Marshall sets new school test records, while Charlie revolutionizes his father's department store. The climax comes when the villains kidnap Marshall and Charlie must find a way to save his father.

CAUTION: There is some coarse language.

GO: This is a terrific film about the value of human relationships and about remaining young at heart.

✗ WATERSHIP DOWN

Warner Home Video
1978
90 minutes
Directed by: Martin Rosen
Starring the voices of: Richard Briers, Denholm Elliot, John Hurt, Zero Mostel, Ralph Richardson
MPAA rating: PG

Fiver, a rabbit visionary, senses terrible destruction (a land development) is coming to the warren, so he and his brother Hazel and a friend called Bigwig go to the chief rabbit to try to galvanize the warren into leaving. They manage to persuade only a few to accompany them, and leave to start a new warren. They are later joined by a survivor from the old warren who describes the terrible destruction. Painfully aware that their warren will not survive without female rabbits, they infiltrate a nearby warren where many of the females with no chance of finding mates wish to leave, but are forbidden to do so. Hazel and some others help them escape, fight a ferocious battle and triumph with

intelligence and ingenuity. In the end, the new warren flourishes and the Black Rabbit of Death comes for Hazel. Based on the novel by Richard Adams.

✗STOP: The story is a social commentary and not suitable for children. Death is everywhere and no effort is made to reduce the tension for young viewers.

CAUTION: The film is violent. Hawks swoop out of the sky, talons extended, striking with blood-curdling shrieks; rabbits are buried alive and crushed to death by construction; combat between rabbits is bloody and graphic; and in the end, the lead character dies.

GO: A fantastic score, great voice-overs and superior animation are the hallmarks of this production.

■

✗ WAYNE'S WORLD

Paramount Home Video
1992
93 minutes
Directed by: Penelope Spheeris
Starring: Dana Carvey, Rob Lowe, Mike Myers
MPAA rating: PG-13

Wayne Campbell still lives with his parents in Aurora, Illinois and has never had a career — although he's quick to point out his considerable collection of hair nets and name tags. The one thing in life that is going well for him is the public access television show he has on Cable 10: *Wayne's World*, a hilarious basement talk show which he hosts with his best friend Garth Algar. But when Benjamin, an ambitious, unscrupulous TV executive, sets out to acquire the rights to *Wayne's World*, Wayne and Garth are tricked into signing the show away for five thousand dollars each and things begin to go terribly wrong. Wayne is fired from the show for insulting the sponsor on the air and Benjamin has plans to steal Wayne's girlfriend. The only thing that can save Wayne's career and his relationship is a special edition of *Wayne's World*.

✗STOP: Viewers who are not yet able to read will miss the rudest elements of this film.

CAUTION: Coarse language, stereotypes and crude behavior abound, but, thanks to all of the hype, it's a major attraction for young children.

GO: Lowe is perfect as the amoral executive, and there are wonderful cameos from Ed O'Neill (*Married With Children*) and Alice Cooper. All in all, it's a wild satire of American life, the kind of entertainment created just for the fun of it, right down to the optional multiple endings.

WHAT ABOUT BOB?

Touchstone Home Video
1991
99 minutes
Directed by: Frank Oz
Starring: Richard Dreyfuss, Bill Murray
MPAA rating: PG

Dr. Leo Marvin is a cold-hearted, career-oriented psychiatrist who's definitely on his way to the top. He has a successful practice and a best-selling book, and he's planned a month's vacation in New

Hampshire, where the *Good Morning America* crew will do a show about him. But fate plays a cruel joke on Leo when a colleague sends him a patient named Bob Wiley. Bob is so crippled with neuroses that he can barely leave his apartment and worse, he's the terror of psychiatrists everywhere. When Leo tells Bob that he's going away for a month, Bob will have none of it. He uses subterfuge to locate Leo's isolated summer home where he finds the egomaniacal Leo, and makes his life hell. Refusing to go away, Bob befriends Leo's family, upstages him during the *Good Morning America* interview and, most astonishing of all, gets better. Leo, meantime, becomes angrier and angrier until he's positively beserk with rage and ultimately needs therapy himself.

CAUTION: This film is not likely to be of interest to anyone under the age of ten. Bob, in order to prove to himself that he doesn't have Tourette Syndrome (which causes involuntary outbursts of obscenity), swears voluntarily. Leo goes mad and his homicidal mania is a little unnerving.

GO: The film touches on the ways relationships can heal.

✗ WHERE THE RED FERN GROWS

Doty-Dayton Productions
1974
90 minutes
Directed by: Norman Tokar
Starring: James Whitmore,
    Beverly Garland, Stewart Petersen
MPAA rating: G

(continued on next page)

Billy Coleman is a young boy growing up in the Ozarks, whose heart's desire is a pair of hounds. He asks his grandfather to explain why it is that though he's been asking God for puppies for as long as he can remember, he still has none. His grandfather replies that God will do His share, but that Billy will have to meet Him halfway. So Billy goes out and works at every possible odd job and finally earns the money to buy the dogs. He begins training them at once and soon becomes a champion coon hunter. Then one night, Billy and his dogs accidentally surprise a cougar. The dogs save Billy's life, but one is killed and the other, crushed by grief, dies a few days later. The dogs are buried side by side, and a rare red fern, the symbol of enduring love from a native legend, grows between the graves.

✗STOP: The dogs die and when Billy fights with two mountain boys one of them trips, hits his head and dies.

GO: This is a terrific film about a boy with grit, determination and the will to succeed. ∎

✗ WHERE THE RED FERN GROWS II

Morningstar
1992
92 minutes
Directed by: Jim McCullough
Starring: Wilford Brimley, Doug McKeon, Chad McQueen
MPAA rating: G

Billy Coleman, now a bitter amputee, returns to Louisiana after a harrowing four years of service in World War II. At home, his grandfather reminds him of the deal he made with God as a child, and tells him to go out and look in the barn; there, Billy finds a pair of Redbone hound pups and his old coonskin hat. At first, Billy doesn't want the dogs, but when his sister tells him that their grandfather has only a few weeks to live, he reluctantly agrees to train them. But the weeks turn into months, and Grandpa is looking better than ever. Even so, Billy turns down a job offer in California because of his grandfather's health. Grandpa overhears this, and on the next coon hunt, when one of the hounds is killed, explains to Billy that if one surrounds oneself with living things, sooner or later, one watches them die. On the way back to the farm he dies himself and, after the funeral, Billy gives the remaining dog to a young friend and prepares to go to his new life in California.

✗STOP: There is much grief in this film. Billy's grandfather dies and so does one of the beloved dogs. Billy is forced to give away the other dog.

CAUTION: Billy's embittered description of battlefield surgery may disturb some young viewers. Also, the concept of running down raccoons may upset some children.

GO: This film is a surprisingly profound examination of the pain and joy of life itself.

✗ WHITE FANG

CAUTION: A third member of Jack's party is killed during the wolves' assault.

GO: Despite the above-mentioned cautions, this is an exciting adventure story with minimal violence.

■

Walt Disney Home Video
1991
109 minutes
Directed by: Randal Kleiser
Starring: Klaus Maria Brandauer,
    Ethan Hawke, Pius Savage
MPAA rating: PG

At the turn of the century, Jack Conroy, a young man on his way to his father's claim in the Yukon, hooks up with Alex Larsen, a friend of his father's. Along the way, they are trailed by a wolf-pack, and during a mishap on some thin ice lose their ammunition. The wolves, as if aware of the fact that their prey is helpless, close in for the attack. One of the she-wolves is killed, and her cub, White Fang, is forced to travel the frozen wasteland alone, living by his wits. Then one day he's caught in an Indian snare and turned into a sled dog. Meanwhile, Alex and Jack reach the Klondike and travel up the Yukon River to the Indian village where, coincidentally, White Fang lives. Jack and the savage wolf strike up a tentative kinship, and each in turn saves the other from certain death — Jack from a grizzly and White Fang from an implacable pit bull in a dog fight. Jack then wins White Fang's love with his patient kindness, and in the end, White Fang repays this kindness by again saving Jack's life.

✗ **STOP:** The fight between White Fang and the pit bull is in agonizing slow motion. Alex is travelling with the corpse of a friend, and at one point the coffin spills open and the blue-faced corpse tumbles out.

WHITE FANG 2: MYTH OF THE WHITE WOLF

White Fang 2: Myth of the White Wolf
Walt Disney
1994
Directed By: Ken Olin
Starring: Scott Bairstow, Charmaine Craig, Alfred Molina, Geoffrey Lewis
116 minutes
MPAA Rating: PG

Jack Conroy has returned to San Francisco to help deal with the devastation of the 1906 earthquake, leaving his friend Henry Casey to run their Alaskan claim. Meanwhile, the nearby Haida Indians are starving, for the caribou that used to come every year have mysteriously vanished. Worse, all the Haida warriors who had set out in search of the caribou have not returned. Concurrently, Henry has assembled a small fortune in gold, and decides to take it to town. But his boating skills are obviously inferior to his mining skills, because he manages to get himself into a tight spot in some rapids and nearly drowns, losing boat, gold and dog in the process. Luckily, Chief Joseph of the Haida has had a prophetic dream, and has sent his daughter Lily on a quest for the White Wolf, a great warrior who will find the caribou. She comes across Henry and saves his life, bringing him back to her village. Lily and Joseph insist that Henry is in fact the White Wolf, but Henry, convinced that they've got the wrong guy, excuses himself and heads back into town. A series of events convince Henry that he should go back to the Haida village. There he is reunited with White Fang, trains as a Haida warrior, and then sets out in search of the caribou with Lily's valiant brother Peter. Very soon the pair discover the reason why no other Haida warriors have returned. Leland Drury, an evil profiteer disguised as a minister, is running an illegal gold mine. The results of his mining have blocked off the canyon through which the caribou migrate, and all the Haida sent to investigate have either been killed or captured and forced to work as slaves in the mine. Peter is killed by the nasty miner-types, but the courageous Lily arrives just in time to save Henry (again). Together, Lily and Henry defeat the evil miners, blow up the mine, free the caribou and save the Haida. White Fang helps and gets a wolf girl-friend; Leland gets run over by stampeding caribou; Lily and Henry tie the knot; and Peter comes back as a raven.

✗STOP: Peter dies (he is, however, killed off-camera).

CAUTION: There is some violence, and a bit of 1906 trash-talking ("get dressed, you pig"). A bad guy sits down on a bear trap. The evil miners hit their Indian slaves. Leland gets trampled by caribou (but we're glad). We get a glimpse of a slain Indian warrior in a state of relatively advanced decomposition.

GO: A good adventure film, with clear delineations between good and evil. Lily is a very positive role model, strong, capable and attractive (as mentioned, she saves Henry's life twice). Henry abandons avarice for true love.

✗ WHO FRAMED ROGER RABBIT?

Touchstone Home Video
1988
104 minutes
Directed by: Robert Zemeckis
Starring: Bob Hoskins, Christopher Lloyd, Joanna Cassidy
MPAA rating: PG

Los Angeles in 1947 is a place where humans and animated beings coexist. The cartoons are an underclass, living mainly in an area called Toontown, where they work in low-class jobs and in show business. A few of the toons are stars, like Roger Rabbit, who's one of the box-office mainstays of media mogul R.K. Maroon. But Roger is losing his concentration and costing Maroon a fortune. The reason, allegedly, is that Roger's wife Jessica is having an affair with Marvin Acme, the novelty king who owns Toontown. So Maroon hires Eddie Valiant, a boozy, down and out human private eye, who agrees to get some dirt on Jessica. After catching Jessica's racy act at the seedy Ink and Paint Club, Eddie photographs her and Marvin playing "patty-cake" in a back room. (They really *are* playing "patty-cake.") When Roger sees the pictures he goes berserk, and the next day Marvin Acme is murdered. Though the evil Judge Doom (inventor of Dip, the only substance which can destroy a toon) is sure that Roger is guilty, Eddie is equally convinced of the rabbit's innocence and sets out to set things right. Then a terrible conspiracy is revealed: Judge Doom intends to secure ownership of

Toontown and destroy it to make room for an expressway. In the end, the characters meet at the Acme Gag Factory for a final confrontation with the Judge, who is not at all what he seems to be.

✗STOP: Judge Doom is slowly run over by a steamroller and is then revealed to be a toon himself, and a real figure of terror. His eyes swirl and glow and his hand turns into a frightening buzzsaw. Roger and Jessica are bound together and are repeatedly in terrible danger of being sprayed with Dip.

CAUTION: This isn't really a kids' film. One preteen we know remarked, "I saw this film when I was eleven, and I had to watch it five times before I understood it." The figure of Jessica Rabbit is cut in the 1950s full-figure girl mold, and her ample charms are prominently displayed.

GO: This is simply one of the most mind-boggling achievements in film history. The combination of live-action and animation used new techniques that set a precedent for films that followed. This film won four Academy Awards including a 1988 Special Achievement Oscar.

WILD HEARTS CAN'T BE BROKEN

Walt Disney/Buena Vista Home Video
1991
90 minutes
Directed by: Steve Miner
Starring: Gabrielle Anwar, Cliff Robertson,
    Michael Schoeffling
MPAA rating: G

Just after the Great Depression, orphaned teenager Sonora Webster and her younger sister are taken in rather unwillingly by their aunt, who already has too many mouths to feed. When Sonora sees an ad for "diving girls" in Atlantic City she grasps the chance to escape being turned over to the state. Arriving in Atlantic City she lands a job mucking out stables with Dr. Carver's travelling show which includes his son Al and the diving girl Marie. Sonora is determined to make it as a diving girl in spite of the dangers (this stunt, very popular in sideshows of the era, requires a horse and rider to dive from a very high platform into a pool of water) and tries to prove her horsemanship by training a wild horse for Dr. Carver. When Marie is injured, Sonora gets her chance. She is very successful at diving, but less so at love, as her romance with Al is stalled when he walks out on his father. He writes, but Dr. Carver doesn't give Sonora the letters. Eventually, there is a reconciliation but Dr. Carver dies soon after and Al is left to manage the troupe before a big show. Sonora is obliged to ride a skittish horse who makes a very bad jump from the diving tower. Because of the accident, she goes blind. Through sheer determination she continues to dive, and the audience is none the wiser. She performs for the next eleven years and marries Al. Based on a true story.

CAUTION: Sonora and her sister lead a hard life, devoid of parents and unwanted by their aunt. Sonora leaves her sister in order to venture out into the world. The film is emotionally intense. The sight of horses diving from high towers is nerve-wracking and may disturb young horse lovers. Although there is no sex, violence or swearing, the film is about a tragic accident that is permanent.

GO: A story of perseverance and courage. Sonora is a good role-model for young girls although stubborn, she is determined to live her dreams. The men in the film are kind and supportive.

AGES 10 TO 13

✗ WILLOW

RCA/Columbia
1988
130 minutes
Directed by: Ron Howard
Starring: Billy Barty, Warwick Davis,
 Val Kilmer, Jean Marsh
MPAA rating: PG

Willow begins: "It is a time of dread. Seers have foretold the birth of a child who will bring about the downfall of the powerful Queen Bavmorda." Seizing all pregnant women in the realm, the evil queen vows to destroy the child when it is born. But when the baby of the prophecy is born, it's spirited out of the queen's dungeons by a midwife. With a pack of Bavmorda's wolves close on her trail, the midwife places the baby on a small raft and floats her down river where she is taken in by Willow Ufgood, an unsuccessful and diminutive magician. He keeps the child until a pack of the queen's wolves falls upon his village, and he decides to take the baby back. On the way he is joined by a criminal named Madmartigan, a pair of Brownies and a sorceress. Together they battle trolls, a two-headed dragon and the queen's soldiers. The baby then falls into the hands of the sinister General Kael, who takes her to the evil queen. And in the film's climax, as the queen conducts the ritual which will banish the baby to everlasting night, Willow dupes her into destroying herself.

✗ **STOP:** This film is violent. The midwife is torn to pieces by hideous wolves, which then run snarling through a village, tearing cradles apart and terrorizing the inhabi-

tants. Combat scenes, though virtually bloodless, are fierce in the extreme. Swords cleave bodies with meaty impact, spears and arrows thud on the mark, fists crunch facial bones and the slain die with their eyes open. Magical transformations are intensely biological, depicted as agonizing and accentuated with sound.

GO: Despite the pervasive violence, the film is extremely well-made. The cinematography, editing, special effects and art direction are superb; the performances are generally strong, and the fantasy world is brought vividly to life. Here, loyalty, courage, perseverence and love allow even the smallest underdog to triumph in the end.

✗ THE WITCHES

Warner Home Video
1990
92 minutes
Directed by: Nicolas Roeg
Starring: Anjelica Huston, Rowan Atkinson,
 Bill Paterson, Brenda Blethyn
MPAA rating: PG

When Luke's parents die in a car crash, he moves with his grandmother to England where they live happily enough until his grandmother develops a respiratory ailment. As part of her treatment, they plan a stay at a seaside resort. But their stay coincides with an international witches' convention, and while Luke is playing in the convention hall he overhears a dastardly plot: the witches have developed a formula to turn every child in Britain into a mouse. Luke knows from the stories his grandmother has told him that witches hate children and he watches in horror while the witches try their formula on an innocent boy. Luke is next. But even as a mouse, Luke is courageous and resourceful. And with his grandmother's help, he steals the witches' potion, sneaks into the kitchen and doctors the soup intended for their banquet. The witches thus disposed of, Luke (still a mouse) returns home with his grandmother and lives in a little model house. Only the timely arrival of a white witch restores him to human form.

✗**STOP:** This film is not for young children! The witches (The Grand High Witch in particular) are hideous, scary allegories of child abductors.

CAUTION: In one of Luke's grandmother's stories, a witch steals a young girl and puts her into a painting, where her parents are forced to watch her grow old, imprisoned on the canvas. When Luke is a mouse, a cook cuts off half his tail; it bleeds. In one scene a witch tries to lure Luke out of a tree with a variety of enticements and this may disturb some children.

GO: Brilliant special effects highlight Roald Dahl's tale of childhood courage in the face of terror and adversity.

WONDERWORKS SERIES

Public Media Video
1986-1991

This is a collection of live-action films produced in a variety of countries including Britain, Africa, Australia and the U.S., that are of interest to children and teens. They are often about issues or situations of concern to young people, or are based on best-selling books. The aim of the studio is to present high quality children's drama with uplifting messages. The films are award-winning and feature well-known actors. Often shown on PBS and the Disney Channel, the Wonderworks series includes comedy, drama, fantasy, adventure and mystery. The titles include:

African Journey

Starring: Jason Blicker, Alan Jordan

174 minutes on two tapes

In this fast-paced dramatic adventure, Luke, a high-school student from Canada, and Themba, an African youth, forge a lasting friendship as each discovers how much they have in common despite their vastly different cultures.

Almost Partners

58 minutes
Starring: Paul Sorvino, Mary Wickes

A comic whodunit about an unlikely duo, a tough New York City detective and a fourteen-year-old amateur sleuth, who join forces to investigate the disappearance of her grandfather's ashes and wind up being friends.

And the Children Shall Lead

60 minutes
Starring: LeVar Burton, Danny Glover

A young black girl attempts to advance the rights of blacks in a sleepy Mississippi town in this dramatic exploration of the civil rights movement.

The Boy Who Loved Trolls

58 minutes
Starring: Susan Anton, Sam Waterston

Based on the play *Otoed* by John Wheatcroft. Fantasy and reality are poignantly blended in this rites-of-passage story about a twelve-year-old boy's struggle to retain his childhood dreams while searching for a mythical troll.

Bridge to Terabithia

58 minutes
Starring: Annette O'Toole, Julian Coutts

Based on the book by Katherine Patterson. A story of the special bond between a young boy and girl who share the joy of friendship in the magical kingdom of "Terabithia."

■

Brother Future

116 minutes
Starring: Frank Converse, Phill Lewis

T.J., an inner-city Detroit youth, is knocked unconscious while fleeing police and wakes up in Charleston, South Carolina in 1822 where he is taken as a slave.

CAUTION: There are scenes in which black slaves are whipped.

The Canterville Ghost

58 minutes
Starring: Richard Kiley, Mary Wickes

Based on the story by Oscar Wilde. An American family encounters the ghost of Canterville Chase in an old English manor house.

■

The Chronicles of Narnia

169 minutes each
Starring: Sophie Cook, Richard Dempsey, Barbara Kellerman, Jeffrey Perry, Jonathan Scott, Sophie Wilcox

Based on the books by C.S. Lewis

■

The Lion, the Witch and the Wardrobe In a strange castle in the English countryside, four children open the door of an old wardrobe and find themselves transported to the magical kingdom of Narnia, which is under the spell of the evil White Witch.

■

Prince Caspian and the Voyage of the Dawn Treader (168 minutes on two tapes) The mystical land of Narnia and the treacherous high seas provide the backdrop for the thrilling adventures of Prince Caspian, who must defeat corrupt King Miraz and restore Narnia to its former glory.

■

The Silver Chair (Starring: Tom Baker, Richard Henders, Camilla Power, David Thwaites; 168 minutes on two tapes)

At boarding school, Eustace and his friend Jill discover the magical land of Narnia behind an old wooden door. Aslan the lion king charges them with the dangerous task of finding the missing heir to King Caspian's throne, and they must battle the forces of evil to free the enchanted prince.

■

(For more detailed reviews of these videos, see individual titles)

Clowning Around

174 minutes on two tapes.
Starring: Ernie Dingo, Van Johnson,
  Rebecca Smart, Clayton Williamson

Based on the novel *Clowning Sim*
by David Martin. Fourteen-year-old
Sim has grown up in a series of
foster and welfare homes. Although
life is tough, he has survived by
dreaming of becoming a world-class
clown. Against the odds and his
new foster parents' objections, he is
determined to make his dream a
reality.

■

Daniel and the Towers

58 minutes
Starring: Miguel Alamo, Alan Arbus

Based on a story inspired by the
work of Sam Rodia. Streetwise
ten-year-old Daniel Guerra forms an
unlikely friendship with eccentric
Italian immigrant sculptor Sam
Rodia, who spent over thirty years
building the Watts Towers in Los
Angeles. Through Rodia Daniel
gains hope and a new set of values,
and he crusades to save Rodia's
lifework when the county slates it for
demolition.

The Fig Tree

Starring: Olivia Cole,
  William Converse-Roberts.

58 minutes

A young girl who is learning to cope
with her fear of death becomes
aware of the cycle of life in rural
Texas. Set during the early 1900s,
this is based on the Pulitzer
Prize-winning story by Katherine
Anne Porter

Frogs!

116 minutes
Starring: Shelley Duvall, Elliott Gould,
  Scott Grimes, Judith Ivey, Paul Williams.

In this whimsical sequel to the
award-winning 1987 movie *Frog*,
Gus, a would-be lounge singer (who
is really a 900-year-old frog prince)
once again disrupts the life of his
friend Arlo. Now Arlo must deal with
a wicked witch and a polluted city
pond in addition to his own teenage
trials and tribulations.

A Girl of the Limberlost

110 minutes
Starring: Joanna Cassidy, Annette O'Toole

Based on the book by Gene
Stratton Porter. The story of a
teenage girl's struggle in the 1900s
to get an education and find a
relationship with her mother.

(See Ages 6-10 for detailed
synopsis)
■

Gryphon

58 minutes
Starring: Amanda Plummer

Based on a short story by Charles
Baxter. A tough Hispanic boy in an
inner-city school gets a taste of the
extraordinary when his life is
transformed by a substitute teacher
with magical powers. (See Ages
6-10 for detailed synopsis)

The Haunting
Of Barney Palmer

> 58 minutes
> Starring: Alexis Banas, Ned Beatty,
>   Meredith Braun, Eleanor Gibson,
>   Michelle Leuthart

Adapted for the screen by Margaret Mahy from her novel *The Haunting*. In this suspenseful tale of the supernatural, young Barney Palmer fears he has inherited the Scholar family curse when he is haunted by the spirit of his dead great-uncle. There is more here than meets the eye. His older sister Troy is guarding a shocking secret.

CAUTION: Spooky old house, apparitions, scary music, nasty family members — this is the stuff of horror movies, and too intense for those easily frightened.

■

Hector's Bunyip

> 58 minutes
> Starring: Scott Bartle, Robert Coleby,
>   Barbara Stephens

A delightful comedy about a child who brings his eccentric family closer together with the help of his bunyip, a giant, scaly, possibly imaginary creature.

Hiroshima Maiden

> 60 minutes
> Starring: Susan Blakely, Richard Masur,
>   Tamlyn Tomita

The gripping story of a young Japanese girl who comes to America for plastic surgery to correct scarring caused by the atomic bomb, and the impact she has on a teenage boy, his friends and his family.

The Hoboken
Chicken Emergency

> 58 minutes
> Starring: Gabe Kaplan, Dick Van Patten.

Based on the book by D. Manus Pinkwater. Young Arthur Bobowicz brings home a 266-pound live chicken!

■

Home at Last

> 58 minutes
> Starring: Adrien Brody, Frank Converse

Billy, a streetwise kid from New York City, is sent to a Nebraska farm to live with the Andersons, who are Swedish immigrants. At first fearful and resentful, he clashes with his new father and family. It takes a crisis that threatens them all for Billy to find his inner strength and realize that he truly belongs. Based on the real Orphan Trains which resettled children in the Midwest at the turn of the century.

The House of Dies Drear

> 116 minutes
> Starring Moses Gunn Howard Rollins Jr.

Based on the book by Virginia Hamilton. A modern-day black family moves into a house haunted by the murdered abolitionist Dies Drear in the days of slavery and "underground railroads."

■

How to Be a Perfect Person in Just Three Days

59 minutes
Starring: Wallace Shawn

Based on the book by Stephen Manes.Twelve-year-old nerd Milo seeks guidance from a specialist in the not-so-perfect science of perfectology.

■

Jacob Have I Loved

58 minutes
Starring: Bridget Fonda, Jenny Robertson

Based on the book by Katherine Peterson. A moving portrayal of a teenage girl's struggles to overcome her jealousy of her twin sister.

■

Konrad

116 minutes
Starring: Ned Beatty, Huckleberry Fox, Polly Holiday

Based on the book *Konrad ode Das Kind aus der Konservenbuechse* by Christine Noestlinger. Konrad, a factory-made instant child, perfect in every way, is mistakenly delivered to the eccentric Mrs. Bartolotti. When the factory realizes its mistake it demands Konrad's return, but Konrad's new mom has other ideas.

(See Ages 6-10 for detailed synopsis.)

■

A Little Princess

177 minutes
Starring: Nigel Havers, Amelia Shankley

An award-winning story based on the book by Frances Hodgson Burnett about the little rich girl who becomes a penniless orphan. Deluxe two-tape set.

■

The Lone Star Kid

58 minutes
Starring: Charlie Daniels, James Earl Jones

Based on a true story. 11-year-old Brian Zimmerman makes history when he is elected mayor of his Texas town.

Maricela

58 minutes
Starring: Carlina Cruz, Linda Lavin, Lisa Marie Simmon

A young girl struggles to find her place in American culture when her mother, who was a schoolteacher in El Salvador, now must work as a live-in housekeeper to an affluent family.

The Mighty Pawns

60 minutes
Starring: Alfonso Ribeiro, Paul Winfield

Chess boards and chess men inspire and rechannel the energies of inner-city kids.

Miracle at Moreaux

> 60 minutes
> Starring: Robert Joy, Loretta Swit.

Based on the book *Twenty and Ten* by Claire Huchet Bishop. In a powerful drama based on a true story, a nun and her young charges risk their lives to protect three Jewish children fleeing from the Nazis during World War II.

■

Necessary Parties

> 111 minutes
> Starring: Alan Arkin, Julie Hagerty

Based on the book by Barbara Dana. A fifteen-year-old boy tries to head off his parents' divorce by launching an unprecedented lawsuit.

■

Runaway

> 59 minutes
> Starring: Gavin Allen, Charles S. Dutton

Based on the book *Slakes Limbo* by Felice Holman. The story of a boy who goes "underground" and lives for 121 days in the New York subway because he blames himself for the accidental death of his friend.

■

Sweet 15

> 108 minutes
> Starring: Karla Montana, Tony Plana.

A sensitive coming-of-age tale about a fifteen-year-old Mexican-American girl who discovers that her father is not a U.S. citizen and may be deported just as she is about to celebrate her "quinceanera."

Taking Care of Terrific

> Starring: Jackie Burroughs,
> Melvin Van Peebles.

58 minutes

A compassionate and imaginative teenager, her boyfriend and a sheltered little boy hook up with a street musician to plan a fun and joyous evening for several bag ladies living in a local park. However, their well-intended efforts get them all in trouble.

Walking on Air

> 59 minutes
> Starring: Lynn Redgrave, Jordan Marder

Based on a story idea by Ray Bradbury. Determined to conquer the odds and prove his own abilities, a boy in a wheelchair fights to realize his dream of walking in space.

A Waltz
Through the Hills

> 116 minutes
> Starring: Dan O'Herlihy

Based on the book by G.M. Glaskin. Outfitted only with courage, two orphans embark on a dangerous, secret journey through the wilds of the Australian outback in a fast-paced adventure story.

■

Words By Heart

Starring: Robert Hooks, Charlotte Rae,
Alfre Woodard

116 minutes

In this evocative, inspiring drama, a black family in the early 19th century lives in an all-white Missouri town. Based on the book by Ouida Sebestyen.

■

You Must Remember This

102 minutes
Starring: Robert Guillaume, Tim Reid

A budding basketball star discovers that her beloved great-uncle, now a barber, was one of the first great black film directors in the late '40s. She helps him to accept his past and, in the process, unearths a rich cultural legacy.

YOUNG EINSTEIN

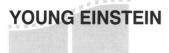

Warner Home Video
1988
90 minutes
Directed by: Yahoo Serious
Starring: Odile de Clezio, John Howard,
Yahoo Serious
MPAA rating: PG

Albert Einstein, the twenty-year-old son of an apple farmer, isn't cut out to follow in his father's footsteps. He's an environmentalist, and a scientist. For example, when a crate of apples accidentally drops on his head, he formulates his first complete scientific principle: for every action there is an equal and opposite reaction. And he proves it, by building a catapult and launching himself sky-high. It's at this time that Albert's father reveals a well-kept family secret: his granddad was also a great inventor; he died in a mysterious accident while trying to put bubbles in beer. Well, Albert decides to continue where his grandfather left off, and bends a beer atom, setting off a miniature atomic blast that does indeed put bubbles in the brew. Armed with his new formula, $E=MC^2$, he sets off for the mainland patent office. On the way, he meets the delectable Marie Curie and the evil snob Preston Preston. Preston has Albert committed to the asylum for mad scientists, steals Albert's formula and begins the process by which carbonated beer will be mass-produced. There's just one problem: Preston Preston has inadvertently created the first atomic bomb. Now Albert must escape from the asylum, get to the award ceremonies in Paris and defuse the bomb before it goes off.

CAUTION: In one scene, the chef in the insane asylum makes a kitten pie with live kittens. There is some sexual innuendo.

GO: Albert saves the kittens. And as for the sexual innuendo, Albert's innocence is cleverly used as a foil; in other words, what he doesn't get, young viewers won't get either. This is a truly off-beat film with genuinely funny moments and something for everyone.

✗ YOUNG SHERLOCK HOLMES

Paramount Home Video
1985
109 minutes
Directed by: Barry Levinson
Starring: Roger Ashton-Griffiths, Alan Cox,
    Earl Rhodes, Nicholas Rowe, Nigel Stock,
    Sophie Ward
MPAA rating: PG-13

In the heart of the Victorian era, young John Watson is sent to a new school in London. There he meets young Holmes, who astounds him by deducing the details of his life from a moment's observation, and Elizabeth, Holmes's true love. The three soon learn that prominent citizens are dying of unknown causes, but only Holmes believes it's murder. He has noticed in the obituaries that victims were all in the graduating class of 1809. However, Scotland Yard will have nothing to do with his theories, and it isn't until Elizabeth's Uncle Waxplatter becomes the next victim that Holmes takes up the case with vigor. His only clues are Waxplatter's last words, and a blowpipe of exotic construction. The friends trace the pipe's origins and discover an ancient death-cult connected to the destruction of an Egyptian village, and to a high ranking faculty member of the school itself. In the end, the cult kidnaps Elizabeth to turn her into a mummy, setting in motion a climactic chain of heart-stopping events.

✗STOP: The hallucinations experienced by the drugged murder victims are *extremely* frightening and intense. When the murderer fires at Holmes, Elizabeth steps in front to shield him and is shot herself. Elizabeth dies tragically in Holmes' arms.

CAUTION: The action is too intense and the mystery too complicated for most young children.

GO: An exciting action mystery in an historical setting, this film is best selected for pre-teens and up and may kick-start an interest in the Sherlock Holmes stories.

AGES 10 TO 13

398

Chapter 7

Videos Listed by Theme

These lists have been compiled over the years from customer requests at our business, The Original Kids' Video Store. Parents, teachers, librarians and caregivers have asked for title suggestions to fulfill specific functions. We hope these lists will be helpful to you in selecting suitable material for parties, get-togethers, sleep-overs or special occasions. These lists are in no way to be taken as representative of *everything* that exists on videotape, only to give a head start in a direction. Only material that is considered by most people as suitable for children and teens has been included.

A warning: since no ratings accompany these titles, please use discretion in selecting the titles for small children. The onus of selection is on the responsible adult.

Some of the titles listed are currently out of print but have been included because they are still available for rental at some outlets.

Many, but not all, of the titles listed here are reviewed in this book. You can refer to individual reviews for further information.

For more extensive listings write to us at:

Children's Video Services Inc.
40 Scollard Street
Toronto, Ontario M5R 3S1
Canada

Animals (domesticated or trained)

A Summer to Remember
Baby Animals Just Wanna Have Fun
Cat from Outer Space, The
Flipper
Flipper and the Elephant
Flipper's New Adventure
Flipper's Odyssey
Ladyhawke
Old MacDonald's Farm
That Darn Cat
Three Lives of Thomasina, The

Animals (wild)

Animals Are Beautiful People:
  The Secret Life of Wildlife
Baby Animals
Baby Animals in the Wild
Bear, The
Big Cats of the Big Top
Born Free
Cat, The
Challenge to White Fang
Charlie and the Talking Buzzard
Charlie the Lonesome Cougar
Christian the Lion
Clarence the Cross-Eyed Lion
Day with the Animals, A: Kidsongs
Doctor Doolittle
Dolphin Adventure (caution)
Flight of the Grey Wolf
Goldy 2–The Saga of the Golden Bear
Goldy–The Last of the Golden Bears
King of the Grizzlies
Legend of Lobo, The
Legend of Black Thunder Mountain, The
Let's Go to the Zoo with Captain Kangaroo
Life and Times of Grizzly Adams, The
Living Free
Lorne Green's New Wilderness series
Monkey Folk, The
Mother Nature Tales of Discovery series
Coastal Habitats series (2 titles)
Forest Habitats series (3 titles)
Mountain Habitats series (3 titles)
Nursery Habitats series (3 titles)
Napoleon and Samantha

National Geographic series*

Cheetah
Creatures of the Mangrove
Elephant
Lions of the African Night
Realm of the Alligator

Reptiles and Amphibians
Sharks
The Grizzlies
The Secret Leopard
Whales
Nature: Leopard A Darkness in the Grass
Never Cry Wolf
Nikki: Wild Dog of the North
Really Wild Animals series (6 titles)
Ring of Bright Water
Sharks: The True Story
Sharon, Lois and Bram at the Zoo
Tadpole and the Whale
White Fang
Wildlife International series
Animal Babies
California Odyssey
Creatures of the Coral Reef
Galapagos Land and Sea
In the Arms of the Octopus
Last Lords of the Bush
Rocky Mountain Glaciers
Sharks of Eniwetok
World of the Canada Goose
Zaire–Tracks of the Gorilla
World of Discovery series (5 titles)
Zoo Babies

Animation and Live-Action, Combined

Bedknobs & Broomsticks
Dot and Keeto
Dot and the Bunny
Dot and the Kangaroo
Dot and the Koala
Dot and the Whale
Dot Goes to Hollywood
Dunder Klumpen
Jack and the Beanstalk
Light Princess, The
Mary Poppins
Pete's Dragon
So Dear to My Heart
The Snow Queen (BFS)
Three Caballeros
Who Framed Roger Rabbit?

Art

Don't Eat the Pictures: Sesame Street at the
  Metropolitan Museum of Art
Draw and Color with Uncle Fred series (3 titles)
Draw Squad with Capt. Mark Kistler series (3 titles)
Hideaways, The
How to Draw Comics the Marvel Way
Let's Draw!
Squiggles Dots and Lines

* note: only the National Geographics that do not
have scenes of violence against animals are listed.

Vincent and Me
Wow, You're a Cartoonist

Balloons/Ballooning

Around the World in Eighty Days
Charlie and the Great Balloon Chase
Fantastic Balloon Voyage
Five Weeks in a Balloon
Lassie's Greatest Adventure
Let the Balloon Go
Mysterious Island
Night Crossing
Voyage En Balloon

Based on Books

5,000 Fingers of Dr.T (Dr. Seuss)
20,000 Leagues Under the Sea (Jules Verne)
Abel's Island (William Steig)
Adventures of Huckleberry Finn (1939)
  (Mark Twain)
Alice in Wonderland (Lewis Carroll)
Angel and the Soldier-Boy, The (Peter Collington)
Animal Fables of Leo Lionni (Leo Lionni)
Anne of Green Gables (Lucy Maude Montgomery)
Any Friend of Nicholas Nickleby Is a friend of Mine
  (Ray Bradbury)
Arnold of the Ducks (Mordicai Gerstein)
Around the World in 80 Days (Jules Verne)
Babar the Little Elephant (Laurent de Brunhoff)
Ballet Shoes (Noel Streatfield)
Bedknobs & Broomsticks (Mary Norton)
Berenstain Bears series (Stan & Jan Berenstain)
Big Red (Jim Kjelgaard)
Black Arrow, The (Robert Louis Stevenson)
Black Beauty (Anna Sewell)
Black Stallion, The (Walter Farley)
Born Free (Joy Adamson)
Call of the Wild (Jack London)
Charlotte's Web (E. B. White)
Chitty Chitty Bang Bang (Ian Fleming)
Chocolate Fever (Robert Kimmel Smith)
Cry in the Wild, A (*Hatchet* by Gary Paulsen)
Curious George (Margaret & H.A. Rey)
Dragon That Wasn't (Or Was He?), The
  (Marten Toondner)
Electric Grandmother, The (Ray Bradbury)
Elephant's Child ("Just So Stories"/Rudyard
  Kipling)
Emil and the Detectives (Erich Kastner)
Encyclopedia Brown (Donald J. Sobol)
Fantastic Balloon Voyage (Jules Verne)
Five Lionni Classics (Leo Lionni)
Gold Bug, The (Edgar Allan Poe)
Granpa (John Burningham)
Gulliver's Travels (Jonathon Swift)
Hans Brinker (Mary Mapes Dodge)

Hardy Boys series (Franklin W. Dixon)
Heidi (Johanna Spyri)
Hobbit, The (J. R. R.Tolkien)
How to Eat Fried Worms (Thomas Rockwell)
How to Raise a Street-Smart Child (Grace
  Hechinger)
Incredible Journey, The (Shiela Burnford)
Island of the Blue Dolphins (Scott O'Dell)
Ivanhoe (Sir Walter Scott)
Jacob Two–Two & the Hooded Fang
  (Mordecai Richler)
Journey to the Center of the Earth (Jules Verne)
Kidnapped (Robert Louis Stevenson)
Knights of the Round Table
  (*Le Mort D'Artur* by Mallory)
Land of Faraway, The (Astrid Lindgren)
Lantern Hill (*Jane of Lantern Hill* by
  Lucy Maud Montgomery)
Lassie Come Home (Eric Knight)
Last Unicorn, The (Peter S. Beagle)
Light in the Forest, The (Conrad Richter)
Light Princess, The (George MacDonald)
Lion, the Witch & the Wardrobe, The (C. S. Lewis)
Lion, the Witch & the Wardrobe, The (C. S. Lewis)
Little House on the Prairie series
  (Laura Ingalls Wilder)
Little Lord Fauntleroy (1936)
  (Frances Hodgson Burnett)
Little Mermaid, The (Hans Christian Anderson)
Little Miss (Trouble & Friends) (Roger Hargreaves)
Little Women (1933) (Louisa May Alcott)
Looking for Miracles (A. E. Hochner)
Lost in the Barrens (Farley Mowat)
Madeleine (Ludwig Bemelmans)
Mark Twain and Me
  (*Enchantment* by Dorothy Quick)
Mary Poppins (P. L.Travers)
Miracle Worker, The (the play by William Gibson
  and *The Story of My Life* by Helen Keller)
Misty (Marguerite Henry)
Moonspinners, The (Mary Stewart)
Mouse & His Child, The (Russell Hoban)
Mr. Men (Roger Hargreaves)
My Friend Flicka (Mary O'Hara)
Mysterious Island (Jules Verne)
Nancy Drew series (Carolyn Keene)
Never Cry Wolf (Farley Mowat)
Neverending Story I & II, The (Michael Ende)
Old Yeller (Fred Gipson)
Oliver Twist (1948) (Charles Dickens)
Paddington Bear series (Michael Bond)
Peter Pan (James Barrie)
Phantom Tollbooth, The (Norton Juster)
Pippi Longstocking series (Astrid Lindgren)
Prince and the Pauper (1984), The (Mark Twain)
Princess Bride, The (William Goldman)
Railway Children, The (E. Nesbitt)

Ramona series (Beverley Cleary)
Rebecca of Sunnybrook Farm
  (Kate Douglas Wiggin)
Ring of Bright Water (Gavin Maxwell)
Robinson Crusoe (Robert Louis Stevenson)
Rupert (Alfred Bestall M.B.E)
Secret Garden, The (Frances Hodgson Burnett)
Secret Life of Walter Mitty, The (James Thurber)
Secret of N.I.M.H., The (Robert C. O'Brien)
Selfish Giant (Oscar Wilde)
Seven Alone (Honore Morrow)
Snowman, The (Raymond Briggs)
Swiss Family Robinson (Johann David Wyss)
Sword in the Stone
  (The Once And Future King by T. H. White)
Thomas the Tank Engine series
  (The Rev. W. Audry)
Three Musketeers, The (1948) (Alexandre Dumas)
Three Worlds of Gulliver, The (Jonathon Swift)
Time Machine, The (H.G. Wells)
To Sir with Love (E. R. Braithwaite)
Treasure Island (Robert Louis Stevenson)
Tree Grows in Brooklyn, A (Betty Smith)
Tuck Everlasting (Natalie Babbitt)
Velveteen Rabbit (Margery Williams)
Watership Down (Richard Adams)
Where the Red Fern Grows (Wilson Rawls)
White Fang (Jack London)
Who Has Seen the Wind? (W. O. Mitchell)
Willy Wonka & the Chocolate Factory
  (Charlie & the Chocolate Factory by Roald Dahl)
Wind in the Willows (Kenneth Graham)
Winds of Change
  (The Illiad and The Odyssey by Homer)
Winnie-the-Pooh (A. A. Milne)
Witches, The (Roald Dahl)
Yellow Winton Flyer, The
  ("The Reivers" by William Faulkner)

Note: The Childrens' Circle Collection of 31
videocassettes contains approximately 130
stories, most of them based on books. The Rabbit
Ears Collection of approximately 39 videos are for
the most part based on books, folk tales or
legends.

Camp

Campfire Thrillers
Day at Camp, A: Kidsongs
Ernest Goes to Camp
Kidsongs: A Day at Camp
Looking for Miracles
Parent Trap, The

Caution List

(These films depict the death of a loved one or
beloved animal, or children or animals abandoned
or in state of duress. This, of course, is not a
complete list of all films that contain these
elements, but it will give you an idea of how many
films contain this premise.)

And You Thought *Your* Parents Were Weird
  (the father has apparently committed suicide)
Anne of Green Gables (her adoptive father dies)
Babar (mother shot by hunters)
Bach and Broccoli (orphan)
Bambi (the mother is shot by hunters)
Bear, The (the baby bear's mother dies)
Benji (child kidnapped)
Benji the Hunted (the lion cub is carried off
  by an eagle)
Black Stallion, The (the father dies)
Boy Who Could Fly, The (the autistic boy's
  parents were killed in a plane crash. The girl's
  father committed suicide)
Challengers, The (the father is deceased)
Dark Horse (the mother is deceased)
Dead Poet's Society (teenager commits suicide)
Dog of Flanders, A (the grandfather dies)
Dog Who Stopped the War, The (the dog dies)
Dumbo (the mother is committed)
Flight of the Navigator (separation of child from
  parents)
Ghost Dad (father dies)
Granpa (grandfather dies)
Land Before Time, The (the mother dinosaur dies)
Land of Far Away, The (the parents are deceased)
Legend of the White Horse (the mothers are
  deceased)
Little Heroes (the dog dies)
Little Princess, The (the father dies)
Looking for Miracles (a father dies)
Moon Stallion, The (the father dies)
My Girl (little boy dies)
Old Yeller (the dog has to be shot)
Phar Lap (the horse dies)
Ramona (the pet cat dies)
Shirley Temple movies (she has had more parents
  die than any other child actor)
Tree Grows in Brooklyn, A (the father dies)
Wizard, The (sibling dies; parents are divorced)
Yearling, The (the deer is shot)
Young Magician, The (child taken away from
  parents)
Young Sherlock Holmes (his girlfriend dies)

Computers

Black Hole, The
Explorers
National Geographic: Miniature Miracle The
Computer Chip
Real Genius

Tron
War Games
Weird Science

Cooking

Cooking with Dad
My First Cooking Video
Kids Get Cooking: The Egg

Christmas

A Year Without Santa
All I Want for Christmas
Alvin and the Chipmunks: A Chipmunk Christmas
An American Christmas Carol
Babar and Father Christmas
Babes in Toyland
Baby Songs Christmas
Bear Who Slept Through Christmas, The
Bells of St. Mary's
Benji's Very Own Christmas Story
Berenstain Bears Christmas Tree
Berenstain Bears: Christmas Tree
Bugs Bunny's Looney Christmas Tales
Cabbage Patch Kids Christmas
Cartoon Holidays Featuring Betty Boop
Charlie Brown Christmas, A
Child's Christmas in Wales, A
Christmas Carol, A
Christmas Eve on Sesame Street
Christmas Sing-Along, A
Christmas Story, A (MGM)
Christmas Story, A (Hanna-Barbera)
Christmas Tree, A
Christmas Toy, The
Currier And Ives Christmas, A
Disney Christmas Gift, A
Dot and Santa Claus
Ernest Saves Christmas
Family Circus Christmas, A
Family Circus Christmas, A
For Better or Worse: Bestest Present Ever
Frosty the Snowman
Garfield's Christmas
George and the Christmas Star
Gift of Winter, The
Gumby's Holiday Special
Hanna-Barbera's Christmas Sing-Along
Here Comes Santa Claus
Home Alone
Home Alone 2: Lost in New York
Homecoming, The
    (premier episode of "The Waltons")
House Without a Christmas Tree, A
How the Flinstones Saved Christmas
How the Grinch Stole Christmas
It's a Wonderful Life

Jack Frost
Jetson Christmas Carol, A
Jiminy Cricket's Christmas
Jingle Bell Rap
Little Drummer Boy
Littlest Angel, The
Madeline's Christmas
Merry Mirthworm Christmas, A
MGM Cartoon Magic "Peace On Earth"
Mickey's Christmas Carol
Miracle on 34th Street
Nativity, The
Nightmare Before Christmas, The
Nutcracker Prince, The
Nutcracker: The Motion Picture
One Magic Christmas
Pee-Wee's Christmas Special
Pink Panther Christmas, A
Pinocchio's Christmas
Prancer
Rudolph and Frosty's Christmas in July
Rudolph the Red-Nosed Reindeer
Rudolph's Shiny New Year
Santa Claus Is Coming to Town
Santa Claus: The Movie
Santabear's First Christmas
Santabear's High Flying Adventure
Scrooge
Scrooged
Shari's Christmas Concert
Silent Mouse
Simpson's Christmas Special, The
Small One, The
Snowman, The
Star for Jeremy, A
'Twas The Night Before Christmas
Very Merry Christmas Songs
Very Merry Cricket, A
Walt Disney Christmas, A
Wee Sing: Best Christmas Ever
White Christmas
Yogi Bear's All-Star Comedy Christmas Caper

Circus/Clowns

115th Edition of Barnum & Bailey Ringling
Brothers Circus
116th Edition of Barnum & Bailey Ringling
Brothers Circus
A Day at the Circus: Kidsongs
Big Cats of the Big Top
Big Top Pee Wee
Cirque de Soleil: Nouvelle Experience
Cirque de Soleil: Saltimbanco
Cirque de Soleil: We Re-Invent the Circus
Mickey's Fun Songs: Let's Go to the Circus
Most Death Defying Acts of All Time
National Geographic: Soviet Circus, The

Ringling Bros. Barnum & Bailey Circus
Featuring the Shanghai Acrobats

Dinosaurs

Adventures in Dinosaur City
Baby, Secret of the Lost Legend
Barney and the Backyard Gang series
Curious George and The Dinosaur
Denver the Last Dinosaur series
Dinosaurs, Dinosaurs, Dinosaurs
Dinosaurs! series (6 titles)
    with Walter Cronkite (4 titles)
Dinosaurus! Stone Age Monsters Return to Life
I Love Dinosaurs: The Biggest Dinosaurs
I Love Dinosaurs: The King of the Dinosaurs
Infinite Voyage: The Great Dinosaur Hunt
Invasion of the Robot Dinosaurs
Jurassic Park
Land Before Time, The
Lost in Dinosaur World
Mister Roger's Dinosaurs and Monsters
Nature Series: Learning About Dinosaurs
Nature Series: Vol. 1
    Dinosaurs, Fun, Fact and Fantasy
Nature Series: Vol. 2
    Dinosaurs, Fun, Fact and Fantasy
Planet of the Dinosaurs
Polka Dot Door: Dinosaurs
Reading Rainbow: Digging Up Dinosaurs
Videosaurus series (6 titles)
We're Back!: A Dinosaur Story
What Ever Happened to the Dinosaurs?
Wonders of Earth and Space, The:
    64,000 Years Ago
World's Greatest Dinosaur Video, The

Dogs

Beethoven
Beethoven II
Benji Collection
Big Red
Bingo
Call of the Wild
Challenge to Lassie
Courage of Rin Tin Tin
Digby, The Biggest Dog In the World
Dog Care Video, Guide
Dog of Flanders, A
For the Love of Benji
Great Adventure, The
Greyfriar's Bobby
Homeward Bound
Incredible Journey, The
Iron Will
Lassie Come Home
Lassie's Greatest Adventure

Little Heroes
Magic of Lassie, The
Milo and Otis
Oh Heavenly Dog
Old Yeller
Puppy Pals
Rin Tin Tin in the Paris Conspiracy
Shaggy D.A, The
Shaggy Dog, The
Toby McTeague
Where the Red Fern Grows
Where the Red Fern Grows 2
White Fang

Dragons

Big Little Ticket, The
Dragonslayer
Dragon That Wasn't (Or Was He?), The
Flight of Dragons
Last of the Red Hot Dragons, The
Pete's Dragon
Puff the Magic Dragon
Railway Dragon, The
Reluctant Dragon, The
Sleeping Beauty

Drugs and Drug Rehabilitation

3 Ways to Keep Your Kids Off Drugs
A Hero Ain't Nothing But a Sandwich
Adventures of Rufus and Andy: The Drug Decision
Cartoon All-Stars to the Rescue
Chemical Solutions
Degrassi Talks
Drug "Dialogue" (Health and Welfare Canada)
Drug Free Kids: A Parent's Guide
High on Life Not on Drugs: A Guide for Teens
It's OK to say No to Drugs
Let's Sing and Dance ("Don't Do Drugs")
Right Thing to Do, The (Captain Kangaroo)
StreetNoise

Easter

Berenstain Bears' Easter Surprise, The
Bil Keane's A Family Circus Easter
Bobby Goldsboro's Easter Egg Mornin'
Bugs Bunny's Easter Funnies
Buttons and Rusty and the Easter Bunny
Daffy Duck's Easter Egg-Citement
Easter Bunny Is Coming to Town, The
Easter Story, The
Follow That Bunny
Greatest Adventure Stories from the Bible-
    The Easter Story
Here Comes Peter Cottontail
It's the Easter Beagle, Charlie Brown
Little Sister Rabbit

Peter and the Magic Egg
Teenage Mutant Ninja Turtles: The Turtles'
    Awesome Easter
Will Vinton's Claymation Easter

Educational Home Videos
ABC School House Rock
Grammar Rock
Multiplication Rock
Science Rock
Adventure of the Scrabble People in a Pumpkin
    Full of Nonsense,The
Berenstain Bears series
Cartoon All-Stars to the Rescue
Clifford the Big Red Dog series (6 titles)
Divorce Can Happen to the Nicest People
Donald in Mathmagicland
Get Ready for Math
Get Ready for School
Get Ready to Read
Ghostwriter series
Who Burned Mr. Brinker's Store?
Into the Comics
Ghost Story
Human Race Club, Vols. 1–6
I'm Not Oscar's Friend Anymore
    (Creole, Hug Me, Birds of a Feather)
Ida Fanfanny and Three Magical Tales
Learning the Alphabet with Professor Playtime
Learn About Living series
How Come? Stories, Music and Fun
Mine and Yours: A Story About Sharing
Never Talk to Strangers
Who Will Be My Friend?
Mathnet: The Case of the Unnatural
Mathnet: Treasure in Monterey Bay
Montessori in Your Home
Mr. Men in the Great Alphabet Hunt
Phantom Tollbooth, The
Polka Dot Door series (5 titles)
Pre-school Power: Jacket Flips and Other Tips
    (4 more titles)
Professor Iris series (6 titles)
Reading Rainbow series
Richard Scarry's Best Videos Ever! (6 titles)
Shari Lewis 101 Things to Do
Shari Lewis: Kooky Classics (intro to music)
Shari Lewis: Have I Got a Story for You
Shari Lewis: You Can Be a Magician
Ustinov Reads the Orchestra
Who's Afraid of Opera?
Working with Numbers
Working with Words

English Not Required
Angel and the Soldier Boy, The

ballets
Benji The Hunted
cartoons
Grandpa
Lyric Language series
Paddle to the Sea
Nutcracker: The Motion Pictures
Red Balloon, The
Sign Me-A-Story
Snowman, The

Extra-Terrestrials
Batteries Not Included
Buckaroo Bonsai
Close Encounters of the Third Kind
E.T.: The Extra-Terrestrial
Explorers
Flight of the Navigator
Forbidden Planet
Last Starfighter, The
Mac and Me
Nukie
Spaceballs
Star Trek II: The Wrath of Khan
Star Trek III: The Search for Spock
Star Trek IV: The Voyage Home
Star Trek V: The Final Frontier
Star Trek VI: The Undiscovered Country
Star Trek: The Motion Picture
Star Wars Trilogy
Supergirl
Superman II, III, IV
Superman: The Movie
War of the Worlds

Fitness Videos
American Junior Workout
Baby's First Workout
Baby 'n Momerobics
Baby 'n Daderobics
Dance! Workout with Barbie
Funfit: Mary Lou Retton Workout
Funhouse Fitness: Ages 3–7 The Swamp Stomp
Funhouse Fitness: Ages 7–10 The Funhouse Funk
Karate for Kids
Kids in Motion
Kidzercise
Lori Oats: Workout for Kids
Me and Mom
Mousercise
Teen Steam with Alyssa Milano
Teen Workout, The
Tip Top with Suzy Prudden: Ages 3–6
Tip Top with Suzy Prudden: Ages 7 and over
Workout with Daddy and Me
Workout with Mommy And Me

Yoga for Children
You And Me Kid Vol. 4

Genius Kids

Computer Wore Tennis Shoes, The
Encyclopedia Brown Collection
Explorers
Little Man Tate
Real Genius
Searching for Bobby Fischer

Ghosts

Blackbeard's Ghost
Canterville Ghost, The
Casper's Travels
Casper's Animals Friends
Casper's Favorite Dogs
Casper's Fairy Tales
Casper's Good Deeds
Escape to Witch Mountain
George's Island
Ghost Chase
Ghost Dad
Ghostbusters
Ghostbusters II
Legend of Sleepy Hollow, The
Lonesome Ghosts
Peanut Butter Solution, The
Topper

Halloween

Boy Who Left Home to Learn About the Shivers,
The
Bugs Bunny's Halloween Special
Buttons and Rusty and the Halloween Party in
"Which Witch Is Which?"
Campfire Thrillers
Casper's Halloween
Disney's Cartoon Classics Vol. 13:
Donald's Scary Tales
Disney's Cartoon Classics Vol. 14:
Hallowe'en Haunts
Ernest Scared Stupid
E.T.: The Extra-Terrestrial
Garfield's Halloween Adventure
Ghostly Thrillers
Grandpa's Silly Scaries
Great Bear Scare, The
Halloween Is Grinch Night
Hocus Pocus
It's the Great Pumpkin, Charlie Brown
Legend of Sleepy Hollow, The
Monster Squad
Spaced Invaders
Watcher in the Woods

Horses

150 Years of the Grand National
Black Beauty
Black Stallion Returns
Black Stallion, The
Courage of Black Beauty, The
Dark Horse
Horsemasters, The
International Velvet
Into the West
Legend of the White Horse
Man from Snowy River, The
Misty
Moon Stallion, The
My Friend Flicka
National Velvet
New Adventures of Black Beauty, The
Phar Lap
Prince and the Great Race
Return to Snowy River
Ride a Wild Pony
Stephanie Powers Introduction to
Horseback Riding and Horse Care
Summer of the Colt
Sylvester
White Mane

How-To Videos

101 Things to Do: Shari Lewis
Baseball the Pete Rose Way
Dog Care Video Guide, The
Gymnastics Fun with Bela Karolyi
Here's Howe! (Hockey with Gordie Howe)
Hey, What About Me?: A Video Guide for Brothers
and Sisters of New Babies
Hockey for Kids and Coaches
How to Raise a Street-Smart Child
Karate for Kids
Ken Dryden Hockey series
Kids' Guitar
Let's Build
Let's Draw
Let's Get a Move On!: How To Cope with a Family
Move
Look What I Found
Look What I Made
Look What I Grew
Making and Playing Home-Made Instruments
My First Activity Video
My First Cooking Video
My First Green Video
My First Musical Instument Video
My First Nature Video
My First Science Video
Neat Stuff to Know and Do

Paws, Claws, Feathers, Fins: How to Be
a Responsible Pet Owner
Piggy Banks to Money Markets: A Kid's Guide to
Dollars and Sense
Shari Lewis: Lamb Chop's Play Along! (8 titles)
Stephanie Powers Introduction to
Horseback Riding and Horse Care
Ukulele for Kids
Wayne Gretsky: Above and Beyond
Wayne Gretsky: Hockey My Way

Knights

Adventures of Robin Hood, The
Black Arrow
Brothers Lionheart, The
Dragonslayer
Ivanhoe
Knights of the Round Table
Ladyhawke
Lionheart
Prince Valiant
Robin Hood the Movie (Richard Greene)
Story of Robin Hood, The
Sword and the Rose, The

Learning a Language

The BBC Language Course for Children
Lyric Language series
Spanish Club: Fiesta!
Peli The Clown Vol. 1–3 (Spanish)
Learning to Read
Disney Sing Alongs
Mickey's Fun Songs
My Baby Can Read
Not Now Said the Cow
Learning the Alphabet with Professor Playtime
Richard Scarry's Best ABC Video Ever
Sesame Street Start-to-Read series
Don't Cry, Big Bird
Ernie's Big Mess
Ernie's Little Lie
I Want to Go Home
Sesame Street series
Getting Ready to Read
Learning About Letters
The Alphabet Game

Life Lessons

Aesop's Fables (4 titles)
Baysitters Club Collection, The
Davey and Goliath: School Who Needs It?
Dust Bunny Chronicles, The
Careful Curiosity
Everyone Is Special
Responsibility Is Cool
Billabong Tales with Uncle Colin and Koala Ted

The Creator's Pet (Learning to Be Grateful)
The Cranky Crocodile (Learning to Be Content)
Human Race Club, The
A High Price to Pay
Casey's Revenge
The Fair Weather Friend
The Lean Mean Machine
The Letter on Light Blue Stationary
The Unforgettable Pen Pal
Humpty
Peter and the Magic Seeds
Teeny Time Tune-Ups
Pleasant Dreams (5 titles)
McGee and Me series (12 titles)
Mr. Button Family series (4 titles)
The Penelope Gang (2 titles)
Spin: Secret Adventures #1
Star Quest (5 titles)
Winnie-the-Pooh: Pooh Learning
Making Friends
Helping Others
Sharing and Caring

Magic

Abra-Kid-Abra
Be a Magician
Blockbuster Magic
Magic Secrets
Magical Birthday Party, The
Magic Party Show, The
Shari Lewis You Can Do It

Making a Difference/Overcoming Difficulties

Amazing Grace and Chuck (global social reform)
Brother Sun, Sister Moon (religious reform)
Challengers, The (sexual discrimination)
Dark Horse (physical handicap)
Free Willy (saves a whale)
Girl of the Limberlost (poverty)
Heidi (illness)
Lady Jane (political and social justice)
Let the Balloon Go (physical handicap)
Lost in the Barrens (racial prejudice)
Love Leads the Way (physical handicap)
Mac and Me (physical handicap)
Mask (tolerance and understanding)
Miracle Worker, The (physical handicap)
Romeo and Juliet (hatred and prejudice)
Secret Garden, The (illness)
Seven Alone (pioneering hardships)
Stand and Deliver (culturally disadvantaged)
Summer to Remember, A (physical handicap)
Walking on Air (physical difficulties)
Wild Hearts Can't Be Broken (physical handicap)

The Making of...

Classic Creatures: Return of the Jedi
From Star Wars to Jedi: The Making of a Saga
Great Adventurers and Their Quests:
   Indiana Jones & The Last Crusade
Great Movie Stunts and the Making of
   Raiders of the Lost Ark
Illusion of Life: Wonderful Worlds of Disney
Inside the Labyrinth
   (the making of the film Labyrinth)
Making of Star Wars, The/SP FX The Empire
   Strikes Back
Making of Teenage Mutant Ninja Turtles, The:
   Behind the Scenes
Movie Magic
Plausible Impossible: Wonderful World of Disney
Secrets of Back to the Future Trilogy
Work In Progress: Beauty and the Beast

Misrepresented Films (or videos with unfortunate titles)

And You Thought *Your* Parents Were Weird
Better Off Dead
Don't Tell Mom the Babysitter's Dead
Girls Just Want To Have Fun: The Movie
Lambada
Last Prostitute, The
Little Heroes
Suburban Commando

Movies Not Made for Children That Children Love

(This list contains titles popular with children from 9 to 13. Interestingly, they all contain similar elements–either a baby or young child as the focus, a bumbling or incompetent adult or an adult not in control of the situation, an animal (preferably a cute one), or a rebel (usually younger) getting the better of an adult. Please note the ratings on some of these films before showing to a young child.)

Arachnophobia
Baby, Secret of the Lost Legend
Batman
Beetlejuice
Better Off Dead
Big Man On Campus
City Slickers
Edward Scissorhands
Ferris Bueller's Day Off
Gremlins
Home Alone
Home Alone 2: Lost in New York
King Ralph
License to Drive

Look Who's Talking
Look Who's Talking Too
Mr. Mom
Naked Gun
Naked Gun 2 and a Half
Princess Bride, The
Problem Child and Problem Child 2
Pure Luck
Raising Arizona
Spaceballs
Splash
Strange Brew
Three Amigos
Three Men and a Baby
Three Men and a Little Lady
Time Bandits
Top Gun
Troop Beverley Hills
UHF
Uncle Buck
Vice Versa
What About Bob?
Who Framed Roger Rabbit?
Who's That Girl?

Musicals

Annie
Babes in Toyland
Bedknobs and Broomsticks
Cannon Movietales
Beauty and the Beast
The Emperor's New Clothes
Puss In Boots; Sleeping Beauty
Snow White
Little Red Riding Hood
The Frog Prince
Rumpelstiltskin
Chitty Chitty Bang Bang
Cinderella (Rodgers & Hammerstein)
Court Jester, The
Doctor Doolittle
Follow That Bird
Glass Slipper, The
Grease
Grease 2
Hans Christian Andersen
Happiest Millionaire, The
Jim Henson's Muppet Video series
Little Prince, The
Mary Poppins
New Adventures of Pippi Longstocking, The
Newsies
Oliver!
One and Only Genuine Original Family Band, The
Peter Pan (Mary Martin)
Singing in the Rain
Sound of Music, The

Summer Magic
That's Dancing
That's Entertainment
Popeye

Mysteries

Almost Partners
Benji
Cloak and Dagger
Condorman
Crystalstone
Double McGuffin, The
Edison Twins, The
Emil and the Detectives
Encyclopaedia Brown series (7 titles)
Ghost Writer series (3 titles)
Golden Treasure, The
Goonies
Hardy Boys (8 titles)
Mathnet
The Case of the Unnatural
  Treasure in Monterey Bay
Moon Stallion, The
Moonspinners, The
Mysteries
  (Sharon, Lois and Bram Elephant Show Vol.1)
Mystery of the Million Dollar Hockey Puck, The
Nancy Drew collection (8 titles)
Oh Heavenly Dog
Quest, The
Treasure, The
Undercover Gang, The
Young Detectives on Wheels

Parties for Girls

Annie
Beethoven
Candleshoe
Challengers, The
Frog
Girls Just Want to Have Fun: The Movie
Grease
Grease 2
Incredible Journey, The
Labyrinth
Maid-to-Order
Milo and Otis
New Adventures of Pippi Longstocking, The
Night Train to Kathmandu
Parent Trap, The
Polar Bear King, The
Rags to Riches
Ramona
Reach for the Sky
Road to Avonlea
Three Lives of Thomasina, The

Three Men and a Baby
Three Men and a Little Lady
Troop Beverley Hills
Trouble with Angels
Who's That Girl?
Wild Hearts Can't Be Broken

Parties for Boys

Adventures in Dinosaur Land
Boris and Natasha
Clash of the Titans
Cloak and Dagger
Defense Play
Dirt Bike Kid, The
Explorers
Gnome Named Norm, A
Godzilla movies
Great Whales, The
In Search of the Titanic
Jason and the Argonauts
King Kong
Mom and Dad Save the World
Monster Squad
Mysterious Island
Rad
Radical Moves
Rookie of the Year
Seventh Voyage of Sinbad, The
Sharks
Sinbad and the Eye of the Tiger
Spaceballs
Suburban Commando
Superman
Super Mario Brothers
Three Ninjas, The
War Games
Wizards of the Lost Kingdom

Parties for Girls and Boys

20,000 Leagues Under the Sea
Adventures in Babysitting
Baby, Secret of the Lost Legend
Back to the Future Trilogy
Beethoven
Free Willy
Home Alone
Home Alone 2: Lost in New York
Land of Faraway, The
Love Bug, The
Mac and Me
Real Genius
Shipwrecked
Short Circuit I and II
Spacecamp
Star Wars Trilogy
We're Back!

Performing Arts

Amahl and the Night Visitors
An Evening with Danny Kaye:
  Danny Kaye Conducts the New York Philharmonic
  with Zubin Mehta
Backstage at the Kirov (ballet)
Ballet Class for Beginners: David Howard
Ballet Shoes
Children of Theatre Street (ballet)
Creative Movement: A Step Toward Intelligence
El Amor Brujo (flamenco)
Flamenco at 5:15
Giorgiotime (first music lesson)
God's Children in a Celebration of Dance
I Can Dance
Land of Sweet Taps, The
Little Humpbacked Horse, The
Nutcracker, The (Baryshnikov and Kirkland)
Nutcracker: The Motion Picture
Professor Iris: Music Mania
Saint-Saens Carnival of Animals
Step Into Ballet with Wayne Sleep
Ustinov Reads the Orchestra
Who's Afraid of Opera? with Joan Sutherland
Vol. 1: Faust & Rigoletto
Vol. 2: La Traviata & Daughter of the Regiment
Vol. 3: Barber of Seville & Lucia di Lammemoor
Vol. 4: Mignon & La Perichole

Pirates

Blackbeard's Ghost
George's Island
Goonies
Hook
Kidnapped
Long John Silver
Peter Pan
Peter Pan (Mary Martin)
Pirate Movie, The
Pirates of Penzance, The
Shipwrecked
The Crimson Pirate
Treasure Island (Disney)
Treasure Island (MGM)
Treasure Island 1990

Pixilated/Puppetmation/Stop-Motion

California Raisins
Dig and Dug with Daisy collection
Dinosaurs!
Fireman Sam
Huxley Pig series
Jack Frost
Jason and the Argonauts
John Matthews Collection (6 titles)
Little Crooked Christmas Tree, The

Nightmare Before Christmas, The
Mysterious Island
Rudolph and Frosty's Shiny New Year
Rudolph and Frosty's Christmas in July
Sinbad and the Eye of The Tiger
Thomas the Tank Engine collection
Three Worlds of Gulliver
Thunderbirds Are Go
Will Vinton Collection (4 titles)
Wind in the Willows, The
Wombles, The
Year Without a Santa Claus, The

Religious Videos

Bible Heroes (Golden Book Video)
Bible Stories
Children's Heroes of the Bible:
  The Story of Jesus Part 1
Children's Heroes of the Bible:
  The Story of Jesus Part 2
God's Children in a Celebration of Dance
Hanna-Barbera's Greatest Adventure Stories
  from the Bible
One Minute Bible Stories (New Testament)
One Minute Bible Stories (Old Testament)
Our Dwelling Place: The Birth of Jesus
Our Dwelling Place: The Trial of Jesus
Oxford Vision Children's Video Bible, The
  (Vols. 1–10)
Superbook series (24 titles)

Robots

And You Thought *Your* Parents Were Weird
D.A.R.Y.L.
Electric Grandmother, The
Forbidden Planet
Konrad
Not Quite Human
Not Quite Human Two
Still Not Quite Human
Robbie the Robot
Short Circuit
Short Circuit II
Star Wars

Safety/Street-Proofing

Baby Alive: Emergency Treatment/Accident
  Prevention (Action Films and Video)
Babysitting the Responsible Way (CCP)
Berenstain Bears Learn About Strangers
  (Random Home Video)
Bicycle Safety Camp (Academy of Pediatric)
Cartoon All-Stars to the Rescue (BVHV)
Child Safety at Home (KSA)
Child Safety Outdoors (KSA)
Childproof: Home Safety Checklist (Prom)

Curiosity Without Tears
David Horowitz Presents:
　The Baby-Safe Home (EM)
Dr. Lee Salk's "Supersitter's Basics"
Emergency Action: When Seconds Count (AMA)
Fire Safety for the Family
Home Alone: A Kids Guide to Playing It Safe
　(Hi-Tops)
Home Safe with Martin Short (FMS Marketing)
How to Raise a Street Smart Child (HBO)
It's O.K. to Say No to Drugs (True North/JCI Video)
Kid Safe
　(Master Digital/ from the makers of Triaminic)
Kids Have Rights Too (JCI Video)
Let's Sing and Dance Music Video (Kards for Kids)
Little Red Riding Hood from the Shelley Duvall
　Faerie Tale Theatre series (Playhouse)
Little Red Riding Hood:
　A Cannon Movietale (Warner)
Mr. Rogers: When Parents Are Away (CBS)
Never Talk to Strangers (Golden)
Right Thing to Do, The (Captain Kangaroo) (MPI)
Strong Kids, Safe Kids (Paramount)
Safety Magic with Philip and Henry
　(Safety 1st Video)
Too Smart for Strangers: Winnie-the-Pooh
　(Walt Disney Home Video)

Scary Sleep-Over Movies

Birds, The
Canterville Ghost, The
Dragonslayer
Ernest Scared Stupid
Fly, The (1958)
Frankenweenie
Ghost Dad
Ghostbusters I and II
Goonies
Haunting of Barney Palmer, The
Indiana Jones and the Last Crusade
Indiana Jones and the Temple of Doom
Ladyhawke
Last Starfighter, The
Legend
Little Monsters
Monster Squad
Mummy, The (1958)
My Science Project
Mysterious Island
Nightmare Before Christmas, The
Raiders of the Lost Ark
Rescue, The
Scrooge
Something Wicked This Way Comes
The Canterville Ghost
Treasure Island 1990
Watcher in the Woods

Willow
Young Sherlock Holmes

Science/Ecology

3-2-1- Contact series (4 titles)
Astrodudes: Shooting for the Moon
Astrodudes: Solar Mysteries, The
Carl Sagan: Cosmos
Earth Day Special, The
Help Save Planet Earth
Ida Fanfanny and Three Magical Tales
Miracle of Life, The
Mr. Wizard's World: Air and Water Wizardry
Mr. Wizard's World:
　Puzzles, Problems and Impossibilities
My First Green Video
My First Nature Video
My First Science Video
National Geographic
　Invisible World
　Miniature Miracle the Computer Chip
　Rainforest
　The Incredible Human Machine
Professor Iris: Earth Daze
Professor Iris: Space Cadets
Tell Me Why collection (Vols. 1–24)
World of Discovery: The Secret Life of
　118 Green Street
Wonders of Earth and Space, The

Sex Education

"What's Happening to Me?": A Guide to Puberty
"Where Did I Come From?"
Goldie and Kids
What Kids Want to Know About
　Sex and Growing Up
What About Sex?

Sign Language

Say It by Signing (Living Language)
Sign Me-A-Story
Musign

Space (real or fantasized)

An Incredible Odyssey
Black Hole, The
E.T.: The Extra-Terrestrial
Explorers
Last Starfighter, The
Mac and Me
NASA: The First 25 Years
Spacecamp
Spaced Invaders
Star Wars
Wonders of Earth and Space, The

Sports

Absent Minded Professor, The
Air Up There,The
Amazing Grace and Chuck (basketball)
Angels in the Outfield
Back to the Future I, II, III
Bad News Bears
Bad News Bears in Breaking Training
Bad News Bears Go to Japan (baseball)
Better Off Dead
Blue Chips
Breaking Away
Court Jester, The
Days of Thunder
Dirt Bike Kid, The
Herbie Goes To Monte Carlo
Hoosiers
Iron Will
Jugger of Notre Dame, The
Karate Kid I, II, III
Ladybugs
Little Big League
Major League 2
Mystery of the Million Dollar Hockey Puck
Popeye
Princess Bride, The
RAD (BMX Biking)
Radical Moves
Reach for The Sky
Robin Hood
Rookie of the Year
Sandlot, The
Teen Wolf
Teen Wolf Too
Three Musketeers, The
Tigertown
Toby McTeague

Submarines

20,000 Leagues Under the Sea
Russkies

Thanksgiving

Bugs Bunny's Thanksgiving Diet
Garfield's Thanksgiving

Trains

Awesome Trains
Cars, Boats, Trains and Planes: Kidsongs
Great Locomotive Chase, The
Ivor the Engine
National Geographic: Love Those Trains
Railway Children, The
Red Express (World of Discovery)
Thomas the Tank Engine
Trains, Trucks and Boats

Valentine's Day

Be My Valentine, Charlie Brown
Berenstain Bears: Cupid's Surprise
Big Screen Sweethearts
Bugs Bunny: Cupid's capers
Courtin' Cut-Ups
Dino and Juliet
Fred Flintstone Woos Again
Rompin' Romance

Vehicles

20,000 Leagues Under The Sea
Awesome Collection, The (10 titles)
Chitty Chitty Bang Bang
Dig and Dug with Daisy at the Factory
Dig and Dug with Daisy on a Building Site
Dig and Dug with Daisy on the Road
Dig and Dug with Daisy on the Farm
Fire and Rescue
Great Race, The
Road Construction Ahead
Those Magnificent Men in Their Flying Machines
Trains, Trucks and Boats
World of Discovery: Tall Ships

Witches

East of the Sun, West of the Moon
Hansel and Gretel: A Cannon Movietale
Hansel and Gretel:
    Shelley Duvall's Faerie Tale Theatre
Lion, the Witch and the Wardrobe, The
Polar Bear King, The
Sleeping Beauty
Snow Queen, The
Snow White: A Cannon Movietale
The Three Lives of Thomasina
Witches, The
Wizard of Oz, The

INDEX OF VIDEOS

FOR THE BABYSITTER
Videos we are saving for your visit

My Neighbor Totoro

Galaxy Express

Giant Robo

FOR THE BABYSITTER
Please do not rent any of these titles for the children

_____   _____

_____   _____

_____   _____

_____   _____

_____   _____

_____   _____

_____   _____

_____   _____

_____   _____

_____   _____

_____   _____

_____   _____

_____   _____